PETER MARK RICHMAN

I SAW A MOLTEN, WHITE LIGHT…

PETER MARK RICHMAN

I SAW A MOLTEN, WHITE LIGHT…

An autobiography of my artistic and spiritual journey

BearManor Media
2018

Peter Mark Richman: I Saw a Molten, White Light…
An autobiography of my artistic and spiritual journey

© 2018 Peter Mark Richman

All rights reserved.

For information, address:

BearManor Media
P. O. Box 71426
Albany, GA 31708

bearmanormedia.com

Typesetting and layout by John Teehan

Published in the USA by BearManor Media

ISBN — 978-1-62933-247-5

Table of Contents

Biography xi

Acknowledgments xiii

Prologue xvii

1   My Childhood 1

2   Growing Up 15

3   The Navy 23

4   Discharged and Home Again 33

5   A Reluctant Pharmacy Student 45

6   A Life-Changing Decision 63

7   New York 71

8   The Commitment 89

9   Hallowed Place 97

10 Hollywood and Gary Cooper 113

11 A Hatful of Rain 129

12 A Volvo Delivery 145

13 Subud—My Spiritual Search Is Answered 151

14 Shooting *Cain's Hundred* 167

15	The Nightmare of Letting Go	191
16	Auditioning for Meredith Willson	209
17	Peter and Helen	221
18	Bapak In Woodland Hills	233
	Photo Section	243
19	My Nudes at the Playboy Club	301
20	*Dynasty*	317
21	Vienna and Leonard Bernstein	339
22	Suddenly, In Charge	341
23	How Do You Spell Purgatory?	349
24	Danger In Manila	357
25	Pitching In the Pentagon	371
26	Hitler Never Envisioned This	379
27	Germany Revisited	391
28	Art at the Essex House	405
29	Ray Badbury On Stage	415
30	New York and a Flawed Audition	421
31	That Molten White Light…	429
32	You Just Had To Prat	441
33	*4 FACES*—The Beginning	449
34	*4 FACES*—Actors Studio—NY	459

35	Subud World Congress In Spokane	471
36	A Grandson Named Max and then, Japan!	477
37	An Amazing Proposal	487
38	The Super Bowl Rams	499
39	Lucas Does Sondheim	511
40	Final Cut	517
41	Father and Son	533
	Epilogue	539

*To my wife, Helen.
I love her dearly,
and she is always there for me.*

Biography

PETER MARK RICHMAN WAS BORN in South Philadelphia and went to Southern High School. He excelled in football and was captain and fullback in The 1944 Philadelphia High School Championship. At seventeen World War II was still going on so he enlisted in the navy and served on an aircraft carrier, *USS Ranger*. In 1946 he was discharged and played for a team for two years in the Eastern Pro Conference. Unfortunately, a serious knee injury terminated his football days.

As an actor, Peter Mark draws from a deep well of experience on the Broadway stage, motion pictures and television. His first New York appearance was in Calder Willingham's *End As a Man*, an Actor's Studio project. This was followed by leading roles in *A Hatful of Rain* opposite Vivian Blaine and toured nationally. *Masquerade* with Cloris Leachman; and on the summer circuit in *Arms and the Man*, *Look Back In Anger* and *The Rainmaker* with Eva Marie Saint. He portrayed Jerry in over 400 performances of Edward Albee's original New York production of *The Zoo Story*.

He also starred in the stage performances of *Blithe Spirit*, *Night of the Iguana*, *Hold Me*, *The Deputy*, *Equus*, *Twelve Angry Men*, *Funny Girl*, and *Babes In Toyland* with Robert Morse.

William Wyler brought him West for the classic film, *Friendly Persuasion* with Gary Cooper and Dorothy McGuire. Among his many other feature films he also starred opposite Sophia Loren and Anthony Quinn in *The Black Orchid*.

Mr. Richman starred as Nick Cain in his own NBC series, *Cain's Hundred* and in over 500 guest star appearances on such shows as *The Vir-*

ginian, *Twilight Zone*, *The FBI*, *The Love Boat*, *Mission Impossible*, *Fantasy Island*, *Star Trek: The Next Generation*, *Beverly Hills 90210,* and *Bonanza: The Next Generation*. He co-starred on the series *Longstreet*, recurred as the funny Reverend Snow on *Three's Company* and as Blake Carrington's attorney, Andrew Laird in *Dynasty*. He created the role of C.C. Capwell on the soap *Santa Barbara*.

As a writer, his play, *A Medal for Murray*, was translated into Hebrew, premiered in Tel Aviv and had a two year run in Israel. He received a Drama Critics award for his performance in *4 FACES*, a play he wrote and starred in, for which he wrote the screenplay and also starred in the film which received a Prism Award commendation. His one act plays have been produced by ANTA, The Actor's Studio and The Richard Basehart Playhouse. He also has written a novel, *Hollander's Deal* and a book of short stories, *The Rebirth of Ira Masters*. In 1990 the Motion Picture and Television Fund awarded the Silver Medallion to Mr. Richman for outstanding humanitarian achievement. He was chairman of the building committee which built their 25 million dollar hospital. Also in 1990 he received the Sybil Brand Humanitarian Award from The Jeffrey Foundation.

Mr. Richman is a graduate of The Philadelphia College of Pharmacy and Science and is a registered pharmacist in Pennsylvania and New York. He resides in Los Angeles with his wife, Helen, and has five children and six grandchildren.

Acknowledgments

I WOULD LIKE TO THANK Jason Duplissea and Loren Lester for their edits and my children for helping me with the photos in the book:

>Orien Richman
>Kelly Lester
>Lucas Richman and
>>the inestimable
>>Howard Richman

Four Richman family members have changed their first names for spiritual reasons.

*Peter Mark was known as Mark
Helen was known as Teddi
Howard was known as Gard
Kelly was known as Stacey*

I want to eliminate any confusion about to whom I am referring.

Prologue

ACTORS HAVE A LOT OF TIME on their hands. It is the nature of the business in between employment, and employment for actors is generally not easy to come by, no matter what stage they are in their career. As you get older, it gets even worse. Thus, time may hang heavy because there is so much of it. What does one do to fill the time of the day? I ask myself that every morning when I look in the mirror as I brush my teeth—the circles under my eyes a little darker, the lines a bit deeper.

After a more than sixty-year career in the theater, film and television, I am one of the fortunate ones. What do I do with my time? I can do what I jolly well please. Actors are always waiting endlessly and impatiently for someone to call, the agent or manager, to tell them what's happening.

They want you! The deal is fantastic! They don't want you… the deal is off! You're hot! You're cold! You're overexposed! I think we can make it work! The new pilot season is just around the corner! The network doesn't think your TVQ is high enough!

Whether it's Stock, Broadway, or Hollywood, it's a process with countless variables that grinds on through an actor's life and never seems to change. It's similar to pulling a slot machine lever and hoping to hit the jackpot, but coming up with two cherries and a lemon. It can wear you down if you let it. Rejection is continual and relentless.

Acting has never been enough for me. I act and I paint. I always thank God for that. It has been a blessing. The writing came much later in my life. It came after I figured out what I wanted to write about and had the facility to express my life experiences. I've learned by doing it, much as I have learned everything in my life by living it. Raising our five children has been no exception. It has been a profoundly joyous, daunting, and powerful experience with all of its heavy responsibilities, and my wife, bless her, has been a superbly wise partner, a safe harbor and a solid foundation through it all.

Six grandchildren were much easier.

1 My Childhood

My father, Benjamin, was born in Lithuania; I don't know the city. No one is alive to give specific answers to my many questions—and when they were I never asked. His brothers and sisters who came with him to America are all gone, their children are distant, and the remaining family who wouldn't leave Lithuania were all murdered during the Holocaust. My father was short, stocky, red-headed, and very freckled—and a good man. He was volatile and quick-tempered and not someone to be crossed (I once saw him, furious at incompetent workmanship, take a sledgehammer and obliterate a carpenter's shoddy efforts), but he was loving and caring to his children and knew instinctively what they would need in their future lives. My father knew that his second child, Harry, who was burdened with a handicap, would need a college education to compete, and so he would let nothing stand in the way of Harry's getting it. Harry had been run over by a trolley car that ran in front of the house when he was five years old. Four fingers had been severed on his left hand, leaving only the little finger and a scarred, but functional, stump. As a quality pharmacist, he never had a problem dispensing prescriptions. Harry revered his father and never tolerated a negative word said against him.

In those days, people in Philadelphia papered their walls with decorative wallpaper every few years and rarely painted. Only the woodwork trim was freshened with paint. The gold printing on my father's store window read: "B. RICHMAN, DECORATOR." He had an experienced crew of paperhangers and painters, sending them all over the city to fulfill commitments. He was a dedicated and dependable provider, and during the Depression years when I was growing up, that was not easy. My mother, Yetta, was born in Lublin, Poland, and she was something else. She must have been very beautiful when she first arrived in America. She had good features, smooth olive skin, rich, dark hair, and questioning brown eyes that always saw the negative in everything she encountered. My parents met in Philadelphia around 1914 and married soon after. They had five children. It has been told that my mother pulled her hair out by the roots when Harry lost his fingers. All of my mother's family who did not emigrate to America were killed in Poland.

When my mother smiled, the chimes tinkled, but most of the time as a kid, I heard an incessantly shrill, brassy trumpet. I was the one who bore the brunt of the animosity she expressed toward her husband, the basis of which I was never quite sure. It was an accumulation of many grievances, and she spewed them forth with paranoid fervor over and over. I was the fifth child and probably unwanted by my mother, although I can't prove it. An accident, they used to say. I heard my sister Fay, the first born, who was a sparkling, blue eyed vivacious blonde and twenty years older than I am, laughingly tell me on more than one occasion about the time she found out my mother was pregnant with me: "Mom, what are you doing, getting pregnant at your age? How can you? You're embarrassing me in front of my friends!"

I was born April 16, 1927, in South Philadelphia's Methodist Hospital; I was the last child in a family of five children, and the age distances between us were vast. The closest was my brother Dave, and he was eight years older. My mother was forty-two when she gave birth to me and she never got over it. I have no idea what she was like before, but my debut may have pushed her off the ledge. I'm not saying I wasn't loved, but I didn't get the focus of concern I should I have had. I was always like this cute little intruder kid wandering around with a bunch of adults who couldn't figure out who I was and what to do with me. I remember playing, or was it hiding, under the baby grand piano in the living room that nobody played. It was my secret hiding place for my pimply rubber ball, two marbles, and stacked wooden Popsicle sticks. I would check it all the time, crawling on my knees on the dusty floor to make sure that nobody stole my treasures away.

Very early on I discovered I had a passion for drawing. It gave me the attention I craved. Showing my family my latest pencil creation and hearing, somewhat indifferently, "Oh, that's good, you have talent" went a long way in boosting my worth.

In South Philadelphia where I grew up, there was a first-rate philanthropic art institution called the Philadelphia Graphic Sketch Club. I first went there when I was nine years old and continued to study there periodically until I was seventeen. The classes were in the evening.

Most of the emphasis was academic so I developed a strong technique in drawing. The teachers were the finest and came from Temple University, University of Pennsylvania, and the Pennsylvania Academy of Fine Arts. As far back as 1875, the great American artist Thomas Eakins taught at the Pennsylvania Academy before assuming his post as its director. Since the beginning, the quality of instruction has never diminished. I suppose the teachers were paid, but I don't remember paying for any of my classes. I do remember having to buy supplies—large, 24 x 30 inch, 100 percent rag charcoal paper at 5¢ cents a sheet! A sliver of charcoal for two or three pennies, and a cut of sandpaper stuck to a small rectangular piece of wood to sharpen the charcoal. I have many of those charcoal and pencil drawings I did all those years ago, of plaster cast busts and half figures. They are preserved in the original black art portfolio, frayed and dusty and shoelace-tied on three sides, with the letters painted in red on the cover by a ten-year-old art student that proudly declares: PHILA. GRAPHIC SKETCH CLUB.

Even at that young age I found it rather tiresome to have to sketch only white plaster casts of people or famous statues. But it served to develop my observational ability, and the instructors were particular and insistent about details. Gradually, as I progressed, I was allowed to draw my classmates. We took turns posing on the platform in front of the class, usually a half hour at a time sitting perfectly still, no squirming.

That was difficult, with all studied eyes focused on you, your breath restricted, self-consciousness exposed. I didn't enjoy that, but it was an obligation I accepted, and maybe a precursor to my eventual profession as an actor. I vividly remember setting up my easel and placing my portfolio at the proper angle to proceed on a fresh, toothy sheet of virgin paper held erect by metal clips, a sharpened charcoal in my right hand. Looking around at the other artists getting ready to attack the subject, the scratching and shuffling sounds, and the muffled voice of the instructor, was a powerful and memorable experience. Most of my art collection of the time consists of the busts of fully clothed adults, so I assume I was one of only a few children allowed to participate in this adult class. I do remember asking the instructor if I could sketch in the life classes and getting a smirking rejection. "You have to grow up a bit, son… children are not to be seen in the same room with nude women or nude men."

That didn't prevent me from sneaking a look or two on the second floor with the door slightly ajar. I did it on more than one occasion and was never caught. I had come to the mature conclusion it was far more interesting and stimulating than cold white plaster. Once or twice a week in the early evening with sneakers on my feet and my art portfolio under my arm, I would go out the front door of my father's paperhanger-decorator store on Passyunk Avenue and take the long adventurous walk past the ominous Moyamensing Prison on the way to my classes. Built in the early 1830s, the huge, impenetrable stone walls towered to the sky, or so it seemed, taking up blocks of city streets—prisoners sadly peering down through tiny barred openings at the top. It was a dreadful sight in the daytime, but in the shadowed evening it was horrifying. I often wondered what it must be like, holed up for life in a place like that? I swore I would never do anything so bad that I would end up in there. The thought would make my scalp tingle. My mood always lightened when I got past the prison, mixing in with the noisy neighborhood bustle and the narrow street traffic of honking cars. I would hurry past the raucous gang in front of the candy store bent over and shooting dice against the wall; the "used tire" store, where the owner was making new grooves on a bald one with a special rubber burning instrument; the Italian bakery with glorious aromas emanating from unknown confections; the kid on roller skates almost knocking me down and laughing about it as he zoomed away; the gas station on the corner with the big Esso sign waving in the wind; the very pregnant woman on worn down high heels pushing a rattan baby carriage of crying twins. I remember it all and more; I will never forget. How can I? It is where I grew up. Where you grow up is sewn into your soul. It is the fabric of your life and you wear it until you die.

The pushcarts on Ninth Street, filled end to end with weighing scales and umbrellas, were always brimming over with fruits and vegetables, dried beans and nuts, pickles and flowers, hand-made trinkets, hats and shoes, and more. There wasn't anything you couldn't bargain for and buy there. If it wasn't on the pushcart, it was in the store opposite. I had to pass all this to finally get to the sketch club, and I was allowed to do this on my own. There were no carpools in those days or pick-ups after school. You walked—and there was never any doubt that you would get to where you wanted to go by walking, even in tough neighborhoods. Th s was South Philly, a tough neighborhood. I had to work my way out of some mean, sweaty situations to survive, but times have certainly changed. Parents would be crazy to let their children do what I did then, alone and unprotected.

I still have in my files a salmon-colored Graphic Sketch Club membership card with my name on it and a big, blue-stamped 1939. 1939! My God, I was twelve years old. About this time, when I started painting in oils, many of my first canvases were not canvas at all, but heavy kitchen wall covering. The back side, where I painted, was a linen-like porous fabric, cut and tacked down. Not a good texture or quality, but so available in my father's store. (The first small wooden palette I used, pressed against my thumb, now hangs in my studio along with several tubes of hard cheap oil paints I saved, and an expensive tube of alizarin crimson costing the enormous sum of 50¢!)

My mother whined and wailed endlessly about all of her hurts, her pains, her frustrations and sufferings, physical and mental—irritations that may have happened twenty years earlier—her children not caring about her; the married ones not coming to see her; nobody calling her on the phone; her husband not coming home to spend time with her. "He's always out playing cards and drinking beer, not giving me the respect that I deserve! Why does he get all the children's attention and love and I get nothing? NOTHING!" She was a broken record that never stopped playing the same droning tune. It was continual, and so were the mood swings and the profuse tears. It was tough to get your bearings, never knowing what would set her off. As long as you agreed with her and were on her side no matter what, you were safe. It wasn't until I was five or six years old that I began to tire of her poisonous rhetoric, my loyalty shifting as I sensed her irrationality. I didn't understand that my poor mother was mentally a bit off kilter, but even as a child I felt that her constant accusatory manner in most cases was unjust. Once, when she was in a rage, I witnessed her smashing every dish and glass in the kitchen and dining room cabinets. Then dropping to the floor, shrieking and wailing pitifully, she continued her rampage by rolling side to side over the broken pieces. I cringed in a corner, helpless and beyond shock, while curious passers-by, alarmed by the commotion, peeked through the store window.

I was always trying to make peace between my parents, a tremulous child's voice pleading, "Please don't fight. Let's go to the park… we'll have a picnic." Every day without fail there was turmoil of some sort. When I innocently expressed a warmer consideration for my father (the warning signals now flashing in my mother's eyes) and tried to assuage the tension that hovered by boldly saying, "Mom… uh… Mom… can you and Pop not fight all the time?"—it was then that I began to get the direct focus of her ravings, verbally and sometimes physically with a solid ear-ringing slap or a jaw rocker. She accused me of being just like all of her other children who didn't love her. I suppose it was because I was the only one in earshot of a lonely and distressed paranoid woman.

Everyone else was married and out of the house, except my brother Dave, and he was mainly indifferent and unaffected, being eight years older and never around. There was so much hollering and screaming between my parents, I wasn't sure there was any other way. It was a daily occurrence. The conflicts permeated everything and persisted with insidious contagion. Harry and his wife didn't speak to my mother for ten years, nor to my sister, Fay, and her husband. Fay avoided seeing my mother for many years too. She couldn't take her rancor. She had an ulcer and it was detrimental to her health. Sister Fay, when provoked, could let loose the demons as well. This went on and on for years with only my father and I visiting everybody, playing both sides and trying to calm the turbulent waters of enduring alienation. When I was a bit older, I once sympathetically talked to my father about the awful situation he was enduring with Mom. He gestured with a half-smile and said, forgivingly, "She doesn't mean it… she doesn't know what she's doing."

To say that my mother was mentally disturbed and desperately in need of help is a simplistic conclusion to a serious problem. In those days, in this family, it was out of the question. It wasn't even thought about or considered. Divorce was an option as unknown as a visitor from Jupiter. I do know this: I have come to realize that I was an emotionally abused child with all the fears and anxieties attendant—it shaped my life. I never held that against my mother. I loved her, and when she was in her normal periods of behavior, admittedly rare, I heard those distant, tinkling chimes of happiness and was cautiously at ease, like treading barefoot around shards of glass.

How I survived that daily dose of pain I'll never know, but it certainly has made me what I am—good, bad, and everything in between. It did give me a short fuse, a volatile nature, and an impatient attitude that wants to cut through all the shit that life is full of. It also has made me a good actor and a compassionate human being, I think, with a sensitive nose to avoid phoniness whenever I see it. In truth, I never knew what the great conflict was between my parents. My mother expressed her discontent with everything my father did. Nothing was ever good enough. She was neglected; the children were against her—she wasn't appreciated for all the sacrifices she had made for us, and she wasn't loved. Of course, to get love you have to give love, and to give love freely, without caveats and reservations, was a problem for my mother. Maybe they had a problem in the bedroom, I don't know. Only God knows the origin of their torment. Looking back, I'm convinced that all the family strife and turbulence, all the helpless heartache I went through helped to propel and stimulate me as an actor and as an artist. It deepened my awareness and firmed my resolve.

Every year, to alter the atmosphere, my father would arrange a rental in Atlantic City, New Jersey, and send my mother, my brother Dave, and me to enjoy a summer at the beach. Sometimes it was a whole house (when I was an infant), then half a house, and finally, because of the Depression, a room with kitchen privileges, which was rather unpleasant because my mother constantly complained. Among other things, she complained that somebody was eating her butter and eggs which she had put in the refrigerator. By that time, Dave, too grown-up to join us, chose to suffer the dreadfully hot summers at home in Philly. My father sometimes, reluctantly, came down on weekends—the sixty-mile drive a big deal in those days. I have a vivid memory of him sitting on a burning hot beach with his clothes on, his stiff, straw hat perched atop his head, his pants rolled up exposing his shockingly white skin. Atlantic City was for his family and not really for him. I have a large oil painting of my father and mother in a rolling chair on the boardwalk that I painted from an old, frayed photograph taken in 1927, the year I was born. When I was painting my father's face I just couldn't get it right. Then when I finally captured the look in his eyes—loving, but deeply sad—I became so emotional that I had to put the brushes aside and stop for a while.

I was a lonely child. I spent most of my time in an adult world amusing myself. From early morning until late in the afternoon I was on the beach unsupervised, digging in the sand with my hands, searching for tiny crabs and clams; making sand sculptures in the wet, the incoming tide lapping at my feet; probing the cool sand under the boardwalk for coins that might have fallen through the cracks above; lingering around the lifeguard stand, and the two bronzed and muscular guards, men I admired and looked up to—especially when they heroically dashed to the ocean for a rescue. When I was older—dangerously taking chances, a dare with myself more than once—I'd swim a quarter of a mile offshore and remaining afloat, treading deep water without a care in the world, the sun searing my skin. Who ever heard of suntan lotion? That was for sissies if they could afford it. It didn't matter that I suffered festering blisters and suppurating burns for the first three weeks of our vacation and was forced to wear an embarrassing shirt until I eventually acquired a protective, golden tan (and oh, yes, pray tell, who was even aware of potential skin cancer in those days?) In the evening, I walked the boardwalk endlessly, that scraping, thumping sound of walkers on wood seared in my brain forever—the pounding waves roaring an approving accompaniment in the windy, salty air. So many things to do and see, and no one at my side. Steel Pier and Million Dollar Pier and all their extravagant spectacles would have to wait for another time. Ten cents in my pocket wouldn't get me past the gate, but it would get me a double-dip, ice cream sugar cone before I went home to sleep.

One summer when I was six years old, instead of the shore, Pop rented a house in Bucks County, Pennsylvania. I have no memory of the house, but I have strong remembrances of several incidents that happened that summer. They are cauterized on my brain in a place where memories such as these will never fade away.

One: A young woman on a deserted road was riding a horse at a fast gait and coming toward me and then she was thrown. She landed with a terrible thud, her dazed look and her head bleeding profusely. As a child I remember standing there, helpless.

Two: I couldn't swim, but I remember compulsively jumping into a swimming lake from a small bridge to see what would happen to me if I sank to the bottom. I remember opening my eyes and looking around while I held my breath, not thinking of the consequences when I would have no more air in my lungs. Thank God, Dave saw what I had done and jumped in to pull me up and save me. "What the hell are you doing, you crazy kid?" he yelled. I had no idea... I was just listening to this strange voice in my head that dared me to do certain things—a challenge to myself and did I have the nerve to do it? It started with simple dares—don't step on the cracks in the pavement! And went on from there. I also remember hearing normal sounds of the day that would suddenly become encased in a repetitive rhythmic pattern and tune—the airplane overhead, the engine of a bus passing by, the slapping surf at the beach. I suppose I was troubled, the chaos in my dysfunctional family affecting me more than I could handle as a child.

Three: My mother had a friend in Bucks County, a Mrs. Fried who was a heavyset, good-natured widow with bulging eyes and an attached sadness. She was also very wealthy. That summer, she invited us to spend the afternoon at her beautiful old mansion. I remember it was huge, all white, and surrounded with heavy foliage and full blossoms of multicolored chrysanthemums. In the evening after dinner we were all sitting on this spacious porch, the fireflies lighting up here and there, the crickets screeching loudly, and the flowers tickling the night air with their intoxicating scents. The droning, amorphous adult conversation, however, was certainly not engaging to a little boy.

I was sitting in a rocking chair, intrigued by a firefly, when suddenly to my right, above the arched doorway to the house, I saw a massive white light appear—a dense molten whiteness that radiated and glowed so intensely I could hardly look away. It lingered and vibrated in its blinding brightness and just stayed there. I don't remember how long, possibly a few minutes. I cannot remember if I told anyone what I was seeing, but I do know that no one else saw it or remarked about it. I just sat there fascinated—shocked, frightened, and absorbed in what I had observed. Imagine, a six-year-old witnessing something like that, and no one to talk to about it, let alone, be believed. This experience has stayed with me all of my life. Later, as an adult I found out the significance and the profound meaning of what I'd seen and witnessed.

There was another trying situation in my family, concerning my sister Gertrude. She was thirteen years older than I and an extremely beautiful young woman with a far-away, Garbo look. Unfortunately, she was quite ill. Gert, as we called her, had a high school girlfriend named Ruth and they were closer than book pages, but Ruth was in a rapidly developing stage of tuberculosis and didn't know how contagious she was. Neither did Gert. My father found out and pleaded for his daughter to stay away: "Gert, please… she's sick… very sick. Stay away from her… please… I don't want you to get sick too."

Gert wouldn't listen. Ruthie was her closest friend. They did everything together, and she couldn't abandon her. Not now! It was too late, and by her eighteenth birthday Gert was also a tubercular. It was tragic. My parents were overwhelmed with grief, especially my father. He tried to do everything he could: doctors, sanitariums, whatever he could afford at the time. In the 1930s, there were no instant cures for TB—just rest, sunshine, dreadful ineffective medicinals, and more rest, while the virulent tubercle bacillus persisted and slowly destroyed more of her lungs.

There was a brief period when Gert seemed to rally and improve. I have no idea of the reason for it, but during that time and being the beauty that she was, she attracted and fell in love with an unusually handsome fella named Jack Feldman. Maybe he was the reason for her determination to get well. He accepted her illness as if it were a case of the sniffles. He was a fine young man and dedicated his life to her. In late 1934, when she was twenty, they married and I was their ring bearer in a full dress suit. I was seven.

Jack didn't work. He just took care of my sister and that was enough. My father didn't object and only helped. He rented and refurbished a little corner row-house for them to live in on 4th and Durfor Street, with a storefront so they could open a hosiery shop. He thought they could accomplish this in an unstrenuous way and earn some money. You can imagine the business they did selling silk stockings in 1935 in that depressed South Philly neighborhood. Gert was the one who encouraged me the most concerning my art creations. She thought everything I drew or painted was special. Of course, it wasn't, but for me, a neglected child, it was buoyant music. When I visited her little shop, she would open the limited stock of boxes on the shelves and carefully extract the pulpy, white paper placed in the folds of the stockings and give them to me for sketching. It was so exciting to have all these clean, new surfaces only for me to use. I have often wished that I had just one of all of the drawings I did then with my sister's smiling patronage. I loved her so, and writing about her now, I have to pause to collect myself, the memories are so strong.

Jack was a fight fan and I remember sitting on the storefront step one evening, drawing, listening to the radio and hearing the roar as Max Bear knocked out Primo Carnera. It is always amazing to me to realize that when I reminisce about myself, recalling events that are buried deep in my past, that they still remain vivid, even though they may have happened so many years ago. As Lee Strasberg used to say, "Memories are the tools of the actor, the raw material he can draw from when needed." It's obviously true in writing. As a painter, I have no doubt that whatever you have experienced in life affects and influences how and what you paint. It has touched your inner life, maybe even scarred it, giving you your gift of individuality.

The hosiery shop was a failure and Gert needed fresh air, so Pop rented a house at the edge of Fairmount Park on Conshohocken Avenue in the upscale "Main Line." It was the closest thing to being in the country, and in 1936 there were no freeways so it was a long trip back to South Philadelphia. We stayed there a year or so, my sister mainly bed-ridden in a back bedroom, spending her time listening to the radio—and my mother cooking the meals and grousing about isolation and loneliness. My father visited on the weekend and Dave… well, he had remained in town with Pop, quit high school, went to work as a paperhanger, and pursued pretty girls. He was very good-looking and quite successful at it. Living way out there was a difficult adjustment for me. I had to go to an ancient public school by bus (the Joseph Leidy, decrepit in 1936). I had to try to make new friends in the neighborhood (impossible), and I wasn't able to go anywhere that wasn't five miles walking distance away, or so it seemed. The contrast was shocking. On Passyunk Avenue there were candy stores on every block and boxes of penny confection smells mixed with cigar smoke and hot dogs on the grill. There were myriad storefront windows to look through, bursting with jewelry, shoes, linoleum, household wares, and tailored goods. There was the organ-grinder lady with the cock-eyed perpetual smile and her jumping monkey, and there were wild games on the street with a tied newspaper as a substitute football. On Sunday, in a somber parade for some Italian Catholic saint, a somber clarinetist played in a shuffling band as the ladies in bare feet or on their knees moved slowly, doing penance—the sainted statue plastered with dollar bills, hoisted and passing by. My passion was the Alhambra movie theater across the street from my house. I attended as often as I could sneak in, or scrape up a dime. It was an old barn of a place, full of marble pillars and burgundy, gold-fringed drapes. Who could ever forget the inspired fantasies up there on the sparkling silver screen that were influencing my life? A young Clark Gable, so manly and noble in *Mutiny on the Bounty* facing such a hateful Charles Laughton! Gary Cooper, so folksy and real in *Mister Deeds Goes to Town*; the lovable Shirley Temple dancing into my heart in *Little Miss Marker*—and when Boris Karloff as Frankenstein looked directly at me, was I ever more frightened in my life?

I miss sitting in those squeaky, worn-out seats. I miss the traffic and the noise. I miss it all terribly. I even miss climbing up the mountain of stacked bundles of wallpaper in my father's store that I once totally collapsed while playing war with Johnny Mazzeo, the barber's son. After that and a crunching slap, I wasn't allowed to climb anymore. That was okay, I could play in the cellar messing around with the wheat paste Pop had delivered to him every week for his paperhangers. I remember the horse-drawn wagon and the delivery man sliding off the enormously heavy, monstrous barrel and rolling it to the cellar door on the pavement, then carefully letting it glide down the wooden planks to the basement floor. The creamy, thick paste had a sweet aroma and looked like pudding. I used to trowel out a glop, thrust it back down, sculpt different shapes, and then smooth it over. It was as routine and mindless as bouncing a ball and I enjoyed it. I was sure it would taste good too, so I tried it once. I was wrong. I threw up.

Next to the barrels and the waiting paste buckets and tools were the wallpaper trimming machines. A long steel shaft was thrust through each roll of paper, then clamped, the cutters adjusted, the motor turned on and the humming machine would make piles of trimmings that looked like ribbons. After the trim, the rolls of paper were ready for hanging. Sometimes the trimmings were as high as the ceiling and bouncy fun to fall on. When it got too flattened out I would fluff it all up again so my father wouldn't notice. Once a week, Dave or I would gather up all the trims and shove them down inside the empty paste barrels for the delivery man to cart away.

The house we lived in at 1617 East Passyunk Avenue was a three-story building with living quarters on all the floors and Pop's store in front. The cellar was a dark, dank congested mess. From the narrow wooden stairs to the furnace next to the coal bin, half-filled with anthracite coal, or the dreadful and gaseous bituminous (which is all we could get during the war), you had to navigate cautiously. The place was over-filled with everything, and most of it should have been thrown out. There were partially empty paint cans left over from a completed job; old, stained and useless furniture, bottles and bottles and cans of turpentine, linseed oil, cleaning fluid, and motor oil. The deep sink area had even more bottles of tightly corked contents and brown laundry soap and empty coffee cans filled with unknown goopy stuff that stank. There were dirty rags on a clothes line and rusting license plates and cobwebs enough for a haunted house. Instinctively you brushed them all away with your waving hand as you walked; otherwise, you might get a spider in your mouth.

It was so poorly lit down there, each step could lead to a disaster. I did have one, but it was of my own making. I had decided to create a Batik design on a white cloth. I had made one in school and thought I could do it easily at home. First you have to melt the wax before you get to the dyeing process, so I swiped some candles from the kitchen cabinet, put them in a coffee can, lit the gas stove in the rear of the cellar with a wooden match, and waited for the wax to liquefy. Not only did it liquefy, it exploded, the flames shooting up and biting at the low ceiling, the rags on the line, the cobwebs—and me! Retreating bug-eyed, I was in a panic as the acrid smoke belched forth and burned my eyes and throat. The cellar was like a bomb waiting to detonate. Somehow, I rushed to the deep sink next to the stove, turned on the water, grabbed an empty coffee can, partially filled it, and tossed the water at the same time. It doused the stove and the gas flame went out, so I quickly turned off the lever. The wax continued to spit and burn, so I frantically flooded it with more water, hoping and praying that if I got out of this, I wouldn't ever do anything as stupid again. Thank God, it finally went out. Luckily for me no one had been home, but I still had to get the smoke and stink out. After a frenzied clean-up and an innocent, artistic explanation when my parents came home from shopping, I got away with it. It was one of my best early performances.

By the end of 1937 the soup kitchen lines were just as long, and the "Pennies from Heaven" weren't falling. My father, struggling with his constant obligations, had to give up the rented house in the suburbs, but he kept paying all the other bills and never complained. (My sister Fay was already married to Phil Kuntz, a painting contractor, and was living in her own home; and so was Harry, with his wife, Faye, and running a pharmacy.) Pop knew Gert needed the time and attention Jack gave her—that her mother was incapable of. Without an attendant nurse, it was considerable. It was decided and quietly accepted that Gert and Jack should move into a newly papered room on the third floor of the house above the store; although, if she chose to, she could spend the day on the second floor in a pleasant room with pale yellow, flowered walls. I remember the look and feel of that room as if it were yesterday. I spent hours sitting and talking with my sister, giggling and laughing, listening avidly to all the popular radio programs of the time: *Fibber McGee and Molly*, Edgar Bergen and Charlie McCarthy, Jack Benny, and the ever-scary *Lights Out!* She was so thoughtful and considerate of her little brother, who was thirteen years younger; helping him with his homework, eager to see his art work, nurturing his talent, and never a harsh word. She was the purest, sweetest, and kindest person I have ever known. Sometimes my mother would stick her head in the doorway and silently motion for me to leave and sometimes not so silently. She was extremely concerned that I would get the disease and I couldn't blame her for that, but I resisted and remained reluctant to stay away. This whole situation was so worrisome for her, it multiplied her unhappiness. Thankfully, I never had an active case, but many years later when a lung x-ray was taken, I was surprised when the doctor showed me a couple of calcified black spots, indicating my body had healed itself from an infection.

Growing Up

IN 1940, WHEN THE WORLD was on the verge of going to hell, my father, in a peculiar move, took over the shaky management (no rent payments) of a large beer hall called The Garden Cafe a couple of doors away from where we lived. I will never forget the time I was with Pop at the bar when the bartender brought a huge bowl of beer out to the street as a parade for "Two-Ton" Tony Galento passed by. He slobbered the beer down sitting atop an open car as everybody cheered, except his furious manager. Regardless, on the next night September 15, 1939, he butchered Lou Nova in fourteen rounds. Pop owned the building and had failed there in previous ventures with misguided attempts at a miniature golf course and a Tucker car dealership. It was inevitable that he would miscarry in his latest effort on the same premises.

Richman's Café at 1621 East Passyunk Avenue in South Philadelphia was a place with a long bar in the front and all the usual beer guzzlers standing with one foot on the pipe railing—Schlitz, Budweiser, and Erlanger beers signs boldly blaring their message; in the rear, the night club with the aproned singing waiters—Lonnie Little, a favorite with a high-pitched tenor voice singing Italian melodies with tenderness; a five-piece band (Ruby Star and his electric guitar), and enough red-checkered tables to seat a small army of drinking patrons. In the evening Dave was the sandwich maker with an assistant before he went into the Army—no dinners, just sandwiches, salads, beer and booze. On the weekends, two sparsely clad female dancers would do their thing. I wasn't allowed to attend, of course, but I did paint Ruby Star's bandstands and designed a colorful R/S logo with gold sprinkles on the letters that pleased my father. Oddly, the rear of the cafe and the back of our house almost touched across an alley; and the female dancers' dressing room had a steel door that faced our kitchen window and was always open in the summertime.

It didn't take me long to discover that fact; at thirteen my curiosity and hormones were running rampant. I watched them undress to the barest, and fan themselves in the oppressive heat. One night as I was leering in the darkness I heard someone coming and had no time to switch on the kitchen light—so I grabbed a chair, jumped onto it and quickly opened a cabinet. Dave walked in and snapped on the light, surprised to find me on a chair in the darkness. "What the hell are you doing in the dark?" he asked.

"Looking for a glass," I said, trapped. Well, that was a laugh for a long time.

Sometimes I would mosey into the cafe and when the band wasn't playing I would change the records for dancing—"I'll Never Smile Again," sung by The Ink Spots was a particular favorite. To this day I can still clearly hear that recording in my head.

My sister Gert got all dressed up once and came down with Jack to the smoke-filled club to see the waiters parade around with their trays of beer, singing the latest pop songs and Italian favorites. My concerned father sat beside her and took her hand.

"Gert... you shouldn't be in here... the air isn't healthy."

"Pop," she answered, "if I can't enjoy myself once in a while... what's the point in living?" Tears flooded his eyes. I guess God heard her plea. Soon after she developed pleurisy, a major inflammation around the lungs, and had to go back to the sanitarium for special treatment. She looked so beautiful in a black, crepe dress with a small white collar as I hugged her and said goodbye. She stepped into Pop's old Hudson and as soon as I closed the door, Jack put it in gear and drove away. She smiled and waved. It was the last time I ever saw her. One month later, March 1941, she had a massive hemorrhage and died. All through the years I often think of her with longing. How much richer our lives would have been with her magnificent presence. I'm grateful for her vividness in my remembrance, and will never forget her and what she has meant to me. The death of Gertrude was devastating to us all; to Jack, of course, who just seemed to fade away out of our lives. My father, overwhelmed and unable to accept the loss of his precious daughter, totally neglected his health and his financially teetering cafe. Everybody was stealing him blind; the bartenders were notorious crooks and so were the waiters—pocketing most of the cash. By the time Dave went into the Army, leaving no one to watch the store, so to speak—it was a disaster. Pop had lost the desire for enterprise and finally closed it down. Strangely enough, he rented the property to the same guy who had bombed with The Garden Cafe! Now the place was a furniture store where the highly-waxed dance floor displayed mattresses and double beds.

Our lives were in chaos—and so was the world. At the end of the year the Japanese bombed Pearl Harbor and America was at war.

I was growing up fast and gaining some bulk. The next thing I knew I was a freshman at South Philadelphia High in 1942 and a starting halfback on the varsity football team. I was an art major too, and had a teacher who said to me once during football season, "You're talented, Richman, I like your work… but you don't work hard enough!" I'm sure he didn't know that football was all I ever thought about—all the time. It was more than an obsession, although I still continued to paint and draw, and was active on the yearbook art staff. I even ink-sketched a whole series of football players in action for the team's publicity release. I also had an English teacher, a Mrs. Swoyer, a lovely woman who thought I had a good voice. She asked me to audition at WCAU and WIP for the dramatic civic radio programs popular at the time about William Penn and Ben Franklin. I soon became a regular doing two or three different voices on each show. Radio was big stuff—television hadn't been born. The acting bug was quietly nibbling at me.

My brother Dave, now married (I was Best Man at his wedding), was drafted into the army and sent to Alaska for two years to build the Alaskan highway. He came home in 1943 for a couple of weeks on emergency family leave after my father died. He looked terrific in his uniform, all trimmed down, and I was so happy to see him, to hug him and feel the warmth of his handsome face against my cheek. It was a great to be together. Terribly sad, but bonding. I told him everything that happened on that awful day and how it all evolved. I remembered how I kept looking at my father in the late afternoon in front of our store—he was just standing there on the sidewalk near the curb, smoking a cigar, his arms folded. He seemed deep in thought, hardly moving. I was inside the house and couldn't be seen, but for some reason I kept staring at him, as if I were taking a long, last look, implanting his memory. Pop had been ill on several occasions, a neglectful diabetic who refused medication— totally at wits end with his disturbed wife and the death of Gertrude. I don't think he wanted to live anymore and certainly made no effort to care for himself. That night, he had been found somewhere in a faint, sickened condition—possibly a mild heart attack—vomiting and weak, and brought home by my uncle, Hyman, my father's brother. Harry, the pharmacist, had come to the house to assist in his care and had brought amyl nitrate capsules to snap under his nose if he fainted again. It was about 1:30 a.m. and it was my turn to sit with Pop as he tried to fall asleep in Gert's old flowered room next to the master bedroom.

"Go to sleep, son…"

"I'm fine, Pop," I said. "I'll just sit here with you for a while."

Then he sat up and tried to get out of bed—and as he did he fell over. I caught him just as he toppled and laid him back down on the bed, gently placing his head on the pillow. I was shocked to see that his eyes were open, his blue eyes staring at me, vacantly. Fearing the worst, I quickly grabbed the capsules and snapped one under his nose to revive him. Nothing happened. I snapped another to no avail. "Pop… please wake up! Please!" I said, knowing in my heart he was dead. I closed his eyes with my fingers. I must have seen someone do that in a movie. Harry, exhausted from concern for his father, was asleep downstairs on the living room couch. He went goofy when I told him what had happened. It was a frantic and highly emotional time. I remember running uselessly down the street to some doctor's house whose address I wasn't sure of and finally ringing the doorbell—knowing full well that nothing could be done. Why we didn't have his phone number I will never know, but that is only a minor mystery. My mother, during all of this, behaved abominably. She even resented bringing my father the pillow he usually slept on, finding an old pillow from somewhere else instead. She was no help whatsoever—and whatever she half-heartedly did, she could be heard mumbling something hurtful as she went about doing it—never expressing one bit of sorrow.

The death certificate listed his demise as coronary thrombosis. He was only 56. It was March 1943, two years after Gert. I was sixteen years old. A boy needs a father and I didn't have one anymore. I loved him deeply—a kind, generous and good man who died and left a cavern of emptiness in my life. He was a man who lived to help his children in any way he could. A man loved by all: Italians, Jews, African-Americans, he had everyone's respect. When I was very young I sometimes would go with him to collect rent on some broken-down houses he owned in a very poor North Philadelphia African-American section. Two dollars a month—$1 a week—or whatever they had, my father smiled and said, "Thank you." If they had nothing, he'd say, "That's all right… I'll see you next time." A gentle landlord with a big heart, that Benny Richman—everybody loved him—except his wife. It was a tragic story and I lived through it—torn between loyalty to two parents, both of whom I loved, but differently.

My only regret when Dave was home was that he never got to see me play football, and in 1943 I was an established member of a pretty good high school team. I was also co-captain with a fabulous tackle by the name of John Sandusky who later became a great pro for the Cleveland Browns. The innovative first year coach, Joe Pitts, a terrific guy, created a new system for us—a fabulous, modified T-Formation that drove opposing teams bonkers with all the options in our game. I was not a fancy runner (we had one), but a hard-driving, reckless fullback at 182 pounds, playing sixty minutes on offense and defense; a linebacker, a short yardage pounder, a good passer and a punter. I took so much punishment they called me the Kotex Kid for wearing taped Kotex padding on my gimpy knees—sponge rubber was not available in abundance in those days. Eli Korn, our team doctor who had a practice directly across the street from South Philly High, would drain my right knee of excess fluid when necessary to alleviate the swelling. His office became a team hangout. He was a wildly dedicated sports enthusiast who loved his Rams (team logo) and sometimes forgot that he was no longer in high school. He would write a doctor's prescription excusing us from class for treatment, and then discuss strategy for the next game on the schedule. I don't think I ever saw the inside of a French or chemistry class the whole football season. A couple of us swiped his prescription pads from his desk and would scribble our own official prescription with the words, in my case: "Please excuse M. Richman from class for treatment on…" For some reason only the gods know, we never got caught.

One day after spring training in 1944, the coach came to me and asked if I would like to go to Camp Happy for the summer, a city recreational camp on the outskirts of Philadelphia. I would be a counselor to underprivileged children who would come there for three weeks at a time. In nine weeks, there would be three different groups. Some of my teammates and other high school athletes would be there also; I would have the opportunity of working out, getting prepared and in shape for the coming fall football season, which had the potential to be a great one for us. Sounded good to me, so when the time came I took the long trolley ride to the end of nowhere and finally got to a dump called Camp Happy. It was a run-down, neglected conglomeration of dilapidated buildings and weedy grounds—a section for the boys and an equal mess for the girls.

Philadelphia at the time was a politically corrupt place with all major improvements put in continual, rathole abeyance. It was not a surprise to find Camp Happy reflective of the city. All the workers and the commissary servers were derelicts from county prison working off their sentences with "good" time; not the most elevating personnel for children to be exposed to. I remember this bored, little squirt of a man, Mayor Samuels, coming to camp for a flag raising one morning, and my civic-minded thinking at the time: Why doesn't this jerk do something to improve this place… doesn't he see? He's the mayor, for God's sake! One incident is still vivid in my remembrance. We were having dinner in the counselor's dining room one evening and we were all chatting away, enjoying ourselves and our company, when I looked down at my gravied roast beef, about to take a bite, and I noticed to my shocked amazement—it was unmistakably moving! Not to wonder, it was full of maggots. Needless to say, we were all outraged and protests were expressed to the camp manager, another political ass kisser. Aside from all the negatives at Camp Happy, we did get into fairly good shape, and it was a valuable learning experience. The kids coming to camp were excited, fun to be with and grateful, especially the African-American children who were the poorest of the lot.

At the end of that summer in my senior year when I was seventeen, we had a potent and powerful team. Next to the "Phillies" and the "Eagles," we were the talk of a "sports-nutty" town. I now weighed 187 pounds, had developing muscles and a thicker neck. We were confident and undefeated when we ran onto the University of Pennsylvania's Franklin Field for the public high championship game; we were in all black uniforms for the first time—and we looked scary. I don't know whether the coach, Joe Pitts, psychologically spooked Northeast High as part of the game plan, but we won, 18–6. I scored two touchdowns and got a fractured nose trying to block an extra point. After a few minutes, with blood-stopping cotton stuffed up my nostrils, I wore a nose guard for the first time and returned to the game. The following week we won the city championship of 1944 in a tumultuous victory over a tough West Catholic, 13–7. It was the first city championship the team had won in twenty-eight years, and I was the captain. The press called me "The Battering Ram" fullback. All of South Philadelphia went nuts. It was a thrilling and unforgettable high and has always been tough to top in anything I have ever done since, including show business.

I am reminded of an incident that happened when I was about twelve years old. In the neighborhood, on narrow streets, touch football was a game we heatedly played all the time, except we couldn't afford a football, so it was played with a tightly rolled newspaper tied with string.

We were wild and crazy kids, usually eight on a side, calling on-the-spot plays and running to score past parked cars and trash cans—or catching a floater while avoiding the telephone pole. I got along fine with most of the players who were all Italian, but one—a tall, wise-ass named Facio who was making it a habit to pick on me, the only Jewish kid in the whole Italian neighborhood where we lived. He seemed to relish saying snide things to get a laugh, like: "Your mother's a Jew, too… right Jew-boy?" Or, "You Jew sonofabitch," or the standard: "You're a mocky-Jew shit!"

This went on for weeks. I wasn't looking for a fight, but it was eating the hell out of me. He was really obnoxious, older and bigger than I was and persistent in his taunting; and since I just took it he kept doing it. One day after I had scored to win the game, he again said something awful and I quietly responded. "Facio," I said, "don't keep saying those things to me anymore… I don't like it."

He walked up to my nose and said, "Fuck you, Jew shit… what are you gonna do about it?" He had topped my limits. Without even thinking, I hauled off and hit him in the face with all of my pent-up rage. He went down like a fizzling balloon, his nose erupting with blood, and then he ran into his house, crying.

Suddenly, his fat mother came running out swinging a broom at my head, "You bastia! You bastia! Looka-whata you-doa to my son! You bastia, sonumabitch!"

I moved away, defending myself and yelling, "He started it… not me!"

I laughed—for the first time in my life I felt empowered and respected by my playmates. I believe it was this occurrence that enlightened me and gave me confidence that from then on I didn't have to take crap from anybody—and I never did—a precursor to my future football exploits.

True to his word, Dr. Korn fulfilled his promise of taking the starting championship team to a whorehouse if we captured the city title. I don't know if it was an incentive for victory, but we wasted no time in bugging him for completion of the deal. He had, shall I say, a special relationship with the madam, since he was the doctor who cared for all of the prostitutes' medical needs. I suppose, of course, that he was able to receive a group rate. I remember sitting uneasily in the living room of an unobtrusive house on a leafy street somewhere in West Philly, waiting my turn. I actually said, boldly, to this statuesque, Venus-like madam, the classic words echoed in a hundred stories and films I've seen since: "Uh… how did a beautiful girl like you ever get involved in a situation like this?" She smiled and answered the way you would expect: "Honey… there's only one thing I know how to do and do well…"

The Navy

MANY COLLEGE SCOUTS HAD SEEN me play and were talking me up to their coaches as a scholarship possibility. The only problem preventing their commitment was that I was approaching the age of eighteen. If and when I was drafted, they wouldn't have my services. I accepted that. I had no other choice. Everybody was making enormous sacrifices and football didn't seem that important in the scheme of things—the war was raging.

After the horrendous invasion at Normandy, Dave was sent to Europe and was fighting somewhere near Germany. Once in a while I would get a letter and a snapshot of him posing in front of some burned-out building. It was frightening to think that he was in the thick of it and might not make it home. A few months after I graduated, still seventeen and unable to picture myself with a rifle on my shoulder and lugging a pack on my back, I enlisted in the Navy. Clean living on a ship appealed to me. I never told anyone I was leaving, and when I got to the bus terminal for pick-up, heading to boot camp in Samson, New York—there stood my sister, Fay. I was surprised.

"How can you do this without telling anyone?" she said, embracing me. "What's the matter with you?"

"I didn't think anybody cared," I said, feeling sorry for myself. "I care…" she said, opening her bag for a handkerchief.

"How did you find out?" I mumbled, regretting not calling her. "Never mind," she said, tears in her light blue eyes. "I love you. I'm glad I caught you before you left…" "So am I…"

We sat and talked and held hands until I had to get on the bus.

My experience in boot camp was somewhat peculiar and disjointed. Although everything was going well as I adapted to the rigors of Navy life, instead of finishing up with my division after nine weeks of intensively hard training, I was one of several hundred sailors who contracted scarlet fever in an epidemic. On orders, the idiocy of standing in a downpour for forty-five minutes waiting for an entourage of late performers to arrive and entertain us, then sitting in soaking wet uniforms during the show was probably the culprit. Whatever caused it, I was sick as hell. After three weeks in the hospital with a sore penicillin-jabbed rear, I had to start all over again for the required ten weeks with a new division—not a stimulus for enthusiasm. Our new chief petty officer, McNerney, a hulking bear of man, was in charge and called us all shitheads. He told us in no uncertain terms that we would be the first wave in the invasion of Japan. "This is serious stuff," he shouted, "and if anyone of you shitheads don't think so, there's an empty space where your stupid brain should be!"

My first naval assignment after boot camp had me placed in a deck division on the light cruiser, USS-some-state-or-other. I was a first loader on a five-inch gun (translation: huge cannon). My job was to insert a fifty-five-pound projectile into the breech many times a minute in firing exercises while we were out at sea in General Quarters (battle stations). After several days of rigorous bending over and lifting the projectiles, I suddenly discovered I had a pain and a lump in my groin area. I saw the ship's doctor, and when we pulled into Newport, Rhode Island Naval base, before I could say: Hold on a second… do I have a choice? I found myself in surgery for a hernia operation.

During the lengthy procedure, the anesthesia wore off from the spinal and I started to wiggle my toes. I'll never forget the warm and considerate officer-surgeon's remarks when I mentioned the pain: "We can't give you anymore anesthesia, son… but don't worry, we'll be finished soon." I bit my lip and rolled my eyes at the nurse as she wiped my forehead. One of the most unbelievable, unexpected moments happened while I was recovering in the hospital ward. I was just lying there half asleep on the pillow, and as I turned my head I thought I saw my mother in the distance lumbering toward me in her slow, rocking arthritic gait. *It can't be!* I said to myself. I carefully raised myself on one elbow and took another look. Sure enough it was my mother. How she ever got there by herself is another mystery that will never be solved. It took several trolley cars and train changes in Philadelphia, then in New York she had to go from Penn Station to Grand Central, then a change in New Haven, a change in Providence and last, a long bus ride to Newport. Hours and hours of travel under wartime conditions, with a box of cookies under her arm. Although she read the Jewish newspapers, for a woman who never traveled and couldn't even read English to help her on the way—that was something. She kissed me and gave me the cookies she had baked, and twenty minutes later, with watering eyes she said goodbye. She walked slowly down the hall and was gone. My mother's love was unpredictable and erratic, but she was my mother. In that moment in time, I appreciated her remarkable thoughtfulness and pursuit. I still do.

During all of this chaos and training, I somehow found the time to sketch and paint watercolors. Sailors were good subjects, patient and respectful, and they always got a big charge out of seeing themselves in the completed work. At one point, I put up a small sign announcing: SKETCHES TO SEND HOME, $2. SEE RICHMAN. One enterprising fella came to me and asked if I could draw an aircraft carrier for $2. Of course, I said yes. He had the drawing reproduced on stationery paper and sold a pack of twenty-five sheets for $5. He did okay. It was my first personal taste of commercial art.

The war in Europe ended in May 1945. After some elated weekend liberty and getting slightly bombed in some forgotten town, I was promptly shipped off to a naval base in Dam Neck, Virginia Beach, for some specialized training in fire control that involved radar and the firing of revolving gun turrets aboard ship. It was an interesting experience and I did find pleasure in traveling to different naval destinations. Following this lengthy exercise, I was sent back to Providence and ship's pool, (unassigned), to await my next designation. Frankly, however, as a seaman second class, after months of all kinds of smatterings of unabsorbed knowledge, the one thing I felt truthfully most qualified for was swabbing the deck and chipping paint. I guess my mind wasn't in it. I was thinking— or should I say dreaming—about football, beautiful women, painting pictures, and the possibility of radio in my future. Going to college was my wish, but in what capacity? Was football the ticket? Could I make it on a college team? I would have the GI Bill, but doing what and where? The days and weeks groaned by. I was in the Navy and the Navy fills your time—not always to your liking—classes and more classes, marching and running, calisthenics, and the ever-reliable guard duty. I liked getting mail, any kind of mail, and there wasn't much personal stuff coming, so I wrote a lot of letters to paint companies for sample tubes of paint and to art and acting schools for brochures. I even enrolled in a correspondence course that taught artful lettering. All the guys were very impressed at mail call when my name was repeatedly shouted. One day I was sitting at my locker in the barracks writing another letter when a sailor came in and yelled—I will never forget the moment—THE JAPANESE HAVE SURRENDERED! THE WAR IS OVER! Everybody went crazy. We were jumping up and down, hugging each other with joyous fervor and excitement that I had only seen at a victorious football game, but at such a momentous occasion as this the joy was much deeper. We knew now that none of us would have to die on a beach in Japan. It was August 15, 1945. I had a weekend liberty coming up, and there was so much confusion, happiness, and goodwill at the base, I had the illicit hankering to extend my free time. I was still in ship's pool and the discipline less restrictive, so in light of our nation's glorious victory I decided to go A.W.O.L. (away without official leave). I took off for Atlantic City from Providence, making connections to the New Jersey Shore Line. The trains were packed with servicemen. It was a time like no other and I wanted to savor every moment.

The sun was shining, the air was salty crisp, the beach was glowing, and beautiful girls were abundant and smiling. Near the Chelsea Hotel I met friends and relatives whom I hadn't seen in years. Everybody was pleased to see me and told me how well I looked. I even ran into an old girlfriend I had known in high school, giving me a slight heart tug. I swam in the ocean, played tag football, carved a face in the sand, and in the evening walked the boardwalk with a sun-lacquered beauty on my sailored arm. The war was over and everything for me was as smooth as silk. I couldn't make a decision about my return. I was taking advantage of the times and hopefully the good will of Uncle Sam when I got back. Days extended to over a week and I began to feel the butterflies tickling. My bravura was weakening. I could be thrown in the brig and discharged dishonorably and I certainly didn't want that. I finally made up my mind to go back. As luck would have it, or whatever you want to call it—maybe the angels looking out for me—when I returned to the base, nobody even knew I was gone! My name had not appeared on any billet sheet. I was ecstatic and thankful for the minor miracle.

My next assignment aboard ship was a miserable training voyage in the north Atlantic on the USS Randolf, a war-damaged flagship aircraft carrier just returned, unrepaired, from Okinawa. It had a 15-degree port list, which means it tilted to the left and made it somewhat difficult to get around easily. We hit a major storm while under way, and now it was like trying to stand up on a roller-coaster. Many of the heads (toilets) were inoperable from extensive bombings, so a dreadful stink permeated the tight passageways. I was on duty way down below in a magazine (ammunition) compartment, the ship pitching side to side, the air as hot and as close as a tomb. I thought if I didn't get some air quickly—I was so nauseated—my stomach and intestines would alter the design of the bulkhead. With permission to go topside I somehow made my way to the catwalk below the flight deck, and threw up everything, including last week's lunch. It was freezing cold and I held on for dear life as the ship rocked and rumbled wildly as the waves smashed against the side. I was soaked and scared. It was the roughest ocean I had ever seen, and I found out later that we had lost two men overboard. They were never found. The aircraft carrier experience aboard the Randolf was a preparation for things to come. When I got back to the base in Providence, I was given my new departure date and destination. I would be traveling on a naval train going south to Pensacola, Florida, to pick up my new ship, the USS Ranger, the oldest aircraft carrier afloat. It had seen a lot of action but now it was only being used to train pilots in their initial carrier landings. I thought, hopefully, that since I had spent so much time taking classes in big gun operation and maintenance, radar and fire control school, that I would be placed in the corresponding division. Wrong! I was randomly stuck in the deck division, the last place I wanted to be—and their job was to maintain the mop and swab integrity of the ship, with chipping and painting thrown in. The deck division also did all the menial jobs that needed to be done, like hauling 100 lb. flour bags from the storage deck to the cook. I was depressed to say the least. The only thing positive turned out to be the watch I was required to serve—four hours on and eight hours off—and that was putting my inexperienced hands on the brass wheel to steer the carrier! Of course, I had to be trained to function as a helmsman. You would think that would be achieved in the best possible way. Wrong again. To train me, they assigned me to another young idiot with only three weeks of experience. That's the way it was: learn by doing and not always well. Just think: I am high up on the bridge, looking down on the flight deck, my frozen hands on the wheel. We are underway, over two thousand men aboard a massive carrier unaware that li'l ole me is trying to absorb how to read bearings and headings, without which you cannot steer a steady course. The ridiculous part of this story is that in a few weeks, after I had mastered the art of steering the carrier, ha!... there I was teaching another young moron the same routine. Unfortunately, it almost led to disaster. It was about two in morning, and I had to go relieve myself, so I asked my seaman student, whom I had been teaching for a couple of days, if he could handle the wheel alone for five minutes.

He nodded yes, and off I went. When I returned my heart said hello to my toes. The ship was swinging right! The moon was bright and I could see the flight deck lights moving closer to the destroyer escort about 200 yards away. A major sea collision was about to stupidly happen. I went into a panic mode, grabbed the wheel from the other idiot, and turned it violently opposite to the doom direction. I watched the lights swing left and the whole hulk of the ship, all twenty thousand tons, groan and tilt to the other side, as if in slow motion. It was frightening. Where the officer of the deck was during all of this I will never know, but that was the last time I ever tempted fate, leaving the bridge when I was in charge of the wheel. I have often wondered how we won the war. One cloudy morning about 1:30 a.m., underway, I was up on the bridge doing my wheel routine and maintaining a steady course, with the officer of the deck standing nearby, when we received a communication informing us of a problem. A freighter had a crewman who needed an emergency appendectomy. We would have to rendezvous at sea for a rescue and bring him to our surgeon. The captain (in his quarters), who is God personified on ship and rarely seen, gave the command to increase knot speed and we were on our way. The navigation officer gave me the new heading and I altered course. I was truly excited by the unexpected development, and the fact that I hadn't been replaced by an experienced helmsman. A couple of hours later, a rather small, fatherly type gentleman quietly entered the bridge. It was the captain, and I had never seen him before. I was so nervous I could hear my heart pumping loudly in my ears. "What's your course, son?" he asked.

I fumbled out the degrees on both dials and he altered them slightly. I repeated his commands as I adjusted the wheel with an accompanying "Yes sir!" When I had completed the change, he said, "Steady as you go, son."

God, I thought… *what a nice guy.* Here am I, a novice, steering a zillion-dollar aircraft carrier with forty or fifty multimillion dollar bombers aboard and thousands of men, and I'm being talked to by the captain like I really know what the hell I'm doing! I guess I do…

It was very quiet up on the bridge, just the monotonous drone of the engines, and in the Navy, you don't attempt small talk with the captain. About a half hour later as the moon broke through the clouds, I suddenly saw a ship way in the distance. It was sideways and we were heading directly for it and if we didn't alter course we would crash into it amidships. I didn't say anything, I figured somebody must be on lookout and didn't need my measly help. However, we kept getting closer and closer and we were moving at a very rapid clip for a huge ship. When we got within a few hundred yards I couldn't take it any longer. I said, "Sir... sir... I haven't done much of this before, but... we're gonna hit that ship!"

"Calm down, son," he said. "Everything is under control."

A few minutes later I heard him say, "Reduce engine speed!" Then there was the corresponding "Engine speed reduced, sir!"

And I thought: *Jesus, we can't be more than 200 hundred yards away and that's too close!* Some more nerve-racking time ticked by and I was sweating, when suddenly the captain said, "Reverse engines!" The officer next to me said, "Yes sir!" then into the phones he repeated the command "REVERSE ENGINES!" There was a roaring sound and an immediate change in dynamics. It was like running down hill and trying to immediately stop. I buckled over the wheel. "ENGINES REVERSED, SIR!" the officer blared. The rescue was completed without a hitch.

Something happened to me recently that was more astounding than this incident so many years ago. I was having lunch with Nancy Dussault during a rehearsal break. We were both appearing in a play in Los Angeles called *Next In Line*, adapted from a Ray Bradbury short story. We were talking about our life as kids and she said she had been a Navy brat. She had traveled a lot, and her father, a captain, had served on an aircraft carrier. My ears perked up and I asked, "Which one?" When she said the Ranger I nearly fell into my sushi. Her father was George Adrian Dussault, and he was the captain I had served under!

During the daily flight exercises I never had duty on the wheel. The old salts did that. Usually, I was on the phones assisting the flight crews in some capacity. We would leave Pensacola with a herd of newly trained young pilots from Corpus Christi air base who had never landed on a moving carrier before. We would be under way in the Gulf of Mexico near Guantanamo Bay with about forty planes aboard—SB2C Hell Divers and SNJ Trainers—when the siren for flight operations to begin would blare from the speakers. The pilots, anxiously waiting in their roaring planes, would be waved to take off one at a time, circle around, and fly in at a reduced speed to land on the flight deck. If the arresting gear missed catching the hook underneath the rear of the plane as it passed there were serious problems; more times than not the insecure pilots would miscalculate airspeed, miss the deck coming in too high, then suddenly pull up and zoom ahead for another go around; or tip their wings too far on a turn and hit the ocean and crash; or miss the tail-hooking arresting gear then bounce hazardously into the horizontal smoke stacks unique to the Ranger. It was hair-raising. One time I saw a Hell Diver hit the stacks on the port side and get stuck between them. I heard the captain angrily say to the salvage crew, "Godammit... dump it!" (pilot rescued— thousands of dollars in the drink). I got so used to the mishaps and the "Whuuup... whuuup... whuuup!" of the emergency signal on the loudspeaker that I hardly went to look. By the time we got back to Pensacola more than half the planes were damaged severely and one or two were lost. It was the nature of the operation. As soon as the carrier was replenished, we were back at sea to repeat the same process with a new class of eager, young pilots. This went on for months.

In my division, the first, there was a boatswain mate, first class, named Kenealy who was in charge, and he was a first-class sonofabitch— and we didn't get along. He was a tough, wiry twenty-year navy man as salty as the ocean. He didn't like enlistees and young men of intelligence. I sized him up the first day I arrived and knew I would have trouble. He was a picayune, anal personality—a scabrous navy man to his toenails. If there was a crappy, menial task to do, I was always on the crew to do it. However, now that the war was over, I was having the overwhelming feeling gnawing at me that screamed in my ear: *What the hell am I doing here?* And this guy's antics were getting stale.

I don't remember where I got the information, but I found out that you could now put in for an honorable discharge if there was a hardship in the family. Well, there was: my mother was alone and in need of assistance. When we got back to base I went to a naval administration office and filled out a form. My sleeping quarters were forward of the ship, just below the flight deck. It was pleasant there—fresh and breezy— the sky clear and very blue. I had finished my wheel watch at 2:00 a.m. and was still groggy after breakfast. As I polished my dress shoes, the dark cloud came to me with a smear on his face. "You better watch your ass, Richman," he said.

"I didn't know it needed watching," I answered. "Don't smart ass me, Richman... I'm warning you."

There was a long pause while I tried to figure him out. Finally, I said, "I know our relationship is... uh, a bit strained, but we could kiss and make up." I smiled.

Steam came out of his eyes and his tight, black moustache bristled. "Listen you civilian piece of shit, I'm going to put you on report for being a wiseass. Just because you put in for a discharge doesn't mean you're back where you came from! You're still here, and I won't let you forget it!" Then he turned and huffed away.

Wow! I thought… *Wow, news travels fast. I might be getting out of here!*

Hallelujah… Soon after this warning incident I was taken off the flight detail and glued into the chipping-painting routine full time. One such occurrence almost put me over the edge in more ways than one. The powers that be had decided that the enormous forward sides of the ship were in need of chipping and scraping. No time would be wasted. It was to be done while we were under way, even during flight operations, and who do you think was chosen to carry out this national necessity? Me, of course. There I was, all muscular nineteen years of me, in my work denims with a hammer and a heavy chisel, being lowered many feet down over the side in a Boatswains chair, the rolling sea snarling at me below. If you remember what a swing in a tree looks like, with a little seat, that's a Boatswains chair. There I was trying to carefully maintain myself, chipping away, when suddenly flight quarters was sounded; and the next thing I knew I was holding on to the lines for dear life as the planes took off and swooped down lower than the flight deck before zooming back up; the wind pressure banging and waving me around like a paper doll. I said to myself: *That sonofabitch is trying to kill me!* After about ten minutes more of this torture, I had had about as much as I could stand. I started yanking on the line to bring me up, my heart racing, my blood beyond the boiling point. Finally, on the catwalk, shaky and livid I found Kenealy and grabbed him by the shirt, my nose against his. "You tried to kill me," I said, "you weasel sonofabitch! I've had more of you than I can take!"

"Get your hands off me, you…." he flustered. "You're in trouble." "When we get ashore, you creepy shit bastard," I hissed, "you pick the place and I'll knock your fucking teeth out…"

Well, before I could sing "God Bless America," I was standing before a portly, first lieutenant with a scowl on his weathered face. He was reading an official document. Kenealy stood next to him. "Richman… it says here that you can be discharged in thirty days. You wouldn't want to jeopardize that, would you?"

"No, sir," I answered.

"Boatswain mate Kenealy says that you have been a troublemaker. Is that true, Richman?" "No, sir," I said.

"You put your hands on petty officer Kenealy and threatened him. I could throw you in the brig for six months. You wouldn't want that, would you?"

"No, sir," I said.

"Tell you what I'm going to do with you," he said after an endless pause. "From now on, 'til the day you leave this ship, you're to report to petty officer Kenealy here. Whenever you go on a work detail, to your wheel duty, or a smoke on the fantail… no matter what, all day long, even when you go to the head for a piss… you're to report first, without fail, to petty officer Kenealy. Understood?"

"Yes, sir," I said, relieved, but not looking forward to the degrading humiliation.

"If you don't do what I say, and I hear about one more infraction, no matter how minor, I will throw you in the brig faster than your eyes can blink."

Following this confrontation, in a peculiar way boatswain mate Kenealy became a bit more respectful and I was on my best behavior. In thirty days, I was sent to Bainbridge, Maryland, and unceremoniously received my ruptured duck (discharge).

 Discharged and Home Again

AT THE END OF MAY 1946, I came home without fanfare to the apartment above the furniture store that used to be my father's cafe. My mother had foolishly sold the other house on Passyunk Avenue for little money and we were now squeezed into this four room, second and third floor walk-up. I had a tiny room facing the roof. It had two windows, the frames rotting and in desperate need of putty and paint. The iron bed I slept on had a sagging mattress on exposed bouncy springs, giving me a constant sore back. The place was stifling, especially in the summer. Mom didn't know what she was doing. She just collected the rent on the furniture store below and couldn't care less that her son Harry held the mortgage on the building. Since he didn't speak to his mother, she never paid any monthly payments out of resentment—and probably wouldn't have anyway, even if they spoke. Of course, that was just another point of rankling contention in a very disturbing scenario. I recall going to the City Hall of Records later to find out about the property taxes that hadn't been paid for a long time—my mother being totally unaware of such things. A bespectacled old geezer brought out a huge, dusty book and leafed through the pages one by one and finally found the listed property. It was a scene from Dickens: the man, the book, and the musty basement of Philadelphia's City Hall. The furniture store property that used to be Richman's Cafe at 1621 E. Passyunk Avenue was still listed as a stable! It hadn't been reappraised since 1923! I didn't want to rock the boat—I thanked the man profusely for his courtesy and left quickly.

It's funny, but I don't remember anybody giving me a welcome home party, let alone a family get-together. They were all still estranged from one another. I did go to dinner at my sister Fay's home and it was caring and warm and equally so at the home of Harry and his wife, who had the same name as my sister but spelled it with an "e" at the end— Faye. Harry wasted no time getting right to the point: "So, what are you going to do with your life? You have to get an education… have you thought about it?"

"Sure, uh… well… I think I, uh… would like to, uh…." "Have you thought about pharmacy college?"

Jesus, that was the last thing I ever thought about! I said to myself: *Who in hell wants to stand around in a drug store lab wearing a white shirt with a stiff collar and a flowered tie, like you, making prescriptions for dyspepsia and diarrhea? I have better things I want to do! But I'm not sure what the hell they are yet.* Of course, I couldn't say those things to him, not now. He was only wanting the best for me, giving me sound advice about a solid profession, trying to be a surrogate father. The thought of spending my life behind the counter selling Kotex and toothpaste to mommy, while junior gets a marshmallow sundae at the soda fountain made me want to puke.

Dave, who was discharged before me, was back into the paperhanging business. One day he asked me if I would like to work with him doing some of the painting jobs he had been contracted for. I figured I could use the cash and it might be fun to work with my brother, with whom I hadn't really spent much time in years. Unfortunately, it was a drag— hard work and boring. After completing three homes, I was given the unenviable task of painting Harry's renovated living quarters above his pharmacy. I had no idea what I was letting myself in for. Harry was always so proper and formal about how a professional man should dress, so I tried for a little levity. However, he didn't find it amusing in the least when I arrived for work one morning in a T-shirt and wearing a tie around my neck. I smiled, but he didn't. It was a portent of what was to follow. Faye, who always made me wonderful dishes to eat and a baked almond cake to take home on occasion, was an attractive, sympathetic woman and a good listener. I adored her. She became an entirely different personality, however, when I was painting her French doors. One coat of paint was not enough. Two coats didn't cover properly—and why was I doing such a careless, lousy job? Sooo… I painted three coats of enamel on all the woodwork, feeling as if I was back on the Ranger hanging over the side. Then, as the fates would have it—frustrated and annoyed, and wanting to get out of there as soon as possible—I made the dreadful mistake of sloppily painting over some of her newly installed shiny, brass hardware. I thought that little mishap would send them off the plank, especially when I said I would quit. Of course, I didn't. I just gritted my teeth and did a meticulous clean up job, steel wool and all. They finally approved and were satisfied, and without hesitation I turned in my brushes and my overalls forever.

I began taking classes again at the Philadelphia Graphic Sketch Club. The feel of a piece of charcoal in my hands and a large sheet of toothy paper in front of me gave me a kick that I had missed. I must admit, it did take me awhile to assume a nonchalant casualness in the life classes when a lovely model disrobed. There were so many desires, creative and otherwise, floating around in my being, not the least of which was the impulse to pursue performing again; developing my speaking voice and getting rid of localisms; auditioning for acting parts on radio, maybe even for an announcer position at a small station. (I did that at WMID in Atlantic City and fumbled over Amadeus Mozart.) It was almost as if I were receiving a revelation, an epiphany of understanding from a higher power that my life should go in an artistic direction, veering from the norm and the conventional. It was so strong that I began sending out requests for brochures from acting schools all over the country. I began to read plays and books about theater. I happened to find Harold Clurman's *The Fervent Years*, about the Group Theater, and it lifted me off the chair, I was so enthralled. I identified with all the young actors in the book who had since become famous: John Garfield, Lee J. Cobb, Franchot Tone, Morris Carnovsky, and Luther and Stella Adler. (Years later I worked with, met, or was friends with all of them except Garfield. He died too soon.)

I had been in several stage productions as a kid, and then in junior high I had the lead in *Swing Fever*, playing a snappy, dancing lover-boy who gets the girl in the end. I was fourteen and this was a major production as a senior before going to South Philadelphia High. What I remember most was the fifteen year old absolutely knockout blonde who played opposite me in the show, whom I had to kiss on her teasing luscious lips—and some mutual extracurricular necking behind the curtain when no one was looking.

The acting desire was getting stronger so I bought a Webster wire recorder with a microphone that I would talk into for hours, altering my voice, then rewinding to play it back. I was intrigued by the sound of my voice and the subtle variations I could achieve. More times than not, the wire would get entangled and the reel would be ruined—sending me into a screaming fit. It was a problem Webster never solved and neither did I. Many times, I wanted to smash the instrument with a hammer.

I knew I had a certain instinctive, natural ability. Now, in the privacy of my room, I had this deep burning in my gut to express myself: to be somebody else, change voices, look at myself in the mirror, make faces, smiling then stern, turning this way and that, jutting my chin, shouting a command like a general—whimpering and pleading like a wounded animal, "Please, please… help me, don't let me die!"

My frightened mother yelled up from the second floor: "What are you doing up there? Is somebody up there with you?"

"No, Mom… it's okay. I'm just messin' around…"

The itch to play football again was still potent, and I was now bigger and stronger. Playing in college and getting an education, too, would be something to shoot for. I had gained quite a reputation as a good football player winning the city championship, so I was rather confident that I could get a scholarship under the right circumstances, even though a couple of years had gone by. Many of my teammates who hadn't gone into the service were now playing at major universities, like Duke and Tennessee. One day the phone rang and when I picked up there was a man talking with a heavy Southern accent. Thinking it was a gag of a friend, I hung up on him. He called back and asked why I had hung up—he wanted to offer me a possible scholarship to the University of Maryland. I apologized to the coach, Jim Tatum, and accepted his offer to visit the campus, all expenses paid. Off I went by train to College Park, Maryland, and an exciting few days working out with the team and getting a feel of college life in the fall of 1946. College football players were in demand, the war had diverted the flow, but being required to take business courses and economics put a damper on my easy acceptance. I remember the coach's raised eyebrows when I mentioned radio communications and theater. He said he would see what he could do. Of course, that would never work in those days. He was disappointed when I didn't matriculate. At least, that's what he said.

One afternoon I was up in my bedroom being Jack the Ripper when the doorbell rang. I reluctantly went down the two flights to see who it could be. A short, smiling guy smoking a cigarette stuck out his hand for a shake and introduced himself.

"Aaaay, kid… it's good to see you," he said. "I'm Bobby Myson. I liked the way you played at Southern High… you're a tough kid."

"Thanks," I said. "What can I do for you?"

"I'd like you to play for me… my team, Passyunk Square. We're gettin' organized for a whole season. First time since the war. Your old coach says he'd like to have you play for us."

I was puzzled. "My coach?" "Yeah, Joe Pitts."

"Uh… you mean… Joe Pitts is gonna coach for you?"

"That's what I said, kid… and he wants you. I'll pay you fifty bucks a game."

I couldn't fathom my football coach in high school agreeing to render his services to the Eastern Pro Conference. It was a semi-professional conglomeration of teams that I used to watch assiduously as a youngster, going back to the thirties. It is where I first acquired the passion for the game, watching teams like the Zuni Indians, the Chester Pros, and Conshohocken. It was really a bastard league a few notches below the NFL—a rough, wild and dangerous kind of play, with not enough practice and little conditioning. The teams had many excellent, experienced players with big names from colleges, many just cut from the major pro teams— but it was not a full-time job. This operation was strictly part time, the players making a living elsewhere. There were three practices a week and games were on Sunday. The National Football League was nothing like it is today. There was no TV and no Super Bowl. The look of sports was not the same as we're used to seeing now, with professional and college games slurping all over every TV channel. Consequently, the Eastern Pro Conference had a large following. Fifty dollars in 1946 was a lot of money, and with an additional twenty for fifty-two weeks, courtesy of Uncle Sam's discharge program, I was bulging in green. I played under an assumed name, a requirement if you still had the intention to play in college—and taking money dumped you out of the amateur class.

Here, I will make a painful confession. My real name is Marvin Richman, a name I've always hated. Even when someone from my ancient past thought they were endearing themselves to me by calling me by that name, I could feel my ears wiggle in disgust. It proved to me that children may suffer their whole lives with a name that doesn't reflect their true inner nature. That is a subject I promise to pursue later.

So, Marvin Rich (I wasn't fooling anybody; nor did anybody care) made his debut in the Easter Pro Conference and passed, ran, and punted adequately through a mediocre season. However, a lot of publicity was generated by a once moribund league of teams finding new life, especially the Battering Ram fullback reunited with his South Philly High School championship coach, Joe Pitts. When we first came out onto the field at historic Shibe Park, home of the Philadelphia Athletics, I remember standing on the fifty-yard line and looking up at the stands in awe. The feeling was overpowering—so many great baseball players had caught fly balls where I then stood. It's amazing how the mind chooses to remember specific moments. In one of the last games of the season, I scored the winning touchdown on a fancy twenty-yard run against the first place Shamrocks and kicked the extra point too. It was a highlight that garnered some additional attention for me. Josh Cody, coach of Temple University, requested my consideration to attend, and Dartmouth invited me up for a visit after our season ended. It was a trip I was honored to accept. On the train ride to White River Junction, Vermont, I had my own spacious bedroom… a real honest-to-goodness bedroom! Looking out my private window as the snow-touched trees drifted quickly by, I leaned back thinking: My God, can this really be happening to me? Or is it only a dream? If it is… don't want to wake up! On arrival, I was picked up by a very friendly Dick Cassiano, a legendary college backfield star at Pittsburgh who was an assistant coach. He took me to the prestigious Gridiron Club for a special luncheon. There were a lot of introductions and speeches, one in particular I remember by a former Dartmouth star who was horribly burned, facially, in the war as a fighter pilot. All the coaches were exceptionally warm to me and I felt surprisingly comfortable in their presence. Tuss McLaughry, the head coach, chatted with me and seemed pleased that I was there. Moreover, when I worked out with the team I felt right at home. I was thinking seriously that Dartmouth was a place I should consider; and wouldn't it be great to live in New Hampshire?

The coaches were more than serious about my becoming a Dartmouth College football player. They locked me in an office on campus for hours at a time—with a secret piece of paper in my pocket—and I sat copying the correct answers to all the questions asked on the ponderous entrance exam! And this at an Ivy League college! Shhh! Don't tell anybody. The highlight of my visit was the privilege of traveling with the team to see the Dartmouth–Princeton game on Thanksgiving weekend. Not only did I see the game, I sat on the bench with the players. I don't remember who won the game, but in the locker room afterward several players said they hoped to see me playing with them next season. Soon after I returned, I was invited by a Philadelphia athletic club to an evening honoring a sports legend. It was an event that I will never forget. I had seen him knock baseballs out of the Phillies ballpark when he was the manager of the Brooklyn Dodgers for a brief time. Prior to the game, he amused everyone by pointing to right field, and then, whack! And now, there on the dais was a shadow of the man called Babe Ruth. He had been diagnosed with throat cancer and, sadly, he croaked a short speech. I don't remember what he said, but when he got up to leave I followed him to the door as he put on his camelhair coat, tied his swagger belt, lifted his collar, and went out into the cold and windy night. I walked outside, too, and watched this bent over, knock-kneed giant of baseball disappear.

During all of this I was still trying to find myself and the direction my life should take, and my brother Harry was still on my neck about going to pharmacy college. He even convinced me that I had nothing to lose if he, as an alumnus, could get me into the freshman class in the fall of 1947. Of course, I would have to take refresher courses in chemistry and algebra and get my high school marks up. I finally acquiesced, thinking that by that time I would be playing football at some university and would have forever ditched the idea of being a pharmacist just to please my brother. Further complicating my situation was a rekindled love affair with a high school sometimes-sweetheart. She was a beautiful girl, blonde and sexy and we had some wonderful times together. The only glaring problem was that she was intent on getting married as soon as possible, and that to me, at my age, was like a sentence to be electrocuted. My life was just beginning; I couldn't turn it off before it started. Her father, a cab driver for years, had a little influence with the company—and I suddenly found myself driving a yellow cab wearing a cabbie's outfit, complete with a shiny, black peaked cap. Of course, for a while I enjoyed the extra change in my pocket, but there I was driving around the dark streets of Philadelphia on the night shift with too much time to think—and when I thought of her father and imagined myself down the road, the relationship was doomed. It was about this time that I met someone who suggested I call a particular producer at KYW, an NBC affiliate, to audition for the KYW Radio Playhouse. Nervously, I placed a call and spoke to a haughty gentleman with a British accent who said he had nothing for me, but to call him next week. The following week I called again and got the same routine. Finally, I lucked out. "I may have something for you," he said. In the late forties, radio was still a big deal. The KYW Playhouse was a long-running successful show that boasted a wide audience on the eastern network. The leading actors had been together for a long time. For me, a newcomer, just to take the elevator up to the third floor and step onto the polished marble floors was quite enough to get the heart pumping wildly—and then to stand in the studio before a microphone, waiting for the countdown to: On The Air!—and finally, waiting to get the cue to speak my few scripted lines—was hair-raising. Eventually, my anxiety diminished and the size of my roles expanded. The producer seemed to like what I did because he kept hiring me. I was a student, a cop, a delinquent, a salesman, and even a Texan, of sorts. Sometimes two voices on a half-hour show. I found out I had a facility to alter my voice quality with ease (the experience of the wire recorder silliness must have helped). The pay wasn't much by today's standards, but $10 a show was impressive when you thought of yourself as being a professional—and a new member of AFRA (American Federation of Radio Artists)—and having an agent who collected 10 percent of my $10!

At the end of December, Dick Cassiano of Dartmouth sent me a friendly letter requesting an alumni rating sheet. Apparently, I had passed the entrance exam with more than flying colors and who would wonder why? Everything was in order with the admissions office except the alumni sheet. He told me to get in touch with a particular alumnus in Philly who knew all about these things and would help me complete the arrangements. He told me also that once I was admitted I could go elsewhere if I changed my mind. For some reason, I never called the man nor did I meet coach Cassiano when he came into town with the wrestling team in January. I just didn't have the conviction in my heart that a college education in God-knows-what, via football, was the correct path for me. Complicating everything even more was this stirred-up theatrical turbulence I was going through. Imagine telling a football coach that you had a feeling that you wanted to go on the stage. "Really?" he would answer. "Well, darling… football is not for you!" Of course, I had the GI Bill and I could really go anywhere my little heart desired. I didn't have to suck around for a football scholarship, which was a gravy train for colleges who accepted GI athletes. They gave the scholarship and the little perks, but Uncle Sam paid the tuition. The matriculation business with Dartmouth just faded away and I didn't pine over it. In a way, I was relieved. Things were changing. My head was swirling with the abstract dream of a life in the theater and radio; but I wasn't sure I knew how to go about it. In my neighborhood and background, it wasn't something you talked about with ease. In this Italian-American community where I lived, people were mainly concerned about getting a job and making a living, and if you were lucky enough to go to college, you better learn something practical! I knew I was way out of the norm. There wasn't anybody in my family that I knew of from here to the planet Uranus who was an actor, but I just felt that I had to immerse myself in the activity of becoming one and not remain a spectator. Philadelphia was, and still is, a try-out town for new plays prior to Broadway. I went to the theater as often as I could, trying to absorb the atmosphere and the professionalism that would help develop my innate sense of critical observation. It was as if I were going to school on my own. I had a keen awareness, I thought, concerning who the quality actors were and why they kept me interested; as opposed to the superficial ones who had no believability and turned me off. I kept a little 5¢ notebook, recording every play I ever saw at the Forrest, the Erlanger, and the Walnut Street theaters—who was in the cast, the director, producer, and the set designer. I derived a private pleasure making my notes and watching the list of plays grow, no matter where the production was performed. I went to the community playhouses, the Bucks County Playhouse and the Hedgerow Theater in the suburbs that ran a repertory program with a group of fine actors. I even had the nerve to keep an appointment with Jasper Deeter, the managing director and producer of Hedgerow, intimating that I would like to be part of his acting company. (Mind you, I had really not done very much, nor had I appeared in a play since junior high.) He was very gracious and said that I could join his acting school, and maybe he could work it out with the GI Bill. It was very tempting, but when I said (hearing the voice of my brother Harry), "I may want to do something that has a little more security," he looked at me strangely and then answered with mild sarcasm, "If you want security… drive a truck. Don't become an actor."

At the time, going to college as a theater major seemed as remote to me as enlisting in the Marines. Playing football on scholarship at Palooka University as a theater major became even less of a possibility, so I made the decision to go to the Bessie V. Hicks School of Drama in town for a summer course on the GI Bill in 1947. It was one of the best decisions I ever made in my life. It was a place with a pretty good faculty where I became pointedly aware of speech, movement, and scene development—and not only that, it was fun. I enjoyed it and looked forward to going to the classes every day. These people had no idea that I had played football, getting mangled every week by 275-pound linemen, or getting my nose broken picking up three yards and a touchdown. I didn't tell them. I was an actor now, and in this group I seemed to excel in doing what was required, and I somehow impressed them with my naturalism and simplicity. Where it came from I had no idea. I just seemed to be able to do it more easily than most. The bug had bitten me deeply; the structured, daily routine seemed to accelerate the weeks slipping by. I knew crunch time was approaching.

We were a friendly bunch and a few of the relationships have lasted a lifetime. One young man in a pinstriped suit and dark glasses looked like a hood when I first met him. He was ill at ease, laconic, very quiet and serious, trying to absorb all he could about the acting thing. He told me his name was Charles Buchinsky when we went out for lunch at our favorite hangout, Horn and Hardart's Automat, where you could slip two nickels in a slot and get a sandwich. Years later he became a major movie star by the name of Charles Bronson. A former student, Jack Klugman, would come by to visit the classes on occasion, and that was where I first met one of my oldest and dearest friends, a warm and appreciative man my family and I always enjoyed being with.

I continued doing my radio performances on the KYW Playhouse and other shows, collecting my $10, but I made the mistake of telling my brother about that astronomical sum. He studied me momentarily as he made a prescription, his straight, dark hair meticulously combed, his rimless glasses reflecting a glare.

"For ten dollars, you'll become a bum," he said, scraping the mortar.

"That's a helluva thing to say… it's only a beginning."

"You have to get an education," he continued, wiping the pestle. "I'm getting an education now. It may not be pharmacy, but I'm serious about this acting thing as a possible career."

"Get a real education first," he said. "Something that nobody can take away from you. You'll thank me later. It's all set at P.C.P. (Philadelphia College of Pharmacy) for September. Don't be a damned fool and let it pass you by. It's important. You'll have plenty of time to be an actor later. You're still a kid."

I resented Harry's relentless and dogmatic approach to everything and, in particular, my situation. I loved him, but it was always tough to present another viewpoint to him. I attribute that to the fact that there wasn't one artistic cell to be found in his entire body. Truthfully, he was only trying to guide me to make the right decisions for my future. He knew the difficulties Dave was having since he came home from the army with a wife to support—no education and no job except settling within the limits of just being a paperhanger. Harry didn't want those uncertainties for me. A pharmacist was a professional man and could always make a good living, support a wife, and raise a family. I struggled, twisted, and turned my predicament over and over in my mind… and in my sleep. I couldn't find a moment of peace. Go to college and get a degree in pharmacy—or float around aimlessly dreaming to become an actor, but having nothing tangible to grasp.

The culmination of the summer's work was a full stage production of a one-act play called *Where 'Ere We Go*. I don't remember very much about it except it was presented at a lovely theater in Rittenhouse Square (a chic section of central Philadelphia), and I had a substantial role. I have a photograph taken on stage and I recall some of those faces when I told them I wasn't coming back in the fall but going to pharmacy college instead. Collectively, a surprised gape—mouth open, eyebrows raised. Charles Buchinsky said, "Are you kidding me?" And Frank London said, "No shit?"

A Reluctant Pharmacy Student
(and a Football Disaster)

DURING THE TIME I DROVE A CAB, since I had been a total goof-off in high school, I had enrolled in a refresher night school course in chemistry and algebra two nights a week to get my marks up. After the classes I hustled the taxi until 3:00 or 4:00 a.m. Now, as I sat in a chemistry lecture at the Philadelphia College of Pharmacy and Science, a freshman with four years to go, I looked around at my eager young classmates, and others—eager but older, very insecure veterans of the war. I felt like an alien sneaking across the border and I said to myself: *What in piss and hell am I doing here? Is this what I want to be doing the rest of my life... jamming my brain with the symbols of matter and chemical compounds? No, no, no, no, no! I don't!* All the classes had the same complex beginning, the professors droning on doggedly, slyly promising that once familiarity with the subject kicked in, the load would lighten. I didn't find that to be true at all. After a class in pharmaceutical calculations, my head felt as heavy as the U.S. Dispensatory (a huge book of all medical compounds) that had been issued to me at the college book store.

Then, as if I didn't have enough confusion and turmoil in my college life, I got a call from the head coach of the Shamrocks in the Eastern Pro Conference, a team I had played against the previous year. I had beaten them on a twenty-yard touchdown run, and now they wanted me to start at halfback for them. Of course, even as an overburdened pharmacy student who had closed the door on college football, I still couldn't get football out of my blood; it lingered there, festering actually, like a disease. I was flattered by the offer and the chance to play another season, so I foolishly and stupidly accepted, telling myself exactly what I wanted to hear: Why not, what's the difference? As sure as bananas rot… you're gonna flunk out anyway.

When my family found out I was playing again, they thought I was foolhardy beyond words, except for Dave, who thought it was great and looked forward to seeing me play. Harry was apoplectic. My mother was unaware, even though we lived together, except for the time I sported a purple-black eye and an oozing cut on my right cheek. She frowned as she looked at me and speaking in her light Yiddish accent she asked:

"What happened with your face?" "Nothing… I got into a fight…"

"A fight… it's all swollen," she said. "Why do you want to fight?" "Mom, it just happened… some guy tried to steal my books." "In pharmacy school… they steal books?" I was squirming.

"No, it was on the street… some guy. I mean, they sell them when they steal them. Oh, forget it… it doesn't mean anything."

That was the extent of our conversation. I was ill-equipped to explain football and pharmacy in the same breath. Getting into details with my mother was something I tried to avoid. Of course, she was happy that I would become a pharmacist. Then, when I opened my own pharmacy, she could visit and proudly sit down in her son's store and have a cherry soda… something she couldn't do with that other "sonofabitch" son!

I had to learn a completely new offensive and defensive system playing for the Shamrocks. Football is football, but methods and variations in carrying it out are extensive, and practicing three nights a week after having spent an exhaustive day studying logarithmic progression and the internal anatomy of the Rattus Norvegicus (white rat), I was goofy-eyed to say the least. Frankly, I don't know how I ever achieved getting through a season of games. My study time at college diminished, and some of my exam marks began to reflect it. Surprisingly, despite all the splitting up of my concentration, I wasn't that far behind. My exams showed that I was lousy in physics and algebra, two subjects that made my saliva feel like chewing gum. However, when I spoke to other veterans who were also stinko in those subjects, I perked up and began to think that with a bit more application, maybe I could do this pharmacy thing. The class that gave me a strong sense of accomplishment and good marks was zoology. I had the opportunity to use my artistic skills, making very detailed drawings of animals that I was required to dissect for study. From the rat to the turtle to the frog to the squalus acanthias (shark), I made a collection of sketches that the professor passed around as outstanding work. At the end of the semester, he asked me to donate the drawings to the college for study purposes. I selfishly refused. (Strangely enough, recently, fifty years later, after a southern California alumni meeting in Los Angeles with Philip Gerbino, the new president of the University of the Sciences in Philadelphia—my alma mater's new name—he asked me if I would donate all of my writings, study notes, and drawings—and I have, happily.) Tim Resnick, Richman, Sal Rinaldi, and Lou Rinovato, the alphabetical quartet, were in every class together—veterans on the GI Bill studying pharmacy. They were older and having a harder time than I grasping all the complicated material. We would jostle around and kibitz each other good naturedly, laughing a lot about our inadequacies. In the lecture hall, if a teacher was particularly boring or left us absolutely lost, we could be counted on to roll our eyes, making faces with clandestine mirth. We were a bunch of guys from vastly different backgrounds, relishing our unexpectedly warm camaraderie. Sitting next to one another in class or in the laboratories, I began to feel that maybe, just maybe, I was a participant in something important, truly sharing a learning relationship and getting a solid, professional education. To my surprise, I wasn't flunking out—I was getting by.

But now, as always in my life, we come to another fly in the ointment jar—or was it a cockroach? The football season was winding down, the Shamrocks were in first place, and we were playing the Zuni Indians. The weather had turned frosty, but there was sloppy mud all over the field from a recent rainy deluge. The players were slipping and falling helplessly, looking like prehistoric animals when they lifted themselves from the muck. Before the second half started, one of the coaches suggested that I put mud cleats on my shoes to give me better traction—a mistake. On an end run to the right, which I rarely ran, I took the toss from the quarterback in our modified T-formation and was fiercely clobbered. I think I was hit by every Indian this side of Zuni and the Navajos. My right leg stuck deep in the mud, the cleats firmly implanted and immovable— my right knee was pulverized. After the pile untangled, I tried to stand and couldn't; I had no functional right leg. It was a rubber band. I had to be carried off the field. I had no idea at the time how serious the injury was, but here is a quote from *The Philadelphia Inquirer* sports page:

"Shamrocks Team Loses Richman for 2 Weeks"

Marvin Richman, one of the club's best blockers and defensive men, is out of the fray with a severe leg injury received Sunday's game against the Zuni Indians. Richman, a former Southern High School athlete, suffered a torn ligament and has been advised to remain out of action for several weeks. Fred Golden, formerly of the Miami Seahawks will replace him.

The damage to my knee was extensive. I knew it was bad and the pain at times was excruciating. I had to get around on crutches, and it was not a fun deal lugging a load of books on my way to classes. After some pointed requests to the team to get the proper medical attention, I finally was sent to see an orthopedic specialist by the name of Dr. Irvin Stein. He had an impressive midtown office. On his desk was a large photo with a signature dedication to the doctor from Arturo Toscanini. I assumed he had operated on the maestro or was married to his daughter. I never asked. After a rather impersonal examination, he told me that I needed an operation to totally reconstruct the knee. Ligaments and cartilages were torn and it should be done as soon as possible. I told him I would have to wait for eight months until classes were over, otherwise, I would lose the year of study. He said he understood but didn't think it was a good idea because other complications could happen during the postponement. He gave me a brace to wear when I was off the crutches, and another prescription for my pain. I have a small pen and ink sketch in my old football scrapbook. It shows a pair of high-top football shoes strung up by the laces and hanging on a large nail. My football days were over. The swelling went down, the pain diminished and I finally could walk without the crutches. Not well, but at least I could get around with the brace holding me tight-legged and stiff. Classes continued, relentlessly, from 8:00 in the morning until 6:00 in the evening. The only new addition was an enterprising English teacher on this campus of potential druggists, who decided he wanted to put on a play and would give extra credit for performing in it. Of course, I volunteered. I also offered to do the makeup. The only problem was that with so little time and the performance date set, he couldn't get any other actors who could say lines and walk at the same time. Therefore, he decided that we would all read the words from a silver-foiled clipboard, pretending it was in the style of a famous Chinese acting company who read from scripts. (The only thing we knew about the Chinese was almond chicken and egg roll.) On the night of the performance, no one complained, but I had used too much black pencil liner on the actors' faces. Instead of looking Chinese, they all resembled a road map to Shangri-La. It didn't matter anyway because only about twelve people showed up and most of them left at intermission. We wound up talking to ourselves, giggling and burying our faces in the clipboards to hide our embarrassment.

I was short on money to function so I succumbed to becoming an apprentice pharmacist at Harry's pharmacy a couple of evenings a week. Actually, it was a glorified title for sales clerk. I sold all of the usual drug store items and occasionally assisted in making prescriptions. It did give me an opportunity to spend some quality time with my oldest brother who was 18 years my senior. He was a master prescription dispenser with all the knowledge and technique to compound any doctor's request with ease. Watching him orchestrate a mortar, a pestle, and a spatula with one hand and a functional stump on the other was a wonder to behold. He was an efficient taskmaster whose laboratory was his sanctuary, but he sometimes forgot that he was my brother. That continual oversight would really piss me off, but mostly, I submerged my irritation out of respect for his good intentions. For someone whose main interests were acting in the theater, playing football, and painting, how in God's name I ever survived the drudge of selling ex-lax, condoms, and bottles of Listerine is beyond my understanding.

The weeks and months passed like a creaky, old grindstone. My head always felt like it was going to fall off my shoulders. I would stay up all night studying until 4:00 and 5:00 a.m., trying to jam and cram the material into my weary brain that I knew would be in the exams. Falling asleep on the trolleys and nodding off in class was the price to be paid, but somehow I continued to show improvement and, lo and behold, I passed my freshman year. During the extended summer break, while my pharmacy buddies were expanding their professional opportunities working full time in labs and drug stores, I went in another direction. I had to get my leg fixed. Dr. Irvin Stein performed the operation at the Philadelphia General Hospital, an old institution that had seen better days when they signed the Declaration of Independence. I remember lying on my back after a spinal and seeing Dr. Stein waving this strange appendage around like it was a flag. I quickly realized it was my leg. Everything went successfully in the surgical reconstruction of my knee, but I was informed by the doctor later that all of my ligaments and cartilages had been torn; there was erosion of the femur condyle, and there were rice bodies (bone chips) floating around in the knee joint. To top it all off, I had developed an arthritis condition due to the long incorrected state. There would be a long recovery and rehabilitation period. I was back to the crutches full-time. The arrangements the Shamrocks had with the hospital must have been political and not financial, because I was bedded in the oppressive general ward, and that was a "delight" that I wouldn't wish on a prisoner of war. I had no private amenities. I remember vividly a sick old man who was dying in the bed next to mine. His son had come to visit him, and I watched as he slipped a couple of dollars into the male attendant's hands and said, "Please take care of my father… make him comfortable."

The attendant nodded as he accepted the money and then, when the son had left, I heard him say under his breath, "Yeah I'll take care of him… I'll give him some ground glass."

In an adjoining room close by, there was a young man who had been horribly burned all over his body. He was in a state of total decay, and the odor from that room was enough to change your hair color. It soon became obvious to me that the general ward was a place for the indigent and the helpless. It was a place that I had to get the hell out of as soon as possible. I thought to myself: *My God… what an awful hole the glorious game of football has dumped me in…*

My sister Fay came to my rescue soon after I was discharged. She took care of me during the recovery time and put me up quite comfortably in her suburban home in north Philadelphia. Her husband Phil and young daughter Elaine went out of their way to provide all the nursing care I needed and the family warmth I craved; and my sister's sincere concern and bubbling personality lifted my spirits. In a few weeks, I was getting around without crutches, a cumbersome leg brace reminding me to tread lightly. Soon after that, I was barefoot on the beach in Atlantic City, brace and all. The breeze was gentle, the sun was hot and so were the lovely females parading around in their skimpy attire. I still had a couple of months before classes began and I felt as if I were just let out of a cage, the clanging metal still echoing in my head.

In those days, Atlantic City was a place, whether on the beach or the boardwalk, where you would meet everyone you ever knew in Philadelphia. You just had to keep your eyes open and sooner or later there they were. Sure enough, I ran into Frank London, one of my actor-friends from the Bessie V. Hicks School of Drama. He told me he was working the Bingo games at the Million Dollar Pier and maybe he could get me a job there. I jumped at the chance and we set up a time to meet later. I showed up at Bingo in the evening, and Jack Klugman was on the microphone. "Number… twenty threeeee!" he said, his voice booming over the intent, hunched-over crowd. "Number… seventy twooooo!" Frank explained that they all took turns on the mike and then they walked around collecting money and handed out the numbered cards. Charles Buchinsky (Bronson) was up next and after him, Ed McMahon (who later became Johnny Carson's TV announcer). Frank chuckled and told me that Charlie loved to hear himself on the microphone, his deep voice reverberating with authority. He told me to hang around while he went to talk to the boss about me. I said okay and walked outside to watch the passing crowd. To me the boardwalk in Atlantic City was a marvel of its time. Just to stroll the boards and hear that unique shuffling-pounding sound of leather against wood was a thrill I will never forget. The peddlers selling their wares: "POSTCARDS! FIVE CENTS! GET 'EM… 3 for 10!" "FRALINGER'S SALT WATER TAFFY! TAKE HOME A BOX!" "TOMMY DORSEY NOW AT STEEL PIER… GET YOUR TICKETS HERE!" The smiling, sun-scorched gawkers taking it all in, hand-in-hand with their children and loved ones, pockets full of cash—it was vacation time!

My friends hawking Bingo were all making very good money, but unfortunately, I never got the opportunity. When Frank came back he had an unexpected frown on his face. I think they had a smooth operation going and were all doing so well, they were afraid that another hand might screw it up. I can still hear Charlie's breathy, deep resonance as I walked away: "Numberrrr… fortyeee niiiiine!"

I really wanted to be doing something else. Setting a task for yourself and completing it is always a tough road to follow, but I was determined that, no matter what, I would see it through. I rationalized that studying a profession I didn't wish to make my life's work would have gratifying rewards in the long run. For the most part, it has proven to be true. While in college my concentration was split right up the middle and I still cannot fathom how in heaven's name I was able to pull it off. Classes all day, generally from 8:00 until 6:00, sometimes later for lab work; working three nights a week at Harry's pharmacy; and finally, on my free nights or a weekend, squeezing in an acting workshop. Of course, during all of this juggling of hours, I had to find the time to really study. In a professional school, you cannot coast. Nobody ever said trying to be an actor was easy. In my case, it was ridiculous.

In the spring of 1949, I joined the Coach House Theater and played one of the leads, a naval officer in Noel Coward's family war drama *This Happy Breed*. It was a good part and a solid learning experience for me. I also learned how to be a little more selective in who I let myself be attracted to. There was this rather good-looking young married woman in the play who stirred me a bit. She always seemed to be flashing her eyes at me during rehearsals, so one night I finally asked her out for a late snack. She was pleasant enough and very charming, but at one point while we were having coffee, holding hands, and smiling a lot, she got a bit emotional about her fading marriage and reached into her bag for a cigarette. That was when a .38mm pistol plopped onto the table with a thud.

"Hello..." I said, shocked. "A friend of yours?"

"Not a friend," she answered, quickly returning it to her bag, "but someone I'm familiar with."

"Do you always carry that with you?"

"I really don't want to talk about it," she said with finality.

Later, when we said goodnight and she stepped into her cab, I heaved a sigh of relief. From then on, during the short run of the play, I was determined to keep my hormones under control. Shortly after, I did eight performances in a short period drama, *Tomorrow Is Important* at the historic Joseph Bonaparte House (named after Napoleon's brother who lived there after his exile from Spain). I was chalking up a continuity on stage that was so invigorating that I found myself getting involved with another local theater group called the Philadelphia Experimental Theater. They had their own small playhouse in the Rittenhouse Square area and produced new plays of variable merit, some passable and some downright ghastly. I did a couple in the ghastly category. My brother Dave and his wife, Shirley, came to see me in *Abou Hassan the Good*. I was all dolled up in dark makeup, earrings, pantaloons, and pointy shoes. When he came backstage to greet me, he called through the door:

"I want to see Abou... I want to see Abou!"

"Who is it?" I shouted.

"This is your brother, Peek-a-boo!" That sums up the evening.

Death of a Salesman was really the first great theater experience of my life. Just before the Broadway opening it played Philadelphia, and I took my sister Fay to see it. We sat in the balcony of the Forrest Theater absolutely overwhelmed by the words of a great playwright and the fabulous actors living them. When the curtain came down we both looked at each other with tears rolling down our cheeks. The acting of this play and the direction of Elia Kazan was so astounding and moving to me that I had a lump in my throat for an hour afterwards. I have never forgotten it. Years later when Lee J. Cobb and I became friends, I told him of my initial reaction to his work. He thanked me, sadly, knowing that all of his important stage appearances were behind him. Even when he recreated Willy Loman for a taped television production years later in which he was marvelous again and I called to congratulate him, he was depressed, feeling it hadn't come up to what he had done on the stage. There were about thirty years in between the two performances, but both were brilliant.

Latin American dancing, especially the Mambo, was the rage in the late forties and early fifties in Philadelphia and Atlantic City. Everybody in the party set, young and old, were seriously learning how to do the Mambo with all of its subtle variations. Leading this pack of devotees like a pied piper was a nutty and clownish band leader by the name of Pupi Campo. He was a sensation at the Latin Quarter in Philly and at the 500 Club in Atlantic City. One of the features of his show was a mambo dance lesson, participants eagerly jumping up from the audience to exhibit themselves and maybe take home a prize. The dance instructor was a vivacious and lovely professional named Penny Davis, who had a sparkle and a warmth that was endearing. We met at a soiree in somebody's home. Thus began a relationship that had my head spinning additional revolutions. To say that I got involved is to ask, what do you call a man, up to his nostrils in quicksand? When our relationship started out, I was quickly ankle-deep, and before too much time had elapsed, I was up to my waist and stuck. Penny was a tremendous personality with a tenacity and a pursuit to keep a young fellow on a silky leash. She seemed to know or have access to everyone who was in show business, at least in Philadelphia—radio personalities, press agents, producers, and phonies. For a wannabe actor it was enticing, and before I could resist even a little, I was off and running to her theater invitations, parties, dance recitals, and social gatherings. It was easy for Penny to open doors, and I was, in a way, stepping lightly through them just to see what would happen. She was a wonderful woman, intelligent, encouraging, gracious, and very loving— she only wanted me to love her. It was all so damned convenient. There was only one problem, and for me, it was insurmountable. She was thirty and I was twenty-two. Eight years is a lot of years to kiss off. I was just beginning to find a direction in my life, and she had already been there. I was always on the verge of breaking off and succeeded a couple of times, but I found our connection so habitual that I couldn't completely cut the string—there were strands always hanging. Then I suddenly assumed an unexpected responsibility.

When Penny opened a new charm school and dance studio in the center of town, I became the designer. I had my brother Dave paper the walls in a chic green and white striped pattern and had all the woodwork painted white. I helped design the school's brochure and the invitation for the opening. I even began assisting her as a dance partner in cotillions all over town, giving the spurious impression that I was a mambo dancer. Of course, she did most of the dancing and I just fooled around. The only thing I didn't do was move into her apartment. More times than not, I was very tempted. I was still tiptoeing up the stairs at 3:00 a.m. to my room on the second floor of a dreary row house in Strawberry Mansion, a section of Philadelphia in rapid decline. My mother had sold the Passyunk Street property, or rather, Harry had, and we were now situated in a place where the owner, an unpleasant man suffering from Parkinson's disease, lived on the first floor, and we resided on the second. Joyful, it was not. I remember one Sunday morning sleeping late after a strenuous night and restlessly turning over in bed. Suddenly, I felt like I was in an earthquake being tossed to the edge, as one leg of the bed crashed through a large knothole in the wooden floor and broke through the ceiling below, chunks of plaster falling into the owner's lentil soup. Screaming and hollering ensued, and it was the only time that I can recall a shaking and twittering man threatening me with a cane. "What-the-hell-are-you-doing-up there, you-sonofabitch... you-you-you broke my ceiling!" I felt sorry for the suffering old man, but I still felt like strangling the irritating bastard. My mother blamed me for the incident and no matter what I said to try to make her understand, it was useless. She still wanted to know why I moved the bed into the knothole. I nailed a piece of plywood over it so it wouldn't happen again.

With my heavy schedule—and Penny—I tried to dole out my time like a miser takes a coin from his pocketbook. Getting organized for the finals was my immediate concern. I decided that I would see Penny only on the weekend if I were free of other obligations. She pouted and said she understood. Victor Rossi and Elias Packman, two genius classmates, liked to study with me. In lectures, I would make illustrative notes and drawings that helped them in our sessions, and they in turn had all the answers to everything that I was shaky on. It was a solid symbiotic relationship. Years later, they both became professors at the college: Victor, a doctor of pharmacology, and Eli, a scientist who also developed the flavor of Trident gum. Working the extra laboratory hours and cramming all the required information into my brain paid off. When the last proctor had circled the aisles and the finals were finally over, I exhaled a sigh of relief and felt confident that I had passed the exams and would be a junior in the fall of 1949. I put down my books, my pencils, pens, and lab coat, and immediately joined a little theater group called The Neighborhood

Players. This pharmacy thing was definitely a part of my life, but it didn't reside where I live.

Milton Jacobson, the dramatic director of the theater, was a warm and chubby fellow with a droopy moustache that gave him a distinctive sneer. It was an erroneous impression. He was a sweetheart of a man, a book-nut intellectual, and a genuine theater lover. He also gave me my first starring role of consequence in a good production of Ferenc Molnár's *Liliom*, playing the wayward carnival barker (the play became the basis for the musical *Carousel*). Milton was patient, helpful, and encouraging in his directing, and I really began to feel my destiny. He surrounded me with a bevy of quality actors. A great set was created by a designer named Bill Fletcher, who was to play an unexpected, but important, part in my life. Handling a large role on stage with all of its complexities and nuances from one scene to the next is a reality that only an actor can know. In this production, I had taken a giant step. My relationship with Penny continued as if nothing had interrupted it. Her school was a success, the wealthy little girls from Elkins Park and West Philly were learning how to be charming, and some even showed promise twirling around in their ballet shoes. She was a fine teacher with a solid reputation and parents were eager to have their kids participate. Penny had a few dance cotillions booked, and I was her reluctant partner again doing the Mambo. I was falling deeper and deeper into the vortex. I am essentially a loner, and it was a peculiar position to be in—being Penny's guy. If you are seen often enough with the same fellow at your side, I suppose it's inevitable that you would be considered a pair. However, I had made no such commitment, so it was stressful. A woman who devotes a lot of herself to a man expects a lot in return. It cannot be helped. I'm not talking only of the physical. There is a thread of feelings and emotions winding around one another that begin to pull on the heart, and when that happens, you either clasp hands and say: I love you! Or you walk away. She was saying it, but I was backing away, sideways.

In my junior year at college everything began to come together. The study of pharmacy was interrelated with chemistry, chemistry was interrelated with pharmacology, pharmacology was interrelated with anatomy, and so on; it began to dawn on me how one course unfolded an understanding of another. I was acquiring a vast amount of knowledge that was specific, useful, and broadening at the same time, even if I never practiced pharmacy. That pleased me, and it was like Harry said, "Once you got it, they can't take it away from you."

I continued to do an occasional dramatic radio show on KYW, and accepted a role in the next production at the Neighborhood Players in a play written by Dalton Trumbo called *The Biggest Thief in Town*. During rehearsals, I discovered that I had a penchant for character work, the one I was playing was a much older man, jolly and droll. Whitening my hair to alter my twenty-two-year-old looks didn't fool anybody in the first few rows, but after the play got moving I guess I passed for at least twenty-nine.

It was about this time that we were all jammed together on the sidewalk in front of a store window, trying to squeeze our way closer to the minute television screen and the hilarious Milton Berle. Outrageously funny and a great performer, he entertained all of America doing unforgettable skits and pratfalls on the *Texaco Star Theater*. It was the beginning of a new era and he, above all, carried the nascent industry to new heights. Little did I know or dream that one day, later in my life, I would not only meet him but think of him as a friend. I will never forget the first time he called me on the phone, prompted by an invitation to a play I was appearing in.

The phone rang and I picked up. "Hello," I said.

"Hello, this is Milton," the voice said. "Milton who?" said I, distracted.

"What do you mean Milton who?" he said, "Milton Berle… how many Miltons do you know?" I felt like a real dumb-dumb, everybody should know who Milton is when he calls.

In the summer of 1950, postage stamps were just 3¢, the minimum wage was 75¢ an hour, the Korean War was about to explode, and, according to Senator Joseph McCarthy, Communists were lurking in every governmental cupboard and must be purged immediately. Times were complex and disheartening, but lo and behold, I was now a senior in pharmacy college at the age of twenty-three with my whole life and future lying ahead. There's the rub. What future?

To be or not to be… that is the question: Whether 'tis nobler in the mind to suffer The slings and arrows of familial pressure, Or, against all odds, stick to my dreams, And by opposing, end the turmoil Blinding my true path…

With apologies to Willy, I definitely felt like Hamlet talking to himself half the time; and although the circumstances were different, a dilemma is a dilemma in any age. My senior classes didn't start until September, and Penny, influential as she was, had suggested me to be the dramatic director of Camp Akiba, an elite recreational summer camp for children and young adults in the Pocono Mountains of Pennsylvania. What did I know about being a dramatic director at camp? Absolutely nothing. Penny must have given me quite a recommendation because surprisingly, the managers of the camp were delighted to offer me a contract, and I vowed to create a summer of camp theater that they never had seen before. It was a fabulous opportunity to put all my burgeoning thoughts about acting, directing, and stagecraft to immediate use. Conscientious and energized, I put together all the raw materials I thought I would need for eight weeks of presentations. I ordered canvas for stage flats that I would build, gels for lights, paint and brushes, tacks, nails, and a saw. When I arrived three days early, with a choice of plays under my arm, everything was waiting for me. I went to work, diligently following all the drawings I had made from books on stage construction—building and painting my first designed set for Eugene O'Neill's *In the Zone*, a one-act play I'm sure they never expected to see at camp. I even built a small wind machine. When the curtain parted and an eerie blue light sliced through the cabin window, a foghorn broke the silence, and in the distance a lonely light house buffeted by howling winds. That was the moment when the camp authorities were impressed and realized that they would get more than they had bargained for. The illusion I had created was successful and my audience, riveted. The campers were curious about this strange guy who had no other camp duties, except for putting on plays. It was rather a unique position to be in. During rehearsals, I quickly realized that I had a sound feeling for directing and handling the children. They responded willingly to my requests and demands. I began to get eager helpers and enthusiastic, talented and promising actors. Even the counselors joined me later in a goofy production of a melodrama called *He Ain't Done Right By Nell*. The boys loved it, seeing some of their counselors dressed up in dresses and bonnets.

I directed a minstrel show, a historical drama for the Fourth of July, and just for diversion, I wrote a silly radio script for my youthful actors so they could try altering their voices. We performed it on a stage set I created to look like a radio station, a light blinking "ON THE AIR," with the letters K-I-B-A prominently displayed.

The girls' camp auditorium, high on a hill and surrounded by enormous pines, was chosen for my closing production because everyone thought we needed more space. Throughout the summer I had been using the smaller boys' theater, but this was to be a showy co-ed effort, so I agreed to the move. I wonder sometimes how it was accomplished considering the horrendous obstacle that surfaced. We were in the final days of rehearsal for the Gilbert & Sullivan comic opera *The Mikado*, and I was staging the song of the "Three Little Maids," my musical director at the piano. "No, no," I said to Yum-Yum. "Just step downstage when you start to sing and then bring your fan…" Then all of a sudden, I heard the blood curdling words yelled from behind the stage: "FIRE! FIRE! THERE'S A FIRE BACK HERE!" We were all startled for a moment at the interruption as smoke quickly filled the air. Then everybody made a mad dash to the outside, the counselors assisting in ushering all the children safely away from the building. We all watched helplessly as towering, spitting orange flames engulfed the dry wood structure in minutes, the choking, black smoke sending us all scurrying down the hill. The Stroudsburg fire department came as quickly as possible, which wasn't very quick at all, but they couldn't flood the flames with water because there wasn't enough pressure to get water up from the lake. It was hopeless. No one admitted it, but one of the teenage stage assistants had been smoking and had accidentally dropped a lighted cigarette in the costume department. Years of silken gauze period dresses, hats, and funny animal garments were gone in a flash. My actors and helpers, shifting about aimlessly, were deeply affected, some with tears flooding their eyes. I was pretty shook up myself.

What to do? The next day, I suggested we all go back to the smaller boys' theater and proceed with the production, and give more than one performance to accommodate everyone. That is what we did. I designed, built, and painted a *Mikado* set which had more perspective and scenery detail than I ever thought I could do in such a limited time. It was a huge painting of an imaginary place with mountains, sky, and a pagoda. On both sides of the stage I cut, ruffled, and painted large expanses of paper to look like trees and leaves. *The Mikado* was a resounding success. Camp Akiba had never seen anything like it, and the following year they would offer me another contract at a higher salary. When I look at a photo of the stage production, the wonderful kids in their hastily made costumes, all smiling, our arms around each other, I can still hear their voices singing—and I still get a tug at my heart.

I had studied so diligently in my sophomore and junior years that by the time I was a senior, I had the slavish routine of knowledge absorption under control. I knew how to devote the time required to achieve the results. I suppose that understanding was an integral part of getting an education; my simplified note-taking at lectures never failed to clarify the complicated wording of a textbook. It was also gratifying to know that my grades were in the higher echelon now, rather than the murky average. Feeling confident that I was keeping pace, I continued to commit to the theater. One evening, after the performance of a barely tolerable play I was doing at the Rittenhouse Players called *Red in the Morning*, a gentleman by the name of James Blair came backstage to see me. He was an executive from an advertising agency and suggested that I was right for a role in a new network television program that would originate from Philadelphia.

I got the part as a young soldier on *Papa Pietro's Place*. I was the guy in love with Papa's daughter. Actually, it was an early black-and-white television soap opera that went on the air in late 1950 through 1951, networked on the east coast. The program was broadcast from the third-floor studios of WPTZ-TV, an NBC affiliate. The successful *Ernie Kovacs Show* originated on the second floor, and *Miss Susan*, starring former film star Susan Peters, confined to a wheelchair after accidentally being shot in the spine, broadcast from the first. This was my initial employment on television in a continuing role. The Dean of Pharmacy, Dr. Linwood Tice, a dear man, granted me permission to miss his lectures every Thursday at noon, and that was quite a concession. They put a TV in the entrance hall of the college and it was turned on during the broadcast so anyone passing by could see it. In my graduation yearbook, beneath his photo, Dr. Tice wrote: "Best wishes to my only student on TV." When I think back and try to recapture my chaotic college days and all the extra non-pharmacy activity, all I can come up with is: How the hell did I do it? I have no answers. Maybe it was the passion and energy of my youth. Then again, it must have been some guiding force, an angel of sorts, tickling my nose to go this way and that.

I continued to work for my brother, and when I would see him the inevitable questions always came up. "So, how are you doing… in class?" "I'm doing okay," I said, nervously fingering the coins in my pocket.

"Are you still doing those… plays?"

"Yeah," I answered, "when I find something interesting to do." More jiggling.

"When do you find the time to study?" He quizzed me while grinding a medicinal powder in a mortar.

"Uh… I just do," I answered. "You know Tice gave me permission to miss his lectures for the TV show. That was pretty gracious."

He frowned. "I went to college with him. He was in my class, but we weren't friends. He was a quiet guy, very brainy." He looked at me hard. "Are you keeping up?"

"I think so," I said.

"What about finals and state boards? If you don't pass the state board exams now, you never will… and the whole four years will be a waste."

"I'll be all right," I said, getting weary.

There was a moment of silence. Then he asked, "What about Penny Davis… are you still seeing her?"

"Yes," I said. "And it's all under control." Knowing in my heart that it wasn't.

She was really serious and clinging with hope, and I was halfheartedly trying to pull away, weighted down with guilt and habitual convenience—a relationship already consuming two years of my young life.

The voluminous and all-encompassing final examinations, dreaded by all, and covering enough specific material to make even the most confident tremble, came upon us like a dense, black cloud in June 1951. Pharmaceutical calculations, identification of 100 raw drugs, botanical origins, toxicity, incompatibilities, dosages, pharmacologic effect, lipotropic agents, emulsions, the precipitation of arsenic, fat assimilation, amino acids… and on and on for several days. When it was finally over, we were all bleary-eyed and numb. Four years of damned hard work for a Bachelor of Science degree in pharmacy. (Today it takes six years to get the same degree.) I won't say that I danced a jig when I saw my name on the degree list with an elevated B average, but I will say that I let out a sigh of relief like a high gust of wind. WHOOOO-EEE! The next immediate obstacle looming before me was the Pennsylvania State Board exams. Without that little passing grade, you don't get to be a registered pharmacist and cannot practice your profession; the only way it is humanly possible to pass it is when you have just graduated college and all the stuff fresh in your skull. I had been thinking ahead, not only about Pennsylvania but also the New York State Board exams. I had been wishfully thinking—or shall I say dreaming—that I would be moving to New York City to be an actor, and if I couldn't get an acting job I could get by until I did by working as a pharmacist. I had it all planned out perfectly, sending them my application and examination fee, even knowing that New York didn't look kindly on "Out of Staters." But when New York turned me down I was furious, and I didn't know what to do.

When I got word that I had passed the Pennsylvania exam, the notice posted at the college, I had a revelation of sorts and a strong impulse to act on it. I knew there was still a week left before the New York exam took place and I thought, with surprising bravado: *What the hell, give it a shot!*

I went to the cafeteria and made an exchange, filling my pockets with coins. Then I went to a phone booth next to the college side entrance. I removed the turn-down letter from my pocket, looked at the phone number, and placed a person to person call to Mr. Leslie C. Jayne, a name I will never forget, the president of the State Board Pharmacy of the state of New York! My heart was pounding. Suppose he won't take my call? What will I do then? After two rings, his secretary answered cordially, "Hold on a moment, please." When Mr. Jayne picked up and said: "Yes, may I help you?" I was off and running.

The words poured out of me like a summer storm. I said, "Sir, I have just graduated from the Philadelphia College of Pharmacy and Science and I just passed the Pennsylvania Board exams... and I am moving to New York City next month, but I have a rejection letter from New York signed by you, and it puts me in a very precarious position. I think it's imperative, sir... that you allow me to take the exam in your state because if..."

When I heard him say, "All right, come ahead, son. I'll make the arrangements," I was ecstatic beyond words and couldn't stop thanking him.

Jack Klugman, Joe Roman, Frank London, and Charles Bronson, all young actors trying to make it, shared a large apartment on the Upper West Side of New York City. Charlie was in Hollywood making his first movie, *You're in the Navy Now*, so when I called Frank and told him I was coming to take my exam, he said since Charlie was away I could stay with them. I accepted his offer thankfully. Five thousand professionals, including doctors, dentists, lawyers, pharmacists, and others, sat down at an endless row of tables in the huge armory near Columbia University to take the state boards. It went on for three gruesome days. I had to go the Brooklyn College of Pharmacy on the fourth day to take the practical exam—the making of ten prescriptions. I remember vividly the tenth preparation I had to compound—twelve suppositories!

Being with my friends, I got an immediate taste of an actor's life in New York City: the freedom, the craziness, the excitement of Broadway, the scratching for employment, and the potential for major opportunities. This was the hub and there was no place like it. This was where it was at. I had done my four years of penance and now I wanted to be here too. How and when I would make the move, I wasn't sure. There was one move I had to make. I was committed to a second year at Camp Akiba and it was time to show up. A couple of days after my exams, I thanked everybody for their hospitality, said goodbye, and boarded a train at Penn Station for Stroudsburg, Pennsylvania.

The cool, fresh mountain air, the gorgeous surroundings, and the delicious food almost made me forget that I was there to produce a summer of theatrics. It took me a while to switch gears, the tremendous pressure I had been under slowly dissipating. I don't think I had the same enthusiasm I had the previous year, but when I finally got focused, I directed several plays that pleased the campers and the authorities. Penny came up for a visit and I had to surreptitiously disappear from camp for the day to rendezvous at her secluded motel. Nothing was resolved in our relationship; we were just happy to see one another and share the private moments. I can't for the life of me remember how I was able to get out of camp and back, traveling the long country roads without a car. My venture in New York paid off. I was one of five from out of state who passed the exams. I was now a registered pharmacist with a license to practice in two states.

When I returned to Philly, I had several new offers for employment. I continued to work a day or two for my brother and at various other labs around the city, sometimes filling as many as fifty prescriptions during my shift. Everything went smoothly, but I was a failure in one thing—typing labels! I had never taken a typing course and it slowed me down to a frustration level. Harry opened a new store and asked me to work for him full-time. He was more than annoyed when I turned him down and accepted a job managing a drug store in Rosemont, Pennsylvania, near Villanova College. I felt that as long as I was going to function as a pharmacist, it would be better to be on my own until I made the move to New York. Finally free from the restraints of academia, I resumed my efforts at the Neighborhood Players portraying Hector Hushabye, a funny character in George Bernard Shaw's *Heartbreak House*. It was a part I enjoyed playing. It gave me the opportunity to develop the confidence of being silly on stage with conviction, wearing a turban and twitching my tailored moustache. Believability is so much a part of acting; if an actor believes fully in what he is doing, no matter how outlandish, without commenting on the character, the audience will accept and believe him too. It was a lesson I have never forgotten.

A Life-Changing Decision

WHILE I WAS APPEARING in another play called *Bonaventure*, I asked Bill Fletcher, our extremely gifted set designer, to get me a job at the Grove Theater, an equity company in Nuangola, Pennsylvania. I knew he had worked there for several years in summer stock. He graciously said he would try. I didn't think about it for a long time, then, in April 1952, after an exchange of letters and a strong recommendation from Bill, I received a telegram from Royal C. Stout, the eighty-year-old director of the Grove Theater: "… you are hired for $35 a week as second business [old theatrical term for second leads]. Please report in Wilkes-Barre for rehearsals on June 16…."

I kept reading the telegram over and over as if to find, somewhere, a hidden nuance that said: "However, don't come; you're fired!" This was what I had been waiting for. This was the professional opportunity and experience that every actor longs for and has to face—getting on a stage to confront a discerning paying audience. I looked at the telegram again and laughed at the offer of $35 a week. I would have gone for less. Professional equity minimum at the time was $55 a week, but I wasn't in the union as yet. As a pharmacist, I was earning $125 for four days of work, which was pretty good in 1952, but it wasn't enough to keep me chained behind a prescription counter. Needless to say, everybody in my immediate family thought I had lost my mind. Harry turned pale and shook his head in disgust, saying: "What a waste… what a waste." Fay said: "Are you sure you know what you're doing?" My brother Dave just laughed, and my mother looked at me blankly, not understanding: "Wha… ? You are quitting a drug store… to go be an actor? You are meshuga!"(A Yiddish word meaning crazy.)

Penny was truly pleased and happy for me when I got the job at the Grove Theater. She had always been supportive and encouraging. We had been splitting up and getting back together again for months. All of the obvious reasons were in play, but mainly my lack of commitment for the future— her future. If I wasn't inclined to commit, then it was obvious that I didn't love her, or not enough to make any plans for our life ahead. Another split. When the cab dropped me off at the Arch Street bus terminal, I went to the ticket counter to check on the time the bus was leaving. I turned around and Penny was there. She smiled but was tearful when she came up to me. "Why didn't you call me?" she asked. I didn't know what to say. We had been through it a hundred times.

Finally, I said, "Penny, why do I have to call? I thought we said goodbye the other night."

"You really don't care, do you?" she said, her eyes filling. "Why do you say that? I do care."

"No, you don't," she said, a handkerchief now dabbing. "If you cared, you wouldn't go away without calling."

"I never said I'd call. I'm going away for three months. I don't know what I'll be doing… what's the sense of torturing each other?"

"Will you write to me?" she asked hopefully.

"Uh… well, if you want me to, I can…"

"Is it such a big deal to drop me a line…?" she said, pouting.

By this time, we were sitting on a bench, the conversation getting repetitive and draining, but when I looked up and saw my Wilkes-Barre bus pull out of the terminal and turn right onto Arch Street, I let out an unreserved: "OH SHIT!" I jumped up, frantically grabbed my luggage, and started racing up the street, Penny in hot pursuit. She was calling after me, "Don't leave like this!" and I was yelling back, "I gotta get that bus!"

I didn't catch the bus then, but I caught up with it eventually by dashing down the steps, falling over my luggage, and finally hopping onto a Broad Street subway to the end of line where I knew the bus stopped one last time before going on to Wilkes-Barre. This whole ridiculous, wrenching scene was straight out of a movie, but the saddest part was that after all we had been through, I never saw Penny again. One chapter closing, another about to open.

Royal Stout, the octogenarian producer with the cherubic face and soiled shirt, picked me up at the terminal and ushered me into his dusty, black Packard limousine. As he was explaining the operation of the theater and rehearsals, I was trying valiantly to hold on to my seat as he negotiated the wild country curves in the road. He was a really lousy driver and I was relieved when we arrived at the playhouse. He stopped for a moment, pointed it out, then proceeded to the little country house where I was to reside during my stay in Nuangola. I walked up the old, narrow staircase, deposited my bags in the upstairs bedroom, sat down on the creaky iron bed, and studied the stained and peeling, flowered wallpaper. The breeze brushed the maple tree branches against the window. I sat there thinking: *My, God... am I really here... in summer stock? I'm sure I'm not dreaming... I'm in a professional acting company and very shortly, I'll be up there on the Grove stage cuttin' the mustard or making a damned fool of myself.* I chuckled.

As instructed, I walked a couple of houses down the road to Ma Whitebread's Place, where the company had their food served. I introduced myself to the chubby and jolly Ma Whitebread, who immediately offered me a sandwich. Then I went to the theater to watch a run-through rehearsal of the first play of the season, *Glad Tidings*, which was opening that night. Royal was still reading directions from the play in his hand concerning who moved where and not much else; the "let the actors figure it out all alone" kind of directing. That was okay in the early stages of rehearsal, but not in the delineation of dramatic moments, when the actors' needs and the playwright's intentions were required. Royal was of the old school of summer stock producers and directors. He had been doing it for many years with his wife, Nellie, and had a successful routine: get the latest Broadway plays available, mix it up with some oldies, hire the best actors you can get for the paltry money, and then let them "act." He had an alumni boasting many big names that got their start at the Grove Theater, including Kirk Douglas and Celeste Holm.

During the rehearsal, I more than noticed a well-endowed, beautiful young woman who had a warm and confident demeanor. She was professional, knowing, and rather sweet in the way she talked to the other actors and to Royal. She was the leading lady and was playing the role Signe Hasso had originally created. I was impressed with her acting. In fact, I was impressed, period! Later, at the evening meal before the opening night performance, we were introduced formally and I realized she was much younger than I had thought, looking adorable with a kerchief around her hair, her red lips glowing. I liked her immediately. I met the whole company of players—and I was spoken of as "the new guy" who would be in the next production beginning rehearsals tomorrow morning. This was summer stock. Play one, and rehearse another at the same time!

The opening performance went well, and afterwards I wandered backstage to knock on the dressing room door of the star. She opened the door and smiled warmly.

"I, uh… thought you were very good… uh, congratulations on a fine performance," I said, self-consciously.

"Thank you," she said, and started to busy herself, not hearing anything more. I lingered a bit, then I said. "Well, I'll see you tomorrow at rehearsal." "I look forward to it," she answered, nicely.

All I can recall about my first appearance in the play *Lo and Behold* is that I did a lot of nervous snapping of my fingers as the character who had a habit, I told myself, of snapping his fingers a lot. After the audience had left the theater and all my makeup had been removed, I was walking down a cricket-cracking country road with Theodora Landess, the leading lady, to get a beer at Spades, the local pub. She was only twenty-two and lovely, and I was beginning to be smitten. I became even more smitten, accompanied by a step-up in my position, when the inadequate leading man was fired after three weeks and Royal asked me to step in to take his place. I would now be playing all the leading roles in an Equity company, and I was not at this point in the union. Teddi (which she preferred being called) and I performed opposite one another in fourteen plays that summer—a grind and a groan away from insanity having to cram all those lines into our heads. She was more used to it than I, having been in several seasons of stock prior to this. I remember staying up until 5:00 a.m. on many marathon study sessions, dousing my face with water and endlessly pacing, trying to memorize the words of Matt, the Irish sailor in O'Neill's *Anna Christie* for the following week—while presently playing the part of Eliot in Noel Coward's *Private Lives*. It was almost impossible to keep my dialects straight, nor the words, which darted elusively around my brain like pebbles.

In *Member of the Wedding* Teddi had to bind her ample bosom to play a twelve-year-old. I played her brother Jarvis, and Nellie, Royal's eighty-year-old wife, performed the Ethel Waters role in blackface! Nellie and Royal's idiosyncrasies had to be forgiven. They had been together admirably doing theater since before the turn of the century, and they were still doing it—their way. In a production of an obscure play, *Pretty Lady*, I saw Royal eating the ice cream prop off stage that he was setting for me to eat in the scene coming up. In that same scene, as I poured the required congratulatory champagne, I clumsily spilled it all over Teddi's glass, her hand, up her arm, and on the floor, prompting us to break up into uncontrollable laughter, the audience gleefully joining in. Standing offstage, Royal admonished us, "Come on boys and girls… that's not the way to play the game!" In *The Rose Tattoo* by Tennessee Williams, the versatile Teddi played Serafina Delle Rose and I was the comical Mangiacavallo. We were both a bit young for the roles, but good, and it gave us an opportunity to stretch beyond the usual stock menu of acceptable drawing room comedies. Bill Fletcher created a fabulous Gulf Coast set design, and the Grove audience was appreciative of the production.

A New York agent by the name of Stephen Draper, accompanied by his client Richard Kiley, saw the show. Every summer Steven would make the rounds of selective summer theaters looking for new talent to sign to his office. Much to my surprise, he was interested in signing me. He gave me his card and told me to come to see him when I got to New York. I was rather flattered at the invitation, and more so when he proceeded to get me a membership in Actors Equity by a mere phone call! Agents could do that in those days, or at least he could, just by his evaluation of the talent and his perception of the actor's future. Royal was not too pleased after I signed the union membership papers—he had to pay me $55 a week, the equity minimum, instead of $35.

Teddi and I were constantly together on and off the stage. I looked forward to seeing her the next day after I had just kissed her goodnight. I was falling in love, but at twenty-five, I wasn't that sure what love meant—especially following a torrid three-year relationship with an older woman. Did I want to be with her? Yes. Did I want to hold her? Yes. Was I physically attracted to her? YES! Did I think she was intelligent enough for me? Oh, yes, she was an Ithaca College graduate for God's sake! Probably smarter than I am. Did I think we were compatible together? There you got me. Uh… I don't know, she's a little artsy-fartsy with the drama sometimes, and she has a stubborn streak of moodiness… drives me crazy. What the hell goes on in her head a lot of the time, I don't know. Do you think she loves you? Uh… I think maybe she's spinning the wheel of fortune… waiting to see what happens like I am.

I was sitting on the porch one day, when a good looking, well-dressed woman approached me and asked if I knew what house Theodora lived in. I smiled and pointed to the white one down the road. I knew that she was her mother because they looked somewhat alike, with pleasant good manners and an air of self-assuredness. As she thanked me and walked away, her posture erect, I actually said to myself, *She's a thoroughbred…*

Teddi comes from good stock. Teddi told me later that her mother had said, "I think that young man is interested in you."

As if I didn't have enough to do, playing one part and learning another, Royal asked me if I would like to be the host of a radio show airing once a week. I would be able to promote the production, possibly bring in some additional ticket buyers, and he would provide the transportation to the radio station in nearby Nanticoke. I accepted and hastily wrote the weekly half-hour program, giving it an arty title: *Theater Marquee*. The jazzy "Slaughter on Tenth Avenue" was chosen as my theme music, segueing into hyped-up talk about the Grove, and the reading of articles and tidbits about Broadway and Hollywood actors that I had purloined from old copies of weekly *Variety*. It was an ingenuous scam—all glued together and saved by more Broadway show tunes in between my gab. Royal liked it, mainly because he got a freebie, but he didn't live up to his part of the bargain. Many times, I had to scrounge to get to the station on time—once, holding on for dear life on the rear end of a speeding motorcycle driven by Jan Peters, a cast member. The summer of 1952 was a foundation on which my development and seriousness as an actor took hold. I notched a lot of roles on my acting belt playing a wide variety of different characters. I have always been an instinctive actor, but because I was working continually, I was learning how a role can be enhanced with specific external character traits—a walk, a limp, dress, makeup, an altered voice, a dialect—the many colors the actor's imagination can weave into the mix to create an interesting living human being. I was also discovering how to use myself on stage—to really listen and think before speaking, and to try to be as relaxed as possible. Learning to be an actor takes a long time. Learning how to be a good actor can take a lifetime. Sometimes during the season, it was necessary for Royal to job-in an additional actor from New York to fill a lead role. The fine actor/director, Paton Price, a tall, lanky balding man, joined us for *Lo and Behold*, and we became friends. He came to visit me once in Philadelphia, months after we had closed, and on an impulse, I invited him to have dinner with me at Harry and Faye's. He was a perfect gentleman, a worldly man of the stage, but he was in a pleasant but hostile environment concerning my career. They thought he was from outer Slobovia when he told them the theater needed my kind of manliness more than pharmacy.

Another jobber came up to take the female lead opposite me as Amanda in *Private Lives*, while Teddi played Sybil, the other female. She was a competent performer but her awareness left a lot to be hoped for. In one scene when Elyot is having a fight with his former wife, she cracks him over the head with a phonograph record. We faked it during rehearsals, but for the opening night, Royal, from his vast collection of ancient props, placed an old 1915, one-half inch thick gramophone record in the spot where she would pick it up. She had never checked it, and in performance at the appropriate moment, she thoughtlessly proceeded to conk me over the head with great force, splitting the record in two. I stood there for a blank moment seeing stars, knocked senseless and bleeding at the hairline. When I got my wits back several seconds later, I was so dazed and angry at her stupidity, I felt like strangling the woman. She apologized with fright in her eyes; I relented, and we somehow finished the scene.

In the orange dusk of evening, Teddi and I walked slowly around Nuangola Lake holding hands, the trees rustling in the warm breeze, the crickets and birds shattering the stillness. The season was coming to a close. Fourteen plays have a lot of words to say. We had memorized them, we had said them, and now it was almost time to go home. She had been a terrific leading lady, and I had established myself as an actor who could take care of himself. As far as the two of us were concerned, our emotions and feelings were deeply stirred. No commitments were made, no lasting bonds were pledged, but there was a sense of all those possibilities. Our situation was not any different than what most young people face when they are attracted to one another. Two young actors with strong egos, high emotions, and nebulous careers—uh, that presents a problem. "I'll miss you," I said. Her eyes sparkled in the shadowed light as I kissed her.

"I'll miss you too," she purred. "You remind me of my brother." "Oh, is that a compliment or do you love me like a brother?"

She laughed. "No, I mean you look like him, that's all. Next subject… are you coming to New York?"

"Uh… I guess so, but I'm not sure when."

"Well, I want to get into Lee Strasberg's class in September," she said. "I'm moving soon after we finish here."

I was surprised. I didn't even know he gave acting lessons. "You mean he'll just take you into his class?"

She nodded.

"Can I do that too? I'd love to study with him. I read all about him and the Group Theater."

"I have his phone number," she said. "We can go see him together."

New York

BACK IN PHILADELPHIA, after a few weeks, I threw together everything I thought I would need, left the remainder with my mother, said goodbye, and boarded a train for the big city. Somebody had told me about an interim cheap place called the West Side Residence Club on West 57th Street. They had a room so I took it for $6 a week and joined my fellow Norwegian sailors sharing the multi-crapper in the hall. Elegant it was not. The first night I was there, twisting on a spring mattress that had escaped the trash heap, I was startled awake by the screaming words: "FIRE!" Barely moved-in and I'm running out in the street in my skivvies, and I don't even know anybody personally. Luckily, the fire was a small one, but the smoke stink lingered for days. With the windows wide open, I wasn't sure which was worse—the smoke or the cooking from the Chinese restaurant next door. For $6 a week, if it didn't bother the sailors, I decided I could put up with it too. Everything in my new life seemed to be on 57th Street. CBS-TV, brick-red and huge, was across the street. Carnegie Hall and my prospective agent were halfway across town, but also on the illustrious 57th. When I called Stephen Draper, he immediately invited me up to his office and seemed genuinely pleased to see me—all smiles, a cigarette dangling from a loose wrist. Steven was an elegant, old queen and a gentleman and one of the best agents in town. If he believed in you he would extend every effort to find you work. He had a fine client list that included the comer, Richard Kiley, whom I had met in Nuangola, and a very important young off-Broadway actress, Geraldine Page. I became his new "potential."

I always liked the name Mark, so when I signed my new professional name, Mark Richman, on the dotted line, I was added to the promising actor list of the Lee-Harris-Draper Agency. It was a big step in the right direction and I was very pleased. In a few days, Steven began lugging me around town to see some of the network casting agents. This was the beginning of the so-called Golden Age of Television and the blossoming of fabulous writers for the small tube, such as Paddy Chayefsky, Reginald Rose, Tad Mosel, and Rod Serling, among others. It was an exciting and creative time for live television. For actors, it was a blessing with the abundance of episodic shows being cast each week on the *Philco/Goodyear Playhouse, Studio One, Suspense,* and *Kraft Theater*, to name just a few. My casting visits with Steven paid off. I was given five lines to say on a *Studio One* period drama with Eva Gabor. I won't say that I felt at home doing my first New York network show, but I didn't have to recite the Declaration of Independence either; and my experience on TV in Philly had given me the confidence to deliver what was required. In the days of live television, before tape and intercuts with film, the medium's immediacy for an actor could be hair-raising. The waiting, and more waiting, the seconds ticking down to when finally the stage manager points to YOU to make your entrance or to speak! There is no going back, there is no other take, THERE IS NO OTHER TIME! It is just YOU—and YOU ARE ON LIVE TV—AND MILLIONS OF PEOPLE ARE WATCHING YOU ACROSS THE COUNTRY RIGHT NOW AT THIS VERY MOMENT! For any actor who has never done it, the first time can freeze your toenails.

The charm of the West Side Residence Club had worn notably thin. I was compelled to find another humble room to lay my head. It was on the third floor of an old brownstone building just like you see in the movies, at 83rd Street and West End Avenue. I paid $8 a week for it. The room was so narrow, I'm sure at one time it must have been a closet. I had to turn sideways to get past the bed and the jutting sink just to carry my groceries to the window. There, I would deposit my milk, eggs, jam, and butter on the outside of the sill to keep it cold. My glorious breakfast was made on a hotplate, but many times I would lose everything to the sidewalk when a strong wind came up during the night. My frustration and anger at the loss and inconvenience was monumental, aside from the fact that I was already squeezing pinched pennies.

Teddi had gone home to be with her parents in Albany, New York. We had been corresponding, writing sweet and goopy letters about our summer together. She was pleased to hear I was now in New York, and we both expressed looking forward to picking up the pieces. One day she called (pay phone in the hallway) and told me she had started sharing an apartment with a girlfriend up on 94th Street near Riverside Drive. I was a bit annoyed at her not letting me know she had been in town, but that was the kind of relationship we had—erratic, warm and fuzzy—and uncertain. When you are young, idealistic, and full of passion—and are actors besides, dreaming of a career—relationships are bound to be up in the air. She did come through with getting an appointment with Lee Strasberg for the both of us and I was impressed. I just couldn't get over the fact that I was going to meet this legend of a man, this guru of acting from the Group Theater and the newly famous Actors Studio. I'll never forget when the day arrived and Teddi and I rang the doorbell at his Upper West Side apartment. Susan Strasberg, his daughter, who must have been fourteen at the time, opened the door, smiled and said, "My dad's watching a baseball game. He'll be with you soon." So, we nervously sat and stared at his enormous book collection, heard the muffled voice of the sportscaster and crowd in another room, and waited… and waited. Finally, Teddi went in first, and I waited some more.

After what seemed an eternity, I was at last sitting in a chair opposite this slightly built little man, wearing a learned Jewish face and glasses. He seemed cordial, but slightly cold, when he quietly asked me why I wanted to study with him. I gushed a whole bunch of stuff about Harold Clurman's book *The Fervent Years*, the Group Theater, and "Method" acting and how much I wanted to be part of that technique since I was instinctive in my own approach, trying to use myself and felt that Stanislavski and the Moscow Art blah, blah, blah… and right in the middle of all that spew, I heard him say, "Okay, you can study with me."

I couldn't believe my ears. I said, "Really, you mean I can take your class and study with you. You mean it?"

For the first time he smiled and said, "Yes." Teddi had been accepted into Lee's class also, so we gratefully hugged and kissed each other, holding hands as we walked out onto the bustling city street and the brisk autumn air.

The first introduction to Lee Strasberg's work was a revelation and a disturbing shock. Lee held his classes at the Malin Studios on 46th Street, which had a small theater with about fifty seats and a stage. Teddi and I chose to do a scene together to recreate the triumph we thought we had had at the Grove in *The Rose Tattoo*. We huffed and puffed our way through it, and when it was over there was a long silence. Then Lee said to me, "Mark, what do you want to tell us?" I tried to tell him what I was working for, talking to this overweight, sexy Italian woman in her bare feet. Lee interrupted. "I don't see any overweight woman," he said. "I see Teddi in a robe, and she's rather nice looking and she has slippers on…

and I don't see any bare feet." That was his initial comment, and there were many more confusing statements to follow. I didn't know what the hell he was talking about, and Teddi felt much the same. We listened and digested and tried to absorb his words of wisdom, but it couldn't get through the density of preconceived ideas and clichés. The fog didn't lift for about a week and then it hit me. It was the beginning of my understanding. All Lee was telling us was that the reality that we see is the reality of real thinking on the stage, and as an actor you must not ignore the truth of what is before you! It was so simple and freeing! To actually see the freckle on her nose, the curvature of her lips, and the length of her lashes… letting those true thoughts register in your brain; it steadies your concentration, and begins to alleviate the concern with "self" onstage. Studying with Lee became almost an obsession. We thought about it, talked about it, fought and dreamed about it. It was an absorbing, brain-consuming dedication to the art of acting by learning the tools available to the actor via the so-called Method. Every actor has his own method, and Lee's work was just an aid to solidifying and expanding it. We saw the progress. There was no other teacher, in my opinion, who ever came close to what he was able to accomplish to help the actor achieve his potential. His classes were cauldrons of hot creativity—the scenes that were performed, the potent dissection, and analysis of what took place—and of what might have taken place if the actors had explored a little deeper. Aside from your God-given talent, it was fascinating to think of yourself as an instrument able to play many notes—all you had to do was find the right key to push. Some keys you don't have to think about, they play automatically, but others may be hard to find. Lee Strasberg's gift was helping you find them. He was a master, and I was grateful to be there witnessing his scholarship and his genius.

Stephen Draper continued to send me out for interviews and auditions, but I wasn't landing anything of consequence. I also reluctantly "made the rounds" on occasion, which entailed stopping in at Broadway producers' offices, leaving my photo and resume, and taking crap from an indifferent secretary who couldn't care less and, more than likely, threw the photo in the wastebasket after I had left. After a few months, trying to make a go of it in New York without a job was a bit of a crunch, and I couldn't face going to work as a pharmacist. I had walked away once and had made up my mind that I wouldn't walk through that door again. However, living off my meager savings and out-of-town unemployment checks where funds were almost depleted forced me to make a decision. I told Lee that I was short of money and couldn't afford the $30 a month for his class. I was somewhat embarrassed, and I don't know what I expected him to say; maybe I thought that by pleading my case he would give me a break and reduce the fee. He just looked at me for a moment then quietly said, "Keep coming." I was astounded. Without saying it, he had confirmed my talent and graciously gave me a scholarship. Gratefully, I kept going to his classes for almost two years without paying him a dime. During that period, he never asked me for any money, nor did his secretary. A few years later, when I was touring in a national road company, I would send him checks in remembered thankfulness.

Teddi and I were seeing each other frequently, but distractedly, in our on-again, off-again relationship. Struggling to be an actor greatly complicated the struggle to maintain a courtship—for both of us. I almost blew it totally one time when I thought something was funny, but actually it was cruel and stupid. She had been called back for the second time by Harold Clurman to read for the understudy to Kim Stanley in a Broadway show that was going into rehearsal. After the reading, flushed with excitement, she told me how Clurman liked her reading and the way she walked and looked on stage. Clever fellow that I am, that evening I called her and passed myself off as Harold Clurman's assistant, telling her she had gotten the job. It was a terrible thing to do to a vulnerable young actress, and I was extremely remorseful soon after the initial levity. She wouldn't speak to me for days and I deserved it. To top it off, she didn't get the job, which made it even worse. (Terry Fay was the casting lady—her sister got the job.)

New York winters can be harsh and bitter cold. This was one of those times. The snow swirled around my head as I walked bent over toward the Hudson River on 94th Street, my coat collar up and the wind stinging my ears. Frozen and shivering, I was relieved when I finally made it to Teddi's apartment building. I shook myself off and pounded my gloveless hands in the hallway. Teddi shared the apartment with Blanche Cholet, an actress she had worked with previously in summer stock, but she wasn't there when I arrived. Teddi's mother opened the door instead, and we greeted each other warmly. She had come down from Albany to be with her sick daughter who was in bed with the flu, bordering on pneumonia. I had come to do what I could to cheer her up.

"Hi, honey," I said, all smiles and good spirits.

"Hi… you didn't have to come out in this terrible weather," she said, looking pale and forlorn.

"I wanted to see you… and I brought you a present." She smiled. "You did… why did you do that?"

"Oh, it isn't much," I said. "Well, what is it?"

I removed a small, wrapped package from my back pocket and handed it to her as she sat up in bed. "Shall I open it?" she asked.

"Sure, go ahead," I said.

She carefully took off the scotch-taped ribbon, then the cheerful red paper to reveal a 10¢ box of Smith Brothers cough drops. She looked at me, her eyes lighting up, and we both had a good laugh until she started to cough with scary intensity.

"You know it's cold in here," I said. "Why don't they send up more heat? You shouldn't be in a cold apartment with the flu."

"We told the manager, but nothing's changed," her mother said.

Now being the enterprising, solve-all-the-problems-guy that I am, I had the brilliant idea that if I turned on all the gas range burners and the oven, it would heat up the place very quickly—and I was right, it did! However, five minutes later, as I was walking around the apartment, congratulating myself, the fire sprinklers in the kitchen area went off with surprising efficiency and flooded the apartment, creating a hell of a mess for my flu-sick girlfriend. Another Good Samaritan effort shot to hell. Soon after her illness and wanting to get away from the lousy weather, Teddi accepted a job in winter stock at the Palm Tree Playhouse in Sarasota, Florida. She was sorry to leave Lee's class, but a job is a job and she was thrilled to have the opportunity to play good roles in a quality theater. I was pleased for her, but in a way, I was depressed and sad to see her go. I would be lonely for our closeness. She expressed pretty much the same feelings in a long lingering goodbye, but I've always felt it's easier to go on to new ventures than to stay—maintaining the sameness.

Janice Mars, a fine actress and a sensitive caring young woman, kept the books and the schedules for Lee Strasberg's classes. She also knew everybody in the theater and what was happening in their lives. She liked my work in class and took a tenacious liking to me personally. Before I knew it, I was escorting her all over town; not that I minded in the least. I was meeting an assortment of known and soon-to-be-known personalities and having a pleasant time besides. One night Janice invited me to a party at the apartment of Maureen Stapleton, who was her close friend. Maureen and I hit it off immediately: "Any friend of Janice's is a friend of mine!" she said. To say that I was disarmed by Maureen's sweet openness and unpretentious manner would be an understatement. There

I was talking to the real Serafina Delle Rose of the *The Rose Tattoo* and she was as genuine in person as she had been on the stage—a switch I was unprepared for. I liked her instantly and we became good friends.

I was milling about with a glass of wine in my hand talking with Janice when the doorbell rang. Janice excused herself and went to answer the door, and I sat down on a couch. The next thing I knew, in walked the trim, young Marlon Brando in a long, black coat, looking as great as you would expect, except smaller, and Janice brought him over to meet me. After our perfunctory introduction, she sat him down next to me, and as he sat I heard him say, "Who's the guy?" And Janice began to explain me, a nobody, to Marlon—who was already an icon at a young age. I got such a charge out of that I've never forgotten it. Later in the kitchen getting a wine refill, I picked up our conversation after watching him playfully squeeze the head of the newborn baby of his sister, Jocelyn Brando.

"Marlon, stop it!" she said. "You'll hurt him." He laughed, really enjoying the baby. Thinking of something to say, I told him how mesmerized I was by his performance in *The Men* (Stanley Kramer's film about a paraplegic) and had the guts to ask him about his preparation. Without hesitation, he simply said that he had spent some time with paraplegics at a veterans' hospital and absorbed what he needed living with them. I asked him what he was doing next and he told me he would be starting a motorcycle film soon on the coast called *The Wild One*. All the time we spoke, he was responsive, friendly, and just plain nice. This young actor was impressed.

Maureen, who was in the process of a divorce, was having an affair with David Rafael, a promising writer. More than once, Janice and I would meet them at Janice's congested village apartment to party and get progressively potted on cheap New York State wine. We would dramatically expostulate about life, love, and the state of the theater—which lead to the genius of Tennessee Williams and Maureen's devoted, inside take on the playwright. Of course, then, every actor inevitably gabbled on and on about Lee Strasberg and his powerful Method influence (we were all his students). Maureen, with her marvelous and contagious laugh, lightened the seriousness of my labored comments and observations. "In the theater, if you don't feel it—fuck it!" she said. "Just fake it!" But some can fake it better than others and if need be, she was the best—and you couldn't tell the difference. I've always been prone to a certain reserve and propriety, but with a touch of a buzz on, these particular qualities were altered somewhat during those mirthful and uninhibited evenings.

Stephen Draper had suggested me for the understudy role to Mark Stevens in the play *Midsummer*, which was going into rehearsal shortly. In the play, he had to dance a soft-shoe and all I could do was the Mambo and the foxtrot and that wouldn't do. So Janice Mars had the right answer and the connection. She made an appointment for me with a dancer friend named Lucille Patton who graciously gave me two lessons free in basic soft-shoe. The narrow room that I lived in was inadequate for practice, so I would continue out into the hallway past the bathroom and back again—the music blaring on my tiny portable record player (a sight only believable in movie musicals about New York). While making my twenty-seventh "Tea For Two" toe trip out of my room, the phone rang downstairs on the first floor. The loud landlady called up: "Mister Richman, it's for you... and turn the music down!" Getting a phone call under these conditions could be life changing, so I quickly turned off the player and dashed downstairs out of breath.

"Hello," I said.

"Hi, it's Teddi... how are you?"

"Oh, I'm fine, I guess... but I'm no Fred Astaire."

"What? I don't know what you mean," she said.

I told her the whole situation about the play and my hallway escapade and my room neighbors thinking I'm nuts.

"And what are you doing?" I asked. "Are you still rehearsing *The Lady's Not for Burning*?"

"Yes, and it is going very well. Everyone seems to be pleased with my interpretation of Jeanette, although I really don't know what Christopher Fry is trying to say. The whole thing is kind of pompous."

"It doesn't matter, you'll make it live," I said with encouragement. There was a pause before she said, "I got your last letter. My... aren't you meeting a lot of celebrities. I am impressed. I hope you won't forget about li'l ole me while you're flitting all over town with name brands."

"No, I don't think so," I said. "I miss you a lot and if I had you here right now I would plant a very juicy kiss on your mouth."

"Do you mean it?" she asked, a sadness in her voice.

"Mean what? The juicy kiss or the part about missing you?"

"Both," she answered.

There was another long pause and some noisy breathing.

"I'm telling you the truth about both," I said. "I miss you and I wish I could hold you in my arms for a warm slobbering kiss because I love you. There, I said it."

"Do you really love me?" she asked.

"No, I'm just saying it to keep you hanging around."

"That's what I mean. I don't know whether to believe you or not." She sounded annoyed.

"Okay, let me ask you a question. It's very simple. Do you love me?"

"I asked you first," she said, "and then you made a joke about it."

"I'm not joking… I love you," I said quietly.

"I love you too," she responded, with a giggle and a laugh. It was a game we played on the phone and in letters - an avoidance of total commitment.

Midsummer opened in early 1953 and Geraldine Page in the lead role became a star. I didn't get the understudy role. I would have to save my scintillating soft-shoe for another show.

Scenes from *A Streetcar Named Desire* had been done a thousand times in class before I attempted my version of Stanley opposite a gifted actress named Joan Potter playing Blanche. I thought it was going pretty well in the breakfast scene, me stuffing myself quite obviously, when suddenly, in a moment of annoyance and impulsive violence, Joan slammed her cup down shattering it and cutting herself badly, the blood spurting profusely and dripping on the floor. It was awful. We tried to carry on but Lee stopped us in a fury. I had seen him annoyed and angry, but I had never seen him at such a pitch. He yelled at us, his peculiar and characteristic glottal stop working overtime:

"Acting is not reality! Acting is an illusion of reality! You have been careless and thoughtless and you have endangered yourselves! You must not allow these things to happen, getting carried away with objects that can be a menace! You have to think about what you're doing… with a cup, a glass, a gun… a knife… before you do it! Otherwise… it is chaos! Not acting!"

All through this tirade Joan was wrapping herself with a handkerchief and a towel and getting first aid attention from another class member.

Lee continued as things settled down: "And you, Mark… don't show us what an animal you are… licking your fingers and eating so grossly. You were indicating. Stanley wouldn't do that. He would try to be genteel, eating with a woman of Blanche's elegant upbringing. Don't try to show character… you have to *be* character."

That was another lesson I have never forgotten. Every class session presented a new situation and new problems to be solved.

It was fascinating to witness how different actors had set tasks for themselves to achieve in their scenes, and how Lee commented on whether the actors had succeeded or failed in their efforts. It sharpened our observations; we weren't just there to enjoy. Of course, Lee gave a final analysis of what the student had accomplished or didn't—and what he or she could have done or should do the next time. The process worked. I saw the incredible growth that sometimes happens when the actor takes the constructive criticism he had received after a scene, and actively uses it the next time the scene is performed. Just to walk on a stage and do nothing is a beginning, but then—to incorporate the reason you are there in the first place, while saying dialogue that is the opposite of why you are there; at the same time experiencing whether you are hot, cold, feeling faint, sick or have to throw up before you murder your girlfriend who is six months pregnant with the knife in your pocket! And just as you are about to, somebody knocks on the door and insists that they want to come in and it changes your plans. If you can do all of the preceding simply and honestly with conviction—that's acting.

Finding good scenes to do in Lee's class was a necessity. However, doing old and tired material that had been done many times before was not the way to go for me. I began reading short stories in new publications as a source for me to adapt, as long as the story had some dialogue. I found one about a newly returned soldier from the war who dances with his date in her apartment, then, because of her rejection of his advances breaks down emotionally. I worked on that scene for weeks with a good actress named Lorraine Kirby, finding many nuances and adding much needed dialogue to the sparsely written story. It was developing nicely and Lee was extremely helpful when we performed it in class. I thought it would be an appropriate scene to do for an Actors Studio preliminary audition.

My one-room jail with the broken spring in the bed that kept jabbing my shoulder when I turned over, and the window sill serving inadequately as a refrigerator was now beyond toleration. As luck would have it, I ran into Paton Price, my actor friend from Nuangola. Over coffee at Cromwell's drug store in the RCA building, I blurted out my frustration about walking sideways in my room to get to the peanut butter. Always sympathetic, his face lit up with the solution. He was leaving on a cross country tour stage managing the Vienna Boys Choir and suggested that I could stay at his place free until his return. It sounded good to me, and as soon as I could, I was happily ensconced in his sixth-floor walk-up on Sixth Avenue below the Village. The rooms were tiny and extremely crowded with an excess of everything imaginable, but it was a godsend—even though my legs felt as if I were back at football practice climbing six flights of stairs several times a day. Unbeknownst to me, he shared the apartment with Don Murray, an actor whom I had seen in *The Rose Tattoo* on Broadway. One night, about 3:00 a.m., I was noisily shocked awake and saw a tall shadow standing near my bed. It scared the hell out of me. I jumped up with a: "Who the fuck are you!"… my heart and adrenaline racing to meet the challenge. He put the light on and calmed me down explaining that he would only be there for the night and was living elsewhere. It was a peculiar beginning of an intermittent friendship that has lasted through the years. Another time, I was in the kitchen making a sandwich when I heard the key turn in the lock and I thought: *Who the fuck has the keys now?!* I stood there at the doorway ready to pounce and the door opened and there stood a young, handsome fellow with a broad grin on his face. It was the young, handsome and unknown Paul Newman.

Don Murray had lent him the keys for a place to stay a couple of nights. He said he had been working all day in a crowd scene as an extra in a film shooting in Central Park and had a hoarse voice from shouting. He told me he had just signed with Maynard Morris of the Music Corporation of America (MCA) and proceeded to show me his new photographs. I thought, *God, how could anyone be so attractive!* We had a pleasant buddy-buddy time together for a few days, sharing the small apartment and discussing the business and our future plans. I found out he had a wife and a couple of kids who weren't with him in New York. I knew instinctively that Paul had the looks and the presence to have a successful career, although I didn't know if he could act or not. I couldn't help but think about myself and where the hell I was at the time, which was somewhere close to nowhere.

After Paul left, I was happy to have the apartment to myself again. I've always had this feeling of the need to be alone—definitely from another male—to pace and to think, to talk to myself and stare at the walls if I have to—and I did a lot of that, trying to figure out what I wanted to do that day, or night, or tomorrow. I've always been a loner. I've never needed the company of the male sex for companionship, solace or the sharing of my private thoughts, except on a very superficial basis. I've never boasted about or revealed my encounters with the opposite sex—as men do. To me, that is almost sacrilegious—to betray intimate moments. I cherish a sense of quietness—to paint, to write, to read or just to do nothing. Doing nothing for any length of time is painful and fills me with anxiety and guilt. I'm compulsive by nature and always have to be doing something—and the more creative, the better.

Teddi's letters to me from Sarasota were frequent, newsy, and enticing. I couldn't help feeling envious of her theatrical activity. It's one thing to prance around on stage in an acting class, but it's quite another to prance and get paid; albeit the honorable goal of my acting development with Lee was still foremost in my mind. An actor keeps telling himself no matter what period of his life, something will turn up that will forever alter his future and career. It's all part of an actor's mindset—or psychosis, as the case may be—having the faith to dog it through until that elusive opportunity presents itself. An opportunity came, but it wasn't one that I had anticipated. During a phone conversation with the leading lady in Florida, she casually dropped a hint:

"Oh… by the way," she said, "my father is coming to visit me next week and if you like, he could stop by and pick you up and you could drive down together."

"Really?" I said, not knowing what to say further. It was a definite invitation to see my girl, but at the hands of her father? That was definitely a different ballgame. A pause continued.

"Hello… are you there, Charlie?" she queried. "Or have you fallen asleep?"

"I'm still here, sweetheart. I'm just thinking, I'd love to see you, but I'm not sure I want to spend a couple of days with your father before I do. I mean, Sammy's a nice guy… or seemed to be when I met him in Nuangola, but I don't know how much we have in common to talk about for two days."

"My mother is already here. She came down by train. It'll be fun to have you all here at the same time."

"Fun… or frightening," I said.

"Don't you want to see me?" she asked, petulantly. "Of course, I do, I miss you."

"Then come," she said.

It was early March and patches of melting snow were still on the streets when Sam Landess, in his blue Cadillac, drove down Sixth Avenue to Paton Price's apartment. I was ready when the bell rang, and after clunking down all those stairs and a warm handshake, we were off. Sam was a kid from New York with a limited education who became a self-made man and president of State Photo in Albany, New York, a photo reproduction company he had founded. He was short, balding, and bow-legged, but he had a sweet smile, a funny laugh that was communicable, and a heart that was almost as big as he was. I liked him and he seemed to like me. Our trip down south was uneventful, but meaningful to him when we stopped briefly in North Carolina to visit his brother. After that, since it was early evening and getting dark, Sam suggested we get some dinner and then stop at a motel so we could be fresh in the morning to continue our journey. I was just taking off my shirt in the motel when Sam asked, "How do you feel about my daughter?" He walked up close to me and asked again, "How do you really feel about my daughter?"

I looked at him and was somewhat off-guard. "What are you asking me, Sam?"

"I'm asking you… what are your intentions?"

"Uh, I don't know Sam," I said. "I'm going down to see her. I've missed her and I want to see her."

"Do you love her?" he asked, gently. "Uh… I think so."

"You think so… is that all?" He was persistent and stared at me. "No… I love her. It's just that I never said I did to anybody else, and it's hard for me to tell her father who is probing my intentions."

"Mark, come and sit down," he said. "We don't have to stand." We both moved to sit on opposite beds facing each other. He seemed to be collecting his thoughts and after a long pause he continued: "I'm asking you questions because that is what a father does when it concerns his only daughter. I love her and I only want the best for her in her life. I don't want her to make dumb mistakes and suffer."

"I can understand that, Sam," I said, as a drop of perspiration trickled down my back.

"Are you serious about her future, I mean, with you?" he asked.

"Yes, I am," I heard myself saying.

"Then you love her… honestly?"

"Yes," I said.

When I said that he reached into his pocket and held it there for a moment and said: "There was this stone… a diamond, that belonged to my mother. The setting fell apart so I had it redone and reset… and I think it might be a nice gesture, if you felt in your heart… compelled to give it to Teddi." Then he removed his hand from his pocket which held a small case, and opening the case he revealed a beautiful diamond ring.

"I can't do that," I said.

"Why not? It's a beautiful ring and it belonged to my mother."

"Then you give it to her," I said.

There was a pause, a surprised, hurt look on his face. "Why don't you want to give it to her?" he queried.

"First of all, Sam... I can't afford a ring like that."

"The cost doesn't matter," he said. "It's the gesture."

"It's hard for me to do that. It didn't come from me. It came from you."

He smiled, then put his hand on my shoulder. "Mark, listen... just put it in your pocket. Sometime, while you are together... if it feels right and you have an impulse... give it to her. Just slip it on her finger. Nothing else has to be said, all right?"

Reluctantly, smiling and shaking my head at his persistence, I took the ring and put it in my suitcase.

A few days later, after dinner at a beach hotel with her parents, Teddi and I strolled along the water's edge, the seagulls cooing and the palm trees swaying slightly in the breeze. It was a beautiful, romantic night, stars in the dark purple sky, blinking like heavenly flash bulbs. Teddi looked radiant and so desirable, her warm, inviting smiles giving me the chills. We held hands and kissed, deep and feeling. Any reservations I had had about our relationship were forever changed when I impulsively reached into my pocket and withdrew the small velvety case. I slipped the ring on her finger and said, "I think this means that we are now engaged... now and forever." Her eyes filled with tears and mine did too.

"Oh, my God," she said, holding her ringed finger high above her head. "Look how it sparkles. It's beautiful, thank you... oh, I'm so surprised and I'm so happy! I never expected anything like this." She hugged me.

"Your father certainly knew what he was doing!"

"What do you mean?" she asked, making a face.

"You put your father up to it, right?" I said, half-joking. "I mean, about resetting your grandmother's ring."

"No, I never asked Daddy to... oh, my God... it's Grandma's ring," she said, staring at it with greater understanding. "What a sweet thing for my daddy to do... but I never asked him to. You believe me, don't you?"

"Of course, I do. But how did he know your ring size?" When she started to cry I knew my jesting was a zero.

"I didn't put him up to it. I wouldn't do that, and you don't believe me. That's terrible," she said, tears dropping on her cheeks.

"I'm sorry, pumpkin," I said, trying to make amends, "I love you and we're engaged and I'm happy about it. Your father did a wonderful thing.

It was so thoughtful of him… and I was only kidding." I wiped her eyes with my handkerchief, then kissed her tenderly on each cheek.

"I know you know I'm telling the truth," she said.

I lifted up her chin with my right hand and looked into her eyes for a long moment. Then with as much feeling as my heart could gather I said, "As long as I have a breath in me… and as sure as the sun will shine tomorrow… in good times and tough ones… my love for you will be there. I'll always be there for you… now, tomorrow… and all tomorrows. You can count on it."

"I'm so happy you came to me, Mark. I love you," she said softly.

When we embraced this time, I felt a sudden responsibility and a deeper significance in our relationship that I hadn't felt before.

I kept thinking while watching The Palm Tree Playhouse production of *A Streetcar Named Desire* that I should have been up there playing Stanley opposite my betrothed who was emoting as Stella. She was wearing puffed-up pregnancy padding because in the play Stella is close to delivery. She gave a very good, sympathetic performance, but watching her at a distance I had an additional perception: I was seeing my future wife in the guise of an almost mother—which stimulated my imagination to freely see myself embracing our future child. It was peculiarly comforting, and I was touched.

In early April, her winter season of stock completed, Teddi drove up from Sarasota to Philadelphia with a friend from the company. I picked her up and brought her to my brother Harry's home in Oxford Circle as part of our plan for her to meet my family. To say that Teddi was a radiating charm flower that illuminated the Richman clan with her light would be entirely too reserved. Harry fell over backwards with joviality, his normal dour cynicism nowhere to be seen. Everyone was so taken with her—her beauty and sweetness—and so impressed with my choice of a future wife, their words couldn't fully express the relief and happiness they felt—and she, an actress yet! Their response was amazing and warmed my heart, and as I look back on that remarkable first meeting, I can still see the smiling faces, hear the gales of laughter, feel the embraces and kisses that never seemed to end. It was a happy time. When Jean and Sam arrived later that evening, the familial good will continued. Then the enthusiastic talk suddenly took on another dimension. "Why not get married right away?" "You're in the same profession, you can help one another." "What's the point in waiting?" "Two can live as cheaply as one!" I thought to myself: *Whoa, just a minute… wait just one friggin' moment. I love you all but you're all going a little nuts! I can't afford to get married… I don't have a pot to piss in!* Nonetheless, they wouldn't be deterred. Through Faye's scrumptious dinner the conversation never veered. Even Sam and Jean got the bug, even though when they arrived, I'm sure they had no intention of forcing a marriage date. Sam, rather taken with me (I found out later that he called me a prince) and without a doubt thinking I was a good guy for his daughter, was already rolling the potential matrimonial event around in his enterprising head. I'm reasonably certain he thought, as any father would, that if I didn't make it as an actor I could always make a living as a pharmacist. Of course, he couldn't know that I would rather hunt for sand in the Sahara than work in a drug store.

Our wedding was booked to occur in six weeks on Mother's Day, May 10, on the second floor of Jack's Oyster House, in Albany (actually a fine restaurant). First, we had to secure a temporary place to live in New York City. That was a chore I wouldn't have wished on any prospective couple who were limited financially, to put it kindly. Teddi and I traipsed all over Manhattan trying to find a suitable place to lay our heads, but things were exceedingly slim. When she finally went back to Albany to get herself organized as a young bride-to-be, I continued to look at newspaper ads and scour the rental possibilities. Only in New York would a hovel pass for a rental. Some of the spaces I saw were enough to make your skin turn green. One brownstone on 49th Street, near Third, had a large room for rent on the second floor. When I entered the building, I knew I should have left immediately. The whole place smelled like a tomb with the corpse still decomposing. As I walked up the musty stairwell, the decrepit landlady followed me and pointed to the closed door at the top of the stairs. Dreading what was behind it, I slowly opened the door. The room smelled of animal and sickening decay, and what light there was came from a darkly draped wide widow. Slivers of light sliced at a double bed that was covered with a dirty spread. It looked as if no one had slept in there since 1922. It was disgusting. As I turned to go I said, "Thank you, but this is not what I'm looking for." When I got to the bottom of the stairs, the landlady yelled, "If this isn't good enough for you… TRY THE WALDORF!"

Maybe I was just worn out, but I finally found something that was half presentable in a pleasant Upper West Side neighborhood, at least to get started. Actually, it was only a very large furnished room with a bed, couch, table, and a hot plate for cooking. It was clean, and the sun washed the room in warm light, softening the depression that I felt, knowing the john was in the hall to be shared with the other guests on the floor.

Painful thoughts were running through my mind: *God, what a hell of a place to bring my bride back to. She'll probably hate it. Why wouldn't she? The john is in the hall?! You've got to be kidding! Is this any way to start a marriage? I can just see the look on Sam's face, or Harry's, if I brought them up here. Shiiiit! Two can live as cheaply as one! Beggars can't be choosers! A bird in hand is worth two in the... stop, stop, STOP! What in hell am I thinking?*

All the fucking clichés kept repeating over and over in my brain as I counted out what little cash I had for two weeks' rental, starting May 11.

When I told Stephen, my agent, that I was going to get married, I didn't expect him to dance a jig, but I was a bit unprepared for his raised eyebrow glum acceptance. I think he uttered something that sounded like: "Ohhh… uuumm…" I think he thought my career would get bogged down before it got started by committing to a marriage. At the time, being free and available was preferable in some show business circles, but I didn't submit to that philosophy, nor did I give a crap about what anybody thought of my objectives—and certainly not my gay agent.

One day after class, Yale Wexler, a young actor whose brother Haskell later became an Academy-Award winning cinematographer, came to me with a surprise offer. He wanted to give the impending marriage couple a good luck party and invite all of our Strasberg student friends. It was a very kind and thoughtful gesture and I accepted. I even invited Lee and his wife, Paula, but they had a previous commitment and couldn't come. He did wish me good luck as we shook hands, a genuine smile relieving the seriousness of his face.

At the party in Yale's spacious apartment, young actors and directors spilled out into the hallway, drinks in hand, a steady flow of show business talk bouncing off the walls. With perpetual grins on our faces, there were toasts and kisses and good-natured jokes, back-slapping hugs, and even a few tears. At one point, Janice Mars came up to Teddi and said in a charmingly envious way, "I congratulate you. You're a pretty smart girl… nailing him." Teddi told me this while I was reasonably coherent. I got so plastered on Yale's strawberry punch, I forgot or didn't care what else was in it. I should have, because I spent more than half of the party in the bathroom with my head in the toilet puking not-so-fresh strawberries.

The Commitment

A COUPLE OF WEEKS LATER, on the assigned momentous day, May 10, 1953, Teddi, at twenty-three, and I, three years older, took the oath of matrimonial commitment. Before I got there, the two rye-and-Cokes I had had prior to the ceremony while conversing with family and guests, and the mellow feeling that accompanied, suddenly and frighteningly disappeared when I started my walk down the aisle. I turned white, I am sure, and cold, clear sober. It had nothing to do with stage fright or the expectant turned heads staring at me. The gravity of the vow I would take and the realization that it was about to happen, and that I would not only be making a pact with my beloved, but also with God—penetrated my soul to the core and was a deeply profound moment for me. When I stood under the chuppa (bridal canopy) in my new pair of Cordovan leather shoes (on which I had spent my last twenty-dollar bill), and I looked at my troubled mother deep into her own fleetingly happy, but insolvable thoughts; my brothers and sister, Fay; Sam, and Jean with tender tears in her eyes—the Rabbi's sonorous voice intoning endlessly–I felt intensely grateful to be standing there with such a prize at my side. (Teddi's brother, Lieutenant J.G. Alfred Landess, was on a destroyer and couldn't be there, but his loving telegram made her cry.) Later, after all the joyous eating, dancing and cake cutting we left Jack's Oyster House in a cab to go a few blocks up State Street to the DeWitt Clinton Hotel for a one-night honeymoon; we couldn't afford any more than that. After all, our New York City residence was awaiting and two weeks were already pre-paid!

Sitting on the bed, we giggled as we tossed the white envelopes filled with checks up in the air. As we retrieved them, opening each carefully, reading the sentiment, and recording the amount of the gift, I had to laugh knowing we would have to wait, maybe a week, for the checks to clear. The total came to $725, a veritable fortune for two young, newlywed actors who didn't have a dime otherwise. Oh, yes, there was a $50 bill in one of the envelopes. It was certainly enough to get us to New York City the next day on the train. I don't remember whether we stayed the full two weeks, but after an attempted hot plate hamburger meal that failed, and our first hollering contest—the hamburger stink still lingering–I knew we had to get out of there sooner than later. We desperately scoured the daily apartment want ads, hoping something affordable would turn up, and it did—a $63 a month third floor walk-up on Elizabeth Street that was a converted cold water flat. That meant there were no doors in between the two small rooms and the kitchen. There was a door on the bathroom, but there was no tub, just a tiny shower stall where you could give yourself a warmish trickle shower if you were lucky. When we first rushed down by subway to see the Lower East Side apartment, Mrs. Impellatieri, the owner, was extremely nice, and her father was still painting the whole place a light shade of pink, so we immediately signed on thinking we had lucked out. I did hear a continual banging noise while we were there, but I assumed it was a guy changing a tire or fixing a fender nearby. My perception would change drastically when we moved in.

We scrounged some furniture and a dresser from Teddi's grandmother's apartment. She had died months earlier in Long Island and the stuff was just sitting there. How we got it to Elizabeth Street escapes me. Paton Price came to the rescue again, donating a double bed that he said belonged to Kirk Douglas when they shared an apartment together (they had originally met at The Grove Theater). After a few days, the odd conglomeration of furniture and kitchen chairs now set in place, and even two lamps for illumination, we felt we were ready to officially move in. We both had slight headaches from the fresh paint, the last of which had been applied that day, but with the three windows open we hoped it would abate soon. With a final look around on our first night, a sheet tacked up to cover the windows facing the alley, we hugged each other and drank an orange juice toast to our good fortune and then exhausted, went to sleep. About 2:00 a.m. I woke up and my throat felt like sandpaper, so I lumbered into the kitchen for some water, opening the wall cabinet for a glass. I was more than shocked when I saw several monstrous-sized cockroaches on their backs, legs jiggling in the air trying to free themselves from the congealed and still wet paint! Oh, shiiiiit! How pleasant!

Then at 6:00 a.m., when I heard the incessant pounding that days earlier I had taken for someone temporarily repairing a car, I was beside myself with rage. Although we screamed and hollered out our window at the horrendous intrusion to our sleep, and the neighbors also yelling back, banging their pots and pans in protest, our ritual was to no avail. The pounding continued daily. We eventually learned that there was a button-press machine next to the window in the building across the alley and nothing would alter that terrible sound. It was part of their manufacturing process and that's the way it was. *Like hell!* I said to myself. *I am not going to put up with this shit!* I decided to get all the neighbors together, hire a sympathetic lawyer, and take them to court. That is exactly what we did. It took months to get a hearing, but we finally did and we won. What did we win? What was accomplished by our victory in jurisprudence? They moved the button-press twelve feet farther away from their window, and the ear-splitting pounding was diminished by half. That was when I began shoving wax ear plugs in my ears. It was either that or move; which I was seriously thinking about. As far as the cockroach problem, that was effectively solved by the deadly insect killer called DRO. The area that we lived in—Mulberry, Mott, and Elizabeth Street—was later glorified in the *Godfather* films. This was Little Italy: colorful, unique, and dangerous. In a way, I was used to the environment, not on the same scale as typified here, but in the fact that I grew up in an Italian neighborhood and felt at home with its people, whom I loved. The fragrance of roasting coffee from the Italian grocery filled the air, and it was exhilarating to inhale on a cold night as I walked up Houston Street and turned right onto Elizabeth. Sometimes you could even see the flakes of coffee falling like snow. Frequently, our friendly neighbor from across the kitchen window would yell, "Ay, Mrs. Richman! You want a piece of pizza?" On the affirmative, she would put the pizza in a bag, then extend her arms across the alley with her broom—a personal delivery service! Outside our door, once a year the festival of San Gennaro took place—a fun-filled spectacle of festivities embracing food, games, music, and religious observance. It was memorable, just to walk out the door and step into a celebration, sharing the good-natured merriment that went on for blocks. It was far different from stepping over the drunks asleep in the downstairs hallway every morning. The "Volunteers of America" on the corner of Houston Street and Elizabeth supplied them with meals, but, unfortunately, no beds.

The place was full of surprises. One morning as we were having breakfast, a mouthful of cornflakes and raisins in my mouth, there was a heavy pounding on our door. We both jumped up, alarmed. The pounding continued.

"Who is it?" I asked, annoyed.

"Police… open the door!"

Teddi looked at me in a panic, shook her head no, and whispered, "Don't open the door!"

"How do I know you're the police?" I said.

"Never mind that crap… just open the door or we'll break it down!"

Teddi was putting on her robe still shaking her head no and me not knowing what to do in my pajamas.

"This is the police so open the goddamned door now!"

Hesitantly, not knowing what else to do, I slowly opened the door and smiled, thinking that maybe I could good humor them or something. I said, "Hi… what's goin' on… what's wrong?"

Two burly, tough guys, looking more like truck drivers than cops, brushed past me and started to look around. One of them, in a leather jacket, had a gun in his hand. It was shocking and very scary. Teddi stood in the doorway ready to scream, her voice shaking when she said, "How do we know you're the police? You don't have uniforms!"

"We're undercover, ma'am… you can call the station," one guy said. He gave us a number and his name and Teddi, making frantic faces, pointed to the phone for me to call. Still looking around, the other guy said that they were investigating bookmaking in this apartment and had received a call stating it was in active operation. I nervously dialed the number because those two guys looked more and more like a couple of pugs that I would be ill-prepared to tangle with. "We just got married and moved in here recently," I said, "and we don't know anything about bookies."

Finally, a voice on the other end of the line said, "Fourth Precinct." When I said the names of the so-called cops and explained our predicament the voice said, "Oh, yeah… they're okay." Apparently our freshly painted apartment had previously been a bookmaking joint, but justice had moved a bit too slow.

My young wife was warm, sweet, gullible, moody, emotional, and very impressionable. I, on the other hand (so I've been told), was warm, sweet, cynical, emotional, and temper-impulsive. It was not difficult to deduce that we were having a rocky period of adjustment. Then, added to the mixture, we had an employment separation; we couldn't decide whether it was good or bad for our relationship.

Regardless, one month after our marriage I accepted a job at the Westchester Playhouse in Mount Kisco, New York, playing Stefanowski in *Mister Roberts*, with the new Broadway sensation Russell Nype (*Call

Me Madam). He was a good fellow and a nice actor, but I think he felt more comfortable singing. It was a pleasant experience for me, playing with a bunch of older professionals and I got to bare my muscles as a tough seaman. The actor who played Doc was Edward Binns. He and I hit it off pretty well and that was to pay off in a show coming up. Teddi had accepted a stock job for several weeks in Malden Bridge, New York to try out a new play. We missed each other and were not reserved in expressing our longing on the phone. Immediately following one production of *Mister Roberts*, I went into another one starring Wayne Morris for three weeks in Fayetteville, and East Rochester, New York, playing Mannion, another muscle-bound sailor. I remember Wayne Morris, still quite young, looking overweight and dissipated, certainly not the ruggedly handsome image of his early films.

I've always been intrigued by the creation of a fictional character on the screen and how much lighting and makeup can alter an appearance, especially in close-ups. Good lighting can also soften or eliminate imperfections—bad lighting can destroy you. Some of the greatest stars in movie history wouldn't start a picture unless their personal and coveted cinematographer was signed on first. That summer, at Fayetteville the production that was closing that week while we began rehearsing was *Peg O'My Heart*, starring Billie Burke. She was not a huge star, but I remembered how wonderful she had always looked in all of her films, some rather recent. She also looked incredibly beautiful on the stage but, of course, it was from a distance. At a closing reception later, I got to meet her and was absolutely mouth-open shocked at how old this woman really was—every wrinkle had a wrinkle. The magic of the movies.

At the party, I met a young actor who was to open in another play while we rehearsed *Mister Roberts*. He wore white bucks and Brooks Brothers shirts and his name was Steve McQueen—his tough guy image was created later. Another fellow in the *Peg O'My Heart* production became a dear friend later in life, but when I first met him he was a very serious character actor—Shelley Berman. When Shelley became a hot comedian, I thought it was someone else. It goes to show that a good actor can play both ends. During the run of *Mister Roberts* in East Rochester, the producer of the theater was a charming guy by the name of George Englund. He was easy to be with, fun, and didn't take himself too seriously. We became good friends and have remained so. Frankly, I feel odd repeating that so and so and I became good friends, but it's true and I have to get over being self-conscious about it. Is there another way to say it without being repetitious? Would ditto work? Naaah. George had a delightful wife who was so pregnant that I thought she was going to pop at any moment, and through it all she was as funny and endearing as a woman could be carrying a child. I think her pregnancy gave me the feeling that it was the best time of a woman's life—the time she is nurturing life. Oh, yes... her name was Cloris Leachman and she became a good...

A week after *Mister Roberts* closed, my agent was pleased to inform me that Edward Binns, with whom I had worked at Mount Kisco, wanted me to come back and play his friend, Joe Feinson, a philosophic police reporter in the Westchester playhouse production of *Detective Story*. Eddie played Detective McLeod. He was wonderful in the part and also co-directed. It was one of the best presentations ever put on at the theater, and I was getting some favorable buzz for my performance. There were so many quality actors in the cast that it was an honor to be among them, including Martin Balsam and Werner Klemperer—both of whom, again, became life-long friends.

There is something about the theater, and films too, for that matter, that generates a feeling of kinship with your fellow actors. You become part of a family—you've shared a creative experience, however brief. If chance, luck, or the fates bring you together again in another production, the relationships are enhanced. This "familial" experience lingers for years, and even though your association may get fuzzy, depending on the circumstances, more times than not real and deep friendships have been formed.

Teddi had a couple of weeks left at Malden Bridge, so hubby eagerly made a visit. I caught her last performance playing a German girl involved in a plot to save somebody or something, but neither of us can remember anything beyond that. The magnificent countryside, the walks, the talks, and the closeness alleviated the tension we had felt before we parted. It had been extremely difficult to separate so soon after tying the knot. Our marriage was still taking tiny baby steps in the right direction, and I was hoping that we wouldn't be forced again to be apart for an extended period. The following week I saw my wife in a dumb melodrama-musical, prancing around, tap-dancing (she was an authentic tap-dancer) in a scanty costume and thought, *My God, she's got great legs!*

The most important information I ever got in my early career came from Teddi. She saw this casting notice in a show business rag sheet: "ACTORS STUDIO PRODUCTION CASTING PART OF LARRENCE

CORGER IN CALDER WILLINGHAM'S, END AS A MAN. JACK GARFEIN DIRECTOR." She had a strong instinct that I should get a reading. I was negative, mumbling that it was probably all cast with studio people already. She insisted and finally convinced me, so I went to a casting call and met the director. He was a diminutive redhead who looked about fifteen years old and who had miraculously survived the terror of a concentration camp. Someone in his office had seen me in *Detective Story*, so when I met Jack Garfein and read, he was immediately sold on offering me the part. The fact that I was a student of Lee Strasberg didn't hurt since Lee was the artistic director of the Actors Studio. First of all, I looked the part. I was supposed to be the upright head cadet at a southern military academy and the boxing champion. The actor who had played it at the Actors Studio workshop was too slight for the role and not believable. His name was James Dean.

We all signed to do the play for $25 a week. The group of incredibly talented young actors included Ben Gazzara, Pat Hingle, William Smithers, Arthur Storch, Paul E. Richards, Albert Salmi, and Anthony Franciosa. I was the only one not in the Actors Studio. In rehearsals, Jack Garfein was a patient, but relentless, pursuer of behavior reality; we all worked diligently to expand our character's life by improvisation and sense memory. The play was about disciplinary problems, hazing, subtle homosexuality, and violence—instigated by an arrogant bully played in top form by Gazzara.

On September15, 1953, we opened off-Broadway at the Theater De Lys in the village to unanimous rave reviews. Some critics even suggested we take the production uptown to Broadway.

"*End as a Man*… one of the most fascinating displays of unfamiliar talent I have ever seen… hypnotic as being shut up in a basket full of cobras… the performances suggest that the Actors Studio, which has already presented us with a number of rising young stars, is getting ready for a new invasion of Broadway."

The play boosted everyone's career. Of course, Ben got the most recognition and deserved it, but it helped us all to get established. After a few months at the Theater de Lys, Claire Heller, the strikingly beautiful young producer, raised an additional $60,000. She had Mel Bourne design new sets and moved the play to the Vanderbilt Theater. Before we opened uptown, Jack Garfein invited Lee Strasberg in as a play doctor to fine-tune the scenes, to cut the long pauses and pick up cues. The cast was pleased with Lee's work; it sharpened the playing. In a couple of months, because of scheduling, we moved again to the Lyceum Theater. I was now on Broadway making $100 a week. At one pre-arranged performance, since I covered for Gazzara besides playing my own role, I went on in the lead as Jocko De Paris. It was a real kick and an affirmation that I could do anything that was required, and possibly more, if given the opportunity.

During the run of the play we all became friends and buddy-buddies, but I became closest to Paul E. Richards, a wonderful actor and sweetheart of a man. I was even able to secure him and his wife, Barbara, an apartment in our building, directly over ours on the fourth floor. The four of us had an after-show routine of midnight snacking. My consumption usually consisted of cake and milk. It was an old family habit, and I always kept an ample supply. A small delivery truck would stop by once a week and the driver would ring our bell. When I questioned him, he said he was supplying hotels and restaurants, but I always thought the stuff was stolen and going door-to-door was his way of unloading it. Regardless, I am a cake maven and the pastries were unbelievably delicious. I remember luscious 18-inch squares of cake, 3 inches high with nuts and raisins and other sweet delicacies. Paul thought I was out of my mind as he ravished pastrami sandwiches and sour pickles in between our fun and laughter. Looking back, it was a very exciting and productive time.

9 Hallowed Place

THE ACTORS STUDIO IS A UNIQUE INSTITUTION. It is a workshop for professional actors to improve their craft. Once you become a member, you're a member for life, and there are no required financial obligations. I had passed my preliminary audition using the material I had adapted from a short story—the emotional breakdown of a soldier. I was partnered with Lorraine Kirby. A couple of months had passed and the final audition was coming up. I don't know if it is true today, but when I was starting out in the early fifties, a rejection by the Actors Studio was like a death sentence for an actor. It meant that you didn't have what they wanted to join the crème de la crème in the upper echelon of the so-called Method elite. In the five minutes allowed for the scene you had to present yourself with all of your abilities exposed. You had to make an impression. That was no small task for anyone. Many actors never got over it, and some highly recognized "names," who weren't names at the time, auditioned repeatedly before being accepted. Some never got in. On the fated day to present yourself, you, your partner, and your props would wait and wait until your scene was called, thoughts of failure hovering in your subconscious like lead. Sitting there in the judgement room, stoic and silent, were the ones who had your future in their hands: Elia Kazan, Lee Strasberg, and Cheryl Crawford, producer of some of the finest plays on Broadway—all of the legendary Group Theater and now, the Actors Studio. A formidable bunch. Once you got past this gang, everything else had to be a piece of cake!

When the phone rang in our apartment, Teddi picked up, and after a moment she said, seriously, "It's for you, the Studio."

"Hello," I said, holding my breath.

"Hello, Mark?" the cheery voice said.

"Yes."

"This is Mrs. Hansen at the Studio. They wanted me to let you know that you passed the final and are now a member of the Actors Studio. You can come to your first session on Friday at eleven."

I thanked her for calling and hung up.

"Holy happy shit!" I said, all smiles and goose bumps as we hugged and kissed and danced around the room. It was gratifying to find out that more than a thousand actors had auditioned during that year, and I was one of only a few who had been accepted. Lorraine Kirby and I had spent so much time and energy working on the scene that got me into the Studio, I thought it would be great if we could showcase it for a wider audience. But how? The opportunity came when The Stage Manager's Club announced they were going to present, *Talent '54* at the Mark Hellinger Theater, a mammoth show embracing promising acting, musical, and dancing talent. Every casting agent, producer, and director in town would be invited to come. It was a showcase not to be overlooked. We auditioned and were chosen. The show was a production nightmare and went on forever, but I was pleased to be included in the pack of very talented people that included Tom Poston, Jerry Stiller, Katherine Ross, and Arte Johnson, all of whom went on to achieve fine careers.

Lee's process of running his classes at the Actors Studio was basically the same as in his private classes, except that at the Studio the actors watching the scenes could comment on what they saw before Lee spoke. Sometimes what was said, based on what the performers tried to accomplish, was constructive and helpful. Occasionally, it was out of line, hurtful, and destructive. When that happened, Lee would get up from his chair and turn to the class, his voice rising explosively, and would come down hard on the perpetrator. "You are here to observe what the actor tried to do! And then you are to comment on whether you think he accomplished it or not! This is not a finished performance… this is work! Actors are working to develop their technique! You are not here as an audience to enjoy yourself and eat popcorn! You are here to work as much as they are… to see and observe… carefully digesting what you have just seen, so you can comment intelligently and be helpful to the actor!"

I looked around the room at the taught, attentive faces. They were some of the most well-known faces of Broadway and Hollywood—now—and soon to be. I was absolutely thrilled and honored to be there, and I'd made up my mind that I was going to work as hard at the Studio as I had in Lee's private classes—maybe more so.

When I first became a member in 1954, the classes were held in the upper floor of the ANTA Theater Building. When the building closed for renovation, the Studio was forced to use a midtown rehearsal hall which turned out to be the same room at the Malin Studios where Lee taught privately. In a way, I felt almost at home in a place I had already spent two years. Home, however, was never like this one particular morning I vividly remember. I walked into class and I sensed a kind of buzz and excitement. We had a special visitor. The Actors Studio had always attracted high-profile celebrities from Hollywood and Europe to sit in on classes. After all, this was the famous temple of the Method—but this particular visitor was causing more than a stir.

I finally saw her, quietly sitting there in her beige camelhair coat, her golden hair casually framing her beautiful face; her luscious lips, provocative and inviting; her eyes looking far way and dreamy. As much as you didn't want to, you couldn't help staring at her. She had that kind of extraordinary magnetic power. She vibrated, and there was a glow around her that wasn't imaginary. Marilyn Monroe was the most seductively vulnerable woman I have ever met in my life. She oozed sexuality and desire. After class, a group of us went to Childs Restaurant for lunch, and Marilyn came with us. I recall Eli Wallach and his wife, Anne Jackson, and Tony Franciosa, but a couple of other actors present have escaped my memory. At one point, before the waiter took our orders, I said, "I think we should go around the table and everyone should introduce themselves!" Of course, it was a wise-ass thing to do, knowing full well that everyone knew who Marilyn Monroe was. Around the table we went, and when it came to Marilyn, she just said, quietly and self-consciously in her childlike voice, "Marilyn Monroe." She was more sincere than I was. I felt like kind of a shit.

Some time after I first met Marilyn, Teddi and I were invited to a party at the apartment of Valerie Bettis, a fabulous dancer and choreographer who was married to the pianist Bernardo Segall. Lee was there with his prize pupil and was as warm and gracious as I had ever seen him. Marilyn was next to him in a halter and sandals, looking as sweet and approachable as a school girl. I thought, *Here's my chance. I may as well make a stab at it.* I approached them with the usual party greetings and a kiss on Marilyn's cheek. "Lee," I said, "I would like to do a scene with Marilyn." Lee made a little twisted smile and glanced at Marilyn, who seemed to be game for anything.

Then he said, "No."

"Why not? I asked. "I would be good for her to work with."

"Not now," he said. "I want her only to do scenes with women. Working with men is not what she needs now… for her development. Maybe later."

"Oh… okay," I said, disappointed, glancing down at the floor and catching sight of Marilyn's round and pink fleshy toes. Then I moved away to pick up a glass of cabernet and joined Teddi who was chatting with Alex Nicol and our host, Bernardo Segall.

This was the beginning era of Lee's possessive handling of Marilyn's evolution as an actress and her maturation. He was her gentle guru, her confidant, her teacher and her father figure. He was so protective of her it was spooky. Lee was poised to transform a movie queen into Eleanora Duse. So enthralled with her, he was deeply involved in every aspect of her life, and when she finally went back to the coast to do a film, he sent his trusted emissary, his wife, Paula Strasberg, to be with her and oversee and approve her acting before the camera—making certain that the higher standards he had set for her would be printed on film (much to the consternation of the director and film executives). I think, as far as Marilyn and the acting was concerned, it was mostly a success. She had improved greatly and Lee was responsible. As to the rest of her life and her psychological state—I'll pass.

We had been spending a lot of time with Phyllis Love and her husband, James McGee, who was a struggling and once-produced, mentally unstable playwright. Teddi had been in stock with Phyllis and they were dear friends. She was now a hot Broadway actress in hit after hit, and later, she and I were the young love interests in the film *Friendly Persuasion*. More about that to follow shortly.

Many evenings we had to sit and pretend rapt attention while Jimmy read us his latest play, nearly falling off our chairs in putrefying boredom. That was how I felt anyway. My wife was too kind to admit it. However, in one quiet conversation after the other victims had said goodnight, Jimmy told me about a method of writing that I should try— writing my thoughts down without really thinking; putting down whatever came into my head, free of constraints (maybe that was the problem with his plays). I tried to do what he said. I scribbled and scratched an ambling piece about a drunken derelict, a bum. I'm sure it had something to do with where I was living. At the time, I thought it had the potential to be an interesting scene for class. There was an open booking date, so I signed up to reveal my writing and acting prowess at the same time. There is even a pencil sketch I made of what I thought I should wear; an old torn coat and pants, scruffed-up shoes, and a cap. On the assigned morning, I went through the whole piece, acting out what I thought the character was going through, and, of course, saying the lines. After it was over, Lee asked me what I had tried to do. I told him. Then he said one of the most profound statements in the form of a question that I had ever heard. It was so simple. He said, "Mark... what do you want to be? An actor or a writer?"

I understood immediately. I had done nothing that an actor has to do to fulfill a role to carry out the intentions of the writer. I had been a writer first, saying his words with a kind of conventional meaning and sincerity, indicating a "down and out" character, but not living one, as the actor must. The writer and the actor are totally separate. The writer certainly can act his own material, but while doing so, he has to forget that he wrote it. He must deal with the material with new eyes, as with any other part. It was a great lesson.

Finally, a permanent home for the Studio was found in a refurbished church with an extended balcony on West 44th Street. It was a place with real character and production possibilities. The balcony projected over the audience on both sides of the stage like a horseshoe. The stage was actually the ground floor; there was no elevation. Feeling inspired and bold, I asked Patricia Neal, a wonderful actress and a statuesque beauty who had triumphed in films, if she would like to play Juliet to my Romeo. We had the balcony, what more could we ask for? She agreed.

"But soft! What light through yonder window breaks? It is the east, and Juliet is the sun!"

Juliet was at least fifteen feet above me. I did no climbing, and I certainly didn't have a ladder. All I remember is, we were both hampered by the distance. I got a stiff neck and we wound up delivering the lines with restricted Shakespearian sincerity. Lee was kind and gave us a positive response for our noble efforts. Soon after, I gave Shakespeare another shot. I delivered the Marc Antony oration speech to the class using them as the "Friends... Romans... Countrymen! Lend me your ears!" I started out fine, declaiming, trying to get the attention of the crowd, their restlessness in my imagination not easily subdued. As I continued, the crowd (class) was dumb-ass silent and indifferent, and I made the stupid mistake of picking up their flaccidity. Instead of manipulating the hostile crowd to my desires, with shades of guile and political cleverness, I wound up delivering a sleepy sermon. It was another good lesson. When you set yourself a task to carry out, you can adjust to the circumstances, but you must not be overcome and abandon your original task. In this case, a class of seventy-five variably attentive actors cannot substitute for a violent crowd of 500 Romans. As an actor, it's all in your head and your intentions. It's not out there. You have to create it.

In the summer of 1954 I accepted a job as the leading man in a stock company in Guthsville, Pennsylvania, and Teddi accepted employment in a stock company in Bolton Landing, New York. We both knew that the separation was going to be a bitch. I had been hired by Tom Bosley, who was the director at the time and also at the beginning of his career. The lead character woman was a fine actress by the name of Eileen Ryan, another one of Lee's students. Tom, Eileen, and I struck up a solid relationship and we did some excellent work. In every theatrical company, there is always a turd in the whipped cream—or in this case, two turds—the ingénue and the juvenile, two no-talents. They were bending the ear and deeply influencing the owner of the theater against us. Why? I suppose it was because the three of us were making $85 a week, and they were making $55, the Equity minimum. We had heard some rumblings, but we didn't find out about the depths of their deviousness until our last show together.

While we were functioning, Tom mounted a fine *Angel Street* with me as the bearded and mysterious Mr. Manningham. I remember the dress rehearsal lasting past 1:00 a.m. My miserable hand-made beard wouldn't stick and kept falling off at crucial moments, sending us into spurts of hysterical giggling. In *The Glass Menagerie*, Eileen was marvelous as the crippled Laura, and I played the jaunty gentleman caller. Solid productions of *Room Service*, *The Family Upstairs*, and *Apple of His Eye* followed. In the latter, I played a role and also had my first opportunity to direct a professional production. After the opening night, we were all fired. Of course, we were upset, but we had to laugh too. The two people responsible would now be in charge of the rest of the season; they were such putrid actors the whole situation was rather silly. As it turned out, my wife, after two shows, hating the atmosphere at Bolton Landing and especially the director—in a huff—just quit. We were back together again quicker than we thought. Soon after our return, Eileen invited us for dinner at her Christopher Street apartment to introduce us to her intended husband, actor Leo Penn. They were soon married and in time produced Michael, Sean, and Christopher. Hmmm... I wonder whatever happened to those talented young adults?

Arthur Penn, who later in films went on to direct the classic *Bonnie and Clyde* and *The Miracle Worker*, hired me to play a sympathetic policeman on a *Philco TV Playhouse*. I was called in to investigate an old lady, Lili Darvas, who was doing strange things in her house and alarming the neighbors. This was my first major role in a prestigious network television show, and it boosted my career to another level. What riveted my concentration and worked for me, and drew everyone's attention to the screen were long lingering close-ups of this cop compassionately studying the old lady, trying to figure out what to do with her. In rehearsal, I had discovered a way to use something Lee had said. It was a simple and basic truth in acting. "When you look at someone… really see them. See how long their eye lashes are, see the pores in their nose… how deep the wrinkles are on their forehead…" I seriously did that on television, it was right for the part, and it caused a stir because Arthur kept cutting to my face and dwelling there for my reactions. Suddenly, I was a new, young actor that was wanted—the parts getting larger and more attention-getting, the activity breeding more activity.

The time that I was active in live TV has been termed The Golden Age of Television. It was also a fertile training ground for a whole list of incredible directors and writers who found their nurtured way first on the small screen. During this time, to name a few, aside from Arthur Penn, I had the privilege of working with Franklin Schaffner who later directed *Patton*, Robert Mulligan who directed *To Kill a Mockingbird*, and Delbert Mann, who directed *Marty*. I worked with Delbert Mann on the television version of Paddy Chayefsky's *Middle of the Night*. It later became a Broadway stage hit play with Edward G. Robinson and eventually a film with Robinson, Del Mann again directing the film version. When I did the TV version, which starred Eva Marie Saint and E. G. Marshall (I played his son), as with all live television shows, during the beginning rehearsal, we would all sit around a table in some sterile rehearsal hall and read the script to see how the words sounded to the author. We had about nine days to put it together before air time. One day, I remember saying a line and Paddy Chayefsky stopped the reading: "Wait, wait… that doesn't sound right… uh, what would you say here, Mark?" For an instant, surprised, I looked at Paddy's inquisitive, intense face and on the spot, from somewhere within me, I hesitantly came up with a line. "Keep it… it sounds good," Paddy said. This situation occurred many times with writers such as Reginald Rose, Tad Mosel, Rod Serling, Horton Foote or whoever the writer happened to be that particular week. With director approval, most writers were receptive to suggestions or dialogue changes. This privileged opportunity as an actor gave me an indication that I had a facility to write and express believable dialogue. It remains one of my stronger points as a writer. Continuing this thought, a few years later there was a wonderful show on the air called *Play of the Week*, where stage plays were adapted for television and done in their entirety with quality casts. In *Therese Raquin*, based on an Emile Zola play, I played Laurent, a painter who plots with his lover, the wife, to murder her husband. I starred with fabled Eva Le Gallienne, a great actress and a past major star and director, who played the mother of her murdered son (Alvin Epstein). The translation from the French was stiff and unsayable and my long speeches were the worst. During the final rehearsals, the director Bill Penn (not related to Arthur) asked me if I would be willing to rewrite the final act before we went on camera for taping the following day. I stayed up after midnight, working my ass off to rework and rewrite my dialogue—which was a fearful confessional, delivered to the wife (Anne Meacham), now married to me on our wedding night. The mother overhears my dreadful admission of guilt and has a stroke. The rewrites went on for several pages, including Eva Le Gallienne's paroxysmal collapse, but she was not made aware that I had done the work—nor anyone else.

The show was very favorably received and I, again, was convinced of my writing abilities—aside from my acting skills. The superb caricaturist Al Hirschfeld did a drawing for the Therese Raquin newspaper ads with Eva Le Gallienne, Anne Meacham, and myself in period costume and me in a moustache. A copy of the ink drawing is on the wall in my den. Years later, I tracked down his stuffy agent in an effort to acquire the original. Inflation had set in. I decided I'd rather pursue a Picasso etching.

I was thumbing through a paperback edition of *Best Television Plays of 1954*, edited by Gore Vidal, and I saw that a show I had appeared in was listed. *Man on the Mountaintop* by Robert Alan Arthur won the Sylvania award that season. Arthur Penn again hired me to play a key role. Also in the cast were Anne Meara and Steven Hill. It was executive-produced by Fred Coe, who became an icon of the Golden Age for his guidance of quality television.

The neighborhood of Houston Street and Elizabeth had ceased to hold its fancy for me. I found a two-bedroom apartment on 20th Street and 9th Avenue in a quality building with polished brass doors and a doorman in uniform! As I painted the ceilings in the apartment on the sixth floor, I could look out our windows at the Catholic seminary across the street and take comfort in the scheme of things. We had made a major step up in our living quarters for $77 a month. I was appearing regularly on television in one show or another and my name was getting known and I was developing the reputation of being a good young actor who could deliver. In another *Goodyear Playhouse*, this time with my friend Jack Klugman, we were clogging our way through the camera blocking process in NBC studio 8H, on the eighth floor of Rockefeller Center. Jack kept shaking his head, both of us laughing, sharing the peculiar circumstances of my life and how it was turning out. He still couldn't get over the fact that I went to pharmacy college, got my degree and licenses, and now I was married and a working actor working with him—two guys from South Philly!

During the lunch break, I was walking through the black marble hallway to Cromwell's drugstore when I ran into Jimmy Dean. We shook hands and chatted. I can still see his bespectacled face, all smiles and twinkles about flying out to Hollywood to begin shooting his first film, *East of Eden* with Kazan directing. He was really excited, like a little kid opening birthday presents. He'd made a splash in a new play on Broadway called *The Immoralist*, and this would be his first film. He had no idea what a huge star he would become, and neither did anyone else, including Kazan. We shook hands again and shared a friendly hug as I wished him good luck. I walked away thinking, *My God… Hollywood… I wonder what that must feel like… going out there to never-never land to star in a movie?*

David Ross, an extremely wealthy fellow who was in Lee's classes and fancied a life in the theater, was a dreadful actor but a dear man and a lot of fun to be with. I once overheard him in a heated phone discourse purchasing thousands of cubic feet of something in Morocco, or someplace, for immediate delivery by ship to someplace else. He was a very enterprising entrepreneur. Teddi and I had seen a play in a cramped little theater on lower Second Avenue and she thought David should see this theater for him to possibly purchase and produce plays. She brought him down there and that is exactly what happened. To overcome the limited space, he created the only two-sided theater in New York. Instead of "Theater-in-the-Round," it was "Theater On Both Sides!" It became the well-known "4th Street Theater." One day he called soon after his play, *The Dybbuk*, opened.

"Mark," he said. "I want you to play Channon."

"David, you already have a Channon."

"He's leaving… I want you."

"Why didn't you want me before?" I asked. "I did, but you're always doing television." "I gotta make a living," I said.

"You can still make a living and be in my production. If something comes up, you can do it and still appear at night. Right?"

"I don't know, David."

"Mark, you'll play with Morris Carnovsky… and Eva Rubinstein, Arthur's daughter. She's a doll. Do it for me, please."

That is the chain of events that led me to appear in a wonderful old Yiddish play about an intended bridegroom who dies in a spiritual pursuit. Then his tormented soul enters his intended wife's body, refusing ever to leave after she is forced to marry someone else. It was a powerful and scary evening in the theater with music and colorful costumes of the Polish Shtetl. I was pleased to be in the production and stayed for a few months at the end of the year and into 1955. Eva Rubinstein was a doll and very beautiful. My only regret is that I never got the photograph with Arthur Rubinstein that we took after a performance. Morris Carnovsky had this distinctive stentorian voice, it vibrated with mellifluous authority. It was a kick to listen to him declaiming as the old and learned Rabbi. Here I was sitting next to an actor who had done much to help make the Group Theater the famed acting company it had become in the eyes of the world; a man who had played some of the finest roles written by one of America's greatest playwrights, Clifford Odets; a man who had also had a long and good career in motion pictures, but was now finding the doors in Hollywood steel-trapped shut. Here we were putting on our makeup in a shared, dreary and congested dressing room on Second Avenue. Morris and I became friends, and I was very sympathetic to his situation.

The only problem was he was always trying to encourage me to come to some leftist rally for some cause or another. His wife, Phoebe Brand, would call us and also try to entice us to attend. One night when we weren't playing, we reluctantly went to some meeting on 11th Street in the Village. It was crammed and raucous, and people were making speeches deriding the government. Woody Guthrie played and sang some exciting songs of the thirties: "… I'm stickin' to the union!" he whined. "I'm stickin' to the union!" I was getting uncomfortable. I then saw a guy snapping pictures and I said to myself: *Whoa… we better get the hell out of here!* So, we left This was a time of turmoil and political unrest. Joe McCarthy's rabid pursuit of communists behind and before every klieg light was still resonating, and the House Un-American Activities Committee was still wreaking havoc in the entertainment industry. Elia Kazan and others had named names and black listing was destroying careers. I knew it was awful, but I was in no position to take a stand, and I didn't want to fight somebody else's battles from the past. I was just a young actor trying to get started and make a life. I didn't want it to be cut off before it began. Soon after this event, Morris left the show and was replaced by another fi e actor from films and a perfect gentleman, Ludwig Donath. I didn't know anything about his political inclinations, nor did I ask. He played the old Rabbi differently, and his beard was shorter.

David Susskind, well-known for being an erudite and loquacious talk show host, was also a successful television producer. In early 1955, I received my initial first star billing on a Susskind-produced TV program called *Justice*. I was very conscious of other "names" on the show appearing with me and how prominent they were or had been in the business, and here I was, getting top billing. It didn't go to my head. In a way, it humbled me. Immediately following, I starred on another quality *Philco Playhouse*, a show that was to alter my life dramatically. I suppose, having been in the hit play *End as a Man*, and having been seen playing a tough, head-honcho cadet, the character was not too far from what I was hired to play on *The Bold and the Brave*. I was again a tough cadet in a military academy setting, but I was also a wise-ass bastard. Eva Marie Saint's husband, Jeff Hayden, directed an excellent cast extremely well. Tom Tully, John Kerr, and I starred, and a collection of other terrific actors included the funny, rotund Jack Weston. In rehearsal (as I have tried to do in all of my work), I was looking for some kind of physical activity in my performance that would be interesting to do that would nail my concentration. I found it, and it opened the show: I sat behind a desk talking to another cadet, and all through our conversation I tossed pistachio nuts into a glass on the desk a few feet away. For some guided reason, I never missed! The program received a lot of attention and critical acclaim and was being heavily talked about in the land of sunshine and palm trees. They were looking at a kinescope (rudimentary film copy of the aired show), particularly at John Kerr, who had starred on Broadway in *Tea and Sympathy*, to play Gary Cooper's son in a major new film. While viewing, they couldn't help but notice me. More about that to follow shortly.

A couple of months later, Jeff and Eva Marie were putting together a summer stock package to star Eva as Lizzie in Richard Nash's *The Rainmaker*. The play would tour the summer circuit for eight weeks hitting the best theaters in Maine, Rhode Island, Massachusetts, and Connecticut. I was very pleased when Jeff asked me to play opposite Eva

Marie as File, the marriage-resistant sheriff who has a warm spot in his heart for her and has some terrific scenes. Aside from the fact that she was one of the hottest and most beautiful actresses of the day, she was also a fine actress as evidenced in *On the Waterfront* with Marlon Brando, winning an academy award in 1955 for best supporting actress. Will Geer, a wonderful character actor and another victim of the blacklist, played her father; Jack Mullaney and Arthur Storch, her brothers; and Sidney Armus played the rainmaker. It was a congenial acting company and everything went smoothly in rehearsals and continued during the tour. The reviews were highly favorable everywhere we went, and Eva Marie was a huge draw and packing them in. It was a pleasure to be on the same stage with her. She was an unpretentious, down-to-earth, nice girl, and when you looked into her eyes, she was there—alive and responsive, emanating someone easy to love (she is still the same all these years later).

Teddi traveled with me for a few weeks. While we were in Falmouth on Cape Cod, we stayed in a cabin by a magnificent lake that was isolated and phone-less. One morning at about ten o'clock I was half asleep in bed when there was a knock on the door.

"Who's that?" Teddi whispered. I couldn't figure out for the life of me who would be at our door, way out in the wilderness at this hour. The knock came again. I got up, wrapped a towel around myself, and went to the door.

"Who is it?" I asked.

"It's Eva," the voice said. "I should have worn my hiking boots!"

I opened the door, surprised to see Lizzie in shorts and pretty in no makeup. "Hi..." I said with a smile. "What's happening?"

"Your agent's been calling for two hours," she said. "What do you mean?"

"I'm sorry I couldn't get out here any sooner. I couldn't find your cabin and you don't have a phone... anyway they want you in New York to meet William Wyler about a film. You better call your agent. Sounds exciting!" Then she turned, and waved goodbye.

"Thanks, Eva!" I yelled, as she quickly disappeared up the path.

I just stood there, not knowing what to do first, my heart starting to pick up a few beats. Then I turned back to Teddi and rushed into the room grinning broadly. "We gotta get to a phone!" I said, throwing off my towel. "Meet me in New York... what the hell does that mean?"

About forty-five minutes later, we finally got to a phone and I found out. "Just get the flight out of Boston at one o'clock," Stephen, my agent said. "It'll get you into La Guardia and I'll pick you up in a limo. Then you can go straight to the St. Regis Hotel. Mr. Wyler will be waiting."

Sidney Armus drove me to Hyannis airport to get the flight to New York. I was surprised to see Jack Mullaney on the plane. He was going to the same place, but not for the same part. The film to be shot was *Friendly Persuasion*, by Jessamyn West, based on her book of short stories about the Quakers during the Civil War. Jack was being considered for the son of Gary Cooper, which they still hadn't cast, and I was up for the young officer in love with Cooper's daughter.

I knew about William Wyler long before I met him. I had been a film nut as a kid and my memory for great films lingered in my head. I knew he had directed some of the finest: *Dead End*, *The Best Years of Our Lives*, *The Letter*, *Jezebel*, *The Heiress*, and *Detective Story*. He was a giant and I indeed felt privileged to be sitting in his suite, waiting for him to appear. When he finally walked in, wearing a robe and his cock-eyed smile, it was like meeting an old friend whom you haven't seen in a year. We had some pleasant small talk, then he said, "You're a good actor. I saw a film of that military school show." He laughed, his funny, impish Wyler laugh. "You were a real bastard." He looked at me for a long moment, then he said simply, "Can you be a nice guy?"

I smiled and answered just as simply: "I am a nice guy, so that shouldn't be too hard."

I think he liked that because when I finally got up to shake his hand and say goodbye he said, "Don't take anything until you hear from me."

As I walked down the hotel hallway to the elevator, the words kept repeating in my brain: Don't take anything until you hear from me. Wow… I arrived back in Falmouth just in time to put my makeup on. It had been a wild day that any actor would be thrilled to have but more of the same was looming—and even wilder. I had made an arrangement with my agent that I would be calling him for the next week just to be on the safe side. A couple of days later, the thought of Hollywood sunshine was getting cloudy, so I called Stephen at ten o'clock in the morning.

"Oh, Mark… I'm glad you called. I was getting nervous. They want you to do a test today at two o'clock."

"Today?" I asked, my heart doing flip flops, and wondering how I was going to make the complicated arrangements. "How am I going to get to New York today and at two o'clock?"

"On a plane, of course… they will reimburse," he said. "Let me find out… I'll call you back."

I called the airlines and got a sinking feeling. There were no commercial flights from Hyannis to New York that day. None! I called him back.

"Get a private plane!" he said. "This is urgent." "Uh… will they pay for that?" I asked.

"Hold on," he said. I waited three minutes and then he said, "They will pay for a private plane. Get one!"

I found out that they had private planes for hire from Hyannis airport. I called and made the arrangements for them to pick me up at the Coonamessett Airport in Falmouth in an hour. Dear Sidney Armus, God bless him, had been graciously driving me around and now drove me back to our cabin to get a clothes change and a cup of coffee before taking us to the airport. Teddi was excited and a bit apprehensive, as I was, anticipating this flight on a small plane. Did I say Coonamessett Airport? It was a cow pasture with ruts in the landscape, and all of the other stuff that cows do. The three- seater Bianca looked like a sick old bird as it landed and bounced, fi ally coming to a stop. Destiny called and I was answering. I kissed and hugged my wife, said goodbye to Sydney, boarded the plane, and sat down in the back—the pilot and co-pilot in front. I belted up and closed my eyes. I guess I was praying. In a moment, we were off, the plane's propeller whirring, the engine roaring. We were picking up maximum speed and were just about to take off when suddenly a tire blew on the left side like an explosion, throwing the plane into a violent rocking, almost turning us over at high speed. It was terribly frightening, and it wasn't until the pilot got the light craft under control that we realized we were extremely lucky not to have been killed or seriously injured. The pilot shook his head and apologized. I got out of the plane and saw Teddi in the far distance. She must have been scared as hell. I remember raising my arms at my side, palms up as if to say, "Thanks God… but do I need this?" I grabbed my small bag out of the Bianca and jogged to meet Teddi. She was trembling when we embraced. I was somewhat numb.

"I gotta get to a phone," I said. Sydney, ever helpful said, "Let's go."

When I got my agent on the phone it wasn't Stephen, it was a smart-ass sub agent in the office who I never took a liking to. He couldn't have cared any less about my near death, all he said was "Get another plane… they're waiting!"

By this time everybody in the Hyannis airport knew there was this crazy actor who wanted to fly to New York, on a stork if necessary. Finally, I was able to hire an air taxi service that picked me up at Coonamessett in a Taylor Cub, then flew me back to Hyannis for a switch to a tiny, suffocating Beechcraft. By this time, I was exhausted, hungry, and perspiring profusely—but at least we were on our way to LaGuardia and would be there in an hour and a half, hopefully. I took out the four pages of *Friendly Persuasion* dialogue that a Wyler assistant had handed me at his hotel in case I was called back for a test. I hadn't memorized the lines. The limo and my agent were waiting for me when we landed, and we immediately zoomed off to Manhattan, finally pulling up to a nondescript brownstone on Second Avenue near 83rd Street. I was ushered up the stairs by a friendly, stooped-over giant of a man who was really only a kid. Stuart Millar was 6-foot 5-inches and twenty-five years old, but he was as sharp about the movie business as anyone I have ever met. He was William Wyler's right-hand man and was actually responsible for getting the kinescope to Willy so he could see my performance. He ushered me up to the makeup room on the third floor to get me ready for the test. I had a good suntan so I didn't need that much. Wardrobe people brought me a Civil War uniform to put on, which I refused, opting instead to wear the Western sheriff's clothes that I wore in *The Rainmaker*, which I had brought with me. I hoped Wyler wouldn't object. It was just too damned hot to wear a woolen uniform. I met the guy sitting in the next makeup chair who was testing for another film and a contract at Twentieth Century Fox. He was young and very handsome and his name was Roger Moore.

Stuart informed me that Phyllis Love had been there testing for the part of Gary Cooper's daughter, and when she heard that I was coming, she requested to do the test with me. I was pleased about that—she was my friend and a relationship already existed. I wouldn't have to break the barrier to create a fictitious one. Stuart also told me that Robert Wyler (Willy's brother) and his wife, Cathy O'Donnell, had gone to see me in *Rainmaker* and had liked my performance, reporting that back to Willy (who had probably sent them). I have always equated shooting a film take to when the curtain goes up on stage—the camera (and director) staring at you like that fellow in the first row, except that the director is more discerning and the camera is much closer. It is the same when the camera blinks red in a television studio. At that moment in time, you are "on," and you can't run and hide. You have to deliver. When I stepped before the camera, Wyler was warm and cordial. This was to be the first and only screen test I have ever made. He set up the shot and we said our lines a few times and before we knew it the camera was rolling—and Mattie and Gard Jordan, a Quaker maiden and a soldier, were falling in love.

After Wyler was pleased with our scene, he asked me to just talk to him, answering his questions as I faced the camera. I was beginning to get the hang of it and then it was all over. I shook hands and said goodbye to everyone and rushed down the stairs to get the limo and then negotiated a mad dash to LaGuardia airport and the air taxi for the flight back. It was now after five o'clock. Up in the air I looked out the small window at the slowly moving landscape below, the shadows getting longer and darker, the engines droning incessantly—all the details of an incredibly exhilarating and trying day skipping around in my head until I dozed off. The smiling face of my wife and a warm embrace greeted me as I deplaned. I felt as if I had just returned from a battle in a distant land, a victorious gladiator, taking my woman. At that moment, I certainly didn't feel like performing in a play. I had to shake off the day and quickly generate a whole different mindset, as dependable Sidney drove us to the theater. We had a performance in half an hour and it was sold out.

The Westport Country Playhouse in Connecticut was one of the best summer theaters in the country—intimate, beautiful, and prestigious. Just to be on that stage, sitting on a couch, twirling my cowboy hat, and staring into the lovely eyes of Eva Marie Saint as I emoted in a slightly Western drawl, was a happening that I will never forget—and a couple of other things too. One: Jeff Hayden had grown exceedingly unhappy with Sidney Armus's performance, so instead of getting a professional actor to replace him, he went on in the part himself! Opening night, no less! Two: Sometime during the end of the week I received a phone call from Stephen Draper.

"Well, Mr. Richman… are you ready for a trip?" "Uh…depends on where I'm going."

"How would you like to fly to Hollywood for ten weeks?" "Oh, my God," I said. "You mean I got the…"

"Yes! William Wyler likes you a lot and wants you in his picture and they are going to start shooting in two weeks. We're working on the contract right now."

"Wow… when do I have to leave?" I asked, chills tickling my neck. "I'll find out. They want you out there for wardrobe and makeup tests before they start shooting. You ride a horse, don't you?" "Sure," I said, never having been on a horse in my life.

"Good," he said. "They asked about that because you'll be doing a lot of riding."

Hollywood and Gary Cooper

WE DIDN'T BLOW A TIRE on the take-off, but after about an hour in flight, I noticed the sun coming through our window was now beaming to the other side. Hello? Are we turning around? I looked at Teddi, who was still holding a yellow rose from the bouquet she had received from Allied Artists. I didn't say anything. Phyllis Love, my friend and test partner who would also be in the film, was sitting with her husband, Jimmy, a few rows ahead. Did they sense something was not right? Finally, the pilot on our flight to Los Angeles said on the speaker: "Ladies and gentlemen….may I have your attention please. We have detected a fire in our left engine. There is nothing to be alarmed about, but we are going back to New York as a precaution and we will be dropping fuel so, please, put out all cigarettes. There will be no smoking allowed. Put out all cigarettes, please." My wife gripped my hand tightly and whimpered something. I tried to comfort her as best I could and said to myself: *On my first flight to Hollywood to make a big movie with Gary Cooper which I may never get to do and I have nothing to be alarmed about? Is he out of his platitudinous fucking mind? And what the hell is it with airplanes and me?* When we finally touched down at the New York runway—back where we began after a two-hour flight—I was now able to exhale, my knuckles returned to their normal color, and Teddi was almost smiling again. We lost another hour waiting and finally boarded a second plane. Crossing our fingers, we were off again, hopefully, to the western land of sunshine and flicks.

There were no jets in 1955. The American Airlines flight to Los Angeles took almost eleven hours non-stop, and we were drag-assed tired when we landed. Paul Price, the Allied Artists public relations representative, had a bunch of photographers bursting their bulbs, and we rose to the occasion. Phyllis, a Broadway veteran of major roles, looking like the young girl she was going to play, and I, in my seersucker suit and growing sideburns for the role, posed and smiled through our first Hollywood photographic episode. Then, escorted into a long black limo, the four of us were driven to our designated living quarters at 3950 Los Feliz Boulevard—comfortable apartments with a pool and only five minutes from the studio.

I was up at 6:00 a.m., but it was already 9:00 a.m. New York time. I was too excited to mope in bed. I wanted to see what the land of paradise was like in the daytime. I quickly dressed and rushed out to go for a walk. The birds chirped loudly in the quietness and the sky was as blue as it could ever be and it was magnificent. The stately palm trees rising to the heavens took my breath away. The sun was shining and it was warm and comforting as I walked the street of manicured lawns, and then, something hit my eyes! I suddenly couldn't see! I blinked my eyes and they were burning! Profuse tears were running down my face! What the hell is this… in this land of dreams and fantasy? I soon found out. It was smog—corrosive, health- threatening, particulate smog. Heavenly blue skies were only a mirage.

Friendly Persuasion was to be the big one for Allied Artists and the Mirisch brothers. It was a major step upward with a three million dollar budget, which was enormous at the time. Their "B" productions were to take a back seat. A few days before we started shooting, I was sitting at a long table in a studio office room ready to read through the script. Willy Wyler, ever warm and smiling, greeted everyone as they entered and pointed to a chair at the table. There was a hush when Gary Cooper walked in, the icon of the industry, tall, erect and with a slight gimp from too many horse falls—a wave of his hand and a shy, self-conscious smile on his face. Then he sat down next to me. After the introductions by Wyler, he reached out his hand for a shake. I loved the man instantly. I had seen him a hundred times on screen, sympathetic, steely-eyed and heroic and now, here he was in the flesh wearing a dark blue sports jacket, white shirt, and a gray tie—your friendly, gentle, unassuming MAJOR STAR. I sat there fingering my script as I looked around the table, feeling privileged and grateful to be among such accomplished screen talent. I'd never thought seriously about myself in Hollywood. It was like thinking about going to the moon; the idea was too far-fetched. I remember returning a long-distance phone call to agent Ronnie Lubin at the Jaffe office in Beverly Hills. I was standing in a phone booth outside of Gimbel's department store on 7th Avenue.

"Hello, Mark... I'm glad you called," Ronnie said.

"Well, hi... uh, what's this about?" I asked, the traffic booming around me.

"Mark, I represent your agents in New York on the coast, and consequently, I represent you. I have some interest out here for you to be in a Burt Lancaster picture. Burt saw something you did and..."

I didn't get the Lancaster film, but I remember thinking how extraordinary it would've been to be shooting it at a time not so far removed from when I was managing a drug store. As it turned out, Ronnie Lubin was again representing me—this time with Wyler, who owned 50 percent of me and Allied Artists, the other 50 percent I had a basic seven-year contract, with two pictures a year and gradual salary increases. Financially, I felt like I was floating on whipped cream.

Dorothy McGuire, sitting opposite me, was a very fine actress. She had a sweet, open face and distinctive, lilting voice. We developed a close relationship and remained friends all through the years. I always felt that I could talk to her about anything, and sometimes I did. She played Cooper's Quaker minister's wife and was lovely in the part, although she told me later that she always felt that Willy never wanted her, hoping for Katharine Hepburn instead. It tightened her up a bit unnecessarily. Anthony Perkins, who played Cooper's son, was long and lean with boney shoulders that had the appearance of a clothes hanger being stuck in there somewhere. He was a very handsome, gifted young man and a bit self-possessed. Dorothy Jeakins, the Academy Award winning costume designer on the picture, latched onto Tony and became his confidant and mother hen. I guess he needed one. Tony and I got along well, but there was an air of detachment about him that was difficult to penetrate. I remember "Coop" getting really pissed at Tony and the only time I ever saw him angry. It was an extremely hot afternoon on location at the Rowland V. Lee Ranch in the San Fernando Valley where the Jess Birdwell Indiana farm and home were created. The three of us were sitting around talking and waiting for the next set up when Tony said, "Coop, what was it like when you were young... and blah, blah, blah, and tell us Coop when you were a young actor... how did you feel playing opposite... blah, blah...?"

Coop had had enough. He dropped his half-smoked Marlboro to the ground and crushed it with his boot and said, "Let's cut out all this youth shit!" Then he got up and walked away.

Phyllis sat close to me and smiled demurely. She had a lovely face, big eyes and a unique cleft in her chin and photographed divinely. A member of the Actors Studio also, she was playing Mattie, the Quaker daughter and was supposed to be about sixteen. I think that concerned her a bit. In the film, I thought she pulled it off with flying colors.

Robert Middleton, a heavyset character actor with a booming baritone voice, played my father. He was a nice man. Sometimes when Willy wasn't getting what he wanted in a scene, he could be tough on you—and he was on Middleton. I was watching him shoot a reaction close-up and it was the 25th take and Wyler was saying, "All right… raise your right eyebrow, drop your jaw… now laugh." I was sweating for Middleton.

There is a story with many variations concerning Laurence Olivier when he was shooting *Wuthering Heights*. They were up to the 75th take when Olivier in frustration said, "Willy, for God's sake! How do you want me to play the scene?"

Willy answered, "Better."

Wyler was a perceptive observer as a director, always open to what the actor brought—never missing anything. He had an uncanny ability to "feel" the scene as it was being played—to cry or to laugh in his involvement. He couldn't tell an actor how to get where he wanted him to go, but when he got there, he printed it. Willy was always open to colorful improvisation and had a brilliant touch for adding delightful moments. He was known for it. Like the time I come down the stairs with Mattie, having been up in the attic playing the organ. It was obvious the wounded civil war officer had his arm out of the sling. When Cooper gently put it back in and dusted my shoulder off, humorously, you knew they had been necking up in the attic.

Walter Catlett, a wonderful old character actor from vaudeville and a hundred films, blinked and chain-smoked incessantly—but when the camera was rolling he lost twenty years, stood erect, and never blinked an eye. He played the organ salesman that forced Cooper's minister wife to sleep in the barn when Cooper bought one. Catlett amused himself by riding out to location every morning, reading *Daily Variety* or *The Hollywood Reporter* obituary column. Ashes falling all over his chest, the smoke twirling from his nose, he would say something like, "Oh, look at that… Gunhilda Gleason kicked off. Great gal. I was with her in '26 on the Keith's circuit. She had a good dance act… with a partner in a gorilla suit." Marjorie Main was a treat, younger and more vital than I could have imagined with a voice that growled—her character, a ditzy farm woman with three daffy daughters. When she said her lines, just sitting at the table, she was already a full-blown character as big as life.

Wyler giggled and laughed loudly, enjoying her every delicious moment with Cooper. I remembered her strangely wonderful performance in the 1937 Wyler Academy Award nominated film, *Dead End*, as Humphrey Bogart's mother (one of my favorite films, I must have seen it ten times over the years).

It was heady stuff being in a room full of memorable legends.

Of course, I cannot forget one other remarkable participant sitting in the room, reserved and quiet and intimately involved—Jessamyn West. She was a delightful, freckle-faced Quaker woman and an important American writer. She had written the screenplay we were about to shoot based on her book We had an instant rapport and she sent us an inscribed first edition of every book she ever wrote from the time we met. Not to be morbid, we received the last letter she ever wrote. It arrived four days after she had passed away.

On my first day of scheduled shooting, I was riding in a bus, going to a distant location in Chico, California, by the Sacramento River. I'd been flown up there to complete a war sequence involving some serious action with the second unit. Wyler remained in Hollywood, working with the first unit directing Cooper and McGuire and other principles—including the goose! That's the way it's done in order to complete a major film in the allotted time with multiple locations and hundreds of extras; otherwise, the shooting could take forever. After a long and bouncy ride through the vast and magnificent countryside, we had finally reached our dusty location and were just about to get off the bus when I heard a wild yell: "STAMPEDE! STAMPEDE!" At that moment, I saw about ten horses running crazily toward the bus and beyond with wranglers on horseback chasing after them. One of the horses hit the bus and continued running but I knew it was injured. Well! I said to myself, *That's an exciting beginning. It's a damned good thing I didn't step off the bus.*

I was thanking God that I had taken two riding lessons at Fat Jones Stable the week before, because the first shot I ever performed in the picture as a Union cavalry officer was leading a contingent of fifty riders at a fast clip on a sunbaked dirt road and then into the river, where the horse reared up as I pulled back the reins. It was all captured in close shots and looks great in the film, but at the time it was scary. I wonder how I was able to ride, pull up and stop at a designated spot, and talk in a close-up—doing it all with only two lessons! Sometimes sheer guts takes over.

Friendly Persuasion is the story of a Quaker family who are pacifists and refuse to take up arms in the Civil War until the son (Tony Perkins) feels in his conscience that he must. This forces Gary Cooper reluctantly to do the same, much to the consternation of his minister wife, when his son does not return from a battle. There is a very tense scene when all the home guard are preparing to face off against the superior Rebel forces attempting to cross the river. Hiding behind logs and bushes, they are waiting my command to fire. At the crucial moment when I do yell "FIRE!," a distraught young Quaker (Tony), crying at the thought of killing someone, takes sight of his target and finally pulls the trigger, killing a young rebel. He is emotionally devastated. It is a beautifully done piece of work, and thanks to the second unit director's patience (Tommy Carr), who gave Tony ample time to prepare before the camera rolled.

Gary Cooper was an impressive gentleman. He was kind, thoughtful, unpretentious, and shy. When you were with him, you couldn't help but feel the history of motion pictures emanating from his every pore. At first it was a little disconcerting. Every look, smile, voice change, or gesture had been experienced by you in a huge magnified presence. It took a while to get used to the smaller image. He was like a brother, a warm friend—at least to me. I will never forget the times he would take me to lunch. I would be walking along the street at Allied Artists in my Civil War uniform and he would pull up in his silver Bentley, roll the window down, and say, "What're you doin' for lunch, Marko?" I can hear that in my head as if he were saying it right now. He would patiently wait a few minutes while I hurriedly changed in my portable dressing room, grabbed a shirt, and dashed back. Then we were off to the renowned Brown Derby on Hillhurst near the studio to settle in for a couple of hours in a secluded booth. Private moments with one of the most famous and respected men in the world. To say that it was an honor to be with Coop is an understatement. It was fun and a real joy. He had a way of putting you at ease because there was no guile or self-importance about him. He was just who he was and that was it. I always felt he enjoyed my company too. He was very conversant on a wide array of subjects and far from a "yup" man. My only regret is that I cannot remember a quarter of it! I have often thought it would've been great to have had a hidden recorder, not to deceive, but just to remember those times. He told me that he always regretted that he'd never been on the stage, and he envied the kind of experience I'd had in the theater. (Can you imagine that?) He was so charmingly humble. "How do you learn all those lines… and repeat the same performance every night?" he asked, as if that was something he could never do. He also said that he was impressed with the work they were doing at the Actors Studio. (He knew that Phyllis Love and I were members and liked our performances in the picture.) At that particular time, it so happened that the Actors Studio was on a fund drive and I had been asked to pitch in. I didn't want to be too pushy, so I gingerly said, smiling to cover the push, "Uh… Coop, would you like to contribute to the good efforts of the Actors Studio?"

There was a pause, then he seriously answered, "Would $5,000 make me a member?"

I gulped my chicken curry, chutney, and nuts, a Brown Derby specialty and favorite of mine, and said, "I think that can be arranged, Coop… and I will personally see to it!" We both laughed. As it turned out, he made a $500 contribution, and we were damned pleased to get it.

At night in early September, we had to sleep around the pool or die in the rooms of our apartment. It was a sweltering 110 degrees and it broke the records—suffocatingly unbearable, that's what it was. In the daytime at the Rowland V. Lee Ranch in the San Fernando Valley where we were shooting, it was worse—especially since I was wearing a woolen uniform atop a sweating horse. There's a particularly poignant scene when I come to say goodbye before I go off to battle and Mattie refuses to see me. Sadly, I ride off. Then she realizes her foolishness and comes chasing after me, barefooted. I finally hear her calls, pull up, and go charging back to her. I dismount and we embrace, declaring our love. I don't know how many times I galloped up and down that road before Willy was pleased—wool and leather rubbing unbearably against my thighs and crotch—but I could hardly walk for several days afterwards. In the weird ways of movie making, we didn't get to shoot the close-ups of our embrace and declaration of undying love until four months later on a sound stage! The magic of the movies.

Willy always kept everyone guessing about what was to be shot each day, even though the daily schedule listed specific scenes. Sometimes he would get a whim to shoot a particular something that was not on the schedule and we just had to hop to and be available in makeup and costume, ready to go. Consequently, the assistant directors who ran the daily activities were afraid to let anybody go home, just in case. Sometimes I would sit around in makeup and costume for a week and never get to work. It took me a while before I realized how to play the game. I was in makeup all right, but the clothes—I learned how to throw them on in a flash. Actually, the shooting was extremely slow and methodical, with plenty of time to dress after the scene had been rehearsed and set. The cameraman still had to go to work and light it to perfection, and in a quality feature the lighting can be endlessly time consuming. I came out to shoot the picture on a nine-week contract and was on the payroll for four and a half months. I wasn't complaining. I counted my blessings with every bank deposit.

Phyllis, Tony, and I did do a lot of that standard fan magazine crap: cooking dinner together, playing cards, and the "hanging out" phony stuff that somebody must enjoy reading about. The P.R. department was always coming up with some peculiar idea to involve us photographically on and off the set. I did begin to realize, however, that the publicity and promotion for selling the picture would concentrate on Gary Cooper, of course, and Dorothy McGuire. In the "new young people" department, the emphasis was not going to be on li'l ole me or on Phyllis. They were going to focus heavily on Anthony Perkins and try to establish him as a major new star. He had the part, the looks, and certainly the potential to be one, and Paramount Studios was already lining up future films for him to do. I was less than lukewarm to my next contract picture obligation that seemed to be in the works. It was called *Hold Back the Night*, about marines battling it out in Korea. Aside from the biggie I was working on, their first, Allied Artists weren't known for quality output and that disturbed me. I still had a lot of work to do before I would have to commit, so I temporarily closeted my feelings.

Gary Cooper was a great listener. He heard every word you said when you were playing in a scene with him. He wasn't just waiting for the cue to speak. Cooper had this large head and deep blue understanding eyes, and when you looked into them he was really present. You could see the thoughts bouncing around in his head and you couldn't help being more concentrated because he gave you his complete attention. He was a far better actor than people gave him credit for. During this time, I'd become rather adept in my off-the-cuff impersonation of Cooper's voice and walk. When Jessamyn West and I were together, she always requested my mini-performance. Years later, she still insisted. I tried, but the gift had grown cold. One night Cooper graciously took his young contingent, Phyllis Love and her husband Jimmy, Tony Perkins, Teddi and me, to the world-famous Romanoff's for dinner. Coop brought his young beautiful daughter, Maria, with him. First, he asked us to come to his home for a drink—a lovely place in Beverly Hills off Sunset Boulevard. We wandered through his spacious estate, marveling at the elegant surroundings, his painting collection, and then his gun room, which he was particularly proud of. He was great dresser. I remember he wore a light color sports jacket and pale silk tie, looking every bit the movie star without trying. Of course, when we finally were seated in a plush booth in Romanoff's, we all experienced the deference shown his presence. Later in the evening, more so, when they rolled out this cart with a huge, sizzling chateaubriand on a tray for him to approve before serving. He expertly sliced a section, tasted it, and then said, "A little bit more."

The waiter bowed obsequiously and replied, "Yes sir, Mr. Cooper!" then wheeled the cart away. I knew I would never see anything like that again.

The thought of staying on the West Coast when I finished *Friendly Persuasion* was getting more difficult to accept. I was an idealist and didn't feel that I was a Hollywood actor, whatever that was, but an actor for the stage and I should be in New York studying to be the best that I could be. I wasn't ready to settle in here. I missed the hot cauldron of Actors Studio activity and learning. I had the sense that if I stayed out here doing films only, my talent would be attenuated, stultified, and would dry up like the desert in Palm Springs. I was too young for that. I had to make a decision—my next film, the one about the marines in Korea, was looming and they wanted an answer. I was under contract and I had to comply or there would be trouble. I talked to my agents and found out that the only way I could forfeit the contract was to plead psychological disturbance from not being free to develop my career on the New York stage.

That is exactly what I did. I turned down my next film and made my agents very unhappy, because in rejecting my deal, I was also reneging on my commitment to Wyler. He would lose the opportunity to loan me out to another company for a higher fee—higher than the one he was obligated to pay me, which is what directors/producers do when they sign new talent, hoping they will get hot and thereby earn them money on loan-outs. Ronnie Lubin thought it was a foolish move, but went along with my wishes.

I was determined to see it through no matter how long it took to resolve. I was psycho on the subject. Several weeks later, after threats, conversations to reconsider, and persistent doggedness, it all worked out in my favor—the contract was null and void. William Wyler was the top of the line, and I had more than a twinge, but Allied Artists, I couldn't have cared less about. Whether I made the right decision is open to conjecture, but at the time I was free and clear and my life was my own. I was happy about that.

After adding a short vacation in Mexico City and Acapulco, we were pleased to be back in our New York apartment after such a long time away. I was gratified to have completed a job in a quality picture, my bank account reflecting the high-caloried intake. I realized I was now in an elevated career position when the phone began to ring with more consistency. I was soon back on live television, appearing in a show about illegal wiretapping on *Armstrong Circle Theater*; and then I flew off to shoot *The Adventures of the Sea Hawk* in picturesque Hamilton, Bermuda, a windswept island with a thousand sail boats and yachts— and all very distinctly British. The most notable aspect of that engagement was the fact that I played opposite George O'Brien, a nice guy and a former huge silent screen star trying to make a comeback in TV. This was a pilot for a series, but unfortunately, Mr. O'Brien had difficulty remembering lines—a problem for a series right from the start. Phil Karlson, an excellent feature director, was in charge and delivered a good film in spite of many difficulties. I remember shooting a horrendous hurricane scene on a sound stage with enormous wind machines going full blast and water hoses so strong that no one could stand against it, and we didn't—falling and flopping in the fictitious raging storm on a sailboat at sea. It was very realistic and also a miracle that someone wasn't electrocuted, compelled as we were to stand around in a foot of water, next to all the sparking electrical equipment and cables.

One of the lighter but annoying situations concerned sleeping. I was staying at the Princess Hotel and at that time they washed all the bed sheets in salt water. The salt would dry into the fabric pores and when dry had the feel of cold rubber—not conducive to a restful night. There was also an extremely active and vocally demonstrative sexual liaison going on in the next room—like wolves in the darkest night, they moaned and howled as long as I was there.

A Hatful of Rain by Michael V. Gazzo, another Actors Studio-developed play about a wounded Korean War veteran who becomes a drug addict, was a major running hit on Broadway. After an audition, Gazzo and Frank Corsaro, the director, and Jay Julien, the producer, were interested in my taking over the addict role, successfully played by Ben Gazzara. I was to go into the production for the last couple of months on Broadway and then tour the country in the national company. Needless to say, I was thrilled to accept. I would be working in a great part, Teddi and I could see the country, and I would be well paid. Nothing is ever so simple. Suddenly, an unknown Steve McQueen was in the equation.

Corsaro, the director, for his own reasons wanted McQueen to play the addict role, while the playwright, Gazzo, and the producer, Julien, wanted me. I didn't get the part, and I was really quite pissed after all the overtures and attention. True to my feelings, I said *fuck it!*, and moved on.

James Baldwin was a dear, gentle man with an air of vulnerability about him. He was soon to be a literary explosion. He had a dramatic reading at the Actors Studio based on scenes from his second novel *Giovanni's Room*, which concerned one man's struggle with his sexual identity. I played David and I can't remember if I was or wasn't.

At this time, the Music Corporation of America (MCA) was wooing me full-time to make a break with my agents and move to them for representation in all fields. Eleanor Killgallen, Ina Bernstein, and Monique James were very persuasive. MCA had enormous clout and lots of fingers in a lot of pies. I held them off for a while, my loyalty to Stephen Draper being the main reason. While all of this was going on, a film version of *End as a Man*, by Calder Willingham, was in the works. It was now called *The Strange One*, and Jack Garfein, the stage director of the play, would be doing his first directorial film assignment. Jack wanted me to play my original role in the film for ten weeks' work to be shot in Winter Park, Florida. I read the script and it was not the play. I was disappointed. I would still be the head cadet, but a lot of the meat and focus had been cut. The movie would be a case study of a psychotic, more than military academy discipline problems as in the play. I didn't think it would be a good career move after *Friendly Persuasion*, which hadn't been released. MCA kept the pressure on. They invited me up to their luxurious offices on Madison Avenue, paraded all the agents in to greet me, and told me how much they could do for my future and that I would be foolish if I didn't put my career in their hands. I finally succumbed, signing on the dotted line for three years. That was the first time I met Lew Wasserman, except that I had to traipse into his office to shake hands. But MCA weren't the only ones on my tail. Jack Garfein would not quit no matter how many times I said, "No!"

"Mark, listen… I know a crucial scene between you and Ben is missing from the play, but Calder is still working on the script."

"He doesn't want to write it, Jack," I said, "otherwise it would be in there already."

"No, Calder knows we have to have that scene. Trust me," Jack said. "If he doesn't write it, we will!"

Conversations like this continued up until the night before the company was to fly to Orlando, Florida. I was driving myself and my wife crazy. Finally, with my billing now second to Ben Gazzara, an excellent salary and per diem, and also getting ten days off in the middle of shooting to fly back to New York to star on a TV show, I reluctantly said okay—much to the dismay of MCA who frowned on it and said it was a definite career mistake. I was worried that it was, too, unless I got that extra scene that Jack had promised.

We all got our hair trimmed to a military cut and commenced shooting at an actual military academy. The surroundings were immensely impressive and couldn't help but influence the characters we were playing. One of my first shots in the picture was to address several hundred cadets standing in front of a microphone. I could have sworn to anyone that day that I was a student military officer. The main contingent from the play was in the movie, except for James Olson, replacing Albert Salmi, who now played Gatt, my stupid roommate, and George Peppard, who was making his screen debut playing an important role instead of William Smithers. Calder Willingham, who was supposed to be doing rewrites, was nowhere to be seen; Sam Spiegel, the legendary producer of this film, was everywhere—a likeable, charming, difficult to figure out, and exasperating personality. We found out that Sam had sent Calder to Ceylon to do rewrites on *Bridge on the River Kwai* and would not be available. That altered the possibility of getting that crucial scene I wanted in the picture. Finally taking matters into our own hands, Jack Garfein, Ben Gazzara, and I figured out a way to include material from the play by a rewrite and a shooting plan. We were excited about it and Jack put it on the schedule. It took two days to shoot and Sam Spiegel was furious. Jack and Sam had not been getting along, to put it mildly. Jack, feeling he was getting royally screwed by a breach of his contract, walked off the set in a huff and the production was shut down for a few days. Sam called us all together and blabbed on for an hour calling Jack "an ungrateful punk" who was overstepping his authority and if he didn't stay within his boundaries, he'd get another director. Jack's agent arrived and after some exceedingly hot negotiating, they both agreed to "make nice" and shooting resumed. The scene we shot opens up with me skipping rope (I'm a boxing champion) down a path, the camera following, when I discover my roommate up in a tree with Jocko (Gazzara). I forcefully tell them to get down, and Jocko and I get into a fight. It was a scene that motivated my character to pursue the court-martial of Jocko, getting him thrown out of school, which happens at the end of the picture. I thought it was a terrific scene and so did everybody else. However, Sam, who held the money reins and the final cut of the picture, said to me in his colorful, mid-European semi- Hungarian accent: "Mark… that scene will never be in the picture!"

"Why, Sam," I said. "It's a damned good scene."

"I'll tell you why, Mark… and this is very important. It is wrong for Benny's character."

"Oh, I don't agree with you, Sam," I said, knowing it was a lost cause. "I think it helps his character and clarifies the film."

He was shaking his head, the long cigar in his mouth dropping ashes on his bulky belly. "But don't worry, Mark," he said, smiling as he touched my shoulder. "I will write you another scene. An even better one."

I do recall some scribbled Spiegel notes and dialogue on a yellow pad that Jack showed me that we both laughed at, but that was the end of it. The scene that we shot was never considered or even cut together.

I flew back to New York for ten days to fulfill the previous commitment I had made to appear on the *United States Steel Hour*. The segment was called "Partners," and starring with me was the fabulous actor Luther Adler, who played my father. He was a powerful Broadway performer from the legendary Adler family and an actor who had created many of the Group Theater's great roles. "Partners" was the story of a son bursting with new ideas, in business with his Dad who wants to hold on to the "old" ways—and the inevitable conflicts that ensue. The only conflicts I had were with the director, Elliot Silverstein, who was difficult and inhibiting. I remember in one rehearsal when I wanted to eat something in the scene and he objected. He said, and I quote, "The only actor I have ever seen that can look well when eating is Olivier… so don't do it. I don't want any Actors Studio mannerisms."

I was pissed—and I voiced this to my dear Luther who said, "Patience, Mark… be patient."

I tried and I was miserable, but several days later before the dress rehearsal, Luther said to me, "You were right, the sonofabitch is driving me crazy!"

Adding to my distress, after the dress rehearsal, the producers came to me in my dressing room with tense faces and asked me to heighten my performance by attacking my father with more passion. This was something I had wanted to do all along, but had been squelched! So, on the air, LIVE, I had to alter my performance, since this was live television and no chance for retakes. At last I could let loose. Thankfully, the show was very well received. I have a letter from Elliot with his praise, blah-blah and: "Thank you for your cooperation and the excitement of working with you."

I thought, *Yeah, sure...*

The one wonderful thing that came out of the "Partners" experience was my lasting friendship with Luther. We became close. He really thought of me as his son and even invited us to a family dinner at Stella Adler and Harold Clurman's apartment (husband and wife) to celebrate Luther's son going to M.I.T. All the Adler family were there and us. No other actors. It was a memorable dinner, and later Henry Morgan and Zero Mostel came. They were the dessert. Over the years Luther and I worked together several times more and it was always an honor. We had a warm, hugging relationship and I think of him often. I miss his vital presence.

Back in Winter Park, the shooting continued, but we had some welcome visitors: Carroll Baker, Jack Garfein's pregnant wife, still looking like the "Baby Doll" she was on screen, except for a rounded tummy; Elaine Stritch, Ben Gazzara's inamorata; and my darling wife. We were all good friends in New York, so the warm summer afternoons around the motel pool kept us all loose and laughing when we weren't shooting. One particular evening when we were doing only night shots, the triumvirate—Carroll, Teddi, and Elaine—took off for a concert nearby to see the blossoming pelvic piston, Elvis Presley. We had more than a few laughs when they related the antics of the singer and the frenzied crowd. Elaine, whose many theatrical triumphs were still to come, was the funniest cut up of the group, her infectious sardonic humor and laugh kept us constantly amused. Near the end of production there was a wrap party and Elaine, Carrol, and Teddi performed a song and dance number doing a parody of some of the lines from the film. Even Sam Spiegel was entertained, although he was the butt of some of the jokes. Elaine, with a wink and a nodding innuendo, had the gift of making any innocuous line sound outrageous and funny.

A couple of weeks before the wrap party I had a very strange phone call. It was from Jay Julien, the producer of *A Hatful of Rain*.

"Listen, Mark... uh, I guess you're surprised to hear from me?" "I'm surprised, but it's nice to hear from you."

"Yeah. Uh, to get right to the point," Jay said, "we made a mistake. It's not working out."

"Oh? What's not working out, Jay?" I asked, as if I didn't know. "Well… Steve McQueen, he's just not cutting it. I'd like you to consider replacing Steve as soon as you get back into town."

I felt like saying: *You can take the play and stick it up your fucking ass and one up Frank Corsaro's ass too after what you put me through!* But I didn't.

"Uh, I don't know, Jay," I said. "I have some things cooking now and I'm not sure I could do that."

"Well, please consider it, Mark, please," he said. "We'll make it worth your while."

Soon after, I got another phone call from Michael Gazzo, the playwright, who basically said the same thing in his raspy New Yorkese except for, "I told those motherfuckers to listen to me… I wanted you, but they wouldn't listen!"

It's always nice to be wanted. I told Mike I had to think it over seriously and I would make a decision by the time I got home. Winding up the schedule, the last two days were concluded with some heavy duty night shooting involving a kangaroo court-martial that my character instigates and presides over—swarming cadets, screeching cars, and a slow-moving train upon which I throw the crazed Gazzara. End of picture. End of our stay in Winter Park, Florida.

Back in New York I discussed the *A Hatful of Rain* situation with my new MCA agents, notably Maynard Morris, an influential gentleman who handled legitimate theater, Eleanor Kilgallen, who was the head of the TV department, and Ina Bernstein, who I was the closest to. They all felt it would be a positive step for my career. We worked out a good contract and I agreed to go into the Broadway show for a month then take it on the road—first stop for the national company, Chicago. I knew they were seeing actors for other roles in the production, so I asked them to give my wife a reading to play "Putski," a sexy, young junky that saunters into the play in the third act. They agreed. She auditioned and much to my pleasure and hers, she got the role! Now she was off the shelf and active in her own career. Not only would we tour the country together, but earn two salaries as well.

A Hatful of Rain

Johnny Pope, the drug addicted husband of *A Hatful of Rain*, is one of the most strenuous roles ever written for an actor. There is enormous tension and suffering in the play as Johnny avoids revealing his desperate addiction to his father and pregnant wife; his wild, hallucination frenzy in the second act is chillingly violent and exhausting. I had seen Ben Gazzara in a fine performance opposite Shelley Winters as the wife soon after the play opened. I decided to observe Steve McQueen who I would be replacing shortly. At the time, he was not a well-known actor or the film personality we all remember him by. I am sorry to say that he was totally inadequate and lost. He did not have a clue in how to fulfill what was required from scene to scene. It was unfortunate, but I understood immediately why he was being replaced. I never did get a satisfactory reason from the director, Frank Corsaro, as to why I wasn't cast in the role in the fi st place, but that's show biz and reasons are never forthcoming.

Working your way into a running hit can be ticklish; the staging has been set and the actors are comfortable and locked in to the way it was. A new actor with a new personality and his own way of doing things upsets the apple cart a bit, but finally the cast adjusts and accommodates the changes if they are valid. I went into the production at the Plymouth Theater opposite Vivian Blaine, a film star who had come back to Broadway triumphantly in *Guys and Dolls*. We worked well together, although I don't believe she had the depth of Shelley Winters. Frank Silvera, who had created the role, was formidable as my father, and my dear friend Harry Guardino was marvelous playing my simpatico brother Polo. Teddi was sexy adorable and weird as Putski; also in the cast was Gavin MacLeod who played Apples, a drug peddler. (He was also my understudy and had an unsightly brown wig tucked away for his bald pate in case he ever had to go on.) The last month of the Broadway run was a good break-in for me, and I felt prepared for the road.

The brutal, swirling winds of a wintry Chicago guarantee a perpetually bad hair day. Just to revolve out of the doors of your hotel tempts you to revolve back in. It was cold and miserable. Fortunately, the opening night crowd for our two-week run at the Selwyn Theater was used to the weather. They were cozy and warm in their seats and their reception was even warmer. The critics, too, welcomed our initial touring company with solid reviews. Even Claudia Cassidy of the *Chicago Tribune*, a feared lady with a razor pen, wrote, "Two powerful performances... when the stage in held by Mark Richman as the addict and by Harry Guardino as his brother... has some theatrically vital things to say."

I was ready to settle in for the long haul. We were a hit show wherever we played, the only difference was audience reaction. You could sense the quality of attention when we played the Royal Alexandra in Toronto, in contrast to the slumbering reserve at the Schubert in Detroit, Michigan, where the coma persisted after the performance because there was absolutely nowhere to go. We would laugh about it, but the desolation was everywhere. Harry Guardino, Gavin MacLeod, Teddi, and I would cab around a dark and dangerous Detroit, getting nowhere in our search for a dining establishment and finally winding up eating oatmeal or French toast in a coffee shop near the hotel. Things perked up considerably when we got to San Francisco, one of the most uniquely beautiful cities in the world—the lazy walks on the slanted streets, the galleries, the cable car ride to the magnificent bay, a boat excursion around Alcatraz, or a luscious luncheon at the Top of the Mark. It was a city to feast the eye and the stomach and warm the shivers from our many engagements in wintry landscapes of the Midwest.

Friendly Persuasion opened at New York's Radio City Music Hall to good reviews and then all over the country. I had begun to feel a sense of celebrity that I hadn't known before, being in a major film and a traveling Broadway hit. When we opened in various cities, the film seemed to follow us around. Many of the critics included a comment on my screen performance with the play's review—the two roles so vastly diverse and well received. In January 1957, *A Hatful of Rain* opened at the Huntington Hartford Theater in Hollywood for two weeks. There had been a heightened sense of anxiety before the opening, the movie industry staring down our throats, but it all went well and the reviews were uniformly excellent. What I remember most about the engagement were my opening night "house seat" guests, Talli and William Wyler. They came backstage after the performance and insisted that they take us to the Brown Derby across the street for a bite to eat. Talli, a sweet and beautiful woman, softened and complimented Willy's naturally dominating presence. He was effusive in his praise, his funny smile and laugh punctuating his comments about how different I was from Gard in *Friendly Persuasion*. I've always had the feeling when I was with Wyler that I was in the presence of a superb artist with rare vision and sensitivity. He was one of the truly great directors of Hollywood, his vast variety of works still reverberate with truth, humor, power and pathos—from *Counsellor at Law*, *Wuthering Heights*, and *The Best Years of Our Lives* to *Ben-Hur*. It was an honor to have appeared in one of his films and I am grateful.

During coffee time, Willy asked if we would like to go for a ride in his new Rolls Royce. He was rather keen on showing it off. So, there we were at 1:00 a.m., riding around Hollywood in Willy's gorgeous tan Rolls while he proudly explained the gears, the exceptional braking system, and the "quietness" of operation. He was as enthusiastic as a young kid with his new red bicycle. When Willy finally dropped us off at our hotel, we exchanged warm hugs and goodbyes, then stood and watched as two lovely people pulled away and waved one last time.

While in Hollywood, many people from the movie industry came backstage to see me and pay their respects, but a little lady I remember most vividly was not a film star or a mogul; she was none other than the most renowned American madam of all time, Polly Adler. The assistant stage manager of the show was a friend of hers, and he brought her to meet me. Polly was not an attractive woman; she was small in size with a basso voice that would stifle a frog, but she was an absolute delight, warmhearted and witty. We hit it off the moment our eyes met. It was like I was meeting a long-lost relative, someone I had known and loved as a child, an aunt who had gone away unexpectedly. (Maybe it was because we had the same birthday, April 16.) She held my hands, like an aunt would, complimenting my performance and wanting to know all about me and my plans for the future. Then she invited me to come to her home for a small gathering if I was free on the Sunday coming up. I had a few days before visiting her to find the paperback edition of her memoirs published in 1951, *A House Is Not a Home*. I devoured it. It was one of the most fascinating and revealing chronicles of a life I'd ever read. According to the *New York Daily News* her name was "synonymous with sin." This woman was a legend of wild and outrageous proportions and there was no way just meeting her that you could ever suspect her amazing past. In the flapper twenties and the depression-era thirties, when New York was wide open and lawless, she ran the most popular and notorious brothels in the Upper East and West sides. Her "apartments" were luxuriously decorated with excellent furnishings and thick carpeting, the walls were lined with bookcases filled with writers of note, and the prostitutes in her employ were of higher quality and individuality—and, of course, luscious. What established her places above the rest was the way she ran them. The girls were available to perform their services, but the atmosphere was more like a club, a place to meet and party—and the partying went on constantly until she quit in 1943. (She made a ton of money selling booze during prohibition.)

She had many close friends in all walks of life, especially government, show people, and mobsters. For years she protected Dutch Schultz, hiding him in one of her houses, shifting him around when necessary, and fearing for her life if she were ever found out. In one of her famous quotes she said, "I am one of those people who just can't help getting a kick out of life—even if it's a kick in the teeth." She was arrested many times but never convicted, paying off law enforcement and crooked judges. For a Russian immigrant who went from a Brooklyn sweatshop to a close friendship with Dorothy Parker, Robert Benchley, and the Algonquin set, her life was truly remarkable. It is said that George S. Kaufman had a charge account with Polly—and he was not the only one she kept a ledger on.

In the late afternoon on a beautiful Sunday, I drove past the house on a quiet, over-hanging tree-lined street in Burbank. I backed up the car. "I guess this is her place," I said, making sure of the address. It was rather small and somewhat nondescript. I parked, we walked to the house, and I rang the bell.

After a pause, the door opened and Polly stood there beaming. "Come in, come in," she said, welcoming us warmly.

In the hallway, looking around and trying to be cordial, I said, "Nice house, Polly."

She looked at me impishly. "Home darling... it's a home."

All three of us laughed. I told her I had read her book and she was flattered. She hovered over us as she introduced us proudly to her other guests. I didn't know or recognize anyone in the group. We had drinks and a deliciously prepared dinner, Polly making sure, true to her nature, that everyone was having a good time. With a glass of wine in hand, we wandered into her den and noticed the enormous collection of books and albums, row upon row of leather-bound volumes. I extracted one from the group and was more than surprised to see that they contained 8 x 10 portrait photographs of Polly's girls! Clothed, that is, and quite elegantly—all spectacularly attractive. There were at least fifty photos in each album, and I stopped counting the albums at twenty when Polly came into the room and said, "That's them… that's all of my girls."

"I see," I said, "and I haven't found an ugly one in the bunch." "Thank you, but even if one was not as beautiful as some," she said,

"they had something else. They had a charm, a feeling, a special quality that embraced you. That's why my girls were desirable." Polly spoke of her girls as one would reminisce of a family, now separated by marriage and distance. It was touching.

"Polly, we're impressed also with all of your books, all those famous authors," Teddi ventured. "You must do a lot of reading."

She laughed. "Yeah, I'm always trying to improve myself, smacking knowledge into my head. That's why I went to college when I quit years ago."

"I read that," I said. "That's remarkable."

"Nothing's so remarkable if you want to do it. You do it!"

"Tell me, Polly," I said. "I know you've been asked this many times, so indulge me… what really made you quit being a madam?"

She took a deep breath, then exhaled slowly. "Well, if you want to know… the war was on and things were changing. New York wasn't the same anymore… and running the kind of places that I had didn't seem to make sense. My heart wasn't in it."

After we said goodbye that day, we didn't see Polly for several years, although we corresponded occasionally.

Johnny Pope, as I have said, is an exhausting role and I was really feeling overly tired and drained; leaving the warm West Coast weather for the freezing cold again only added to my discomfort. I was beginning to lose the desire to continue after six months. By the time we had opened in Minneapolis and the temperature hovered around ten degrees below zero, I had had enough and decided to give notice if they could replace me. The tour still had many cities to play, including Philadelphia, but I thought it was right thing for me to do at the time. Teddi agreed with me; she knew how fatigued I was. Ben Gazzara was eager and willing to take over in the next city and the unknown Diane Ladd, getting a good break, auditioned to replace my wife as Putski. Teddi had understudied Vivian Blaine and was a bit sorry that she never got to go on as Celia, although she had come close once in Detroit when Vivian had been nipping a bit too heavily. We held the curtain until she finally showed up a half-hour late, the audience noisily restless, Teddi was reluctantly compelled to remove the garments of the leading lady.

Leaving the show was a wrench, but I never regretted it. We flew to Miami Beach to unwind and get some sun, settling in on Collins Avenue in a furnished apartment near Teddi's parents who were vacationing. One day, while stretched out absorbing the glorious warmth and tanning rays of the sun, I noticed a spectacular-looking elderly man in skin-tight pink swim briefs feeding the pigeons swarming around him. His muscular body was so well proportioned and beautiful he could have been the model for Michelangelo's *David* in another time. In the afternoon I saw him again, and this time he was wearing pale blue swim briefs. I couldn't resist finding out who the guy was. I walked up to him, introduced myself and we shook hands. He was a "dems" and "doze" guy with a warm smile and appealing personality and his name was Nick. I soon found out that Nick was *the* "Charles Atlas," immediately recalling his photographs in a thousand magazines as the "I was a 97-pound weakling…" fame. His exercise routine, labeled "Dynamic Tension," stresses one set of muscles against another and is still practiced worldwide. I have used the principle myself for years and I am pleased to say that it works. He told me he had sold the franchise and retired to Miami. I suppose he was in his early 60s, but he had the body and the muscularity of a thirty-year-old. The "97-pound weakling" became my beach buddy for the week, and he even gave me some personal tips on how to get the most out of his Dynamic Tension. (I've often wondered if he'd ever cheated with heavy duty weights and bar-bells.) Teddi and I posed for pictures with "Mister Atlas," my father-in-law doing the snapping, and I still get a kick of amusement whenever I look at them.

Live television in New York was dying a slow and gurgling death; it was moving to the West Coast and being shot on film. Series TV was blossoming and they couldn't get enough good actors to carry the load in Hollywood, so they were flying actors out from New York. I became one of those commuting thespians, zooming in for a week or four days, then rushing home only to be called back again in a week or two. It all began in 1956 and it continued until I moved out to California to do my own TV series in 1961. I cannot begin to count the number of flights I took to fulfill my TV obligations. It was exciting, exhausting, and fun, and the future held all kinds of career possibilities.

The cross-country propeller flights were long and tiring. This was before the jet engine shortened the travel time considerably. I'd worked out a plan to simplify my life once I landed. I'd rent a car, drive to the Montecito Hotel in Hollywood (the place was full of New York actors), register for a suite with a kitchenette, and drive to the Hughes Market to buy my groceries. The first time I met Clint Eastwood, he was staying at the Montecito and shopping at the same market. He was an unknown contract player at Warner Bros. and hadn't made his big splash. I remember thinking, looking at this tall, handsome, blonde dude: This guy can't miss. The actor folks who came to Hollywood to work with their noses tilted slightly upward usually stayed at the Chateau Marmont, but the more down-to-earth ones stayed at the Montecito. I met so many prominent theatrical people there, I started to keep a list. One of the funniest experiences I had from that group came out of my relationship with Brendan Behan, the former I.R.A. bad boy, renowned writer, and alcoholic. At the time, his hit play *The Hostage* was mounted at the Huntington Hartford Theater. He was enjoying his success and even showed up to greet the audience on stage at the curtain call the night I was there. He had stopped drinking and carrying on, but he was in every sense a gregarious, warm, and delightful extrovert.

Sitting around the pool one day I said to him, "Brendan, would you mind if I got my camera and shot some film of you with my Bolex?" He looked at me and smiled broadly.

"Go get your camera, me boy," he said in his heavy brogue. "I'll wait for ya."

I dashed up to my apartment and rushed back with my Bolex and Rollicord, then proceeded to shoot slides of him as he cavorted about, posing like a primping seal. The other guests at poolside were enjoying this strange fellow with an enormous belly and a peculiarly large, convex belly button. At one point he said, "Get ready for this, me boy!" and jumped into the pool with a huge splash. I grabbed the Bolex just in time to catch him going under again and coming up to moon me—doing it more than once! Consequently, I have a five-minute "collector's item," a piece of priceless film—Brendan Behan doing his uninhibited thing.

Not every experience at the Montecito was pleasant. Something happened that I would consider to be lucky, or maybe even providential. I was again at the pool sitting and talking, this time with Roddy McDowell. Ray Walston, of *My Favorite Martian* fame, was at the other end of the pool and had fallen asleep. His two-year-old daughter was playing in the shallow water and having a splashing good time. I turned to Roddy to finish a comment in our conversation; many seconds later when I turned back, I sensed out of the corner of my eye that the little girl wasn't there anymore. She had disappeared. Alarmed, I sat up and then jumped up to see her face down in about two and a half feet of water! I immediately jumped into the pool with my clothes on and pulled her up and out as she began violently gasping for air and regurgitating water. It was a very scary moment. A few more seconds and she would have drowned. Years later, whenever I would meet Ray with his now-grown daughter, he'd say, "Honey, this is Mister Richman and…" and she would finish, "He saved my life! Dad, how many times do we have to repeat this?" Ray and I would look at each other and laugh.

Jane Wyman was one of the first major stars in films to venture into television. A gracious and considerate woman on and off the screen, she welcomed me on her show on two occasions. The first time, I played opposite her as an army officer dealing with a serious problem at a military base; it was a privilege and a joy. The second time I appeared on *The Jane Wyman Show* was in a script titled "Roadblock No. 7," playing a wrongly accused murderer opposite Margaret O'Brien, for years a delightful child star and now a self-effacing, beautiful young woman. I especially enjoyed a working relationship with the sheriff who was chasing me, the veteran Robert Armstrong, whom I'd seen as a kid pursuing the original King Kong! Back in New York at the Actors Studio, I worked up a scene with Phyllis Love from *Anatol* by Arthur Schnitzler. Lee Strasberg leaned on me for being superficial and not digging deep enough. Following that, I did two rather successful and funny scenes. One was with Doris Roberts, as a newlywed couple on a train to their honeymoon that I adapted from a Dorothy Parker short story called *Here We Are*. Lee especially liked how I had the train movement in my body during the whole scene and thought that my character comedic abilities should be utilized professionally. The second, with Rosemary Murphy, was from another adaptation I did of a short story called *Return to Kansas City*. I played a young fighter preparing for his next fight in his apartment—which was pretty silly to begin with. I exercised, skipped rope, and shadowboxed while the wife nagged him continually. I finally sat down and played the ukulele, singing off key, "Who's Sorry Now?" It was hilarious. All the physical action we did together was totally improvisational and added in rehearsal to enhance the dialogue, giving a "life" to the characters, which is really what the Actors Studio is all about.

At home on West 20th Street there was another "life" developing. My wife informed me that she was pregnant with our first child. I was thrilled, just like you see all those smiling "Dads to be" in the movies. We'd been married five years through a bumpy period of adjustment, but it was time; we loved each other and we were ready. We couldn't have been happier. When I was about twelve years old, I had actually made a vow that when I got married and had children I'd never treat my kids the way my mother treated me, giving me such a lousy, miserable childhood, and have them suffer the way I did. I'd always let them know how much I loved them and how important they were to me. I was going to get the chance to fulfill my vow.

An example of just how crazy this cross-country jaunting could be presented itself when my agent called and said, "John Frankenheimer wants you on the West Coast for a *Playhouse 90*." John was one of the hottest directors working in television. I flew out to star with Kim Stanley and E.G. Marshall on a TV adaptation of Clifford Odets' *Clash by Night*. At the first rehearsal, while we were reading the script aloud at CBS-TV to hear how it sounded and played, I couldn't help but notice that they were slicing my part, here, there and everywhere out of necessity for time. Joe was an important role and suddenly it was disappearing under a blue pencil. To say that I was displeased would not be true—I was really pissed. Back at the Montecito, I called Eleanor Kilgallen in New York and said, "Get me out of this!"

In about ten minutes the phone rang and it was the casting director of CBS, Ethel Wynant. "I'm very sorry, Mark," she said. "It was the only way we could cut the show, it's too long. John [Frankenheimer] wants to have you out here again as soon as possible."

I flew back to New York trying to forget my irritation and the fact that I wouldn't be doing a classic Odets drama with someone I truly admired, Kim Stanley. As far as Frankenheimer wanting me out there again soon… yeah, sure.

When Teddi was almost seven months pregnant, bursting at the seams, and looking as adorable as any almost-mother could be, the phone rang. It was Kilgallen, who said, "Guess who wants you on the coast?" I told her that I didn't want to leave my wife alone at this time. Not in the least deterred, she said, "Can Teddi act?" Of course, I said "Yes." Ten minutes later I was set to star in another Frankenheimer *Playhouse 90*, a Western called *The Last Man* with Sterling Hayden, Carolyn Jones, Hurd Hatfield, Lee Phillips, and Wallace Ford—and Teddi was set to play Sterling Hayden's very pregnant wife! That was what I call quality agenting. We flew out to the coast and settled in at the Montecito, my home away from home. This time I let my wife do the shopping at Hughes Market! I didn't know this when I signed on, but Carolyn Jones's husband was a scrawny young man by the name of Aaron Spelling, and it was his script that we were going to do. They were one of the first to send us a pre-birth gift. I must admit that I was more than astounded in later years when Aaron became this gigantic television icon. I applaud him for it. He had the pulse of America's tastes in TV entertainment and was responsible for producing more hit programs, for a longer time, than any other mogul that preceded him. I performed on many of his shows, but more about that later.

Sterling Hayden was a shy, insecure, withdrawn sweetheart of a man. I really liked him and the feeling seemed to be mutual. I played a gunslinger, one of the gang he recruited to rob the gold in the small town he felt was responsible for the death of his pregnant wife. We were a fine ensemble and Frankenheimer was a stimulus to creative and free development of character. He allowed me to add all kinds of unusual touches such as every time I was to kill someone my hands would sweat, so I would ritually wipe my fingers with a kerchief up my sleeve before withdrawing my gun and firing; when Sterling finally kills me, the last of his recruited gang, I smash against the wall and slide down adding a line I suggested: "I didn't know it hurt so much." For years afterward, whenever John and I would meet he would smile and say, "I didn't know it hurt so much." Two of the most hair- raising and technically crucial scenes in the show were the opening and the bank robbery. I was involved in both. Remember, this is live TV, millions are watching, and there are no second chances. In the opening, I am in a ten paces duel as the camera pulls back and dollies with me as I walk the count. At the count of ten the camera is now behind my hand as I pull the gun out of my holster and fire—the gun EXPLODES, and twenty paces away we see my adversary blown away! (Just think how stupid it would have been if the gun hadn't gone off, or if I couldn't have gotten the gun out of the holster.) That was why I spent several hours taking lessons from Rod Redwing, a Native American and expert in quick gun withdrawal. I practiced endlessly, walking around with my holster and gun, repeating a fast "two- finger" draw, as per Rod's instruction.

The second complex scene concerned the robbery. It began with my killing a shopkeeper, dousing his small store with kerosene, lighting a fuse, walking out the door and the whole length of the studio with the camera following me all the way to a tight close-up. I stop, withdraw a wooden match, strike it with my right fingernail—and when it lights up at the tip of my cigarette, the building that I doused behind me EXPLODES! Then I step forward and tip Hurd Hatfield's hat, signaling the robbery to begin as the townspeople run to put out the fire. This was another precision-timed, directorial touch by John Frankenheimer, who went on to become one of Hollywood's finest film directors of taut dramas like *The Manchurian Candidate*.

During a break in the dress rehearsal, a few hours before we went on the air, I had a telephone call on the set from Martin Ritt, a wonderful director I casually knew from the Actors Studio. I had read for him once for a film with Sidney Poitier that I didn't get.

"Hello, Marty… nice to hear from you," I said. "How's it going? What're you doing?"

"Well… uh, *Playhouse 90*. I'm just about to go on the air…"

"Oh, great… listen, Mark… I'm doing a picture at Paramount called *The Black Orchid*, and I've got a part for you. I want you to come in and meet the producer, Marcello Gerosi."

"Marty," I said, "when you say you have a part for me, does that mean I have the part… or Gerosi has to approve me first?"

"Shmuck, you got the part. I just want you to meet him!"

When I hung up, I was elated with the fact that what took place had never happened to me before; the prospect of doing a feature film and being handed the role.

My wife was pleased too, but the picture was set to start in a couple of weeks. How would we work out this baby business being on the West Coast?

The ninety-minute show went on the air without a hitch. I was pleased to have worked with so many exceptional people, especially Wally Ford, another old-timer. I had seen him so many times in fine films. Hurd Hatfield was a delight and had a self-deprecating wit that kept Teddi and me laughing whenever we were together, telling us stories about his first films, including *The Picture of Dorian Gray*. Seconds before we went on the air, Teddi, sitting high in a Western wagon next to Sterling as his sickly, pregnant wife, whispered to me as I passed her to go to my opening position, "He bought me a beautiful present!" Sterling had given her an expensive, oversized carpetbag in the style of the teleplay, leaving it in her dressing room with a lovely and touching note. She still has it today and it is a treasured remembrance. I will never forget the wonderful day we spent with him and his kids at his spacious Sherman Oaks home. At the time, he was going through a strenuous divorce, but he was warm and gracious and expressed a sincere interest in us. A former marine, he'd become a film star on his spectacular good looks, but he was untrained as an actor. He was fascinated by the process of acting and told me he was startled when he watched me work by how I could gear up an emotion of anger so spontaneously. I told him, without getting pedantic about it, that it was all a kind of a method, to get yourself free and expressive—dropping inhibitions and allowing yourself to follow impulses. I told him, "Anger is easy… it's the other emotions that are hard."

One of the most incredible-looking women I have ever seen in my life without the slightest reservation is Sophia Loren. The first time I saw her, I was talking with someone on a street at Paramount and she slithered by. Wearing jeans and a tight sweater, her movements as she walked reminded me of a panther—they were so smooth, supple, and sexy. She was the living embodiment of feminine attributes all the great sculptors could only dream of.

I had been signed to a good role in *The Black Orchid* starring Sophia and Anthony Quinn, with Ina Balin playing Quinn's daughter—the girl I was in love with and about to marry. We sat around for a week on a sound stage reading through the script with Marty Ritt listening intently and making notes. I was mesmerized by Sophia, who would look at me, smile, and then bat her beautiful eyes. She was twenty-three years old at the time and with the way that she looked, I couldn't figure out for the life of me why she was married to an old guy like Carlo Ponti—who was, of course, only responsible for her career and co-producing this picture. Every day I would mention the allure of Sophia in one way or another to my very round and pregnant wife, who didn't appreciate it one bit. I wonder why I didn't realize at the time how dumb that was? During the week of rehearsal, I met Joseph Stefano, who wrote the screenplay. (Later, he wrote *Psycho*.) There is an interesting story attached to his script and his wife—who wasn't his wife at the time. In 1953, when we lived on Elizabeth Street, there was a young woman who lived across from our apartment named Marilyn Epstein. We were quite friendly, and one day she said to me that her boyfriend, Jerry Stevens, a musician, had written a TV script called "The Flower Maker," and there was a part in it that I would be right for. Jerry never got it off the ground, but years later—now 1958, and I am working on a picture called *The Black Orchid*—the author is Joseph Stefano who used to be Jerry Stevens, but he is now married to Marilyn Epstein, and the part of Noble that I am playing is the same part! It was a happening that has always astounded me. Whether it was fate, chance, or destiny—Marty Ritt told me he wanted me for the same kind of nice guy performance that Wyler got out of me in *Friendly Persuasion*. Later Joe Stefano told me that Marty had said to him when they were discussing casting that he was thinking of Mark Richman for the role of Noble and Joe answered: "That's exactly who I had in mind!"

Sophia, playing a Mafioso widow who made artificial flowers, was made up to look older, wearing a wig and drab clothes. Tony Quinn, living next door, falls in love with her, but his daughter is jealous and, having psychological quirks, hides in her bedroom, refusing to come out. Sophia comes to the rescue, solves the problem, and we become a happy Italian family. During the weeks of shooting, Sophia and I became good friends. One day on location she was a good sport and patiently let me shoot a whole role of film of her (thirty-six shots). Unfortunately, she was coiffed in the ugly wig and drab clothes. Sophia was one of the most genial people I've ever met, certainly for someone who was the focus of everyone's attention—and the most relaxed actress in front of a camera I've ever seen. She was thoughtful and considerate and never said a negative word about anyone. Whenever we weren't shooting, we would spend hours talking to each other in her dressing room on the set, her high-pitched giggle sometimes punctuating her amusement. She once told me to have my eyelashes dyed darker to make my eyes stand out. She laughed when I said I would ask Tony Quinn's opinion. Tony was another fine actor I enjoyed working with. He was easy at adjustments and changes and always allowed my performance to fit in comfortably with his, in moment-to-moment playing. The only one I had a bit of a problem with was Ina Balin. She was playing a troubled girl, but I felt she was rather cold and detached unnecessarily in our scenes, causing me to work my ass off to maintain a level of loving her. Another infuriating annoyance happened when I asked my makeup man (a fine one) Karl Silvera if he knew how to trim hair—I needed one on the back of my head. He said, "Of course," and then proceeded to butcher me unmercifully. The next day I had to take publicity photos and every shot has this utterly stupid haircut—forever! I learned a good lesson: Always make sure the person you enlist is the specialist he says he is. Released in early 1959, *The Black Orchid* turned out to be lovely film—warm, emotional, and absorbing. Under Marty's direction, the performances were first-rate and the critical reception was favorable.

I've always had a deep belief in God. I'm sure this feeling of a divine entity was always there inside of me. It had nothing to do with organized religion, which in a strange way had turned me off the adherence to the religion I was born into, Judaism, ever since I was a little boy. I mean, I participate, and go through the motions on sacred holidays and such, but religion has never been enough for me—any religion. I've always felt this way because I've never been comfortable having an intermediary between me and God—to preach and pray for me in a broad sense. Religion is good, good for the heart and mind, but I wanted something more. All my life I have been seeking a personal relationship with my creator, just the "Big Guy" and me—He is telling me what it's all about, guiding me in my life—and nobody in between. Teddi felt somewhat the same as I, she was a seeker too, but was far more devoted to Judaism out of respect and ritual, and doing what's always expected. By 1958, these "feelings" were at an apex. We'd already gone to many lectures embracing various pursuits, but hadn't found a true enough belief to say, this is it! During this time, I even attempted to practice yoga to reach a level of higher consciousness, but I quit all that when I passed out cold and split my head open during a deep breathing exercise. Our quest for enlightenment continued, however, with some peculiar twists. Teddi had been helped by a chiropractor when she had back problems as a young girl, so when her back acted up again, she found a good chiropractor in New York and was relieved of pain. I was resistant, having had a medical background, which disdained at the time any other pursuit of healing; but when we returned from *Hatful*, I was a wreck and finally succumbed to her insistent suggestion to see her man. To my surprise and joy, he began to alleviate my aches and pains, subtly altering my physical body to correct all the damage I had suffered earlier as a young football player, which was the source of my problems. I immediately became a devotee of chiropractic.

When we came out to California, we wanted to have another chiropractor available to us who practiced the same "non-force" technique we were used to. Dr. Vincent Messina in downtown Los Angeles was suggested to us, and thus began a long and meaningful relationship with a dedicated professional. He was not only a fine chiropractor, but he was also a man of great faith and spiritual pursuit. Of course, we were curious to know what he and his wife were involved in, but they were rather secretive about it. After much coaxing, he finally gave us a book to read called *The Path of the Master*. We were fascinated and couldn't wait to read it. I remember sitting down together at the Montecito Hotel, eagerly opening that thick book and each of us reading aloud a page at a time, hoping for answers to our sincere pursuance of the Almighty. By the time we finished page 463 two days later, we disappointedly closed the book. There were no answers, only more questions. It was depressing. It would be a noble effort, but there was no way that we would meditate two and a half hours every day, become vegetarians, and dedicate ourselves to some guru in India or someplace. This wasn't it; there had to be another way— but how do we find it? How?

A Volvo Delivery

Looking ahead before the baby's arrival, I had made arrangements to have two adjoining suites at the Montecito. The baby's nurse and the baby would be set up in one and we would be in the other. I also had the urge to buy my first car. When it was time to go back to New York, I could find someone eager to enjoy a cross country road trip to drive it back for me. A young woman getting a divorce had to sell her 1958 Volvo quickly, so I plunked down the cash for this three-month-old, terrific looking, black PV444 classic with red leather seats. Eagerly I drove to the Montecito to show my ready-to-pop wife our new toy. She loved it, of course. About ten o'clock that evening, I felt like showing off the car to some friends at the hotel (Teddi said that I should do it tomorrow), so Martin Balsam, Val Avery, and I drove around Hollywood, with me extolling the car's virtues. We finally wound up at Bobbie and Lee Phillips's house on Olive Drive. Olive Drive is a very steep hill, so I pulled the emergency brake, exited the car, and stepped into Lee's hallway. About ten seconds later, we all heard this tremendous crash that sounded like a hundred glass milk bottles breaking. I turned back and peered outside. My car was gone; the emergency brake had slipped and down at the bottom of the hill was my Volvo with red leathered interior, ignominiously smashed into a parked station wagon. *Oh, shiiiiit!* I muttered, as I ran down the hill in a panic, continually saying to myself, *I shouldn't have material things… I shouldn't have material things!* I just couldn't believe it was happening. I was in shock. It was like a horrible dream. The Volvo had hit the rear of the actress Phyllis Avery's car, and its front end had been totally demolished. We all had to agree to lie about when the accident occurred, so we stalled calling the police because my insurance with triple A didn't start until midnight and it was only 11:30 p.m.!

Meanwhile, I had to call my wife and tell her the bad news. I shouldn't have, because as soon as I did she immediately went into labor! Val Avery drove me back to the Montecito and graciously offered the keys to his car for the inevitable trip to the hospital. I thanked him and dashed up to our suite. Teddi's strong contractions had subsided, but were continuing erratically. I began recording the times and the duration and placed the pre-packed suitcase in the ready-to-go position. We called our obstetrician, Dr. Alfred Heldfond, to inform him of the situation, and the next morning at about 10:00 a.m. with the contractions the strongest, we were in the parking lot and I couldn't find Val's car. I thought I would have a baby myself I was so frustrated, and then I saw his car and we were finally on our way to the old Cedars of Lebanon Hospital in Hollywood. In the pre-delivery room, Teddi was doing very well under the circumstances, especially since her husband continuously excused himself to make phone calls to the police, the insurance agent, the towing company, and the repair shop. It's laughable now, but at the time it wasn't. Her travails before delivery came to be known as "Teddi's Volvo labor." It went on for a long time, the anticipation mounting, but at five o'clock in the afternoon, April 30, 1958, she gave birth to our firstborn, a son. Not long after that I wrote the following:

The first time I saw him, my bare newborn son, all pink and blotchy and wriggling with healthy uncertainty in a plastic bassinet, his navel covered with the simplest patch of adhesive white gauze, he was yelling, bellowing defiantly his freshly-filled lungs out. As I stood there, awestruck and smiling outside the delivery room, now left conveniently deserted except for him and me, my breath came short and stuck in my throat, and my eyes swelled with thankful, joyous tears. *Oh, my God*, I thought... and then I said out loud and unashamed for anyone to hear... "I have a son! A son! Me! Just like my father before me, and his father before him. A son!"

And then, moving in closer and bending down to study his precious, delicate likeness, his discontent suddenly lifted and he became quiet, calm and still... as if my presence, I like to think, had softened his discomfort and alleviated his fears. And still bent over, as I watched his long black eyelashes flutter, and the curve of his doll-like mouth smile at some mysterious provocation, I said to him in a whisper... "Hey, I love you. I'm your father and you're my son. We're a family now... your mother, you, and me...thanks to God. We're a family. Isn't that something?"

And then, convinced that he understood, his tiny mouth now grinning broadly, or so it seemed, I turned to greet the kindly nurse who informed me that I could see my wife now. As I walked down the corridor, I remember the eagerness in my heart to share the tender moments of grateful thanks with her and for our dream fulfilled… and the dreams and hopes and prayers for his God-given future of untold blessings and joys.

When we came back to the Montecito, carrying our baby, there on the brass mounted sign listing the guests was an addition—Gard Bennett Richman, newborn son of Teddi and Mark Richman. Gard was the name of the fella I played in *Friendly Persuasion*, and my wife liked it most of all the choices. It was a beautiful and extraordinary time to suddenly have this new little person in our lives, healthy, adorable, and a neat fit in my left arm when I carried him—like a sun-warmed football.

A few days later, I flew to Tucson, Arizona, and then small-planed it to Nogales to join the shooting company of a new TV Western called *Rawhide* as a guest star. Eric Fleming and Clint Eastwood were the series stars and the actor Richard Whorf was directing, who was also a fabulous designer and artist. Appearing with me, playing a padre in a long robe, which is pretty funny to begin with, was my friend Martin Balsam. In one scene, I sacrilegiously knocked him to the ground. The segment was called "Incident at Alabaster Plain" and I was the "incident," playing a colorful but dangerous gunslinger who kills his own father. The locations were fantastic, riding and shooting in Nogales, Mexico, and Nogales, Arizona, only borders apart. We spent a lot of time in scenes with the Native American Hopi Tribe and their children in an unforgettable church and mission that was built in the late 1700s. They were all part of a frightened congregation as I was pursued up the narrow church stairwell to the bell tower where I met one of my many film deaths—this time, the massive bell unexpectedly knocking me off the tower during a gunfight with Clint and Eric. This show, as if I needed it, established me indelibly as an actor who could play a miserable bastard with ease. Some producers thought I couldn't play anything else, memories being so short in television. In my small screen career, I have been killed so many times and in so many ways, I've always thought it would be a fun piece of film if I could ever put them all together and call it "Deathly Sequential." A sad note: Eric Fleming, shooting a film in South America a few years later was horribly killed. He fell into a river of piranhas.

Three weeks later, setting up Gard's room in our two-bedroom New York apartment was fun. The dark wood dresser with brass knobs looked attractive against the blue walls. I built a pine bookcase in the corner of the room for the books he would need a little time getting to. We could look out the window at the Catholic seminary across the street as we changed him and hear the church bells many times during the day. It was peaceful and pleasant on the sixth floor. Sometimes when my in-laws visited, we all went up to the tiled, twenty-third floor roof and relaxed on beach chairs, sunning and taking turns nuzzling the baby. It was a productive time and the future had promise. I was a working and developing actor, but I now had a deeper purpose in my life—I was a father. In early 1959, director Alan Schneider cast me as the leading man in a Broadway bound play by Sigmund Miller. It was called *Lovely Star, Good Night*, an insipid title if I ever heard one. It was later changed to *Masquerade*, not that it mattered much. I was a Connecticut doctor whose wife had a problem with frigidity in our young married life and it was screwing up the relationship. Marjorie Steel, Huntington Hartford's wife, was the wife rehearsing, and since he put up the money for the production everything seemed cool. I thought she was okay, but Richard Krakauer, the producer, a Runyanesque Broadway character, didn't like her; neither did Alan Schneider, who quit the production because he couldn't have Patricia Neal. He was replaced by a gay untalented director-dreg named Warren Enters, who was not a perfect choice to explain the problem of frigidity in marriage. I suggested Cloris Leachman, whom I adored, to replace Marjorie, and she got the part.

Since she was my friend, I thought it would be helpful to get a head start as soon as Cloris arrived from the West Coast. I remember sitting in a Plaza Hotel suite trying to explain the play and the sexual difficulties between the characters, with Warren Enters looking on somewhat embarrassed and offering zilch. Then, during a rehearsal break one day, he asked me to have lunch with him. He said to me in all seriousness, and this is the God's honest truth, "Mark, in your scenes, when I watch you… I can't tell when you're acting and when you're not acting." It was not meant as a compliment.

Glenda Farrell played my chic and adoring mother, wearing long, lavender chiffon robes that nobody ever wears except in 1935 movies—but with foxes supposedly running across the lawn, she looked great gazing out the French windows. Donald Cook, a wonderful farceur and Cloris's Dad, got a lot of laughs in the second act, but it didn't quite fit this particular play. While we were out of town, I found myself rewriting the play because it needed it desperately and Sigmund Miller couldn't or wouldn't do it. By this time, having left New Haven and now in Boston, Warren Enters was fired (but not soon enough) and our new director,

Jed Horner, a protégé of Moss Hart sensing a bomb on his hands, was encouraging my valid script changes.

There were many problems that weren't so solvable, but at least I could help make the dialogue easier to say. Even the set worked against us. At one point after an argument, Cloris smacks me in the face, I pick her up and threaten to throw her off a high balcony, except that it looked as if she would land in the garage on the first floor. On a humorous note, although it wasn't very funny then, I couldn't get Cloris to learn how to smack me on the face, upstage, with an open hand. She couldn't do it. One night she hit me so hard with the stiff part of her wrist and thumb, I almost flipped out. It was such a shock and I got so angry, I picked her up and carried her to the window with such a thrust, she thought she was going into the garage. (The audience probably hoped we'd both disappear). On Broadway, we opened and closed in one night at the Golden Theater, although Cloris and I received good notices. All that work gone to hell. The next morning, I went to retrieve my makeup and utensils from my dressing room. It was depressing, the powerful fragrance of dozens of roses in Cloris's room still permeating the air.

Suddenly, I was in demand to play the lead opposite star actresses who were, shall I say, a bit older. I suppose it began with Vivian Blaine, but it continued for a long succession of live and filmed television programs. I was more than pleased when I committed to appear in a *U.S. Steel Hour* titled "The Shame of Paula Marsten" with Anne Baxter and Gene Raymond. Anne played a trembling nutcase in a hospital and in my dedicated psychiatric doctor way, I was able to solve her problems and cure her. Oh my, how all the complexities of life and their miraculous conclusions give us hope to carry on—all wrapped up and packaged neatly, with a product to purchase to help us along the way. Anne was a wonderful actress and a fine human being. When I went to the Coast to do my first TV series, I rented a house in Pacific Palisades and had no beds. Anne immediately came to the rescue and supplied us with two bedrooms full of furniture that were in storage from her divorce from John Hodiak. I met her in a warehouse in Pasadena and had a choice of what I needed. Extremely gracious, indeed. Soon after, I starred on another *Steel Hour* called "The Hours Before Dawn" opposite Teresa Wright, one of the sweetest women I have ever met. Also starring was the powerful Colleen Dewhurst. A spooky domestic story, I was protecting Teresa from that bad Colleen, who was our housekeeper living up in the attic. During that time, I had a problem sleeping at night, noise disturbed me. (Maybe it was my son? Naaaa!). I do remember Teresa thoughtfully sending me a special box of cotton-wax ear plugs only found on the West Coast. I became addicted for a while, but then I couldn't stand the sound of my own heartbeat!

The June Allyson Show for DuPont was shot in Hollywood. I flew out to appear in "Ruth and Naomi" with June and Ann Harding, with whom I had worked in *Playwrights '56*. I must say it was a real charge to work with June and be her love interest, and whose wholesome image had been implanted in my mind from all the films I had seen of her. Actually, there was little difference between the screen persona and the one in the flesh. She was a genuinely nice person, friendly and warm, and maybe a bit insecure. I found it interesting and rather true to form that no matter how elevated you become in this business, under certain circumstances there's an unmistakable touch of insecurity—which doesn't take anything away from the talent of the artist. The shooting went well, and when I finished I visited the chic and hallowed halls of MCA on Burton Way in Beverly Hills. The place was so beautifully appointed and so damned intimidating, you would think you were visiting the King of Siam; then you realized you were only seeing another shlumpy agent in a dark gray suit. Things were brewing, I was told, but not imminent enough to keep me West, so I flew home to my wife and child in our little haven on West 20th Street.

Then something happened that was to change my life forever.

13 Subud—My Spiritual Search Is Answered

WHILE I HAD BEEN GONE, Phyllis Love, my girl in *Friendly Persuasion*, had spoken to Teddi about an English gentleman, John Bennett, who was going to give a talk at the French Institute about a new spiritual pursuit called Subud. He was a physicist who had written a book on the subject called "Concerning Subud." Teddi was fearful that I would reject her wish to attend, but I was immediately willing. At the lecture, attended by about a hundred people, the Englishman droned on and on about this new way to receive a contact with the power of God, first received and brought into this world by a man from Indonesia named Bapak Subuh. When exercised, this power acquired by the contact would awaken your inner life or sleeping soul. I was astounded. Awaken my sleeping soul? I found that extremely interesting, so much so that I fell asleep. When I woke up, Bennett was answering questions from the audience. For some reason, I had a compulsion to ask a question so I raised my hand and when called blurted out, like I knew what in hell I was asking: "Uhh… in Subud… uhh… what about your karma?" There was a pause, then in a polite answer that bordered on dismissal, the evening was over. Teddi was beaming and ready to sign up, but since I never jump at anything, I took a bit longer to scribble my name, signifying that we were candidates for the spiritual brotherhood, group or organization of something called Subud. As it turned out, it was the most momentous decision I have ever made in my life—and I have never doubted for one second that it was the right one for me to make.

That evening we also learned that Bapak Subuh was born on June 22, 1901, in Semarang, Java, and his full name was Bapak Muhammad Subuh Sumohadiwidjojo. ("Bapak" is Indonesian for father and is informal like saying Mister. "Subuh" means dawn in the Indonesian language and it is the time when he was born.) In 1924, Bapak, who worked for the municipality and was also studying bookkeeping, usually went for a walk at midnight for some fresh air to clear his head. One evening while walking, something quite strange happened unexpectedly. He saw a brilliant light above him that turned everything into day, and this light, as bright as the sun, suddenly accelerated and entered his head and filled his whole body. He started to shake violently and thought he was having a heart attack. He managed to get back to his home and immediately went to his bed to prepare to die. He didn't die; he fell peacefully asleep. Then he heard a voice inside of him that said: *Awake... rise... walk.* He didn't understand, but was not afraid. He was a Muslim so he was made to do his Muslim prayers. He didn't know who was making him move and talk, but he had faith and felt at peace and surrendered to this power—the power, he thought, must be the power of God. This experience went on for a thousand nights and changed him completely and was the origin of Bapak's Opening and the beginning of the latihan. Later, Bapak realized that according to God's plan, he was meant to pass on this contact to anyone who wished to receive it and that it embraced all religions and all peoples.

Whaaaa? Hold on there a second! Whooa! Are you kidding me? The Opening... the latihan? What in the hell is this all about anyway?

Well, here goes, and I'm going to try to keep this as simple as possible. If I offend anyone I will say beforehand that I'm sorry, and please forgive me. We found out that the candidate had an obligation to attend a meeting once a week for a three-month probationary period to talk to the "helpers," who would further explain what this Subud stuff was all about. (Helpers were people who were in Subud for a while and doing the latihan and were qualified to give answers to any questions that we may have.) After having all our curiosity and questions satisfactorily answered, we could be opened and receive the Contact if we wished to.

The latihan? What is that, pray tell? Can't you be a little more specific? I'm really curious about that...

Latihan is an Indonesian word that means training or exercise. It is the spiritual training in Subud once you have been opened. To be graphic, it's like getting the switch turned on... letting your soul breathe so that you can get in touch with your real self.

Indonesian? Why Indonesian?

Only God has the answer to why Bapak Subuh, an ordinary young man in Indonesia, was chosen to be the first one to receive the latihan in our time.

Okay... well, how do you get this latihan?

When the new candidate is ready to be opened, he stands in the middle of a group of helpers, or it may be only two or three helpers, who then proceed to do the latihan around him. If the person is willing to surrender and let go, this contact is automatically transferred to the new person like a fissionable chain reaction. Once opened, you then do the latihan twice a week for about thirty minutes.

Who trains you or exercises you?

Here's where it can get a bit sticky and weird sounding, but bear with me. The training or exercise that you do in the latihan is granted to you by the great life force... or, to put it another way, the big one Himself... GOD! God has opened you by way of the helpers, and He will now train you in the latihan.

God will? Really? Uh, huh... Oh, well... hmmm... whew, this is tough to digest. Well, okay. Tell me what happens in the latihan?

Lots of things happen. It's the reality of Subud controlled by God when you are in submission to Him. It's a direct personal experience of a higher power in our everyday lives. God knows you better than you know yourself, and certainly He knows that other person inside of you, the sleeping one, which truly is your soul—and once awakened, a whole process of cleansing away accumulated impurities, illnesses and sins, even ancestral sins... and then positive growth is triggered because the teacher inside of you, God, can now guide that newly alive soul. Once you have felt the latihan, it is unmistakable. You may move, walk about, dance, yell, exercise, speak in other tongues, sing ancient songs, and even say gibberish... but you are not doing it—it is the "other" you who is expressing himself, your inner life who is having a workout. You can stop the latihan at any time. It's not a trance, but worship. God has allowed you to worship Him. In this process of worship you are being cleansed and every part of you is being improved.

Holy cow... I've slugged along with your autobiography until now, but this is too way out. I'm not going to get proselytized into some spooky cult thing, for goodness sake!

No, no... there is no proselytizing in Subud, that's why you haven't heard of it, but I'm writing about my life and Subud has been a major part of it for forty-four years. I'm expressing my experience in Subud, my point of view and what it has meant to me. Teddi and I were early initiates into Subud and we've been helpers for the forty-four years we've been in it, so you could say that we're a couple of elders. And by the way, Subud is not a cult, nor is it a religion. It is before all religions. You may keep your own religion. It is important to do so and continue to practice it. Subud gives sustenance, understanding, and a new dimension to your chosen religion because it is the source of all religions. The power of God was there before religion.

What does Subud mean?

I thought you would never ask! Subud is a contraction of three Sanskrit words and is part of the original human language: Susila, Budhi and Dharma. Susila means a man's character, a humane person having truly human feelings toward his fellow creatures; someone with good behavior who lives rightly. Budhi is the essence, force, or power within all of us given to us by God—the soul. Dharma means the surrender to that force, which is submission to God who has awakened you. Scholars and researchers have unearthed scrolls, stones, and ancient historical documents relative to many faiths. Tons of books and zillions of words have been expressed concerning religions, their origin, spiritual perspectives and their varied conclusions. It's all valid and good, but maybe a bit slanted here or there to arrive at a desired objective. But truly, there are more questions than answers in all of that, profound questions, in my opinion, that cannot be answered by accepted practices and conventional thinking.

Oh? Are you setting yourself up as some wise-ass, know-it-all?

Heavens no! I want to share what I've come to understand. Now, I just want to say a few words about my filtered analysis of spiritual history in an overly simplistic way. As an actor, I always like to get to the simple essentials and avoid complications, which only muddy things up. Besides, and I'm smiling when I say this, this is my book and I can say anything I want!

Here's my take on the subject, which has been gestating in my brain for a long time (again, I'm sorry if I offend anyone):

Before the present time, I believe God gave the gift of His latihan only to his messengers, enlightened men like Abraham, Moses, Jesus, and Muhammad—prime prophets all, and the most revered. They had the gift, but they were not permitted to transfer it! God didn't wish for them to transfer it at that time, it wasn't needed. So, when these prophets died, man made a religion out of what they had brought. They had brought the words of God, and it was enough, and it was good, and humankind could live by those words when life was simpler—but it is not enough for today. Today, in the age of cynicism and modern chaos, when we have the ability to destroy the world with our tremendous technical advancement, we are truly at the edge of the abyss. So, God, in his infinite mercy, sent another messenger for the present time (it may be our last chance), but this fellow had a different job to do than all the other men who had preceded him. Bapak Subuh had the tremendous task of passing on the latihan to anyone who wished to receive it in almost every country of the world— and he has traveled the world over many times (Subud is in 81 countries), designating helpers to help him so that each person, individually, could be opened and experience true worship through the power of God and begin to understand and give credence to the meaning of the religion he or she was born into, because the Subud latihan is the foundation upon which all religions are based. The power of God was there before man was ever formed.

There, I've said it and I'm glad.

Uhhh, that's pretty interesting. I have never heard of anything like that before. What does it feel like when you do this, uh... latihan?

How do you explain the taste of a strawberry unless you have tasted one? Subud is there for you to taste if you want it. It is all up to you.

I want to get back to the night that my wife and I received the opening in Subud. We had been candidates for the required three months, finding out what it was all about by talking to the male and female helpers in the New York Subud group. The male helpers were an eclectic bunch: a retired executive, a book dealer, a salesman, and an actor. They were renting the second floor of an office building on Seventh Avenue and 27th Street to do the latihan. I spent most of my time discussing Subud with the elderly actor, whose name was Reynold Osborne. He was a dear man, very patient and helpful. Subud was so new to the West, it's of interest to note that he'd been opened only three months prior to me; in less than three months after my opening, I became a New York helper. Subud was spreading rapidly around the world and helpers were needed quickly to satisfy the requests for explanations and openings. Bapak Subuh was supposed to open me and several other candidates, and his wife, Ibu, was to do the same with the women, but his plane was late from Mexico. Consequently, I was opened by the physicist John Bennett, who I'd heard lecture, and his wife opened Teddi.

In a large, semi-darkened room, I was told to stand with arms at my side and relax; after hearing a statement read which basically said that I was willing to accept God's grace in submission to his will, Mister Bennett said, "Begin." I had my eyes closed, which I was supposed to do, and in the latihan I began to hear soft singing with words I couldn't distinguish, sounds and grunts, and the noises of people shuffling about. This went on for a few minutes and I didn't feel a thing happening to me, but there were all kinds of goings on around me. I didn't know what to expect and maybe I wasn't supposed to expect anything. Suddenly, I felt like I was being pushed backwards. *Uh, oh… hello… what the hell is that,* I said to myself! I kind of resisted and tried to stand still in my place. Again, I was pushed back as if a powerful gust of wind was propelling me. It was definitely happening, so I just went along with it and stopped any resistance. I was moved continually backwards and the strength of the push kept getting stronger—feeling almost as if I would be thrown over on my head, but I wasn't. Finally, after thirty minutes I heard Mister Bennett say, "Finish!" and the latihan stopped. I was now officially opened in Subud and I was mystified and more than ecstatic by what I had just experienced. Since that time, I have come to believe that this is what it truly means to be reborn—when your soul is awakened from a deep sleep and begins to stretch and thrash about. And every soul is different—so the coming alive varies with each person, but it is really you coming alive. Our openings had taken place on April 30, 1959 at 8:00 p.m. We don't know what it means, but our son, Gard (later given a Subud name, Howard) was born April 30, 1958 at 5:00 p.m., Los Angeles time. Exactly one year earlier to the hour! (*An Important note: Bapak Subuh was a practicing Muslim when he received the opening in Subud. His religion has nothing whatsoever to do with the crazy, murderous Islamic fundamentalists and terrorists who later have cruelly and totally distorted and corrupted the religion of Islam to their own insanity.)

Soon after joining Subud, I felt so grateful for my good fortune that now, in the present time, I was getting a taste of what the messengers of God had felt. Not to the same degree, of course, but a taste… an itsy-bitsy taste. (I was beginning to get a glimmer of what the molten white light I saw as a child may have meant.) Because of this, I wanted to tell everyone I met. I would corner someone I knew and say, "Let me tell you about this fantastic thing that happened to me" and before I was through, I could see their eyebrows go up and their eyes glaze over and then the inevitable: "My, that is interesting… listen, I'm supposed to meet my wife so forgive me for rushing off." I remember elaborating a bit to Frank Corsaro, the director of *A Hatful of Rain* who I had just gotten an apartment for in our building. Frank was a practicing Catholic and I don't know if what I had said was too challenging or sacrilegious, or both, but he wasn't buying my story. He appreciated my conviction, but it was with a typical Corsaro laughing dismissal. I wasn't trying to snare anyone, I just had a compelling desire to share.

At one point we visited Philadelphia, and aside from the good and less-good feelings always generated when visiting my family, I couldn't help but tell them about Subud. They were used to hearing way-out things from their unconventional, "artistic" brother, so this was more or less another fairy tale like a Disney movie. I saw faint momentary sparks in my brother Dave's eyes, but they were quickly extinguished. My mother, I couldn't even begin to approach, and my sister, Fay, strangely enough, came to visit us many years later and was opened in the Los Angeles group. In 1970, my niece Laura and her husband, Alan, visited us and wanted to hear all about Subud, eventually joining a group in Philadelphia. Everyone else I encountered was stone deaf. I had surely found a way to deaden the air and turn people off, so I decided to give it a rest. As for myself, I was thrilled having this joyous secret going on inside of me.

Getting back on stage was a need of mine that gnawed at me like an itch. Shooting film is a "fits and starts" kind of acting that is not completely satisfying for an actor. I have always felt the compulsion to find a way to work on stage with an audience, just to keep the instrument tuned up. I'll never forget a famous film actor appearing in a play on Broadway and how uncomfortable he was. He'd been doing films for so long, he looked as if he were shooting close-ups the whole play, having become so restricted in his body that he couldn't move and talk at the same time. John Osborne was a hot playwright and his blistering "anti-everything" was well expressed in *Look Back in Anger*. In the summer of 1959, I put together a package with Phyllis Love (now in Subud too); my wife, Teddi, to play the other woman; and Lou Antonio, a good young actor who later became a very successful TV director. We opened at the Capri Theater in Atlantic Beach, Long Island, and ran for a week, with me ranting and raving as Jimmy Porter. It was a good play to get the creative juices flowing again. Doubly so, when we found out after an evening performance that Lee Strasberg, surprisingly, had come to see us. All four of us were his students, and he thought we all had done good work, which was very gratifying and made our egos soar. Praise from Caesar is indeed praise! Reflecting on that, I had become acutely aware since doing the latihan (this secret inside of me) that it helped my concentration and relaxation on stage.

Earl Holliman had a Western TV series called *Hotel de Paree*, so I flew out to the coast to play another elegant bad guy with a sly smile and a black heart. In every show I worked on, I tried to create a little different element about the character, so that each appearance might seem to be someone else playing the part; this was especially true in Westerns, where a regional dialect, a moustache, a beard, or a particular choice of clothing could alter your look dramatically. I was always very fussy with the costumers and wardrobe department about the clothes I wore—the cut of the garments and the complimentary accessories. I once went through Western Costumers and Twentieth Century Fox's collection of hats before I found the right one for another Western character—an Australian wide-brim straw hat, with a bandana coming down to cover a fire-scarred face. I suppose it was appreciated because the costumers invited me to speak at a Universal Studios meeting once about how important I felt their contribution was to the actor's portrayal.

I was still in Los Angeles working with Earl Holliman, a good actor and a perfect gentleman, when I found out that Bapak Subuh, on his limited tour, was coming to town to open new candidates, give a couple of talks, and do the latihan with the developing Los Angeles group. This was only a few weeks after being with him in New York after my introduction to Subud. I was very pleased to be able to be in his presence again. Although he was a very ordinary looking Indonesian with a gracious manner, you couldn't help but sense his profound depth as a human being. And even though I was new to the experience, doing the latihan with him in the room was of a full-blast higher quality. This was a man chosen by God, a messenger, to bring the gift of the contact to everyone who wished to receive it. (Every time I say that, I hear in my head somebody's retort: What the hell kind of gushy spiritual stuff is this guy handing me! But, the truth of my understanding is what I am writing about.)

One evening I remember going out to a junior high school in Alhambra, California, a sleepy suburb on the edge of Los Angeles. There, it seemed to me, were hundreds of people waiting patiently to be opened. Word had gotten around that when Bapak was present you could be opened immediately—with helpers you had to wait the three months. That evening, it had to be done in shifts to accommodate the crowd, and I thought: *Where does Bapak get the energy?* Later, as I walked away toward my car after doing the latihan, I looked back at the school and heard these prayerful utterances, raucous noises, and melodious reverential singing coming from the second latihan that had just begun. I have often wondered, what did the neighbors think and whatever happened to all those opened people?

The *U.S. Steel Hour*, performed live in New York, beckoned once again in a show called "An Act of Terror." In a locale simply identified as a Latin American country, I was a wannabe Castro type with an intense passion for the revolution. "We'll have time for justice after we've won!" I say to the effete intellectual played by George Grizzard. It was a grim and brutal story, well written and received—and I looked fairly menacing sporting a bandolier and a military swagger.

Out on the Coast again, I starred on an *Alfred Hitchcock Presents* in "Man with a Problem" with Gary Merrill. I played a police officer who's called up to a high floor hotel room to prevent a guy from jumping off the ledge. When I have almost succeeded, he takes my hand and manages to throw me over. I had no idea who he was, but I'd been playing around with his young wife, performed by a lovely actress appearing in one of her first television jobs, Elizabeth Montgomery.

The *Play of the Week* produced out of New York did quality plays adapted for TV. In Joseph Forsythe's play, *Emmanuel*, I was pleased to land the part of Joseph in a biblical interpretation of Mary and Joseph's trek to Bethlehem for the birth of Christ. It was a beautiful and moving two-hour presentation. Lois Nettleton endowed Mary as a woman you couldn't help but honor as Christ's mother. My Joseph, in a long beard and flowing hair, was a man who was concerned for the safety and care of his pregnant wife and who knew less of the magnitude of their mission. The scene between the two just prior to delivery, when Joseph assures Mary of his love and that all will be well, is one of the most beautiful and moving scenes I've ever done and that I'm most proud of.

One of my favorite actor friends is Nehemiah (Nicky) Persoff. We worked together in early 1960 in another Alfred Hitchcock show called The Cure, a black and white film shot on the back lot of Universal Studios. I played a stud working for Nicky on his Brazilian plantation or some exotic locale, and I'm fooling around with his roving-eyed wife who entices me to run away with her. Of course, everything works out Hitchcockian—I get stabbed by the native servant who is keeping an eye on the wife and then he slices off her head! This turns into a headhunter size trophy for his master! She is cured permanently of her headaches.

*A note: There is something that I feel necessary to mention here. As an actor client of MCA, whenever I would fly out to do one of these shows that were produced under the banner of Revue, an MCA subsidiary company—and the Hitchcock show was one of them—why was I asked to accept less money than I would normally get? I was eager for the work, so I didn't complain, especially with Eleanor Kilgallen telling me that these shows were good exposure and would lead to something better. I often wondered why, if MCA owned the show, and they had their hand in many shows and were making a bundle, why was it necessary to crimp the actors that they represented? The Federal Government was wondering about that too, and it led to an antitrust case, but more about that later.

One night I went to see a friend of mine, William Daniels, in a one-act play, *The Zoo Story* by Edward Albee. Performed at the Provincetown Playhouse, it was preceded by *Krapp's Last Tape* in an unusual double-bill evening. Bill was wonderful playing Peter, an uptight, rigidly conventional gentleman. He is sitting on a bench in Central Park when along comes a crazed and lonely guy named Jerry, who has a dangerous and menacing purpose in striking up a conversation. During a fight, he forces Peter to "accidentally" impale him with a knife and then dies on the bench, his mission accomplished. The fellow I saw playing Jerry was an inadequate understudy, but I still found the play workable. George Maharis had opened in the part a couple of weeks earlier but had stayed for only ten performances before dashing off to Hollywood to do his star-making turn in *Route 66*. When I went backstage to see Bill after the performance, he told me that Richard Barr, the producer, was very interested in me taking over the Jerry role.

I said, "George got all the reviews… why would I want to do that?" "It would be fun to work together, Mark," Bill said, "and it is a hell of a role."

It was a hell of a role indeed.

I thought about it, weighing my options, then I called Barr and accepted. Milton Katselas had been the director, but I never saw him. I worked with the stage manager for the moves and Bill for our give-and-take. I went into the play in a week, and it was a monster undertaking. Just one of Jerry's speeches, about his dog, was nine pages long. Of course, I had my own interpretation of the part, and after I got rolling it was one of the most important, satisfying, and attention-getting roles I'd had up to that point. The evening was an off-Broadway sensation. Everybody came to see us: Arthur Miller, John Huston, Hume Cronyn, and even Lee Strasberg, to name a few. I received an effusively complimentary letter from somebody named Carroll O'Connor who had come to see the play with Cyril Cusack. I wrote back and thanked her for such a lovely letter. Of course, Carroll wasn't well known then, but years later Carroll and I laughed about that one. I vividly remember an overweight Josh Logan coming backstage to our hovel of a dressing room in a sweat, eyes beaming as he said, "This is the best thing I have seen in the theater in ten years!" I must have felt the same way because I stayed with the production for 400 performances, constantly moving to different off-Broadway houses. After Bill Daniels left the show, I had a variety of "Peters" to contend with—some good, some lousy—and still we went on and on successfully. At the time, I think I was the highest paid actor working off-Broadway at $150 a week.

We had Edward Albee to dinner in our roomy new apartment on West 84th Street and Central Park West. Ed was a tough one to know. He was amiable, but somewhat withdrawn, quiet and reserved. No matter what he said, you never really knew what he was thinking. He was to become one of America's most important playwrights, but at the time he was just struggling along like the rest of us. One night I even ran my little films for him that I had been shooting with my 8 mm Bolex, and he was reasonably impressed, marveling at how I was able to accomplish so much with a hand-held camera. We only had one point of contention about my performance in Zoo Story. When I slumped over in death on the bench with a knife in my gut, I kept my eyes open and had a smile on my face. It was a chilling and profound moment at the curtain. Maybe it was my newfound purpose and faith in God that instinctively moved me to play it that way. Ed didn't like it. I don't know whether he believed in God or not, maybe it just offended him for some unknown reason, but that was the only segment he questioned. I didn't change my performance. Forty years later I was browsing in a book store with Teddi and I came across a new book, a biography of Edward Albee. I said to myself, *Oh, let's see what it says about* The Zoo Story. Lo and behold, I found the section and I read to my utter surprise and disbelief that dear Ed said in effect that I had negatively altered his play with an inadequate performance! (After having kept it alive 400 times). I have come to the conclusion that in this wonderful business of show, some people are ready, willing and waiting to stab you in the back—even if it takes forty years.

Soon after the birth of my son, I'd become a camera enthusiast—zealot was more like it. I had a father-in-law who sold cameras, developed the film, and did the photo finishing! Need I say that I had cameras coming out of my ears? I suppose I was preparing myself for a career as a director. I studied and knew more about a frame of film than most actors did, but it was something for the future, I thought, having made up my mind to dedicate myself to the acting career. But with my little Bolex always at the ready I learned and crammed an extraordinary amount of information about how to shoot film and direct through the lens. It doesn't matter about the size of the negative, the principle is the same. Whatever I would shoot, I would edit in the camera for cutting purposes—to make a story—so that I had less editing to do with my white gloves and tiny moviola. I began to understand the terminology and the continuity of film and was eager to try out my creativity with a script, even if it was only in my head.

Paul E. Richards, a dear friend from *End as a Man*, was the "star" of my first effort—a man going crazy in the city who gasses himself in his apartment. I filmed him in the street walking and running, in a church praying (two priests asked us to leave), and in his apartment stuffing towels under the doors—and with his gas-sucking head spinning in tight close-ups. When I edited it together with gas escaping from the range, children's toys moving, and tops spinning, in stop frame photography, it was extremely effective. Next, I shot a powerful twenty-minute film titled *There Are People in the Park*, about a rape. I enlisted two good actors to be in my experimental movie, Joan Potter and Albert Paulson (who had driven my Volvo cross-country). They graciously followed me around in Central Park for four months whenever time permitted in surprisingly good spirits as if it were a major enterprise—with me lugging my camera, tripod, and homemade reflectors, dreaming up shots and locations. At one point, Bill Daniels agreed to drive my Volvo while I hung off the rear on a rope shooting park people and their activities as we slowly drove by. There is a charming sequence when I captured close shots of Joan feeding a squirrel, the squirrel nibbling at her hand. I must have filmed twenty squirrels to get the proper takes. One day, in a secluded bushy area with camera in hand, I was lying under Joan, who was spread out above me on a folding chair, to get the proper angle of Albert about to rape her, when a New York City policeman came upon us.

"What the hell are you people doing?!" We froze. Joan was mortified and changing colors as I spoke.

"Uh… we are, uh… shooting a movie," I said sheepishly, on my back. "Yeah?" (I'm sure he was thinking kinky sex). "You got a permit?" "No, it's just a little home-made experiment."

"An experiment, huh? Get the hell out of here before I take you in!" he said, and he meant it.

The film turned out remarkably well for what it was—a major learning project. When I reviewed it for people I always ran the music of Leonard Bernstein's "Fancy Free" along with it, and it had an amazing synchronization! Lee Strasberg had heard about my film and asked me to show it to the director's group at the Actors Studio. I readily agreed and couldn't believe that I would be showing my silent, primitive 8 mm movie to a bunch of working professionals. After the screening and some fine comments, Guy Tomajohn, an assistant to Elia Kazan, came up to me and asked if I would be amenable to shooting it again on 35 mm for commercial possibilities. I was very pleased, but told him it would have to be put on hold. I was going to the coast to shoot a pilot for MGM—a new TV series I would star in called *Cain's Hundred*.

My son Gard was doing great and was the thrill of our lives. A large cab always accommodated us so we could take our stroller to Central Park for the afternoon—letting Gard run around, and me with my Bolex recording the joys of my wife and son for a fragment of the eventual nine-hour film *The Richman Saga*. Teddi and I actually enjoyed being parents. We enjoyed it so much another joyous event was well on the way. Teddi had the most peculiar habit of informing me that it was time! Time to conceive, that is.

I continued to do *The Zoo Story* in the Village right up until I was expected on the Coast for the shooting of my pilot. I was expected to return in three weeks and go back into the play. *Cain's Hundred* had an interesting premise for a television series. I played Nick Cain, a savvy lawyer for the Mob who was so brilliant he got them all freed from their transgressions. However, he was fed up with the dirty job, was getting married, and wanted out. That didn't sit too well with the big guys—knowing all the secrets—so they try to kill him, accidentally murdering his fiancée. Nick then works with the government to indict and prosecute one hundred top criminals. I never did bag that many, but I nailed thirty of the suckers. Irvin Kershner, a fabulous director who later helmed *The Empire Strikes Back*, the second Star Wars film, was capably in charge, with Paul Monash producing the MGM project. It was a strenuous night and day shoot in a six-day work week; in those days overtime was a thing of future Screen Actors Guild contracts. The pilot was a gutsy episode dealing with murder, drugs, violence, and a deep conviction that a moral correction was necessary. David Brian, a fine film actor from the big screen, played the first Mafia figure, and our scenes together were tense and sizzling. The texture of the picture was rough-hewn and believable; it had a "high reality quotient," a phrase I heard many times during filming. I couldn't help but feel excited about my efforts and the good reaction to the dailies that were reported to me every day, which I was averse to viewing for fear that it would inhibit me.

A day after I returned to New York, I decided to go back into the play. I'd been performing *The Zoo Story* for several months, but I hadn't really thought about the part until I blithely walked on stage confident that I would just pick up where I had left off. Surprise, surprise... I didn't know where the hell I was and had a ghastly time remembering my lines. It was a horrifying nightmare. I kept going absolutely blank and had no idea what followed what. I learned a big lesson and have never done that again in any play I've ever been in. When I make an entrance on stage I'm as prepared as I can possibly be, no matter how long I've been in it.

Having a car in New York City was a blessing and a curse. Garage parking? No way—it was street parking and frantic changes all day long to conform to the posted hours. One little goof and there on your innocent windshield, an exasperating ticket—the bastards! But when you can take your wife and little boy out for a fun excursion across the George Washington Bridge and picnic in a New Jersey park along the Hudson, it was worth it. Just to get away to anywhere was refreshing. I even felt brave enough to drive the car to the theater. I changed my mind after an incident. One night the finicky twin carburetors just died on the West Side Highway going downtown. I pulled over, lifted the hood, and smelled gas fumes from the flooded carburetors. It was very dark, so what did the dummy do who had twenty minutes before his entrance on stage? Naturally, I wanted to see what was going on, so I thoughtlessly lit a match—and the carburetors burst into flames! Well, I was shocked, bug-eyed and frenzied—and, of all things, I instinctively, like the "huff and puff" character in the fable, inhaled a monster breath and exhaled with all my power at the fire and the damned thing went out! I couldn't believe it. I just stood there thinking, someone is looking after me! Then I jumped in the car, started up and sped away to make my performance praying the car wouldn't die again.

Teddi, in the meantime, was enlarging with great regularity and was almost ready to let fly. One night we went out to a spaghetti dinner at a friend's apartment and afterward I dashed off to do the play. At the curtain, there was a message for me: "Don't go home, come to Mount Sinai maternity!" Just to make sure that I wasn't playing favorites, I wrote the following piece after my daughter was born:

A VERY SPECIAL BEING (Born: September 10, 1960)

I was sitting in a stiff uncomfortable chair, my feet propped up and resting on a lamp table piled high with stale newspapers, overstuffed ash trays, and half-empty paper coffee cups—the accumulated refuse of the prospective father's waiting game. It was early morning and still dark outside. It had been raining heavily, and through the Venetian blinds I could see the silvery streaks of water glistening on the spotted window pane. It was quiet and still except for the symphony of night noises drifting up from the city streets below. And down the hall I could hear the muted busyness of hospital activity. My head bobbed a few times. I was tired. It isn't easy to become a father for the second time—it isn't difficult, but it isn't that easy either.

I think I was asleep when I felt a warm squeeze on my arm. Startled, I looked up into a smiling face inches from mine. "It's a girl," the doctor said, "a healthy six-and-a-half-pound girl, and she's a beauty, and your wife is doing fine."

"Thank God," I said, "thank God." Jumping up and embracing him then taking his hand to shake, happily. "Uh… they're both fine? You're sure? Everything's okay?"

"As good as it could be," he said, nodding with quiet assurance. "Thank God," I said again, my heart suddenly racing with excitement and joy. To be a father is one thing. To be father of two, and one a daughter… well, that's something else. A daughter is a very special and divine being.

Minutes later in the recovery room when I saw my groggy but beaming wife, her eyelids drooping heavily, her hand firmly in mine, we shared those very personal, private moments of deep understanding and quiet grateful thankfulness. Then when I finally saw her, my newborn infant daughter, swaddled loosely in a white downy blanket, her round sweet peaceful face turned toward mine, her long curly lashes fluttering like a baby chick's wings in a soft breeze, my eyes swelled with happy tears. I was so proud. "Hey," I said. "Hey, I'm your daddy, me… I'm your dad… and I love you. And I always will."

Now, years later, as every father knows, the tender isolated memories linger in my mind's eye as vividly and as fresh as ever. In so short a time, a little girl becomes a young woman with a mind of her own and a destiny to be fulfilled; as a father, an acquiescent participant and witness to God's miraculous plan. Yes, a little girl is a very special being, and as a parent I'm thankful… oh, so thankful that I have one. We named her Stacey, but later received her true name from Bapak Subuh and liked Kelly even better; Gard (which he never liked) was given his true name, Howard. They say that children brought into this world bring gifts to their parents. It has always been so for my wife and me.

After much jiggling and hassling at the network, NBC chose *Cain's Hundred* to represent the highly competitive ten o'clock time slot on Tuesday night. To say that this was a big deal, to be suddenly thrust into the national limelight with my own weekly show to be seen by millions, WAS A BIG DEAL! And my life was changed completely; the press was plastering me all over the papers, there were more interviews than I could handle, and people I couldn't get on the phone before were calling to offer syrupy congratulations and "Let's have lunch." I was still doing *The Zoo Story*, but there was an added kick when I walked onstage. It was an exciting time. I even indulged to have a couple of suits custom-made by my favorite New York haberdasher, Alfred Norton of Rockefeller Center.

14 Shooting Cain's Hundred

I CHECKED INTO THE MONTECITO and began to gear myself up for the heavy publicity appointments and shooting schedule. My first priority, however, was to find a home suitable to rent for my family. No problem. In those days MCA even had someone to find you a house! Every day for a week, this lovely lady would pick me up at the hotel and drive me to the prospective choices. I must have seen thirty homes before I saw the one I wanted, and it was spectacular. The only home high up the hill on Will Rogers State Park Road in Pacific Palisades; it had five bedrooms, a sunken living room, and a den, in a ranch style design expansively landscaped with lovely green grounds and an incredible view of the ocean in the distance. On the phone, I had mischievously told my wife it was just a so-so joint and hoped she wouldn't be too disappointed when she arrived. When she did, with our two children in hand that June of 1961, it was a joy to pick them up at the airport and to see so many changes in the little ones in so short a time. Driving to our new residence I asked for her patience, hoping she'd be happy and accept the place I found, even though there were detriments to contend with. "What? What are they?" she asked, her face pinched and worried. The thought occurred to me: Maybe I was going too far.

When I drove up the driveway still making excuses and Teddi giving me a sideways glance as if to say: Are you kidding me? I cut out the goofy stuff and said: "This is your new home, honey… and all the toilets work, all four of them." Carrying my daughter as we walked in the front door, my little son's hand in mine—and seeing the astounded look on my wife's face as I watched her step from room to room overjoyed and so happy with what I had secured for us—was surely one of life's most satisfying moments. I slid open the glass doors in the living room, the view almost make-believe, and the cool, fresh ocean breeze blowing in our faces as we hugged each other. We were all here now in California—it was a new beginning—and New York seemed to fade into nothingness—or somewhat farther than Timbuktu.

One of the most charming men I've ever met was Robert Weitman, the head of MGM-TV. He was a kindly gentleman who graciously tried to accommodate all of my needs while I was shooting the series. He couldn't do anything, however, with the rigidity of the wardrobe department who insisted that I wear a particular blue Oxford shirt in all of my scenes. (I think they had purchased a ton of them and wanted to save face under the guise of "It is best for the lighting.") This was 1961, the show was shot in black and white, and studio bureaucracy was immovable, especially at MGM. This was a venerated "Movie" studio where some of the greatest films in history had been shot and television was still a little, sniffling cousin who had just been allowed to sit at the table.

Paul Monash, the executive producer (who later produced Butch Cassidy and the Sundance Kid) and creator of the series who said that I saved the studio thousands of dollars by my professionalism, assigned the everyday producing chores to a nervous and always-smiling Charles Russell. There were hordes of writers and directors, story consultants, editors, production managers, and assistants galore. There were so many people involved with putting *Cain's Hundred* together, it took me weeks to figure out who did what. I'll never forget the makeup department headed by the famous William Tuttle, after looking at film, coming to me with serious concern about the natural cleft in my nose suggesting that I add a prosthetic piece at the tip to hide it. I thought they were out of their minds and said to them, "Hey, I'm sorry, that's me… forget it!"

Earlier in the year, before the series went on the air, the Federal Government stepped up its push to pursue organized crime; in fact, it was reported that Attorney General Robert Kennedy vowed to target 100 top criminals—just like Nick Cain. When I asked Paul Monash who had the idea first, Paul smiled that impish grin of his and walked away without answering. I never did find out. (I often wondered if Bobby Kennedy watched the show.) I was the sole star of the series. I suppose that's why since then, a series always has a couple of stars or as many as an army. I worked my ass off day and night. I was heavily involved in every show so there was no let up, getting to the studio at 6:30 in the morning and sometimes never getting home until 1:00 or 2:00 the next morning; then I would get a forced call and have to be back at 7:00 a.m. Occasionally, I was locked into performing in two episodes at the same time, doing a frantic shuttle act between the two. Sometimes I slept at the studio in my dressing room on the lot. My kids thought I was a stranger. If the overtime rule of the guild had been in effect then, I might have owned a large premium share of MGM. It was a grind, but as they say, "That's showbiz."

Chasing after bad guys that I had represented earlier and then nailing them for their nefarious deeds afforded the writers a rich smorgasbord of possibilities to explore; drugs, prostitution, gambling, booze, crooked sports, the race track, political malfeasance, dishonest judges, the works—and it certainly gave rich and varied acting roles to a select group of guest stars, even from Broadway. Martin Gabel, a diminutive actor with a powerful presence and a deep, boffo voice, came out from New York to play a Mafia leader and my employer in the two-part premiere. When I informed him of my decision to quit representing the Mob, I can still hear the unique sound of his refusal to accept it. "Nick… Nick… don't do it!" I enjoyed working with him immensely. *Cain's Hundred* was an actor's show, with fine directors, stories and production. And the most interesting fact is that so many of the stars appearing soon became stars of their own series or had big screen careers. On one show, I had Charles Bronson and Jack Lord to work with; another, Ricardo Montalban, Robert Blake, and Keir Dullea; then Telly Savalas and Barbara Eden; Robert Duvall and Edward Andrews; James Coburn, Dorothy Dandridge, and Ed Asner; David Janssen and Kent Smith; Jack Klugman and Gavin MacLeod. Each week another terrific cast member and his cronies to manipulate to the clink, or save, as the case may be—and when the feelings were right, even develop a new and lasting friendship. My only problem was keeping Nick Cain interesting within the restrictions of the part, a government "goody two-shoes" who was a bit sanctimonious and preachy. The bad guys had meatier roles!

Dorothy Dandridge and I hit it off immediately. She was an unusually striking, African-American beauty of a woman with a disarming smile and a touching vulnerability. Burdened with a shaky marriage, she'd been through some tough times and doing my show was a hesitant, but grateful, step back into the film business. She was very insecure and I felt a responsibility to help her in any way I could, whether it was continually running lines or a discussion about her role. We spent a lot of valuable time together and it paid off in the episode. The show, "Blues for a Junkman," about a drug-addict singer being released from prison, was one of the best of the series. It was ably directed by John Peyser and the cinematographer Bill Spencer captured her special beauty. Dorothy was just wonderful. When Donald Bogle was writing his well-researched biography of Dorothy, he called me for my remembrances, and our warm relationship is told in his book. She was one of the most memorable women I have ever met, and I treasure the moments shared in the evenings we spent together with her husband in her home and mine.

Ed Begley, a fabulous character actor, was one of my favorites. He was short and stocky with large, gripping eyes and a unique basso voice, and when he stops me in a district court hallway and says: "You're lookin' good, Nick," you knew right off it was a challenge with dangerous innuendos. I finally took care of him, but several powerful scenes were needed to do the job and I enjoyed every minute. Sam Jaffe, a bushy-haired, lean wonder of a man with large protruding teeth and a quiet, infectious manner, was "Dr. Zorba" on the medical show, *Ben Casey* with Vince Edwards. But who can ever forget his performance as the bugle blowing Indian in the classic film *Gunga Din*? On *Cain's Hundred* he was a garment manufacturer threatened by the Mob and of course Nick Cain came to the rescue. It was a kick to stare into his face and recall the unforgettable image of that subservient Indian buglar in a turban. Sam, an ardent vegetarian, was married to a lovely young actress named Bette Ackerman. I had known her in New York and she was at least thirty-five years younger than Sam. I don't know if vegetarianism had anything to do with it, but they were a loving and devoted couple. A few years later, Sam invited us to a luncheon at his home, wanting me to meet another fellow painter, Edward G. Robinson. Sam introduced me: "Ed, I want you to meet Mark Richman… an actor, a writer, and a painter."

As we shook hands, I'll never forget what he said to me, with that distinctive Eddie G. voice: "Spreading yourself a little thin, aren't you?"

Sammy Davis Jr. guest starred on an episode with Robert Culp and was a standout, even in a small role. He was a very talented actor. I wasn't surprised. I can honestly say without reservation that Sammy was the greatest entertainer I've ever seen in a live performance. He could do everything. He had a great range in his voice, his dancing was beyond superb, and his stage personality was so electric you could feel the tingle sitting in your seat. I was always amazed that a man with such a diminutive stature, one goofy eye, and a convert to Judaism no less, could achieve so much. I recall with fondness our warm relationship that extended beyond his guesting on my show.

Gavin MacLeod, a dear friend from *Hatful of Rain* days and who later sparkled as the captain of *The Love Boat*, was the rotten bastard who kills my fiancée on the premiere episode of *Cain's Hundred*. I forgave him for his dastardly deed, so he also appeared as a good guy in another show with Jack Klugman called "Women of Silure." Jack played a violent Mafia kingpin ensconced in an Italian mountainous town, and I had to travel to Italy to bring him to justice. Fortunately, I didn't have to make any complicated travel arrangements; it was all shot on the backlot of MGM and you would never know the difference. Our relationship on film is solid, strong, and believable, and those attributes were evident when I guested later on his successful show, *Quincy*.

*It is interesting to note that Sydney Pollack, who later had a major career as the director of such films as *The Way We Were*, *Tootsie*, and *Out of Africa*, directed two of my shows and very well. I remember telling Sydney while shooting "King of the Mountain," with Robert Duvall and Edward Andrews, that he needed to cover another angle in a scene, but he didn't want to do it; then when they saw the dailies we had to come back and shoot the additional shot. (I couldn't help thinking about my little hand-held camera and the squirrels in Central Park.) Robert Altman, the Hollywood director-icon, was just developing his mystique when he had a turn at directing *Cain*. This was well before doing the classic *M*A*S*H* and *McCabe and Mrs. Miller*. Working with the good and the not-so-good was a continual learning experience. My directing discernment and awareness was heightened considerably. The opportunity to try my hand at directing a segment came up, but I turned it down, maybe too hastily. There never seemed to be a script that I was light in, where I thought I could handle the acting and directing chores at the same time, and commitments had to be made far in advance of the written page. And in those days, unless you were in a long-running hit, there was the quietly said onus: "What are you… an actor or a director?" So, at the time I let it pass to save my sanity. Robert Weitman, the white-haired boss of MGM-TV, came to dinner one night and brought the novelist, screenwriter, and director James Clavell, a warm and amusing raconteur. After a pleasurable Italian dinner Teddi had prepared and some exceptional Cabernet, I had the audacity to run my little Central Park film of squirrels and rape. They were extremely gracious and respectful of my directorial efforts, and I am sure that it was the only, and probably the last, time an MGM executive was subjected to an 8 mm film.

On a Sunday afternoon, someone I adored came to pay us a visit. She called me on the phone and said, "This is Aunt Polly, I want to see the children!" We hadn't seen her for three years, but when the long black chauffeured Lincoln limo pulled into our driveway, we went out to greet our revered Polly Adler. My family never flew out to see us during this time, so it was warm hugs and kisses and the joy and excitement of showing off our two kids to "Aunty Polly." She was happy for my success and blown away by the children, never having had any of her own. She told us she was writing a little bit and reading a lot, "like sucking in knowledge through a straw." We laughed at that one. In our conversations, she never complained about her past or regretted anything she'd ever done, although we knew that she was extremely lonely and getting older was intensifying the loneliness. It was a lovely day of warm feelings and sharing and it was the last time we ever saw her. When the limousine exited the driveway, I had a thought: "... when comes such another?"

Months later, I had a call. It was Polly, her voice more croaky than before. "Mark, can you believe this?" she said.

"What?" I asked. "Believe what?"

"I got a big lump… under my arm. Sonofabitch, it's cancer. I'm in the hospital. This is it. I'm gonna die… it's all over."

She didn't want us to come see her. I asked her to keep us informed, but we never heard from Aunt Polly again.

One morning in November, while getting my makeup touched up, I received a call from my wife; she sounded extremely agitated. "Have you heard the news?" she asked.

I like questions like that with a Pan Stik sponge dabbling under my nose. I waved John Sylvester, my makeup man, away and said, "Uh, honey… what news are you talking about? Are the kids okay?"

"Yes. I'm talking about the fire… the fire!" "What fire?" I asked, alarmed.

"There's a huge fire that started early this morning in Sherman Oaks," she shrieked, "near Mulholland… and it's burning out of control."

"Well, uh… don't worry and calm down… let me find out about it and I'll call you back." I hung up and put on the radio. I found out that ferocious winds of 55 to 100 miles an hour were fanning the flames and it was jumping all over the place and moving west, creating deadly "fire storms." Homes were being threatened and some were already lost; people were evacuating because the wind was shifting the flames toward them unexpectedly. I kept thinking: If the flames were moving west on Mulholland and fanning out to Mandelville Canyon… that was getting close to our place in Pacific Palisades. This was serious, and it began to scare the hell out of me. I found out that an additional 400 county firefighters were called and a dozen airplanes were dropping a water-borate solution for containment, but it wasn't working. I had a hard time concentrating on the day's shooting. I kept calling Teddi to assure her that all would be okay, but in the afternoon as the raging fires continued, I arranged for the MGM wardrobe department to send a truck out to the house to pick up all of our clothes and valuables just in case we had to evacuate. I was able to leave the studio earlier than usual, and driving home the sky was black with smoke and the smell was suffocating. When I got to Will Rogers State Park Road, I was stopped by a state patrolman who wasn't letting anyone pass. I had to convince him that I lived up there.

I had my arms around my wife, and the little ones gave me a hug and a smooch as Marcella, our dependable housekeeper, nodded a worried grimace. The sun was going down and it was a fireball—red and orange and purply through the smoky haze. I walked back outside and peered at the sky toward Mulholland Drive—a red glow as far as the eye could see. It was hot and ominous, matching the sun, and ashes were swirling all over the place like large snowflakes. It was early evening and I wondered how long we could stay there safely before wisely evacuating; the fire was only a half-mile north of us. I was sure we would be notified by the authorities if we had to go. We were ready.

During the sleepless night, the winds had shifted, the inferno moving farther west to Topanga Canyon, and thankfully, the firefighters were making a successful thrust for containment. We were riveted to the TV to keep abreast of the situation. Over 3,000 people fled and 350 homes were burned to the ground. The "Bel Air Fire" was classified as the worst in history covering an area of twenty-one miles and losses totaling millions. It was a horrifying, unforgettable mess and thank God it didn't get any closer to us. We escaped, nervous and jittery, but unscathed.

Thoughts of home ownership were beginning to dominate my plans for the future. No matter what would happen with the series, I was convinced I could make a living on the West Coast. After fully experiencing the freedom and luxury of living in a home, the possibility of raising two children in an apartment in New York turned my stomach. I began to call real estate offices, scour the newspaper ads, and visit potential neighborhoods perchance to see a For Sale sign. In Beverly Hills, Westwood, Brentwood, and Pacific Palisades, I saw an endless conglomeration of "dogs" that needed extensive work or were too expensive to consider. One day in *Daily Variety* I saw a full-page ad for twenty Summit Hills Estate homes being built in Woodland Hills—some with five bedrooms, four bathrooms, and lots of land for a terrific price in comparison to what I had seen. Woodland Hills? Where the hell was that? It was in the San Fernando Valley, and the construction was taking place on "Chalk Hill," where we had passed by every day in the limo on our way to shoot *Friendly Persuasion*. We drove out to see what was available and were so impressed, I immediately gave them a down payment for a home in the final days of completion that I could alter a bit to my liking. It also had the largest lot and best view of the north valley. Teddi was thrilled. She thought it had the right number of bedrooms and the kids could walk to Taft High at the bottom of the hill. The only problem was that it increased the time to get to MGM by way of the old Sepulveda Pass through the mountains—and the 405 freeway being extended to the Valley was months away from completion. In January 1962, Los Angeles had one of its monsoon-like rain storms. We hadn't occupied our new home as yet, but I was waiting there for the delivery of the refrigerator, the water coming down as if Noah and his ark were due any moment. The sky was a blackish-gray and the street was a river, and after my refrigerator was in place, I was glad to leave. There is nothing so loud as a heavy rain on the roof of an empty house. Manipulating my way in the downpour back to the Sepulveda Pass was a nightmare. Buckets of rain on the windshield made it extremely difficult to see as I wound my way from the valley up the mountain to the other side. One thing that I will never forget: After I had just passed the apex of the mountainous drive, I heard a tremendous rumble behind me and it really frightened me, so I pulled over. When I looked back, the road that had been there wasn't there anymore—it had washed away! I didn't want to think where I would have been only a few seconds earlier. Someone is watching over me…

A few weeks later, the sun was shining brightly, the birds were chirping their melodies, and our sparkling new residence in Woodland Hills was fully occupied. My father-in-law, Sam, bless his heart, had closed up our New York apartment and had all the furniture shipped to our new address. I can gratefully say after all these years, we made a good choice. Our home has served us well. While most people in California change homes like changing their cars, we have been in the same one for forty-two years. The television season lives or dies relative to the Nielsen ratings. It was an insane system then and still is. A meter-device is put into a select and willing person's home (plus a viewing diary) and the device is analyzed as to the viewing habits of the household. We're talking about a very minute sampling—1,000 electronic devices for the whole country then… and 5,000 people-meters today! This, for a country of millions and millions of people. If Mr. Homebody or the Mrs. turns off the TV for an extended visit to the john—their goes your Nielsen! The Nielsen ratings were and still are the most powerful governors of television viewing tastes in America. No matter the inaccuracy of their conclusions, they live in an unanswerable, ethereal atmosphere high up on the mountain-top—supreme Gods of this material world. The networks genuflect in obsequious obeisance. In 1961-1962, there were three one-hour prime-time network shows competing on the Tuesday, ten o'clock time slot. Always No. 1 in the Nielsen ratings was *The Gary Moore* Show with Carol Burnett. In the No. 2 position came *Cain's Hundred* and in the No. 3 spot was *The Fred Astaire Show*. Being No. 2 or No. 3 is shaky-time U.S.A.

The executives at the networks are always sweating their tinsel balls off to be No.1, and if you ain't… it's GOOD-BYE CHARLIE, IT WAS NICE TO SEE YA! Aside from the fact that the government and all the savers of our morals were into an anti-violence kick at that time, and *The Untouchables* running concurrently was setting a bad example for our youth—which didn't help us. Sooo… being a gangster show, we got the axe at thirty in the can. All the phone calls, hopes and prayers, and letter writing didn't mean a diddly-do. We were terminated, finished, kaput! We were so dead that Kent cigarettes, our sponsor, who had been delivering me a carton of cigarettes every week for my smoking pleasure for a year, terminated the gesture immediately! My God, the indignity of it all… hey fellas, I was just on the cover of TV Guide!

No matter, pick up your shoes and get the hell out of here!

Cain's Hundred for the most part received excellent notices when it went on the air, and the same can be said for me personally. It was a quality effort. I occasionally view an episode on video today and it stands up surprisingly well. Soon after the cancelling, I flew back to New York to appear again on the *U.S. Steel Hour*, this time with Shirley Knight. It seemed that everywhere I looked, my photo in *Cain's Hundred* ads were plastered all over billboards, delivery trucks, and newspapers. The show had secured a fast syndication deal and was on TV twice a week.

While in New York, I spoke to my theater agents. I was eager to get back on stage again and summer theater was the best way to do it. Three possibilities and eleven weeks of work were in the offing if we could paste it all together. I even had a meeting with Cheryl Crawford who wanted to chat with me about the impending Actors Studio Theater and my availability to participate if it happened.

After the *Steel Hour* I flew back home, and one morning while eating breakfast I had a call from Paul Monash, the producer of *Cain's Hundred*. "Mark, I'm out at 20th and I'm going to produce a new television show. I'd like you to be in it."

"That's nice to hear," I said. "Actors like to work." "You'll be in it for about three months," he said.

"What do you mean?"

"Well, it's a running character, a doctor who'll be around for about three months and that's it. The show is innovative for nighttime TV… like a serial, a half-hour a couple of times a week."

"What's it called?" I asked.

"It's called *Peyton Place*… like the film."

As it turned out, we couldn't come to a satisfactory financial agreement and I thought the character seemed indeterminate so I turned it down. Another one of my foolish decisions. *Peyton Place* became a huge success.

Write Me a Murder, a frothy mystery was all set. Peggy Ann Garner, a friend and a fine actress, would join me, along with the wonderful English character actress Ethel Griffies. We would play Ogunquit, Maine, and Dennis, Massachusetts. Then I would go to Philadelphia's Playhouse in the Park to star in *The Best Man* by Gore Vidal as a guy running for president with Ed Begley. After that, my strength holding up of course, I would do *The Desperate Hours* as an escaped killer in Harrison, Maine.

Peggy Ann Garner was a piquant, short-cropped blonde and a doll. She was married to Albert Salmi, my *End as a Man* stage buddy, so our relationship had already been established. We worked well together, with professional ease, solving all the problems that actors face in a limited rehearsal period. *Write Me a Murder*, directed by Christopher Hewitt, was a prop nightmare, meaning all the intricate gimmicks had to click and work and the gun had to fire without fail. Because of it, the dress rehearsal in Ogunquit was running well past 1:00 a.m. and would have gone on longer, when suddenly from the audience we heard a plaintive voice singing a World War I song with a cockney accent: "I want to go 'ome, I want to go 'ome… I didn't ask to come into this war, I don't want to go to the front anymore… I want to go 'ome!" A very senior Ethel Griffies was exhausted and so were we all. The rehearsal was over. The play opened the next night and everything worked well. It was an audience pleaser and the reviews were good.

But of all things, I had a problem, an agent problem—I didn't seem to have one! For several days, I kept calling the MCA coast office and there was no answer. Then I tried the NY office and again no answer. MCA, the largest theatrical agency in the world, not answering the phone? Why not? I had enormous details to work out for the next engagement in Dennis, Massachusetts and then the new production in Philly. What the hell is going on? I was shopping in a local store and I picked up a weekly *Variety*. There on the front page I was shocked to find out my agent problem. MCA had been put out of business by the Feds! You couldn't be a producer and represent the talent too. It's called a conflict of interest and ripe for an antitrust break-up. I mentioned it earlier and that is exactly what MCA was doing—paying actors less on shows (Revue) that they owned and produced. So, MCA made the choice of getting out of the agency business altogether and into production as the new owners of Universal Studios. It didn't matter that their clients were stranded and drifting towards a rocky cliff—not a phone call, a telegram, or even a letter, no sir! Fuck you and tough apples—you are not our concern anymore!

I also read in *Variety* that some MCA agents had moved to the Ashley-Steiner office and one of them was Ina Bernstein, whom I liked a lot. I called her and became her client immediately. After completing the successful engagements of *Write Me a Murder* in Ogunquit and the Cape Playhouse in Dennis (occupying the little house that a messy Tallulah Bankhead had just vacated), I was in Philadelphia for *The Best Man* at the beautiful playhouse in Fairmont Park. Ed Begley had a scheduling conflict, so Phil Bourneuf, a good actor, replaced him to play my adversary. Going to my hometown after starring in a TV series and seeing family and friends was a particular kind of excitement.

After one performance, my sister told me that our mother was telling everyone around her, rather loudly: "That's my son, the star!" I was happy to bring some measure of joy to her life. I was also pleased that *The Best Man* had one of the highest grosses of the 1962 season. *The Desperate Hours* at the Deertrees Theater in Harrison, Maine, was the last leg of an exhaustive summer journey. Wearing a putty bump on my nose, I menaced a household of innocents before I met my timely demise—and none too soon. I was eager to get home.

I don't remember how I found this oddball Mexican Indian man who told me he had worked as a valet for Rudolf Valentino, but he became my cement layer, wall builder, sprinkler system planner, and landscaper. His name was Peter Amezcua and he was an unbelievable character. He performed amazingly good and amazingly lousy work. But the good is still standing, the plum tree is still bearing fruit; and the huge, hand-crafted stepping stones still show my son Howard's hand prints as evidence of the fun he had as Peter's willing little helper.

I received a letter from Lee Strasberg, Cheryl Crawford, and Roger Stevens informing me that "the Actors Studio Theater will be going into production sooner than had been anticipated." They asked that I let them know before I commit to an outside contract. I sure would have liked to be in a Studio play, but I had already committed to star in another Richard Krakeur pre-Broadway production called *Have I Got a Girl for You*. It was to have a Los Angeles opening before proceeding to New York. I had initially turned it down, but they persisted and I finally said okay if the many changes I had requested were done—but so far, the author, Irving Cooper, wasn't coming through.

The play had potential, but it needed an overhaul and I strongly felt I had an insight in how to do it. I was a pretty hot actor at the time, and Dick Krakauer wanted me so badly he gave me a lot of power. I wanted my friend Leo Penn (father of the unborn Sean) to direct, and he accepted, then bowed out when he got a job on the *Ben Casey* TV show as a director-observer. I then turned to Malcolm Black, an Englishman who had directed me in *The Best Man* in Philly. I then decided to go to New York to cast the other parts. In the comedy, I would play a thirty-five-year-old high school football coach with a kvetchy mother who wants him married. All of my casting choices were accepted. Mabel Albertson (Cloris Leachman's mother-in-law) was to play my mother; Doris Roberts (scene partner from the Actors Studio, and later in *Everybody Loves Raymond*) was set to play my sister; and Gail Kobe, my girl. I was sitting in my hotel room reading the play again when I impulsively began to rewrite the stilted dialogue—and adding funny lines. I was so excited by what was happening that I called Teddi to get her reaction. She liked it. But I made the mistake of calling the author who hadn't rewritten a single word. I read him what I had completed, hoping for a little titter, at least, but there was nothing, only silence.

"Hello, Irving… are you there?" I asked. "Hello?"

More silence.

"Irving… these are some of the things I asked for….and I think what I've done works and will be fun to play."

"Well, I don't know," he mumbled. "We'll have to talk about it. I'm not convinced. And I don't want you to rewrite my play."

"Irving, it needs it desperately. I've been asking you for a month and I've seen nothing."

All I was trying to do was make the play better and funnier and I wasn't asking for writing credit. When I showed what I had written to Malcolm, he agreed with me and liked it. Thus began the saga of the surreptitious rewrites. I also had to do major alterations in dialogue concerning the football team—it was obvious Irving knew absolutely zilch about football. I was turning out multiple pages of changes and funny lines and having them copied and inserted into the script as if they were coming from Irving Cooper who, peculiarly enough, did not interfere. We were opening in a week and there were still problems with the final scene. As God is my witness, I rewrote the denouement of the play, improvising all of the parts— with Malcolm writing down the words as I said them, and Irving sitting there stone-faced and lost. And that was the final scene that we opened with at the Biltmore Theater in Los Angeles to excellent reviews for the play and for me. We were building an audience and New York was getting closer by the day. The play was being held over for three more weeks and we were ecstatic. We set about making necessary changes and cutting the excess. I kept writing funny jokes for Mabel Albertson and they were slipped to her by Malcolm. It really irritated me when I overheard her complimenting Irving for the "new one" just given her that we were putting in that night, but I kept mum. Then something happened that screwed up everything— all the newspapers in New York went on strike. We just hoped it would be over soon. It wasn't. We closed in Los Angeles after the extended three weeks and waited. And waited. The strike went on for three months! In the meantime, I was guesting on various television shows.

One day Richard Krakeur called and wanted to talk to me about picking up where we left off and opening in New York. Irving Cooper had done a little work on the script and he wanted me to read it. In shock I said, "What? Irving has done a little work… how come he couldn't do any fucking work before?"

"It's just a little," Dick said, trying to placate my anger. "When can I bring you the script?"

We set a time and Dick showed up at my home and handed me the "reworked" play. I walked out into the garden and Dick followed. I spent about ten minutes reading through Irving's play and realized he had done nothing—it was the exact same play I had seen originally. All the work, everything I had done—the play we had opened with—was not there. I looked at Dick and said, "Are you kidding? You've got to be kidding."

"Well… Irving wanted to make a few changes. He's entitled, no?"

I think I turned green. I took the script and threw it as far as I could up my pink-blossomed hill and said, "You can tell Irving he can take his putrid script and shove it up his ass 'til his nose bleeds. I don't want to have anything to do with his… amateur bumbling script! I wouldn't piss on it now!"

Richard Krakeur, the producer of ten or more Broadway plays, was shaken at my anger. He pleaded, "Please, Mark… please don't be so upset. I want you in the play… you did so much. You've been such a gentleman… we can work it out."

"Dick, we cannot work it out. That ungrateful moron doesn't know what the fuck is going on. I worked my ass off fixing his crappy outline of a play and he has the gall to say he's done a little work? He's incapable, the dumb shit, and I've had it!"

"Please, Mark… don't say that… I'll give you a piece of the play, a piece of my share and you can direct it if you want! I don't want to lose you. Please, Mark."

"Dick… you're a nice man. I appreciate your offer but it's too late," I said with finality. "It wouldn't matter if Irving stood on his head and pissed lemonade in his ear, it's over. I've reached my limit. It's over!" But it wasn't over. Dick kept calling me for my suggestions about cast members and directors. I still tried to help him, but he didn't listen to my choices. He hired a TV director who was all wrong for the project and a leading man who was much too old and heavy for the lead I played. They opened in New York with Irving's version and closed in one night. I remember reading the headline of the review from the New York Journal America: "*HAVE I GOT A GIRL FOR YOU*! BADLY MISCAST."

The sad addendum to this story and the strangest took place several years later. I was guest starring on some TV show and Irving Cooper was the script supervisor. He came up to me during a shooting break and sheepishly said, "Mark, would you like to do something with my play… for television maybe?"

I tried to put the play and the torture of putting it together out of my mind. After all the responsibility of trying to handle so many areas of production, it was almost as if I were going on vacation when I jumped into a heavy television schedule. Joe Stefano, my dear friend and author of *The Black Orchid* came through with a wonderful part on a new program that he was producing called *The Outer Limits*. The "Borderland" segment, written and directed by Leslie Stevens who co-produced, has become a classic. I played a zealous scientist pursuing a fourth dimension who accidentally alters his own anatomy creating two right hands! I had the pleasure of having Nina Foch, a fine actress, play my adoring wife, and an incredible supporting cast including Barry Jones, Gladys Cooper, Gene Raymond, and Phillip Abbott. It was the first show of the series, and peculiarly enough two years later, I starred in the last black and white segment of *Outer Limits* called "The Probe" with Peggy Ann Garner. In that production, several of us became quite ill with walking bronchial pneumonia. Before every take we were sprayed with water and a special effect fog to surround us. Unfortunately, the continuous fog generated with a mineral oil and water mist was the culprit that affected our lungs. Actors are always subjected to hazards the public is never aware of. Shooting on Back Lot #3 at MGM was an adventure. There were so many extraordinary exterior sets, streets, homes, buildings, roads, bridges, villages, and a county square still standing from all the films created there over the years—you could travel the world in fifteen minutes. Even the set of Tara from *Gone with the Wind* stood majestically on an artificial hill. It was wonderfully eerie. As a blonde Nazi S.S. officer in a *Combat* episode, there was no question that I was in an authentic German town when I loaded my American soldier hostages into an ambulance to deceive the enemy at the front lines. Ted Post, a wonderful director, helmed this segment with great skill and visual fluidity. One sequence that I stupidly insisted on doing myself could have ended my career. My captive driver violently swerves the ambulance causing me to almost fall out, but I catch and hold onto the swinging passenger door as we speed by (much too closely) several burning vehicles and tanks. I just missed getting seriously injured or crushed by inches each time the door swung open as we passed. There was another incident I had no control over that happened when I was filming a *Bonanza* episode. Shooting on a ranch near Thousand Oaks, I was on my horse leading a pack of bad guys—about 30 horses and riders going at a very fast clip—and of course, they were all stunt guys and wranglers. As I approached the camera, the speeding horde was pushing me towards a low and massive overhanging oak tree branch. I tried to rein the horse away from it but couldn't, the other horses were too close—all I could do was duck and hold on. It was a frightening moment. I remember the camera crew and the collective: "OOOOOOHHHH… uuhhh!" The horse missed by an inch, and if I hadn't ducked, I would have been decapitated. Coming up to me after I dismounted, Lorne Greene asked me if my life insurance was current.

Sometimes during a heavy shooting schedule, you get involved doing things that you shouldn't, especially if an insistent director keeps telling you with a coaxing whine that he has to have the shot, otherwise it would look false if a stunt man did it. I had a lot of those requests over the years and I learned how to handle them. I would think of my wife and children and simply say: "I don't do that anymore." I was shooting an episode of *The Virginian* called "The Gauntlet" as a hard-nosed rancher. The scene was a crucial duel between James Drury and myself, who is the Virginian, which led to a dangerous climactic riding fight over winding, treacherous roads. At one point, I grab my whip and start violently swinging at him as we are galloping side by side following a camera car speeding in front of us. Just to stay mounted was a task—falling off was easy, which I almost did. I mean, we are going at one another as if our lives were at stake—and they were; that is—mine was. Thomas Carr, the director, who had been the second unit director on *Friendly Persuasion* and an experienced hand in the action department, begged me to do the scene in close-up after we had done the master. "Mark, I have to have the shot, I am following you with a 200 mm lens."

"Tommy," I said. "If you're following me that closely we can do it another way. I don't have to ride crazy like that."

"Well, the horse's head might show when you swing the whip so it's better my way... trust me," he said, not to be deterred.

Foolishly, I trusted him. Galloping along swinging my whip and holding on to the reins was a tough assignment, and at one dip in the road I lost the whip and almost went sailing into a rock. I finally pulled up and dismounted and said to Tom. "That's it! I'm not doing it again! If you got the shot, great... if not, tough!"

The stunt man came up to me and whispered, "Mark... that's what I get paid for... taking chances. You shouldn't have done the master. I thought you were you were out of your mind." Just in case it was needed, we got another take of the scene by me sitting on a tall stool strapped to a truck as we rode the terrain, the camera framed above the horse head. The rest was acting.

Another dangerous occurrence happened while I was filming a two- part episode of *The Man from U.N.C.L.E.*, later released in Europe as a feature film. In one sequence playing again an elegant, international hood—you see me firing my machine gun out of a third story window at the good guys, then I jump out the window (stunt man) and land on an awning below, and jump again into an open sports car where my girl, the beautiful Eleanor Parker is waiting. We zoom off at a mad clip to escape the pursuers, but we must get through the huge iron gates before they close and trap us. Eleanor, a fine film actress and star, was rather nervous about taking off and driving like that because the closing gates were real and it was dangerous, but she accomplished it in fine form after several takes. Mind you, we would just get through the gates in time. A camera operator with a hand held 35 mm camera was posted on the other side of the gates as they closed to film the car chasing us. Unfortunately, in the closer shot, the pursuers just couldn't break in time so their car hit the massive, tall gates full force crunching and lifting the cameraman behind the gates as they violently opened, throwing him about ten feet in the air as we all watched in horror. He landed with a sickening thud, unconscious, the camera still in his hands, and was seriously injured. Shooting was cancelled for the rest of the day.

One evening we were invited to the home of Shirley Jones and Jack Cassidy for dinner. Jack and I were friends from New York. When we pulled into their driveway, we thought we'd never get out of the car—we were attacked by their two huge, black, ferocious slobbering dogs, barking and baring their teeth and jumping all over my car. It was scary—and before the age of cell phones—so we just sat there wondering what the hell to do. Afraid to open the door we sat staring at a couple of vicious monsters ready to tear us apart. It was horn blowing time, and after several minutes, Jack finally came out to rescue us and apologize. Shirley has always been a lovable doll, but that evening we were pleased to meet an exceptional beauty from an earlier age, a sweet delight with no pretensions, Jeanette MacDonald. She radiated a warmth and loveliness that was truly endearing. I had already worked a couple of times with her husband, Gene Raymond, a fine gentleman. (Years later when I joined Gene as a trustee on the Motion Picture and Television Fund, I was in charge of the art collection at the Country Home and Hospital. Gene asked me to have restoration done on a lovely oil painting of Jeanette after she had passed away.) Also present at the Cassidys' was an agent with a quiet manner by the name of Jules Sharr from the William Morris office. He said he admired my work and wanted to represent me. In the following weeks, he pursued me rather relentlessly to become a client and I eventually made the move.

In July 1963, The Playhouse in the Park in Philadelphia asked me back to perform in *The Night of the Iguana* by Tennessee Williams. Vicki Cummings and Irene Dailey (Dan Daily's sister) were my co-stars, and it was directed by the very talented George Keathley. I played the volatile priest on the verge of a nervous breakdown; it gave me the opportunity to evolve a many-colored performance. The production was exceptionally fine and many people from New York came to see it. Ernest Schier, *Philadelphia Evening Bulletin* wrote: "Mark Richman pours all the intensity of a tortured man into a performance that shapes up as one of the best ever to grace the playhouse stage."

In August 1963, Bapak Subuh was on another tour that embraced many countries came to Los Angeles. The Subud community was prepared and eager to welcome him and his wife, Ibu, and their small entourage with an outpouring of love and affection. Bapak Subuh was a revered spiritual leader in his own country and the understanding of who he was definitely affected all of us in Subud. He was a messenger, I believe, in our time, who had brought a contact with the power of God that was to be given to all of mankind—if they wished to receive it. There had been no proselytizing, but Subud had spread quickly to eighty-one countries in the world of vastly different peoples—all children of God seeking a contact to awaken their dormant and sleeping souls. At this point we'd been in Subud four years and unquestionably had realized the slow but subtle changes in our daily behavior. The latihan had begun to promote a deeper meaning to our relationship as husband and wife and our responsibilities as parents—and the acceptance of the life handed us with all its ups and downs. On this trip, Bapak Subuh and his wife were the guests of John and Asa Lake in their home in Santa Monica. Bapak was a film buff and it had been arranged for him to view a television broadcast of *Friendly Persuasion* since Phyllis Love and I were young Subud people in it. I remember it being a lovely experience, sitting quietly with him as we watched the film about the Quakers and their pacifism during the Civil War. When it was over, he said something quite startling. He said that the Quakers had the latihan and that was why they used to quake! Then, as time passed, they thought it more dignified to sit and mentally pray in silence, doing what is known as their "silent" prayer, as seen in the movie. Subsequently, they lost the latihan. (My conclusion, don't alter God's gift.)

The Lakes suggested that I shoot a film of Bapak's visit. Knowing it would be difficult and somewhat unprofessional because I only had an 8 mm Bolex, I accepted the challenge after Bapak gave me permission. For as long as Bapak remained in the city, I followed him around making a nuisance of myself. I never thought I'd be shooting Bapak in Disneyland, but there I was with him in the submarine, the train ride, the boat excursion, and in a horse and buggy shooting over his hat. He really seemed to enjoy himself and I know we all did; and what was so wonderful about the venture, aside from the privilege of being with him, I have a historical little film with appropriate titles that I shot prior to showing him the results five days later! How I put it all together with the editing of hundreds of splices in such a short time is a mystery. Since that time, I recently added my son Howard's piano music, and hundreds of video copies have been distributed around the world.

During Bapak's visit I became more aware that my wife looked particularly beautiful—radiant and beaming—despite pregnancy blahs and fatigue. She was the one who always said: "It's time… to have another."

And me? I love kids so I just said, "Okay."

I have always thought that a woman carrying a child is a most wondrous time—a gift from God growing inside with all of His special favors, talents, and blessings about to unfold and blossom.

One of the more interesting and challenging roles I've had in a TV series was playing a kind of a black-clothed, death figure on the modern Western, *Stoney Burke*. Leslie Stevens, who had conceived the series, was pissed off at the networks for cancelling it; so, he wrote and directed a script with my devious character, a horse buyer, metaphorically leading aging horses into the slaughter house (TV shows) as useless poundage fit only for pet food. The segment was called "The Journey," and the highly respected cinematographer Conrad Hall captured the dynamics of the horse's life and their handlers. At the end, Jack Lord as Stoney and Warren Oates (a fine actor who died too young) defiantly set all the horses free before they enter the slaughter house—and I stand there, watching them flee into the hills, defeated, but maniacally laughing my head off as if to say, "I'll get you later."

Ben Casey, the medical series starring Vince Edwards, had premiered in the same season as *Cain's Hundred* and had become a monster success. Fractured hips, kidney stones, and heart problems apparently had enormous appeal when accompanied by a good story, and Casey consistently had them. The first time I worked with the very beautiful and gifted Barbara Rush, I guest-starred as a doctor, with her as my psychiatrically troubled wife. It was directed by Mark Rydell, who later received an Academy Award nomination for *On Golden Pond*. Ted Voigtlander, one of Hollywood's terrific cameramen, made us all look good. He was a cinematographer in the tradition of early Hollywood. Light your principles so they look their best… that's where the money is. I have seen my face on the screen so many times and in all angles possible, I know when a cameraman has taken care of me. Lighting and enhancing a face and the eyes with shades and nuances like a painting requires the skill and awareness of a painter. Ted Voigtlander was a master.

I continued to have trouble with my leading ladies—in the scripts, that is. This time I was a guy running for the U.S. Senate who had the lovely Kim Hunter for a wife who was also cracking up. The show was called *Breaking Point* and the segment was again directed by Mark Rydell. More than once, as I looked into Kim's eyes, I found myself thinking—here's Kim, playing my wife in a TV show and I'm the object of her troubled focus desperately appealing for my attention… but I remember her playing Stella so beautifully in *A Streetcar Named Desire* opposite Marlon Brando, desperately appealing for…

The first time I worked with the fabulous, award-winning director, Ted Post, I played a sheriff's deputy inspecting strange goings on in the *Twilight Zone*, created by Rod Serling, the most imaginary writer I've ever met. It was a two-character show titled "The Fear," and I was called to help the beautiful red head, Hazel Court. Shooting my revolver at this enormously frightening giant that seemed to be five stories high, the punctured intruder loses air rapidly and falls to a heap of nothing. Nearby, we discover a small space ship and when we look through the window we are surprised to see frightened, tiny aliens. We are the giants! Serling's collection of films are just as impressive and as morally provocative today as when they were written fifty years ago.

On January 31, 1964, at Cedars of Lebanon Hospital, Lucas Dion Richman, our third child, made himself known. Dr. Alfred Heldfond, our obstetrician, hadn't experienced anything like this birth before. I stayed with Teddi in the pre-delivery room, but when she went into heavy labor I waited in the hall, doing my usual pacing and a little praying. My wife, in a state of total submission to the latihan, suddenly began to sing at the top of her lungs. Standing outside the delivery room, I heard her and knew what was happening and I remember saying, "Oh, my God…" There were no painful groans and cries, only beautiful operatic singing, with varying melodic rhythms throughout the whole delivery. Nurses and doctors from other stations were intrigued and stopped in for a glance at the unusual happening. They, too, hadn't ever heard of a woman singing her lungs out at the birth of her baby. When Dr. Alfred Heldfond came out to tell me that we had a new son and Teddi was fine, he was smiling and shaking his head, convinced that what he had just witnessed was indeed unique in all the years of his practice. I had given a gold bracelet to my wife with a charm attached, denoting the birth date and name of our first child when he was born. I have done this for all of our children, adding charms to the bracelet. Lucas's charm is inscribed: "Jan.31, 1964 Lucas Dion… In a burst of God's song!" Years later, we were invited by Dr. Heldfond to a special doctors' dinner and film showing. We were introduced as his guests and he related the story of the singing and Lucas's birth to the full body of doctors, chuckling and shaking his head as if he still couldn't believe it. Then he said again, "I wish I'd had a tape recorder!"

Lucas, at the present time, is the music director/conductor of the Knoxville, Tennessee, Symphony Orchestra, after six years with the Pittsburgh Symphony.

Norman Corwin, the brilliant writer and director of some of the most memorable dramas in the history of radio during the thirties and World War II, wrote a poetic book called *Overkill and Megalove*. I was honored to be part of a special program at the Lindy Opera Theater under the auspices of World Peace Study Mission honoring the survivors of Hiroshima and Nagasaki. I read a sardonic chapter titled "Killing with Kindness." Afterward, it was painfully ironic to be sipping tea in the Japanese Gardens in Beverly Hills with the maimed survivors.

I have always felt that *Combat*, the ABC-TV war series, was exceptionally well produced, with more visual production and reality squeezed into a one-hour format than most shows on the air at the time. I was pleased to have the opportunity to play another S.S. German officer with a dialect; but this time I was also deceptively double-dealing the American army as a French partisan fighter and ally—with a French accent on an episode called "Counterplay." Vic Morrow, the series lead, finally wises up to me and in a fight, I am forced to accept another grisly death—this time my head is crushed as I'm flipped over onto a rock. Emmett Bergholz was the cinematographer, a favorite of mine. He'd been a camera operator on *Friendly Persuasion* and was deservedly elevated.

Going from show to show I would meet so many people I'd worked with previously—a prop man, a makeup person, an electrician, or a cameraman. Seeing a face you knew warmed the atmosphere and made the shooting a bit friendlier.

*A sad note: Years later, Vic Morrow, a fine actor and a friend, was horribly killed shooting an exterior scene in the Universal feature version of *The Twilight Zone* when a helicopter flew too low and decapitated him. As I've said earlier the public has no idea how dangerous the action can be on a movie set. To continue my point about how danger lurks while shooting, and in spur of the moment decisions, I will relate an incident

I experienced on *The Fugitive*, the second time I guested on the Quinn Martin-produced show. It was called "The Last Oasis," and I was playing a fervid deputy with a compulsion to kill as I pursued David Janssen all over the Arizona desert. When I am close to nailing him in the story and have to go up in a helicopter to finally zero in, the director, Gerald Mayer, asked me to do the helicopter shots live because he wanted to see me in the frame as we flew and over my face as I looked down. It sounded peculiarly the same as being on an erratic horse, but again, under the pressure of making a quick decision and the director saying it was perfectly safe, I stupidly said okay. I am up there flying, acting away, seriously peering out the doorless helicopter, the camera operator shooting my profile and getting shots over my head, when the pilot, next to me, probably pre-arranged with the director, suddenly does a left, 45-degree swerve and roll—where I am totally on my side, looking down at the tall pines with nothing to keep me from falling out—nothing but centrifugal force and my right arm frantically grasping for anything to hold onto! I remember the operator accidentally conking me in the head with his hand-held camera, and the feeling of sheer helplessness—and thinking that when and if I get down, I will conk the director on the chin. "Cut this fucking shit!" I yelled. "Level her out!"

When we landed, I confronted Gerald Mayer angrily. He apologized profusely and told me that he didn't know the pilot was going to do what he did. He said he hadn't asked for that radical a shot. There was no point in checking it out with the pilot—I just swallowed my irritation and vowed never to agree to this kind of directorial coercion again.

My long and close relationship with Harvey Hart, a Canadian director with enormous talent, began when he hired me to appear in *Profiles of Courage*. I played the Secretary of War under Ulysses S. Grant. When I was choosing the wardrobe to wear at Western Costume, everything I tried on for the period had Clark Gable's name on the inside label, designed by his personal tailor—all of Gable's clothes, including the gray cutaway jacket from *Gone with the Wind*! NBC did a story on me for publicity, posing me in Gable's outfits to promote that particular *Profiles* broadcast.

Harvey Hart had been one of the top young directors of the Canadian Broadcasting Company who had migrated to Hollywood to chance the film world after so successfully conquering the electronic medium. He was a special human being—warm, kind, and bursting with genuine enthusiasm. We shared many interests to bring us together; our young children, his wife, Helena, and mine truly liked each other, and, of course; our serious professional feelings concerning quality work in film. He would also laugh uproariously at some of my sillier antics, which I thought was rather endearing, except for almost choking on the cigarette he always had smoldering.

Harvey directed a black-and-white, one-hour pilot for a TV series to be called *The Dark Intruder*. Leslie Nielsen starred as a San Francisco occult investigator in the late nineteenth century, and the show promised to be a scary winner. Harvey asked me to play the friend of Leslie, which was a terrific part. In the film, I actually played two roles, the normal friend he has known, and the conjoined, ugly twin monster brother who had been separated at birth and always thought to have been destroyed. As the picture progresses, the good guy and friend is about to get married to a beautiful woman, but unfortunately, he is slowly being taken over by the forces of the evil brother who is still alive and wreaking havoc; after many mysterious murders, the transformation has completely taken place. Before each grisly event we see a rustling black cape, long, tearing claws, and we hear fearful animal panting that brings a chill to the skin—and the spooky lighting and eerie music by Lalo Schifrin made your blood freeze. In the cemetery, when I kiss my intended and she realizes with eye-popping fright that I am not her Robert, she screams as I slowly become the monster now inhabiting Robert's body—setting off a chain of events where I am finally cornered and killed and then filmically, in death, transform again into the fellow we all know and love.

One of the requirements for doing a film like this is getting a full head "death mask" made. That is the name given the process by the most illustrious of all the Westmore makeup clan, Perc Westmore. It's one of the most dreadful experiences anyone has to go through and I've had to do it twice. With eyes closed, a slowly hardening substance, not unlike plaster of Paris, is heavily applied all over your face and neck as you sit rigidly in a makeup chair. Not moving any part of your face and neck for almost an hour is tough enough, but the fact that your only way to breathe is a straw stuck up each of your nostrils, the mouth being sealed, has panicked many actors. In my case, while the makeup people were doing their job, one of the straws fell out my left nostril and became sealed with the goop. You can imagine how I felt as I was frantically gesturing and pointing, trying to breathe with only one nostril while they tried to solve my problem. On the wall at Universal, in Bud Westmore's workroom there was a collection of famous frozen faces and every one of them had an expression of discomfort or near terror—even Laurence Olivier.

The mask was used to create the many prosthetic makeup pieces necessary to film the gradual change from normal to monster, and vice versa—each application, a few seconds in the finished film. To photograph the transformation, I spent fifteen hours in a makeup chair, going from normal to monster and monster to normal—each completed addition and subtraction filmed to rigidly required placement of my head. I was one of the last to go through this ordeal where every prosthetic piece was applied with thick spirit gum and removed with alcohol and acetone. It was the same application that was done on Spencer Tracy in the 1940s for *Dr. Jekyll and Mr. Hyde*. Today, this whole change would be done on the computer. In the process, I had six makeup men work on me, including three of the famous Westmore family: Bud Westmore, who had designed my scary face; young Mike Westmore; and Perc Westmore, who did my hair and in the past had created the makeup for Paul Muni in *Louis Pasteur* and for Charles Laughton's memorable *Hunchback of Notre Dame*, among many others. At the end of the day, my face felt as if it had been pelted by sandpaper marshmallows. I am honored to have been worked on by so many wonderful artists at the top of their skills. (Frank Westmore gave me a copy of his book, *The Westmores of Hollywood*, and inscribed it, "To Peter Mark… it's been great working with you all these years. Hollywood will never be like this again.")

15 The Nightmare of Letting Go

About this time, Harvey Hart and I expressed how much we enjoyed our friendship and our working relationship. He then said that we should find a book, a film property we both felt strongly about and produce it ourselves. We could write the screenplay; he would direct and I would star. The idea was instantly exciting and extremely appealing. Soon after, he asked me if I'd read *Letting Go*, the first novel by Philip Roth. I hadn't, but I picked up a copy. It was the story of a compulsive and indulgent college professor at a Chicago university and his painful relationship with two women. He was a fine writer but I wasn't crazy about it, especially Roth's anti-Semitic tenor. He was a real kvetch. It's too bad I didn't adhere to my initial instincts and avoid involvement. But Harvey thought we could make a terrific film out of the material and Roth was a published author to get committed to us. So, in 1965, after much agenting horseshit and legalese, we signed an option deal with Philip Roth, guaranteeing him money every six months for two years. In that time, we were sure to have a screenplay and, hopefully, a production. Harvey and I agreed that he would break the book down to the film story we wanted to tell, and I would write the screenplay, even though we were up to our necks in professional responsibilities. It was also true that I always seem to have twenty different immediacies pulling at me from all directions. With so much going on, it was a monstrous task to sit in my den, analyze Roth, and then write in long hand on a yellow pad. Computers were a thing of the future, and I hadn't yet learned to type! (Years later, my wife insisted on sending me to an old retired school teacher who sat me down like a child and, bless her, forced me to learn.) There I was, like Job, facing the wrath of a tidal wave of forces from all sides, scribbling away whenever I could to write a screenplay that some entity would hopefully finance to allow us to make a brilliant film.

What a process. What a chain of lead weights I was wearing around my neck. What a fucking torture chamber of horrors I was letting myself in for—and I was paying for the privilege! Little did I know in my innocence that there was a craggy range of mountains in the near and far distance growing higher and tougher to climb, no matter my equipment and qualifications. I suppose, in retrospect, what kept me going was the dream of starring in a meaningful film with a sensitive director capable of achieving it. And that is no small thing.

My life wasn't standing still for the sake of Philip Roth. I had to get away from him every chance I could or I might have become a raging maniac. I felt a compulsion to begin to paint again. From the window of my studio as I mixed my paint, I could watch my children play on the swings and in the sandbox. Many times I would interrupt my painting, turpentining my hands as I ran to get the Bolex—Teddi and my three children, with their bubbling smiles letting me know what's important in my life; precious moments not to be ignored or forgotten.

In the fall of 1966, Harvey, breaking away from his plenteous TV shooting schedule, brought me up to Toronto to shoot a ninety-minute special on The Canadian Broadcasting Corporation's *Festival*. It gave us an opportunity to show what we could do if given the "go-ahead" on *Letting Go*. The TV program, similar to our *Playhouse 90*, was called "*David Chapter III*," by Charles Cohen. It was the humorous and heart-tugging story of a lawyer selling out his soul to materialism and sexual passion, losing the guidance of his inner voice. It was a fantasy and I played a variety of characters—even a woman. Harvey and I worked together with such ease it was joyful, and the reviews reflected that. The *Hamilton Spectator* of Ontario called it "a fantastic adult tour de force, it had daring imagination and a thoroughly spectacular performance by Mark Richman."

The show had created quite an excitement in all of Canada and ebullient reports kept coming in. Harvey was able to get a kinescope and we began having screenings hoping to stimulate interest in our talents for *Letting Go*. The response was very favorable. We then decided to hold a screening in a larger house with a seating capacity of two hundred. I remember that I was shooting an *Invaders* at the time and was worried about getting to our screening by 8:00 p.m. I made it with little time to spare and the place was packed. My heart rate was up a bit, but the reaction was fabulous and the applause at the end was heartwarming—and we were only viewing a 16 mm kinescope! At one point, I went up to the projection booth to tell the projectionist to increase the sound a touch and looked at the film from the booth's window. I was struck by the fact that I was really looking at a film with a potential for release to theaters. I said to myself: *This is a movie!*

When I sat down again, my wife whispered to me: "This is a movie!" Maybe it was the electricity of the evening, but Harvey felt the same way and so did our lawyer, Gunther Schiff. He flew to Toronto and miraculously made a deal with the CBC about a theatrical release and a 50 percent ownership, Harvey and I owning the other 50 percent.

Then, much to my delighted surprise, knowing how we felt about Subud, Harvey suggested that I write to Bapak to ask for the name of our production company. In a couple of weeks, the name arrived in a letter from Indonesia: Noble Light Projections, Ltd. We both thought it was a pretty cool name, so we went ahead and became a legal corporation in the state of California. (I had already asked previously for my true spiritual name and had received Peter, and my wife's new spiritual name was Helen, but it took us several years to get around to using them. In Subud, it is beneficial for you if the name you go by is in harmony with your inner life. I believe that is true even if you're not in Subud.)

When the deal was set with the CBC, the original tape was sent to us and we took it to the Technicolor Corporation to transfer it to 35 mm film. At the time, they were the best at doing transfers and cleaning up technical glitches which entailed a highly complex electronic dickering. In our partnership, I hadn't expected to spend four months at Technicolor lab with the executive in charge, Joe Bluth, completing our film, but I did, enthusiastically. It was a unique undertaking and worth the effort and considerable expense. I was bleary-eyed from seeing TV monitors and full screenings, carefully checking the clarity and contrasts before I tentatively approved a print with our new feature titles. Then Harvey came in for finishing touches with his keen observation.

Our product was now ready for sale. NOBLE LIGHT PROJECTIONS and the CBC present: *DAVID CHAPTER III*. It looked pretty damned good. We acquired the services of Mike Beck, one of the best producer representatives to sell a film. We had high hopes, even though it hadn't been done before, a release of a TV show as a theatrical film. But Mike's enthusiasm went a long way to give us encouragement, even though a black-and-white picture was becoming a difficult sell—everything was now being shot in color.

I wasn't going to stand still, waiting for something to happen so I jumped into the mix. If I can show an 8 mm movie to a studio head, I would stop at nothing! I had seen a film that Artie Shaw, the great clarinetist and ladies' man, had acquired and released for his Artixo company—a black-and-white spooky picture titled *Seance on a Wet Afternoon* with Kim Stanley and Richard Attenborough that had become a cult classic. With extra chutzpah, I called him on the phone, convinced him of the merits of our film, flew to New York with the kinescope under my arm, and met him for lunch. He was still the charming and good-looking band leader, only grayer around the edges. We then went to some crappy, badly equipped screening room on 7th Avenue and watched *David Chapter III*. The sound was distorted and the print looked dark and unappealing. It suddenly became what it was—a 16 mm kinescope. Artie was gracious, but he wasn't interested. I'm not sure that Mike Beck would have done any better in this screening room with the new 35 mm version. At least I can say that I had lunch with the man who had survived marriages with Lana Turner, Ava Gardner, Kathleen Winsor, Doris Dowling, and Evelyn Keyes! After months of meetings, screenings on both coasts, wires and letters from Mike in New York, he let us know that he had great interest in a sale that was possibly imminent. The company that liked it, well known for distributing quality art films, was about to put the pen to the dotted line, but wanted a little more time to decide. They were also considering another film that they liked, John Cassavetes's *Faces*. He asked for our patience. We waited and hoped.

It took them thirty days to make the choice. It wasn't our film. All during this venture, any time I was free I was slaving away with my sharpened pencils trying to complete a credible screenplay of the Roth book. Finally, after two years of drafts, endless fits and starts, and tedious tobacco smoke-clouded meetings with Harvey, I had a screenplay ready to be seen. A lot of Mark Richman was on the printed page and the best of Philip Roth. I'd made a mensch out of his main character. Of course, we had to have our lawyer, Gunther Schiff, renegotiate our contract and the options were increasing in dollars and ball tightening. The script was now being shown selectively around town and the response was a passively warm… "Uh, maybe," to the standard: "I pass…" It would have been a slam-dunk with Robert Redford or Warren Beatty attached, but it couldn't have been made with the modest budget we were talking about. Whenever I sensed that I wasn't wanted in the production if it were to be made (although Harvey in kindness tried to keep it from me), I felt my jaw tighten and my fists curl, as if I were ready to pounce again as a linebacker in a football game. Hey! I own the property and I wrote the screenplay, so it's only right and proper that I star in the fucking picture! You don't like it? Take your bucks and fuck off!

The process of torturous rewrites, fine tuning, and submissions painfully continued as we doggedly pursued that shiny, but elusive, brass ring. When someone is reading your script and you're laboring with the unrealistic hope that they're going to like it, more times than not, they won't, and will give you some dumb-ass critique about the script's faults and how to correct them. It's easy when you're uninvolved and an all-knowing expert in bullshit. Almost everyone who reads a script in Hollywood, with few exceptions, is an expert in bullshit. It's the nature of the game. It's always easier to say no. No one in his right mind has the guts to say: I don't have a clue as to whether this script will make a good picture with the right director and cast. No one. It takes a director or a producer or an actor or whoever it is that has the belief and the faith that the script he holds tenaciously to his bosom is a quality piece of work and a winner— and tirelessly scrapes and crawls ahead to get it made.

In 1967, Harvey signed a multiple picture deal at Twentieth Century Fox and had completed his first film there called *The Sweet Ride*, which Joe Pasternak produced and Tom Mankiewicz wrote. I was really pleased for Harvey. It gave him additional clout as a director and it would be helpful to get our picture made. Suddenly, however, I found out that Harvey was talking to Tom Mankiewicz about producing *Letting Go* and possibly to do some rewrites on my script, never having informed or consulted me with his intentions. I was pissed off and hurt that having such a compulsion to get the film made he wouldn't even discuss his actions with his partner. It took me quite a while to get over that one, especially since I always seemed to be advancing Roth's option money and Harvey's share at the same time because he was low in funds. There were many irritations like that, but I guess that's true in most partnerships. I don't like to harbor grievances; they can linger and fester if not brought out into the open. I would much rather have them all on the table, sticky and prickly, where I can see and deal with them and make the best of it.

In the spring of 1969, after nearly four years of perpetual rejection and another extension of our options with Roth, the sun was beginning to glimmer through the dark clouds. We had growing interest in a possible production. Julian Roffman, a dear man and an enterprising Canadian who was a close friend of Harvey's, had shown the script to the Canadian Film Development Corporation. They liked it and were giving warm indications of coming in for $300,000 in an $850,000 budget if we shot the film in Canada. No problem. I would change the locale from Chicago and New York to Toronto and New York. There were to be about $200,000 in deferments for our script payments, our producer-director-actor salaries, and much more. Julian and his company (Taylor-Roffman) would defer payments for laboratory and technical facilities to the tune of about $75,000 in return for Canadian distribution. We needed an American company to come up with another $325,000 that would guarantee international distribution and also furnish a completion bond. Things were beginning to look rosy. Lawrence Gordon, who later became an executive producer on many huge money-making films (*48 Hours, Die Hard, Field of Dreams*) worked at that time for Sam Arkoff and James Nicholson at American International Pictures. He was V.P. in charge of project development, looking for the property that would elevate the company to a higher level of picture making. He found it in our screenplay. By this time, four years after we plunked down our first option money, when Philip Roth was relatively unknown, he was now basking brightly in the klieg lights with the Paramount picture *Goodbye Columbus*, from his second novel. Another book, *Portnoy's Complaint*, his ode to reaching nirvana by jerking off, was also in the movie hopper. Roth was now a hot property. "Larry" Gordon knew what he was doing when he said to us as we sat in his office at A.I.P., "I'm recommending this to Sam, this is the best script I've read since I've been here." Harvey and I looked at each other and smiled. Our chests were bursting. It felt damned good to hear some positive words for a change and not a lot of soupy bullshit. It felt even better when Sam Arkoff agreed to give the green light for the $325,000 needed to complete the equation. The moment we heard the news was almost too overwhelming. Oh, my God! We can now make the picture! We were walking around ecstatic, our feet never touching the floor. Is it any wonder? After four fucking years it was really going to happen. I was going to star and co-produce a film that I had written! After all that pain and suffering and loss of blood, after all those sleepless, interminable nights of twisting and turning and sweating and groaning, there had been a miraculous change. Noble Light Projections was now unexpectedly illuminating the heavens! It was a wonderful time and we reveled in it.

We needed an executive producer with smarts and Hollywood know-how, so we brought in Leon Mirell, who'd been at Selmur productions making all those TV *Combat* shows. He would be co-executive producer with Canadian Julian Roffman. This rounded out the production team.

Although the contractual complexities and percentages were still being pondered and resolved by the lawyers, we were eager and ready to get the project finally going. On a lighter note, I'll never forget how we sat quietly around Sam Arkoff's pool at his home in Studio City one very hot afternoon, waiting. He had invited us to celebrate the impending production and toast its good fortune. Harvey and I and Leon Mirell were sportily dressed, but Sam, looking like a beached whale, still floated in his pool with an enormous cigar stuffed in his mouth. It was a tableau for a comic book.

I couldn't take the silliness any longer. I walked to the edge of the pool. "Sam," I said, smiling. "We're here and we're roasting."

"Uh… oh… Oh! I'm sorry," he said, coming out of his reverie, splashing about. "I'll be with you in a minute. I think I dozed off."

A few days later Sam and all the involved parties came to my home for the cutting of a large cake with a single lighted candle on top and the words *Letting Go* in a pink confection. Raising our champagne glasses, we toasted our association and good luck for the future. Harvey and I blew out the candle and then we hugged each other.

There was another celebration to be deeply thankful for. We received another blessing. On June 15, 1969, my wonderful wife gave birth to our 4th child, a boy! Bapak had given us his name and we loved it: Orien. It's from the Greek. It means: "To rise from the mountain top, as the sun rises." My God, I was now the father of four!

I was also a full-fledged producer now going to our offices at Columbia Pictures on Gower Street. I had a desk, a phone, and a pencil and pen—and oh, yes… I carried a black briefcase, and inside, a script that had my name on it. I remember running into Rona Jaffe, a hot novelist, in the hallway and we hugged each other. She also had a film in pre-production and was happy for my success. We were deeply involved in casting, the agents and managers calling endlessly. Leon handled all of that extremely well, giving us memos and suggestions about the appointment schedule. Months earlier, before anything was happening, we'd had a preliminary casting session at my home. Harvey had worked with Melvyn Douglas previously and wanted him to play the father in *Letting Go*, and also to meet me. Mr. Douglas graciously came for coffee and surprisingly brought his lovely wife, Helen Gahagan Douglas. It was an A-plus night, having a wonderful star from another era who'd worked with so many film legends, including Greta Garbo, and his wife, a legend in her own right who'd been an actress too, but had only performed in one film. When I told her I had seen her in *She* in 1935 when I was eight years old and it had scared the hell out of me, she was astonished and couldn't get over it. I then related my compulsive childhood movie-going when we lived opposite the Alhambra Theater in South Philadelphia. Melvyn Douglas turned the part down. It wasn't big enough, but in my eyes he was very big.

We had sent a script to the American Airlines representative in New York for them to consider if we could use their facilities. A week later, I placed a call to Bob Edgerton. The first thing he said when he answered the phone was: "I liked your script."

"Great!" I answered, making another thrust. "You like it so much that you'll let us shoot in New York and Toronto at your terminal and with mock-ups too, right, Bob?"

"Yeah, I think we can work it out," he said.

I gulped my heart and said, "Oh, that's terrific, Bob… and how about some cash for in-film plugs? You know, on screen "American Airlines" always on view in the background?"

"I think I can do that," he said without hesitation. "How about $15 to $20,000… would that be in the ballpark?"

"Uh, I was thinking more… but that could do it."

Chills were running up and down my back as I wiped the perspiration off my chin. We talked further about the script and a tentative start date. By the time I hung up, sitting there in a creaky old studio desk chair shaking my head as to what just happened, Leon stood in the doorway with a smile on his face. "I heard your conversation, Mark. You're a born producer!" We were about five weeks away from a shooting date and it was a heady time. Our production manager had even begun to lay out a daily shooting schedule. We were lining up commitments for all the required equipment and personnel for our two locations. It was a mammoth operation—sending scripts, telegrams, and lengthy phone calls with heartburn personalities; it was a wonder that we were progressing so rapidly. There was no doubt that Leon Mirell was a godsend, the man to keep it all flowing with organizational clarity. I remember something he said to me, as if it were an hour ago, and forty-four years have passed. We were strolling outside after a meeting at his home. "Mark, when you get this picture made," he said, "it will put you in a whole different category. You'll be a producer who made a quality film for under a million. You and Harvey will be able to do that as many times as you want…"

Dyan Cannon seemed to be disgruntled as she sat facing Harvey and me, her agent, Sue Mengers, nearby. We were discussing the film to be, and the more we talked the less I thought she was right for the part of Martha.

There was something too hard about her. I was sure she was thinking: Who the hell are you to be interviewing me? The next actress we saw was Karen Black. She was pleasant and sweet and was considered a possibility. Judy Collins, the singer, had read the script and liked it and was also interested in doing Martha. The agents and managers were vigorously pushing their clients for the plumb female role; the dialogue was rich in real talk and the situations were emotionally powerful. All the parts were exceptional and the potential for whoever played them would be attention-getting. It wasn't surprising that the phone never stopped ringing. The list of good actresses we were talking about went from Shirley Jones, Candice Bergen, Yvette Mimieux, Connie Stevens, Elizabeth Ashley, Maggie Smith, Barbara Eden, and Suzanne Pleshette to Leslie Caron. Even Sherry Lansing, who eventually gave up acting and became a studio boss, wanted to be considered for the part of Libby, the troubled second woman.

I would be sitting in my office chair, or driving home, or lying in bed… and I would think of all the female possibilities available, imagining how it would be to play with each one—to hold and hug and kiss the choice we would make to bring alive Martha and Gabe's torturous romance. Who did I feel most comfortable with? Who was it that had a presence I would love? Leslie Caron, of course. It would be advantageous besides, a French girl in our new location, Canada—a place full of Frenchmen. We had just made an offer to Tuesday Weld to play the part of Libby. Our first choice for the part of Martha, Leslie Caron, who liked the screenplay, was seriously considering doing the film even though it meant short money. Her agent, Mike Medavoy at CMA, was emphatically telling us that she'd received $120,000 plus a percentage of the gross in her last picture, *Head of the Family*. We couldn't pay anything near that, but I was beside myself with hope that she would have a mind of her own and come through for us. In the meantime, I was going to talk to my friend Lee J. Cobb about playing Gabe's father. He probably would think that the role was too small also, but I would give it a shot. Joseph Cotton, Van Heflin, and Ed Begley were possibilities too. I had worked with Patricia Medina on my show *Cain* and she was Mr. Cotton's wife. It could be a good introduction, I thought.

On July 15, 1969, a long article written by A. H. Weiler appeared in *The New York Times*:

"ROTH'S '*LETTING GO*' HEADS FOR FILMING:

'*Letting Go*,' the Philip Roth novel published by Random House in 1962 will be filmed by American International Pictures in association with Leon Mirell Productions and Noble Light Projections… it will be produced by Mark Richman, who will also star, and Mr. Hart who will direct from their adaptation of the novel… scheduled to go before the cameras on location in Toronto and New York…"

To say that the doo-doo hit the fan in globs when the column surfaced would be like saying World War II was only a skirmish. All fucking hell broke loose. Philip Roth and his lawyers contended that American International Pictures was not capable or worthy of fulfilling the contract's "assumption agreement." This was a clause that our lawyer Gunther Schiff had put in when we extended our option. It listed examples of studios or entities who could assume financial responsibility for our production and distribution. Because he hadn't initially listed AIP (nor fifty other companies), Roth was using it as a ploy to renege on our deal after accepting four years of our option money! AIP was an extremely solvent filmmaking company and besides, had successfully distributed quality pictures such as *The Pawnbroker* and *The Umbrellas of Cherbourg*. Actually, AIP was only one of the investors, it was to be a Canadian picture, a good portion of it funded by the Canadian Film Development Corporation and also Taylor-Roffman Studios of Toronto.

Sam Arkoff, at one point in the miserably enervating and hostile negotiations, was willing to put up his personal assets of $25 million as a guarantor to satisfy Roth's piss-green greed that he would get everything he deserved as contractually stated. But no, that wasn't good enough. Roth considered himself a star novelist now, entitled to gobble up tons of money from whomever he could for the rights to his book. All he had to do was fuck the trusting and faithful Hart and Richman who'd carried him along when he needed it—and was so happy to get the every-six-months option dough with the increasing numbers. A more despicable sonofabitch never was born. No matter how many complicated communiques and phone calls were made between our lawyers, Leon, Harvey, me, Arkoff and Roth's legal contingent, the acrimony increased. After a couple of weeks, it was becoming obvious to all concerned, much to our dread, that the production would be forced to shut down. Mr. Roth was continuing to "unreasonably withhold his consent to the rights" of *Letting Go*. It was so painfully disheartening I was walking around in a daze, and so was Harvey. Paying for something for four years, studying it, dreaming about it, visualizing it on the screen, laboring to put into an actable form, fighting to get it financed and finally made, and then to be told that you didn't really own the rights and cannot complete the act is like the vilest form of coitus interruptus.

Philip Roth was indeed lucky that we were always a great distance apart. I've never been in trouble with the law, but he is one individual I could have easily without hesitation for a second sent back to his ancestors, who he wasn't too crazy about I gather.

This man with the inner life of a roach caused me such pain and heartache and financial loss that when I even think of him all these years later, all the anger and desire for violent retaliation still burns in my throat. Harvey and I were honorable men who would have created an honorable and memorable piece of work and we weren't allowed to. I resented it greatly—and I still do. Instead of a creative production, we went into a debilitating lawsuit. The papers were a half-inch thick, spelling out in detail all the grievances and misdeeds perpetrated against us and the financial penalties we were requesting. We had a solid case. Roth didn't have a tum for the bile in his heart. My share, as the damaged plaintiff, was $510,000. Of course, this was in 1969 numbers. I have no idea what that would be today. I was the co-author, co-producer, star, and I would own 15 percent of the film.

During the case, which dragged on for years, I had to go to New York for a deposition. Somewhat naive as to the procedure, I let this turd of a lawyer get to me with insinuating lies and falsehoods, and our New York lawyer for the case, Egon Dumler, had to restrain me. All my frustration aimed at Roth almost got his lawyer's jaw cracked. I was absolutely a crazed individual concerning Roth, and I couldn't get rid of him no matter how I tried! I will explain: suddenly, this illustrious parasite of an author realized that he would get his head handed to him and that he would lose his shirt when we went to trial, which was finally approaching. So, what did he do? He put out a feeler to settle the case. Now? After having closed our production down? Now? After all the time and expense and the heartache? Are you kidding me? I wanted no part of it and neither did Sam Arkoff or anybody else—except Harvey. I wanted to go to trial and make the ungrateful worm suffer like we did. Harvey wanted the property back. He still wanted to make the film! Arkoff indicated in an itty-bitty way that under the right circumstances he might be flexible. I couldn't believe it, and it caused a great deal of friction between us. Harvey felt that I was preventing him from making the picture he longed to make—even though now, I was too fucking old for the part. Somebody else would have to play the role.

"You could still co-produce with me, and it's our script... and if Arkoff does the picture, you'll be guaranteed your actor's salary," Harvey said seriously in a letter, resting on our friendship, playing that tune like a funereal fugue. "Mark, we've come so far. Let's not give it up now." (My brain felt as if it was being pelted with rocks.)

"*Letting Go* can't be held responsible for the success or failure of our respective careers, the traumas, although not equal, have been there for the both of us... but that much responsibility is too much weight to put on any one project. But *Letting Go* can be held responsible for drawing us closer—in deeper friendship... for thousands of marvelous times together. What else have we got? Tell me, what single person has shown more faith in your acting talents than I have? Or more loyalty to you as a person?

"There's no guarantee even now that we can put a new deal together, but I'm sick and tired of being destructive about the project and I want to go forward. The only revenge I'm interested in now is proving that we can make one hell of a picture! Is that so bad?

With all my love, Harvey."

So, on January 1, 1974—again, against my better judgement—almost ten years after first optioning the book, knowing it would be an even harder sell, especially after being tainted with litigation—I let Harvey talk me into having his way, submitting myself to reluctantly plunge into the perpetual well of misery again. I agreed to a new deal with Roth for two years and the privilege of paying him more option money! In retrospect, it was disgusting. There were revisions and more revisions... submissions and more submissions. I believe I had written one hell of a good script that would have made a fabulous picture, one that would have been the defining one for Philip Roth. But, always the hidden, underlying bug-a-boo that turned up sooner or later—the lurking contagious dread... litigation disease. It withered away all interest, killing initial enthusiasm. As David Brown (executive, Zanuck/Brown Co.) wrote when he returned the script: "I like this and I know it has emotional power, but I'm frightened to death of getting involved..." Even Sam Arkoff and AIP folded their tent. I ran into Paul Monash at the Academy of Motion Pictures one evening. He had produced my series, *Cain's Hundred*, and then the film *Butch Cassidy and the Sundance Kid*. He called me after he'd read *Letting Go*. He said, "I liked it, but... it's past its time. The two years went by and nothing happened." It was January 1976. After twelve years of effort, all I had to show for it was a pile of useless scripts in my garage with fading covers.

It was getting clearer and clearer. Actually, it was quite obvious. Nothing in my life has ever come easy. I have grown so accepting of that fact that I have a built-in, unshakable wariness and cynicism tugging at me in whatever I do. It is a preordained pattern cut from my ancestral cloth. I will have to wear that suit until it fits perfectly, taking in a little here or there as we go along. I don't mean that I am devoid of positive possibilities, but I do mean that whenever I get involved—in what I would consider a worthwhile venture—the endeavor to accomplish it will usually be a climb up "Mount Treacherous." With some people, it's always clear sailing; with me, the sail is torn, the boat is leaking, and there's a fearful storm brewing on the horizon. But through it all, there are lessons to be learned and stored experiences that cannot be had any other way; and in the end, for whoever is keeping record, it's the struggle to create that tunes the instrument and sharpens the talent. As I said later through an elderly character that I wrote, "How we solve our problems... that's what God sees."

On August 13, 1965, just getting started on my *Letting Go* ordeal, Los Angeles confronted its first massive taste of communal racial chaos and eruptive anarchy—the Watts Riot. It was the beginning of widespread tension and urban violence. A minor incident with a black motorist and a white policeman escalated in the summer heat to a full-scale rebellion. The ty- four people were killed in the five-day riot and over 1,000 were wounded, which caused an estimated $200 million loss of property. The 35,000 African-Americans who participated directed their anger at the white shopkeepers in the area and the police. Over 16,000 National Guardsmen, city police, and other law-enforcing deputies were called in to finally quell the disaster.

We didn't know this as actors when the curtain went up on the first Theater Group production at UCLA's Schoenberg Hall. We were deeply concentrated performing another dreadful period in history where a total loss of humanity caused the extermination of 6 million Jews. The German play we were appearing in was called *The Deputy*, by Rolf Hochhuth, and was directed by Gordon Davidson, working from the translation that had opened earlier on Broadway. The play is an indictment of Pope Pius XII for his complicity in not raising his voice to protest against the Nazi wholesale slaughter. It was a fabulous production with a cast of top quality actors. I had originally gone in to see Gordon about playing the idealist Jesuit, a man who wears a yellow star in protest and dies in the gas chamber, but he asked me instead to assume the role of the doctor, a man of horrifying evil based on the real Dr. Mengele. I couldn't resist; the part had many areas worth exploring. I had read a translation of the original German version and I asked Gordon if he would approve my lifting a section of the text for my first entrance. He approved, so in the play I walked in with a large pickle-size jar under my black SS cloak, plunking it down on the table, telling my subordinate in absolute self-satisfied delight as I pointed—that I had just dissected the brains from a set of twin Jewish children.

The audience gasped, guaranteeing their hate whenever I was on stage. Near the end of the play, after a "good versus evil" discourse between me and the saintly priest, I point my riding crop for him to go to the gas chamber, and then I step downstage to berate the audience for their complacency and indifference to the suffering. Well, when the audience started to throw their folded programs at me, I knew they wouldn't invite me home for dinner. But, speaking of dinners, several months later, my wife and I were invited to dinner at the home of my children's piano teacher, Adela Gebr, who had escaped from Czechoslovakia during the war. Sitting opposite me, as we ate was a psychiatrist who seemed to have an inherent irritation with me, provoking a mild argument about drug treatment for illnesses, but since I was a pharmacist and knew the subject, I held my ground and resisted his conclusions. After we said good night for the evening, Adela told us the next day that the doctor had said, "I just don't like that man… there is something about him… he's like a Nazi!"

Adela laughed and replied, "Silly, we sat next to each other when we saw him play one in *The Deputy*." Apparently, my characterization had seeped into the doctor's subconscious.

The reviews were excellent and extended the run for twelve weeks. Cecil Smith wrote in the *Los Angeles Times*: "… Stage center stands the diabolical doctor, the black angel of Auschwitz, the director of the death factory. His uniform is immaculate, his boots shine like midnight suns, his darkly handsome face wears a disdainful smile, a lip-curled, contemptuous smile. He lights a cigarette. He strides off stage. The play ends. Richman is superb." Since I didn't appear until the second act, I was able to sit backstage almost every night, doing quick ink sketches of all the performers. Everyone was in black, the Nazis, the priests, and the victims. My drawings titled "Backstage at the Deputy" were included in my first one-man art exhibition at The Orlando Gallery in 1966.

Our children were blossoming. They were good kids—easy and happy. My first son, Howard, an eager helpmate around the house, was exhibiting a more than ordinary aptitude at the piano. He didn't have to be coaxed to practice his lessons, and he showed a peculiar ability for a child of seven to transpose original keys into many musical variations.

For Howard, this was the beginning of a life in music. It's been fascinating as a parent to watch how, with encouragement and guidance, aside from an innate talent, a child can find his true profession. It's a far cry from the way I grew up, where everything was a trapped trauma of guilt and obligation, and the only way to pursue a change was to come out swinging with a spiked club. I did a lot of that as a child, and it shows in my personality—still protectively ready to pounce when provoked—I'm afraid nothing has changed. Oh, well... maybe a little.

From 1965 to 1974 during the run of the popular *FBI* series, I appeared nine times, playing a variation of guest star criminal. Sometimes I was Mafia bigwig, a communist operative, or just a sleazy, purposeless hood. One of the more interesting segments I performed was called "Breakthrough." I was an organization gangster getting released from prison but who is targeted by the Mafia for extinction. Once outside, I rent a room from a young landlady who, oddly enough, owns the building. Unexpectedly, we fall in love, a tender twist for such a grim story. Dorothy Provine played opposite me and was an absolute delight to work with and so was her husband, the director Robert Day. Our scenes together were a joy, and when the killer comes for me and sadly does me in—the hopeless, emotionally touching, love relationship really paid off.

Quinn Martin was one of the best and most loyal producers of television in Hollywood. He continually hired the actors who had worked successfully in his shows, and he never forgot you if you had come through for him. I was fortunate to have been one of those actors. Whatever Quinn produced, sooner or later I would be on it. This relationship began when I appeared on the first show he ever produced, *The Jane Wyman Show*. Over the years I guested on many of his TV series innumerable times, including *The Fugitive, Barnaby Jones, 12 O'Clock High, Bert D'Angelo/Superstar, Cannon, The Streets of San Francisco, Banyon, Caribe,* and *The Invaders*. In 1968, I guested on a QM-produced murder mystery movie for TV called *The House on Greenapple Road*, and I was a suspect. My first day of shooting required me to be in bed with Janet Leigh (in a flimsy something) to perform that first moment after we just had sex! Sitting on the edge of the bed, as beautiful and as provocative as she could possibly be, she lights my cigarette and shyly asks me how she performed. I assure her that she was okay. After some more sexual innuendos, when I try to recruit her for a friend of mine, she becomes incensed and throws a small statue at my head, hitting me in the jaw. The funny thing about all of this is that Janet and I had met for the first time only an hour before shooting the scene. After we were made up we got together to run our lines and rehearse a bit before stepping onto the set. A few minutes later I was in bed with her, the camera was rolling and the director was saying: "Action!"

Talk about an actor's preparation for a scene! There wasn't enough time to change your socks, let alone get in the mood for sex.

Somehow, we fooled everybody. Since that time, Janet and I would address each other with our clothes on all the time. We were both Trustees on the Motion Picture and Television Fund Board, and were so together for over twenty years.

During a period of the early 1960s and 1970s I was appearing on many television programs with a religious premise. I was a character always going through some internal turmoil, struggling to find my way to a higher understanding—eventually doing the right thing for myself or someone close to me. It somehow paralleled my real life and gave me a deeper grasp into my portrayals. The most interesting aspect of doing these shows was the fact that they also gave me an opportunity to play roles with problems all human beings face—roles that I wasn't getting in commercial TV where I was generally hired to torment people or blow them away. On shows for a branch of the Lutheran Church, called *This is the Life*, I brought enlightenment to a wayward girl who had tried to harm me by touching her heart with my goodness. The girl was played by a very talented and young Sissy Spacek (who later won an Academy Award for *Coal Miner's Daughter*). On another, I was a businessman intent on ripping off an associate, but my son shames me into changing my materialistic ways. Really good stuff.

The Reverend Ellwood Kieser, a Paulist priest from Philadelphia, originated a television series called Insight. It was the most successful of all the "God" shows on the air. I guested on the program a number of times. In one, I was a distraught husband to Vera Miles who had just given birth to a special needs child, causing their marriage to be severely shaken, but finally salvaged by a spiritual realization. In another show, Robert Alan Simmons, a renowned writer, came up with a powerful story of revolutionaries capturing a hostage and their dilemma about killing him. It was called "Cry of Terror", with Andrew Prine and myself as the head of the gang. It was an extremely tense drama and when I finally make the painful decision to kill Harry Townes, who played the hostage—

morally and psychologically, it was sweating time. It was directed by Ralph Senensky, who years later directed me in the pilot of *Dynasty*, which, believe it or not, was first called *Oil*. Father Kieser hired me again for "Damn the Human Race," by David Karp. In the story, Jack Albertson, playing my older brother, offers me some stirring advice, hoping to change the way I treat my sensitive daughter, which was nicely realized by sixteen-year-old Barbara Hershey.

"Even though you're a do-gooder for many world organizations," he says, "what good is it… if you don't have time for your own family?"

While I was rehearsing another *Insight*, with Geraldine Brooks playing my wife, I didn't know why, but I was feeling terrible. It was one thing to act trying to solve a wrenching problem in a fictitious marriage, but how do you solve the real grinding pain in your gut accompanied by feverishness and nausea? About 4:00 in the afternoon, Ted Post, who was directing the opus said to me, "You look awful… I think you should go home."

We were scheduled to tape the episode the next day and he wanted me to get some rest. I thought I was possibly having a problem with something I'd eaten and surely, it would blow over, but it doggedly persisted. When I got home, my wife insisted that I call a doctor, but I resisted. The pain got worse. Finally, I called my next-door neighbor who was a doctor and told him how sick I was. He refused to see me and gave me some lame excuse about having to go to a meeting! My next-door neighbor? What ever happened to the Hippocratic Oath? I knew another doctor acquaintance up the hill, a half block from my home. Maybe he would come? Naaah! Wishful thinking. He wouldn't come either!

I'd heard that a character actor, John Bleifer, had children who were doctors, so I tracked him down and called Dr. Selvyn Bleifer in Beverly Hills. He immediately responded and said he would show up as soon as he could. Can you imagine? Even then, house calls were not the normal way of doing business; it was rare. Today? Forget it! Dr. Bleifer arrived about 9:00 in the evening. He suspected my problem, and in the examination pressed my stomach area and I nearly flew out the window, but the good doctor caught me and held on. He then informed me that I must have a blood count taken right away to analyze the infection—it could be dangerous to wait any longer. Still resisting, I excused myself and went to the bathroom, but before I got there I fainted, hitting the floor like a laundry bag. Ted Post was made aware of the drastic situation and was successful in getting William Shatner to replace me for the taping.

At Cedars of Lebanon Hospital, my white blood count was off the charts. By the time surgeon, Dr. Joel Zisk, performed an appendectomy at 7:00 in the morning, I had peritonitis and my appendix was about to burst á la Rudolf Valentino. I was indeed a lucky fellow. Strangely enough, the doctor next door who didn't want to come to see me didn't do as well. It's a peculiar fact, but a month after this little episode he had a heart attack and died.

Auditioning for Meredith Willson

ONE OF THE MANY REGRETS I HAVE in my life is that I never learned how to sing when I was young or even thought about it. During the first year of representation by Jules Sharr at the William Morris office, he said that he thought it would be a natural for me to sing and so he set me up with a teacher. Lillian Goodman was a heavyset, funny, old and old-fashioned voice coach who'd taught half the old stars in Hollywood at one time or another. She'd had a record released called "I Say You Can Sing!" that was still popular and gave me a copy, signing it with a flourish. Eventually, I painted a study of her that I still have in my collection. I can't vouch for how successful she'd been with me, but she got me going and I was a semi-serious student with a purpose—I wanted to do a musical. Janis Paige, a friend and a fine singer/actress with whom I'd worked on a *Fugitive*, had taken lessons from Lillian on occasion and was very encouraging. Lillian and I kibitzed and conflicted a bit, but I diligently worked on her exercises and even on an obscure Italian opera solo that she forced on me to develop my technique. About two months later, Jules Sharr called me to tell me that I had an appointment to sing for Meredith Willson. "He has a new musical in the works and you're perfect for it!" How ridiculous! I said to myself, *Sing? I just started to open my mouth!*

But, game fellow that I am, on the appointed day I geared up my courage and drove to Mr. Willson's home in Beverly Hills. I rang the bell, the door opened and I was greeted by a somewhat grim and bored woman who happened to be his wife. She ushered me into the study to meet the great one. He was an absolute gentleman, telling me that he'd seen me on television, and how much he'd heard about my potential as a singer for musical comedy. Then he sat down at the piano and I courageously began. First, I sang an inept Broadway tune that he followed to my music…

and then, naively, I proceeded to warble my Italian opera ditty. Can you imagine? I did notice the wife sitting in stone-faced rigidity. When I finished, the pleasantries abounded and he even walked me to my car. We shook hands with a smile and I drove away—uncertain, but pleased with my effort at least.

A couple hours later an agent, who I didn't know, called me to tell me that Meredith Willson had said that I was "lousy and sang flat." That was all I needed to set me off. I screamed into the phone, "You sonofabitch, who are you to report to me what Meredith Willson said? What kind of a fucking agent are you? I don't know you, you tactless bastard... and where the fuck is Julie Sharr? I shouldn't be auditioning after two months anyway! It was stupid and you can go fuck yourself!" It took me an hour to calm down, but it was the first indication that I was destined to leave the William Morris office.

In 1967, I had a one-man exhibition of my paintings at the American Masters Gallery in Los Angeles. I had been working in acrylic paint during that time almost exclusively, fascinated by the quick drying time and the adaptability to impulsive renderings. Most of the work was quite large, with many background layers of transcendent color bleeding into a foreground figurative study. I also had oil paint monotypes and figure ink drawings included. The show ran for a month and was fairly successful—which means some paintings were sold.

In August, I flew up north to Sacramento, California, to play Nick Arnstein in the Sacramento Music Circus production of *Funny Girl*, under a sweltering tent. It was a first for me and a wonderful venture. By this time, I was fairly secure in my singing, and I had gotten over my nervousness when I knew I could consistently come in on cue with the orchestra. That's the scary part for a novice, coming in on time. At one point while I was performing—with beautiful young dancers moving all around me, their bosoms bouncing as they swirled, the orchestra blaring, the choral voices rising—and center stage, there I was in a full dress suit, high hat and a cane, grinning, and enjoying the spectacle, saying to myself, *My God... I'm really in a musical!* One of the weirdest incidents happened as I was making my first entrance on opening night. As I moved quickly down the inclined aisle, the cane I was loosely carrying in my left hand got stuck in a patron's chair arm as I passed by. It just stuck there. So, what did I do? I gave it a yank and it broke in half! I must have looked silly walking on stage in my top hat and riding crop. However, the strange part of all this was that I found out the cane broke in half in a newspaper critic's chair!

William C. Glackin, Sacramento Bee wrote: "... *Funny Girl* wins standing applause... Mark Richman's Arnstein is the big difference." In the fall of 1967, I was one of four stars to shoot an entertaining Columbia picture titled *For Singles Only*. I was the married ringer in a group of single guys who was playing around with the unknowing younger chicks, all residing at "sexual haven" Sans Souci apartments surrounding a mammoth pool. The gorgeous one I was making it with was Natalie Wood's sister, Lana Wood. She falls in love with me, but, of course, occupied elsewhere, I have to disappoint her. The running gag in the film entailed a bet that several oversexed males made with John Saxon—that he couldn't make it with former Miss America, prudish Mary Ann Mobely. There were scanty swim suits, heavy breathing from all, and oh, such risqué conversation! In comparison to today's "anything goes" standards, the picture was as sweet and innocent as a chaperoned junior high school prom. Milton Berle was a special guest star. Playing the entertainment and activities director, he was at his charming, leering best. He was a dear man, warm, funny, always "on," but compelling when quiet and reflective.

I was as busy as any Hollywood actor wanted to be, going from one television show to the next as a guest star. I wasn't always pleased, however, with the category I seemed to be locked into—the dangerous bad guy you don't mess around with. I kept telling my agent, who was now Ronnie Leif at Contemporary Artists (Lew Wasserman's son-in-law), that I wanted to do feature films. I felt that's where my career would take off from if I was given the right role. On more than one occasion I said, "For God's sakes, get me a feature. TV leads nowhere… it's a dead end. It's only a repeat of the same crap!" Work and more work is what brings in the money for my agent and for me, and the avenue that provided acceptability and the most remuneration at the time was the small screen. Consistency of exposure that would come with a successful weekly series to help instigate the transition to the big screen just wasn't happening. I kept telling myself I would have to bide my time. *Letting Go* could be my big splash in features if it was meant to be—I would just have to finish the script and get a production going. We all know how that turned out.

After a luncheon meeting at MGM for some prospective film, I was walking to my car when I ran into Lloyd Bridges. He was strikingly handsome and always emanated warmth and genuine friendliness. He asked me if I would be available to guest on his successful series *The Loner*. Of course, I said, "Yes." His series was created by Rod Serling, and the episode was called "Incident in the Middle of Nowhere" and Joe Pevney directed with a sure hand. I've always enjoyed doing Westerns and in this show, I played a high class stagecoach robber who'd been a Shakespearean actor until one side of his face was hideously burned in a fire. Always fussy and particular about my costuming, I found exactly what I was looking for at 20th Century Fox wardrobe after much searching: a wide-brimmed Australian hat with a scarf coming from the inside of the hat and tied under the chin that would cover my scarred face. It was very effective. When I pulled it off, finally revealing to Lloyd my facial condition, which had motivated my life of crime, I punctuated it with a shortened oration of Hamlet's soliloquy at Yorick's gravesite! As expected, after a chase and a gunfight up a rocky hillside, I finally got my just desserts. The makeup man had to be at my home at 4:30 in the morning to begin the work on my face before going on location. It was a complex application of scars and needed more time than usual for me to be ready to begin shooting. Beverly Garland played my wife, and Lloyd Bridges' twelve-year-old daughter, Cindy, played our daughter. Years later she told me that it was the only acting she'd ever done. Her brothers, Beau and Jeff Bridges, also perfect gentlemen like their father, have had great and deserving careers. I was successively appearing on such shows as *T.h.e.Cat*, with Robert Loggia; *Voyage to the Bottom of the Sea*, with Richard Basehart; *The Iron Horse*, with Dale Robertson; *Ironside*, with Raymond Burr; *It Takes a Thief*, with Robert Wagner; *Gunsmoke*, with Jim Arness; *The Name of the Game*, with Anthony Franciosa; and *Mannix*, with Mike Connors. I even flitted off to Hawaii to guest on *Hawaii Five-O*, with Jack Lord, the high potentate of the Islands. On that trip, Teddi was with me and it made it all worthwhile, visiting glorious and dreamy Maui, having Hawaiian custom shirts made in Lahaina, flight hopping to Kauai and Molokai, and getting a firsthand look at Pearl Harbor in Oahu where a dastardly deed can never be forgotten. I even impulsively purchased ten acres of property on the always-drenched area of Hilo on the east coast of the big island of Hawaii for a prospective Subud development. (It didn't pan out.)

Going from one show to the next was an enviable position to be in, and I could continue to say, "I've played a lot of characters, but I have never played an Indian in my life!" That changed when I accepted a job on *Daniel Boone*, starring Fess Parker and Ed Ames, to play a killer Indian whose hate for whites knew no bounds. I certainly scared the hell out my three children when my wife brought them to the set for a visit at the 20th Century Fox ranch in Malibu. I kept leering at them without saying a word until they realized it was their dad and just couldn't believe the transformation.

In August 1968, I flew up to Sacramento, California, with Howard who was then ten years old. I wanted him to be with me for the opening of my art show at the Crocker Museum. It isn't often that one can say they had an exhibition in a museum, so it was rather a prestigious and exciting event, especially for someone who earned a living in another profession. Because of that, some people refused to take me seriously. They thought that if I'm an actor I must be only an amateur painter—a dilettante. The truth is, I'm just as dedicated as a painter as I am as an actor. I remember walking slowly through the two spacious galleries where my work was displayed and I was a bit overwhelmed. Howard said to me, "It looks really good, Dad." We had a wonderful time together, tender and loving—a memory to hold on to. Richard Simon of the Sacramento Union wrote, "… an artist of considerable originality… Renaissance man."

Waiting for a phone call from my agent about prospective employment has always been tough for me to take. The free time between jobs can be briefly rejuvenating, but for an actor it's an extremely difficult and vulnerable time. That's when all the doubts and insecurities about your place in this fickle and erratic business come slithering back to bite your neck. The longer the in-between time persists, the deeper the bites. Unfortunately, it's also the time when some actors get involved in negative pursuits that can be detrimental to themselves and their careers. That's why I feel blessed and grateful for my aggressive compulsions to create—this tingling, sensual need to express myself another way, to put it all down on canvas or paper. In April and May 1969, I had an exhibition at the McKenzie Gallery on La Cienega Boulevard in Los Angeles. It featured large figurative studies in oil of people and their endeavors, some with theatrical content, and water colors of nudes. At the time, I was using a vibrant green underpainting that bled through and outlined the final figure, giving it a luminous glow. I was always experimenting with different underpaintings to see what was most effective for my figure work and how it might influence the finished painting. It's fascinating how the work changes over the years without even trying, but no matter what you do, it always remains you and what you are as an artist. It's a reflection of your inner life at that time, where, I believe, all creativity comes from. Even if a conscious effort is made to disguise your work, telltale signs will remain—like a thumb print or a signature.

Many international Subud visitors came to Los Angeles, solidifying our understanding that Subud was a spiritual movement that had touched the world. One guest in particular became a dear and memorable friend. Varindra (Tarzie) Vittachi, a short, bald, smiling dynamo, was from Ceylon (now Sri Lanka), but traveled extensively as a reporter from his home base in London with his wife and four children. Tarzie wrote the award-winning *The Fall of Sukarno*, as well as several books on Subud. His stories of being with Bapak were deep, refreshing, and delightfully witty. When I listened to him speak, I always had the feeling that I was getting the real scoop, an insight into the profundity of who Bapak really was. Prio Hartono, an experienced Subud helper, was sent by Bapak to live in Los Angeles for an extended period of time. Bapak felt that we needed some hands-on guidance for the Los Angeles group to function properly. He was warmly welcomed and his advice and patience were truly an enormous help to all of us. One of the things he did was enlighten us to the power of fasting and what it could do—with God's grace, of course. Periodically, Bapak Subuh would leave Indonesia to travel on a partial world tour, and we were extremely grateful whenever he came to California. In the spring of 1968, leaving the children with our dependable housekeeper, Teddi and I drove up to San Francisco, Bapak's first stop, excited about being with him. A joyous, almost festive atmosphere always permeated the preparations being made for his visit. There was a large Subud group in San Francisco and also active centers in Marin, Carmel Valley, and Palo Alto. We would visit them, all doing latihan with Bapak and his traveling entourage, and then settle in to listen to his penetrating talks, which are actually a receiving from God. It is interesting to note that sometimes Bapak would speak for five minutes or longer in his native tongue, and then the translator would express what he thought he had heard; if he goofed in expressing the true meaning, Bapak, who didn't speak fluent English, would correct him! (With a laugh.) Or his granddaughters, Muti and Tuti, or his daughter, Rahayu, would suggest a correction. His wife, Ibu Siti Sumari, beautifully attired in Indonesian garb, would smile and just listen, an aura of total quiet emanating around her. Being with Bapak has always been a booster to our faith and purpose in Subud—a supercharged rejuvenation of knowing first hand that the power of God is in our lives here and now—and how graced we are to have received this miraculous blessing. One of the highlights of our trip was a motorboat ride around San Francisco with Bapak and some other Subud brothers. I have a photograph of myself in a raincoat smoking a Bing Crosby pipe, and in the background, a low angle view of the windy Island of Alcatraz looking institutionally serene from afar, but scary.

When we arrived back home, our children were as thrilled to see their parents as we were to see them; there were hugs and squeezes and kisses to fill another cup running over.

I was doing so many bad guys on television, I thought the only way I could keep my sanity and not repeat myself was to alter the performance with a dialect. I suppose it all started when I was performing multiple voices on those radio shows in Philadelphia so many years ago. It has been enlightening to me how much a character can change with an inflection of speech. The modification of vocal delivery by a serious attempt at an authentic dialect can greatly influence the body language, posture, look, and characteristics of a performance. I appeared a few times on *The Wild, Wild West*. In the episode titled "The Night of the Dancing Death," I played an imposing prince of some foreign entity who was a great kung fu expert. I chose to make him a Hungarian, sporting an attractive moustache along with his princely attire. I had a producer-writer friend in New York who was Hungarian and his speech had always stuck in my head. I became Prince Gio in the flesh. I think if I had played the part without a dialect it wouldn't have worked for me, or had been as colorful. I remember doing a number of guest star bad guys on *Fantasy Island*. Ricardo Montalban and I would joke about this. "Back for another one," I would say, as we shook hands and laughed. I first met Ricardo when he guest starred on *Cain's Hundred* playing a Mob gambler related to the young Robert Blake in a school basketball scandal. Ricardo, a kindly, unpretentious man and a fine actor, unfortunately suffered greatly from an injury to his spine that happened years before in a horse fall. As a devotee of chiropractic, I sent him to my doctor to see if he could help alleviate his constant pain. For a while he was relieved and thankful, but the extensive damage was beyond chiropractic treatment.

One time on *Fantasy Island* I chose to make a particular international slimeball a Frenchman. On the first day of shooting, I opened my mouth with a French accent and the surprised director accepted it and went along with me. It was an Aaron Spelling show and when they saw the rushes they complained to my agent. "We hired him to play a Mafia guy... why is he suddenly French?" He didn't have an answer. They weren't going to reshoot the footage, so I remained forever a Frenchman. As it turned out, when the producers saw the final cut they were very pleased and so was I. It gave the character an added dimension—a worldly sexiness—especially in the suggested intimacy with my co-star, gorgeous Britt Ekland. It was one of the better episodes I ever shot for Aaron and only solidified my relationship with him. In a *Mission Impossible* segment I altered my speech with a variation of a Brazilian accent—or shall I say, a reasonable facsimile of one. However, the varying density of the accents surrounding me made the origin of our country somewhat suspect.

In early 1970, I flew to New York to begin filming a pilot for Universal called *McCloud*. I was to play Peter Clifford, the hard-nosed chief of police, and Dennis Weaver was set for *McCloud*, the irritant, out-of-state cowboy. We were to be the co-stars for a future series that had "sure thing" written all over it. A few minutes after I had seated myself and buckled in, a familiar gentleman sat down next to me. He happened to be a friend and neighbor, the great actor Lee J. Cobb. To say that it was a surprise is one thing, but when he asked me why I was going to New York—what was more than bizarre—he told me that the part I was doing in the pilot was the same part he played in the film *Coogan's Bluff* with Clint Eastwood! (*McCloud* was based on *Coogan's Bluff*.) Why we were ordained to sit next to each other on a flight to New York under those circumstances is another one of life's perplexing little mysteries. To top it all off, when the stewardess asked me what I wanted on the menu and I told her I wouldn't be eating, Lee looked at me curiously and asked, "Why?"

"I'm fasting," I said.

"What do you mean... you're fasting?" he asked, warily.

"Uh... well, I'm doing a spiritual fast," I said, not really wanting to go into it.

"What's a spiritual fast?"

"Well," I answered, hesitantly, but with a smile, "it's a fast where... if you deny the lower forces... the material and vegetable forces their sustenance... you can elevate the higher forces."

I could see that this was too much for Lee to take. The wrinkles in his forehead were squeezed. After a moment, he asked, "Uh, how long are you doing it... this, uh... fast?"

"Before sunrise and until after sunset," I said.

"Are you kidding me?" Lee asked, eyebrows raised.

"No, I'm not," I said, and we didn't talk about it again until his food arrived.

Then he said, politely, "Are you sure you won't change your mind?" I nodded no.

Lee was a rather cynical fellow and I'm sure he must have thought I was cuckoo, but I knew a long discussion about Subud would have been a clunker so I let it drop.

Universal put me up quite comfortably in a suite at the Diplomat Hotel on Park Avenue. This was a far cry from my meager beginnings in an $8 a week room on West 57th Street eighteen years earlier. The *McCloud* shooting went well and everyone seemed to be pleased with the rushes. Later, it was seen as a TV movie on CBS titled *Portrait of a Dead Girl*, produced by Leslie Stevens and directed by Richard Colla. Also in the cast were Craig Stevens, Raul Julia, Diana Muldaur, and Julie Newmar. Dennis Weaver and I got along extremely well and the adversarial relationship on film worked to the advantage of the story as planned. However, for me, there is always a beetle in the butter. Universal and CBS were screwing around with the *McCloud* format. Even though the contracts had not been signed, I had agreed to do twenty-four one-hour shows a season, a fee for each episode, and co-star billing with Dennis. Now, they were talking about doing only eight shows a season, each one in a ninety-minute TV movie length. Universal wanted me to accept the same fee per show, but for doing the lesser amount of episodes, one-third of my promised potential income. Much to the chagrin of my agents, it didn't take me long to decide which way I would go. I don't like getting hustled or deceived by anybody. We had an agreement.

McCloud was a very successful series and I was pleased for Dennis's good fortune. It was not easy for me to do, and as it evolved I turned down seven years of work. It may have been foolish in some people's eyes—I had four children to support—but I felt that I had to adhere to my principles of truthful negotiations and commitment. I have never regretted it. Strangely enough, years later, in 1978 after *McCloud* had gone off the air, Universal and CBS came to me again to make a pilot with Dennis Weaver, who was to play a fellow who had purchased a hotel in Hawaii. This time I was Lieutenant Larkin of the police doing what police lieutenants always do, except that now I wore a Hawaiian shirt. In a way, shooting in the islands was the closest thing to being on vacation. Of course, having my wife with me again was an added treat. She became very friendly with Dennis's wife, Gerri, and they had lots to share while we were working. It was so beautiful everywhere you looked, the air so invigorating and smogless—it was indeed a kind of paradise. The show was called *The Islander*, written and produced by Glen A. Larson and directed by Paul Krasny. Sharon Gless rounded out the trio of stars. There was the sun, the magnificent Hawaiian surf, and lots of intriguing stuff going on at the hotel, which guaranteed a great potential for a series. Also in the pilot was the raspy-voiced Sheldon Leonard and the diminutive delight, Bernadette

Peters—one of my favorite performers. She is such an unusually sweet and attractive woman with an extraordinary face. I impulsively asked her to pose for me so I could shoot 35 mm stills for a future painting. She graciously obliged, and I eventually completed a large oil based on the photographs. It's one of my most prized paintings.

CBS was high on *The Islander* and a sale looked good for the coming season, but something was indeed stalling it. Another fungus on the porridge? Later, Glen Larson told me that Jack Lord had threatened the network to bolt his successfully running *Hawaii Five-O* if another Hawaiian series was put on the schedule. Ah, yes, dear Jack Lord… a man who took his last name seriously. CBS, counting the dollar signs, buckled and *The Islander* died a "pilot's death" - the potential income of hundreds flushed out to sea, off Honolulu.

In December 1970, I received a letter from Lee Strasberg saying that he would like to have a meeting with me. I had no idea what the purpose of the meeting would be, and when he came out to take over the classes at Actors Studio West during January, I still didn't find out. He wasn't someone you could corner for immediate answers. Lee and Anna Strasberg invited us to dinner at his rented home, and it was fun to see the master in an apron intently cooking his specialty—a Chinese dinner, the pea pods and condiments expertly tossed into the mix. Anna, vivacious and much younger than Lee, was the perfect hostess, eager to please and an up-tempo counterpoint to Lee's relative quietness. That enjoyable evening prompted a reciprocal invitation to our home a couple of weeks later. We were honored to have our mentor, one of America's greatest acting teachers, as a guest. Of course, sitting and facing him at dinner when you were used to sitting behind him in a scene class was a bit disconcerting at first, but Lee was just a man after all, except for the perch we all put him on.

Lee saw my artwork plastered all over the walls while Howard played Chopin and Kelly nonchalantly prodded the keys for a short Mendelssohn piece. Anna whispered to me: "I have never seen Lee so relaxed," which surprised and touched me. Lee hinted at what he what he wanted to talk to me about, then skirted it by telling me he would write me a detailed letter. It wasn't until April that a three-page letter arrived, which fully expressed his frustrations:

"Dear Mark: Since my return from California, I have given the following a great deal of thought and should like to share my thinking with you so I hope you will bear with this lengthy letter. From time to time, I have wondered whether the Studio was in the mainstream of what is happening in the theater today—and I also wondered whether we hadn't been running fast and standing still. On at least two occasions within the last ten years I have been ready to call it quits at the Actors Studio. One was the elimination of our possible participation at Lincoln Center, and the other was the closing of the Actors Studio theater which we had expected to continue."

He went on to say that for all of the recognition in the world arena that the Studio had received for its approach to acting, the individual brilliance of its actors, playwrights, and directors, Lee felt that the organization had been run abominably, financially and otherwise, and wanted to embark on innovative changes to guarantee the Studio's longevity. I was one of a select group asked by Lee to (1) become a member of the Board of Directors; (2) join the new legal corporation of the Actors Studio; and (3) contribute a certain amount of funds each year. Without a long deliberation, I was quite pleased to accept the invitation, and Lee responded with a letter in kind. Then, at the end of the year, with great reluctance and a heavy heart, I had to bow out of my good intentions due to the Philip Roth *Letting Go* lawsuit that was pressing on my head like a worsening migraine.

I had written several one-act plays and decided that I should work on them at the Actors Studio, get them on their feet, and see how they played. Lonny Chapman, a good actor and director moderating at the Studio at the time, liked what I was doing and enjoyed the material. He suggested that I submit the plays as a "Studio Project" and invite an outside audience when I felt the work was ready. I asked Martin Brooks, a studio stalwart, to direct, and he suggested Tracy Roberts, a wonderful actress and teacher of acting, to play the woman opposite me. The first play was called *Heavy Heavy What Hangs Over*. I was a pompous movie star, so self-possessed and insecure he wouldn't leave his palatial bathroom. We observe him expertly trimming his own hair and going through his daily workout routine—all accompanied by bickering with his tolerantly witty wife doing her nails. Then the strange, uninvited spiritual doctor shows up in the bathroom and hilariously changes their lives, beautifully played by Don Hamner. I must confess that the doctor was my theatrically comic way of suggesting the possibility of Subud—and how it could affect us all for our betterment.

The play was well received and stimulated me to mount another one-act play called *The Place* with Tracy and me and with Marty directing. Again, it was a comedic approach to a very serious subject and reflective of my personal feelings about the sanctity of motherhood. The play opens in a private hospital room. The man in bed recently had a serious heart attack and his loquacious wife pays him a visit. She never stops talking. Finally, with his eyes closed the man says, "Charlotte… do you remember that I recently had a heart attack? I'm trying to remain calm… I recently had a heart attack."

"I know you had a heart attack, Roger," she says. "Why do you have to bring that up? Actually… it was only a little heart attack, it wasn't a big one, thank God… you're not paralyzed or anything…"

We find out in the continued verbal assault between them that the buried resentments can no longer be subdued. Years before, Charlotte had had an abortion unbeknownst to her husband which led to complications and a hysterectomy. The sufferings explode. She asks his forgiveness, but he cannot give it, having lost the right of fatherhood being too much to bear anymore. Emotionally, he says, "A man can only put it there… that's all he can do… but a woman has the place… the place. It's a gift inside of her… there is no other place. Why did you let them take away that place?" Soon afterward, I directed another one of my one-acts called *The Party List*; it was an evening presentation as part of ANTA, the American National Theater Academy in Los Angeles. The play is about a World War II veteran putting together a party for his wife's brother, a sailor returning from Vietnam; they didn't get along, and he's trying to make amends. The veteran was played by Vic Tayback and the wife by Eileen Ryan (Sean Penn's mother). When she receives a phone call from the brother who reveals on the phone that he has a Vietnamese wife and an eleven-month-old son, Eileen's handling of the news and the complications it engenders with her intolerant husband was a gem to watch. Teddi thought the plays could be a successful commercial venture and I could play the three male roles with three different women. Eventually, I put the three one-act plays under one cover and called them *Heavy Heavy What Hangs Over. An Evening in the Theater*—Three plays about marriage.

17 Peter and Helen

EVERY SUMMER I WAVED GOODBYE to my wife, children, and the housekeeper before they boarded a plane for Albany, New York, to visit Sam and Jean, the best grandparents any child could ever hope for. There were camp activities for the kids, joy and freedom for the wife—and utter misery for the guy remaining in California. As a domesticated homebody, I missed my family desperately when they weren't there. They would be gone for about eight or nine weeks, and when I couldn't take my bachelorhood any longer, I would join them for a week or two later in the summer. After visits to the kids' camps—Kelly dancing gracefully in a blue tutu; Sam's barbecues in the yard; an embarrassingly, rusty nine holes played at their country club—we were more than ripe to take off, driving farther up north to Provincetown on the Cape, or Kennebunkport, Maine, or to Stowe, Vermont, for a mini respite. In the summer of 1970 we went in the opposite direction, driving south to Front Royal, West Virginia, in the magnificent Shenandoah National Park area; from there found our way to the Subud gathering at Skymont, a wooded conference center that was to accommodate hundreds for this special occasion. Bapak Subuh would be visiting for a week of latihan and talks before continuing on to another country. Subud people from all over the United States and Canada and farther away would find their way there as we had. It was a glorious time of warm pleasantries and genuine camaraderie, a feeling of sweet peacefulness falling on all of us like a summer's misty rain. Every time Bapak came there was a perceptible degree of calm and comfort that enveloped us, but the Skymont conference was indeed a milestone. Maybe it was the mountain air or the fact that my beautiful wife was three months pregnant, but we were becoming more acutely aware that spiritual changes in our lives were taking place and getting stronger. It was at this time that I felt I had to start using my true spiritual name, Peter, in all of my professional endeavors—the name that Bapak had given me. I couldn't skirt the issue any longer. Teddi felt the same way about her true name, Helen—so from that time forward, it was to be Peter and Helen!

Also, Ibu, Bapak's wife, spoke to us about Eva Bartok, a European movie star opened in Subud and considered hopelessly ill during pregnancy. She had been miraculously cured by Bapak in England, allowing her to give birth to a healthy girl, Deana. (Eva Bartok wrote a book about the experience, *Worth Living For*, published by Putnam in 1959.) Now, after living in Indonesia for a long time, Bapak and Ibu felt it was important for Eva, a Subud helper, to be in America and gave us the challenge of carrying it out. We told Ibu we would give it serious thought and discuss it thoroughly with the Los Angeles group, because apparently, she was without funds. I had agreed to finance her flight to Los Angeles, but her accommodations were to be the responsibility of Subud Los Angeles. One of the first things I accomplished on our return home was the inevitable phone call to my agent. "Ronnie," I said. "I'm changing my name."

"To what?" he asked, after a strained pause.

"I'm just adding Peter. From now on it'll be Peter Mark Richman." "Oh, that's not bad," he said. "Peter Mark Richman has a nice ring to it. I like it, but it may be a bit difficult for people to adjust. It isn't like you're just starting out in the business. You've been established a long time."

"I know," I said. "They'll just have to live with it."

The word was out. Now I had to change my identification with the unions, driver's license, social security, bank, and everything else that had my name on it. Helen did the same. I even sent out a card to all of our friends informing them that my wife would no longer be referred to as a miniature bear, but by her true spiritual name, Helen. It confused a lot of people, but they eventually adjusted. Some old friends still insist on calling me Mark and that's okay too. Of course, our families thought it peculiar.

As far as Eva Bartok was concerned, we found her a pleasant apartment in the Valley not far from us, and when she arrived she was able to move right in. She was an exceptionally attractive woman, warm and gracious, exuding a decidedly European theatricality. I brought her to my agents who quickly signed her as a client, convinced she still had good earning potential. A few weeks after her arrival, feeling too isolated in the Valley, she moved to a Brentwood apartment off Sunset Boulevard at a much higher rent. At that time one of her past husbands arrived in town to shoot a film—the fine German actor Curt Jurgens, who was a perfect gentleman and a powerful presence. He may have assumed paying some of the rent, but I cannot vouch for that. Eva's daughter, Deana, carried his name. One evening Eva asked me to explain Subud to Curt. She felt it was better coming from a man. I did my best, but it never got beyond his pleasant curiosity. Years later, Eva, who had been married four times, unexpectedly revealed to me that Deana had been conceived with Frank Sinatra in a rather casual affair, but she had never told him about the pregnancy or birth. When I first met Deana as a twelve-year-old, she was extraordinarily beautiful and had the look of a teenage Nancy Sinatra. When Deana grew up, longing to know her blood father, but not wanting anything from him, she tried to inform Frank that she was truly his daughter. Rebuffed on all accounts, it saddened her deeply.

My mother periodically would bake us strudel, a magnificent concoction of dried fruits, raisins and walnuts, encased in a crispy dough. The only problem was that she would wrap it in wax paper, shove it into a "Mothers Oats" box, get some good Samaritan to address it on brown paper, tie a string around it, and then take it to the post office for mailing. It was always a mess when it arrived in New York, but shipping it to California was another matter. It took a month to get to us—the paper torn to shreds, the box broken, and a surprise it was even delivered. But inside, the strudel, crushed and crumbled, was as preserved and delicious as if it had just been freshly baked. I can still taste it and my mouth waters. As my mother aged, the burden of maintaining her in an apartment became an impossibility. Although I contributed to her upkeep, she needed constant attention and care and it had become too much for my sister, Fay, to handle. I had been away for years; my brother Dave lived with his family in Hartford; brother Harry wouldn't even speak to her, so it was the same miserable alienation and indifference. My mother was now in a home for the elderly in a leafy section of old Germantown, a suburb of Philadelphia. I hadn't seen her for a while and decided it was time to pay her a visit. Helen and I and two of our children, Kelly and Howard, flew east. When we landed, the sky was a smoky gray and threatening to unload its snow-laden clouds. Walking through the hallways of a repository for old people, even though this place was better than most, wasn't pleasant under any circumstances. Although the personnel were courteous and helpful and the place was clean, it was depressing. I was sorry to have to subject my children to the reality of aging in this way—

some people in wheelchairs asleep, others sitting and staring listlessly—and the momentary, but unmistakable, whiff of human excrement.

My mother was sitting on the bed when we walked into her room. Her face lit up with a smile and tears filled her eyes as she rose with difficulty to greet us. My eyes were wet too. Enthralled with my kids, she was as soft and as sweet as I had ever seen her. She had shriveled, and the dominant edge of smoldering anger was quiet now—almost as if the fire had gone out. I had the feeling that in her old age—she was now eighty-four—there had been an acceptance of her situation, knowing it wasn't going to change no matter what.

She didn't complain much about her ailments, and there were many, but was very sure that one of the nurses was stealing her candy out of the closet. Nothing Helen and I said would assuage her conclusions. After letting a nurse take my children to a waiting area to watch television, Helen and I sat with my mother and talked about our lives, our home, what it was like being an actor in Hollywood, and the obvious five-month pregnancy of my beautiful wife. She was smiling and shaking her head in approval and expressing how happy she was for us. All the time I kept looking at my mom, remembering—some of it very unpleasant. *My, God… how old she's become… a troubled, shrunken woman in the last days of her life. My mother… so much pain and anguish she caused herself with all her compulsions and craziness… almost enjoying the chaos she created. Now… it's so strange… she seems almost peaceful. Is this what happens? The turmoil and misery no longer matter when life is slipping away? Is this God's way of preparing us for death… quieting us?* I couldn't answer that question, but I was grateful for having made the trip and the opportunity to be with my mom, who had carried me into this life.

Four months later, at the end of February 1971, my mother passed away. On February 6, 1971, two weeks before my mother died, we had another little gift from heaven. Our fifth child, Roger Lloyd, was born at Cedars of Lebanon Hospital, weighing in at an impressive seven pounds, six ounces. Helen was doing well, except for a very scary period just as she was about to begin a breastfeeding session early in the morning. Suddenly everything in her room began to shake and shudder—bottles were falling off the shelves and shattering, and the wall television crunched to the floor. Los Angeles was hit with a 6.7 earthquake that crumbled freeways and structurally deficient buildings all over the city. A lot of people got killed. The most horrible fact for me, aside from knocking me out of bed and everything tumbling and my young children running down the hall screaming, "Daddy, Daddy! Daddy!" (while Orien, the youngest, not two years old, slept soundly in his crib) was the loss of the phone lines. After comforting my kids, I tried and tried but couldn't contact the hospital. All day long, while chaos reigned all over the city, my main concern was, of course, Helen and our new son. Not knowing how they were was driving me frantic. I considered driving to the hospital in Hollywood, but the radio broadcasts continually advised that freeway travel was unsafe. In the afternoon, I finally got through. Helen and the baby were okay and doing fine, and there wasn't a scratch on any of us. Thanks, God. But there was no doubt in my mind—reflecting on the fires, riots, and earthquakes I had witnessed—Los Angeles could be detrimental to your health.

In 1971, *Yuma*, a television movie produced by Aaron Spelling and shot in Tucson, Arizona, was the first professional film that listed my name as Peter Mark Richman. Everything before that carried Mark Richman in the credits. *Yuma* was a pilot for a Western series to star the muscularly huge, handsome, and good-natured Clint Walker—a nicer gentleman I've never met. The film also starred Barry Sullivan and Edgar Buchanan, the most authentic and comically endearing character ever to pull on dirty dungarees and a floppy hat, with a voice like low octave static. I played a captain of the Union army trying to settle a violent family murder and land dispute. The antagonist was the stern and steely-eyed Morgan Woodward, another dear friend. The film was directed by one of my favorite people, Ted Post, a severely wounded World War II veteran, who walked with a limp and who certainly knew his way around the dry mesquite and saddled horses. In fact, he knew his way around anywhere and everything, having directed with distinction more series episodes and films than most directors only dream about. I had already worked with him on *Twilight Zone* and *Combat* and several other efforts, and it was always a creative joy to put myself in his hands because of our mutual respect. We were destined to work together again on a major project that I wrote and produced, but more about that later. During all of this professional activity, the anchors of my life continued to be my wife and my children. Howard's dexterity at the piano seemed to be a serious sign of a potential career as a concert pianist. He had a long way to go, but the inclinations and talent were there. He had other talents too. I'll never forget the time he came to me when he was twelve and said he wanted to make an art table for me in wood shop. I drew up the plans, and in a month, he delivered a quality, custom-made "drawing" table on wheels that I still use in my studio today! One summer we sent

Howard to Interlochen National Music Camp in Michigan where he continued his piano study in addition to composition and choral singing. The following two summers he attended The Saratoga Potsdam Choral Institute in Saratoga, New York, culminated by singing Beethoven's Ninth Symphony with the Philadelphia Orchestra under the baton of Eugene Ormandy. After high school, Howard entered UCLA as a music major studying piano for two years with the exacting Aube Tzerko—one of the most rigid technicians of piano any student has ever had to face. Howard credits him with learning a proficient technique, but it was like coming out of a dark storm into the sparkling sunshine when he began piano studies with Johana Harris, the first faculty member to receive the UCLA "Distinguished Teaching Award." She was also a fabulous recorded pianist and wife of a renowned composer, the deceased Roy Harris. Howard continued his choral singing too, in grand fashion, he became a member of the highly respected UCLA Men's Glee Club.

Years later, I had the impulse to paint an oil study of Johana. I knew she hadn't the time to pose for me, so we arranged a day for me to photograph her, and from the photos I would be able to paint a definitive Johana Harris. I shot a roll of 35 mm film as if I had a brush in my hand, made enlarged prints, and presented her with a selection of the best ones. She was pleased and I set about preparing my painting study. At the time, she had just completed a mammoth recording of the complete piano works of J.S. Bach for MCA Classics. One day she called and told me that MCA was going to use one of my color photos for the album covers, and I should call them in New York and demand compensation. "MCA didn't like their own photographer's work!" A ridiculous hassle with MCA followed, until I finally said, "Pay me what I want and give me signature credit on the album or forget it!" I must say, it's a lovely photo of Johana and above her it says, A LIVING LEGACY… JOHANA HARRIS plays BACH. I finally finished my oil of Johana and it truly is Johana—her warm smile and powerful hands prominent.

When Lucas was three years old, I asked him, jesting, "Lucas, what's the secret of life?"

Without hesitation he replied, "Joy!"

I was astounded. I looked at his beaming, sweet and innocent face and realized then that Lucas was an old soul with special gifts who would be guided by God to do important things. When he was five, he began tickling the piano keys. Helen would provide Lucas with children's books about the lives of the classical composers. Fascinated, he had thought that all composers were dead, and when he read about Aaron Copland and found out that he was still alive, he was ecstatic. He then wrote a long letter to Aaron Copland, with a drawing representing Copland composing "El Salon Mexico," and told him that he wanted to be a composer too. He asked me to mail it to him. At first I resisted, telling him that I didn't know where Copland lived, but Lucas insisted. I had no other choice. I finally called the secretary at the Actors Studio in New York and surprisingly, she had his address in Peekskill, New York. Off went Lucas's letter. Well, in about ten days, a beautiful, picture post card arrived (a guardsman outside tower of London), addressed to Lucas. Copland wrote: "Dear Lucas: I received your letter and I thought it was just fine! Best of luck in your composing. Your friend, Aaron Copland."

When Lucas was fourteen, and for two years afterward, he was a violinist in the Young Artists Orchestra, conducted by Victor Yampolsky—a music program of the Boston University Tanglewood Institute, in Tanglewood, Massachusetts. The guest artist one week was Aaron Copland. I have a lovely photo of the two of them together in 1980, all smiles. We were visiting Tanglewood the summer Lucas was sixteen and had been chosen to conduct the eighty-piece Young Artists Orchestra for "Tanglewood on Parade," a yearly festive happening for parents and guests. It was a warm but breezy autumn afternoon, the cooler air blowing in through the open- sided chamber Music Hall, past the towering pines and blooming acacia trees. We waited with the rest of the packed house, sitting in the third row in nervous anticipation. We were looking at the stage where great conductors had thrust their batons—Leonard Bernstein, Seiji Ozawa, Gunther Schuller, André Previn, and many others—when suddenly the audience hushed its restlessness and applauded as this kid in a blue corduroy suit (that I had recently purchased for him) walked briskly onto the stage. He stopped at the center acknowledging his reception, smiled broadly and bowed. He then turned to the orchestra, took a moment of silence, raised his baton, and began to conduct, with surety and ease, Brahms' "Academic Festival Overture." To say that I nearly fell off my chair would be an understatement. I gulped in awe as I turned to Helen and said, "Where the hell did he learn to do this?"

In the fall, he entered UCLA as a music major.

My daughter, Kelly, who was getting more beautiful daily, was also at the piano with regularity. When she was eleven, she discovered the guitar and began to strum it and sing. Guitar lessons followed, of course, but the sweetness of her voice and her vibrato was emotionally touching to listen to. On more than one occasion as I watched her perform, her long chestnut hair blowing in the wind, I said to myself: *My God, this kid will be a recording star by the time she's twelve!* It didn't work out that way, but as she matured she became a fine young actress, concentrating on musical theater with a mellifluent lyric soprano voice. In the summers, we sent her to the Brianski Ballet camp at Skidmore College in upstate New York, and the New York State Music Camp in Otsego. At UCLA, as a theater major, she won a Carol Burnett Musical Theater Award and starred in an original musical called *Hurry, Hurry, Hollywood* written by students Sam Harris and Bruce Neuberg. And who was the seventeen-year-old orchestra pianist playing in the pit who had also done the arrangements for the show? Why, Lucas Richman, of course! Kelly graduated but never attended her UCLA graduation exercises, and neither did we—she was appearing at the Barn Theater in New London, New Hampshire, playing Aldonza in *Man of La Mancha*.

For the 1971–1972 season, I signed onto a new ABC television series called *Longstreet*. Shot at Paramount, it starred James Franciscus as a blind insurance investigator; me, playing "Duke Page," his boss, sporting my 70s haircut and a wiry moustache; and a lovely Marlyn Mason as the girl involved in everything. There was another young fellow in the cast for a few shows who has since become a legend, Bruce Lee—a fresh-faced, eager kid, somewhat insecure in the acting department who was zealously perfecting his Oriental arts techniques. I always thought he was as tense as a steel wire, but maybe that is a requirement if martial arts are to be your way of life. The premise of the series, to me, seemed patently stupid—a totally blind man investigating nefarious activities, who is able to overcome gun, knife, and physical combat by his metaphysical will and skill. Ridiculous. Of course, he's learning all this other-worldly know-how stuff from Bruce Lee. In one show, I walk in on a session and jokingly challenge Bruce to an old-fashioned "put-up-your-dukes" fight, and he almost flattens me with his superior method. It's a pity that he died so young after becoming such an international phenomenon from his feature films. There have been many Bruce Lee television documentary specials since that time, and our so-called fight scene is in two of them.

One of the dumbest things I ever did in a series was to allow the wardrobe people to dress me in the same suit getting out of my car. We shot all exteriors in New Orleans where the series is supposed to take place, and when I drive up and exit my car and enter Franciscus's office I have on a brown suit. Grant you, it was a beautifully tailored suit, but for the life of the series in most scenes shot at Paramount, because I originally drove up in a brown suit, I was stuck wearing the same clothes! Also, in a distant dolly shot of walking through the park with Jim used in many episodes, I'm still in that lousy brown suit. The only change was the different dubbed dialogue over the picture. Of course, nobody noticed or cared but it irritated the hell out of me.

One of the big plusses of doing the series was the cementing of my relationship with Joel Rogosin, the active producer. Joel and I had worked together many times at Universal on varying shows, but on *Longstreet* we became quite close. He's one of the most talented writer/producers I've ever had the privilege of working with, extremely adept at coordinating all the elements—the script, casting, director, music, and the final editing. He later produced a series called *Ghost Story* and wanted to buy a spooky script I'd written for a segment. I foolishly turned him down, thinking I could get it done as a feature film. Another one of my many goofs. I often wondered if Joel thought the premise of *Longstreet* was as dumb as I thought it was, but I never confronted him on it. It didn't matter, the show was cancelled after shooting twenty-four episodes. In the overall scheme of things, it certainly seemed quite clear that I couldn't land a successfully running series—even if my life depended on it. Thankfully, it didn't.

Whenever I have a problem and want to resolve a situation, I dislike wasting time with underlings. I always try to go to the guy at the top who can get things done. I initiated a correspondence with the president of Permanent Pigments concerning their acrylic paint, and he responded immediately; it continued for quite a while. The reason: during the sixties and early seventies, I was experimenting in that medium, extensively diluting the paint with water; testing the binding qualities with other materials; how it worked in collage, and the drying time limits without using a retardant. I had discovered a fungus in the paint under certain conditions when exposed to air. I wasn't sure if it came from the water diluent or the paint itself. I happened to attend an art show where I saw a painting that I was sure the artist had used a barium orange paint manufactured by Permanent Pigments, and it had turned brown while drying. Knowing something about the chemistry of paint, I informed the company of my discovery that barium sulfate had turned to barium sulfide, modifying the color. Since I sounded fairly credible, it alarmed the executives. Colored wood slats and tubes of paint arrived monthly for me to carry on my primitive investigation. I came to the conclusion that ordinary drinking water had been the culprit in both instances. A trace of a contaminant sulfide in the water was altering the color of the barium orange. In my case, a fungus growth had already been present in the water I used. I suggested that painters should try distilled water as a diluent when working in acrylics, and I believe they changed the chemistry formula for making the barium orange paint which solved the undesirable "browning." My pharmacy background came in very handy there.

In 1971, I had an expansive art exhibition at the Rasjad Hopkins Gallery in the heart of Beverly Hills, including oils, water color and ink drawings, and oil monotypes. Gladys Lloyd Robinson, Edward G.'s ex-wife with whom he shared a multi-million-dollar art collection, and had acquired most of it in their divorce, got out of a sick bed to come to the opening of my show and purchased two paintings. I had first met Gladys Lloyd when Edward G. Robinson Jr. brought his mother on the set to meet me. I even sketched her in a large black hat sitting near a makeup table and gave it to her. She was so pleased, and told me how much her son liked me. We were shooting some TV show, and he was playing my assistant bad guy again. It had happened on a few shows, and he'd become attached to me—like a father figure, or something. He was a very troubled young man, good-looking, and sweet-natured but screwed up with drugs and alcohol. His relationship with his parents and especially Eddie G. was greatly lacking. Sometimes he would call me at 3:00 in the morning, drunk or high, and tell me his troubles. Having a famous father and not having the talent to reach his heights was an enormous burden on such a sensitive young man, especially with a Jr. at the end of his celebrated name.

He had a young daughter, Francesca, that Gladys commissioned me to paint, but before I could get started, sadly, Gladys died. Years later, Francesca, now a married woman, invited me to the dedication and luncheon for the official Edward G. Robinson U.S. postage stamp—his replicated, unmistakable image now a miniature collector's item. She knew all about the painting I'd never painted of her and my relationship with her deceased father. She had also inherited the paintings that Gladys had purchased at my exhibition.

Another purchaser of my art at this particular show was a friend of the great American artist Thomas Hart Benton. He asked me if I would mind if he sent Benton photos of my work. I said, "I would be honored." A few weeks later a letter arrived from this gracious man and I think it's profoundly to the point.

Dear Mr. Richman:

As I told Bob McDonnell, I don't go in for making judgements of another artists work. There is no doubt that you have talent. But lots of other people have too. You come out an artist by applying that talent day after day, year after year—10—20—30 years. It's a kind of voyage of adventure where you don't know where you're going or where you're going to land.
Best of luck on your voyage.

Sincerely yours,
Thomas H. Benton

18 Bapak In Woodland Hills

IN EARLY 1972, Bapak Subuh Sumohadiwidjojo was on another worldwide tour. Helen and I couldn't resist joining him and his entourage in San Francisco, then traveling with him as he visited all the centers in northern California, doing latihan and listening to his talks as we had done before. We had become quite friendly with the man who was now translating Bapak's talks as he spoke—his name, Sharif Horthy, a brilliant young fellow who had been born in Hungary, studied physics at Oxford and who had lived in Indonesia for many years. In one of our chats after latihan, I suggested to Sharif, knowing that Bapak was a film buff, that I would like to extend an invitation to Bapak and his group to visit my home when they came to Los Angeles, and that I would screen a print of *David Chapter III*—if it interested him. Sharif said he would discuss it with Bapak.

We'd been away for almost a week and the phone calls to the children made our hearts tug, so we left the group in Carmel Valley and headed back home via Carmel and the picturesque route down the coast, one of the most splendiferous marriages of landscape and ocean anywhere in the world. After several days at home, I received a call from Sharif telling me that Bapak wouldn't be able to see my film this time but he would be pleased to pay us a visit—in about three hours from now! Well, all pandemonium broke loose—Helen frantically trying to get the house in welcoming shape with the help of our housekeeper and taking our children out of different schools so they could meet Bapak. Somehow, everything was accomplished, and when the large entourage arrived, somewhat car weary from the long drive, they were as ready as we were for a comforting respite. We were honored, grateful, and exhilarated to open the door to our home to Bapak, who had brought the power of God into the world for us. While we were enjoying soft drinks and snacks, I happened to mention to Bapak (who was always interested in whatever you wished to talk about) that I was having a problem with gophers in the garden. He laughed and said that he would like to see them. I asked, surprised, "You would?" When he nodded yes, we all descended the stairs to my den and then outside, walking past the bronze-flowered hibiscus bushes to inspect the green, gopher-pitted lawn. Regrettably, Bapak never saw the gophers. I said to him in jest, "Bapak… they know you're here and they're hiding!" We all laughed. Then then I snapped some memorable photographs of Bapak, Mastuti, his new wife (Ibu Sumari had died two years earlier); Muti and Tuti, his granddaughters; Rahayu, his daughter; Sharif; and Eva Bartok. Helen and I are in some of the photos and I'm grateful for that; otherwise, the remembrance of the lovely afternoon would only be like a distant dream.

I met Hans Burkhardt one day, who was a powerful expressionist painter with a huge reputation. He graciously invited me to come and paint with him and several other artists. I jumped at the chance. For a period of months, I concentrated on large ink and watercolor paintings of nude models in various poses. Sometimes Hans would comment on the other artists' work. I remember his saying to me in his Swiss-tinged accent as I was painting a voluptuous nude, "A little more red in the cheeks!" In 1973, I presented the efforts at the McKenzie Gallery. William Wilson,

L.A. Times wrote: "… Drawings and paintings by Peter Mark Richman abound with bright patches. Pen and watercolor studio-study nudes hint the obsessiveness of Jules Pascin. Vigorous simplifications of pose and paint lend certain paintings the directness of Picasso's blue period… From classroom discipline to conceptual self-knowledge, he has the edge of natural strength."

Another far-fetched TV series of the early 70's was called *Search*, and behind a massive console of computers sat the intensely sincere Burgess Meredith, surreptitiously relaying vital information to the hidden earplug of Doug McLure-who knew exactly where, how, and what to do! It had alternating leads-McLure, Hugh O'Brien, and Anthony Franciosa exerting fantastic efforts to prevent catastrophe and save the universe. On this particular episode, I played a martial arts devotee and international Mafia leader ensconced in Switzerland, where I cleverly abscond with $25 million, aided by a reputable but shady banker, my dear friend, and fabulous actor, Luther Adler. We had been close ever since I had played his son on a *U.S. Steel Hour* years before. The first day on the set we greeted each other with warm hugs and nice words. Then he said to me, "I have a present for you."

"A present?" I answered. "What is it?"

He gave me an impish smile, his velvety, camel hair coat hanging loosely around his shoulders. "Walk with me," he said. So, we walked the whole length of the sound stage, past the crew setting up the next shot, in and out of partially constructed sets, talking about what my children were doing and how drastically the business was changing.

Finally, I stopped because I couldn't stand the suspense any longer. "So, Luther," I said, "what's my present?"

He turned to me with a big smile on his face and said, "The present is… from now on I am going to call you Peter!"

I appeared on *The Streets of San Francisco* several times, and working with Karl Malden was always a joy. I greatly admired him. When playing with him, he rooted you in a scene with his convincing presence and immovable solidity—like a rock you couldn't go through or get around. The young Michael Douglas was a pleasure too, eager and receptive and growing rapidly as an actor working alongside his "old pro" partner. On location one day, chasing around the hilly streets, I received an urgent call from my voice agent, Don Pitts, relayed to me by an assistant director. When I finally returned the call, Don informed me that the agency handling the Oldsmobile account wanted me for several voice-overs to be recorded that day. They knew I was shooting a film and I told them that the earliest I could fly back to Los Angeles would be on an 8:30 evening flight and hopefully begin recording by 9:45 p.m. Strangely enough, they accepted and reserved the unusual studio time. Thus began one of the most tension-filled, awful commitments I've ever made while already contracted to fulfill a TV obligation. *The Streets* schedule had a list of required scenes to shoot with me in them that had to be completed that day and there was no getting around it. I just had to finish on time before even considering a jaunt to the airport. Time was pushing along. It was now 6:30 in the evening and I still had several pick-up shots to complete. While shooting in the streets, anything can happen. Everybody was made aware of my situation and were as accommodating as possible, but I was still sweating my butt off looking at the clock, knowing I needed at least a half hour for the airport scramble. I had arranged for a savvy driver to be ready to drive the shortest route once I jumped in the back seat. At 7:55 p.m. on the second take of my last cut—a staring, suspenseful close-up—I heard the director say, "That's a print!" and waved me goodbye. Waving back, I started running like a frenetic gazelle, pulling off my wardrobe as I made my way to the portable dressing room. How I changed in thirty seconds was a minor miracle, and before I could catch a breath, we were speeding madly on the freeway to grab an 8:30 flight; if we didn't make it, it wouldn't be my driver's fault! He scared the hell out of me. I remember running down the airport corridor to my gate at 8:27 yelling: "I'M HERE! HOLD THE PLANE… HOLD THE PLANE!"

It was a good thing that I made the session. I became the voice of Oldsmobile and eventually recorded over one hundred TV and radio commercials. I remember how pleased I was when I first saw an article in *Variety* that stated Oldsmobile sales had risen 15 percent in the campaign. Then, unfortunately, the oil crisis hit during the Vietnam War, instigating terrible lines at the gas pump. All the commercials were pulled off the air and that was the end of that. When the crisis was over, I was called in to audition again for the new Oldsmobile campaign. I didn't get the job. Go figure.

There was something so cogent and riveting about "old time" stars whenever I met them through the years. Perhaps it was the fact that I had seen their images plastered on the screen a thousand times in every angle and mood imaginable. It was a peculiar truth: they had become an intricate mini-composition of my subconscious. I'll never forget the time I met Greer Garson. I absolutely adored her work in films and when we shook hands, her warm smile and genuineness nearly knocked me over. I was Mister Chips and Mister Miniver, touched by the sweetness of my fictional wife, the feelings were so profound. When I met Ginger Rogers, now somewhat matronly and white-haired, she was still as beautiful and sparkling as ever. I told her straight out, without gushing, a true utterance from an admirer of long standing that I first fell in love with her in the film *Kitty Foyle* when I was a kid and that she was the epitome and a lasting impression of enviable femininity—someone I wanted to marry. She smiled at my words and said, "Oh my… tell me more!" And I did.

Robert Young had a face you would never forget. It was a wonderful face: clean, strong, and extremely handsome, even in his later years. I had seen him in so many films that he was like an old friend when I worked with him on his series *Marcus Welby, M.D.* Before each day of shooting began, he liked to have a harmonious atmosphere and requested a moment of silence on the set. I thought it was a nice touch, and it certainly didn't hurt to quiet yourself down prior to all the incessant busyness and noise on a sound stage. He'd made arrangements for your name, as a guest star, to be painted on the canvas slip-on-back of the director's chair you sat on; when you finished shooting, the "slip-on" was presented to you as a gift. Another nice touch from a nice man.

James Stewart had a television series called *Hawkins*, and I was a guest on his lawyer show in 1974. In his later years, he'd lost his definitive features and it was difficult to recognize him without his hair and makeup. He was sensitive about it. Bill Tuttle was his personal makeup man and he was very secretive about application. I knew Bill and had worked with him on several occasions, but when I approached Jimmy's dressing room to discuss some lines, Bill closed the door in my face because he hadn't completed his makeup. In the show, I played a devious sports executive whose boss had been murdered; Jimmy, representing the accused, comes to question me. James Stewart was a fine gentleman and a consummate professional. It was a kick to play in a scene with him. How many times had I seen him do that stuttering pause, that momentary look away, that high-pitched change of voice implying a challenge; now he was doing all those characteristic things with me—and I was standing toe to toe with him in a confrontation fraught with pregnant meaning. It was delicious.

James McArthur, a good actor and a likable young man, was our nearby neighbor in Tarzana. He wanted me to meet his mother, who was none other than Helen Hayes. Needless to say, Helen and I were thrilled and honored to come to dinner with Jimmy and his wife, Joyce Bulifant, an actress I had worked with in New York in *Therese Raquin*. The night of the event, we couldn't wait to meet such a huge personality. I had seen her on the stage and in showings of old films, notably with Gary Cooper in *A Farewell to Arms*, so I was prepared to converse and say complimentary things.

Helen Hayes made her entrance to meet us and she was as unpretentious and delightfully disarming as any icon of the theater could possibly be. Here was this little lady of great and vast repute telling me as we shook hands and before I could open my mouth, how much she had admired me on my show *Cain's Hundred*, what a fine show she thought it was, and how she had looked forward to seeing me every Tuesday evening when she came back from touring a play in Europe! I was astounded, floored, and humbled—my mouth agape. I melted in my shoes. The uniqueness of that evening has never been topped.

William Wyler had his 75th birthday party at his sumptuous estate on Summit Drive in Beverly Hills. Willy was the perfect host and Talli, his wife, who always looked lovely and fresh, couldn't have been more welcoming. It was truly star-studded, a "who's who" afternoon celebration. Everybody who was anybody was there, with roving musicians and multiple booths of mouth-watering ethnic foods to munch on. Helen and I felt as if we had entered a splendacious storybook land that at any moment might vanish into the breezy, pale blue sky. Bette Davis walked up to our table and said, "May we join you?"

It grounded me as I swallowed my pasta and answered, "Please, it would be a pleasure."

She sat down with a female friend as we introduced ourselves and then the conversation limped along on crutches. Finally, she said, "You were in one of Willy's pictures…"

"*Friendly Persuasion*," I answered.

Then she said, "Oh, yes… that was a nice film."

A few years later I was asked to be the Master of Ceremonies as a last-minute replacement for the yearly National Film Society affair, a black-tie gala that honored older stars. I was called upon to introduce untold numbers of famous faces, say something interesting about them, and then call them up on stage. It was an impromptu improvisational nightmare, but luckily, I had worked with many of the stars on television. Bette Davis was the final and "pièce de résistance." I gave her a flowery and respectful introduction.

We wandered over to join our dear friend Jessamyn West, who wrote *Friendly Persuasion*; Dorothy Jeakins, the costume designer; and Richard Eyer, who played Cooper's little son who always tangled with the goose. He was now a grown young man and a school teacher but with the same freckled face. There were hugs and kisses all around and then Willy joined us for a remembrance photograph. I am pleased to have it in my collection—everyone smiling, a moment to cherish. I will never forget the conversation I had with another illustrious guest, Henry Fonda. It wasn't about Willy's famous film Jezebel, with Fonda and Bette Davis. It was about painting and a No.6 sable brush that his friend Andrew Wyeth had given him. He was enamored of that brush and thrilled as a painter that he could accomplish so much in his realistic watercolor technique with that blessed, special instrument!

Before we left I asked Willy to sign my copy of the book by Axel Madsen, *William Wyler, the Authorized Biography*, which had recently been published. He wrote on the inside: "To Mark Richman—who did a great deal for *Friendly Persuasion*. Best wishes, Willy Wyler."

I was surprised to see Frank Capra at some affair I attended, sitting alone at a table, looking lost and lonely among all the social activity surrounding him. This great director of the past with so many memorable films to his credit was being totally ignored. I couldn't resist saying hello. I introduced myself as we shook hands, and then I sat with him. His face lit up when I told him how much I admired his films and that *It's a Wonderful Life* was my favorite.

"Why do you like it?" he asked, sincerely wanting to know as if it had just been released.

"Because it has such humanity," I said, "and values you just don't see in films today."

He seemed so appreciative, especially when I told him his autobiography, *The Name Above the Title*, was an extraordinary work. It was truly an honor to meet him. We corresponded a few times and I treasure his letters. When I think of all the powerful personalities I have had the privilege of working with or have met—each one unique and memorable, their vibrant presences etched permanently on my brain— I realize how grateful I am to have had such indelible experiences in my life.

My agent called one day and asked, "Do you want to play a homosexual?" I said that I had no objection if it was a good part. I would play a ballet dancer if the costume fit, but I'm afraid my shaky football knees would give me away. When I read the script, I realized the character wasn't only a homosexual—he was a killer of homosexuals, slashing and mutilating them with a knife. The show was appropriately called "The Ripper," and it was a segment on *Police Story* with Darren McGavin, which I had done a few times before. I accepted the role as a well-known fashion designer, with inordinate guilt and hate in his heart, who frequented gay bars searching out his victims and creating havoc in the city while disguised in a blonde wig, glasses, and moustache. Winding up the show, when I'm finally cornered in my design studio removing my makeup, and the cuffs are on me, the camera moves in tight to my face and I quietly, but defiantly, accuse the detectives, "… you're arresting me and leaving the streets full of those people… whose continued existence offends the purity of nature… narcotics addicts, homosexuals, prostitutes! I know decadence when I see it." It was a very spooky and convincing scene, the meat on the bones that convinced me to do the role in the first place.

It was fascinating through the years as a working guest star actor to observe how a successful show on television sometimes can breed a kind of operational "this is the way we do it and that's it!"—a locked-in kind of thinking; and the crew, assistant directors, makeup and wardrobe people complacently contribute, giving them a modicum of power they enjoy and don't want to give up. What I'm getting at is, for instance, on *Gunsmoke*: "Oh, no… Jim Arness never does the off-camera lines with guest stars."

When I heard that from the A.D., I just smiled and said, "Really, is that the way it works? Well, you tell Jim that I'm going home if he isn't there when I do my close-up."

Of course, Jim Arness, being the gentleman that he is, appeared on set to complete my shots. I suppose nobody had ever complained before; it was so much easier and faster for the star and assistant director to just say no and move on.

It was the opposite working with Raymond Burr, a perfect gentleman and a fine actor. I guested on his show *Ironside*, and when it was time to do his close-ups, he said it wasn't necessary for me to be there off camera. I've never seen a more masterful technique in the use of a teleprompter. He'd been doing it for so many years it was his preferred way of working, talking directly to the teleprompter. His studied thinking processes and concentration were amazing.

I was in the makeup chair for an appearance on a particular *The Virginian*, and I said I wanted to wear a moustache as the rich river boat gambler I was playing. The makeup man, comfortable and lazy and the star of his own domain, said in a huff, "Oh no… no moustaches on this show!" (Of course, he would've had a little extra work to do making sure before each take that the moustache was secure and of necessity, cleaning it after use.)

I said again, quietly, that I didn't think it was an unreasonable request. "I want to wear a moustache… show me a selection."

He again said, rudely, "No moustaches!"

I got up from the makeup chair to face him and then said in a tone that was quiet, but unmistakably pointed, "Now listen, just get the producer down here, and don't fucking tell me what I can or cannot wear on my face!"

When I stepped on the set to shoot, I thought I looked quite proper in my cutaway coat, vest, and elegant, curling moustache. I've always thought that an actor should have whatever he wants or needs to play a role, as long as it doesn't infringe on anyone else's rights or space for them to perform theirs.

During the 1970s, I was fortunate to keep working on all the primetime shows, guesting repeatedly on various series like *Mission Impossible*, *Police*

Story, *Streets of San Francisco*, *The F.B.I.*, *The Name of the Game*, *Cannon*, and *Barnaby Jones*, where I enjoyed being with a dear old friend, Lee Meriwether, who played Buddy Ebsen's assistant. I had first met Lee, who is an extremely beautiful and talented woman, on a *Philco Playhouse* that was shot live out of New York when she was appearing in the commercial as Miss America of 1954. Robert Wagner always had a show on the air. Working with him was a pleasant experience; aside from the fact that we liked each other, he was always warm and amiable, and even though we kidded around a bit, he was a serious professional. I appeared with him a couple of times on his series *It Takes a Thief* and then again on his next opus called *Switch*. Following that and much later, I guest starred repeatedly on his series *Hart to Hart* with his lovely co-star Stephanie Powers. I couldn't begin to recall the various plots—they all seem to run together, a momentary glimpse in a dulled memory. Sometimes when I'm casually clicking channels, I see myself in action on an old show. It's peculiar, but it is almost as if I am watching another person.

Nick Mayo, a gifted producer and director, called me in the summer of 1975. He had written a play called *Hollywood Freeway* under the auspices of the National Playwright Company and wanted me to play the lead. I read it and thought it was wonderful. It was free, loose, and a great role for me to do—a hackneyed screenwriter who is cracking up and beginning to hallucinate, experiencing again all the people he had significantly been involved with in his life. He never left the stage and never stopped talking, but it was funny and poignant. I immediately said "Yes," and Nick began casting the other roles for an August opening at the Group Repertory Theater in the Valley. He had to cast a car, too, because it is center stage and prominent when the curtain goes up, and my character is cursing and kicking the flat tire on the Hollywood Freeway that has delayed his attendance at an important film conference. When he finally gets through to the studio he's told that he's been fired and replaced. High strung and shaky to begin with, he is now devastated; and thus begins his gradual flip- out as his adversarial wife materializes, played by the lovely Madlyn Rhue; his father, a gentle and fabulous Cliff Norton; his mistress, a knockout-sexy Barbara Rhoades; a stupid cop played by Allen Case; his whiny children; and a couple of threatening African-Americans who try to steal the car.

Each scene is purgative and powerful, and at the end we witness his final disintegration. Facing the audience, all smiles and obsequiousness, as if accepting an Academy Award for his masterful writing, he suddenly changes. Cursing the attendees for their shallowness in granting him the coveted award, he tells them to shove it as far as it will go and makes a triumphant exit! It was a hell of a tour de force and a privilege to perform and the reviews were satisfying. I had high hopes for this play. It deserved a major shot but didn't get it. Nick Mayo expected the money people to move it to a larger theater immediately and rejected playing in another small house for a longer run. It was a mistake. All the kinks could have been corrected and the play refined. Several years later, after Nick had passed away, I spoke to his wife, Faye Nuell Mayo, who'd produced it, and received a smiling vagueness. It's too bad. I believe the play is as valid today as it was then.

Photo Section

At age 17, I was captain and fullback of the South Philadelphia High School "RAMS" football team, and helped them become the 1944 city champions.

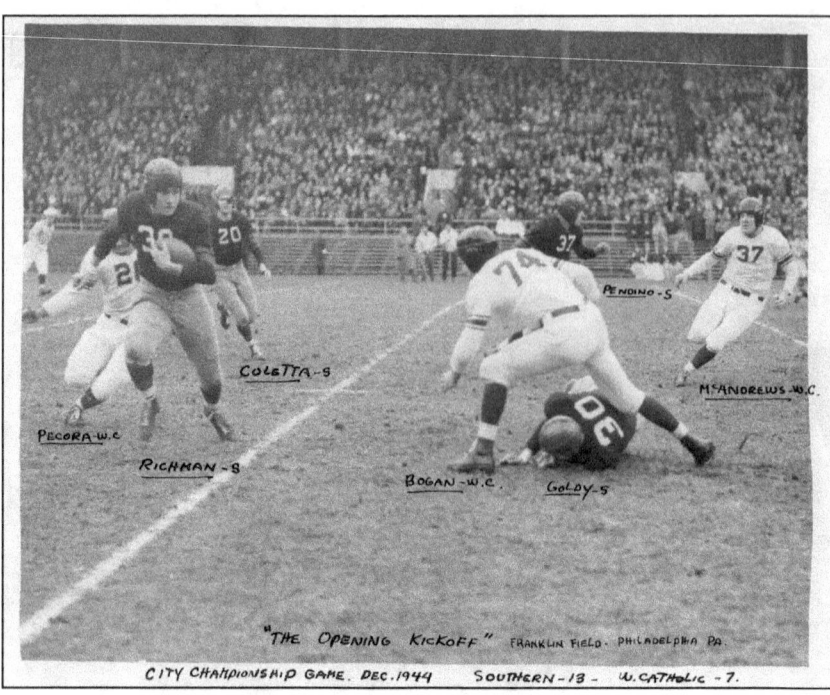

On Philadelphia's Franklin Field, I carried the ball towards our victorious city championship win: Southern 13 – W. Catholic 7.

Gary Cooper and PMR in a scene from *Friendly Persuasion*. "Coop" always wanted to hear about my work at the NY Actors Studio.

William Wyler brought me to Hollywood in 1956 to play the Methodist soldier, Gard Jordan, in *Friendly Persuasion*.

In this *Friendly Persuasion* scene I am shaking hands with Gary Cooper. Standing by are Anthony Perkins, Dorothy McGuire and Phyllis Love.

The Quakers were forbidden to play music, but Mattie and I found the organ that her father had bought and we tried it out in the attic.

Phyllis Love and I did our screen test together for *Friendly Persuasion* and we were cast as the young lovers, Gard and Mattie.

I starred as Johnny Pope opposite Vivian Blaine in Michael V. Gazzo's *A Hatful of Rain* in 1956 on Broadway and in the national tour. Frank Silvera played my father.

Helen was with me in *A Hatful of Rain*, both on Broadway and the national tour playing Putski, the little dope addict and understudy for Vivian Blaine.

Helen and I spent our summers in Albany, NY, visiting Helen's parents, Sam and Jean Landess. Here we are in the 1960's enjoying the pool.

I Saw a Molten White Light... ❖ 249

Gordon Davidson directed me in "The Deputy" at UCLA before he moved his Theatre Group to the Mark Taper Forum.

The movie *The Strange One* was based on the play *End as a Man* by Calder Willingham. Helen and I are attending the premiere with the director, Jack Garfein and his wife Carroll Baker and the producer, Sam Spiegel.

During the filming of *The Strange One* in Orlando Florida I hung out at the pool with Pat Hingle and Elaine Stritch.

I Saw a Molten White Light... ✢ 251

In the 1964 *Twilight Zone* segment of "The Fear" I am investigating scary noises on the roof.

My *Twilight Zone* co-star Hazel Court and I did not know that we had nothing to fear from our very tiny aliens.

Off Broadway at the Provincetown Playhouse in 1960. I did 400 performances as Jerry in Edward Albee's *The Zoo Story* with William Daniels.

My first performances were on live TV. Nancy Berg and I co-starred in "Act of Terror," a segment of the *United States Steel Hour*.

Bela Lugosi was Helen's co-star in a stage production of *Arsenic and Old Lace* at the Green Hills Theatre in Reading, PA in the early 1950's.

Eva Le Gallienne and I co-starred in "Therese Raquin," a segment of the TV show *Play of the Week* in 1961.

A lovely story inside this February 3rd, 1962 issue of *TV Guide* about me and my family.

My series, *Cain's Hundred*, had wonderful guest stars. Here I am with one of them, champion heavyweight Jersey Joe Walcott in his acting debut playing a hoodlum's bodyguard.

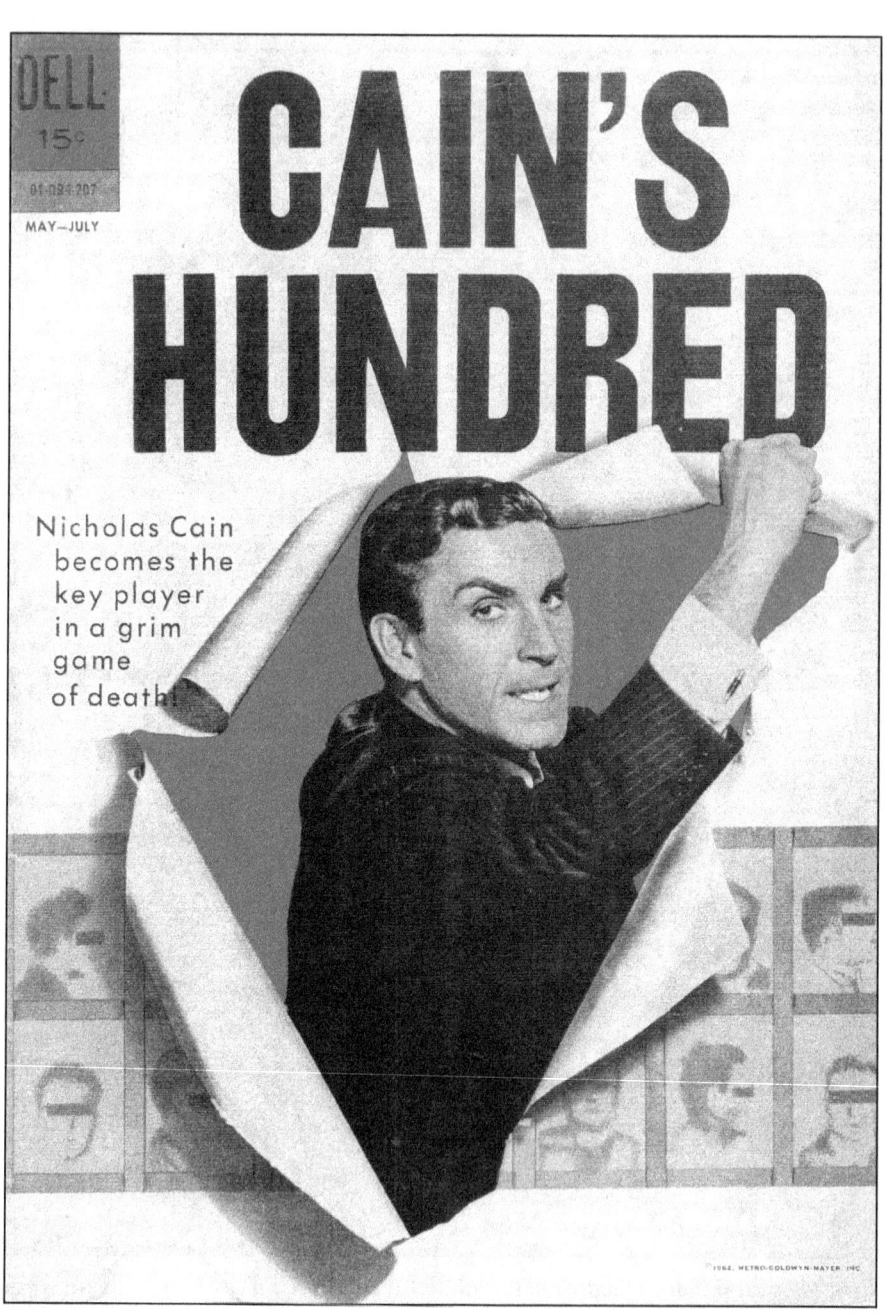

In 1961 I starred in my own NBC TV series as Nick Cain in *Cain's Hundred*.

Audrey Hepburn visited the Chatsworth set of *Friendly Persuasion* and chatted with me and William Wyler.

Joined by William Wyler, Jessamyn West and Richard Eyer at Willy's 75th birthday party in the garden of his Beverly Hills home.

Eva Marie Saint and I co-starred in the stage production of "The Rainmaker" in a summer theatre tour. It was directed by her husband, Jeffrey Hayden.

Jack Klugman and his first wife, Brett Somers, join Helen and me at the beach.

June Allyson and I co-star in "Ruth and Naomi" segment of DuPont's *June Allyson Show*, also starring Ann Harding.

Michael Westmore did my monster makeup for the Universal feature, *The Dark Intruder.*

Miss Israel, Alizia Gur in a scene with me from a Universal feature *Agent for H.A.R.M.*

I Saw a Molten White Light... ✣ 263

Taking aim as I starred in *Agent for H.A.R.M.*, a 1966 Universal International film.

Martin Ritt cast me as the future son-in-law of Anthony Quinn in Paramount's 1959 feature *The Black Orchid*, written by Joseph Stefano.

Sophia Loren is serving me dinner in this scene from *The Black Orchid*, along with Anthony Quinn and Ina Balin.

Chris Noel and I in a scene from Columbia Pictures feature film *For Singles Only*.

Dancing with Lana Wood in a scene from *For Singles Only*.

It's always nice to have Helen by my side.

Another one of our many beautiful summers in upstate New York.

Cloris Leachman, one of my favorite co-stars and me in the TV show *Lancer*.

This is from the *Lancer* segment titled "Angel Day and Her Sunshine Girls" in 1969.

Eleanor Parker and I in *The Man from U.N.C.L.E.* segment titled "Seven Wonders of World Affair," a 1968 two-parter.

I co-starred in the 1971 TV series *Longstreet*, produced by Joel Rogosin, with James Franciscus and Marlyn Mason. Photographer/© ABC/Getty Images

In this *Longstreet* segment Bruce Lee teaches me how to fight.

Nina Foch and I are exploring the 4th dimension in "The Borderland" segment of *The Outer Limits*, 1963. Photographer/© ABC/Getty Images

In the TV series *Heroes of the Bible* I played King of Sodom and Gomorrah.

My recurring role as Chrissy's father the Reverend Snow in the TV series *Three's Company* with Suzanne Somers in the segment, "Chrissy Come Home."
Photographer/© ABC/Getty Images

John Ireland and I on location in Lake Tahoe on The Ponderosa shooting *Bonanza: The Next Generation*.

Playing the bad guy again in *Bonanza: The Next Generation*.

Tommy Lasorda and I on the set of *Hart to Hart*.

Stephanie Powers, Robert Wagner and I working on *Hart to Hart*.

I Saw a Molten White Light... ✣ 275

Helen is with me and Coach Chuck Knox and Rams team owner, Georgia Frontiere.

My character Andrew Laird is the attorney for Blake Carrington played by John Forsythe in *Dynasty* with Linda Evans and Pamela Sue Martin.
Photographer/© ABC/Getty Images

I premiered the character of C.C. Capwell in the daytime soap opera *Santa Barbara*.

I Saw a Molten White Light... ❖ 277

My son Lucas Richman with Leonard Bernstein at the Southern California Harvard Radcliffe Alumni Association *Bravo Bernstein!* event September 13, 1987. Lucas conducted The Young Musicians Foundation Debut Orchestra.

Helen and I are with Lucas Richman and Leonard Bernstein. Among the pieces Lucas conducted on the evening of *Bravo Bernstein!* was the overture to Candide which led to Bernstein selecting Lucas for the 1988 Schleswig-HolsteinMusik Festival tour.

Helen and I were pleased to spend some time with Nancy and President Ronald Reagan.

As chairman of the building committee for the Motion Picture and Television Fund hospital I welcomed George Burns in 1985 for the unveiling of his plaque along with Janet Leigh and Edie Wasserman.

Helen and I were always together.

Friday the 13th Part 8: Jason Takes Manhattan.

Milton Berle, Steve Allen and I were among those enjoying a screening of *The Great Re-Run* at the Academy of Television Arts and sciences in June of 1996.

At a 2002 Warren Cowan event. I wonder what I said to Aaron Spelling?

Marlo Thomas and I at a Rams game in 2004.

My first born son Howard with his son Oliver his wife Cherie, and their daughter Danica.

My son, Maestro Lucas Richman with his wife Debbie and their son Max.

My daughter Kelly Lester with her husband Loren and their three daughters, from left to right, Julia, Jenny and Lily—all performers.

The Richman family before all the weddings from left to right Peter Mark, Helen, Howard, Kelly, Lucas, Orien and Roger.

This made a nice Christmas card clock wise from the left Orien, Howard, Lucas, Kelly, Roger, Helen and Peter Mark

I Saw a Molten White Light...   285

The author, Peter Mark Richman painting in his art studio.

The artist sitting next to his paintings.

Peter Mark in front of his painting "Pregnant Helen Sitting in a Rocker" – oil on canvas – 36" x 24"

Peter Mark at one of his one man art exhibitions standing in front of "The Old Peddler Woman" oil on canvas – 36" x 30"

Helen and Peter Mark sitting below his painting entitled, "Mom and Pop in Atlantic City" – oil on canvas – 39½ x 33½

"The Actress in a Lavender Hat" – oil on canvas – 27½" x 19½"

"The Conspirators" – black ink and water color on rag paper – 12" x 9"

"Actress in a Robe" – oil on canvas – 27" x 19"

"Touch Up" – oil on canvas – 27½" x 19½"

"The Old Woman and Howard" – oil on canvas – 49" x 36½"

"Take the Bus" – oil on canvas – 35½" x 19½"

"Woman in a Red Chair" – black ink and watercolor on rag paper – 12" x 9"

"Before the Take" – oil on canvas – 35½" x 23½"

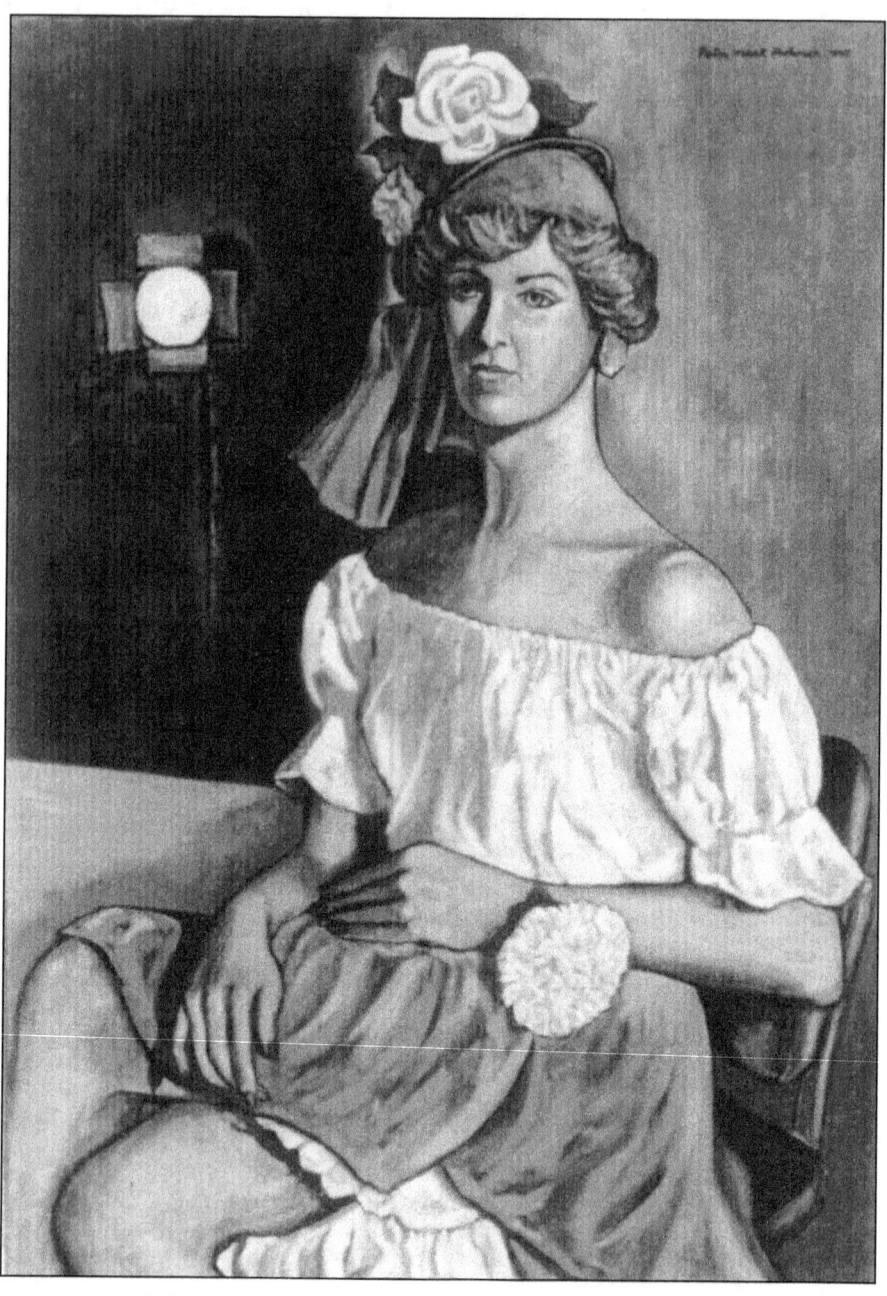

"The Actress on Stage 19" – oil on canvas – 35½" x 24½"

"Bernadette" – oil on canvas – 30" x 20½" While shooting a pilot called *The Islander* in Hawaii I photographed some poses of Bernadette Peters which then became the source of this painting.

"The Feeding of Orien" – oil on canvas – 40" x 30"

"Backstage Dressing Room" – black ink and water color on rag paper – 12" x 9"

"The Magic Make-up Man" – black ink and water color on rag paper – 12" x 9"

"Kelly Holding Jenny" – oil on canvas – 30" x 24"

"The Application" – black ink and water color on rag paper – 12" x 7"

"Helen Holding Roger" – oil on canvas – 35½" x 23½"

"The Loved Child" – oil on canvas – 40" x 30½"

19 My Nudes at the Playboy Club

BURTON TAYLOR, THE DIRECTOR of customer relations at the Los Angeles Playboy Club, called me and asked if I would like to have a one-man art exhibition at the Club. It was an offer I couldn't turn down, and it led to something that was quite unexpected. I must say it was somewhat startling to have some of the most beautiful and physically endowed bunnies gawking at my twenty-five large oils of nude studies hanging in the club. After seeing my art, Sitmar Cruise Lines proposed a show of my paintings on their ship The Fairsea for their first cruise to Alaska, but for some reason we couldn't work out the exact time for the paintings to be put aboard. I kept getting ship-to-land calls from faraway places, the gentleman in charge apologizing for the delay in arrangements until one day he called and said, "Forget the art show for now… just meet the ship and be our guests!" The fourteen-day cruise to Alaska in June 1975 was one of the most memorable experiences and vacations we have ever had. We became friends with the captain and the purser, and they treated us royally, personally giving us a private tour of the ship—its eleven decks, engine room, and impressive bridge, even showing us the wine tank for the 490-man Italian crew. Captain Ferruccio's only request was for me to host a captain's party. The ship's main entertainment was none other than one of the great singers of all time, Tony Martin. I remember seeing him at the Latin Quarter in Philly years ago, pin-spot in profile and raised top hat, with a voice made in heaven. He was still terrific and in one of his shows he introduced me and unexpectedly called me up to sing! In an early conversation, I had mentioned that I had done a musical, so I suppose that's what prompted it. I did get up and make a silly ass of myself not being able to remember the lyrics to anything, although the audience seemed to enjoy it. Occasionally, we run into Tony at some charity affair and chat amiably, while his wife, Cyd Charrise, smiles with a distant look on her lovely face.

Every time I would run into Robert Blake, whom I have always liked, the first thing he would say to me, good-naturedly, was "The Kotex Kid!" Then he would break into a big smile and laugh. I once related to him that when I played high school football, sponge rubber was scarce due to the war and the only available padding was Kotex, which I abundantly taped over my gimpy knees. He never forgot it and the greeting persisted for years, including the last time I saw him at the Golden Boot Awards, a yearly Western tribute benefitting the Motion Picture and Television Fund. This was just before his arrest for the alleged murder of his wife. I first met him when he appeared on *Cain's Hundred* years earlier. He was a withdrawn, quiet but very gifted young actor with a list of credits going back to the *Our Gang* comedies. His performance in Capote's *In Cold Blood* was chillingly memorable and fulfilled the promise of a superior talent. Later, to see him carry on as the wise-ass *Baretta*, his series that I appeared on a couple of times, I wasn't sure if he knew what was real and what was fictional, playing this muscular, strutting boneheaded character that unfortunately influenced his off-screen personality. I'm sure it was all an act, but it was a transformation that startled and irritated his studio employers. This is a weird and unforgiving business. People you've never met form an impression of you—good, bad, or indifferent. If it's bad, they'll lurk in some unsuspecting corner somewhere like buzzards, waiting to attack and do you dirty if they can when you least expect it. I have no opinion on the outcome of Robert Blake's situation. I am not a judge of guilt or innocence, only God is. But he is someone I know and like and I wish him peace. (In early 2005, he was acquitted, and I'm glad.)

It brings to mind someone else who was a close friend who also had a shocking and tragic twist to his life. Albert Salmi, a fine actor who had appeared with me in *End as a Man*, on and off-Broadway, had his career jump-started in that play—the same as had happened to Ben Gazarra, Anthony Franciosa, Pat Hingle, and me. Albert was a big, goodhearted character actor with a blushful face and reddish hair who wound up playing bad guys and oafs in Hollywood but had a much deeper unused talent. He had been married to Peggy Ann Garner, and they had a daughter; the marriage didn't last long, and years later he married again, choosing to live in Los Angeles where his career flourished for a while in films and TV. The last time I saw him, he and his wife, Roberta, came to dinner and we had a warm and gemütlichkeit evening. Albert had become fed up with

Hollywood and "the phony bastards who inhabit it" and had made the strange decision to move to Sandpoint, Idaho.

"Idaho?" I asked. "What about your career?"

"They know where to reach me," he said, "and if they want me, I'll come. But I gotta get away from this place."

We toasted them goodbye, wished them every good luck, and promised to visit them some day—knowing in our hearts we never would. Not too long afterward, we heard the terrible news. Albert had killed his wife and then taken his own life.

The nature of the business and what it can sometimes do to the psyche of an actor is appalling. The actor is always subject to the extremes; the exhilarating highs and the morbidly, gruesome lows, and the endless rejections, which can lead to interminable unemployment and inactivity and wreak deep and irreparable damage to an assailable, insecure individual. Without a calming influence or some pacifying inner quiet, the demons of uncontrolled rage can be unleashed and sow their seeds of chaos. I'm saying that a creative artist is different and unique. He has the capacity to utilize his specialized talent to believe in a fiction and produce instantaneously, by whatever means, the subtle or volatile emotions of love, joy, hate, anger, loss, and suffering—and all the sensations that a human being is subject to. When the curtain comes down or the camera stops rolling, the actor has to go back to reality, turn himself off to what he had created just a few moments earlier. This duality is what makes acting exciting and sometimes profound, but it is also why it can be so disturbing to the overly vulnerable.

In the summer of 1976, I flew to Atlanta, Georgia for a week's rehearsal to prepare getting a two-character comedy in shape for the opening night of *The Owl and the Pussycat*. One week is never enough time and especially for this engagement. It recalled the old days of summer stock, trying frantically to learn the lines and who the character is you're playing. This spicy play by Bill Manoff was not the most thrilling experience of my life, but it wasn't the worst either. After we got it going, the ticket buyers seemed to enjoy themselves. I had a good actress playing opposite me, making the best of a whore moving in with an eccentric writer—and not unexpectedly, we both fall in love. Gail Fisher had won a couple of Emmys on the series *Mannix*, and she knew her way around a stage, but the Midnight Sun Dinner Theater was giving us a tough time, playing to martini-softened brains, stuffed bellies, and tardy waiters noisily scurrying around at crucial moments. Atlanta was a city in transformation and redevelopment in 1976. The charm of the Old South was maintained by the magnificent homes and stately wisteria trees vividly capturing another time, the era of the Civil War. However, all the extensive sightseeing and the twice-visited incredible miniature of Lee's Burning of Atlanta couldn't cover the longing for my family; the five-week engagement was almost painful. I was grateful when Helen came for a visit near the end of the production and lifted my spirits.

A definitive indication of what playing in Atlanta was all about, at least at that time, suddenly became clear to me one night. During the first act, I noticed four guys sitting at a table up front all dressed the same— short hair, long-sleeved white shirts, and black ties. My instincts implied that they might be members of the Ku Klux Klan; their expressions, scary. When the play was over I had four visitors come to my dressing room. They were pleasant but cold when we shook hands. Then a man about forty-five, the tallest of the group with sweat dripping off his chin said in a heavy southern accent, "Mr. Richman… I wanna ask you a question."

"Sure, go ahead," I said, somewhat uneasily.

"The question is… how does it feel to kiss a nigger on stage in front of all those people?" It was said with quiet venom and contempt.

I weighed my answer, and after a pause I said, "Well, I guess it feels the same as kissing anybody else…"

He held his ground without altering his course. "You must be a pretty good actor to do that… you looked like you enjoyed it."

I smiled and then said, "I'm an actor. That's what I get paid for."

That tense evening was one of the most unpleasant I have ever spent in the theater, far different than the evening Coretta King came backstage to see Gail, and Gail brought her into my dressing room to meet me. It was an honor, and the lovely and gracious lady had some very complimentary things to say about our working together with such dignity and professionalism.

I had written plays, short stories, and a couple of screenplays, so I figured, what the hell, why not a novel? So, with my Praxis typewriter fighting me at every push of the keys, my younger kids driving me to distraction, and my wife yelling, "Be quiet… Daddy's writing!," I proceeded to pound away, incorporating the tedious cut and paste method (a laborious and painful process prior to computers) to amass 700 pages concerning a young producer fornicating his way through Broadway and Hollywood in the late 40s. Hence began the saga, the interminable epic of trying to get a novel published. If there is another definitive way to invite and expand the exposure to suffering, I haven't found it. First off, I needed an agent to represent it. The initial office I enthusiastically called, certain he would respond to my authored jewel, was Irving "Swifty" Lazar. Making millions elsewhere, he never got back to me. Not discouraged, I brought it to another highly reputed literary maven in Beverly Hills who weighed the 700 pages in his hands like a chicken ready to be cooked and said, "It's too heavy." He then dropped it on his desk with a thump and continued, "This is what a novel should look like," and handed me a scrawny book of 217 pages. I had no idea that books were sold by the pound. I thought he was an idiot. The next office I ventured to was a famous Hollywood literary powerhouse of earlier days on Sunset Boulevard, H. N. Swanson & Co. I never met the man or ever saw him. There was even a question of whether H.N. was still alive; he had handled the greats and most of them were dead. Another agent in the firm, a friendly, elderly gentleman by the name of Ben Kamsler, eagerly took my novel, read it, and liked it enough to represent it. However, he felt it was necessary to have a New York agent handle it since all the publishing was done out of the major houses situated on the East Coast, and H. N. Swanson would share in the proceeds. I agreed, so Ben sent my first novel, *Falling Up*, to Roslyn Targ, a highly respected author's rep in New York. In three weeks, she let me know how much she liked it, thought I should think about doing some trimming, but was high on the possibility of a sale. I was floating and a little voice in my ear said *Wow!*, but I wouldn't let myself get too carried away lest I stir the bugs in the bottom of the ointment.

On one of my summer trips to Albany to see the kids, I made a side visit to New York City and took Roslyn Targ to a chic bistro on Madison Avenue for lunch. She was pleased to be seen with such a recognizable face and I'm sure it was part of her selling pitch, "… a stirring, sexy first novel by a well-known television star." By this time, we had had several rejections from some major publishers—comments ranging from "talented" and "brilliant first effort" but no sale. She was still encouraging, but the rejection slips continued to mount, and every time I opened one of her letters, I had a heart flutter.

On the stage, I have done many leading roles in sophisticated comedies and consider myself fairly adept at playing character humor. But I don't think there was a living soul in television at the time who thought I could play anything except Sam Sourface or George Grim. In 1977, to counter that impression, I went into the stage production of *Hold Me*, by Jules Feiffer, at the Westwood Playhouse. The play was a series of zany vignettes based on Feiffer's comic strip. I was featured playing many characters with an off-the-wall pursuit, but honestly played. At one moment, I was a baseball player talking to himself while trying to strike out a batter; in another I revealed a compulsion to dance like Fred Astaire, sporting a high hat and cane. It was quite hilarious and so satisfying I stayed in the play for several months. During this time, I had acquired a manager, Arlene Dayton, and a hot new agent, David Shapira. One of the positives, in light of my desire to do comedy on TV, came to fruition when Arlene brought the producers of *Three's Company* to see my performance in *Hold Me*.

They were impressed. I was now the strait-laced, but funny, Reverend Snow, the father of Chrissy (Suzanne Somers), who made his unexpected and troublesome visits to the threesome's apartment. There I was wearing my religious collar in front of live audiences, getting big laughs with my pontificating righteousness and silly double takes and enjoying every moment. I also had a contract that guaranteed an increase in salary for each show, and it was beginning to look as if I would be included in the future planning of the smash-hit series—the character was that successful. Lo and behold, another worm in the jello—Suzanne Somers went loony-greedy asking for $150,000 an episode (at the time, exorbitant), and the curtain came down on Reverend Snow. She was fired and her father was never heard of again. It is interesting to note that of all the shows I have done—more than 500 episodes of different series—the public seems to remember me more quickly for *Three's Company* and I appeared in only three programs! Of course, it has been repeated endlessly in syndication.

In 1978, while the three older over-achieving children were startling us with their musical accomplishments and, in addition, Kelly's acting and singing abilities, the two younger ones were showing an inordinate interest in sports. That suddenly stimulated mine, which had been dormant for years. We became Dodger fans and especially ardent devotees of the Rams football team. Hallelujah! Through my younger kids I was having a passionate rebirth. At least once a week during the season, I would take Orien, nine, and Roger, seven, down our street to the Taft High School football field and gleefully throw the football around and teach them the fundamentals of the game—play quarterback in a T-formation and show them how the ball is handed off, faked, or passed. I even taught them how to punt and kick a field goal. They loved it—and no more than I did. We still talk about our football workouts that went on for years while they were growing up. It's a memory I cherish (Hey Dad, you wanna throw the ball around?).

One year, after many disappointing and frustrating seasons, the Rams were again in the playoffs under head coach, Chuck Knox. We were ecstatic. The crucial game was to take place at the Coliseum against the dreaded Dallas Cowboys. I immediately purchased four tickets on the fifty-yard line for that Sunday so that we could cheer our heads off. But Friday afternoon, my agent called and said they wanted me on location in Utah to start shooting *The Greatest Heroes of the Bible* on Monday, playing the evil king of Sodom and Gomorrah. I had already recorded many of the shows in Hollywood as the voice of God for the series (insisting in gentle exasperation to the producer in my first recording session that God doesn't have to shout, he whispers in your ear!). I had won that argument, but now they were insisting that I do my stuff on-camera as evil King Bera—and my agent had already committed. I was trapped, and my kids were deeply disappointed. There were no flights directly to Page, Arizona, where the company was headquartered, so on Saturday I reluctantly flew to Phoenix and there, waiting for me, was another one of those little two-seater mosquito jobs that I detest flying in. Unfortunately, I couldn't back out now. Little did I know there was a bloody blizzard in Page, and the only way to get there was the way I was going, privately. There were no commercial flights. It was too dangerous!

Sitting behind the two pilots with no room to spit, the wind buffeting the craft like a feather and looking out the windows on either side, seeing a dancing wall of solid white, I thought to myself, *Why in heaven's fucking name am I subjecting myself to this? Is it written down somewhere that I have to kill myself for a crummy TV show?* I held my breath the whole trip and my heart was pounding its muscular self off. I swore as I'd done many times before, but this time I meant it… I'm never going to fly in another pissy private plane again—squashed like a cockroach, my stomach bringing up the taste of yesterday's lobster bisque! My little prick agent should be the one subjected to this! When we thankfully landed, I'm sure I was as white as the snow swirling around us. It was freezing cold and standing around on a barren runway waiting to be picked up was a drag. Finally, a car arrived and I was driven to a motel outside of Page with a complex Native American name. The first thing I did at the registration desk was to ask about the next day's Rams-Dallas playoff game. To my shock, they had no television hook-up! The friendly clerk with a large wart on his nose and pipe-brown teeth said, "The Holiday Inn about thirty miles from here has a big TV in the bar." The following afternoon I took a taxi to the Holiday Inn. I instantly realized that the crowded bar was filled with raucous Dallas fans, and I was a lonely intruder. I thought I would have a problem being the only Rams person, but I endeared myself to the crowd when I called housekeeping for some blankets and tacked them up over a window preventing the outside light from hitting the large TV screen. In fact, they cheered. When the Cowboys beat the hell out my team 25-0, and my boisterous bar companions were going crazy, I faded out of the room and taxied back to my motel, depressed.

All the sets for the production of this series were built against the magnificent Buttes of Utah, near Page. There was no studio. It was a blessing for the exteriors but a curse for the interior shooting. There was a layer of white mud on every inch of slippery interior surface, and there was no heat, except for small electric blowers which accomplished little. Comforts for the actors didn't exist; it was a wonder we survived the inclement, cold weather on the long shooting days. It did give us a dramatic sense of what it must have been like in the time of Jesus. I wore a full beard and a wicked scar on my face to compliment the crown on my head as King Bera. My costume, of rough, black fringed leather and gold adornments, contrasted with the simple robes that Ed Ames wore as Job and Dorothy Malone wore as Job's wife—before she disobeyed and was turned to stone! Gene Barry was Abraham and Rick Jason played my leering confidant as I scheme to get Job to do my wishes. Of course, I fail and righteous Job escapes with his family while Sodom is turned to rubble.

One day when we weren't shooting, Ed Ames and I and another actor who knew his way in Native American lands decided to go exploring. We thought it would be a great idea to sneak onto a Navajo reservation and look around—which is verboten. We drove for miles and finally saw a sign that seemed to imply we were close. We drove for another couple of miles on a desolate dirt road, when out of nowhere a Navajo man dressed in western gear with a rifle flagged us in no uncertain terms. "STOP!" he said, "STOP!" It was nervous time as he approached us menacingly. He asked us what we wanted on the reservation where trespassers were not allowed. Clever as we could be, we said that we were just looking to buy some Navajo jewelry, got lost, and did he have any? He looked at us for a long questioning moment and then he said, surprisingly, "Follow me." We followed his truck to a small cinder block house and a yard with a couple of chickens strutting around near a goat eating weeds. There was also a Navajo hogan nearby with a hanging row of drying meat. "Wait here," he said. He then went into the tiny house and came out with a handful of beautiful, handmade turquoise and silver jewelry.

I knew Helen would love them, so I bought every piece for a rather modest price and said, "Do you have any more?" He gave me a big smile of rotten teeth and asked us to come to the cinder block house. Ed and I were thrilled as we looked at each other chuckling inside. I found out later that it was kind of an honor to be invited in. The Navajo opened the door to this roughly made building of two rooms that couldn't have been more than fourteen feet square. Sitting on a bed was an old woman who looked eighty but was probably younger. This was a rough way to live. A young Navajo woman in a shiny blue blouse and beautiful dark eyes suddenly appeared with a box of magnificent earrings, necklaces, pendants, and rings—all of quality Navajo workmanship. Ed and I and the other fellow went crazy buying almost the whole collection. I also purchased an authentic Navajo wedding basket from the old woman for $40, who wasn't too eager to part with it. I asked her if she would come outside so I could take a picture with her. She refused and had to be coaxed, then reluctantly agreed. But first she wanted to put on her new shawl and I couldn't convince her that I wanted a photo with her wearing the old Navajo blanket on her shoulders as I first saw her. Vanity on a reservation won out. The photographs with the old woman and me are rare and wonderful memories—and the soaring flight home to Los Angeles on a Lear Jet owned by some Arab prince who was in love with one of Job's daughters isn't too shabby a memory either.

In 1979, my oldest son, Howard, who was twenty-one, was already a junior in music at UCLA and deep into perfecting his piano technique. Kelly, nineteen, was also at UCLA studying in the theater department with a developing singing voice of major promise. Lucas, fifteen, finishing Taft High School, was into everything—his violin study, violinist in the Youth Symphony of the California State University at Northridge, composing, piano playing, and even acting in the school's musical, On The Town. Lucas asked me to please come and tighten the staging before they opened. I did, gently, much to the stiff-necked chagrin of the teacher-director. Thomas Osborn, conductor of the Youth Symphony, asked me to appear as the narrator in a performance of *Through the Looking Glass*, by Lewis Carroll, with music by Deems Taylor. He suggested that if I wished to, I might expand and adapt the texts appearing in the score. I was pleased to selectively incorporate more of the author's words, and I believe it was the first time the original text had ever been touched for enhancement. It worked so well that a long-playing record was released of the live performance. I was the story teller and acted all the roles, and Lucas, sitting behind me, played the violin with the orchestra.

Cesar Romero, that tall and very handsome man with the toothy grin that I had seen a hundred times in films, was my Mafia adversary in an episode of *Vegas* shot in Las Vegas. Even though we despised each other when the camera was rolling, we became friends. Always accessible, courteous and kind, he was a fine actor who had seen it all, a gentleman I respected and admired. I was depressed playing so many bad guys on television and since nothing much of consequence was being offered to alter the situation, it seemed that the best part of my day's work was the drive home to be with my wife and kids. When I think of my children growing up, one of my most wondrous memories is the sound of them practicing or having a mini-concert in the living room. As I drove into the garage and parked my car, I could hear them playing, sometimes with a group of friends, bringing alive the chamber music of Mozart or Schumann—the beautiful, vibrant sounds reverberating off the walls. It warmed my heart and immediately changed my grumpy mood. From an observational point of view and as an involved parent, I've come to the conclusion that children deeply involved in good music (my three oldest) and the friends they attract with similar interests, will have a more serene life overall. Of course, indications of a child's interests (coming from his inner life) begin to manifest early and should be encouraged, not deterred or squashed. You never know where it may lead for their future, and it's worth a serious try to provide an environment that nurtures their development and happiness.

If you've ever been to Texas in the summer time you know what it's like to fry while you're still alive. I flew to Dallas in August to appear on *Dallas*, and I dreaded leaving the air-conditioned hotel every morning to go on location. Actually, you can scramble eggs on the sidewalk. I was playing a crooked senator and Morgan Fairchild was my babe. All I remember about my nefarious carryings on is Morgan's mother cornering me at every opportunity pleading with me to tell her daughter to gain weight! Why she felt that I had any influence on her child was beyond me. I guess she figured that since I was sleeping with her in the episode we were filming, I could certainly, intimately, tell her to eat more. Her arms were a little thin, but I thought she looked pretty good in a nightgown leaving my bed, so I finally said to her mother, "Dear, I think you should take her out for a rigatoni and meatball dinner… and just express yourself." She gave me a starched, unappreciative look.

John Dean, a justice department attorney who was appointed special counsel to President Nixon, wrote a tell-all book called *Blind Ambition* about the administration's obstruction of justice in the Watergate cover-up. It was made into a television miniseries of four parts and aired on CBS in 1979. Everybody and his uncle was in it, including me. I played Robert Mardian, one of the inner circle of personalities involved in the questionable deeds of the hierarchy. I met John Dean and we chatted. It was odd playing a character that the man had been on intimate and confidential terms with, but he didn't offer me any Mardian information and I didn't ask for any. If there was a quality I remember about Dean it was that he was somewhat shy, but friendly—and I wouldn't have trusted him with my daughter's piggy bank. Martin Sheen played Dean and George Schaeffer directed.

Helen and I flew to Toronto, Canada, for the sixth International Subud Congress, an occurrence planned every four years in varying countries. One thousand six hundred Subud people from all over the world came to spend a week with Bapak Subuh, doing latihan with him, listening to his deeply profound talks, and discussing world Subud organizational activities and charitable endeavors. The experience always made me think of myself staggering off a sun-parched desert and finding an oasis of clear, cool water to drink and plunge into. We stayed in an old theatrical hotel next to a lovely Victorian park where every morning I forced myself to take a short morning jog, with the deceptive notion that I was staying in shape. Seeing many old friends and doing latihan with hundreds of people—the power so strong—was like getting a shot of adrenalin. By the time we left, we felt refreshed and replenished.

In the fall of 1979, my brother, Harry, had a heart attack and died instantly. He was nineteen years older than me. He was a favorite of my father and when Pop died, Harry was so overwrought with grief he wasn't someone I could go to assuage our loss, and my mother couldn't have been happier, so I couldn't look for comfort there. Although I loved him, there was always a distance between us. I suppose it had more to do with age separation than anything else. He tried to be a surrogate father when I came out of the Navy, but I was too resistant to his conventionally staid suggestions. The times, the war's end, hormones, and totally different interests were the driving forces in my life, that is, until he finally convinced me to submit to pharmacy college at his alma mater. I still can't fathom how I put my chosen profession in abeyance for four years to study pharmacy, acquiring a license to practice in two states and then abandoning the whole effort like a rotten tomato to embrace a dream. Years later, Harry and I became much closer. He reveled in my accomplishments as an actor and loved Helen and the children—especially Kelly, whose loving warmth touched him profoundly. Helen and I flew back to Philadelphia for Harry's funeral. It's always sad and difficult to accept a family death. All those moments of a life remaining in your head forever—the smiles and the sounds of laughter, the memories that roll over you like the lapping ocean at the beach's edge. Laura, his daughter and my niece, was rational and accepting. Faye, his dear wife, a good woman and a sympathetic soul, was inconsolable.

Ken Moscowitz, owner of the American Masters Gallery where I had a show in 1967, Eddie Goldfield of Goldfield Galleries, and Terry DeLapp, another fine dealer, were instrumental in stimulating my sometimes frenzied interest in collecting. We had become good friends and a gallery of art is a very special place to study and discuss—with knowledgeable people, sometimes heatedly—the merits of a particular painter. I began to acquire an eye and an awareness of the quality of the artist's work, especially of the twentieth century. Over the years I've purchased and sold a variety of known painters and sometimes wish I hadn't been so hasty to sell—their value having increased considerably. Sometimes I would stumble into an auction in some isolated place or city and find a painting of importance waiting to be snatched up. My heart would pump a few more beats and sweat would dampen my armpits, and I would wonder whether anyone else knew what I knew about the artist. It was exciting and nerve-wracking. Once, I found two valuable oil paintings that way—exposed to an unknowing audience. I purchased them both with the highest bid, a pittance of their true value. An Henri Lebasque and an Hippolyte Petitjean. On one of my searching jaunts, I found a large oil painting in the window of a junk shop in Albany, New York. My heart almost stopped. I knew it was something special, a painting of an 18th century woman in a flowing dress and beautifully done. I bought it for $200. When I got back to Los Angeles, all my dealer friends were impressed, but since it was an unsigned painting the provenance was uncertain. I took it to the Los Angeles county museum and when the two authorities first saw it they immediately said, "My God... it's a Gilbert Stuart!" I nearly fell over. At the time, a painting by Stuart, who had painted George Washington, would be worth about $300,000. On closer examination, their noses and magnifiers close to the canvas, they finally said, "It is not a Stuart... brush strokes are too modern. Sorry." Then they just left the room leaving me standing there as if I were contagious. Not giving up, I called the curator of the Huntington Library in Pasadena, whose collection of American and English art is profound. He responded quickly after my description of the painting. Schlepping it to Pasadena was a chore but once there he studied it extensively then excused himself for about twenty minutes. He came back with a book in his hand opened to a page that showed my painting in a black and white photo!

He told me that the painting was a masterful copy of a George Romney who painted at the time of Gainsborough and was just as famous. It probably had been copied many years ago judging by the deteriorating, unlined canvas but it was still a copy. I sold my almost-a-treasure at a Sotheby auction in Los Angeles. I certainly didn't lose any money selling the unsigned work classified as "In the school of Romney."

At another time, I was shooting a commercial on a desolate beach in the Bahamas for a new revolutionary air-conditioner with the letters "S.S." (silent service) following the company name. I was the spokesman, but I knew it was absolutely hopeless with those letters. One evening I drove into Freeport and went to their main art gallery searching for goodies. Nothing on the walls impressed me, just native second-rate stuff, so I asked the gallery director if he had any important artists' works. He came back with an Alfred Kubin drawing, an Austrian surrealist, and a Picasso etching, *Tête de Femme*, done in 1905 and a famous piece. I feigned dumbness and bought the Kubin, haggling a bit, for $60 and the Picasso for $235. He was happy and I was overjoyed. The seeking out and pursuing of art works in isolated barns, farms, dusty attics, and bankruptcy estates became my passion. It had become almost an incurable disease. It was taking over my life and consuming me, so much so that I had to cool it and declare a collecting moratorium.

Eddie Goldfield, whose girth had increased with the size of his enormous collection of fine American art, gave me a major exhibition in 1979. Having a show at the Goldfield Galleries in Los Angeles, where accumulated treasures included the works of Thomas Hart Benton, William Merritt Chase, Childe Hassam, and Robert Henri to name a few, was definitely a step up in the credentials of Peter Mark Richman. I was also extremely pleased with the presentation of the twenty oil paintings and twenty watercolor/inks that were mounted. Knowing my works were hanging on the walls of a gallery where in the room adjacent hung the paintings of Reginald Marsh and George Luks—figurative artists I greatly admired, was an honor. As they say, "You judge a man by the company he keeps."

In 1921, Mary Pickford, Charles Chaplin, and Douglas Fairbanks founded the Motion Picture Relief Fund, which eventually became known as The Motion Picture and Television Fund. They had a purposeful vision, and to this day it has never faltered, now situated on forty acres in Woodland Hills, California. It's a unique and fabulous organization that provides charitable assistance, residential living, medical treatment, and quality care, supported by everyone who works in the entertainment industry. The Fund has always interested me and its motto "We take care of our own" sends out a powerful message that still echoes as potently as the day it was first phrased. I have always had an innate feeling for the elderly and when I had been asked to participate in functions at the country home or hospital I responded immediately—as a master of ceremonies, an informal photographer, a celebrity attendee on special events, or just as a visitor to patients I had worked with in films. Every year, William Campbell, a former actor who was then an executive Fund worker, put on the comedic "Ding-a-ling Show," with resident performers and invited celebrity guest artists. It was one of the highlights of the year mounted on campus in the beautiful Louis B. Mayer Theater. In one production, the wonderful Eleanor Powell tap danced, in another, Gordon MacRae sang, and a spectacular Fayard Nicholas (of the Nicholas Brothers) did amazing things with his nimble feet—even after a double hip operation! (It scared the hell out of his doctor.) In March 1980, while attending the show, I was suddenly called up to the stage to greet everyone. When I got there, the executive director at the time, Jack Staggs, surprisingly introduced me as the newest board member of The Motion Picture and Television Fund! I stood there smiling self-consciously and slightly befuddled as the audience loudly applauded my unexpected assignment. Going with the moment, I took the microphone, accepted the invitation and said it would be an honor to serve an organization that does such fine and noble work. I have been a dedicated trustee ever since.

Also, about this time, I became involved with the Jeffrey Foundation, a remarkable charity that cares for children with multiple disabilities. It was founded by Alyce Morris, a resilient and dedicated woman, who lost a son, Jeffrey, to multiple sclerosis. No other agency provides as many services for the handicapped, abused, and special needs children and their families. I have served as a celebrity ambassador and master of ceremonies on countless occasions. I am honored to do so.

Several New York publishers liked my novel but wouldn't commit to taking it on, suggesting it would be an easier sale if it were shorter. So, after much deliberation and painful acquiescence I forced myself to excise a lot of meaty, colorful stuff. Of course, this process went on and on until I finally said to myself with no trumpets blaring and I meant it: *This is it, I shall not alter thee again!*

Work-wise, 1980 started with a burst of activity which is always heartening for an actor. I flew to Las Vegas to guest on a pilot for Aaron Spelling, a spin-off from the show *Vegas*—the stars, two gorgeous girls who were really undercover cops. I thought the premise was weak and the girls too startlingly beautiful, but I wasn't Aaron Spelling, and anything can happen in Las Vegas and usually does. I was pleased to have the opportunity to work with Tony Curtis again (I had done *Vegas* previously). He was always professional and fun to work with, although, story-wise, I was done in rather quickly, playing a detective blown up in his car turning on the ignition. We spent some time talking about writing and painting. He was serious about both endeavors and was quite glib in extemporaneously describing the landscape as we drove to location. It impressed me. I think his autobiography, published in 1993, which he wrote with Barry Paris is an exceptional book of its kind.

20 *Dynasty*

EARLY IN 1980, I flew up to San Francisco and then was driven to San Mateo to begin shooting another new Aaron Spelling-Doug Cramer television pilot. The show was called, of all things, *Oil*, written by executive producers Richard and Esther Shapiro. A bunch of star names were attached, including George Peppard, Linda Evans, Lloyd Bochner, Bo Hopkins, Dale Robertson, and many more. I came into the project late and was told that they didn't want to have any more "names" as running stars, so I was granted the consolation billing: "Special Guest Star Peter Mark Richman as Andrew Laird." Their rationale was that since I was playing George Peppard's lawyer, my character was uncertain as to its development the way the scripts were evolving. If the show were to be picked up, I would not be assured every episode. It was an annoying pain in the ass, but I accepted it. For the most part, shooting the pilot was a pleasant experience. The location was extraordinary because all the shooting took place on the splendiferous Filoli estate (formerly of the Matson Line family), comprising a magnificent mansion, incomparable grounds, and over 400 acres of quiet privacy representing the home of Blake Carrington—the richest Denver-based oil baron this side of Saudi Arabia. He was played by Peppard. "Knowing where all the bodies were buried," I was the guy who was going to protect him and his multi-layered assets, even with Blake's impending second marriage to the lovely, blue-eyed Linda Evans—getting her to sign a marriage agreement before the wedding. My friend Dale Robertson, a genuine sweetheart of a man played an oilman that Blake Carrington had financially screwed, so there was plenty of conflict and intrigue to go around, including the messiness and plot twists concerning Carrington's closeted homosexual son (Al Corley) and the daughter (Pamela Sue Martin) secretly bedding the family chauffeur.

I thought the location was so spectacular that I called Helen and asked her to fly up with our youngest boys, Orien and Roger. They had a wonderful time exploring the grounds, meeting the actors, and going riding with a stable of horses kept by the company wranglers. George Peppard had his son with him and he and my boys got along and played well together. After the shoot, we spent a fun time in San Francisco riding the cable cars, taking in the sights, and capping it off with an Italian stuff-fest on Fisherman's Wharf. The only problem during the shoot was that George Peppard was being difficult. I had known George for a long time, going back to our early Actors Studio days and the film *The Strange One*. He had a tendency to let his ego burst the bubbles of his success with an irritating and pompous attitude. He was unhappy with the script and wanted changes… no, he demanded changes. I remember sitting in his trailer discussing the show, the script, the way the shooting was going, and his discontent. Suddenly, he showed me a telegram that he was going to send to Tony Thomopoulos, the president of the ABC network, expressing all of his harsh gripes. I read the wire and was aghast. To me, it was unnecessary and he should have been talking to Aaron Spelling to straighten things out, not the network.

"George," I said, "don't send this telegram. It will only cause problems and make you look petty."

"I don't give a shit, they're not listening to me," he answered smugly.

"George, you're going to screw yourself… don't send it."

Well, he did send it and it was the beginning of the end for George. A few months later *Oil* was changed to *Dynasty* and the new Blake Carrington was John Forsythe. Everything that George had filmed would have to be shot again with Forsythe. I knew it sent the production and the network into a spinning nightmare. The costs were mounting wildly. There were high hopes for the success of the pilot and so many people were involved aside from the actors and their lucrative contracts. Six months later, I began re-shooting the unfinished pilot of *Dynasty* with the new leading man. In a sense, we were doing everything over; it all went exceedingly well. The characters were established, relationships were melded, and the foundation for a new hit series seemed to be resting on a stronger foundation. There was one particular scene when I am moving along in the reception line after the wedding with handshakes, hugs, kisses, and congratulatory wishes, when Pamela Sue Martin (the daughter) says a fresh remark to me and I respond with a short throwaway quip (mine) that broke everyone up viewing the dailies. After that, the supervising producer, Duke Vincent, said to me, "Peter Mark… you're locked into the series!"

As it turned out, I thought that John Forsythe was better casting. He gave the part what you would hope to expect of an attractive, wheeler-dealer-money-bags—maturity and a believable presence. The network liked what they saw and the show was picked up for thirteen episodes, guaranteeing at least a full late entry season. There was an excitement in the air and the feeling that we were involved in a classy show that had the potential to be a blockbuster. I can say without reservation that no expense was spared in trying to achieve that determinacy. Aaron Spelling, a powerhouse producer for the ABC Network and a track record second to none, seemed to have another impending notch on his belt. On a personal note, when we returned to a shooting schedule at Twentieth Century Fox Studios, I enjoyed seeing my name painted on a designated parking place outside stage #8. Parking my new silver and black Cadillac Biarritz (a modest indulgence) was definitely in character with the nature of the show.

While the Carrington family and their associative appendages were doing their emotional and clandestine carryings on, I was always called upon to give solid and protective advice to my friend and employer, Blake Carrington. He didn't always agree with it, but valued my assistance. However, in the final analysis I was to carry out his wishes no matter what potential complications it caused. John Forsythe and I had a good working relationship. It was warm, easy, friendly, and respectful. There was a powerful interplay in our scenes, two pros setting off heated sparks. We also enjoyed being with one another, kibitzing, telling ribald jokes, and talking of our families, sometimes revealing very personal things while we waited endlessly, sipping coffee between set-ups. In one of the early episodes we were going to shoot, I had a scene to do with John and had memorized several pages of involved dialogue concerning oil shipments, foreign countries, and what we should do about it. During the rehearsal, while we were moving around and setting up for the camera with the director, much to my surprise, John suddenly got agitated and forcefully said, "Why do we have to have all this crap in the script… and who cares about it anyway?" Then he proceeded to cross out my dialogue without consulting me as if I didn't exist—the first sign of star pomposity and arrogance that made my linebacker blood begin to boil, and then when it sizzled:

"Hold on a second!" I said, my voice rising. "Just hold on one damn minute! Who the hell are you to be so frigging cavalier in crossing out my dialogue? It would have been nice if you had discussed it with me first! And maybe the producer has something to say about it!"

That's when John stormed off the set. I never found out what was eating his ass, but it took me a while to calm down. There was no question that John and Linda Evans were the main stars of the show and that was where the focus was pointed. It was his manner that bugged me. If there is one thing I cannot take and never could, it's someone assuming they can diminish me to my face and get away with it. Never. My fuse is too easily ignited. The producer came to the set, calm was restored, and we finally shot the scene with some minor changes that satisfied everybody—but I was sorry to see this strange, unnecessary conflict take place. It never happened again. John knew the parameters of where he stood with me. I liked John and I am happy to say that our relationship eventually became warm and friendly again—although, in my heart, I often wondered if he still harbored resentment over the incident.

On January 2, 1981, *Dynasty* made a three-hour debut on the ABC Network and a new monster hit was born. Money, power, and unharnessed passion played well in Peoria and Poughkeepsie. It was the talk of Hollywood and the whole country. People were entranced by the look of the show, its beautiful people, the adult themes, and the dreamy escapism. After a few weeks, feature film attendance dropped to alarming numbers on Wednesday evenings. Audiences stayed at home glued to their TV screens as *Dynasty* became the heralded evening soap opera. There were so many unexpected quirks in the story line that the burgeoning and loyal audience was kept on the edge trying to determine where it all would go. Then a thunderbolt gripped the *Dynasty* advocates. In an angry confrontation with his son's homosexual lover, Blake pulls him away from his son and violently pushes him. He accidentally falls over backward and bangs his head at the marble fireplace. The young man is dead! Blake is accused of murder in the first degree, and, of course, in my self-assured manner and pinstriped suit, working my professionally wily ways against the prosecuting attorney, Brian Dennehy, I defend my client with all barrels blasting. It was a sensational trial, beautifully directed by Don Medford, with more twists than a German cruller, but none more startling than the sudden courtroom entrance of Blake's first wife, Alexis. When we shot the scene, which was in the last show of the half season, the part hadn't been cast, so they kept Alexis (an extra) in a long view, her monstrous, wide-brimmed hat hiding her face, and everybody aghast and whispering: "It's Alexis Carrington!" A cliffhanger for the new season if there ever was one.

I had a meeting with David Obst in his Paramount Studios office, one of those dreary rooms on the lot in the old writer's building. David was a literary hotshot who somehow would get books published and have a caption on a separate page that read "A David Obst Book." I really never knew whether he was an agent, a producer, or a procurer. He had read my novel, was excited about it, and wanted to represent it. He also thought it had great potential to be a major film. We were getting along extremely well, the meeting dragging on for almost two hours as we discussed all the characters involved, my "authentic" dialogue and that it was an enjoyable, easy read. We were running into a problem however, and it just wouldn't go away. He wanted me to rewrite one of the main characters—the head of a movie studio and his relationship with his troubled, over-sexed daughter—insisting on a case of continuous incest. That would have changed the whole book and I felt strongly it was totally wrong. He was smiling and I was smiling through our disagreement, but we were making no headway in the daddy-fucking-daughter department. Since I was so adamant, at the meeting's conclusion he said he would submit it to Simon and Schuster without the changes and he'd know in a week. I followed him down the stairway to his car, shook hands, and said goodbye.

Before he pulled away I asked, "How many books that you submit to Simon and Schuster get published?"

He answered, confidently, "They all do."

I stood there and watched his car go out the Paramount gate, the late afternoon sun warming my face. It felt good and I was thinking: Wouldn't that be something? He sure does seem to have a lot of clout.

Two weeks later I received a form letter from Simon and Schuster. No thanks. Another bullshit artist on a list of many.

Before starting a feature film or a series, the actor is required to get a physical examination for insurance purposes to make sure that he is capable and healthy to fulfill his contract. When I arrived at Dr. Michaelson's office to get my exam for the new season, I saw this attractive woman, quiet and forlorn, sitting in the corner of the empty waiting room. She looked up at me and shyly smiled. I walked over to her, we shook hands, and introduced ourselves. She knew who I was, she had seen the show. I knew who she was—it was Joan Collins, here from England to play the mysterious Alexis Carrington, Blake's first wife, without the face-covering wide hat. She was so disarmingly sweet and pretty and surprisingly insecure, I thought she was kidding when she asked me to take her to lunch because "I don't know anyone."

After the examinations, I took the lonely beauty to the Fox commissary. We sat and talked for an hour over salads and a glass of wine, breaking the ice, and establishing what I thought would be a solid working relationship. She even revealed to me her unhappiness about the lesser money her agent (my former agent, Ronnie Leif) had her contractually committed to for playing such a major role. Well, that didn't last long—neither the money she was getting nor her sweet and tender personality. When the new season's programs went on the air, her character exploded on the small screen like an earthquake and the response to her was enormous. She was damned good, and, of course her salary was renegotiated skywards. Needless to say, her glamorous presence enhanced the show and solidified her position and the direction the series took. No more Little Miss Insecurity, though. She became Alexis Carrington in person, a snooty, hoity-toity Hollywood star. A couple of times I couldn't abide her attitude and had to cut her down to size. It was startling to see, when faced with a "no bullshit" opponent, how quickly she reverted to the vulnerable little girl persona. Nevertheless, everybody genuflected to her whims as her life and career were rejuvenated beyond her dreams.

Of course, after much tribulation, tension, and suspenseful courtroom theatrics, my superior lawyering (in the script) removed Blake Carrington from the murderer designation. He was set free to resume his enviable life, confronting a former and a present wife attacking each other's throats, children you want to drown, and a business associate who wants to destroy him. It was great TV and the ratings, which the industry worships, hovered at the very top and stayed there.

At the completion of shooting, the exclusive *Dynasty* wrap party was given at the Beverly Hills Hotel. There, everyone gave thanks to everyone for the success of the show, except God. I was also called upon to speak. I was totally impromptu in my delivery and made everyone sit up with an attentive smile or giggle, but I did catch a few troubled and sour looks. I said, "… in the new season you are all going to be rapturously surprised… because, while Blake Carrington is in his office selling oil to Yugoslavia, he will soon discover that his wife Krystle (Linda Evans) and his ex-wife Alexis (Joan Collins) will both be carrying my child." The applause and laughter that followed wasn't particularly appreciated by Eileen and Robert Pollock, who wrote the story line, nor by Esther Shapiro, the executive producer. They had absolutely no sense of humor, but Aaron Spelling smiled broadly and chuckled as we shook hands on the way back to my table. Joan Collins came up to me afterward with a questioning grin.

"Is it true?" she asked.

I shook my head yes, then answered, "Naah… I was only kidding."

I suppose in an unconscious and unsubtle way I was suggesting a direction the series could follow that would be of lascivious interest and would certainly enhance the participation of my character—but I had no buyers.

One of the plusses that season was the opportunity to meet a young football player I greatly admired, Vince Ferragamo of the Rams. Vince came on the show as an actor in bandaged, wheelchair incapacitation as one of Blake's football stars playing on his fictitious team. Vince and I hit it off immediately; the Rams were my passion and here, before me, was the starting quarterback in the flesh! A gentle sweetheart of a young man, he was tall, muscular, and so good looking it was startling. I said to myself, *how can anyone take the pounding he does and still look like he belongs in the movies?* I told Vince how I'd followed his admirable career and how we had suffered through the 1979 Super Bowl loss to Pittsburgh, 31–19, my sons Roger and Orien crying with inconsolable sadness at the loss. After shooting that day, when I told my sports-obsessed younger kids that we were going to the Ferragamos' for a Christmas party, they were ecstatic. Thus began my close association with the Rams when they were in Anaheim. At his party I met the players, the coaches, and some executive personnel, and, of course, Vince's darling wife, Jodie, who had been his college sweetheart at the University of Nebraska. That evening, I also met one of the great defensive coordinators in football, Fritz Schurmer, who became a special friend who I will never forget. A kind and thoughtful man, he invited me to the Rams' practices, a privilege I continually pursued with diligence up until the move to St. Louis. I became sort of a Rams "celebrity" person, dedicated and loyal to the organization. For years I would drive down to the sports complex at Fullerton, not far from Los Angeles or the University of California at Irvine, for pre-season practice. Sometimes, I would bring Roger and Orien, who were goofy with excitement, especially when Fritz provided us with a golf cart and opened his personal refrigerator full of soft drinks for our use at any time, and the PR representative slipping us Rams hats and T-shirts. Those were glorious times watching practice on the sidelines as they grunted through violent combat, followed by privileged conversations with stalwarts like Eric Dickerson, Jackie Slater, Kevin Greene, and Jack Youngblood.

I will never forget the time Vince Ferragamo and his wife, Jodie, came for lunch at my home and then threw a football around in the courtyard with Roger and Orien. The quarterback of the Rams throwing a football to my kids! One day at one of the early practices, Marshall Klein, a Rams executive, invited me to be a guest in Georgia Frontiere's suite. She owned the team and I became spoiled for life—a privileged Rams person, viewing a game in the best seats and feasting on a gourmet catered luncheon. It was heaven. Helen enjoyed it too, and more so, the kids. However, being a Rams fan was synonymous with suffering. For years the team couldn't get beyond playoff contention, and each game became as crucial a one for me as if I were still a player—some psychologically entombed absurdity. I cared so much about my team winning. At the kickoff my heart rate would go up at least ten beats (it still does) and my physical tension would become "game-like"—ready to take on any opposing rat bastard standing in my way! I'm definitely in the game, intensely concentrated, energized and vocally expressive. I remember once while sitting in the seats of Georgia's suite, a referee made a bad call and I boisterously let loose with a string of explosive and colorful expletives. I happened to turn around and saw the Reverend Robert Schuller sitting behind me, eyebrows raised, smirking. I knew I must have been damned to hell that day—and the Rams lost.

I will always be grateful for having become friendly with so many incredible sports figures over the years because of my association with the Rams. The list is endless but some of the most memorable are: Chuck Knox, a superior coach I greatly admire who tried to resurrect the glory days, but couldn't; John Robinson, another fine coach who brought Eric Dickerson to the Rams and built an offense around him and almost got to the big one; Ernie Zampese, an extraordinary offensive coordinator who had a great influence on younger coaches who still use his methods today; and Deacon Jones, charismatic and humorous, was one of the most ferocious defensive ends of all time as a member of the Rams "Fearsome Foursome," and is in the Hall of Fame. We were up in San Francisco in a bar grousing after a Rams loss and I asked him, "In the days when you played, Deak… what went through your mind when you charged a quarterback about to pass?"

He looked at me as if I were stupid, then said, with a laugh, "I'm gonna kill that sonofabitch!"

Then, referring to Steve Young, the San Francisco quarterback and how to take care of him (missing me by an inch), he said, "Give him a forearm and call 911! This game is violence! Knock their fucking heads off then drink their blood!" Jiggling the ice in his glass he shook his head and shifted his powerful body. "You know, in my day… there was discipline and dedication to the team. Now, it's changed… it's rough… a lot of these kids get confused. Too much money. They see dollar signs dancing in their head."

Jack Faulkner, a warm bear of man with a golden heart, has been with the Rams for an eternity as a coach and administrator. He became a close buddy and confidant. He still sits in his office in Santa Ana, studying opposing teams on videotape, then ships his brilliant and invaluable analysis to the Rams, now in St. Louis.

In the spring of 1982, during a *Dynasty* shooting break, I flew to Austin, Texas, and St. Edward's University to begin rehearsing the play *Equus*, a sexual-psychological drama about a psychiatrist and his young stable-boy patient who mysteriously blinds seven horses. Peter Shaffer's stylized play probes the boy's innermost mind with disturbing pursuit, and the eventual revelations are compelling and shocking. As the only professional working with a totally student cast it was an extremely rewarding experience, and Donald W. Seay, director of the university's theater program, did a fine job of staging. I've always enjoyed being with young people interested in the theater—their eagerness and budding potential, their vulnerabilities, and willingness to accept helpful criticism if it isn't laid on with a hammer. I was able to impart an approach, a way of working, giving them ideas on how to fulfill their tasks as actors. That, of course, is what the university had in mind when I was hired. I was also invited by the University of Texas Theater Department to give a lecture on acting. I've done it many times at various schools and I really enjoy talking to students and answering their provocative questions. To see young talent begin to develop, molded into an acceptable and sometimes extraordinary performance, is very gratifying. There's so much talent buried in all children. If the inclination is there, it's only a question of how to stimulate and encourage it to the surface. At the last performance after a two-week run, I found a collection of their notes and letters on my makeup table, thanking me for coming to St. Edwards and helping them. I was very touched. B. Lochlin, Westlake Picayune, Austin, Texas wrote "… as Dysart, guest artist Peter Mark Richman was superb. His performance had depth, spontaneity and a natural flavor, as though he were saying the lines for the first time."

When I returned to Los Angeles, I quickly resumed the niche I was known for—the bad guy personified with all possible variations. I've always enjoyed playing with Ricardo Montalban and his hit show *Fantasy*

Island. Emmet Bergholz was the cinematographer (a camera-operator on *Friendly Persuasion*) and always gave me the attention he would have given Clark Gable. I was never photographed better. This was one of several appearances I made on the show; this time I played the cowboy manager of singer Linda Blair—a truly nice kid who was growing up and whose head didn't spin around as it had in *The Exorcist*. In the story, she's making a recording comeback and finds out that the song she is singing was written by her dead boyfriend. However, he isn't dead, but horribly disfigured from a car crash that I, the despicable bad guy, was responsible for. In the end, I get my head bashed in, his disfigurement disappears with a kiss, and all is right with the world. It's a fantasy, right? Following that episode, just before resuming *Dynasty*, I guested on my favorite "couple" show, *Hart to Hart* with Robert Wagner, whose hair was never out of place nor was his sense of humor, and his fictional wife, the always gorgeous Stephanie Powers. Gabrielle Beaumont, who had directed me in *Dynasty*, helmed this "Western" story with a sure hand and a pleasant English smile. I was bumped off appropriately, but I did spend some time gabbing with Lionel Stander who was a running character on the show with a voice almost as low as Polly Adler. He revealed the dreadful predicament he'd experienced being blacklisted during the heyday of the wayward House Un-American Activities Committee, in surprisingly humorous terms. He also told me how weird it was to hear himself quoted in his actual testimony when he saw the play *Are You Now or Have You Ever Been?*

One day, my sixteen-year-old son, Lucas, called me from UCLA where he'd been a freshman for two weeks as a music major. "Dad, what's my social security number?"

"Why do you need your social security number?"

"They want to put me on staff as a piano accompanist (he was a violin major) and I'm getting a staff parking place!"

For four years Lucas didn't have to worry about the nightmare of parking on campus and was paid besides. By the time he graduated he was quite a budding conductor-composer, conducting campus musicals and operas (Puccini's *Johnny Scicci*)—and with a Fritz Zweig conducting scholarship in his pocket to study with Daniel Lewis at the University of Southern California (USC) where he received his master's degree in orchestral conducting. My eldest son, Howard, a piano major at UCLA, received a scholarship after graduation to the Disney-created California Institute of the Arts in Valencia, California. Then, to his surprise and ours, at his final recital after acquiring his master's degree in music, Leonid

Hambro, a fabulous pianist and his master-teacher at Cal Arts, asked Howard to join the faculty as a piano instructor. It was quite an honor; Howard taught there for three years before hanging up his own shingle.

Every day as I looked around me—at my life, my wife, my children—I was grateful and thanked God for all my blessings. Subud and the latihan had had such an influence on our lives, it was indeed beyond conventional measurement. The simple fact that since I had been opened in 1959—and now I was staring at 1983—the surge of God's power experienced in the latihan was still as awesomely mind-boggling and sweet as the day I first witnessed it. Of course, Subud is not a panacea, an immediate spiritual cure for all the difficulties of living. Subud is not that. It's a slow process, and slowly everything begins to change as the inner debris we are tenaciously holding on to is thankfully cleansed away. Sincerity and patience is required. I have always been sincere—patience is the tough part. Artistically, I was frustrated as hell—what creative artist isn't? All of my efforts always seem to go so far and never with the extra push that garners real recognition, and I belched a lot of complaining (to my wife, who was a constant reservoir of empathy). Despite all the obstacles, impediments, and negations of my endeavors, which always seemed to show up in one way or another, I felt blessed, protected, and guided to pick up and carry on. Every indifferent turn-down or brick wall rejection was just another hurdle to jump over, another test of my strength, as if to see how much I could take and how easily I could laugh off another door closing in my face. I'd begun to realize with a deeper understanding that life is a never-ending lesson. I became more and more willing to submit to being in the hands of my supremely patient, all-powerful teacher—God.

Dynasty continued to be a smash hit and the ratings swaggered at the peak. I was pleased to be part of its success, but I knew that my lawyer character wouldn't be expanded storywise. I would just maintain my position as Blake Carrington's confidant and friend and move the plot along. I was a recurring character contractually, and I knew that when I committed to the series. But now, in light of the show's enormous acceptance worldwide, it depressed me to have a limited participation. An actor always wants more to do in any project; it isn't a question of just picking up a check.

In 1983, during another lull in *Dynasty* shooting, I rashly jumped into a last-minute replacement for Robert Reed in a production of *Blithe Spirit*. We were to open at the Lobero Theater in Santa Barbara and I had less than a week to learn the complex farce-fantasy, Noel Coward lines.

The pressure was monstrous and during rehearsals I was wondering why I'd been so hasty to get back on stage under these exasperating conditions. But there was a plus—working with Barbara Rush again, who played my ex-wife, the ghostly, gray-faced, departed Elvira. When I got my words down as a harassed Charles, I enjoyed spouting Coward in a cultured British accent. I hadn't done Noel Coward since playing Eliot in *Private Lives* years before in summer stock and it was a kick. *Blithe Spirit* turned out to be a good production and an audience pleaser. Getting the juices flowing again full time in front of an audience does have rejuvenating rewards. As soon as we closed the show, I began shooting *Dempsey*, a television movie, playing Tex Rickard, the manager of Jack Dempsey. Treat Williams, a good young actor playing the champ, was a bit soft in the killer instinct department, but did a credible job overall. I've always felt comfortable wearing period costume as if I'd lived in that era, but walking into the massive, very run-down, turn of the century hotel in Pasadena where we shot many of the interiors gave me the creeps. There was an "old time" oppressive smell to the place—the green color of the walls; the hanging photographs of men in derbies, beards, and long moustaches; women in flowing dresses and bustles; prancing horses and ornate carriages. It was a dead atmosphere hovering around us like lead. I had to walk outside to the garden every so often just to breathe fresh air. It had happened to me before, an overpowering sense of the past—all those forces still hanging around and making themselves felt, trying to influence the present with their aura. It gave me a chill and made my hair stand on end.

Dynasty kept rolling along, counting over sixty episodes already completed in August of 1983. It was a phenomenon and looked stronger than ever. My periodic freedom from the show gave me an opportunity to get back into my studio and paint; when the muses tickled, I even found the time to write—or rewrite, I should say—my novel. I had had so many variations of rejections I was compiling a file for future reference. After Rosilyn Targ and I split, I put the book on the shelf, but now I was getting involved with a new agent, a lawyer by the name of Harold Lipton who was excited and eager to handle it, re-titled, as *Hollander's Deal*. He had all kinds of ideas and also thought the material could be a miniseries à la *Dynasty*.

In January 1984 I went to work again for my most consistent employer at Universal, Glen Larson, on a two-parter *Knight Rider*. I played two roles and two look-alikes. It was interesting when they put the film together to open the door as one character and stare at myself looking the same on the other side of the door. David Hasselhoff and Edware Mulhare tried desperately to solve the mystery of my two identical faces—one dastardly and the other a peach—and, of course, they finally did. Joel Rogosin, who had produced Longstreet, did the same for this hit series.

Samuel Landess, Helen's father, had gone through a trying period suffering with prostate cancer, but thankfully, surgery had granted him seven years of remission and appreciated time. Then the cancer returned and metastasized with a vengeance. Helen and I flew back to Albany to be of comfort and assistance. Sam was someone I truly loved. Sammy. What a guy—what an extraordinary, loving father-in-law who couldn't do enough for us and our kids and always found absolute joy in doing it. He knew he was dying and had accepted his predicament, but it wasn't a slam dunk—it isn't for anyone. How do you say all the things you want to express to someone you love who is leaving, never to be seen again? There are no simple answers. You wing it, and maybe find a way for some humor, and pray that God will bless and ease his last journey. A few weeks later, Sam died. And I lost another father.

In July 1984, a lucrative offer came my way that was difficult to turn down even though I had sworn I'd never perform in a daytime soap opera. A new NBC show called *Santa Barbara* was about to go into production immediately and the only other star they had signed was Judith Anderson. I thought if Miss Anderson, with her reputation, was willing to do a daytime soap then who was I to quibble? Aside from the fact that Jeffrey Hayden (Eva Marie Saint's husband), with whom I had worked before and was an old friend, was the director of the initial episode. I was to star as C.C. Capwell, the richest dude this side of a Lubbock, Texas—an oil baron who was not unlike Blake Carrington of *Dynasty*. On television, big money living big with screwed-up families playing out their lives in ostentatiously grand mansions was the rage of the eighties. So, after soulful deliberations concluding I'd gone as far as I would go on *Dynasty*, I opted out of my contract and signed on to *Santa Barbara*—unexpectedly taking on a whole set of other problems. Taping an hour show a day is a monstrous undertaking, at least under the conditions I was confronted with. There were young kids in my family and their friends, and due to union priorities they had to be photographed first. So, getting into makeup at 7 a.m., then rehearsing and blocking scenes for the camera, I would then have to sit around until the youngsters taped their scenes before getting to mine—usually not until after dinner! By that time, I was tired and looked like crap. Imagine—twelve hours after arriving at the studio you are just getting to perform! In addition, the night before shooting the next day's work the technical crew lighted the sets; they did not light the actors. Many days I worked until 1:00 or 2:00 in the morning before they called it quits, the grind beginning again at 7:00 a.m. for me. Once, while sitting around during the interminable waiting process, I had a conversation with a dear friend who had a featured role on the series—a now matronly, but still attractive, Virginia Mayo. She had been one of the most knockout beautiful of Hollywood leading ladies who could really act when given the opportunity. We were griping about the sacrificial waiting while the kids worked and wondered if it would ever change.

Of course, *Santa Barbara* was on its break-in run and Jeff Hayden was trying to work it all out, but there were too many difficulties. After a few weeks, my enthusiasm, hope, and interest absolutely disappeared. I don't believe my performances suffered, but I felt as if I were serving a jail sentence. I hated doing it with a passion and came to the conclusion (I knew it before) that I was not a soap actor and never would be.

On a lighter note: Once, during the early days of shooting, I remember being made up with Judith Anderson in the chair next to mine. I turned to this petite, great stage star who was getting up in years and said, "Judith… I really look forward to working with you."

She looked at me with a funny half smile and answered, "You better hurry."

We never did work together; she was in the opposing family and the scripts didn't involve us. I did enjoy working with a lovely young actress who played my daughter, a really sweet kid. I knew she was destined for stardom and it wouldn't take long. I was right; her name—Robin Wright (she also married Sean Penn). Three months later I was out of *Santa Barbara* by mutual agreement. I felt as if I had just crawled out of a suffocating tomb and I could begin to breathe again. Now after four years of *Dynasty* and an abortion in *Santa Barbara*, I was out of a job. I knew something would turn up, especially in episodic television, so I wasn't overly concerned.

Glen Larson hired me to appear in another Universal running hit with Lee Majors called *Fall Guy*. What kind of a character was I playing? My standard hard-as-nails, sneering, tough guy sonofabitch, of course. Shall I wear glasses, sport a moustache, or attach an itchy Van Dyke? I could lower my voice, come from Brooklyn, or maybe be a recent gangland transplant from London—just for variation. Always fussy, I had reached the point of getting over-particular about my wardrobe. Shall it be a pinstripe suit or a dark solid with hand-stitched lapel?—the sleeves slightly puffed at the shoulder, the jacket waist, tailored and trim—and please, take the bagginess out of the trousers rear-end. Anything to alter the appearance, the sound, and the mien of another bad guy! Then, there I am appearing in another Aaron Spelling-Doug Cramer success, *The Love Boat*, looking très elegant in a tuxedo and making lurid advances to a young beauty while we're dancing. If that wasn't bad enough, I'm observed by my wife, played by the lovely Florence Henderson, who was naturally distressed. In a later scene she tells me so, and then, of all things rotten, she accuses me of sexual improprieties with our teenage daughter! Heavens to Betsy, what a mess I'm in. Not even my good old friend Gavin MacLeod, the captain, could get me out of that one. Aaron Spelling and Doug Cramer, spectacularly prolific producers, had hit on a winning formula: multiple stories involving as many guest stars as possible in the same episode. *Fantasy Island*, *Dynasty*, *The Love Boat*, and *Hotel*—all with different tales running concurrently and beautifully wrapped in a satisfying golden ribbon at the conclusion. Of course, *Dynasty* was an evening soap opera not confined to an hour wrap-up, but many continuing involvements entangling the principle characters.

In early 1985, I guested on *Hotel* and it was like old home week seeing dear friends. Anne Baxter, with whom I'd worked in New York twenty-five years earlier on a *U.S. Steel Hour*, was now a running character and a classy addition to the series. We had a warm reunion and a pleasant lunch together. Barbara Rush, my fictional wife on many shows over the years, is now passionately kissing me on the ascending hotel elevator and elsewhere. Why? I'm wooing her away from her husband whom I'm representing as a lawyer—a very confused Howard Duff giving a pained and suffering good performance. Martha Scott, one of the most caring and gentle women I've ever met, was also a fine actress and a dedicated theater producer. She had co-founded the Plumstead Theater Society in 1968, a non-profit foundation to produce limited engagements of American classics. Her co-founders were Henry Fonda, Alfred de Liagre, and Robert Ryan. With Mr. de Liagre she had produced *Our Town* and *Front Page* starring Henry Fonda and Robert Ryan and then Fonda in *The Time of Your Life*. It was indeed an inspiration for Martha Scott to premiere a Plumstead Theater production for the opening of the newly named Henry Fonda Theater (originally the Carter DeHaven Music Box and then the PIX) on Hollywood Boulevard after his recent passing.

The play was *Twelve Angry Men* by Reginald Rose. It had been a highly successful television show in the 1950s and then a prestigious film with Henry Fonda in the leading role. Twelve impressive actors brought a sense of real Broadway to Tinseltown. I was privileged to be a part of this fine production directed by Robert Lewis, who was a founder of the Group Theater with Elia Kazan and Cheryl Crawford in the 1930s and the Actors Studio in the 1940s. He wore his overcoat of "Method" history in good humor and was fun to work with. I did catch him dozing off once or twice during the grueling rehearsals, but I won't hold that against him—I just smile in remembrance.

This jury-room drama is about twelve diverse white men with their own problems gnawing at them, locked in a stuffy room, all too eager to convict a black defendant on shoddy evidence and quickly go home. Only one man stands up against this bunch of bigots and semi-prejudiced humanity pleading for decency, a defendant's rights, and patience in getting the facts straight. The story is told with raw, blistering emotion, their personal lives unexpectedly laid bare before the elusive vote to convict or not is finally taken. I still suffer from a partially torn rotator cuff injury when, in the action, I had to get in between and prevent two violent jurors from slugging one another.

Six days before we opened, Jack Klugman, playing a bullying bigot, had to drop out of the show; cancerous polyps had been discovered on his vocal cords, a shock for all concerned to say the least. Vic Tayback replaced him and went on for the scheduled premiere, a task for any seasoned performer. Ken Kercheval played the Fonda role and brought a certain charm and honesty to the part. Other jurors in the remarkable cast were Howard Hesseman, John Randolf, David Opatoshu, Whit Bissel, Adam Arkin, and Jack Riley. I was Juror #4, a wealthy stockbroker and had my moments of "thoughtful perception and cutting furiousness." At one moment after a long, wandering speech, there was a shocked "OHHuhhh!" from the audience when I dramatically pulled a knife from my pocket and violently stabbed it into the table to make a point. The knife, similar to the defendant's knife and easily purchased anywhere, began to convince the group of his possible innocence, as I, a staunch "guilty" advocate, moved to the "not guilty" side.

The reviews were uniformly good.

In 1985, Helen and I and my youngest sons, Orien and Roger, flew to Philadelphia and settled in comfortably at the landmark Bellevue-Stratford Hotel. I had accepted the South Philadelphia High School

Alumni Association's invitation to receive the Athletic Hall of Fame Award. As captain and fullback of the powerful 1944 city championship football team, it was quite an honor, even though forty years had passed. Fifteen players from my team showed up—and what memories and feelings it evoked in all of us. After my acceptance speech, I read a short essay that I'd written about how the excitement and gratification that I'd experienced winning the championship had been a high point in my life that has never been equaled in anything else I'd ever done since. There was silence and a long pause when I finished, then the 550 dinner guests at the Centre Hotel exploded with applause. I was moved and had to dab my eyes. Later, I got a kick out of hearing one of the players tell my sons, "Your dad was a helluva football player!" Seeing their beaming faces, their arms around me, was worth the whole trip. Earlier in the day I'd taken them to the Philadelphia College of Pharmacy and Science to show them around. As we walked up the path to the entrance, a strange happening—we ran into Dr. Linwood Tice, the retired emeritus professor of pharmacy who had given me permission to skip some of his classes to appear on TV. Now an ardent fan, he was so pleased to see me and meet my family that I invited him to the banquet, seating him at the front table with Helen and the boys with a contingent of Philly relatives. When we left the college that day, driving down Spruce Street in the heavy traffic, looming before us was the University of Pennsylvania's Franklin Field where the championship had been won. "Dad, take us on the field!" the kids yelled. "Please, Dad… we wanna see where you played!" I made a sudden, jerky left turn into a stadium driveway without getting a ticket and parked. A few minutes later we were on the field in a deserted stadium, my excited kids running and jumping, catching imaginary passes and crossing the goal line victoriously. It was an incomparable feeling to stand there recalling the tension and the cheering crowd and explaining to my boys where and how it all happened—the playoff and championship games and the touchdowns I scored—remembering and sharing the vivid moments of an impassioned seventeen-year-old. On another day, I brought them to Passyunk Avenue to show them the neighborhood and the houses I'd lived in and my father's store, now a run-down furniture repair shop with "B. Richman, Decorator" still in the mosaic tile step. We were allowed in and made our way past stacked chairs, tables, and boxes, climbing the creaky stairs to the second floor. The once shiny hardwood floors were now scruffy and worn. Everything was a grimy, depressing mess, even the white, tiled bathroom with the luxurious sunken tub that was once very grand. I remembered my weekly bath and the remaining scum-ring where flowers would grow if planted, and I used to stand on my toes just to see myself in the mirror above the sink. I brought them into Gert's room, where she would sit up in bed listening to the radio and where my father had died in my arms—the wallpaper now peeling from the walls. Everything seemed so small and insignificant. We stood looking down on Passyunk Avenue from the bay windowed master bedroom. Here, stirred memories of my sister and my parents welled my eyes with tears.

We walked the streets where I'd lived and played as a kid—Mazzeo's barber shop where I first became fussy about my hair and how it should be cut, old man Mazzeo passing me off to his son, Ben, more sympathetic to my demands; Krutzke's Jewelry store, where I played with my skinny friend Warren; and the old Alhambra Theater, still standing, where I saw all those great films. I even showed them the smelly alleyways, still unstoppable—a far cry from anything they'd ever been exposed to. Then surprisingly, we ran into an old neighbor's daughter who recognized me and excitedly invited us all to her home for a spaghetti dinner. Every look and step brought a charge of remembrances that can never be erased from who I am—this place where I come from.

Lucas was the conductor of the Young Musicians Foundation Debut Orchestra from 1984 to 1986. During that time, he studied and worked with Leonard Bernstein and Michael Tilson Thomas at the Los Angeles Philharmonic Institute—and also as a conducting fellow in master classes with Pierre Boulez, André Previn, and Herbert Blomstedt. (I have a collector's item of a 45-minute video of Lucas in a conducting session with Leonard Bernstein, just the two of them.) I first met Lennie when Lucas was a violinist in the Hollywood Bowl Institute Orchestra for gifted young musicians that Bernstein conducted. Lucas had invited me to a rehearsal, and when it was over, I went up on stage to meet the famous maestro. He was very cordial, and putting his arm around my shoulder he said, "Your father is noble and patrician." I got a big kick out of that—in fact, I wrote it down.

In the fall of 1987 the Harvard-Radcliffe Club of Southern California presented a lifetime achievement award to Leonard Bernstein. The "Bravo Bernstein" evening was a celebrity-packed festive occasion. John Green, the revered composer ("Body and Soul"), produced the event with Charles Champlin who at that time was the entertainment editor of the *Los Angeles Times*. John was also a former president of the Young Musician Foundation and had asked Lucas to conduct a program featuring Bernstein's music.

During the dessert (we were sitting with Dudley Moore), the curtain parted and the resounding overture to *Candide* knocked us out of our seats. It was spectacular. I looked over at the next table to see the beaming face of the honoree and tears came to my eyes. Helen and I shared a proud look and held hands. My God, Leonard Bernstein was watching my son conduct his music. Of course, afterward there were hugs and kisses and lots of photo bulbs flashing. It was one of those memorable evenings for a couple of proud and grateful parents. John Green adored Lucas and in a humorous way thought of him as the son he never had, parenting only daughters. When he passed away, he willed Lucas his baton and stopwatch.

In 1988, Lucas received an important opportunity. He called from Europe and told us that he was one of four out of the original sixteen young conductors from around the world chosen to share the podium and tour with Leonard Bernstein and the Schleswig-Holstein Festival Orchestra. As a result, Lucas conducted in Germany; in Moscow, Russia, at Tchaikovsky Hall; and then in the "Proms" concert at Royal Albert Hall, London, where he raised his baton for the Brahms "Academic Festival Overture." That was a very big deal. Lucas told us that Bernstein would sit in the bassoon section, watch him (along with 6,000 in the audience), and then later in the dressing room quietly give him his critique! On occasion, with very little provocation, I will play the videotape of the London event for guests at our home and revel again in the performance of this young man. Also, while he was in Germany, Lucas received a call from Louis Spisto, executive director of the Pacific Symphony in Costa Mesa, California, who offered him the job as assistant conductor. He was thrilled and accepted his first position with a professional orchestra. The *Los Angeles Times* column headline declared: "Bernstein Protégé gets Pacific Symphony Post." We never missed driving down to see him conduct the "Pops" concerts and the children's concerts at the magnificent Orange County Performing Arts Center—proud parents marveling at the poise and professionalism for someone so young. I remember saying to him with a kiss and a hug when I first saw him conduct, "Lucas, you are major." Everything was beginning to happen for him.

I finished out the 1985 shooting season with another *Knight Rider*; an appearance on *Crazy like a Fox*; and finally as a dying Mafia boss taking his last, hoarse breath for *T.J. Hooker*—alias William Shatner in a police uniform. On the Fox show, a medical series playing a shady doctor (what else), I had a humorous conversation with John Rubinstein (Arthur

Rubinstein's son), who was the series lead. I told him he'd better listen to me carefully this time—because last time when he didn't, there were terrible consequences. He played Jesus on the *Heroes of the Bible* series in one episode and I was the voice of God.

Ted Knight had appeared on my show, *Cain's Hundred*, years earlier as a very straight and serious FBI agent. In 1986, the first TV show of the year I worked on, taped in front of a live audience was *The Ted Knight Show*. He had achieved fame as the zany news broadcaster on *The Mary Tyler Moore Show*—and now, deservedly, had his own spot. For me, this was only the second time I'd ever guested on a comedy series. The first was well received as Reverend Snow on *Three's Company*. The producers in this constricted business thought of me only as a serious actor, never fancying the thought that I was an actor of many colors, comedy included. Oh, yes, I did play a goofy pharaoh on *Electra Woman and Dyna Girl* awhile back, but that was a character oddity in the cartoonish class. On Ted's show, I played a distinguished French underwater explorer à la Jacques Cousteau (spouting a French dialect) with a charming manner. I try to enlist Ted's wife, Nancy Dussault, an amateur photographer, to travel with me and take pictures of our exploration, causing hilarious stress for Ted and getting big laughs by the innocent misunderstandings. It was an extremely successful segment and it remains an enigma to me why I wasn't tapped to do more comedy shows. Unless you're seen doing it by the people who are hiring or an agent takes the film or videocassette under his arm and says, "You gotta see this!"—you're destined to stay in the box you've created and are known for. The box was choking me.

Stephen J. Cannell, a prolific writer and producer, had another successful show with *Hardcastle & McCormick* starring Brian Keith, a fine actor and a friend. I guested as a… uh, bad fellow, a very bad fellow with some terrific scenes of festering violence with my former associate, Stuart Whitman (I am stealing his wife, too—played by Abby Dalton) and a nasty punching fight with Brian, who is a retired Judge! Of course, I lose.

I enjoy doing voiceovers for commercials, and recording a voice for an animated television series was equally gratifying and lucrative. However, playing the Phantom with my breathy, lower register on the cartoon *Defenders of the Earth* led to other consequences. There was a young actor in the recording sessions, playing the voice of the young Flash Gordon who was a gentleman, a good actor, and had a warm personality. I liked him, and occasionally during the time of completing sixty-five shows that took almost a year and a half in 1985–1986, I would say to myself, Loren

Lester is a nice kid… and he should meet my daughter. Well, at the wrap party after the production ended, Helen met Loren and said to me, "He should meet Kelly."

I said, "I'm working on it."

The next day I called Loren and said, "Loren would you like to meet my daughter?"

"Wait a minute," he said. I waited and then he got back on the phone and said, "Yes!" He had gone to get the family photo holiday card we send out every year and after taking another look at Kelly, he jumped. They hit it off on the first date and in October 1988 they were married! Walking down the aisle with my only daughter, so beautiful in her bridal dress, was a moving experience I shall never forget. It's just amazing what the Phantom can accomplish!

Vienna and Leonard Bernstein

IN 1986, ON A "GOVERNMENT AND ARTS TOUR" organized by Tarky Lombardi, a New York State Senator, we Pan Am'd to Munich, Germany, and then a tram to Salzburg, Mozart's birth place. After climbing four flights of his cold, narrow stairwell, I was thrilled to touch his piano! This was the beginning of a privileged trip of seeing the sights and being wined and dined sumptuously. The high point in Vienna included Leonard Bernstein's *A Quiet Place* at the Vienna Opera House and then being escorted back stage to see Lennie himself. When he saw us, he hugged me and kissed Helen and said, "How's your brilliant son?" (A moment not to forget). As it happened, two years later, Lucas shared the podium with Bernstein, at his invitation, touring with the Schleswig-Holstein Festival Orchestra in Russia, Germany, and England. The view from our room at the Budapest Hilton overlooking the city was breathtaking, although the not-so-blue Danube looked ordinary, snaking out before us under the many bridges separating Pest from Buda. We participated in all the tours and VIP festivities in the gray, drab communist city where everything seemed to have stopped in 1897 when they celebrated Hungary's one thousandth year. If I saw the interior of one more church I was sure to faint dead away, but the people were friendly and warm with an abundance of old world charm. After ten days on our travels, we were so close to Paris, how could we not visit? So, we decided to fly there while the rest of the group journeyed home. It was raining heavily when we arrived at the DeGaulle Airport and taxied to the Grand Hotel—Paris was even looking good in the rain. On the following day, April 16, 1986, it was my birthday and I was suddenly… uh, fifty-nine years old. There and there was no doubt that I was looking at senior citizenship sooner than I ever expected.

A special day was being planned by my adorable traveling companion. After a charming breakfast, it was museum time at the Jeu de Paume and the Orangerie where all the Impressionists have been enshrined. In the evening, we had dinner at the internationally famous Lasserre Restaurant with Yves Montand sitting at the next table, who smiled and waved at me as the pianist played the musical theme for *Dynasty* while we were having our coffee. *Santa Barbara* and *Dynasty* were running on TV at the same time, so I was very big in Paris at that moment—people sticking a pen and paper in my face saying, "Deenasty! Deenasty!" A telegram from my kids—"Happy birthday, Dad. Do you love Paris in the springtime? Cole Porter sends his love to you and Mom and so do we." Lucas, Howard, Kelly, Orien, Roger got me all soppy. Helen too.

The apogee of my photographic talents was reached at the Louvre, not necessarily by snapping away at the glorious Delacroixes, the Davis, and the Gericaults but by capturing Helen looking at the *Mona Lisa*, her reflection immortalized on the painting's plastic encasement.

We said goodbye to Paris as we boarded an Air France eleven-hour flight to Los Angeles, very concerned about the possibility of Libyan terrorists planting a bomb on our plane. That was then; today, there are more than Libyan crazies to worry about.

Suddenly, In Charge

TO BE A MEMBER of the Board of Trustees of the Motion Picture & Television Fund, serving people in the entertainment industry is an honor and a responsibility. I was already actively involved on the Hospital Committee (Accreditation and Quality Assurance), the Case Committee, and the Building Committee. As the Board's "art expert," I had instituted an inventory and evaluation process for whatever artwork had been gifted to the fund. Valuable paintings were now appraised and sold at auction rather than kept in unsafe storage. As an example, the estate of Charles Laughton and Elsa Lancaster had several paintings I put up at Christie's that brought thousands of dollars to benefit the fund. I also had some of our hanging collection cleaned and restored and even reframed a beautiful Norman Rockwell oil painting of Judy Garland, a gift of Gregory Peck, which now hangs in the medical library. My responsibility jumped seventy notches when Jack Dales, the board president, appointed me to be the chairman of the building committee that was to oversee all design, architecture, planning, and construction for the fund's ten-year building master plan, which would eventually double the occupancy of the country house and hospital on the grounds in Woodland Hills. It would be a 50-million-dollar campaign. The first order of business was the construction of a new 25-million-dollar, eighty-one bed skilled nursing facility. I was slightly flabbergasted by my assignment, but I recovered enough to shake the congratulatory hands of my high-powered committee. They were dynamic men in lucrative executive positions at every studio, and there I was, an actor not knowing when his next job would surface, in charge of the whole bunch. In June 1986, Eastman Kodak donated $500,000 for a therapy center in the hospital, and I was the emcee for the event. In my opening statement I said, "Forty-five years ago Jean Hersholt, Louis B. Mayer, Mary Pickford, and Ronald Reagan stood near this very spot to break ground for the first buildings of the Motion Picture Country House and Hospital. Ours is the only industry in the country to provide health care, social welfare and retirement facilities for its own workers…"

In November 1986, at another festive show of support attended by many celebrities, there was a dedication of the George Burns Intensive Care Unit for which he'd given a million dollars. I again emceed the event and commented on Burns' recurrent role in films as an anthropomorphic God: "We had a problem with the weather earlier, but we called George and you see what happened." (The sun was shining.) I welcomed him as a witness "to the dedication of his own special place on Earth." When the bronze plaque was unveiled of George smiling, holding a cigar, he was in good form at the microphone and had us all quickly laughing.

Then in December, the long-awaited groundbreaking ceremony took place. Several hundred residents and members of the industry were present, including film stars, Charlton Heston, Janet Leigh, Walter Matthau, Cesar Romero, and Edie and Lew Wasserman (who had given $5 million). Mae Clarke was there too (a resident who had been squashed in the face with a grapefruit by James Cagney). I was again the master of ceremonies, and when I introduced Bob Hope, who had contributed another million, I said, "I am very happy today. I've always wanted to be on the same bill with Bob Hope and now I am!" He was delicious in his humorous and gracious commentary. Then, in a chosen spot underneath the enormous temporary tent where the guests were seated, a select group of us took turns with a shovel in our hands to lift a symbolic pile of dirt—the photographers snapping away. Construction had now officially begun, and with my wonderful committee I was Adam's apple deep into everything. There wasn't a square inch of any part of the hospital being built and underground that we didn't meditate, ruminate, digest and act on. Later in the finishing stages—personally, working with the architect, decorator, or freely on my own—I became the artistic guide for the way the building would look in almost every way. I found myself becoming the final word on the choice of fabrics, tile, paint, carpeting, and even furniture for hospital rooms. I basically had very little opposition because, thankfully, my choices and colors were tasteful and attractive. I remember well how I nixed mahogany wood as the choice for hand-rails in the corridors, half-moon headboards in the rooms, and all trim to accentuate the wall coverings. "Too dark and depressing," I said, insisting on light oak for all wood used. It remains today, beautifully coordinated throughout the building.

During and after all of this I was also asked to redecorate. Yes, redecorate, reupholster club chairs, and re-carpet the corridor and twenty-seven rooms in the Frances Goldwyn Lodge; do the same (select roof tile, paint, doors, and lighting fixtures) for a new cottage funded by another movie icon, Howard W. Koch; repeat the effort totally in the old Alzheimer wings, funded by Kirk Douglas that is now called "Harry's Haven" after his father—where earlier I had requested special funding and received ($75,000) from the full board to build a new façade and entrance to the Alzheimer unit. Later, at another Motion Picture Fund facility, the Bob Hope Health Center in Hollywood, I performed my usual stuff, including a pleasing exterior paint job. I was so deeply involved in so many projects, one night sitting in my den with decorator books, plans, sample fabrics, and tiles spread out before me, Helen walked in and asked, "Are you going into a new profession?"

Just two days before the official opening dedication of the eighty-one bed skilled nursing facility in Woodland Hills (a full hospital with two operating rooms), there were exclusive decisions that had to be rendered only by Lew and Edie Wasserman—where to put their designation plaques and signage. On the phone after an exhaustive effort, I finally got Edie and Lew to commit to meeting me at the hospital—their long black limo pulling into the driveway on a Saturday morning. They were both helpful and accommodating. With that accomplished, after they left, I was again standing on a ladder in the lobby of the hospital with a ruler in my hand (my wife's eye helping) attaching bronze letters to the wall with an arrow pointing that read: "The Edie and Lew Wasserman Wing." Voluminous accounts have been written about the life of the Wassermans and unfortunately, in some people's eyes, not always favorable. Personally, I have always found them to be warm and responsive, kind, caring, and considerate in our relationship—and extremely generous in their efforts for the Motion Picture and Television Fund. Enough cannot be said about Edie, with whom I have sat on the board for years. She has been absolutely relentless pursuing affluent film personnel to contribute time and money for the needs of the Fund and hospital—successfully. Without her pursuit, so much good wouldn't have happened.

There was an oblivious chain-smoker puffing away behind me that was making my nose and throat sore and my eyes runny. I wanted to strangle him and I may have if the 747 hadn't landed in Madrid, and none too soon. How did we endure all that smoking? It was April 1987 and we were again included on the Government and Arts Tour, this time to Spain with New York State Senator Tarky Lombardi, Carol and Alfred Landess (who had arranged it for us), and twenty-five legislators and their spouses. We were all a bit groggy and eager to settle ourselves at the majestic Palace Hotel, one of the leading hotels of the world built in 1912—elegance to the extreme. On the way to the American Embassy for a briefing, we had a chance to really see Madrid; a beautiful city, not unlike Paris; well laid out, clean, and cared for with parks bursting with flowers. The American ambassador droned on and on about Spanish-American relations and I was a goner in five minutes, almost falling out of my chair. Helen jabbed me awake, but when I looked around, several senators also had their heads askew, eyes closed, and mouths wide open.

That evening we were hosted to a delicious dinner at Posada de la Villa—lamb roasted in a huge brick oven open fire. Then about ten o'clock, my enterprising wife convinced a bunch of us to go looking for "tapas" (specialty dishes). A whiskery taxi driver took us to Old Madrid and a celebrated hole in the ground that I'm sure hadn't changed in 200 years. Helen got her tapas, with lots of laughter and Sangria to wash it down. It was a kick being with these politicians and lobbyists—not talking politics, really, but just sharing the company of energetic and friendly people. On the way back to the hotel, we passed through a huge square, picturesque and charming, the pigeons bravely nibbling at our shoes as we sat. I fell in love with Madrid.

For twenty-five years I've looked through my art book on the Prado. Now I was there, viewing a collection of incredible works by El Greco, Titian, Murillo, Tintoretto, and Velasquez. The Goyas knocked me out—so fresh, loose and modern. I'm convinced that Goya influenced the German expressionists and the great Egon Schiele—Degas, Manet, and Picasso for sure. I see people on the streets of Madrid that are in his paintings—men with drooping mustaches, their black eyes piercing the distance; full-faced women with bright smiles and hair pulled back in a knot. They are all there on canvas. Goya had an uncanny ability to catch life in the face—a superb, innovative, and provocative genius.

The Royal Palace was so lush, spacious and golden; it defied your sense of reality that such spectacular luxury was even possible. Just the porcelain outer entrance to the king's toilet was mind-boggling, and to see the potty itself for his royal butt with its red velvet cushion was a definite giggler. Seeing the vast display of Spanish armor, several violently pierced, it wasn't difficult to imagine how horribly some combatants died in the fifteenth century. In the late afternoon, we gathered at the Delegates Building (congress) for a photo session with the Minister of Culture and a lecture about how Spain was now a democracy. They showed us the bullet holes where a coup had been attempted and thwarted. The present king refused to accept military rule. He was not going to be another Franco! Now that's nobility!

It was my birthday, again in another foreign country. I was sixty years old and feeling pretty damn good for an old fella. Helen presented me with a lovely card at breakfast, a photo attached of her holding our son, Orien, as a little boy. I became a bit juicy through my smile. (Helen always knows my tender spots.) We had been married now for thirty-four years and our marriage had been a good one, solid, and spiritually deeply satisfying and meaningful (she had brought us to Subud). I knew I had a rare woman who had carried our five children. I told her again how much I loved her and appreciated her mommy-hood and her sweetness through it all. Then I opened a fancy package containing a blood red silk tie created by a Madrid designer—very chic.

That morning we all took a bus trip to the ancient city of Toledo. Our guide, Pepe, assured us that it had remained much the same since the 12th century. We visited a cathedral with an amazing gothic structure that took 500 years to complete, the first stone having been laid 250 years before Columbus discovered America. The church had an astounding collection of towering religious paintings by El Greco. It was humbling to be in the presence of such magnificent work. My favorite was *Espolio* (Christ being stripped of his clothes), a huge masterpiece. One of the most intriguing tours of the day over cobblestones and narrow, twisted streets was the visit to the Synagogue of the Transito, which dated from 1366, showing the harmonious mixture of architecture when Arabs constructed buildings for the Jews and the cedar wood was transported from Lebanon. It's interesting to note that some writers credit Toledo being founded by Jews in 590 B.C. Prior to 1450, the Moors, Jews, and Catholics lived harmoniously here before pandemonium hit. King Ferdinand and Queen Isabella, prompted by the frenzied Catholic Church, expelled the minorities out of Spain when they wouldn't convert. It was the beginning of chaos and the horrible Inquisition.

After a delicious partridge luncheon at Parador Del Conde de Orgath, the whole group toasted me and sang "Happy Birthday." When the cake arrived, I ad-libbed a humorous speech about reaching thirty-six and blew out the few candles. In a private chat with Tarky Lombardi about the New York State legislature, he said, "It was such a pleasure to have you with us." I complimented him for bringing such a divergent group of personalities together and added, "Please come to California and do the same for that antagonistic bunch up in Sacramento!"

In the evening, Carol and Alfred, whom I love dearly, hosted us for a birthday dinner at the famous Horches restaurant. I was mortified when the designer tie my wife gave me that morning suffered a thick layer of onion cheese soup.

In our hotel room, we watched a fervent Good Friday procession from our balcony, a spectacle from the Middle Ages. The devout crowd of thousands was riveting—tears in women's eyes as a saint's statue passed, prayers on their lips, strings of beads turning in their hands. Some walked barefoot in the procession with long, clanking symbolic chains on their ankles. I remembered similar parades of penance I had seen as a boy in South Philadelphia, also frighteningly devotional and gloomy. The following day, we flew to Seville and checked into the fabulous Alfonso XIII Hotel—old world splendor with Moorish architecture. Alfred and I went to Easter Sunday mass at the Seville Cathedral, the largest gothic structure in the world, the building begun in 1402. It was so incredibly ornate and rich, with canvasses hanging by Murillo and Zubaran. I couldn't believe it but there I was—standing at the tomb of Christopher Columbus, four imposing statues at the corners as protective guardians.

I was sitting with Alfred among all the worshippers, hundreds of them in these medieval surroundings fervently in prayer during the ritual service—the resurrection of Christ (a Jew), the organ blasting away, and I had the feeling that the Phantom of the Opera would come swinging down by rope and steal away one of the nuns, a pretty one—if there was one. I was touched by the two nuns who sat behind us, one in black and the other in gray. They were in their middle eighties, fingering their beads, occasionally reading, glasses on their noses, and bent over permanently from all their deep commitment and devotion. So many years of belief and trust in the Catholic Church. Why did I find it so depressing and this service so distant from the people? Maybe… as in all organized religions, the real content was missing. Only the ritual remains.

The afternoon was a radiant 86 degrees and since we were in Sevveeya, how could we not go to the Plaza de Toros, the finest ring in the world to see the bullfights, especially the first bullfight of the season? I swear, it was the Super Bowl but they weren't playing football. What a spectacle! Magnificent Hedy Lamarr-looking women, some with tiaras in their hair, wealthy, well dressed men, all cheering their favorite matador. I felt transported and thought I was watching Tyrone Power making his "Veronicas" in *Blood in the Sand*, the fantastic color and excitement and roar of the exultant crowd pounding my heart. We had great seats in the third row and Helen had her hands over her eyes the whole time and couldn't wait to leave. I understood; it was violent and messy, but what a thrilling experience—this ballet of artful killing. I loved Seville. There was so much going on—not only in the bullring, but in the streets, the restaurants and bars. You could feel the vibrancy, a city of life in the here and now. (While strolling in Seville I ran into Bob Shapiro, a former agent of mine, and John Malkovich. They were shooting a film nearby.)

The next day, I was again appalled by the condition of some of the masterpieces hanging in a small museum in another chapel we visited. All the great ones were there. I mean, I'm talking about a twenty-foot high Goya! If a Van Gogh recently sold for $40 million at Christie's, what were these paintings worth? Unfortunately, they were uncared for, needed immediate restoration and cleaning. For many it was too late, they were just rotting away. (My remembrances of 1987—God knows what they're like today.)

We went to the massive Alcazar (Palace) of Seville, built in 1326 by the Moors (Hebrew writing and a Star of David in the window glass), and walked through the breathtaking gardens. I wonder if the composer Manuel de Falla had this place in mind when he composed "The Gardens of Spain?" We took a bus ride through the fertile, rolling hills wine country of Jerez de La Frontera to the Domecq Winery, 285 years of producing the finest sherry of Spain. After the tour and wine tasting in a mammoth building that housed enormous barrels of wine, each one the size of a truck, I noticed on one of them the signature, Placido Domingo. The Domecq representative suddenly asked me if I would like to sign their celebrity barrel, but he would have to get a special marker. By that time everyone was moving outside and boarding the bus so I just smiled and said, "When I come again." On the way to Granada, we stopped in Cordoba, an ancient city with an astounding history of conquests and defeats. Standing inside the massive Mosque, the epitome of Spanish-Muslim art, I secretly scratched a mark on an alabaster column that was 2000 years old. It was most peculiar to go to the respected Jewish Quarter and at the entrance see a statue of Maimonides, the great Jewish philosopher, then visit the empty shell of the Synagogue of Cordoba knowing there are no Jews in Cordoba and there hasn't been since the Spanish inquisition of 1492. Convert to Catholicism or be damned and banished, you Jew bastards!

Millions of spaced and uniform olive trees were in continual view for two hours as far as the eye could see as the bus rolled on to Granada. Olive oil countryside, where it all began, before reaching your dinner table salad dressing. We finally arrived and settled in comfortably at the Victoria Hotel. In the morning, still half asleep, we went to The Alhambra to see the fortress and castle built in 1236 by the Arabs, an architectural marvel. The splendor of the "Gardens of Allah" and the erotic concubine quarters stir the imagination. Another example of the Jews and Arabs having lived harmoniously together in the past was an imposing fountain given by the Jews as a gift; a copy of the fountain in Solomon's Temple depicting the twelve tribes of Israel.

With hardly any sleep, again we were on the bus at 5:00 a.m. for a three-hour, bleary-eyed bus ride to Malaga for an Iberia Airlines flight to Madrid and then on to New York. After all the changes and switching of flights, we arrived home with zero bags. All were lost and it took days to retrieve them. It didn't matter. Hugging and kissing the kids was all we needed.

How Do You Spell Purgatory?

I HAVE ALWAYS PRIDED MYSELF on being a man of smarts who has had complete and knowing control of my finances, my investments, and expenditures—wisely enough to maintain a monetarily secure marriage and to comfortably raise five children with their multiple needs and education. Then, I made a mistake—a bad one. I entrusted someone else with my money. I thought it was time in my life to have a financial advisor who would protect and guide me to financial security for the future. After having had such a memorable trip in Spain, it was the perfect time to get shocked to the core. Imagine what it feels like when the day after I get home I receive a phone call from this broker who tells me, rather matter of factly, like dropping a quarter in a slot machine, that I had lost thousands and thousands of my hard-earned dollars—just like that! They were gone—in a whiff—up the chimney, irretrievably like heat and smoke. I froze.

"What? What the hell are you talking about?"

I found out very quickly. This evil, conniving-rat-scum-lowlife-sonofabitch, who relished other people's money and used it to enrich himself, had been churning and arbitraging my account with options, pocketing huge commissions, and was driving me to ruin very quickly. Reeling and in a daze and so angry, the veins in my neck looked like ropes—tied ones. It was panic-scary-time, and I had to stop the bleeding immediately. I called a lawyer friend who turned me over to a couple of other lawyers who handled this sort of thing. They were able to put a lock on my account before it disappeared completely; then we instituted a lawsuit against the brokerage house and the manager who was in cahoots with the broker. This episode was one of the worst in my life. It took over a year to resolve and on the advice of counsel, I settled. The firm wrote a check, but I accepted a loss of $400,000 plus legal fees. To pursue the lawsuit further would have taken years and there were no guarantees. I remember sitting there, staring at these parasitic, corporate bastards in their Brooks Brothers suits and striped ties who had flown in from New York, waiting for me to sign on the dotted line—and thinking, what if I kicked the most arrogant one in the balls, would that affect the settlement? We also had a criminal case against the broker if we wanted to pursue it, but Helen talked me out of it. She didn't have the strength nor the stomach for it. "Do you?" she asked me. "And all those legal fees?" We tried to put it all behind us. The broker in question will get what he deserves some day, and maybe he already has. I learned a hell of a good lesson: Never turn anything over to anyone else what I am very capable of doing myself.

On June 22, 1987, Bapak Muhammad Subuh Sumohadiwidjojo completed his remarkable autobiography, and the next day he died. Subud members the world over were deeply saddened and mourned his passing, but were indeed filled with extreme gratitude for who he was and what he had brought to them, my wife and I included. It had changed our lives completely and continues to do so.

Bapak, an ordinary Indonesian who was extraordinarily blessed by the grace of God, had been given a great task to bring what he had received to all of humankind—a literal contact with the Almighty, if they wished to receive it. Bapak had been given this contact, the same contact received by the spiritual messengers of old—Abraham, Moses, Jesus, and Muhammad. The only difference was that the contact Bapak brought can be passed, one to another, unlike the days of old when it died when the messenger died. If all this sounds peculiar and far-fetched, I'm sorry... and please forgive me. After all these years of doing the latihan, I don't carry a speck of doubt. It's the truth as I know it.

I wasn't alone as a devoted Rams football follower. Michael Wayne, now deceased, John Wayne's son and a dear friend of mine, was also a Rams booster and on their executive board. Michael and I were both trustees on the Motion Picture and Television Fund Board and one day after a meeting at the hospital he said to me nonchalantly, "Would you like to go to London with the Rams?" It was like asking me if I wanted to take a temporary trip to heaven to see if I liked it. Travel with the Rams to London? Even my wife who, up to that point, was not a football advocate, suddenly had her ears perking up and paying attention to my every word.

In August 1987, the 747 charter to London with 9 million pounds of Rams was a long and pleasant flight to remember, except I don't know how these enormous guys could sit in such miserably cramped seats without requiring medical attention afterwards. For me, it was a feast of football—hours of relaxed conversation with the players, the coaches, and the executive personnel. Everybody knew my face from television, but I was the one who felt more privileged in the exchange. I had a warm chat with coach John Robinson, who had had up and down results with the team. He invited me to practice in London and said he'd give me a ball to throw around! Had some nice words with the great running phenomenon, Eric Dickerson, and my favorite offensive lineman, Jackie Slater, a gentle giant. Ernie Zampese, the new offensive coordinator and an innovating genius, chatted with me about Jim Everett and what a fine passing talent he was carrying out his schemes. Fritz Schurmer and his wife, Peggy, were happy to see us. Fritz, one of my favorite people of all time and a great defensive coordinator, expressed great enthusiasm for the coming season "and playing in a foreign country will be fun." Dick Bass, former Rams backfield star, stopped at my seat for a friendly few words before I dozed off for a few minutes watching a flickering *Maltese Falcon*. I think I had twenty minutes of sleep the whole trip. Barbara Rush, sitting behind me with press agent Warren Cowan, was out cold, and so was my partner for life sitting on my left.

Stretching my legs, I said hello to Gil Haskell, the backfield coach. He talked real football to me about different teams in the league, where we stood, changing a player from a guard to a tackle, and the difficulties of player development. Wonderful inside stuff. He was the one who first invited me to come to Fullerton to watch the Rams preseason practice and to bring my sons. A gentleman sitting a few rows in front of us with Gene Autry turned out to be James Roosevelt, son of Franklin D. and Eleanor. He was with his wife, Mary, who has since become a friend. While we were waiting for our bags, Helen told him the story of how, when she was an apprentice in summer stock, his mother had invited the company to Hyde Park and had posed for a photograph with her—both in bathing suits. James was shocked and smiled when he said, "I never saw a photo of my mother in a bathing suit!"

After we checked into the Britannia Hotel, I scurried around to get my pounds and pence. Then we were so exhausted that we fell asleep in our room like the dead for a couple of hours. When we woke up, we didn't know what time it was, we just wanted to get to the theater—any theater!

At the very last moment we were just being seated as the curtain went up in the old Garrick Theater, built by W.S. Gilbert in 1889, and despite our fatigue from the time changes, we proceeded to laugh our asses off at a farce called *When Did You Last See Your Trousers?* The English do this sort of thing so well; it was a lesson for any actor. Following the show, we wandered around enjoying this vibrant, historical city full of theaters and creative activity, finally settling in for some lamb tandoori at a little Indian restaurant on Irving Street. The next morning, we had breakfast at the hotel with Andy Fenady, a film director, and his wife, Mary Frances. Then with our walking shoes raring to go, we sauntered through Berkeley Square, memorialized in so many English novels, and then to Piccadilly Circus. Talk about Los Angeles smog—the carbon monoxide here was so thick it took up residence in our tonsils and hung around unwanted all day. We cut across to St. James Park, so green and lushly beautiful. It was August 4 and the Queen's birthday, so the crowds were out and we stood among them and watched the changing of the guard and military parades at Buckingham Palace. My God, what tradition, a heartfelt show of patriotism and faith fully expressed. I'm always touched by that. I loved it and the people—their civility and politeness. I photographed a smiling Helen with two Bobbies, courteous but ill at ease, at the gate guarding #10 Downing Street, the essence of Great Britain embodied in so many books and films. It was a thrill just to stand there. It started to rain heavily so we hailed a taxi back to the hotel and ran into John Shaw, the Rams executive and advisor to Georgia Frontiere—one of the shrewdest men in football I've ever met, who later was responsible for the Rams' move to St. Louis. We have a warm relationship and he is always more than interesting to talk to.

That evening a lovely party was given by Georgia at the Hurlingham Club by the Thames. Strolling the historical grounds, we chatted with everybody. The young Rams players were thrilled to meet a face they had seen a hundred times on TV. They're star nuts and I'm Rams nuts. John Robinson and I had a wonderful conversation talking about our kids, art, and, of course, football. I told him my theory that sports and acting are related—the performance aspect, and the volatile risibility of an actor's emotions being similar to that of a football player—at least in my case it was. In the morning, I was reluctant to get on a bus again for an all-day-affair-Rams-party beginning with Westminster Abbey where the coronation takes place, but I was glad I did. It was something you do once in a lifetime.

Fascinating stuff to stand in the tombs of Rudyard Kipling and Lord Byron—and to find out that Ben Johnson was only given a foot of space and is the only person ever buried there standing up. We also visited the tombs of Queen Elizabeth and Mary Queen of Scots. We were then off to the Tower of London. Climbing the circular stairs, we stepped into an isolated room where prisoners were shackled who'd been condemned to die by beheading or being drawn and quartered. Their names, still visible, were scratched on the walls. The confined premises and atmosphere were shockingly brutal, and after observing more than I cared to absorb, I needed some fresh air. Where did we end up? Standing on the spot where Ann Boleyn had her head chopped off.

The next day Helen crapped out on me so I cabbed it to the National Gallery alone and went through one of the great art galleries of the world. I lingered long in the modern wing with Degas, Renoir, Manet, Monet, and the many Cezannes. I then viewed about twenty major Rembrandts and Reubens, astounded by the play of light and subtle color changes. To stand in front of such masters and knowing what an effort it takes to create such brilliant work always thrills and humbles me. It was an absolutely wondrous place and I hated to leave, but I had to meet Helen at the Palace Theater for a performance of *Les Misérables* at 2:30. The musical was fantastic, one of the finest productions I'd ever seen. Everything about it was just fabulous. Tears were rolling down my cheeks and Helen was wiped out. I was so impressed with London and what a bustling theater city it was. There was so much going on—and what a place for an actor! We called home and spoke to all the children. It was sweet and heart tugging. Lucas was conducting the UCLA production of *The Boys from Syracuse* at the Doolittle Theater and told us, "John Green came to the opening and loved it!"

In the evening, we bravely took a confusing subway ride to Shepard's Bush, then walked to Uxbridge Road and the London Subud house. It was good to do the latihan and to meet and share lovely moments with our English brothers and sisters. Afterward, a traditional salamatan or party was being held to commemorate forty days since the death of Bapak Subuh. My son Orien, who had reached his eighteenth birthday in June, had been opened in Subud and was now doing the latihan. He wants to be an actor and will be entering Pierce College and then will transfer to UCLA in two years as a theater major. My children can pursue whatever they wish as long as they're sincere about it. So far, Howard and Lucas are in Subud and now Orien. Roger is not old enough for the latihan and my daughter, Kelly, is resistant.

I went to the Rams practice at Crystal Palace and got all pumped up talking to the players in the locker room while they were getting taped and ready. Looking at the players from afar or on TV, their massive bulk and pads adding to the mistaken impression, you forget how young they are. They're kids, most in their twenties and still wide-eyed and vulnerable. I watched them go through a full team bump-and-go, non-scrimmage practice with the Denver Broncos. Eric Dickerson looked great. On the Broncos, that fella John Elway wasn't too shabby.

That evening we went to the Comedy Theater to see *Breaking the Code*, an intriguing play based on a true story of a homosexual man who broke the German code during World War II. My life hasn't led me there, but I feel I could be on the London stage and flourish. So much theatrical history and dedication. I haven't felt that way since I left New York. The next morning Helen and I taxied to the fantastic Tate Gallery. So many superb works—it was a meal too rich to digest. Surprisingly, some "story" paintings of the Victorian period were also knockouts. We scooted out of there at 1:45 to Her Majesty's Theater to try to find somebody to sell us tickets to *The Phantom of the Opera*, but the scalpers were unreasonable, so we dashed across the street to the Haymarket to see *Melon*, a play about infidelity, with Alan Bates. He's a good actor, but he remained external, only skimming the surface of what this interesting play was about.

When we got back to the hotel after a quick dinner, the coordinator who provided services for the Rams suddenly asked us if we'd like to see *Phantom* for free and handed us tickets! Wha? We jumped into a taxi and coaxed the driver to "push it along, ole boy!" enabling us to only miss the first twenty minutes. We had excellent seats and it was entertaining, but it wasn't *Les Miz*, but for what we paid it was tremendous. What a day, we were reeling, but it was wonderful—and tomorrow—the big game!

There was a vibrating tingle in the air. American football at Wembley Stadium in London—the Rams against the Denver Broncos! Georgia F. gave a huge luncheon at the Wembley Conference Center and I think half of England was there. The weather was overcast and there was a sudden downpour. Uh, oh… but then all the adorably sexy Rams cheerleaders came over to our table to have a photo taken with Reverend Snow from *Three's Company*. One of them asked the Reverend to pray for the rain to stop. So, he did and—lo and behold—it stopped! In the mammoth stadium for the "American Bowl," 80,000 ferociously enthusiastic fans were cheering everything—even the warm-ups—some wearing the Rams blue and gold. Football had caught on in this soccer-crazed country and looked good for the future. The game was a nerve-wracking uncertainty until the Rams came back to win it in a thrilling climax in the last thirty seconds, 28-27! With an earpiece stuck in my ear, I thought the game was a comedy sketch as the English sports commentator excitedly tried to explain the game to his mystified radio audience: "... the player in the back has the ball now and he seems to want to run with it to the far side.. no, no.. he has stopped and seems to want to throw it... oh my, the opposing team... that would be Denver, has jumped on him, several of them... and he is down now! He is down, but has retained possession of the ball. My, my... that was quite a turn!"

Danger In Manila

Two weeks after landing in London I was on my way to Manila, in the Philippines. I didn't mind; I was pleased to be starring in an independent film called *Judgement Day*, with Cesar Romero and Monte Markham and directed by my friend, Ferde Grofé Jr., who had also written the script. It was a challenge and it intrigued me. I was to play two roles: a priest and in his transformation, the devil. Every year on the same day, the peaceful town of Santana becomes a hellish nightmare when Satan assumes total occupation. All the inhabitants must leave before that day or face horrific consequences. In Los Angeles, before I left, I had my own horror. I had to have another full-face mask made and subject myself to being buried alive for an hour while the goop hardened. Satan in all his frightening facial parts would now be designed to fit my dimensions.

The light was just peeking over the horizon when we landed at the Manila International Airport at 5:45 a.m.—a fifteen-hour time difference—losing in the process a whole day. Jack Weaver, co-producer of the film, picked me up and drove me to the beautiful Manila Gardens Hotel in Mikati, a section of Manila. I thought the city looked extremely run down and the heat and humidity was ferocious, worse than Dallas in August. I checked in and then joined Jack Weaver and Guy Coombs, the rugged, wealthy financier of the film and owner of the DHL Courier business, in Manila for a drink. Just before my head hit the table, I excused myself and retired to my room for a shower and short sleep.

Ferde, on a shooting break, was his portly, ebullient self when I greeted him on the set at one o'clock. He was happy to see me and enthusiastic about my participation. He'd already completed a good portion of the film before my arrival, but the meat and potatoes depended on my performance.

I hate being cooped in a hotel room. I had to get out on the streets to soak up a bit of the atmosphere, be among the people, and at these ridiculously low prices maybe do a little shopping (Helen would have had a ball). Since the demise of Fernando Marcos, the new government in power was still on shaky political ground as evidenced by the heavily armed police on every corner and doorway. They were everywhere, checking packages and cars and whatever people were carrying. I suppose they were looking for bombs. The Marcos remnants, the communists, and the NPA (New People's Army), a virulent, armed guerrilla bunch, were still trying to do damage to their first female president, Corazon Aquino. From what I've a read she was facing an insurgency at any moment. It was more than a bit unnerving. I was up all night in a fitful sleep doing somersaults with a rubber pillow and a concrete stuffed nose. I turned on the lamp and looked at the airlines map and realized I had flown 8,400 miles, plus the London trip, about 15,000 miles in a week, and when this gig was over I would have flown over 30,000 miles in two weeks. To the ends of the Earth—and look at all the fun I'm having. I had a Sunday breakfast at the hotel with Cesar Romero, an amazingly handsome man who had played a 16th century ghost in the film and was now ready to fly home. Eighty years old and still going strong, but his back was hurting him and he was pissed about the shooting conditions, hating every moment. "It's not Screen Actors Guild, you know," he said. "I worked a lot of overtime hours I won't be getting paid for." He wished me luck as we shook hands and left hurriedly to catch his plane. Later, Jack and Ferde insisted on ushering me around Rustan's, one of the great department stores in Manila. There I went a little nuts and started buying a variety of stuff. A couple of shirts I couldn't resist and a silver necklace with delicate and intricate filigree work for Helen. Walking around looking for things to purchase, I again became aware of the police carrying shoulder-harnessed machine guns. It was not a relaxed atmosphere. In the afternoon, I met Guy Coombs who liked to chauffeur me around in his Mercedes. Driving through the mad streets of messy Manila was exhausting with its disorderly assemblage of misshapen, crumbling buildings, new construction, and squatters in tin and cardboard hovels. Then along Manila Bay we passed a maze of massive government buildings that Mrs. Marcos had had constructed on a swamp that was filled in for an international congress. The grotesque size was way beyond necessity and was done for showing off. It was a sad sight; the structures now sinking. Guy then took me to the famous Manila Hotel on the bay, with a panoramic view of where Admiral Dewey had invaded in 1899. Strangely enough, several years ago when in the process of reframing a mannerist, Italian watercolor that I own, before I took it to the framer I removed the old French frame, and behind the painting was a crumbling and yellowed 1899 newspaper that blared a headline: "Dewey invades Manila!" I thought it an eerie coincidence to be sitting there recalling a historic event that had been recorded and encased behind an art work at the turn of the century—and in my possession since I was twelve years old! (My father had been owed money for work he'd done on a wealthy man's home and had taken me along to choose two paintings in the man's collection to pay off the debt.)

It started to rain heavily again, but Guy wasn't about to call it a day. His face lighting up, suddenly he said, "I gotta show you something. You'll get a kick out of this, come on!" Off we went to another part of Mikati to an establishment called "Dimples." It was early and fairly empty, but seemed to be an upscale bar and eatery. I found out quickly that this was really a high-class hooker joint. We were sitting at the bar when a young English gentleman with exquisite manners and diction came over to greet us and Guy introduced me to the owner and pimp. There was a large TV screen above the dance floor that suddenly lit up with a risqué slide show. There were beautiful fifteen- to twenty-year-old hookers in provocative positions, wearing helmets and army gear and carrying rifles, and all in a state of mostly undress. Every soldier had a name and rank and was available. In a few minutes, "sergeant" Anita appeared in the flesh, wearing a flimsy, short dress, and sweetly came on to me, nuzzling close and touching my thigh.

"Hello, sir... what's your name?" she purred. "Peter," I said, inching away, slightly embarrassed.

"Oh, Peter... I'm yours," she said, her seventeen-year-old groping more determined. "You can have me. Take me with you, Peter."

"No, Anita," I said, smiling, pushing her hand away. "Come on, Guy... it's time to go."

I learned that Mike Hampton, the pimp, got 300 pesos ($15) if you took one of the girls, and the next morning you gave the girl another 300 pesos. He told us he did disease testing on all the girls, including AIDS, which they didn't have "because this is not a tourist place." Later, I talked to one of the young members of the cast and found out that he's had a different girl every night since he came here—some as young as fourteen. I thought, *What a foolish boy... jeopardizing his life. It's like Russian roulette... one goof is enough.*

My usual day of work was preceded by an hour's drive through Manila and then through the wet, deep green countryside to Baras, passing swampy rice fields and caribou pulling carts, magnificent scenery and utter appalling poverty—shacks, grass huts and tin dilapidated hovels. I had chosen the most experienced makeup lady of the Filipinos, who was gap-toothed, gentle, and responsive to my wishes. But the heat and humidity were overwhelming, shooting in this Franciscan "Church of Baras" that was built in 1652. I was in my black, down-to-the-floor priest's garment kneeling at the altar before Jesus in devotional prayer—the camera grinding away—and then Ferde said, "Cut! Print!" Immediately, the clattery activity of the crew set up the next shot, perspiration dripping off their noses, the smoke pots for added effect clouding the tepid air.

It wasn't Hollywood conditions, to say the least, but everybody was trying and so eager to help. There were over a hundred people hustling to do their best. I enjoyed working with Ferde—a good-natured, enthusiastic and hearty "artiste," although I didn't know about the quality of the work under these conditions. Just getting it in the can seemed to be the order of the day. I had to assert myself to get proper coverage and to simplify shooting movements so it would work for both of us. Ferde was buying my ideas and pleased with the results. These were long days. We were still shooting at 12:30 a.m. I was asleep on a pew when Ferde woke me up and said, "We're quitting tonight. We'll pick it up tomorrow." On the drive back to the Manila Gardens, I was aware of all the dim, flickering lights in the shacks as we passed—maybe 15 or 25 watt bulbs the only illumination these poor Filipinos had. It seemed to me that with all the dreadful conditions they lived under, there was an innocence and openness about these people, a sweet-tempered inner life that was purer and more loving than most people you meet, and they were a happier lot than most.

On my last shooting day, Evan Brainard, the talented makeup man at the Berman Studios in Los Angeles who had designed my external facial applications from my death mask, was now applying them. It took three hours to achieve "The Devil," and as the moments passed I became more horrifying to look at. The smelly glue took a lot of time to set and made me nauseous and light-headed. Then the oculist put in the contact lenses—yellow with red on the rims, which didn't bother me as much as I had anticipated, but the face mask was thick latex and hot and the horn head piece and hair were an additional discomfort. The makeup completed, I put on the heavy robes. When I walked on the set, I scared the hell out of several people, especially the women who got on their knees and crossed themselves in prayer, totally psyched out. They were a religious lot and the sight of Satan himself was deeply unnerving. During shooting, sitting on my devil's throne, I spoke in my evil voice with an incantational rhythm—low, breathy, and weird. A bare-breasted little Filipino girl was placed on a cross, who I proceeded to burn with an extension of my hand, and I did the same to Monte Markam's chest. It was frightening stuff. Ferde was ecstatic and the crew applauded. It took an hour, but I was pleased finally to get all the crap off my face and discard the devil's garments. Got to bed at 4:00 a.m., exhausted after a seventeen-hour day. The next afternoon I said my farewells to Ferde and Jack at the airport and was finally airborne at 5:00 p.m. As we climbed above the rain-drenched city, I was hoping, as all actors do, that the film would cut together well and be successful. I knew my son Lucas, who had already been hired by Ferde, would compose a wonderful score. It would be a long flight home—twenty-two hours—but I wouldn't have missed this trip for anything now that I had experienced it. The following morning (gaining fifteen hours in time) when I turned over in my own comfortable bed, bleary-eyed after the interminable flight, I saw Helen standing over me checking to see if I was still alive. "Good morning," she said, kissing me. "You won't believe what's in the *LA Times*." And there it was in the headlines; discordant factions had tried to assassinate president Corazon Aquino, causing chaos, but the attempt had failed. However, hundreds of people had been killed and the hotel I was staying at, The Manila Gardens, had been bombed. There is absolutely no credence to the statement that somebody once said, "An actor's life is safe, lush and easy."

Helen and I went to the Capitol Records Studio in Hollywood to watch Lucas conduct his first film score—beautiful and "otherworldly" music he'd written for *Judgement Day*, a complicated procedure involving perfect timing to incorporate music to picture. Twenty-five musicians under the baton of this twenty-four-year-old kid-—so cool and all-knowing, as if he'd done this in another lifetime—and probably had. The score enhanced the film immeasurably, and Lucas's handling of his choral singers adding another chilling effect. Guy Coombs, who had flown in from Manila for the session, whispered to me, with a smile, "Maybe we could turn off the picture and just listen to the music…"

Over the years I've been represented by many agents. But it was never like the old days when I first signed with MCA, a powerhouse and career-building organization. They had many faults, but at the time, as a young actor, I knew I was being represented for the potential of my future.

In 1962, after the government antitrust case put MCA out of the agency business, I kept moving around, seeking to recapture the confidence and security of a new ten percenter. I never really found one. I spent years going from the Ashley-Famous office, the William Morris Agency (who tried real hard to make an unknown of me), Contemporary Artists Agency (who undersold me), and then many individual agents, some good and some not worth their office rental space. It was a dilemma. I was raising five children and had always done well, and in most cases, it had had very little to do with the agency involved. As far as managers were concerned, I'd had a couple that hadn't work out. They became too intimately involved in my personal life, and since I'm a rather private person, their over-involvement irritated me.

For over thirty years I had never read for a part in a television show, not even a series. I was requested based on my previous respected work. Everything has changed drastically. In the late 1950s, and then the 1960s, 1970s, and 1980s, a producer, through his casting personnel, would call and say they wanted my services and the agent would book me if I approved the script. That was when actors were more respected, and television wasn't controlled by the networks in their sardine-can-cookie-cutter operation. Now everyone involved in a show and his aunt Suzy wants to hear you read for every role, no matter the size, and during the interview some have the temerity to smugly ask, "Tell me, what have you done?" These incompetent morons, just free of toilet training or selling shoes, are now passing judgement on professional actors who've made a living doing quality work before they were ever born or even read a *TV Guide*. On the two occasions that I submitted myself to this process, I found it so insulting, degrading, and undignified, and it angered me so that I refused to ever do it again. I would read for a film or a play, but never for television. Needless to say, it has hurt me professionally, but as a matter of principle I wouldn't change. I'm reminded of a story when Shelley Winters was called in for a role in a new film.

The young, insipid producer asked the usual, "Tell me Miss Winters, what have you done?"

Whereupon Shelley removed two Oscars from her bag and clunked them on his desk and said, "Tell me, what have you done?"

Tom Sarnoff, son of the late David Sarnoff of NBC fame, is a television producer and a warm and jovial gentleman. He was going to produce, with Alan Courtney, a two-hour movie-pilot for a new TV series of *Bonanza* based on the old one. It would be called *Bonanza: The Next*

Generation. He wanted me in the new version as the guest star heavy, and so did David Dortort, the creator of the original that ran for fourteen years. I had already appeared on a couple of *Bonanzas* with Lorne Greene and Michael Landon, but now his son Michael Landon Jr. would be in the pilot along with Lorne Greene's daughter, Gillian Greene. John Ireland would star as the owner-protector of the Ponderosa, taking Lorne's place who'd recently passed away; Robert Fuller, John Amos, and Barbara Anderson would also star in the cast. I was excited about the venture that would all be shot on location in Lake Tahoe, California, one of the most magnificent scenic areas in the United States. I was to play the character Dunstan, a mining speculator who has a lot more on his devious mind than providing jobs in a depressed Virginia City. He convinces Ireland to allow him to dig in a remote Ponderosa area and then proceeds to hydraulically search for gold, destroying timberland.

While we were on this three-week shoot in the cold and brisk winter air, I thought everything was going fair to middling, but the direction by veteran William Claxton seemed rather uninspired and static—cliché, "Western" formula stuff that had worked in the earlier series, but seemed tired now. Personally, I was dissatisfied in the writing with my character's development and having a problem because his motivation was totally unexpressed in the script. One night while I was having dinner with David Dortort and his wife, Rose, I told David of my concerns, especially in a town hall scene when I have been found out and am confronted by angry citizens and the Cartwright family—and I just stand there like a lump. "Well, what would you say?" David asked. I looked at him for a long moment and then unexpectedly let loose with a torrent of improvisational angry words that I had been stewing about for days.

"Let's stop all this damn pussy-foot'n around! We're talkin' about gold here! Gold! One hundred percent pure, shiny gold… the kind that can make everybody rich… all of you rich! Mr. Cartwright, it's time you learned about the facts of life. You're holdin' up progress. It is time for you to be, I believe, a little more cooperative!"

David, somewhat shocked and surprised, had his mouth open and after a moment said, "Can you write that down?"

"Yes," I answered.

"Well, when you finish… just slip it under my door."

The next day I said those exact words and more against the irritated opposition of the director who wondered why there were these sudden extensive rewrites that he would have to restage. Of course, it didn't end there—the good guys have to fight the bad guys—and in a Western, the bad guys always lose. I was finally shot off my horse in an exciting chase and the Cartwrights saved their Ponderosa ranch from the dastardly intruder.

I had brought my sketch pad, pens, and watercolors and I had plenty of time in between shooting to do some serious studies. John Ireland, Robert Fuller, John Amos, Barbara Anderson, Michael Landon Jr, and Dabbs Greer all sat for a quick ink and watercolor sketch. Women extras in their long, lacey dresses, high shoes, large hats and bonnets were particularly appealing to paint. I have always found location shooting to be especially fruitful for impromptu artwork. My room at the Hyatt Hotel had a large glass-enclosed balcony, enabling me to do continual water color sketches of the distant and snowy mountainous landscape—the changes every few minutes surprisingly different as heavy clouds and sun altered the shadows of trees and sky. When Helen came up to visit, her presence and her smile took the chill out of the frosty, winter air.

In early 1988, I worked with another legend in the film business who was a gentleman and very professional. Jackie Cooper was the director of a new series segment called "Supercarrier," dramatized personal stories aboard the Navy's mammoth fighting machine. On this particular show, I was an admiral. It certainly was a far cry from my actual aircraft carrier days aboard the USS Ranger during the war as an eighteen-year-old seaman second class. Jackie and I got along well, but it was a bit unnerving to discuss things with this middle-aged man when I would look at his face and see that impish grin and tousled hair on Skippy that I grew up loving.

In March 1988, my one-man art exhibition premiered the opening of the "Galerie des Stars" in Century City, an area next to Beverly Hills. Michael Schwartz, the gallery owner who also had the prestigious Galerie Michael on Rodeo Drive, was pleased when more than 400 people attended. So many wonderful guests arrived that I was overwhelmed. They included Jack Klugman, Margaret O'Brien, Cesar Romero, Sybil Brand, Martha Scott, Arthur Hiller, Morey Amsterdam, Edward Mulhare, Jane Greer, Don Taylor, Hazel Court, and even coaches John Robinson, Dick Coury, and Artie Gigantino of the Rams. The most thrilling surprise for me was the appearance of my daughter, Kelly, who'd flown in from New York with her intended husband, Loren—both young actors trying to make their way. It was a large show of my work featuring forty oil paintings and many watercolor and ink drawings. The location sketches of *Bonanza: The Next Generation* were of particular interest to the film community, and many were sold that evening. A photographer was vigorously snapping away, but when I lined up all my children and Helen for a special shot, the best and most creative aspect of my production was now recorded.

There was another "next generation" to contend with and that was *Star Trek: The Next Generation.* In an early segment of the series, I was contracted to play a rich financier, a sourpuss guy who'd been frozen for 400 years and suddenly gets defrosted. During the shooting in the scene when I'm first discovered, I remember being encased in a plastic tube like an anchovy that was a bitch to get into and worse to get out of. The scene took a long time to shoot, so I just stayed in my tube and tried to fall asleep. It was weird, and I got a feeling of what it must be like being constricted for outer space travel. I was deadly serious as an actor, but I found it amusing when just coming out of my defrost I become indignant, insisting on talking to my lawyer and wanting a *Wall Street Journal.* I didn't even remember the character's name until I attended a couple of those *Star Trek* conventions where the fans buy your autographed photo and know everything about you—even the kind of toothpaste you use. Please sign the photograph, Mr. Offenhouse... just above yours, Mr. Richman."

"What?"

"Offenhouse... that was your name."

"Oh," I said, "how interesting... how do you spell that?"

In 1988, President Reagan went to the Soviet Union for a strategic meeting with Gorbachev. At a luncheon in the Kremlin, facing a bevy of grim communist notables, the president astonished everyone there when he started to expound on the film *Friendly Persuasion*, directed by William Wyler. He talked about the film's moral strength, its significance for a struggling nation during Civil War, and the hope for its survival under dire circumstances. He also emphasized that the two countries that week would negotiate with FRIENDLY PERSUASION, and then he presented Gorbachev with a copy of the movie. The conference was shown on the ABC-TV news with Peter Jennings on May 30 (Memorial Day) at 9:00 a.m. At one point in his speech, the president mentioned the character I played—the "gallant soldier" in love with Gary Cooper's daughter. I received a lot of excited phone calls asking me if I'd seen the news. I hadn't, but eventually did and thought it would be a good idea to write to the president and thank him for a mention in so important a setting. I asked Jack Dales, the president of the Motion Picture and Television Fund, how I could get a letter directly to Reagan. Jack had been close friends with him at the Screen Actors Guild. Following is a copy of what I said:

Dear Mr. President:

I am sure that William Wyler would have been very pleased with your gift of his film, *Friendly Persuasion*, to the Russian leader. Your genuineness and good will was deeply felt by all who witnessed the presentation. I, especially was affected because I played the Civil War lieutenant you mentioned. It was my first film and I have always been grateful to have had a part in a film of such high moral purpose and values. Now, too, I feel that I am a small part of the history between two nations. I thank you for that, Mr. President. And I pray that your sincerity, heartfelt understanding and God-given vision for world peace will transcend all difficulties and problems.

Most humbly, and with all best wishes,
Peter Mark Richman

A week later, I went to my mailbox and there was a package from the White House. It contained a photo of the president and beneath, some warm and personal words. This experience once again proved to me the power of film and how it can persist. *Friendly Persuasion* was first released in 1956 and Reagan's conference in Russia took place thirty-two years later.

In November 1988, I committed to appearing in a California Music Theater production of an all-new version of Victor Herbert's *Babes in Toyland*. I would star with Robert Morse, a wonderful performer, who would play the narrator-toymaker. I was thrilled to be in a musical again. Before we went into rehearsal—before I could even protest—they cut my one song! How inconsiderate. Of course, I was the bad guy again—only this time I was stylishly bad as the evil Barnaby, now a fellow in a long silver cloak and handsome gray suit, a cane and a Stetson, devilishly planning to murder his niece and nephew for their inheritance—certainly not the guy from the 1903 version.

Babes was written and directed by Toby Bluth, a talented animator who also created and designed the imaginative sets and costumes. It was a Disney fantasyland out of a Mother Goose book, with Humpty Dumpty,

The Three Little Pigs, Little Bo Peep, Mother Hubbard, and the wooden soldiers parading in the superbly executed "March of the Soldiers"—firing their weapons in a spectacular finale of strobes and smoke, finally sending the heinous Barnaby to the pit of no return. The music, some of it lifted from other Victor Herbert musicals ("Naughty Marietta," "Sweethearts") was delightful and beautifully sung by Stacy Sullivan and Timothy Smith, the love interests. The dancing was vigorously fresh and delightfully visual. I've always marveled at the stamina of dancers—how they do what they do, rehearsing endlessly without collapsing, their sinewy muscles stretched and pulled and jerked to the limits and beyond without stop. We opened to mixed reviews at the Pasadena Civic Auditorium, a huge barn, then moved to the Orange County Performing Arts Center in Costa Mesa. By then, scenes and numbers were cut, the show was tightened, and the reviews reflected the improvement. It is very difficult to open a show cold, but to open a new musical, with enormous and elaborate set changes without an extensive tryout, is nearly an impossible undertaking.

There had been considerable interest in moving the show to the Kennedy Center in Washington, but, unfortunately, there was a feud going on between Toby Bluth and the California Music Theater executives that killed the possibility. What a shame—the show was worthy. The *Pasadena Star News* said, "Peter Mark Richman as the evil Barnaby performs with great style..."

Blessed with four sons and one daughter, the time had come for the marriage of our one and only. Under the best of circumstances and even cloudless sunny weather, the planning and preparations were plentiful enough to drive most parents over the edge, but not us—we were only moderately stressed-out and goofy. So, on the fateful day, October 1, 1988, with relatives flying in from many faraway places, Kelly became the wife of Loren Lester, that wonderful young man that the "Phantom" had introduced her to. When I walked my lovely daughter down the aisle, her white, satiny gown a fabulous knockout—my tuxedo jacket was busting buttons—and I was thinking, too, that hopefully in the not-too-distant future we might be blessed, God willing, with a sweet and tender grandchild. It was a joyous wedding at The El Caballero Country Club in Tarzana, and an exuberant time was had by all—including my brother David and his wife who were so happy to be with us. I insisted on flying them out from Hartford for the affair, to be in our home and share, however briefly, the brotherly love of his kid brother. I was so glad I did. It was the last time I ever saw him. In February 1989, my brother went under the knife for quadruple bypass surgery and didn't survive. He died on the operating table at seventy-one years. It was a shock for all of us, but a devastating one for his wife, Shirley, and their three sons. Helen and I flew to Hartford, Connecticut, the next day. He was a handsome man, a warm, fun-loving guy, who, unfortunately, had never pursued a higher education to possibly change his station in life—carrying on his shoulders a kind of unspoken inferiority-complex, I believe, because of it. He had to work hard at what he knew best, although his heart wasn't in it—a craft he'd learned at an early age while employed by my father. He was a skilled, top-quality paper-hanger who could always make a good living, but he couldn't seem to get beyond that—either by design or his tendency to fritter away his income at the racetrack. I found out at the funeral, and it disturbed me, that his grown sons resented their father's frivolous attitude concerning financial security, leaving them in a bind to provide for their mother. I loved my brother dearly and had always felt close to him, my senior by eight years. A brother is a brother. I think of him always—and in my memories, vivid and constant, I see his handsome face and warm smile and wish I could embrace him.

Friday the 13th, in all its versions, has been a theatrical money maker for Paramount Studios. When *Friday the 13th, Part VIII: Jason Takes Manhattan* came up, and the director-writer Rob Hedden wanted me for a leading role, I was in no position to raise my proboscis haughtily and say it was beneath me. It wasn't *Gone with the Wind*, but it was a good spooky script, and nobody else at the time was offering me a feature worth a damn. Work is work—and at a fine fee too. I flew up to Vancouver, the coastal seaport at the western tip of Canada that has since become the mecca for Hollywood runaway production. The weather was constantly drippy and damn cold during all of the seven weeks of shooting, except for the final week when Helen brought a total change as her plane landed. The sun suddenly appeared and the rain ceased to fall for the week she was there. She has a peculiar tendency to do this. I played an uptight school teacher who was taking a group of teenagers, from God knows where, on a trip to New York City the hard way—aboard an old freighter, not knowing that the undead Jason Voorhees in his grotesque goalie mask was a stowaway. All of the shooting was done at night. My calls usually started at 5:30 p.m.—a pick-up at my hotel, then an hour's drive to a commercial seaport where our ship was docked, a rusting, stinking old freighter on its last sea legs, but certainly perfect for a horror shoot. I rarely returned to the hotel before 8:00 a.m., hopefully to get some sleep before the grind began again. The company had been given permission to shoot only at night so it wouldn't interfere with business and sea traffic. The ship was unheated. We were all freezing. This was early March and it was so cold below deck that I had to wear thermal underwear, and on top of that a full plastic cover-all to keep dry. That's before I put on my regular clothes: three pairs of socks, boots, shirt, tie, sweater, and a tweedy jacket. It was the only film I ever shot where I gained twenty-five pounds without eating. I had another problem to contend with, my film niece, a lovely Jensen Daggett. Since I was her over-protective guardian, I was dismayed at her presence. These complications didn't matter when Jason begins eliminating us one by one, his steaming gross presence—stabbing, ripping, garroting, beheading, and in my case when finally was in New York, and we're all running around in disgusting alleys trying to escape his repulsive grasp, he dumps me upside down into a barrel of rat-putrid, filthy water until I'm drowned and very dead.

Pitching In the Pentagon

I HAD KNOWN BOBBI FIEDLER, at least tangentially, ever since she had been a member of the school board in Los Angeles. She was an ardent anti- busing stalwart and so was I. As a father raising five children in troubled times, I could never see myself under any circumstances taking my kids away from our quiet good school area and putting them on a bus to faraway places just to prove a social point. It made my blood boil, and in the final outcome years later, the experiment of forced busing was a proven, costly disaster. Bobbi Fiedler's gutsy stand on busing contributed to her election to the House of Representatives, serving from 1981–1987. She was no longer a congresswoman when she called me about a project she had in mind. "Would you meet me for lunch and we can talk about it?" she asked. "I would like to get you involved." Although reserved and cautious by nature, I'm always interested to at least listen, so we made a date. A tall, matronly, school-teacherish woman with a certain amount of charm, she quickly got to the point. She wanted to get involved doing something in television about the Pentagon and all the thousands of possessions entrusted to its safekeeping. In other words, how do we tell a story about the treasures of the Pentagon? She related a lot of vague, disjointed and amorphous comments concerning the different departments in Washington having all these collections of "things" of historical importance going back to the beginning of our country. It enthused and fascinated me, but I told her in order to pique interest the series would have to dramatize events around the objects; for instance, using the desk in Lincoln's office when he signed the Emancipation Proclamation, etc. I agreed to put it all together and write a premise and a functional idea for a TV series. A couple of days later, I sent her a copy of my concept and sent a copy to the Writer's Guild. Below is a very shortened version of what I wrote:

THE TREASURES OF THE PENTAGON
A one-hour television series concept created by Congresswoman Bobbi Fiedler and Peter Mark Richman. A new series for television that will dramatically depict the history of this great nation—its creation—its struggle for freedom and unity—from the turmoil of its origin to the present day.

HOW WILL THIS BE DONE
There are over 16,000 individual pieces of military paraphernalia, artifacts and art treasures housed in the "Not for public view" basement of the Pentagon. Each unique object has its own dynamic story to tell, having played an indigenous role in our country's vivid history. These priceless national possessions will be made available for study and research to stimulate specific story development. The Pentagon, the guardian of our liberty is entrusted with the preservation of these treasures.

The creators of this series will have the full cooperation, approval and participation of the Pentagon. This series will glorify love of country, good deeds and above all, patriotism. Most importantly, THE TREAURES OF THE PENTAGON will be a TV series of personal stories, with depth of feeling, heartfelt conflict and resolution. It will portray the history of this country by virtue of its people—strong men and women of character and faith against insurmountable odds—all pursuing their own individual American dream.

Bobbi called to tell me that she loved it, and asked if I would be amenable to going to Washington. I told her I would, of course, but first we had to get the professional and legal commitments clarified. I told her that ideas are a dime a dozen, but putting the ideas to paper is the consummate act and needs to be protected. She agreed and said that we complimented each other. She had the connections in Washington to grease it along, and I would provide the creative role and connections in the industry to get it going. I even thought of the idea of being the host and narrator.

I sent a copy of my concept to Myron (Mickey) Slobodien, a friend and top theatrical attorney, for his advice and also arranged a meeting with Bobbi and Vicki Light, my ineffectual agent at the time. Nothing was put on paper at this stage, but we loosely agreed that the project was a 50-

50 ownership deal and we would retain creative control. First off, before anything, we had to get the exclusive rights from the Pentagon.

Enthused by the possible project, I had an idea to explore the story-rich South and take a short vacation at the same time. I called the film commission of South Carolina and told them I would be filming in an area near Charleston and asked if I could have some assistance in finding locations. They were extremely accommodating. In April 1990, Helen and I flew to Savannah, Georgia, picked up a rented car, and drove to the Marriott Hotel in Hilton Head, South Carolina, for a glorious week of fresh air and relaxation and to see a wealth of places to shoot with the appropriate storyline.

A couple of days later, Cindi Hobgood, a young woman from the film commission, met and guided us enthusiastically around the area. From Savannah, Georgia, where Union General William T. Sherman made his final push to end the Civil War, to the historic waterfront of Charleston, South Carolina—and all else in-between—there was enough background here for a thousand episodes of our country's history. None were more potent and heart wrenching than our visit to a vast, authentic slave plantation; the rows and rows of small, brick slave quarters with dirt floors still standing, while all around, as far as the eye could see, lush green acreage and huge majestic trees accentuated the owner's mansion in the distance. My mind was racing with ideas and I photographed everything.

In May, Bobbi and I flew to Washington D.C., getting us both upgraded with my TV face and friendly smile. Bobbi liked that, but we were still a bit tentative and cautious in our relationship. I talked about getting the "rights," but she said, "the Pentagon won't assign rights, but we'll be able to get what we need when we need it." *Oh, I thought, Will it be enough to take on a big production company and the networks?* The parents of Bobbi's husband, Paul Clarke, picked us up at Dulles Airport and drove us to their home in Rockville, Maryland. They were really nice people and I appreciated their hospitality. In the morning, Bobbi and I and Brenda, Bobbi's secretary, who would take notes, drove to Washington on a long, laborious route to the Navy Art Museum. Bobbi had prearranged this tour with the curator, and I was knocked out with the quality of the works that were stored here and relatively few people ever see—war-themed art by Thomas Hart Benton, Joseph Hirsh, and many other acclaimed painters who had done military art during World War II. It was astounding, just tons of stuff. We went to a warehouse where discards are stored from all over the world for God knows what purpose—art, motors, bells, propellers, knives, and all kinds of equipment. It was like a Citizen Kane warehouse and just as vast. There was a story in any one of these objects. A gentleman by the name of Jack Dyer showed us through the Marine Museum—exhibits of Marine history, diaries kept by various officers; a meeting with Lincoln, the daily battles they fought, etc. Fascinating story material to say the least. The collection of original poster art that included works by James Montgomery Flagg, Joseph Leyendecker, and Howard Chandler Christy (I had restored a Christy oil painting of Jean Hersholt for the Motion Picture Fund) was beyond anything I had ever seen anywhere. We also went to the Navy Museum where uniforms, guns, and cannons were stored—even Admiral Dewey's personal belongings. In the office of Henry A. Vadnais Jr., the head curator of the Naval Historical Center, we unloaded our ideas for a TV series. I improvised a possible scenario of using the hat that U.S. Grant wore—and the scissors that was used to trim his moustache! By the time we got back to Rockville I was dead.

The next day we drove to Alexandria, Virginia, and the U.S. Army Center of Military History. There were heavy security and identity checks, then the army art curator, Mary Lou Gjernes, showed us the fabulous collection of war art, mainly World War II. Abbott Laboratories, apparently feeling guilty about making money on drugs during the war, decided to fund artists to record the war activity. Their collection, on movable racks, was remarkable and the value, limitless. There were about eighty Reginald Marsh paintings and watercolors, wonderful Aaron Bohrod works, Fletcher Martin, Ogden Pleissner, and Millard Sheets, and so many more—all in excellent condition; an art lover's paradise. Bobbi wanted to show me around the Capitol. There again was heavy security, but when she said, "I'm retired Congresswoman Fiedler," that usually did the trick. Walking through all the chambers and hallways was thrilling, and in a peculiar way, I felt that I was a part of all the government activity swirling around me—or maybe it was just the actor in me adapting to the hallowed environment. (After all, I had been in the TV version of *Blind Ambition!*) Bobbi wangled me through security into the House of Representatives, which was in session. It was truly a "once in a lifetime" experience—Congressmen declaiming their speeches to the Speaker of the House. One, passionate about getting out of the Philippines; another about getting a soldier an honorable discharge who'd been beaten up in Honduras; and on it went. Such theater.

Bobbi and I then walked through the many rooms and places of historic importance. She introduced me to senators and congressmen.

The Honorable Dan Burton of Indiana said, "I've seen you on TV many times. I'm pleased to meet such a fine actor." It was a fun experience and a bit weird when someone automatically handed me their business card. Bobbi then took me to the Senate where I sat and watched Orrin Hatch present a speech on AIDS: "... the monstrous rise in cases, up 13 percent." In response, a senator vehemently questioned why AIDS was getting so much attention and cancer wasn't. Ted Kennedy sat stoically on my left, looking sleepy or bored. On the way to the car, we met many of her former colleagues who were cordial and respectful to her and to me. It was quite an experience being that close to Washington procedures—the real thing. At a famous restaurant for politicians called "The Monocle," I met more of Bobbi's former staff who came for a drink and a dinner on her— wonderful young people, bright, informed, and very friendly. I thought, *It must be painful for Bobbi to be in the company of her staff and not be involved with them anymore.*

At the Pentagon, we went through heavy security before being guided through the maze of corridors past the Secretary of the Navy, the Department of Defense, and the Army Chiefs of Staff to David O. Cooke's office, the director of administration and management of the Secretary of Defense. Whew! Mr. Cooke was a genial, heavyset guy with a big smile and a larger belly. He greeted us amiably and sat us down while four of his underlings, like robotic mannequins with clipboards and pens at the ready, sat down and grimly stared at us. Of course, Bobbi had already set the scene, but they all loosened up as we explained our mission. They were extremely attentive and were willing to help. During the conversation, Cooke happened to mention General Pershing's desk, and I immediately picked up on it, moved my hands and improvised:

"We pan the camera up from the unique ornamental carving on his desk, slowly past his desk sign, and then reveal Pershing's hand writing. He puts the pen down and picks up his hat, and in a wider shot he puts it on his head and rises from his chair and stands there, prepared and determined to carry out some notable event in our nation's history as we follow him out the door..."

They were all intrigued, and I must say, I was too. I'm in the PENTAGON, making a pitch! It was pretty heady stuff, just being in this meeting. Frankly, I couldn't believe it. It was really like I was waiting for the camera to stop rolling and somebody to yell, "Lunch... take an hour!" After the meeting, one of the gentlemen became our guide as we walked the endless corridors before turning us over to a seaman in uniform driving a large golf cart who continued to give us a privileged tour in comfort. We traveled down the Eisenhower Corridor and saw his magnificent, dedicated display. Then the George C. Marshall Corridor (he carried the same briefcase for fifty years, and there it was!) The General McArthur Corridor, the General Bradley Corridor. Just amazing stuff. General "Hap" Arnold's presentation in the Airforce Corridor was nothing short of inspiring. We went through the "Medal of Honor" area and the corridor devoted to women in the military. All the time we were goggling at this stuff, uniformed male and female officers were snappily walking past us—25-30,000 people actively engaged in uncountable offices on these monstrously complex levels and corridors. What a place!

After an excellent lunch, we were escorted to the Arlington Cemetery to watch the Changing of the Guard: soldiers trained specifically for this purpose, a precision, puppet-like ritual performed with devotion and honor for the dead. It was a fantastic and moving experience. We then visited the Robert Kennedy and John F. Kennedy gravesites as rain began to fall heavily. It didn't disturb the peaceful tranquility of these magnificent grounds. That evening, Bobbi and I had dinner together in a quiet restaurant in Bethesda, Maryland. Just the two of us, a getting-to-know-you theme. We picked up on the project and what the next steps might be. She's questioning me and I'm questioning myself and she's finding her way. I wasn't sure that she appreciated what I had put down on paper, developing her very vague ideas and fragments into a cohesive concept that could be developed and accomplished. I was beginning to see that she thought that what I had created and put on paper was everything that she had done. It was a little strange. Some of the things I enlightened her on, stories and ways to do them, she was now telling me that she always knew that. I liked her, but there was still caution on my shoulder whispering in my ear: Watch out, buddy! When I spoke to her originally, she was gabbing on about Pentagon film footage, photos and artifacts and how to use them in some way. Now, she kept mentioning her husband, Paul Clarke, a political consultant, and how he could take this material and put it into a "presentation" package to intrigue takers. The worms in the ointment were stirring and the hairs on my neck were tingling. I'm thinking: There's trouble brewing in River City. Paul will not be taking this project any fucking place if he alters my concept.

The following day we were on our "pulling-teeth" drive to Washington via old Georgetown to the National Archives. They wouldn't let Bobbi park under the building so we had to park in a miserably run-down neighborhood over a mile away. I came to the conclusion that Washington, once you've left the government buildings area, was really kind of a mess, which surprised the hell out of me. The Archive visit was a waste of time. We didn't know what we were looking for, so in this vast repository of photos and film, we glumped our way through World War II catalogs, the Civil War, and the Panama Canal. Bobbi had a thing about the Panama Canal so we viewed some drecky stuff in 35 mm, and I picked some German shit from the Kaiser's era that was as useful as Rhinoceros turds. After about three hours of dreary viewing and more unfruitful searches, we left for Rockville to get ready to fly home. Bobbi's in-laws graciously drove us to the airport through a driving, torrential downpour. When we arrived in Los Angeles at 7:45 p.m., I was pleased to see Kelly and Loren who had come to pick me up. They asked me how it went and I answered, "I think it was productive, but I wish I knew what it all meant. God knows, but I'm not sure I do…"

After a few days, Bobbi and I met at the Whitehouse Inn. She had a pinched face and sudden demands. She wanted creative control and final say on everything. She wanted to be the boss and resented my position. I looked at this rather rigid, unknowing novice giving me attitude and behaving stupidly with greed in her eyes, and I was getting more pissed off by the second. I had a hard time controlling myself from letting loose a stream of my choice epithets, but somehow, I did. I told her, in as calm a voice as I could muster, that putting creative ideas to paper as I had done in this case is the act of creative writing. It's a creative act—not dreaming— and that she didn't have a clue before I put it all together. I wasn't getting through to her, the density was too thick. We parted on a cold and testy non-resolution.

A week later, I told her I would not participate in the project. If she wanted to continue alone, or with her husband or the Romanian cousins of Sam Goldwyn, she would have to settle with me since I was the co-creator. All future dealings without me, all percentages, a cut of the earnings for each show, etc., based on our earlier 50-50 ownership basis would still be in effect. Plus, I wanted my flight and legal expenses and other costs incurred in Washington and elsewhere reimbursed. She got the message quite clearly and it all faded into nothingness. Another episode of utter futility. I have often wondered why I am plagued with these barren, fruitless adventures—though not devoid of unique pleasure and excitement—where the rewarding next step is always continually squelched.

26
Hitler Never Envisioned This

IN AUGUST 1990, we were on our way to Berlin, Germany, to see the Los Angeles Rams play the Kansas City Chiefs in a preseason game. Many friends were aboard, including Walter Grauman, a TV director I had worked with, and his woman, Peggy; Mickey Slobodien, a lawyer friend, and his wife, Doris, who had given guitar lessons to my daughter; Walter Schacht, chiropractor to the Rams, with his wife, Rebecca, daughter of actor Ross Martin; and my buddy Michael Wayne and his wife, Gretchen. I knew it was going to be a great trip. Mike loved to hear my German accent when I kidded around, but I told him I would have to cool it in Berlin. It was so weird—forty-five years ago we were bombing the crap out of Berlin and here we were on our way to play in Hitler's Olympic Stadium. What a world. We finally arrived in Berlin after eleven hours and a brief stop in Shannon, Ireland. Our suite at the Schweizerhof was lovely, but there was no air conditioning to alleviate the humidity. We thought we would melt. We were also across from the zoo on Budapester Strasse and could hear the lions roar. We went for a walk to the Inter-Continental Hotel where the Rams and Chiefs players were staying. We were envious—it was air conditioned. I also noticed that the Chiefs were enormous. They all seemed to be 6-foot 7-inches and 300 pounds. We were definitely smaller, and I was hoping, better.

The following morning Doris and Mickey Slobodien joined us for buffet breakfast. I've known him for a long time. A sweet and kind man with enormous motion picture knowledge, he is Georgia Frontiere's legal consultant for the Rams. The Schachts joined us and then we all traipsed over to the KaDeWe, the largest department store in Berlin. While we were in the candy shop, a sales woman recognized me and excitedly declaimed, "Zie bist Schauspieler!" and kept repeating it as she insistently offered us chocolate samplers (the perks of celebrity). Afterward we walked up the Kurfürstendamm Strasse for a couple of miles among the crowds of people, passing shops and inviting outdoor cafes—the atmosphere reminding me a little of Paris. We stopped for a beer at the famous, old-world Kempinski Hotel, but along the way I was unable to resist buying a couple of pieces of the Berlin wall and a Russian belt buckle—definitely designated for my special drawer: "crap to forget." Walking these Berlin streets, we saw that some of the old buildings were still standing. I couldn't help seeing people leaning over the protruding balconies, waving flags, and fervently cheering Hitler as he drove by in his caravan of killers. Everything was so deceptively modern now and almost completely westernized, but lurking in unexpected corners, in architecture and just a "look" in the surroundings, I could feel the Nazi presence and remembrances flashed in my mind. I must admit that I'm on guard for that tone of cold arrogance that can suddenly appear. Aside from some disgruntled misfits, the people had been mostly pleasant and accommodating. But, there was always a sense, a feeling that grisly darkness lurked beneath their thin epidermis and it would spring at you in a split second. Achtung!

It was pretty weird to see Hermann Goering's Air Ministry still standing as a functional government building, but it was no more chilling than standing on the exact spot where all the infamous book burnings took place. Hitler's bunker, where he committed suicide, was no longer there and neither was the old SS headquarters. In its place, they intended to build a park. I hoped so, but nothing could erase the depravity that permeated that space. We stopped at the Brandenburg Gate and the Reichstag—ineradicable Nazi history. On a lighter note, we stopped at the Marx-Engels Forum, an outdoor market area with rows and rows of push-carts. Helen went into the public toilet, run by the emigrant Turks, and surprisingly returned with a roll of East German toilet paper—brown, thick, and sand-papery coarse. I was immediately convinced that having been deprived the amenities of the west, the East Germans were blessed with cast-iron assholes.

We were supposed to hear the Berlin Symphony that evening, but when we returned to the hotel, Georgia had invited us to a fancy dinner party at the Grand Hotel. We taxied to East Berlin, our young, studious driver expressing he was against the unification of east and west—afraid of being one country and its tendency for war. "Two major wars in a hundred years!" he said, shaking his head. I agreed with him. I'd like four Germanys.

He dropped us off on Friedrichstrasse and there it was—The Grand Hotel, an unbelievable restored palace and one of the finest in the world. We took the elevator to the top floor and were directed to the Silouette Room overlooking a great view of East Berlin, and right below was the Komicha Opera House There was a five-piece orchestra playing badly and the first selections were Jewish, beginning with "My Yiddisha Momma!" I couldn't believe it. Marshall had seated us with Walter Grauman and Peggy Parker, a pleasant woman whom he later married. I'd known Walter for thirty years and had done many TV shows with him directing. He asked me the same question he'd asked me twenty years earlier: "Why did you add Peter to your name?" Somewhat reluctantly I ambled into a gentle discourse about Subud, gazing out at the sky and an orange sherbet moon while I enjoyed an elegant dinner. They were fascinated, but I was sure that would be as far as it would go. When you talk about God you can see people's eyes glaze over, especially when you're oiling a rusted and very locked door. God on a silver platter is much too hard to take.

Arthur Rand, a former Ink Spot, was sensational as he sang the old favorites—"If I Didn't Care," and "I'll Never Smile Again"—with Earle Weatherwax, Georgia's jazz pianist beau, accompanying beautifully. Georgia joined us a bit late, but she greeted everyone personally, even mentioning how our son Lucas had played piano for her and how pleased she was with him. I tried to get her to sing, but she shyly refused. Seated at the next table was an extraordinary couple we got to meet and with whom we've since become close friends: Donna and John Crean. After being introduced, I said to him, "Hey John, that's a hell of a belt buckle you're wearing… can I see it?" He stripped it off and handed to me, solid-gold heavy and diamonds sparkling. Donna and John are the most philanthropic, unassuming, down-to-earth individuals I've ever met in my life and it's a privilege to know them. He was the founder of Fleetwood Enterprises, a huge recreational vehicle and prefab home building company, with sales in the billions. In a later chapter, I will elaborate on what he proposed and did for me.

This hotel was the most eye-popping, luxurious dream of a place you could ever imagine, with a magnificently fashioned marble stairway that almost promised a step to heaven. It was indeed odd in poor East Berlin to see such enormous wealth displayed—abetted by the Japanese shelling out 120 million dollars to reconstruct a new Grand Hotel on the grounds of the original. Feeling mellow, warmed by good food and wine, we danced, holding each other close and giggling at the thought of where we were—and isn't life strange… The band played sweetly on—a little bit off key, but what do East Germans know about Broadway and the tender lilt of a show tune? After dinner, Earle invited us up to see their suite. The San Souci #53. It was incredible… a movie set with Garbo entering at any second. When we said goodnight and brushed a kiss, Georgia was particularly warm. She'd heard all about my ardent Rams feelings and vociferous dedication. She even knew about my attendance at team practices. Having an advocate who cares can be comforting, even for an owner of a team (she and Helen bonded). As for me, to be friends with the woman who owned the team I love was a privilege, aside from the fact that I really liked her. It had truly been a "grand" evening.

We had to run to catch the bus, gobbling down breakfast, because we'd overslept. Going through the notorious "Bravo" checkpoint to East Berlin where guards were absent now, but lest we forget, there was a Russian tank ominously hoisted on a cement pedestal. We were on our way to Potsdam, an old military town dating back to Frederick the Great and before, now infiltrated by the East German and Russian armies. We walked the Potsdam grounds in front of the famous place where Stalin, Truman, and Churchill signed the Potsdam Agreement after the war, attempting to solve the future of Berlin. We couldn't enter the building because some fascist-terrorist bastards had bombed the interior the week before. Every day and everywhere there are misguided, soulless vermin wreaking havoc, who justify their horrific Godless causes with slogans and banners.

That evening Georgia gave a fabulous dinner party aboard an old steamboat, The Pavel Queen, its water wheels turning on Tegal Bay as we sailed to Wannsee—the infamous place where the Nazis at their conference concocted the "final solution," sealing the fate of the Jews. Unfortunately, names recall events that may never be altered. But this was a night for enjoyment on a wonderful cruise.

Fritz Schurmer introduced me to Bill Walsh, the great coach who had guided San Francisco to Super Bowl Valhalla. A nice man. I'd suffered through countless Rams losses when the 49ers were unstoppable, and I said, kiddingly, "Bill, now that we've met, I have a few things I want to say to you!" Then Fritz jumped in: "Bill, you'll never meet another Rams guy like Peter Mark." We then sat talking football and I was on cloud nine. During a quiet moment, I asked Bill if he missed coaching. "No," he said. "There's too much pressure. If you win a Super Bowl everybody feels you have to win another one. It never lets up." The next morning I went to a privileged video reviewing session that Fritz had invited me to, all the coaches commenting on the players' performances in yesterday's practice against the Chiefs. It must be tough to see yourself screw up; just like an actor seeing his own lousy performance in a film. I almost felt like a coach sitting there. I just seemed to fit in, feeling conversant and comfortable with the players. On the bus ride to the stadium, I sat with my good friend Jack Faulkner and offensive guard Tom Newberry talking football—but he really wanted to talk about acting and what was coming up in my career. All these young guys are a bit taken with show business. The Olympic Stadium Hitler built for the 1936 Olympics is a fantastic sports complex and the massive, selectively placed male statuary representing German virility was still standing, their aura undiminished. I snapped pictures of everything, even Hitler's wall plaques. I then walked over to the practice field near the stadium where the Chiefs and the Rams were working out. It was an enormous space the size of about four football fields. I was standing talking to Ahmad Rahshad, who was there to do the color commentary for NBC, and Red Cashion, the veteran NFL referee, when I heard this voice yelling my name: "Heeey, Peeeteer Maaark! Come on up heeere!" I turned and saw Jack Faulkner waving to me from the elevated concrete viewing area. I quickly climbed the steps and moved to where Jack sat scouting the Chiefs through his binoculars, an ability of specific perception for which he is a known master.

 Suddenly, shocked at the realization, I just stood there, my blood turning to ice water. It had hit me like an arrow in the brain, a thought that nearly knocked me down. I was standing in the exact spot where Hitler had stood years before!—making guttural speeches or viewing his troops and the many special Olympic events. I was overwhelmed. Jack turned to look at me and said, "What's the matter?" I told him what I had realized, and he said, "Really… how about that…" and returned to his binocular viewing, concentrated and mumbling about "Number 27 breaking outside when the guard pulls…" After practice, I met Ron Labinski, the famous architect who had built Anaheim Stadium. On the bus back to the hotel, I had a few laughs with Jack Youngblood, a great defensive end, who always reminds me of those ruggedly good-looking men in the old "Gibson Girl" drawings. He invited me to have lunch with the team and I accepted.

 When I returned to The Schweizerhof, Helen wanted to go for a walk so we strolled through an utterly lovely Tier Park, adjacent to the zoo. The flowers, trees, and special plantings bursting with colorful blooms were all so civilized and so thoughtfully laid out. How could a country with such expressed beauty do what it did not so long ago? It was still so difficult to even begin to understand.

That evening a group of us taxied to East Germany and the expensive Moskau Restaurant where the bigwig communists used to dine. The atmosphere was Russian, staid and formal, the grim-mannered waiters in tuxedos not unlike pallbearers at a state funeral. I wish I could say the food was worth it, but I can't. It was extremely mediocre and we almost didn't get to it. While sitting, waiting to be served, our party of eight were appalled as a very large cockroach slowly traversed the starched white tablecloth. We all looked at each other and rolled our eyes, but for some reason we decided to stick it out. When we got back to the hotel, I had a message that my agent, Vicki Light, had called. It was 12:30 a.m. We'd been in negotiations with Entertainment Berlin about doing a TV series in Germany, which had nothing to do with my Rams trip. I called Los Angeles. Vicki said she'd just had a meeting with the German reps and they said that I could shoot all of my stuff in three weeks and it would be inserted into the twenty-six segments. There were many things to work out, but it sounded exciting. It's always nice to be wanted. The woman who ran Entertainment Berlin, Doris Zander-Kramer, had been a fan of mine ever since she was a little girl and wanted me for this production. We met at 11:00 a.m. in the lobby of my hotel. She was a bright, lovely girl of thirty-two and Jewish. She said that the only time she faced anti-Semitism was when she wore a Star of David. *Mystery of the Keys* was to be her first dramatic venture and was intent on hiring me. She thought I was perfect for the role. I'd scared her on a TV show and she'd never forgotten it. I expressed my ideas about the character and what could be done with behavior; a man richer than rich intent on evil doings that would affect the world. She wrote down every word—especially the part when I said, improvising, "He is not a vampire… but suppose Madros is ageless and may even have lived for centuries, he never dies… and instead of a yacht, he lives in a castle..?" I do believe she was more interested after our meeting than before, but she had to go to the German network ZDF for final approval. Her associates in Los Angeles were talking to Universal for additional money, but they were screwing around with complex contracts—an ocean and a language in between.

Ever since high school, I'd heard about this museum with a weird name. I thought we were pretty courageous taking a subway in Berlin to find the Pergamon Museum, asking for directions while underground and getting confused blank stares and giggles instead of answers. Helen's brief German studies were of no help. Once top-side, it started to rain heavily and we got lost and soaked, darting under any shelter we could find, seeing a lot of bombed out buildings on our way. When the rain stopped, a kindly English-speaking gentleman finally directed us to the Pergamon. It's just impossible to digest how this magnificent building from the Greek culture dating from 180-160 B.C. was excavated and transported piece by piece to Berlin in the late nineteenth century. The reassemblage took twenty years. It's beyond amazing because the Pergamon Altar is about a half block long with approximately thirty-five steps, columns and impressive friezes of giants in battle, which were stored in bomb-proof shelters but still suffered heavy damage in the war. To see the artistic emanations of people expressed all those years ago is glorious and inspiring, some antiquities and statuary going back 5,000 years. The sculpture and art objects of the Greeks and Romans began to give us a sense of their culture and society. There was also a dominating theme depicted in many of the friezes of the times before Christ and after—the family. The warrior bidding farewell to his sorrowful wife who is holding a child. He is off to war to fight in some distant place and may never return. How many times have we seen that scene through the ages in art, photos, and films? The more we change the more we stay the same. August 11, 1990. Game day. Helen was too tired to come with me, and thinking it was my last chance, I decided to see some things myself. I took a taxi directly to the synagogue on Oranienburger Strasse in East Berlin, which had been destroyed during the infamous "Kristallnacht" rampage of Nazi violence and humiliation against the Jews in 1938. There it stood, a shell—just as it had been left fifty-two years earlier. Scaffolding had been erected in front, but very little had been done. It was just weird and frightening to stand there and look around knowing what had taken place in the Jewish quarter. I'd seen many documentaries of this scene, its vividness locked in my brain, and now, as an interloper to the past, I was in that same spot. The same eerie clanging trolley car passing behind me gave me the chills. In the distance, I could hear an ambulance with that same screaming high and low pitch that terrified the Jews as they were carted away. Sounds have lingering emotional power. I went around to the side of the building through an alleyway where the Yeshiva (school) had stood. The stairway had been destroyed and all that remained were the few concrete steps and a pile of black debris about twelve feet high—fragments of rags, their faintly distinguishable colors now blackened in ashes, charred pieces of wood, stones and brick—a collapsed testament to horror; a time warp. Time had stood still here. Nothing had changed in fifty-two years! I reached into the inner pile and removed some wooden fragments to take for remembrance. It is not difficult to sense the terror felt by the Jews here at that time. It is visibly obvious. Bullet holes in walls, the battered doorways chipped and scarred, their brass numbers tilted or punctured—a signature to madness. People are living here now in this courtyard, not Jews, but poorer class Germans—their memories alive, but from a vastly different perspective, I'm sure. I walked the rain-slicked streets photographing bombed-out areas that were never restored; shattered, black buildings four and five in a row, pulverized concrete and sand—some with wild trees growing from the third floor!

Thankfully, I found a train station W.C. as I desperately dashed up and down the stairs looking for "Herrin" (men) and was saved at the last possible moment. You can't pee in this country without paying for it. A lady or a man sits nearby with a tray and a price card: 30 phenning for a pee and a wash—and many go the cheaper route: no wash. What does this do for the public character? No phennings, no toiletten! I'm sure the Germans have a warm spot in their hearts for the Turkish toilet police.

I started walking toward the Brandenburg Gate that separated east and west, crowds of people milling around, energized youngsters in western T-shirts and haircuts cutting up and carrying on, some listening to a boom box. I passed all kinds of flea markets and stands, every object and food item under the sun for sale. Zesty long sausages on a roll with cheese, and a beer. I stopped an old couple asking, "Iss Das… (pointing) Brandenburg?" They mumbled, not understanding. Then I said, "Checkpoint Charlie?" "Yah! Yah!" And I scurried off with a "Danka." At the wide square of the gate there were hundreds of natives pulling their children along, souvenir seekers and over-smiling tourists impatiently waiting to be snapped. I bought a Russian hat emblem for 3 marks, a red star, hammer and sickle— another item for the "crap" drawer. To the left of the gate the Berlin Wall was being demolished, chipped piece by chipped away piece with chisel and hammer—all sizes and all prices. I asked someone to take a photo of me in front of the spray-painted, steel-rodded concrete buttress. It was an interesting sight—all these people wanting a small piece of Germany's additionally dreadful history. I hopped a cab back to the hotel exhausted, but felt I had accomplished something. It was, as always, more meaningful and enlightening to experience things personally. After a quick shower and decked out in my

Rams shirt, I was ready to join Helen for the main phase of the trip—the game! The sleek German busses were on their way to the stadium and at one point Michael Wayne, smiling broadly, asked me to relate what had happened last night at the hotel front desk. So, I did, standing up in the aisle and holding on. About one o'clock in the morning, a group of us, maybe twelve people, were waiting quietly, but impatiently, for their room keys. However, the desk clerk was on the phone laughing and conversing in his native tongue for an inordinate amount of time, totally ignoring us. Standing at the elevator with Helen, I impulsively piped up and said loudly in my intensely best, authoritative German dialect, "You will get off the phone… und you will give the keys to the guests NOW!" All those close by laughed at my story and applauded loudly, and Michael gave me a pumping thumbs up. I sat down, and after a few minutes on this air conditioned bus, Helen said, "It's getting awfully warm in here." I reached over and felt the vent. The driver had put on the heat and it was blowing very hot air. I was furious. The driver had heard my story, was insulted and wanted to burn us alive. I stormed up to this guy on the wheel, (who had his windows wide open) and said: "Turn the heat off!" He looked at me defiantly. I growled, "Turn the fucking air conditioning back on… far-shtayin-zee, you bastard" He knew I meant it and I got my way, but I realized again that some of these people still resented losing the war and hated us with immeasurable passion.

We arrived late for the enormous private party being given by Volvo in the stands and on the practice field adjacent to the stadium. We waded through the crowds and the concessions of food and beer on the field while a thunderous rock concert was splintering our ear drums. On the top deck of the stands we finally settled at a table to enjoy the sumptuous buffet dinner and meeting all the V.I.P.s: Paul Tagliabue, the football commissioner; Lamar Hunt, the Chiefs owner; and Jack Kemp, who was Secretary of the F.H.A and a former Buffalo Bills quarterback, to name a few.

Now, the irony of all times: All the food tables at this private party were set up on Hitler's viewing balcony, where Hitler had stood observing his troops and had declaimed those "dishes of hate" speeches. In that same spot where I'd stood with Jack Faulkner, a server in a tall white chef's hat was now dishing out globs of delicious ice cream! That's a story that has never been written.

With our stomachs full and our hearts beating excitedly, we walked among the thousands to the stadium and our fabulous seats on the fifty-yard line. It was thrilling to see the teams work out—the color, the spectacle of marching bands, the Rams cheerleaders and baton twirlers with flaming ends, and the U.S. parachuting jumpers, with magnificent control, dropping down on the field before kickoff. As I looked around the stadium it was absolutely bizarre to think about who built this stadium. The familiar landmarks were obvious from the documentaries of the period and especially Leni Riefenstahl's *Triumph of the Will*. Moreover, this date of August 11 was the anniversary of the 1936 Olympics and of Jessie Owen's tremendous victory—when Hitler refused to congratulate him. Helen was extremely moved when the German band on the field played "Deutschland Uber Alles." It has such terrible connotations and calls forth deep, emotional distress. At that moment, she felt she had to pray—an apology to all the people and Jews murdered under the umbrella of that anthem. The game started at 7:00 p.m. Berlin time and was broadcast by NBC. The fact that this was happening forty-five years after the war was amazing and very positive—an American game of colorful conflict with a dominant theme of sportsmanship, respect, manliness, and fun. There was no more mesmerizing moment for us than when Arthur Rand, an African-American man from The Ink Spots, sang our National Anthem a cappella brilliantly. It wasn't the most thrilling game, only a preseason workout, but the Rams beat the Chiefs 19–3. Rubbing shoulders with all these players recalled the camaraderie and excitement all those years ago when I played. There seems to be a deep need that never leaves me—a reliving of all those high emotions week to week—a lesson in survival; a personality trait of who I am. Up in the press box, following the game, there was another party for the privileged; and then the capper—they set off a spectacular show of fireworks that I'm sure Hitler would never have expected during the reign of his 1,000-year Reich. There was something definitely nutty and wonderful about all of this.

On the 747 charter flying home, I tried to sleep but couldn't. Restless, I walked the aisles talking to everyone, the players, coaches, and friends. I had a chat with another Rams fan, Art Todd, a former singer who had replaced Sydney Chaplin on Broadway in *Funny Girl* with Barbra Streisand. I told him that I had auditioned for the same part and Ray Stark, the producer, after the audition told me that, "It wouldn't work with Barbra because you've never done a musical before." Strangely enough, soon after, I did the musical at the Sacramento Music Circus, getting good reviews playing Nick Arnstein. We landed at 6:00 p.m. setting our clocks back nine hours. We'd been in transit almost twenty-four hours. A white limo I'd ordered was waiting for us. It's nice to go, but it's better to come home—where my heart is. (However, I did return to Germany nine months later to shoot the TV series, *Mystery of the Keys*, which eventually was titled *My Secret Summer* for Entertainment Berlin.)

In the fall of 1990, I was truly grateful to receive the highest honor given by the Motion Picture and Television Fund. I became the 43rd recipient since 1941 of the Silver Medallion Award for humanitarian achievement in the entertainment industry, joining notables Mary Pickford, Jean Hersholt, Edie and Lew Wasserman, Gregory Peck, and Jack Warner, to name but a few. Fund president and executive of the William Morris Agency, Roger Davis, kindly cited my ten years of service on the board and my work as chairman of the building committee: "Peter Mark not only helped coordinate the entire construction of our Motion Picture & Television Health Center… but created one of the most aesthetically pleasing health care facilities in the country." I had asked Georgia Frontiere to be the presenter of the Silver Medallion and she, of course, had nice things to say: "… truly a Renaissance man who has mastered nearly everything he has ever attempted… acting, painting, a registered pharmacist and… football!" Then, aided by Marshall Klein, her operations assistant, she really surprised me, proceeding to pull out of a huge athletic bag a complete Rams uniform with my name and old No. 38 on the jersey! It was indeed a special moment and I enjoyed it immensely—and so did my wife and children, beaming back at me in the main dining room of the Country Home.

I began working at Paramount on *Naked Gun 2½*. The producers wanted me for a cameo performance as head of the "Key Atomics Benefits Office—K.A.B.O.O.M." on President Bush's cabinet. Get it? Leslie Nielsen and I were old friends from way back and I thought it would be a kick to be involved in one of his funny theatrical capers. It definitely was. It was hard not to laugh and ruin a take at one of his antics. Leslie's exploits as the bumbling detective who screws up everything and miraculously solves it all. O.J. Simpson was also in the cast and he and I chatted a bit while shooting, but when the stuff hit the fan, several newspapers and TV news programs, assuming a deeper relationship, called me for hot information. I told them, "I don't know anything… but he was a helluva football player."

Germany Revisited

THERE COMES A TIME in negotiations when a rock has to be moved or you take another path. The international gobbledygook between legalities handled in Hamburg, then sent to Berlin Entertainment and the German network ZDF (Zweites Deutches Fernsehen), and then to Los Angeles with complex translations, was a bit much. I told my agent, Vicki Light, who had been totally ineffective in resolving the German *Mystery of the Keys* contract—what I wanted *period*, listing fourteen amendments, or *forget it*! They got the message; everything was agreed to and my fee was deposited in an escrow account at my bank. So in May I was flying again to Germany, this time on a Luftansa flight to Frankfurt just nine months after my previous trip. I was so pleased to have Helen with me (one of my amendments), a sweet, loving girl and the joy in my life who, on May 10, toasted thirty-eight years of marriage with me.

Based on conversations with the producers, I was confident I'd made considerable improvements in the script's rather stilted dialogue concerning the character I was to create—the mysterious Madros, who is searching for the "stones of the universe" that will give him the infinite power he seeks. My adversary, the good guy and co-star in the series, was the fine actor Richard Dysart, who sides with a group of kids from all countries to free their scientist parents whom I have imprisoned in my castle and to guard the "stones" from my grasp. It was, in truth, an international kids' show. We landed in the enormous Frankfurt Airport and then made a mad dash to catch the flight to Berlin. Jens, our assigned driver, picked us up in a Mercedes and off we went to the InterContinental Hotel—opposite the Schweitzerhof where we'd stayed previously, a lovely suite on the tenth floor awaiting us.

I had a meeting at Entertainment Berlin to attend to all the necessary obligations before shooting. The wardrobe designed by Andrea Schirmer— my suits, fancy billowy-sleeved silk shirts, white tuxedo, and black cape— were impressive. The co-producers, Kaj Holmberg and Jutta Rabe-Suttinger, told me how pleased they were with the changes I'd made that complimented John Hunter's script. They called me the "missing link" for the production, which had already been shooting in Russia, Finland, and Yugoslavia for months. My scenes were to be inserted into all the segments. I'd given them the idea for Madros being a man who'd lived for centuries and John Hunter had incorporated it into the script—and surprisingly, as I'd requested, they had secured a centuries-old castle near Dresden to be Madros's domicile and operations center. I was more than pleased.

Later that day, Helen and I left for Dresden with our driver, Jens, enjoying the luxuriant countryside as we skimmed along the Autobahn at 80–90 kilometers per, passing those dreadful little Russian-built Ladas, every twist and turn over verdant hills like every beautiful landscape painting I'd ever seen. When we arrived in Pirna and approached the 400-year-old Castle Weesenstein, jutting powerfully against the sky, I was overwhelmed by its majesty. The producers showed me around my "platz," which declaratively authenticated Madros's worldliness and deathless life. High on a hill, it was everything you'd expect of a castle (now a museum)—extraordinary rooms, bridges, cultured grounds and gardens, a brook, and even a functioning mill.

The suite I was given at the Hotel Gohrischer Hof in Königstein near Dresden was more storied and fabulous than I could ever have imagined. Situated in a separate building it had been the retreat for Willi Stoph, former president of the East German Parliament, who later was one of the six indicted for manslaughter in connection with the Berlin Wall slayings during the Cold War. There were so many rooms, I stopped counting. Light birch paneling, hardwood floors, rich wall coverings, and lush furniture with a Russian-fringed look. Sneaky Willi and his cohorts had taken good care of themselves during their communist grip. One of the strangest and most shocking things about the suite was the entrance. You had to step into and lock the door to a paneled security closet 2 feet square before opening another door leading to the suite. It gave me an idea of the fear these nice people had to live with.

At dinner time, Helen and I dashed through the rain to another building surrounded by a small forest, the cold air fresh and invigorating with the aromatic scent of cedar and pine. The fireplace was roaring in this elegant "old-world" dining room—an exact copy from an MGM movie about Bavaria. There is nothing simple to eat in Germany—so much meat—and everything is with sauces and toppings, but it was good and our waitress in long blonde braids looked like Rapunzel.

It was 5:00 a.m. under the heavy German feather-down quilt, in a bed that Willy had slept in, and the woodsy quietness was deafening except for a few twittering birds. I couldn't sleep anymore—it was to be my first day of shooting. I had learned my lines last night sitting and fidgeting at Willi's desk... *Oh, Villi, Villi*—but my thoughts that morning lingered on my children so far away. My oldest son, Howard, was now teaching piano privately and had a company (Sound Feelings) producing music tapes for health. Kelly had been happily married for three years and was still pursuing an acting and singing career. Lucas was the assistant conductor of the Pacific Symphony, conducting, composing and advancing rapidly in his field. Orien was a theater major at UCL, and Roger, our youngest, was at Pierce College trying to find out who is Roger. Private moments of each child, a look, a smile, a turn of the head, the sound of their voices continue and echo in my thoughts—always.

The first day of shooting is always tough, but everyone was courteous and helpful. After a discussion with Oliver Schwerdt, the makeup man and his application, I was ready to work. The mixed crew from all over Europe and England were professional and the young director, Joe Coppoletta, was friendly and responsive. My first scene with Richard Dysart, a sweet guy, went very well as we jibed one another—two pros in control of their game. It was amazing to be shooting in this palace where some parts had been built in the twelfth century. I realized why all the rulers died young and consumptive—they froze their bunions off in these hallways of ice where the walls were covered with valuable art. I had asked for hand warmers to put in my pockets, but they had none. The crew rigged up a battery device that worked for a while, but I still shivered. I was in every setup that day and by the time we wrapped, my eyes were drooping as we drove through the superb, blossoming countryside back to our remarkable hideaway.

All the dialog I had rewritten worked well that day—especially a particularly long take of Madros at his desk, the camera moving from profile to front view and then in close as I sip wine and study one of those precious "stones," musing about St. Petersburg and my friend, the Czar! Later, while shooting a scene with an uptight German actress who I was trying to seduce, the director suddenly got testy about the dialogue and the way it was flowing. It had all been approved and now he was getting weird about a couple of words. I'm always ready to adjust—nothing is written in stone, least of all this venture, but his attitude was annoying and I felt myself getting increasingly irritated. He had a confrontational personality—and I know if I'm pushed I'm not a shrinking violet. I called him aside for a calming chat and a slight dialogue change, resolving the situation, which could easily have gotten out of hand. I was leery of him and his direction from then on.

Shot another wonderful scene with Richard Dysart in my incredible dining room at a monstrously long table (maybe 500 years ago the king of Saxony, or whoever, feasted on "schwein und sauerkraut mit apfels!") Richard and I went at each other with silent snarling—games of mental jousts and challenge. Jost Heider, a German actor who plays my henchman, was jumping out of his skin (enthusiastic type) with excitement and compliments, and the reports from the silent dailies (they cannot match picture with sound here) were also very positive. But I remained a bit skeptical. It was strange; here, I was a star, the way I was treated and appreciated, but in Los Angeles I'd become a neglected corpse ready for embalming. I had a late call the next day, not until 2:00, but I was still up at 6:00. Jess picked us up at 9:00 and we were off to Dresden for a few hours, through the beautiful countryside and the industrial town of Pirna, the factories now closed because of new anti-pollution laws. This area was East Germany and controlled by the Russians for forty-five years. The people don't really know how to *be*. The young ones especially are confused and full of hate for foreigners. The unification has created havoc; they're losing jobs and their past salaries don't buy much since they can't compete with the West Germans who have a democratic work ethic and a higher standard of living. And there is a resurgence of Nazism—violent and uncontrollable skinheads and dingbats running rampant. It's a serious problem.

Driving along the Elbe River, the green hills laden with yellow flowers, is a sight to behold, and the stucco houses, their mixed colors of fading, gray-green and gray-ochre is like a finely realized painting. In fact, the whole country looks like a painting.

Dresden was bombed to hell during the war and 100,000 people were killed—many places still untouched, the ugly, twisted black scars sorely visible. We took photos in front of the reconstructed Semper Opera House. It was eerie to stand there—where Wagner and Strauss had conducted their glorious music—imagining the wrathful devastation that had taken place in the raids.

Holding hands like a couple of young lovers, we crossed the bridge and walked the breathtaking promenade along the Elbe before entering the Albertinum Museum, where, at the top of the stairs—I could only say, *Wow!* Four magnificent Canalettos, each about 6 feet wide, depicting the scenes we had just stepped from. Sheer genius. Of course, all the greats were there—Degas, Monet, Lautrec, Van Gogh, Renoir—and the Germans, including Max Leibermann, Lovis Corinth and provocative anti-war works by Otto Dix, whom I admire greatly; plus a train load of all the important classical painters. The museum alone was worth the trip to Dresden.

We returned after lunch in time for my makeup. I had a major scene to do up in the stone tower of Castle Weesenstein where I had imprisoned Dysart. A large room adjacent to the prison—from the year 1455 on— had been "The Room of Judgement," the judge deciding "halt und hans"—translation—"you get your neck sliced or your hands chopped off!" This was an *authentic* horror chamber and a truly frightening place to be in. It didn't take much to be the scary Madros on the attack, my black cape flowing as I gestured threats to my shackled prisoner. I had chills every moment I was there and couldn't wait to get out.

It was raining, snowing and hailing—and miserably cold. This is a German May? It was Saturday and the schedule got all screwed up and we were shifting scenes and locations all day, but good things were accomplished. Joe Coppoletta hugged me and said, "Great work! It's so good to work with you. You should be doing features… you have such a strong presence." Well, I wouldn't argue with that. We'd settled into a fine, simpatico rapport.

Kaj Holmberg stopped by and handed me a gift, a book on "Schloss Weesenstein" with a lovely inscription, and then said: "The network wants fifty-two more! That's why we don't kill Madros in the twenty-sixth episode. He flies off in a helicopter! It all depends on the money people." "Uh, huh", I said, but I was thinking: *Don't get carried away… I've heard all of this stuff before.*

Helen had been driven to see Prague that day with Cathy Dysart, Richard's wife, who is a fine painter. On the way, they passed the Theresienstadt Concentration Camp. She said it was weird, and she asked if I had been with her, would we have visited? Frankly, I don't know whether I could have taken it. Once in Prague, that charming old-world city trying to free itself from the oppression of communism, they had a dreadful experience. They turned into a street and were stopped by two surly Czech cops under a pretense, declaring it was illegal to drive there and then threatened to arrest the driver and the women. Of course, they wanted a bribe and until money was presented they were trapped and scared. It was a lousy feeling for a couple of innocent tourists.

On Sunday, it was freezing cold and raining heavily as we loaded our bags for the long drive back to Berlin. I was so tired that I slept practically the whole way. When we arrived, the Hotel InterContinental had set us up with a lovely suite on the eleventh floor with a spectacular view of the city. I was developing a tickly sore throat, but I didn't let it prevent me from taking a long walk up the Kurfürstendamm with Helen. There were swarms of people—mimes doing their white-faced thing, pamphlet passers, gambling hustlers with a version of the peanut game, acrobatic performers, skinheads, and punkers with defiant, orange flaming hair. Berlin was a lively, exciting city—it had everything. You name it—you got it.

I had a lousy, restless night fighting my flu, or whatever it was. That freezing palace had taken its toll, coupled with a heavy schedule and little sleep fighting that fucking feather blanket and always losing. Kaj called and we made a dinner date for Italian food at La Luna. The young, intense woman and co-producer Jutta Rabe-Suttinger, who had spearheaded the project, joined us. I got something off my chest. I told them I was disheartened by the cuts and lack of violent action in the scripts, which John Hunter had written. I felt that it was *necessary* for an adventure show; a bunch of kids just running around in different countries chasing their tails isn't going to cut it. There's just too much talk, and *my* scenes were not heightened and dynamic enough with threatened mayhem to overcome others that seem to *talk* you to death. They disagreed and assured me that because this was a children's show, we definitely had the proper mix and everyone was excited about its potential. I wasn't convinced, but it was a pleasant evening and I forgot about my maladies for a while.

Monika, our new, attractive driver, picked us up to see some sights (one of my perks). She suggested we visit the Kreuzberg area and Katzbachstrasse, where the Nazis' upper echelon had lived. So, there we were walking around in a beautiful park with gorgeous kindergarten children laughing and playing happily, all escorted by their guardians. It was heartbreaking to think about the little Jewish children that never got beyond their age in this same area fifty-five years ago. Then we took off for the Martin-Gropius-Bau where the art exhibits were fabulous.

Directly across the street was an exhibition of an unearthed prison called *Topographie des Terror*. The whole area under Prinz-Albrecht Strasse and Wilhelm and Anhalter Strasses was where the Nazi headquarters and Himmler's office had once stood—a network of SS interrogation rooms of subhuman brutality and torture of the Jews before being sent to concentration camps. One of the buildings had been converted from an art school to another chamber of horrors, the remains of the glazed, tile rooms still evident—and how easy it was to hose blood off the walls. Directly behind it, just a few feet apart, were the remains of the Berlin Wall. Two monstrosities together!

After a coffee pickup in the Gropius, we viewed *The Jews of Berlin*, an impressive collection of Judaica, photos, and the art of Jewish painters and Jews who had served in the military years back in time. There was a huge poster that Monica translated for us from the years 1933–1945—of laws passed, year by year, systematically eliminating the rights of the Jews, restricting them in every possible activity. No degrading pettiness was overlooked: in 1938, they were allowed only one hour in the day to purchase food.

That evening I took Helen and Doris Zander-Kramer, the young woman responsible for my doing this series, to dinner at the très chic Castel. She straightened me out on one thing: Berline Entertainment was the sole money source—Russia, Portugal, and Finland, etc., only giving service for certain rights. She also told me that Gorbachev himself had stayed in my suite, in *my* bed—not only Willi Stoph! And another wonderful story: Raisa Gorbachev had asked her couturier, Slawa Saitzew, to design the clothes for me as Madros and he agreed. There is a German newspaper photo and article of Slawa holding a photo of me at his work table calling me "America's Klaus Kinski" (because I always played bad guys). I had given them all my sizes and was originally supposed to fly to Russia for fittings, but when Doris flew to Russia and saw his poor-quality fabrics, she realized she would have to fly him materials from Paris or Germany increasing costs, so the whole thing died.

We shot the "Russian" scene on location in Berlin at the Sylter-Hof lobby, set dressed to look very Russian as we sat sipping Vodka—Madros conniving a surreptitious deal with a couple of mediocre German actors playing Russians doing their lines by rote. I'd done some rewrites and they seemed to work, giving the scene some character by putting in Russian words which I had trouble with except for *Nostrovya*! I had a Russian translator who kept giving me contradictory pronunciations, but after screwing up a few takes I finally got it right.

A LATIHAN IN WOLFSBURG

We had planned to visit our Subud brother in Wolfsburg, about three hours away. Monica, my driver, picked us up, and shortly after we were flying on the Autobahn at 140 kilometers an hour, whatever that is. I told her to slow down, the hair on my head was elevating. Wolfsburg was a town created by Hitler in 1936 to build the factory for Volkswagen production. Now, with unification, the community was booming once again. Richard Engel lived on an old farm and was outside his house waiting, so happy to see us. Lunch had been prepared even though his wife, Helma, seventy-eight, was ailing. We sat and talked for a long time, we had so much to share—this wonderfully sweet man who I'd known for twenty-five years, and who'd been one of the first people in Germany to be opened to the latihan. He'd created a Subud community in Wolfsburg. All the people who lived at the farm had been opened. There was no other way I could've been his friend if not for Subud, a man who'd been a conscript in Hitler's army and terribly wounded in the fall of Berlin. After lunch, he showed us his studio, stacked deep with finished canvases. He was a fabulous surrealist painter who created his fantastical images from his inner receivings without physical references. He showed us his tiny sketchbook full of paintings from his walks in the woods, with his quotes and writings; a treasure.

It had been arranged for Helen to do the latihan with some local Subud ladies while Richard and I did latihan in his studio. Feeling relaxed and grateful, I submitted to the comforting power within. It was amazing; Richard and I live so far apart in so many ways and yet we share so much, united by a granted connection with God.

We walked the lovely woods adjacent to his studio, soft breezes blowing, the birds singing their songs. When we said our goodbyes, Helen, for some reason, while hugging Richard, became strangely overwhelmed with emotion. We drove through the East German countryside and towns, taking note of the neglect and disrepair from forty-five years of Russian domination. Finally back on the Autobahn, we zipped our way to Berlin. (Two weeks later we were surprised and saddened to find out that Richard Engel had died.)

I was up at 5:30, mulling and rewriting a scene for the twenty-sixth episode that I thought would solve Madros's problem for the conclusion of the show. I needed words with balls that I could sink my teeth into. The writer, John Hunter, had written such impossible and incomplete shit for me to say, it was disheartening. I wasn't getting paid for my writing efforts—*it's for survival*. As an actor, I didn't want to be standing there when we shot with my thumb up my ass hoping my ears would spin and fly me away. I was hoping the producers would approve what I had done. I had tried to keep it as nonviolent as possible, but at least—probable.

Two interesting people, Gudrun Gloth and Franze Georg Schulze, came to my suite to photograph and interview me for a magazine article. They'd lived through the war and had fascinating stories to tell. Gudrun told me that there were still miles and miles of absolute rubble where this hotel stood, twelve years after the war's end. Nobody considered investing—there was a desperate fear that a major conflict was on the horizon between Russia and America. Franze told me a bizarre story concerning the time he snuck up to the Berlin Wall when it was coming down, but not officially. He stuck his nose into a slit in the wall and an East German soldier stuck his nose in the other side, shouting, "What do you want?"

"I want a piece of the wall," Franze said nervously. The soldier reached down and picked up a piece and slipped it through. Franze looked at it and said, "I don't want this… it's all white. I want a piece with color and graffiti on it!"

The annoyed soldier responded, "Don't be stupid… on this side it is *only* white, so we can see anybody escaping! Any other color is forbidden!" He then gave the soldier 5 DM for a larger piece and it was so much money to him that he said, "What *else* do you want?" He wound up buying the officer's epaulets and hat, slipped eagerly through the slit of the crumbling wall.

Monica drove me to the Gemäldegalerie Berlin, the state museum they call "The Dahlem." I wanted to see the Rembrandts, and I think I saw 40, including "Moses Smashes the Tablets" and "Man in the Golden Helmet"—all extraordinary. When I see the quality of the work the masters created, and I think of the crap that passes for art today, I get nausea cramps.

When I got back, Helen and I had dinner at Mohring's on the K'damm, a fine, historic restaurant that had survived every turmoil since the late 1900s. Sitting near the large window watching throngs of people passing the sidewalk tables, it was easy to envision the flag-waving crowds of years before as they cheered the military, goose-stomping by. I had to laugh at the silliness of it all, when two ladies came over to our table and asked for an autograph—*The Denver Clan*, as *Dynasty* was known, was a hit on the German tube.

Back at the hotel, I received a call from Kaj. They wanted me to shoot the scene in question the next day as is. I told him it was illogical, out of character, and why it wouldn't work. It was nerve-wracking. Then I read him what I had written, and after some mumblings of resistance, he began to like it—finally loving it and thanking me for my hard work, telling me… "we think along the same lines…" and I said to myself, *Like hell we do.*

I was driven to our new location near Spandau—an incredible military complex of bunkers and underground quarters built during Bismarck's time. It had been a weapons manufacturing plant all through the years, but in 1929, when taken over by the Nazis, it eventually became an anti-aircraft training ground. After the war, the Russians took command and occupied it for forty years. Although it had been spared destruction, when they left they indiscriminately bombed many sections. Young neo-Nazis had recently begun camping there, remnants of their *verboten* presence evident by the recent stomped-out fires still smoking.

I will never forget the first approach as we drove down a long, narrow dirt road—twisted tree overgrowth obscuring the tunneled, red-brick buildings. Then, at the ominous entrance, there, above the underpass I saw it, the symbol still embedded in stone—the sprawling Nazi eagle and swastika, and above it in large German printing: Fort Hahneberg. It made me shudder. I was forced to spend a week there and it was the scariest place I've ever visited in my life; it was a nightmare of tunnels, lightless and narrow, and secret passageways with unexpected dropping twists and turns. With stupid adventurousness, I went into one with a flashlight, and after fifteen minutes in a space less than two feet wide, I was damned sorry I had. I was a shook-up mess when I finally made it out, finding myself a long distance away in another isolated area.

There was a six-foot round grate in one of the buildings with a rusted metal ladder going down into the darkness. I was told it was an escape route for Hitler, his tunnel back to Berlin. I asked an electrician to shine a klieg light down the hold, and when I looked I couldn't see a bottom. I dropped a rock through the grate and waited—I heard nothing.

After shooting several scenes in my candle-lighted lair, I told my assistant, Jost Heider, my demands of the day. I insisted they had to get some blowers in there—frosted breath from our mouths looked ridiculous. The set was several layers down underneath a bunker, and it was freezing cold. The best they could do was a small electric heater, which didn't help much. Jost was having a dreadful backache and suddenly became immobile. He was taken to the hospital where he received an injection to alleviate his pain and immediately went into shock. We had to shut down for three days. There was nothing else to do; he was involved in all the scenes I had left to shoot. I'd have time now to do some more *Berlin* sketching.

Earlier, in August, before I had committed to do the series, I had suggested to Doris Zander-Kramer that she use my friend Myron Slobodien to help her solve a problem with Entertainment Berlin. She did—and then when I wanted to use him for *my* legals he couldn't; it was a conflict of interest! I was pleased that it had worked out for her; sometimes I think I better curb my eagerness to open my big mouth to help people.

The concierge got us tickets for Bernstein's *West Side Story* at the Metropole Theater in East Berlin. When we arrived, a sweet, elderly attendant showed us to our box on the loge. It was *the* box! She opened the door with a key and in the anteroom there was a dining table, six chairs, a cloakroom, and a private john. Then she parted the curtain and revealed about twenty high-backed upholstered chairs, but we were the only guests. I asked her why and she said in German, "Too expensive". It was the *only* private box and I'm sure it had been used exclusively for dignitaries. There was no doubt in my mind that Hitler and Goering had been there—and later, the East German contingent.

The production was superb and absolutely nothing had been lost in translation. I was again reminded how Leonard Bernstein had touched our lives because of Lucas and how the memories of him were so intertwined with our son. When we came out of the theater, Jork, our driver, was waiting for us, the car only a few steps away—service I couldn't begin to dream up. Of course, I had the car thing in my contract, but I didn't expect a constant chauffeur at my command. I dare say, I could indeed become spoiled.

Jost was still sick. I would not finish on time. They would have to pay me lots more money. At Helen's suggestion, Jork dropped us off at a reconstructed Berlin Museum that used to be the supreme court building destroyed in the air raids—the façade still standing. Another memorable exhibition of Berlin Jewish history going back three centuries—each room a different era. The whole violent and oppressive Nazi period was explored—Hitler posters, anti-Semitic signs and memorabilia; even the original plans of the "Kristallnacht" synagogue I had visited on my last trip. Then Jork took us to Der Brucke (the bridge), where a showing of the German expressionists Eric Heckel and E. Ludwig Kirchner were on display.

Following that, after a security guard checked our bags as we walked in, we had a kosher lunch at Arche Noah in the Gemeinhaus de Jüdischen, formerly a synagogue that the Nazis burned down on Kristallnacht, the two original portals now part of the new modern building.

That evening, in my whirlwind desire to absorb as much East German culture before it dissolved, we saw a fabulous premiere of a ballet at the elegant Komische Opera. It was called *Frauen—Manne—Paare: Woman—Men—Pair*. It was a remarkable production of highly skilled, precision-like, dynamic and discordant movement—with seemingly homosexual implications—danced to American blues; dramatic and sensual.

The next night, again seated in our private box at the Metropole, we enjoyed a flabbergasting, seventy-person performance of *Die Fledermaus*—the same company that had performed *West Side Story*! It was so wonderful I was tongue-tied with superlatives—their superior acting and singing, bringing such freshness to a rather silly opera. If they accomplished nothing else, the East German communists sure put together amazingly dedicated theater companies.

I did an interview on the German network ZDF, and the question was always the same: "Why do you always play such evil men?" I was thinking: *Because they offer me a job with lots of money.* But I didn't say that. Instead I said, smiling, "Oh, I don't always play a bad guy... Sometimes I play a... blah, blah, blah..."

Afterward, we picked up Helen and dashed over to the Kathy Kollwitz museum to see a whole panorama of her tortured work: a great graphic artist of deathly sad, suffering people during the inflation-starvation time of the 1920s. A communist, she saw the Nazi period coming and was overt in her anti-fascist creations. She did an enormous amount of self-portraiture—all her other women looking like her too; not attractive or pleasant, but powerful.

I must mention the miraculous Galerie Nierendorf, where we were personally escorted by the pretty guide, Plishki. Four floors of great expressionist work stuffed to the gills—G. Marck, Ernest Barlach, Mueller, Beckmann, Dix, Kirchner, Grosz—and everybody else. It was a fantastic warehouse, each floor double-locked for security before going on to the next. I'd never seen anything like this in my life. *This city is just saturated with extraordinary art.*

It was raining again, and I had to do all those running, escaping shots through the claustrophobic Nazi tunnels and bunkers—my flying cape blown by the icy wind. It was so cold that my teeth were chattering and

Antje, my wardrobe girl, wrapped me in blankets between takes. I chatted with Ruth Maria Kubitschek, who was visiting the set—a star in German films and a beautiful woman. She played the guardian of all the kids—a kind of loving grandmother. A painter too, we had a lot to talk about.

The next day we were out at the fort again, surrounded by cavernous bunkers and dense foliage for the final scene—the interrupted pistol duel with Dysart, and then the hypnotic mind zap I get from the kid, Jelena, which overpowers me. We were behind, and I had the feeling that Joe, the director, hadn't done his homework. Facing time pressures, it became tedious and exhausting to stage a complex scene with eighty-nine people—and I had to explain to Joe what was happening since I rewrote the sequence that culminated with my powerful incantation:

"I call upon the winds of the sacred mountain… the fires of Vesuvius… the ashes of Agamemnon… the power of the stones… grant me your infinite grace!"

I thought the poetry of the words fully expressed my character at that heightened moment with Jelena, but the girl playing the part wasn't much help. She was fourteen years old, inexperienced, and not concentrated for the high drama.

Finally, after a fierce look over my shoulder in a tight close-up, I had a sense of relief when I heard the words: "Cut and Print! It's a wrap!" I was now officially finished, but the company had to really hustle before packing up to shoot in Hamburg tomorrow.

The crew congratulated me on my performance, and Richard Dysart even called Helen to say nice things about the day's work—a fine gentleman.

"We will miss you," Joe said, and then told me he enjoyed working with me and with my professionalism, all the good things people say when saying farewell. Jork rushed me back to the hotel to change and transport Helen and me to Wannsee (the name always makes me shudder). Kaj and Jutta had arranged a screening of my scenes in a private school. I saw thirty-five minutes of film and was pleased for the most part. A couple of cut-together segments with Dysart were very exciting—and I felt the writing I'd done had greatly improved the character of Madros. I was glad the venture was over. What followed was out of my control.

After Germany, one of the first pleasures I had back in Los Angeles was seeing my one-act play, *A Medal for Murray*, which had opened at the Richard Basehart Playhouse in Woodland Hills. I'd given Cynthia Baer, the artistic director, permission to direct it while I was away. When

I finally saw it, I thought she'd mounted it well and had done a fine job. It's about an old woman in a Jewish home for the aged whose forty-five-year-old son comes to visit. The two main characters—Eugene Butler, the son, and the mother played by a wonderful character actress, Connie Sawyer—were exceptional. So much of my mother was in the old lady and there was a lot of me in Murray. I was unexpectedly touched with emotion and affected by the humor I'd written. The production was a success, and it gave me additional confidence in my writing. Years ago, Jack Klugman read it and said it should be developed into a full play. It took me a long time to get to it, but I finally worked on the short piece and I've expanded it into a full evening in the theater. I think it works, and someday I hope to get it produced.

And oh, yes… my novel. Eileen gave her husband, Leo Penn, a surprise 70th birthday party out at their sprawling Malibu home high above the blue Pacific. We had been close friends ever since our early days as young New York actors. It was always heart-warming to be with them and share our children and their stories and to revel in the progress of their lives as they grew up. At the party, I presented them with a video copy of our kids together on various occasions; in Central Park (toddlers, Michael Penn and my son Howard), and even a blonde, cherubic Sean pushing my daughter, Kelly, on the swings on her second birthday party at our home in California—a heart tugger. I was chatting with Sean, now hotter as an actor than the Sahara sun, and I told him about my unpublished novel and what a good film it would make, and the lead character, a part he might like to do. He was immediately interested and asked me to send it to him. I sent it to his home in Malibu that he'd purchased with Madonna. After the turmoil and demise of that relationship, he was now with a very pregnant Robin Wright, a lovely, wonderfully talented girl who, oddly enough, had played my daughter on the soap Santa Barbara. I waited patiently to hear from Sean, knowing how jammed he was in his schedule. Then I forgot about it. When his home completely burned down—and everything in it—in another Malibu fire, I figured that was it. I never spoke to him about it again. I'm still confident the book will be published and made into a fine film.

Art at the Essex House

A COUPLE OF WEEKS AFTER coming back from South East Asia, including a visit to Red China on another "Government and Arts Tour," and after having taken care of all the domestic crap pleading for attention and catching up with our children's activities—and with no work looming—we flew off to New York. It was the end of October and the refurbished Essex House was flying in selected "celebrity artists" for a gala week of entertainment, leading up to a dinner in our honor in their new Les Celebrités Restaurant. The walls were to be adorned with our paintings and I was to have several prominently on view. Elke Sommer, a gorgeous blonde film star and a fine painter, had invited me to participate in the Essex House show after seeing my work at my home. Her beau, Wolf Walther, was the hotel manager and had made all the arrangements for the stars, even the shipping and the framing—a first class operation in every way. I found out later that Hisashi Ito, former president of Japan Airlines and now head of the Nikko organization and the new owners of the Essex House, had spent 145 million dollars in art deco renovation and was, of course, behind the public relations event.

We finally toured Les Celebrités Restaurant and were blown away by the beauty of the room; the artistic hanging of the paintings was a knockout. I was more than pleased with the display of my oils in the main room: Actress, Before the Take, and The Guard at the Louvre. Later, while having dinner in the Botanica, another restaurant at the hotel, Elke introduced us to Wolf, a gracious and charming gentleman. They were very much in love. It was a bit odd. She'd been married to Joe Hyams, a Hollywood columnist, for many years and Joe and I were old friends. He'd first interviewed me thirty-six years ago while I was shooting Friendly Persuasion and he was still married to his first wife. I complimented Elke for the fine job she'd done hanging all the works in the Les Celebrités and for her large work on the wall in front of me. She beamed a beautiful smile and hugged and kissed me while Wolf shyly watched. Helen took it all in stride. I was so pleased to have Helen with me—a sweet loving girl and joy in my life, who on May 10 raised her glass and clinked mine to thirty-eight years of marriage—and that, as they say, is more than a little something. The next day we again had a quiet breakfast in the Botanica while we gazed out a window at picturesque Central Park South, the wind blowing the scarves and hair of huddled-over people scurrying by, while passenger-less Hansons clip-clopped along. It was not the New York I remembered. If I'd lived at the Plaza or the Essex House and had had all my expenses paid daily, New York would've been so much easier to take in those days.

It was fun wandering the city where we'd lived for nine years so long ago. I walked 57th Street and over to Madison Avenue, stopping in for a leisurely look in the galleries. Later, I picked up Helen and we rushed to the Martin Beck Theater for the matinee tickets which had been arranged by Zina Bethune, an old friend, who was starring in *Grand Hotel*. I'd first worked with Zina, an extremely gifted actress and dancer, when she was sixteen years old in the TV series *The Nurses*. *Grand Hotel* was a terrific show, imaginatively staged by Tommy Tune, and Zina was wonderful acting the ballerina with great believability. Enjoying the show, I remembered dining with Georgia Frontiere on the top floor in the authentic Grand Hotel in East Berlin.

In the evening, in our trés chic suite, we freshened up and dressed for dinner. On our way, at Helen's insistence, we stopped for a glass of wine at "Journeys," the elegant bar on the ground floor. I was glad we did, and I gave Helen another gold notch for her unfailing instincts about meeting people. Wolf came over and joined us, and then I said I would like to meet the Japanese "owners" who were sitting nearby. That was how we first met the Itos—Hisashi, the delightfully warm chairman of the Nikko Board, and his adorable wife, Cookie. To say that we hit if off would be factual, but it was more than that. Our relationship began budding and flowering quickly. Dinner at Les Celebrités was an event—magnificent and elegantly gourmet, the ambience and service, tops. During the meal, Patricia Morison stopped at our table—a beautiful woman with tight, braided hair who was a fine artist, and her painting hung close to one of mine. I told her how much I admired her (*Kiss Me Kate* and many other Broadway shows). Then she said she was a fan of mine—and looked so lovely saying it.

Halloween—even the Essex House had hanging ghosts. Helen stayed in while I went for a long walk again, the briskness of approaching winter invigorating. I stopped at the Art Students League where many great American artists I admire had taught in the early twentieth century: Robert Henri, George Bellows, John Sloan, Reginald Marsh, and others. It was inspiring just to walk the premises and observe the paintings and all the activity. Again, I felt this prodigious heart tug about my painting and the need to paint—the aching in my hands just to hold a brush and feel the paint smear the toothy linen. It was sensual, this need to express. Painting was immediate. With tools in my hands all I had to do is execute... not wait around subconsciously like a dithering dolt for an agent or a producer to give me permission to paint. Jesus, sometimes I just felt like chucking this whole ridiculous acting rat race and lock myself in my studio, turn off the phone, and spend the rest of my life devoted to sketching and painting. Was it realistic... or just a fantasy?

Helen looked like a movie star in her long gray gown and white mink stole, and I was pretty snazzy, too, in my tux. We were ready for the gala evening—the grand opening of the new Essex House, but first... The Grand Era of Swing! Bucking the wind, dignitaries and stars all traipsed over to Carnegie Hall a block away to see Skitch Henderson conduct the New York Pops and hear Maureen McGovern sing. Skitch did his thing, charmingly, but what I remember most is how pleasant it was to just relax and listen in that fabulous old hall. In the whispery lull before the music started, we had a funny chat with Phyllis Diller, another painter whom I adore. A down- to-earth straight talker, she liked Helen in her mink stole. "I'm glad you're wearing fur," she said, "you look great. What is it with these people who are against wearing fur? The hell with those suckers! They eat meat and carry hand bags and wear leather shoes and belts... I'm sick of them!"

I laughed and said, "Phyllis, I agree with you... screw 'em!"

The festivities at the Essex House were wall to wall. Eight hundred-fifty people were invited, and all the ladies received a Tiffany silver jewel box. In the grand salon, Sammy Kaye's orchestra with a new conductor, of course, had us all moving nostalgically to the familiar tunes. Helen and I were cheek to cheek when Dick Gautier cut in and gave Helen a professional jitterbug twirl around the ballroom. A good friend and an exceptional artist, he was working on an art book with Jim McMullan, published a year later, called *Actors as Artists*. In the book, I got a kick out of my alphabetic placement between Burt Reynolds and Edward

G. Robinson. We sauntered over to Les Celebrités and sat in the booth beneath my large oil *Actress, Before the Take*. It looked formidable in a thick gold frame. Cookie and Hisashi Ito came by and joined us, graciously thanking me for my participation. Photos were snapped of us all in front of the painting. It truly had been memorable night.

The next day after breakfast, we decided to walk all the way to the Actors Studio; crosstown to 9th Avenue and then down that congested, weird- people street—so many unfortunate types and alcoholics without end. The walking was good except for my ever-aching football knees, but that's an old story—the one about the folly of youth following you for a lifetime. New York City smells of the streets: coffee and hamburgers cooking, garbage and urine, oil-stinking car exhaust, dog shit and soft pretzels, roasted chestnuts and a wisp of the sewer with every step. It must have been twenty years since I'd walked through that door and I hardly recognized anyone, except for old-timer Salem Ludwig. We shook hands, and then I said hello to Lee Richardson, an old friend and a good actor. I looked around and noticed that the premises had been spruced up a bit and had a more pleasant atmosphere. But it was more than strange not to see Lee Strasberg take his usual seat and begin the session. He'd been gone for almost ten years. Frank Corsaro was now the artistic director and before the first scene he asked for a moment of silence to honor Joe Papp who had just died. In 1954, Joe called and asked me to play Romeo in an off-off-Broadway production of *Romeo and Juliet*. At the time, I was in *The Dybbuk* with Morris Carnovsky. It was just after *End as a Man*, and I turned him down. I wanted to go up, up to Broadway, not off, off. His company became The New York Shakespeare Festival. He never forgave me. I never worked with him or ever came close to doing so. That's life—and you live with your choices.

We watched three scenes, one good, one fair, and the third a boring disaster from a Wedekind play. While watching, my mind drifted back to more youthful days when I presented my work before the master, orating, "Friends, Romans, Countrymen!" from *Julius Caesar*; playing Romeo to Patricia Neal's Juliet; acting Joe in *They Knew What They Wanted* opposite Maureen Stapleton; and a scene from a Dorothy Parker short story I adapted, *Here We Are* with Doris Roberts (two people just married on a moving train), with Lee expounding on my special ability to do "character" comedy.

The brick walls at the Actors Studio have absorbed a multitude of wonderful and awful stuff. In the process, some actors have suffered desperate insecurity and confusion. Then, suddenly, an acting revelation enables him to develop his talents and direction, and, in a way, his (or her) life—not always in that order by any means. The studio has been a cauldron of incredible creativity for a lot of people for a lot of years, and God willing, it will continue. I profited greatly with Lee's teaching. After the session, we had a "good-to-see-ya" hug with Frank Corsaro, a dear friend who had lived in our building on 20th Street in an apartment I had helped him get. An extremely talented man, he was now directing opera for the Met. As we exited, I said hello to many people I had known and introduced Helen to all. On the steps as we left, there stood tiny, dynamic Sondra Lee. We looked at each other and she yelled "Mark!" and then we reveled in hugs and kisses and picked up on our conversation as if thirty years hadn't intervened. An incredible dancer (Tiger Lily in *Peter Pan*), director, and coach of actors, she was a joy to be with and brought us up to date with all the people we'd known while we reminisced over lunch. Back in our suite, we discovered that Laura Wechsler had called, my brother Harry's only child. She'd gone back to college after raising four children and now had a doctorate in psychology. In town for a Karen Horney conference nearby, she came over and it was just great to see my niece, now a full-fledged practicing psychotherapist. Because of us, she'd been opened in Subud with her husband, Alan, and had been doing the latihan for a long time. I told her again how important it was for her to continue doing the latihan, especially after absorbing a lot of negative stuff from her clients. She agreed.

The atmosphere of the room was sensational—all the paintings shown to great advantage with special lighting and placement. The press and TV interviews were endless and the snap flashes by photographers made us all a bit blind as we ambled around shaking hand and kissing and hugging all the artist participants and guests. I chatted with Sally Kirkland while the cameras popped, and then I wandered over to Van Johnson who was sitting in a booth with his manager. Funny, charming, and boisterous, Van told me he was seventy-six, and I hadn't even asked him. I told him I'd gone to see him in *Showboat* in Pasadena but he had gotten sick and didn't perform. He apologized profusely, kissing my hand and then my face. I backed off a bit, laughing. A small painting by Jimmy Dean called *Portrait of Tommy Gunn* was in the show; it stirred up memories of his tragic death in 1955 after he had finished shooting *Giant*. I was still working in *Friendly Persuasion* when Jack Garfein (Carroll Baker's husband) called to tell me of the loss.

There was more table hopping and congratulations for my paintings. Hisashi Ito wanted another photo with me, this time as I signed the handsome art brochure for the event. The next morning in the lobby, as we were ready to depart in the limo, we were surprised when Hisashi and Cookie, looking lovely in traditional Japanese regalia, were there to wish us farewell, then followed us out to the curb, waving as we pulled away. We knew we would see them again. On the MGM Grand flight home, we were chatting with Phyllis Diller and Dick Gautier in the lounge when John F. Kennedy Jr. walked by. What a striking young man he was, better looking than his senior. I must say, I've never been overwhelmed by the Kennedy myth, starting with their father, Joe. Gloria Swanson in her autobiography had more than a few startling and ignominious things to say about the patriarch and their relationship—a man who'd fathered eight children and was doggedly screwing everything that walked. Like father... like son?

I fell asleep next to Helen in a comfy lounge chair—we were both exhausted—and when I woke up, Dick Gautier did a good pencil sketch of me with my sleepy, staring eyes. It was a fitting conclusion to a rather profound art adventure.

Orien picked us up at LAX. I'm not sure if he's 6-foot 3- or 4-inches, but he looked good, the handsome kid. Sometimes I find it startling to see a child of mine in a different setting and from another perspective. It's somewhat similar to when I'm painting in my studio. I always look in a large mirror strategically placed behind me which faces the painting. It gives me the reverse of what I'm used to seeing. Orien was a senior at UCLA, studying theater, and I felt he could have a career in this lousy business if he applied himself.

In the last few years we'd become very close with Georgia Frontiere, a beautiful woman and one of the warmest and most gracious human beings I've ever met. She was involved in so many philanthropic endeavors and fundraising events I couldn't begin to count, but without fail she always wanted us to be seated at her table the night of the charitable affair. It was tough to turn her down, and with major talent performing, the evenings were mostly terrific. I've lost count of the nights we frantically limo'd down to the Dorothy Chandler Pavilion to take our seats just as the curtain rose on *La Boheme* or *La Traviata*. At the intermission, as we sipped a glass of wine, it wasn't unusual for a Placido Domingo or another musical great to visit with Georgia and her guests in the Founder's Room. Aside from special events, there were intimate dinners at her lavish estate in Bel Air that we attended, sometimes with our children, and where we could quietly talk of many things, including the Rams football team. She knew how devoted I was to the team and respected my opinion, and she shared many privacies that you wouldn't read about in the *Los Angeles Times* sports page. They were always taking potshots at her for the unbearable fact of being a female owner of a major team franchise. She was knowledgeable, tough, and took it well, but it must have hurt her deeply. John Shaw, Georgia's lawyer and team executive, gave a private birthday party for her at Chasen's. A group of her friends were invited and, of course, her children, Chip and Lucia, with her husband, Lupe, and Georgia's handsome fella, Earle Weatherwax. During the dinner, I made a toast and said some heartfelt things and hoped she would find the book interesting we had brought as a gift. It was about Subud.

David Dortort, the creator of the super successful *Bonanza* and of *Bonanza: the Next Generation* that never got beyond the pilot (I was in it), had seen Lucas conduct and had heard his musical compositions. He was impressed and asked Lucas to write the score and lyrics (gratis) for a Broadway version of *Bonanza* and assist in the book. My talented young son couldn't refuse. What an opportunity! He then proceeded to compose about twenty-five musical creations in a three-year period that were astounding. I can say that as his father, but as a professional I will repeat it—the songs and music were astounding.

There was one problem and it was huge. One of the reasons Lucas had to re-lyricize his music so much was that the book of the musical was not good. Frankly, it was lousy. It had been written by David and his partner, George George (I'm not kidding), a producer in New York. After reading it twice, I sat down one day and for the hell of it rewrote a couple of long scenes. I fleshed out the characters and had them say believable, talkable dialogue. I read it to Lucas and he loved it, but said, warily, "You better read it to David."

I called David and set up a meeting and read the scenes to him with Lucas present. David loved what I'd done and was excited by the potential, but cautiously said, "I'm gonna have to discuss it with George." I knew trouble was looming. I wasn't expecting anything. I was just trying to be a helpmate to my beleaguered son, and if they liked what I was contributing we could've worked something out, I'm sure—but that was not my original impulse. However, George George was incensed. How dare I infringe on his creation! He basically told me to get lost. David was sadly upset. And, of course, Lucas was in the middle.

One day, almost two later, I came home and was unprepared for what was taking place in my living room. It isn't often that you walk in and sit in the comfort of your own home and witness "live" a run-through of a potential Broadway musical. Lucas, at the piano, had assembled his cast for *Bonanza*, with top performers George Hearn (a coup in any presentation) and Karen Morrow, supported by a cast of many that included Gary Imhof and my daughter, Kelly, and husband, Loren, in featured roles. Helen and I were mesmerized. Hearing George Hearn's rich baritone ring off the walls singing Lucas's lyrics and music, the physical and vocal embodiment of the Ponderosa legend, was an unforgettable happening. Then, a few days later at a small theater in Los Angeles, Lucas conducted a performance for an invited audience. The music and songs were powerful and moving, and so was George Hearn singing the rousing "Welcome to the Ponderosa." As George said, "They don't write 'em like that anymore… so masculine and a pleasure to sing."

It was a wonderful evening with only one problem. The book was still putrid. Thank God, Lucas retains the rights to the music.

Our social lives during my career have been rich and full and in a way storybook, with special events with famous and interesting people constantly part of the mix. Sometimes, I found myself locked in to three or four consecutive evenings filling our calendar. One night we were invited to the home of Mrs. Jack Hupp, who is really Marie Windsor, a former film star who sat on the Motion Picture & Television Fund Board with me. She was giving a dinner in honor of the legendary Stella Adler, who was thin and frail at ninety-one, but still amazingly beautiful as she walked in firmly holding on to a cane and her assistant, Irene Gilbert. Having met her before, I took her arm and helped her to her seat, and during dinner I tinkled my glass and made a toast: "It isn't often we have an opportunity to have dinner with a true legend…" She beamed. Later, Norman Lloyd, sitting next to film director, Burt Kennedy, told stories about Orson Welles, John Houseman, and the Mercury Theater, with Stella making pointed comments. Still feisty and opinionated, she was suddenly expounding on the "Method" and her trip to Russia to visit Stanislavsky, and how Lee Strasberg had misinterpreted his work. I found myself holding court telling Stella, quite strongly, how Lee had taken the so-called Method beyond Stanislavsky, and the proof is obvious by how many actors in America have benefitted from his pursuits. Oddly enough, she listened intently and didn't refute me. After dinner, I told Stella about my relationship with her brother, Luther, and the charming story of Luther and my name Peter. She laughed and took my hand. The next thing I knew we were attempting to sing a particular Yiddish song, but neither of us could remember the words. At the evening's end, I walked Stella and Irene to their car. Stella turned to me. "We should all see each other soon," she said, "so we can sing Jewish songs… but first we should learn the words!" I made up my mind right there that we would have her for dinner and told her so. "Oh, yes!" she said smiling. "I'm so tired of being with goyim in this fucking town… I long for some Yiddishkeit!" Unfortunately, we could never work it out.

The next night we were the guests of John and Donna Crean who were being honored at the "City of Hope" gala affair. Huge philanthropists, I believe they gave a million to the worthy cause. At our table, I was chatting with Buzz Aldrin and Helen was going at it with Lois, his wife. Buzz, the first man on the moon with Neil Armstrong, told me he was seeking agent representation (later was grateful when I set him up with my voice and theatrical agents). Then Richard Blackwell asked if I could arrange for him to entertain at the Motion Picture & Television Hospital. I told him I would have someone call about available dates. Donald O' Connor, one of the sweetest human beings alive, whispered to Helen after we'd danced, "Helen, I was watching you… you dance beautifully." She melted and it took her days to recover. Jane Withers, another warm friend at our table and always eager to help a cause, once flew to Dallas with me when I asked her, on a fundraiser for the Motion Picture and Television Fund.

Buddy Ebsen, two seats away, suddenly asked me when I'd received the last *Barnaby Jones* residuals. Surprised, I thought, *Hmmm, he was Barnaby… shouldn't he know what's going on?* He was also pissed at Blackwell for giving him a lousy review years ago in a legit show, his animosity clearly showing. All this while Norm Crosby was up on stage making funnies and finally presenting a plaque to the generous Creans. On the following night, I was attempting to be humorous as the master of ceremonies for the Jeffrey Foundation at the Beverly Hills Hotel, a favored charity of mine supporting special needs and multi-handicapped children.

On the evening of April 16, 1992, I walked into the El Caballero Country Club, where we are members, for an intimate birthday dinner with my wife and family. In a state of oblivion, I began recognizing people I knew sitting at a long table, and there I was saying hello to them, wondering why they were all there at the same time—and all so jovial. When they raised their glasses to toast me on my sixty-fifth—the official senior citizen milestone, or millstone as the case may be, it finally dawned on me that my wife had successfully pulled off a wonderful surprise party. Lots of nice things were said by a lot of nice friends, but the fact that I was now eligible to collect a social security check gave me a jolting realization that at least three-quarters of my life was over.

I wasn't depressed by it. I felt alive and actively creative, no matter the frustrations, and that whatever was to happen in my life, God would give me the guidance to do whatever I needed to do—thanks to Him and the pathway of Subud. At April's end, Jack Faulkner invited me to Rams Park for the first meeting of a vitally important new Board, on which, surprisingly, I was included. John Shaw was there and former NFL players and people of influence who'd expressed interest in establishing a retirement home for ill and aged retirees. It was a noble effort and I had a few knowledgeable words to contribute about the "Fund" and how "We Take Care of Our Own." Money, of course, was an absolute necessity and they had to have a "place"—one to be built or a structure to renovate. Jack Kemp, a former player himself, now in Washington and the head of HUD, was present at the meeting and said he might find a suitable unused property that the government might want to unload. That sounded promising, but it still looked like a long haul. When I glanced around the room and saw the many football greats I'd admired and respected, men now in responsible positions and station, I became acutely aware how dreadfully destitute some former players were. In the early days, the salaries were sadly low, and there were no guaranteed medical benefits in later life for having sacrificed their bodies. It wasn't like today when a player can earn countless thousands or many millions in a season.

A retirement home was sorely needed, and I was particularly disturbed that the insanely rich and powerful National Football League hadn't ever initiated the undertaking. In a way, it was shockingly deplorable. Individually, Georgia Frontiere, bless her, didn't need much prompting. She was an initial heavy contributor, but, unfortunately, rigor mortis has set in and the old guys are still suffering.

29 Ray Badbury On Stage

RAY BRADBURY, A PROLIFIC WRITER with great insight always dancing on the edge of fantasy, is the personification of a truly gentle man. I've always admired him as a person and as an artist. He'd written a rather famous short story called *Next in Line* and the premise was developed into a play by S. L. Stebel and Charles Rome Smith. Bradbury had agreed to finance the production. Of course, a story is one thing and a play is another. To coin a phrase, it is a horse of a different color. In one, you are privately imagining the author's words, and in the other, actors have to bring the story alive in front of an audience. It's no small task. Charles (Chuck) Smith, an old friend who'd directed several of Bradbury's plays, called and said he wanted me to play the leading role. I read the play and it wasn't good, but I thought it had possibilities if rewrites could clarify the relationship with my wife and if the spooky elements were motivated for the stage. We discussed the writing and he agreed that it needed changes. I committed to do it and an actress I like a lot, Nancy Dussault, was set to play my wife with a good supporting cast.

We began rehearsals, and before long it was abundantly clear that the leading thespians had to get their parts straightened out or they would be in embarrassing doo-doo. Chuck was more receptive to my suggestions, but his partner, S. L. Stebel, was resistant. He didn't have to spout the stilted lines, thinking they were sprinkled with gold. To save my ass, I had to start rewriting my dialogue or my mouth wouldn't work at all. It helped a bit, but the scenes having to do with "The Day of the Dead" (Mexican holiday) celebrations were ridiculously unbelievable and false. I kept telling the authors that the man I was playing was having a nervous breakdown and he had to have the words to express his impending dissolution. I was finally getting through, but not enough. This was a play about a conflicted married couple who take a vacation in Mexico and arrive on the festival day. She had just written a published novel and he, an art dealer and jealous of her success, is dissatisfied with the alterations he instigated and developed in his Pygmalion wife. He is at her constantly, complaining about everything. As written, I was such a kvetching, disagreeable pain-in-the-ass, it wasn't too disturbing that he finally winds up as one of the mummies hanging there in the tombs, while the wife spouts her last monologue showing little remorse.

We opened at the partially renovated Ivar Theater in Hollywood in May 1992 after two good previews, except that the scenery, too ambitious and clunky for this play of many scenes, didn't work, and the grinding sound when they did gave the impression that huge wild animals were mating backstage. An additional disturbance—we were right in the middle of another horrifying race riot. Rodney King had had his head splattered, and from then on it was terribly dangerous all over the city. Nice time to open a play. A lot of my friends came to see me including Jack Klugman, Rod Steiger, Harvey Korman, Patricia Morison, Irv Kershner, Arthur Hiller, Diane Ladd and Laura Dern (who sent me 100 roses), Lee Meriwether, Norman Corwin, Juliet Prowse, Gloria Allred, Ann Jeffries, Stan Freiberg, Henry Silva, Del Mann, and Phyllis Diller. They were kind. Ray Bradbury loved it. The reviews were unthrilling. The Hollywood Reporter wrote: "Richman has the evening's juiciest part and makes the most of it playing the sort of husband most women have nightmares about."

Near the end of April, UCLA put on a fabulous musical production called *Working*, based on Studs Terkel's factual stories of people and their jobs. Lucas, now on the faculty, was also the musical director and conductor, and Orien, who had just turned twenty-three, played a leading role. We'd seen him on stage several times; he was good, and I thought he could definitely have a career if he took acting more seriously. Theater in college is fun, but it has nothing whatsoever to do with the real world. Kids get caught up in the Hollywood syndrome of glossy photographs, trying to get a theatrical agent and doing commercials. Their time would be better spent if they perfected their craft by working with a quality teacher, putting to use what they've learned on the stage—anywhere—so that when called upon to deliver, they know what it's all about and can do it convincingly. Basically, that was the premise of my lecture, No. 963, that Orien half-heartedly listened to and then said, "I've heard this before, Dad… and it's still boring." So much for fatherly advice based on experience. He was inspired by Jack Valenti's rousing speech at his graduation. A couple of months later, as a graduation gift, we sent him off to England for the summer to study Shakespeare at the British American Drama Academy (BADA) at Bailliol College, Oxford. When he came back, he had us on the floor gasping with laughter—exclaiming Hamlet as William Shatner's captain on *Star Trek* would do it (with all the mannerisms and inflections). Witty kid, my son, Orien… but he didn't go to college for that.

In June, we flew to Montreal, Quebec, to a Subud Congress and were pleased to have our son Howard with us. The day before there had been a series of earthquakes originating in distant Joshua Tree, California, but we still felt it. I was outside watering flowers when the second jolt hit and I felt the earth roll, the trees rock and the windows shake. We had been through it before and Helen always gets a bit spooked when it happens. Our suite at the Sheraton Château Vaudreuil was lovely and was only had a short drive to St. Anne de Bellevue and John Abbott College where the congress would take place. Meetings and workshops are not my bag (no matter Helen's prodding), but I would attend Helper's gatherings and, of course, the latihan, which was the main impetus for me to attend the congress. Lucas arrived from Albany, New York, where he'd been visiting his grandmother (Helen's mother, Jean), Carol, and Alfred and after another fruitless *Bonanza* meeting in Connecticut with George George. Later, our friends Art and Adrienne Stone, a delightful couple who own the workout clubs "Total Woman," arrived also. (They'd been opened in Subud through us.).

It's of special interest to note that after hearing us talk about Subud on various occasions, and mostly at her prompting because she found the subject so fascinating, Georgia Frontiere said to me, "Well, when do I get opened?" So, a week later at the elegant home of the Stones, with the aid of a couple more female helpers, Georgia received the latihan.

The area surrounding the college campus was especially attractive, and so were the people, speaking French with an indigenous twist. I was saddened to hear about the persistent conflict—the French Nationalists wanting to assert their rights to secede from Canada. We were in the English sector of Quebec and in the midst of a "Canada Day" celebration, with flags and banners flying—but underneath the joy, a palpable hostility was present. This is a great country. I hope they always stay united.

It was wonderfully heartening to see old friends in Subud, some I hadn't seen in twenty years, and I was so grateful to do the latihan with my two sons and several hundred men from all over the world. It was powerful. Then Varindra (Tarzie)Vittachi arrived, a very dear friend and Bapak's emissary for years; a UN representative, a fine writer and a raconteur who told unique stories with gusto and charm. It was always enlightening and fun to be in his company and we spent a lot of time together. One evening, I invited Tuti (Bapak's granddaughter) and her husband, Sharif Horthy (Bapak's translator for several years), and Varindra to join us for dinner. Varindra again regaled us with his insider tales, his voluminous cigarette smoke making his eyes tear, and ours too. I've never forgotten a story he told about his wife. She was dying of cancer and the doctors said she had five weeks to live. He called Bapak, told him what was going on, and Bapak sent him a "Raja" (a piece of paper with Bapak's drawing of the illness revealed by a scribbled ovary). Varindra was to burn it and give the ashes to his wife to drink in a glass of water. She did and the cancer disappeared. Of course, the doctors were astonished. She lived three years longer.

One evening, Subud Montreal made arrangements for me to show a video of my vintage 1963 film of Bapak. I had followed him around with my Bolex in Los Angeles and Disneyland. I was surprised how good the picture looked projected onto a large screen, now enhanced with my son Howard's piano accompaniment. It has become a collector's item. After my film, a video was shown of a talk given by Bapak in England, in 1986—a year before he died. He looked quite old, but ethereal and remarkably vital. For years we'd been with him and had heard so many of his talks—and there he was again, just an image, but his penetrating presence was deeply felt—and what he said—just as deeply meaningful.

How could I be on the East Coast and not pay a visit to my dear mother-in-law, Jean, who I've always adored? I thought she was a classy lady the first time I saw her in her prim gray suit, her blonde, bobbed head slightly tilted as she inquired of me her daughter's whereabouts—that summer stock season years ago. She was now eighty-six and had just moved into a senior citizen's retirement complex. I looked forward to laughing a lot with Alfred and Carol, two special people I feel especially close to. It was slow, careful going as the pouring rain, sometimes like a monsoon, persisted all the way to the Canadian border. There is no more glorious a landscape anywhere in the world than the Adirondacks area of upper New York State. It is breathtakingly beautiful, the mountainous ridges overwhelmed by majestic pines. When we finally arrived at Jean's place, a cluster of old ladies and a few old men were sitting on rockers and benches. They were watching me curiously as I unloaded a suitcase full of stuff we'd brought for Jean. "Don't worry," I said. "I'm not staying long." Only one white-haired lady with a walker got it and giggled.

When she opened her apartment door, Jean was overjoyed to see us and Helen was like a little girl, excited and teary-eyed. I wasn't surprised, Jean was a wonderful woman with all of her faculties who looked terrific. At Jean's insistence, we moved some of the furniture around, and I hung three watercolors I'd painted when Sam and Jean had lived in their own home. Later, after dinner, we went down to the recreation room and met her friends. I enjoyed meeting them, kidding with them, and listening to their stories. There was one old guy wearing a straggly wig that was priceless. He'd been a dancer in Milwaukee and was their dance instructor. He liked to feel up the ladies, but Jean was aghast at his behavior and stayed away from him. She always loved to dance and was so elegant and graceful to watch. To the delight of her friends, my boys and I took turns giving her a twirl around the floor, which generated a heartfelt applause. Then they were all mesmerized when Howard beautifully rendered Chopin and Lucas played the music of Broadway, capping it all off with a community sing-a-long of "God Bless America"—our voices rising above the rest.

Something touches me deeply when I look into the faces of the elderly, their lined, craggy faces and wispy hair only the outer definition of a life lived. Underneath, I sense what they must've gone through to reach their longevity—the joys, the pain, and the numbing grief. Life is difficult no matter what station, and the inevitable someday will have to be faced for all of us. I suppose that's why I became involved with the Motion Picture & Television Fund—to assist in my way so that members of the entertainment industry will always have an island of refuge, dignity, and respect when they need it most.

Back on the coast, we were waiting at the hospital with eager anticipation. Finally, the doctor, all smiles, walked out of the delivery room and told us that Jenny Luisa Lester, my daughter Kelly's first child, had been born. Soon after, when we saw her—this tiny infant swaddled in a thin blanket, her beautiful face a heavenly sculpture—we were moved to tears; and when I held her, this divine little thing making me a grandfather for the first time. I said an inner prayer of thanks for such a wonderful gift from God. Kelly was radiant and happy, and Helen was a picture of what a grandmother should be on such a glorious occasion— and my industrious son-in-law, Loren, a joyous Daddy, was videotaping every moment.

Subud California purchased a three-story building on Wilshire Boulevard in a superb location opposite the Los Angeles County Museum. Lorenzo Music, a dedicated Subud member and television producer who'd found the building and had wisely pursued the purchase, asked me to be in charge of the decorating after the construction phase was completed. I was reluctant to get involved. I know what committees are like—every member suddenly has a ferocious and opinionated taste bud to be a designer-decorator. At that time, I was still doing the decor of the Bob Hope Health Center for the Motion Picture & Television Fund and didn't need further aggravation. I turned Lorenzo down. Nevertheless, as Los Angeles Subud Chairman he insisted, coaxed, and cajoled, telling me I could do what I felt was good for the building and could make all the choices. I finally succumbed. I realized I was meant to do this, having acquired so much knowledge and expertise as the Building Chairman of the Fund. So, after Subud member Art Stone, who had done so much construction work on his Total Woman Health Clubs, had completed the savvy fix-up of our building, which had once been an Arthur Murray Dance Studio, I took over. Bringing three floors of a neglected property to life and getting it to look tastefully spiffy with limited funds was no small task. I was thankful for my professional supplier contacts. My decisions about the combination of specific colors were extremely important for our needs in the long run. The paint and the carpeting had to be durable, attractive and restful—and quietly soothing in the latihan rooms. I was pleased with the final outcome and grateful that most Subud members agreed. It was a rewarding and a comfortable feeling to do our first official latihans in our new Los Angeles home.

30 New York and a Flawed Audition

WOLF WALTHER, MANAGER OF THE ESSEX HOUSE, invited me back to New York for a huge celebrity art auction to benefit charities. I couldn't believe a year had gone by since the Essex House Les Celebrités opening. As I expected, it was first class all the way, including our suite on the twelfth floor with a fantastic view of Central Park. Later, we stopped in the Botanica for tea—and there was Elke waving us over, hugs and kisses ensuing. She'd just come back from Germany touring a play and was unwinding. Wolf joined us for a pleasant time together, and it was evident they were edging toward the final commitment. He'd made Les Celebrités room one of five best restaurants in the world—our celebrity paintings, of course, a major contribution. The next morning, I rushed out to meet a reputable New York agent that Budd Moss, my Los Angeles rep at the time, had arranged for me to see. In a dumpy building on 28th and Fifth Avenue, in a dumpy office, I met a nice gentleman named Michael Hartig. "It's an honor and a pleasure to meet you," he said. "I saw you the first time in *End as a Man*. You're such a fabulous actor! I'm sure I can get you into something here if you want to be in New York."

"Okay," I mumbled, "but not forever… like six months, max." I was serious when I said that. I couldn't see myself locked down in this city, living a caged life in an apartment like an animal scrambling up the walls behind closed doors ever again. I needed to be able to walk outside any time I wanted to—and I don't mean via an elevator—to smell the grass, pick a weed, and plant a rose bush. This city smothers me.

In the early evening, we went to a party at Rita Gam's apartment. She'd called earlier, insisting we come, and since she lived on the next block, we found ourselves squelched among 150 other guests—all the top people in television and Broadway. Rita, a classy lady and still gorgeous, was now producing and interviewing stars in various countries for a show on PBS. We were getting pooped. We hadn't stopped for a minute since we arrived—so much energy expended and craziness. Had a nice chat with Lee Grant and Anne Meara. Anne had successfully done my *A Medal for Murray* at the Actors Studio when it was still a one-act play, directed by Sondra Lee. We ran into Arthur Storch, who'd became a very successful Broadway director. I hadn't seen him in thirty years. We were in *End as a Man* together and the film version, *The Strange One*.

The next morning, we were sitting in the Botanica having breakfast and had just mentioned Phyllis Diller and we should be calling her because she'd made such an effort to see me in *Next in Line*—and, surprise, in walks Phyllis Diller. She joined us with her secretary and we had lots of hugs and laughs. What a delightfully sweet and interested person to be with—so down to earth and real. She went on about how wonderful I was in the play, "You couldn't be any better and you and Nancy (Dussault) had such a great relationship and played so well together." I thought that was so nice coming from an old pro. Later, Eli Wallach joined us for a long, enjoyable lunch. It was an absolute joy to sit with this old friend whom we both adore—a wonderful guy and a tremendous actor on stage and in films. The day before, he'd celebrated his seventy-fifth, and he reminded me that I was the one who informed him about his SAG pension! He'd lost thousands unnecessarily, unaware of his entitlement. Bursting with stories he told us a couple worth repeating.

One: John Huston was directing him in a scene in his film *The Misfits*, and Eli was supposed to be drunk. After a few takes, Huston called him over and said, "You know, last night I was the drunkest I've ever been in my life."

"I was with you last night," Eli said, "and you didn't look drunk at all..." Huston just sat there not adding anything. Eli got the picture. Do less.

Two: During the same picture shoot, Clark Gable told Eli a Hollywood story. Gable was touring in the play *The Last Mile*, playing Los Angeles. He'd had an offer to do films and was worried that the producer wouldn't let him out of the play contract. He called the producer and the producer asked, "How much are they offering you?"

Gable said, "$400 a week."

The producer on the other end of the line said, "Stay there!" That's how Gable began his picture career.

Eli loved my play *A Medal for Murray* and wanted to do it. I gave him two more copies. He gave one to the Roundabout Theater (where he did Arthur Miller's *The Price*) and the other to The Manhattan Theater Club. We gabbed about so many things, even Lee Strasberg. I told him I had a tape of him arguing with Lee and his criticism after a scene he'd done with Anne Bancroft. He laughed, remembering. When he left, he said, "It's been a wonderful afternoon… and I hope things work out for Murray." I was thinking, Having Eli in a play of mine… that would be scrumptious.

The tickets for *Crazy for You* at the Schubert box office that the star, Jodi Benson, had arranged for us through Lucas, weren't there (he'd conducted her in a UCLA production). We were sent backstage to see Jodi, and it was all sweetly straightened out. Bruce Adler, in the cast, overheard them page Jodi and knew that I was there, so he came over to talk to us. He was the son of the wonderful character actress, Henrietta Jacobson, who'd passed away. He said his mother always talked about me when he was a kid. I'd seen her in a Yiddish play in Philly on a rare occasion with my parents when I was nine years old, and the man playing her husband (her real husband) kept walking around hysterically yelling, "Tzim-possible!" Even as a child, the way he said it was very amusing to me, and Henrietta's playing always stayed in my memory—a quality actress in any language. When I wanted her to play my mother in *Have I got a Girl for You*, I went backstage to see her in the touring production of *Come Blow your Horn* in Los Angeles. I related my childhood story to her, and she excitedly called her husband from the next room just so he could hear me shout, "Tzim-possible! Tzim-possible!" We all laughed heartily in remembrance. Unfortunately, she had a long-term contract, so I cast Mabel Albertson, Jack Albertson's sister and Cloris Leachman's mother-in-law! But that's an old story I've already sufferingly related.

Michael Hartig, Tyne Daly's agent and the fella I had seen the other day, arranged tickets for us to see *The Seagull* at the Lyceum. It was a Tony Randall Production of his National Actors Theater, directed by Marshall Mason. He'd directed me in a reading of *Whispers of the Mind*, by Robert Lee and Jerome Lawrence on the Coast. The first act was lousy, and it was the director's fault—the actors having no activity or behavior, just standing there talking endlessly like sticks. The second, third, and fourth acts were much better. Tyne Daly was a strong Madame Arkadin and Jon Voight was good as Trigorin. A lovely girl playing Nina was excellent, Laura Linney, and so was Ethan Hawke as Constantine—both very talented kids whose careers deservedly took off. We went backstage to see Tyne and Jon Voight to congratulate them. It was weird sitting in the Lyceum. Thirty- seven years earlier on that stage I was drugged for a month in *A Hatful of Rain* before opening in Chicago.

Early evening in the Les Celebrités Room, we were ready for the onslaught of photographers and press. I was immediately interviewed by a German television crew and then, standing in front of my painting, *The Guard at the Louvre*, I blabbed away for Entertainment Tonight. Walking around and greeting everyone, I was especially pleased to meet Claire Trevor, an actress I'd admired ever since I was a kid. I can never forget her heartbreaking performance in Wyler's *Dead End* as Humphrey Bogart's former girl who'd become a prostitute. She had a unique quality that was so feminine and touching in whatever she did. She beamed as I complimented her. Squeezing my hand, she smiled and said, "Tell me more…" (Ginger Rogers had said the same thing to me.) I chatted with New York Mayor David Dinkins who said to me, "Nice to meet you in the flesh. I've enjoyed you on the screen so many years." It's always a surprise to me, and quite humbling to realize people you don't know have been touched in some way by your performances; as the years go by, as an actor, there's a tendency to forget that the impression you've made on screen is cumulative—compounded with each exposure.

After dinner in the Grand Salon and much too many speeches and entertainment, the auction for the New York Children's Health Fund began late, and people were tired. It was exciting, but a bust. The auctioneer from Christie's wouldn't sell below the top sale price for the paintings, which was foolish. My painting, *The Guard at the Louvre*, opened at $3,000 and went to $6,800, but it didn't sell because I'd given a sale price of $7,500 a year earlier. For a charity auction it should've been adjusted, but there was no communication with me. Every star's painting ran into the same problem—a pass. I remember talking with Peggy Lee who I was disturbed to see in a wheelchair, had her painting for sale at $40,000, but it didn't get there. A lot of money was lost unnecessarily. It was really dumb. Elke and Wolf were very disappointed, although the charity made about $120,000 for the evening.

Carol and Alfred joined us to see Judd Hirsch in *Conversations with My Father* and he was excellent. It was a good Herb Gardner play, and the Jewish element was dynamic and up-front concerning hate, prejudice, religion, and the holocaust. It was raining hard when we went backstage afterwards to see Judd. I caught him in the alley as he passed. I yelled, "Judd!"

He turned around and crossed to me and said, "Richman? I thought that was you… he paints, he acts! Are you still drawing?"

I introduced him to everyone as we tried stepping out of the increasingly heavy rain. He then informed me that he was leaving the show in two months and a couple of replacements had dropped out. I thought, *It's a tour de force role… I certainly should tell Michael Hartig about that.* (He probably knew.) We dragged ourselves through the heavy rain looking for a cab and, completely soaked, we finally found one on 8th Avenue. They dropped us off at the hotel. In the morning, I called Michael Hartig to tell him of my conversation with Hirsch. In a nice way, he informed me that I was too old for the part. He said that he'd tried to place Elliot Gould in the role and he was considered too old. All the time I was thinking, Judd Hirsch looks younger than me on stage? Peter Mark, your professional life… it is a-changing…

All packed and ready to go, we were now concerned with the heavily falling snow and violent winds. White chaos had hit the city; it was the worst winter storm in years. We were lucky to get over the 59th Street Bridge, which was supposed to be closed. Once aboard, we still had to wait while they de-iced the wings, the glycol stink permeating the cabin and making some people nauseated. We finally took off at 12:50 p.m. through the snowy muck—a comforting glimpse of blue, high above the leaden grayness breaking through like an unexpected smile on a sour face. From then on it was clear, pleasant flying all the way home.

I had met her about twenty-five years earlier, but it was certainly time to see her again since she was now one hundred years old! Beatrice Wood, a fantastic ceramist and sculptor with an international reputation, still worked in her studio four hours every day. A fledgling actress in Paris and New York in her rebellious teens, she became friendly with many well-known artists of the day and had an affair with Marcel Duchamp (Dada) in 1917, which she wrote about extensively in her autobiography, *I Shock Myself*. She also had translated Stanislavski—and not many people can say that. After traversing the winding roads above Ojai, overwhelmed by the picture-book scenery near her mountaintop home, we finally arrived. Ram Pravesh Singh, her associate and manager, greeted us with his lilting Indian dialect and ushered us into the showroom. He informed us that she was resting and would be seeing us in fifteen minutes. It gave us an opportunity to view her marvelous work and her unique drawings. One ceramic piece in particular caught my eye and kept me studying it from all angles. She finally came in wearing a long colorful sari, white-faced, dark red lipstick on her lips, bare-footed and Indian jewelry dangling from her neck. Her hair was pulled back and she was smiling. I realized quickly that she was quite deaf, even though I was enunciating my words slowly and carefully. She was very warm and gracious, but as I was snapping away with my camera, she hadn't lost her vanity, resisting me from getting too close. She loved the attention and sitting next to her on a window seat, I got her talking freely of her work and how she begins and achieves her incredible glazes. "I have a strong idea about what I want before I start," she said, "but what baffles and eludes me are my glazes… the consistency and certainty of the result." Then she giggled mischievously. "What keeps me going are chocolates and young men!" I knew she must've used that line on many occasions, but she was amazingly responsive to my questions answering them fully. I was so impressed with the clarity of her vision and dedication. Here was a quality artist still working at one hundred years and still turning out quality pieces. It crossed my mind more than once: Her art is keeping her alive (she lived to be 104).

I couldn't resist the ceramic I'd been eyeing earlier—a blue and gold, museum quality glazed urn, with nude male figures all around the top, heads down; a magnificent work. Beatrice had commented "… and I'm not just saying this because you're interested in it… but it's one of my favorite works and I'd hate to see it go." (Later, I was asked to put it into a Beatrice Wood exhibition in New York, but I refused for safety reasons.)

She wrote in one of the books we'd purchased: "To Helen and Peter… who walked off with *Meeting of the Minds*." Next to her signature, she made a colored pencil sketch of her face with big tears rolling down her cheeks. Afterwards she took us through her studio to see the works in progress, her vast quantity of glazes and her powerful kilns. As we were leaving she kissed me and thanked me for the interrogation. "I'm sorry I didn't have it taped," I said, "people would have enjoyed it."

She laughed and said, "I'm glad you didn't. It will remain just between us!"

Getting back in the car, my Beatrice Wood unpacked in the trunk, I thought, *My God… what a wonderful and special day this was…*

I was involved in so many endeavors and wearing so many hats, I had a hard time figuring out where to devote my energy for the day. Of course, I'd discovered—and it wasn't a mysterious revelation—but slowly and insidiously, the older I became—the opportunities for work had become more elusive. It hadn't been given an official name as yet, but in any color, shape or form it was eventually identified as, Ageism—

and it permeated the film and television industry like a disease. So, while stewing and festering with the hand I'd been given, compulsive as I am and have always been, I tried to fill my time in a creative capacity with other abilities I'd been graced with and was damned serious about fulfilling. I'd given my play *A Medal for Murray* to James Dolittle, an influential producer who called and said, "I like it… it has merit. It's well written, funny and poignant… and has some interesting lines. Just let me think about it some more…"

Possible? I knew he was tied up with three ballet companies, the Joffrey and Baryshnikov's (but it prompted me to call Eli Wallach). My novel in manuscript form was still making the rounds—another major agent had read it, liked it, and was giving it a shot. I was finishing another oil painting in my studio of an old woman asleep on a city bench, and I'd been writing six different monologues of people that intrigued me: Two of which were a preacher and a former Nazi officer. Sometimes I seemed to get the two mixed up.

After walking three miles on the beach in Oxnard, ankle deep in splashing water having succumbed to Helen's favorite pursuit—collecting small, shiny rocks (and watching the grunions run too), we were comfortably settled in our suite at the Mandalay Beach resort, a glass of chilled white wine in our hands. The view of the Pacific Ocean from the balcony, the cool breeze and the quiet were profound. It was May 10, 1993, and we were there to celebrate our fortieth wedding anniversary, periodically shaking our heads in wonderment that it couldn't be. Forty years, it seemed, had passed in a flash. At the appropriate moment, I gave her a carved "40" year gold charm with the engraving: "You were Heaven sent to me," to be added to her heavily laden bracelet of charms, each one a birthdate of our five children. I'll never forget how touched and surprised I was a few days earlier when having dinner at the El Caballero Country Club, all of our children suddenly put on straw hats, rose from the table, and began singing a Mother's Day tribute to Helen. Even the other diners were knocked out. I've been more than lucky to have married a beautiful young woman who was now a beautiful older woman—wise, thoughtful, and loving, and my spiritual companion and soul mate. We'd survived some rough times—the ups and downs, joys and sorrows, and the "whatever is to be's." We were happy to be two people meant for each other, gratefully worshipping God through the Subud latihan. Just ten days earlier we'd celebrated our thirty-fourth year in Subud, the source and blessing for our continued love, health, and good fortune. I can't even begin to imagine my life without Subud and the worship of God. To me, it's the foundation and sustenance of everything.

"My cup runneth over," as they say. I sat enthralled as my son Lucas conducted the Los Angeles Performing Arts Orchestra in The Loren L. Zachery 21st Annual National Vocal Competition. He guided eleven different singers in twenty-two different arias at the Ambassador Auditorium to a packed house. The event lasted close to four hours and the singers were magnificent. Afterward, all were gushing their praises of Lucas. When Licia Albanese, a judge (*the* Licia Albanese), saw me backstage she said, "Oh, I know you!" When I told her the conductor was my son, she said, "He was just wonderful… so considerate and sensitive to the singers." This, from one of the greatest sopranos of all time. When Max Herman, former head of the Los Angeles musicians' union (who got Lucas the job), asked the concertmaster what the orchestra thought of Lucas, he replied, "He's the best we've ever had."

Not to be outdone, in another venue a few days later, what a joyous heart-thumping thrill to see my beautiful young daughter, Kelly, of blessed talent and easy presence, stand up there and sing "The Music of Harry Warren" with a style all her own. I'm not ashamed to go on like this because it's all true. As a supportive Dad, I just hope they have their dreams and hopes fulfilled, at least some of them.

That Molten White Light...

AT THE END OF MAY, my son Howard joined us on an Alaska Airlines flight to Seattle for a weekend National Subud Congress, joining people from all over the world tied together with this remarkable golden thread of the latihan—God's cleansing energy and unlimited restorer. We settled in at the Marriott Hotel, the manager sending up a basket of goodies and a bottle of wine. After the evening latihan, I found out an amazing fact and met the man who achieved it: Seth Aronie, a Subud helper who took it upon himself to go to Russia and the Ukraine and open new people to the contact. It was more than astounding to me that in a communist country for over seventy years that had glorified the state and honored atheism. There were now small, but enthusiastic, Subud groups in Moscow and Kiev worshipping God through the latihan. We were quite moved when he gave a slide and video presentation of Russian men and women joyously expressing themselves (translated) about the "gift" that had come to them by this man named Seth. These vivid moments were a supercharged reminder of how people of different countries and beliefs can truly be touched by the one creator of us all. After the large film screen was removed from the ballroom stage and replaced with a grand piano, Howard played two Chopin études beautifully and then accompanied an extremely gifted cellist, Hamilton Cheifetz, in a concert that was more satisfying than cherry cheesecake.

At this congress, I had a major revelation in the latihan concerning the incident I wrote about in the early part of my book when I was six years old—the time I saw that molten, white light hovering above the doorway of Mrs. Fried's home. It has always stayed with me and is still as vivid as if it happened yesterday. I had been given a clarification and a profound and deep understanding. The white light was an awakening of my soul as a child and preparation for my life prior to receiving the opening in Subud later as an adult. I had received the Kadar (Indonesian word) which is a great blessing from God and a protection for my life—the white light actually entering into my body without my awareness. The light, a manifestation of God's power in the realm of the material world. It has strengthened my faith in God and deepened my convictions. I'm cognizant, finally, that my life is guided by God, and all I have to do is accept it and get out of the way and not throw impediments on the path He has created for me.

There I was sitting on the beach at Sears Point in Brewster, comfy in a short-backed canvas chair, the sun strong and the slight wind a cooling alteration—and all was Cape Cod gorgeous. The silver-green tide was moving out—now dark blue at the horizon touching a pale blue sky. Small sailboats, their sails like sharp shells slicing through the water, an occasional motorboat disturbing the quietness; or a clunky old biplane pulling a long banner advertising a movie—reminding me of the banner pulled across the sky years ago in Atlantic City: Tommy Dorsey now at Steel Pier!

I can still see it, hear it, and feel it as I walk on the boiling hot sand with 10 year old feet; experiences seared in my sensory memory like a brand on a steer, transporting me back in time instantly and without warning: the scuffling sounds of walking feet on the wooden boardwalk; the ocean's lapping waves; the dark, cool refreshing dampness underneath the boardwalk where lovers fool around; the grittiness of the sand between my toes; the efficient clunking of the "Fralinger's" taffy-making machine; the soreness of my unprotected shoulders and sun-peeling skin; the wet sand as I dig my big toe deeper in near the water's edge; the shiny, broken shells all around; my father's white legs as he sits with his pants rolled up, his straw hat perched on his head, his stiff white collar still buttoned and his tie pulled tight in place. I remember it all and more.

This is Edward Hopper country. He painted here, and every beach tower and house looks like a Hopper painting. I hoped to get to it, at least a sketch. We were visiting Carol and Alfred again in their summer place, so tastefully done with Carol's artistic eye. Being together has always been warm and satisfying—poking fun, sharing love; a sense of family in the best possible way. Helen was zealously patrolling the beach again for her little rocks. Plenty of time to think and I was thinking, I suppose I didn't get the job or I would've heard from my agent by now.

Before I left, I'd interviewed for an independent film and they seemed interested, but I guess it's just another dud. I know it's the nature of the business, but I'm finding it difficult to accept—66 years old and still looking for a job. How undignified and degrading. Relaxing in this wonderfully lazy atmosphere, I couldn't shake the thoughts that continually dwelled in my stewpot of a brain. What shall I spend my time doing when I get home? Paint? Yes, I can do that and probably will. Write? I do have a commercial play, *A Medal for Murray*, collecting dust on a shelf. I've been told by a lot of people that they like it—but nothing happens. James Dolittle had expressed interest, but he kept stalling me for weeks. Act? Well, I wrote a one-man show for myself, the beginnings of one, at least—a bunch of different colorful characters that would be fun to bring to life, but I couldn't seem to get off my rear to get it going. I wondered, *What's stopping me*? Am I lazy or just bloody tired of the whole fucking business—the agents, the producers, the networks, the PR hype, the critics—the whole sorry, self-serving corrupt bunch.

Or is it just my age? Inner changes, perhaps? I do know that the view from where I sit is a bit different than what it used to be. My perception and understanding have been altered considerably. The question is: Is it maturity or just plain stodginess? Well, I will say without fear of contradiction that the business has changed so much it's unrecognizable—and nobody, save for a few kindred souls, seem to give two shits in a garbanzo bean can about how low it has sunk. All you have to do is watch television and—except for a few shows—most of what's on view is utter time-filling crap, far inferior to what was offered twenty years ago. Perhaps it's the quality of life that I see represented which offends me—of course, TV only reflecting what's going on around us. But who wants to see all this putrid stuff constantly? The mayhem, serial killings, the abused wives and abused children, AIDS, bestiality, cannibalism, and the excess presentations of man's inhumanity to man. It certainly isn't me. Who wants to see another dysfunctional family with dreadful little monsters running around taunting their divorcing parents? Is it any wonder we have kid monsters growing up to be bigger monsters who taunt and mug the citizenry and shoot the teacher at school? No respect for anyone or anything; no convention, no institution, no governmental entity—and certainly not the police. We're in a helluva state. The whole problem, as Bapak said a long time ago, is spiritual. Unless there's a major spiritual enlightenment, I'm truly afraid that we are in for the shits to continue.

It was raining hard in the morning, the horizon far off from the condo's porch, a maze of varying shades of gray. The raindrops were splashing on my bare legs, but I didn't mind. I delayed moving. On the stairway there was a hanging flowerpot bursting with little purple flowers—and right in the middle, a bird's nest and four tiny eggs the mother sat on. Every time we'd go up or down the stairs she'd scurry away and return when we were out of sight. It's amazing how God has given the female of every species the inbred duty and need to nourish, protect, and care for her young.

The weather cleared and the drive to Chatham, the most chic of all the areas, was definitely "Cape Cod"—the sprawling white homes with their gray, cedar-shingled roofs; the lavender mums, the maroon climbing roses; the glorious ocean front and the rocky beaches; the birds, the seagulls— all spectacularly idyllic. Walking through the town of Chatham, so quaint and charming—the trees, thickly painted with silver-green lichen on the bark; a rainbow of flowers along the way; and the smell of freshly cut grass permeating—the air was almost intoxicating. I had a wish to bottle it all and take it back to Woodland Hills. The one thing I did do was stuff some sand from the Brewster beach into a plastic box, which I swear was definitely lavender in color. But when I got home, the lavender was gone! It was just plain old sand. Another unanswerable phenomenon.

In the evening at the intimate Bramble Inn, we indulged ourselves—lobster and white fish and a lemon soufflé! Then prompted by our mellow feelings, the four of us raised our glasses to a toast—Alfred and I stating that we loved each other, and in forty-one years we'd never expressed a hurtful word to one another. Al, who'd been through hell with his three older children from an earlier marriage, shook his head affirmatively when I said kids today are overindulged and had no concept of what life was like when we were growing up in the depression years and how it had shaped us. I certainly know that the flavor of my personality was simmered and stewed by the stresses of a tumultuous childhood. I don't know why I was destined to go through it, but as an actor it had carved me a bit differently.

The following night they invited three friends to join us for one of Carol's gourmet dinners. Dr. Jang Singh, his wife, and the doctor's brother Ma-Mon' Singh, a wealthy business man. They were Sikhs originally from India, both men with impressive beards and turbans. Warm and personable, they responded easily over coffee and dessert when I asked them something I've always been curious about: "Why do you wear turbans?"

"Like the Jews," Ma-Mon said, "because of persecution… Sikhs were not allowed to wear the headdress for a hundred years, and in defiance they did… and thousands were slaughtered."

According to Jang, now they wear the turban traditionally, identifying and honoring their brothers of the past, but it has no spiritual significance. It all began around 1500 by an Islamic-influenced Hindu who was against idolatry and caste. The Sikhs believe all people are created by God, and there is only one God. I absolutely agree. I walked out on the porch to observe the spectacular color changes in the sky as the orange-red sun began to slowly set—looking like a monstrous, neon ping-pong ball sitting on the horizon. I thought about what our guests had said and how all people have fiercely determined their own comprehension of God and what God means to them. It's terribly complex, and when you express yourself and your beliefs, care has to be taken not to offend while extolling your convictions. When I try to explain Subud, for instance, people don't easily understand—they just don't get the concept. It's so simple that it's unacceptable. The mind prevents getting past the stone barriers of preconceived religious and spiritual "God" convention. There's a block and it's almost impenetrable. Everyone has their own "thing" and way to do it… this, getting to God—but they don't really know how to do it, and they're not really sure who or what they're trying to get to. I certainly don't have all the answers, but I have one—the Subud way—and it has worked for me. I know that whatever happens, in submission to God's will, guidance for my life is a constant. Not that I comprehend what God's will is, really, but I do know that I'm protected, healthy, rational (mostly), prosperous, and blessed with five children and a wife of rare quality. I've never questioned the verity of the latihan and its power. Once experienced, how can you? Helen feels the same way. With so many people the world over searching for God sincerely and assiduously, we feel grateful and blessed that true worship was given to us… in a moment, in a flash—just like that. I'm still in awe after forty-six years, and the wish to share it is strong.

Sometimes in company with friends or with new acquaintances, I have the overpowering impulse to pull away from the boring blah-blah conversation of inconsequential indulgence by saying, Hey, let's talk about real stuff… you know, God. Like, how do you find him and what is worship and what happens when you die? Of course, you can't do that very often; there's no receptivity or readiness. So, you skirt real talk with pretty patter and acceptable bullshit to pass the time—the latest films, TV, the weather, politics, a juicy article in some magazine—small talk leading nowhere. It's a dilemma.

Taking my excited sons Orien and Roger to Rams preseason practices gave them enough stories to tell their friends to last a month.

It warmed my heart to see their sparkling enthusiasm and optimism about the coming 1993 season. Lunch with Jack Faulkner and Jim Hill, a local CBS-TV sports personality there to do interviews, was an added plus. Sports, and football in particular, was one interest that found fertile soil with my youngest kids that was somewhat distant in my three older children; where the smell of the freshly cut grass and seeing the players in full pads ready to go at it gave me an adrenaline pop like no other. It was an Orange County hot day, the club was scrimmaging and we were sitting next to my friend Vince Ferragamo, former Rams quarterback. The sweaty pounding was loud and furious and when a massive Kansas State rookie offensive tackle got into a brawl with our starting linebacker, I said to Vince, "He's a tough kid… I hope he makes the club."

"Yeah," Vince said, nodding in agreement. "They could use him."

That kind of privileged presence, witnessing the molding and selecting of the elements that produce a good team always fascinated me. It was a kick to be an "insider," talking to head coach Chuck Knox and all the other coaches as if I were someone whose opinion counted. In a funny way it did—the players and coaches were, in turn, appreciative of a guy with a known face who regularly showed up at practice to cheer them on. After all, aren't sports just another way to perform? A different format, perhaps, but still—out there, hoping to excel in front of crowds of people doing whatever you're trained to do, getting applause and a salary.

I have vivid dreams, and in most cases I remember them in detail. Here's one about football. I was in this open area, similar to a practice field, and I was supposed to play a game that day. We were running around, throwing and kicking the ball. I knew game time was drawing closer, and that Joe Pitt, my old high school and Eastern Pro League coach, was hovering around—somehow mixing him up in the dream with Chuck Knox as if they were the same person. I knew I had to get ready for the game, taping my ankles, etc.—but when I looked in a mirror, I saw that I was wearing a suit and tie! *Hell*, I thought, *I gotta move fast!* I went up to another player and said, "How are you going to play? You're wearing a suit just like me."

He began to remove his clothes. "I have my uniform on underneath," he said. "We all do."

Then I started to panic. There was no time left and I didn't want Joe Pitt-Chuck Knox angry at me. Suddenly everybody was moving up some stairs to get a bite to eat and I was being ushered along and I thought, *Here's my time to change… I'll run back to the locker room and do it now!*

I am dashing—and on either side of me are rocky hillsides with people now (game fans) milling among the rocks looking for their seats. I have the feeling I know where I'm going and I finally come to a street corner and a three-story building that looks familiar. I go inside the marble stairway and dark wood bannisters seem like a school and three people are coming up the stairs. "Do you know where the locker room is?" I ask. They look at me blankly, then as I turn to go one African-American guy says, "1332!" I turn and run out the door as fast as I can, passing all sorts of row houses and when I look at the address numbers I see #1380! So, I rush back to #1332 and like a camera zooming in to the number, I dash up the steps to confront a locked door! I shake the door hopelessly, knowing all is lost and the coach will be furious at me and I will miss the entire game. I will never find that locker room! I take off toward the field thinking I can borrow someone else's uniform—although I hate that; the uncleanliness, the perspiration, and the body odor. But I have no choice! It's better than the wrath of the coach. I'm crossing the street running like hell, knowing the kickoff must be imminent, when suddenly—I can't lift my right leg! It's paralyzed! It's stuck in the mud, immovable! Holy fuck, what am I gonna do now? I've got to get to that game! Oh, shit! I've got to lift my leg… it's so painful… it won't move! Sonofabitch! Come on, come on… lift it up… the coach is counting on me! Then with all my strength I violently wrench myself free of the nightmare—and wake up in a sweat. I've had variations of this dream countless times as an actor facing mountainous impediments trying to get to a performance and then not knowing my lines once I arrive on stage or even what play I'm appearing in.

In late August, I signed a contract to guest star on several *Beverly Hills 90210* segments, another Spelling monster hit, as the father of a young man intent on marrying Shannen Doherty. On the first day of shooting, I was amused to suddenly find myself giving unscripted "asked-for" advice to the young woman, dedicated dad that I am, concerning an automobile accident she'd just had with her new Mercedes. Though she had a reputation for rebelliousness and inability to get along, she listened intently and appreciatively as I suggested an approach to her problems—her beautiful eyes absorbing my good intentions. I was sorry that we didn't have any extended scenes together to shoot—the relationship would have worked well.

Helen had pointedly said to me in one way or another that all the monologues I'd been writing needed an audience—"work on them at the

Studio… sitting in a drawer isn't going to get it done." My wife is a wise woman and I was definitely getting weary of her calling me "The Man in the Drawer." So the first piece I worked up was called *The Preacher*, a southern fundamentalist giving a sermon to his flock. Unfortunately, he had a little problem with some of the young ladies in his congregation. He had enjoyed them sexually, but his misdeeds had been exposed. It was about a man who'd lost his way spiritually, and in the sermon he denies his transgressions and declares his innocence. It was a complex piece, and I was eager to try it out. I learned the lines, trying to forget I wrote them, and got it up on my feet before presenting it to the acting workshops of good friends Tracy Roberts and Gene Butler. After the run-throughs, I asked for feedback and was able to utilize some of the useful comments for rewrites. In the next few months, I presented *Pastor Harlan Gregory* four times at the Actors Studio with progressive success and encouraging commentary from moderators Tony Franciosa, Susan Peretz, and Salomé Jens. It was coming together.

I stood center stage, the lights came up and I gazed at the grim, but attentive, faces in the half light and began, addressing an imaginary trio of singers who'd completed their part of the service: "Thank you, dear sisters for that lovely hymn. Give us thy strength indeed, oh Lord… Amen! Good mornin', brothers and sisters, I'm so happy to see you all here this bright Sunday mornin'…" Keeping my performance loose and improvisational, I let it fly, following impulses wherever it emotionally took me, my voice, quiet or projected, varying suddenly. The studio was extremely attentive, absorbed and even shocked—with slight fits of unexpected laughter. The response was very complimentary. "Dynamic and powerful." "… The writing impressive…" One actor said, "I believed you and your sermon. You're in the wrong profession!" Shelley Winters was there and her comments were also heartwarming. "I forgot what an extraordinary actor you are," she said, "because you've been out here working and making money. You should have stayed in New York because you're a giant as an actor."

"Thank you," I said, somewhat surprised.

She continued. "Seeing you work gives me hope. I've not been pleased with a lot of what I see here. I can't wait to see the next character."

I was grateful and had learned a lot by their reaction, but I knew that I had to clarify and bolster the ending of the scene, which caused some confusion. It was interesting to note that no matter how convincing I was in squirming my innocence, everyone still thought I was guilty! It was now obvious to me after all the positive appraisals from the group that I had the foundation for a one-man show. I just had to decide how many more pieces I needed and what characters would work for an evening in the theater.

John Crean and his wife, Donna, founders of "Fleetwood," the leading recreational vehicle manufacturer in the world, invited us to be their captive guests in Las Vegas for a few days—along with 800 dealers from all over the country! It was John's way of saying thanks for their dedication to quality customer performance. John, an absolute sweetheart of a man, whose assets were in the zillions, enjoyed having us with him and said, "What good is all this if we can't share it with our friends?" Most of the time at dinners we sat with Mary Roosevelt, who we'd first met on the Rams trip to England (James, her husband, had passed away). Also at our table were Lynne and James Doti, president of Chapman University, who unexpectedly invited me to lecture there on art or theater. Of course, I said that I would. Another welcome guest and friend of the Creans arrived to liven things up considerably—Milton Berle and his beautiful wife, Lorna. We'd known each other for about twenty-five years or so, and being with him was always full of interesting conversation if not always a laugh-fest. He reminded me that he wrote the lyrics for the movie we did together, *For Singles Only*. Included among his prolific output, he also mentioned he wrote the lyrics for "Mairzy Dotes and Dozy Doats"—an oddball hit years ago. We first met on the set of *The Fugitive* with David Janssen when I guest starred. He told me that David's mother was quite a "nutty toots" and he'd taken her out in 1926. He said that she was a real "show-biz mom" and had driven David to drink. Then, shaking his head sadly, he told me that Dean Martin was a basket case, sitting in a chair so drunk he hardly moved. Kibitzing with a legend is an enterprising feat of fun and kept me on my toes. He was also a "zinger" tease, saying at one point that he knew all about me and my varied and "checkered career." I suppose what he wanted to say was, What the hell happened to it? "All Jews in this facacta business know when another Jew comes on the scene and gets attention!" he said. He once asked me, "What's the story on this 'Peter' business?"

I started to go into a whole detailed explanation, then changed my mind and simply said, "I did it for spiritual reasons."

"Oh... okay," he said, nodding his head in thought.

On our way to view the tons of RVs on display, Milton had his arm in mine as we walked, and I could feel the trembling and frailty of an eighty-five-year-old man—this comical genius and icon nearing the end of his life who I'd first thrilled to years ago on a tiny black and white television screen. I was grateful to share these private moments and to be a friend to someone the whole country admired.

For a Rams football fan, no boundaries exist, so three days before a Sunday game, we traveled to Tempe, Arizona, to see the Rams play the Arizona Cardinals. But first, at Georgia Frontiere's invitation, we flew to Phoenix, picked up our rented car and drove to the Canyon Mesa Country Club in Oak Creek, near Sedona, where Georgia was renovating her new home. Our unit at the club was a spectacularly furnished small abode, and the red hills view from our porch was gasping gorgeous. That evening, we met Georgia and Earle at a charming Swiss restaurant for dinner—Earle, living his fantasy, looking more like a cowpoke every time we saw him. Georgia, always comfortable in our company, felt free to unwind about her situation in Anaheim. She was going through tremendous stress and turmoil losing bundles of money with poor game attendance—not even selling out when the teams were good. The renewal of her lease was fast approaching and she had to make a decision. Baltimore and other cities were screaming to have the Rams, and she was eager to be somewhere that loved and supported the team. Anaheim had done zilch to entice her to stay. The National Football League was extremely political and made it ferociously difficult for a team to move, but Georgia implicitly trusted John Shaw, the brilliant Rams president and administrator, who would digest all possibilities and target the best. I would be unhappy, of course, if the Rams moved to another city, but that's life—nothing remains the same. Our old friends Art and Adrienne Stone arrived the next day.

We'd introduced them to Subud and to Georgia and they were now in her inner circle of friends. A terrific couple—Adrienne, a dark-haired, svelte beauty, and Art, a red-headed, pugnacious personality who was a pushover for a good joke. With zany Marshall Klein in the mix, we were holding our sides continuously. Later, Richard Fredricks joined our party, a Metropolitan Opera singer who was coaching Georgia for her infrequent charity performances. That evening, we came back to our place and Georgia did the latihan with Helen and Adrienne while Art and I were in another room doing ours. Afterward, in front of a crackling fireplace, we listened to a 1981 Bapak tape, when he basically said that in every age God sends what is needed (Subud and the latihan) and we are past listening to words, and that the lower, negative forces have become so strong, nothing will change unless mankind receives the influence of the real power of God.

Georgia had practically taken over the place. Italian food with a Chinese bent was served to about forty people. We sat with John Shaw and Rebecca and Walter Schacht (team chiropractor) and nearby was Maureen Reagan and her husband, Dennis. Suddenly, I remembered one night, a while back, at a Georgia Thanksgiving dinner when John said to me, "I heard you and Maureen had a little tiff…"

"Oh, and who is the spy in our midst?"

He laughed. "I have my sources…" Then John and I kidded about the "nothing" event. Maureen and I had been warm and friendly for a long time, but one day we had a slight altercation after a Rams loss. We were watching Chuck Knox's press conference on closed circuit TV in Georgia's stadium suite when Maureen made some derogatory comments about the coach. I didn't like that, my loyalties run deep, so I said in a nice way, "Maureen, I don't agree with you." And she shot back in very un-nice way, "WELL, THAT'S YOUR PROBLEM!"

So, I shot back, pissed: "No, that's your problem!" That was it. Nothing more was said, but at the time I was so annoyed I was sorry I had contributed to her congressional political campaign. After dinner, Georgia invited us to see her new home in Scottsdale, just completed. When I walked in, the first thing I saw was a watercolor I'd painted in 1970, *Backstage Dressing Room*. Then she took us into the dining room and showed us three more PMRs—a nude from the Lake Tahoe series and two others, *Rose in a Box* and *Flowers for Mulanka* that I'd painted in Vancouver. In the bathroom she proudly displayed a large sensuous nude, *Mila*. Georgia is my biggest collector—she owns fourteen of my paintings.

The next morning was game day. I had to drive to Tempe, Arizona, get to the hotel where the Rams were staying, return our rented car, and get back in time to board the last Rams bus to the stadium. It was no small feat—and thank God, the Stones were friends, because following me in their car they confessed to thinking I was absolutely out of my mind—especially when I went the wrong way. After our crazed journey, I remember Helen emphatically saying to Adrienne, "I really do need a drink!"

Before the game, we ran into Fritz Schurmer, my old Rams buddy, now defensive coordinator for Arizona. The Rams sure could have used him that day because we got creamed 38-10 and looked like crap. Looking down from the owner's suite through tinted sun screens, which was as close to the clouds as flying, the players small as bugs, I became extremely depressed and I felt badly for Georgia having to suffer through that season. As we boarded the charter plane going home, Chuck Knox said to me, "We're going through bad times…" Poor guy, it was not the way he planned it—a revival of past greatness was not in the cards.

32 You Just Had To Prat

HELEN AND I WERE SOUNDLY ASLEEP. When the earthquake hit, it was so violent and scary that the only thing you could do was pray, and we did until the twenty-second rumbling stopped. We'd been through many earthquakes before, but the quake on January 17, 1994, at 4:30 a.m. was something else. It was part of the periodic chaos of living in California, like the riots and fires—but until then, we'd never experienced such unleashed monstrous power. Not only was it a "rocker," it was a terrifying "bouncer," compelling us to hold on to our beds while everything around us was falling down—shelves, books, bottles, and a large TV.

"Helen, are you okay?" I asked in the blackness. "Yes... yes," she answered, her prayers still echoing.

I was like a blind man opening his eyes to nothingness, not a speck of light anywhere. I stumbled out of bed and made my first mistake. I stepped on a pile of jagged books and painfully banged my bare foot into the television set that was now displaced at the bed's edge. "Oh, shiiiiiit!" I muttered. "Helen, don't move... it's dangerous in here."

I crawled to where I thought the door used to be and tried to open it, but furniture and bookshelf debris were blocking it. I sat there trying to get my bearings, slowly pushing, pulling, and lifting stuff so I could open the door to get out. I finally did. Slowly, I made my way down the stairs to click off the alarm system, which was now on batteries, and went back to the foyer to open the front door, which I could hardly move, it was so off kilter. I heard some people running, their flashlights making eerie streaks against the foliage. Someone shouted, "Make sure your gas is off! Look out for live wires!"

A sliver of daylight was beginning to show. I went back inside, trying not to step on broken glass and picture frames. Making my way into the kitchen, I found a flashlight and could see the two built-in ovens hanging out of their cabinets on the floor, their electrical cables dangerously pulled to the limit. The smell of booze was overpowering. All of our glassware, dishes, and liquor bottles had fallen out of the cabinets. Whiskey and elegant liquors were splattered all over the floor, mixed with the Gerber's baby food I occasionally fed my grandchild. I suppose I was in shock. When my concerned kids arrived, unable to reach us because the phones were down, they found me on the floor leaning against a cabinet scooping up oatmeal mush and Jack Daniels—actually sitting in it.

"Dad, what are you doing?" Kelly worriedly asked. "Uh… I have to clean up the mess," I answered, dazedly.

We live in a five-bedroom home on a hill. The house is actually on four levels. The master bedroom on the top level used to have an enormously tall brick chimney above the cedar shake roof, each brick weighing eight to ten pounds. During the quake, the chimney came crashing down. If it had fallen on the fragile roof directly above us, where we sleep, we would have been a memory. Thankfully, the whole pile—a ton and almost six feet high—went in the other direction, next to the house in the garden. This 6.7 earthquake, which was upgraded to 6.8 on the Richter scale, was the first to strike an urban area since the Long Beach earthquake in 1933. The epicenter originated close to us in Northridge, another section of the San Fernando Valley, and caused tremendous devastation. Major freeways, bridges, and office and apartment buildings collapsed or suffered irreparable damage. Twenty-five thousand dwellings became uninhabitable and twenty-two thousand people were left homeless. There was $44 billion in damages, the costliest disaster in U.S. history. Fifty-seven people were killed and 9,000 injured, 1,500 seriously. We considered ourselves lucky—or shall I say, protected? We suffered no injury and neither did our children, their apartments were only slightly affected. The quake was selective in its crazy pattern of execution, zigging and zagging leaving some structures totally untouched. I was grateful to have earthquake insurance. The damage was over $300,000—every room had suffered heavily. It was impossible to stay there; it was just too dangerous. We moved out for ten months, putting all our possessions in storage until the major renovation was completed. During that time, I was grateful to move into a condo we owned nearby which, surprisingly, only suffered minor cracks.

I was diligently at my home every day for a year overseeing my contractor and all his workmen. They quickly became sick of me. As chairman of the building committee for the Motion Picture and Television

Fund, it seemed as if I were just continuing a job I'd been performing for a long time—only now I was writing the checks too with all my demands. It was enervating. In the end, even with the dreaded aftershocks sending us scrambling everywhere looking for new damages, our residence turned out more spiffy than it was before—especially with a new addition. It was a separate building of my design—a sky-lighted, spacious art studio. Somebody once said, "From all the bad, something good happens…" In my case, it was true.

The second monologue for a one-man show I had been writing depicted a man reminiscing about his childhood, his mother, and his vivid remembrances of watching the sun rise over the mountains and the tall pine trees swaying in the wind. The more I wrote about him and his close relationship to his mother, who was deeply religious, the more he seemed to evolve into a little German boy asking profound questions:

"Tell me momma, how does the sun come up every day and why does it go down behind the mountain?"

After a pause, she kisses him and says, "The sun comes up because God makes it happen, liebchen… he does all these things. Everything that we have no answers for… that is what God does."

"And who is God?" he asks in all innocence.

Putting her arm around him, she continues gently: "God is who… God is why… and God is where. Wherever you look, that is where God is." She touches his forehead. "God is here also." Then pointing to his heart, "And here too… and if you have a good heart, God is with you always in this place. But if you have a heart that is selfish and mean… then God goes away and doesn't come back again… and you live with a heart that has nothing inside. It remains empty and cold."

For some peculiar reason, an exquisite irony (the mystery of creative impulses), the inquisitive little boy developed into an elderly man named Gerhardt, a former Nazi SS officer, now living somewhere in South America and whose grandson is visiting him and asking him profound and disturbing questions about his participation in the "Final Solution"— questions that could be decidedly dangerous. Again, it was time to take Gerhardt off the printed page and let him express himself fully, with an added authentic German dialect to deepen the presentation. The response at the Actors Studio was very positive, in particular, Ray Walston, who, enthused by the writing and Gerhardt's details said, "… in the tradition of the finest work ever done at the studio," and likened me to Michael Chekhov in what I had achieved. To some, the material was scarily disquieting.

I was not surprised—rounding up and sending innocent people to the gas chamber indifferently. "We had a job to do and we were authorized to do it!" was not easy to take in a charmingly hateful character who unabashedly loved his God-fearing mother. I knew the scene worked and felt it would be a good contrast to the others I was writing.

We've always had a weighted social calendar, and actually, it was a godsend to get away for an evening and put aside the worrisome responsibilities of reconstruction and renovation. We saw my dear friend Theodore Bikel perform Tevya again beautifully in *Fiddler on the Roof* at the Pasadena Civic Auditorium. (We'd seen him play it twenty-six years earlier in Las Vegas with my sleepy kids at our side. The only wide-awake child was a four-year-old Lucas.) After the show, we went to a party for a celebration of his seventieth birthday and toasted our champagne to a very special fellow. Another evening we joined Georgia Frontiere, who was involved in everything, at an affair for the American Air Museum to be built in Duxford, England. I chatted with Bob Hope, who was honored, and Charlton Heston, who was co-chair with Georgia; I even conversed with Lord Bramwell as the photographers snapped away.

We went to a luncheon honoring Poldek Page (Pfefferberg) whose Holocaust story prompted the book that eventually became the Spielberg film *Schindler's List*. We became friends with Poldek and his wife, Mila, both concentration camp survivors. Later, after they saw a performance of my one-man show, they wrote me a touching letter concerning Gerhardt and my fictitious holocaust survivor, Daniel. I then included it in my theater program. Attending a dinner at the home of Lynne and James Doti, the president of Chapman University in Orange, we were surrounded by people of enormous wealth: John and Donna Crean, Judi and George Argyros, and Doy and Dee Henley. During the evening, Jim Doti offered me an art show at the university, which I certainly agreed to. We went to see Cloris Leachman, a fellow Actors Studio member, in *Joyride: The True Story of Grandma Moses* at the Westwood Playhouse. She was brilliant. Afterward, over drinks and coffee, she humorously related a ridiculous incident when she and I opened on Broadway in *Masquerade* years ago. In a serious and dramatic moment as husband and wife, she slaps me and I was supposed to slap her back, but instead she ducked!—sending the audience howling (I was furious with her). Then, in a quiet moment, Cloris recalled something else she'd never forgotten. During our pre-Broadway rehearsal, she said that I said to her, "Cloris, did you forget how to work?" At the opening of the new Stella

Adler Theater and Workshop, we saw director Peter Bogdonovich and an actress read the intimate letters of Stella and Harold Clurman. We had a friendly chat afterward, and Irene Gilbert, who ran the place, expressed interest in having me do my one-man show there when completed. At a St. Jude charity affair where Natalie Cole performed with such heart, I had a conversation with Buddy Rogers who told me he would be ninety in August, and when he said that to George Burns, George quipped, "I have underwear older than that!"

Georgia Frontiere, even with the unpredictable Rams season gnawing at her, invited us to a gala opening night dinner party at the Music Center; where we chatted with Frank Corsaro, the director of *Faust*, which we were about to see, genially commenting on how our lives had changed since *A Hatful of Rain* and how quickly life gallops by.

On top of a small mountain, surrounded by a picturesque panorama at the Brandeis-Bardin Institute in Simi Valley, a Lucas Richman wedding ceremony composition could be heard echoing softly against the hills. It was a lingering, late summer scorcher of a day September 25, 1994, when Lucas and his beautiful bride, Debbie, joyously agreed to their vows of marriage. The kids were ecstatically happy and we were too—and so were Debbie's parents, Lester and Clara Zive, fine people. The joining of newlyweds is such a special time of expectant hope—all the wishes and prayers of their family and friends sending them off with an encouraging beginning to confront, God willing, a bountiful and fulfilling future.

As a pharmacy student, one of my pet subjects was the pharmacological effect of narcotics and other brain altering substances on a human being. In-depth analyses had clearly shown that drug use led to the denigration of the brain and body and were a one-way ticket to hell. When times changed and drug indulgence suddenly became fashionable, I was shocked and appalled by the rampant misinformation spread by the advocates of marijuana, amphetamine, and cocaine—hooking foolish, gullible people, especially the young, to insufferable addiction and fried brains. I thought it was a worthy topic to explore theatrically, and my attempts at a one-man show might just be the avenue. Improvising with myself, a pencil in hand, I began expressing all the thoughts that were troubling me—and in the doing (coming from South Philly), I eventually evolved a situation where I was an Italian-American father telling a drug intervention group about my troubled young son and how I had initially warned him.

CARLO

"… Dominick, if you don't watch your ass, somebody's gonna stick a foot up your ass and it's gonna stay. And no matter what you do then, nobody is gonna be able to get it out. And this foot from somebody… it's got your name on it, on the sole of the foot… and it's gonna stay inside of you for the whole time of your life."

Further, in the development of the narrative I had the opportunity to become the other characters I was talking to: his wife, a cop, the priest… and a funny take-off on the state of television and how it influences our behavior and the kids especially—for instant satisfaction—leading to experimenting with drugs.

CARLO

"I dunno… kids growin' up in this country today… it's crazy. Too much, too fast… and everything is now. You gotta have it now! It's all over the TV… all those fuckin' commercials. Now! Now! Buy it now! Drink it now! Eat it now!"

Then, a few years later in his confessional, he reveals that after all he tried to do for the kid there was only deception and lies in return—his wife begging him to get the boy professional help, which he refuses, telling her:

CARLO

"… let him sleep it off… when he wakes up maybe we can talk to him… maybe we can reach his fuckin' brain… which right now is like linguini…"

Finally, when they do try to wake him up they realize their son is dead from an overdose—a powerful, heart-wrenching conclusion.

I'd completed the basic writing for three characters except for fine tuning and was about ready to mount the fourth at the Actors Studio. I'd found a forgotten short story written years earlier, still in penciled longhand stuck in the back of my desk drawer; a likable old man with a philosophical bent sitting in a park who starts up a conversation with a stranger. The more I "talked" to this old man, the more I found out about him—and his amusing concept of the importance of "walking," and eating properly for good health, his desperately missed dead wife, and his past as a young opera singer and singing teacher in the old country. Finally, he evolved into an eighty-three-year old Jewish holocaust survivor with a Viennese accent kept alive by the Nazis only because he amused them—but always within a hair's breadth of annihilation.

DANIEL

"I had to sing for my life. All the guards loved to hear sentimental German songs. All kinds of songs. I sang them. I sang for them… I survived. Yeah, yeah… I survived." (He sadly shakes his head, remembering, and then he smiles with hope in his heart as always.) "Everybody has problems… big ones, little ones… but how we solve our problems… that's what God sees."

I now had four different scenes of four totally different men who were in somewhat of a crisis and all of them in the writing—one way or another—had a tangential relationship to God. The Pastor; The Father; The Nazi; and the Holocaust Survivor. I called the one-man show to be *4 FACES*.

33
4 FACES—
The Beginning

I WAS HAVING LUNCH IN THE DINING ROOM of the president of Chapman University in Orange, California. True to his word, Jim Doti had invited me to discuss presenting a one-man show of my paintings. Everything was progressing smoothly—talking about dates, how many works to be included, and the duration once the paintings were mounted. Six months in the future seemed like a good option. I certainly had enough work for a large show. Then, in the middle of my mouthful of mashed potatoes, he asked, "Tell me, Peter Mark… what are you doing now?"

"You mean professionally?"

"Yes."

"Oh…just some stray television," I said. "But most of my concentration is spent on writing a one-man play… about four people."

"Really," he said, without missing a beat, "how would you like to premiere it here?"

I looked up from my juicy roast beef and into his smiling, inquisitive face and said, "Uh… you mean, open my show at Chapman?"

"That's exactly what I mean."

"Well, uh… when… are you thinking about?" I asked, now intrigued. "Do you have a specific time in mind?"

"In two months, maybe… or three… whenever you like."

My God, I'm thinking, can this be really be happening? Come down here for an art show and get an offer to do my play! "Jim, I'll be frank with you," I said. "I didn't even know you had a theater."

Tossing his napkin aside as he eagerly rose from his seat, he said, "Come on, I'll show you."

The next thing I knew I was ogling the beautiful, on-campus Waltmar Theater—a fully equipped facility with all the amenities that seated 250 people. Impulsively, I jumped up on the wide stage and suddenly began addressing Pastor Harlan Gregory's congregation with the opening words of my show: "Thank you, dear sisters for that lovely hymn…"

Jim Doti sat down to listen in the back of the theater with a big smile on his face. Fifteen minutes later with a handshake, we agreed to premiere *4 FACES* in this theater—three months away!

I booked several sessions at the Actors Studio, performing the characters that I felt needed the most refinement. I concentrated on Daniel, the Holocaust survivor, his persona being the most complex for me to achieve in transition—age, manner, simplicity—in addition to a believable Viennese Jewish dialect. I had concluded that the first act would open with "Pastor Gregory," followed by "Carlo," the man with the addicted son.

The transition between the two—changing clothes, attitudes and physicality—would take place on stage in front of the audience bathed in a soft blue light. The intermission gave me time to alter my appearance to "Gerhardt," the SS Nazi, for the opening of the second act followed by a blue light, quick change to the eighty-three-old "Daniel." Going from a meticulous SS officer with an exacting German accent to a humorous old Jew was just another task I assumed, like putting on his warn, woolen cap and sweater.

Thankfully, I didn't go outside my home to find the director I'd wanted all along. I asked my very capable wife, who knew me better than anyone and whose perception I trusted. I'd seen her fine direction of a scene from *Orphans* by Lyle Kessler at the Richard Basehart Playhouse and was impressed. Reluctantly, she agreed with one condition: I had to listen to her suggestions with openness and consideration before I plowed ahead stuck in my own ideas. We made a pact with a kiss, but that didn't prevent us from getting pissed at one another on several occasions, probably only because of my hard-headedness. Now that the director situation was solved, there was someone else in the family I turned to. I asked my son Lucas to write a score to introduce and represent each character and at the conclusion of their scene, transition to the next character while I was changing clothes. A few weeks later, I was moved to tears when he played me what he had composed on the piano: four distinct musical identities setting a perfect mood for each of the *4 FACES*. In addition, he'd composed appropriate and lovely music for the hymn I'd written that preceded the Pastor's sermon. I thought his work was remarkable. Following my approval, he arranged to conduct and record the music with twenty-five student musicians and singers at Chapman University. Also at Chapman, I met with the college scenic designer, Craig Brown, and discussed building a set with four movable flats, each with a "face" in profile. It was an exciting, creative time and I was more energized than I'd been in a long time.

On February 24, 1995, while my wife was guest of honor at a pre-theater private dinner for college bigwigs given by John Crean for opening night, I was putting on my makeup and double-checking with my stage manager all the last-minute details before magic time. I took a last look in the mirror, dabbed my chin with a tissue, straightened my tie, and then picked up my bible. I was ready to greet my congregation—and the sold-out ticket holders sitting in anticipation. The lights dimmed, then went out. When they came up came again, I made my entrance, the audience acknowledging me with a gracious applause. Standing center stage, I listened to the last refrain of the women's choir singing my hymn until it finally ended. I put my bible on the rostrum, rested quietly for a long moment, and then began in a light southern accent: "Thank you, dear sisters for that lovely hymn… give us thy strength, indeed, Oh Lord…" Robert Kohler of the *Los Angeles Times* wrote "Peter Mark Richman brings an honesty to the characters in his one man show. He proves his artistry as a performer—and reveals what's on his mind. Writer Richman has carefully linked all four pieces… tying them together in the human quest to understand God." Paul Hodgins, *Orange County Register*, said "Peter Mark Richman has created four memorable characters. He conveys a master's touch in the detail and depth he brings to them."

During the run in Orange County, I tried to get people to come down to see my work. It has always been difficult to get anybody to the theater in Los Angeles, but asking them to come to Orange County was like dragging them by chain to Lubbock, Texas. I would just have to open in Los Angeles, which meant finding an interested party with bucks and a proper theater in which to mount it. But I was exhausted and needed a break.

In a ribbon cutting ceremony for the opening of the beautiful Toluca Lake Health Center in Burbank, I was surprised, as a building committee member, when I received a plaque from the Motion Picture and Television Fund for my efforts in choosing the architect, John Cambianica. Another totally unexpected surprise—while telling my friend and board member Michael Wayne (John Wayne's son) about possibly putting together a Los Angeles production of *4 FACES*, he suddenly said, "Would $20,000 get you started?"

"Are you serious?" I asked, shocked by his generous response.

"Of course, I am," he said, smiling. "Call me when you're ready and we'll have lunch at the Lakeside Country Club and I'll give you a check."

From then on, I began to pursue forming the whole package necessary to open my play in Los Angeles: a producer, small theater, publicist, crew and a set and lighting designer. Rather than seeking additional outside financing, I decided I would personally put up the $15,000 that was necessary. One of the most interesting moments for me turned out to be the day Michael Wayne handed me a check at his club after a three-hour lunch. It was Bapak Subuh's birthday.

There was a reception at the Motion Picture and Television Hospital for the renowned silent screen star Buddy Rogers (Mary Pickford's husband) who was to receive the Silver Medallion award from the Fund. Since we both arrived at the same time, he took my arm and I escorted the strikingly handsome octogenarian inside as the photographers snapped away. It was a star-studded afternoon that included Bob Hope, so I was surprised when Paramount Pictures executive A.C. Lyles, after his lengthy discourse, suddenly introduced me to speak about Buddy Rogers. In an impromptu speech I said, "I am honored to be in Buddy's company, a man who has done so much for the Motion Picture and Television Fund. I was the forty-third recipient of the Silver Medallion and Buddy is the forty-fifth... it only makes mine shine brighter."

I hired Judy Arnold, a respected and knowledgeable producer on the Los Angeles scene, to come aboard *4 FACES*. I asked my old friend Dale Olson, a highly reputed publicist, to work for me. I then called Craig Brown and Ron Coffman at Chapman University to ask if they again would do the sets and lights. Both agreed. All we needed was the venue. I'd seen several theaters, but they weren't appropriate. One day Judy called and said, "Let's meet at the Ventura Court Theater... it's in Studio City. I think you'll like it."

I was very impressed and felt it was the perfect place to open my play. "Feels good," I said, and after some dickering signed a contract for a month.

Carroll O'Connor and Nancy were at a dinner party in Dale Olson's home. We hugged and expressed our condolences. They were still grieving over the tragic loss of their drug addict son, Hugh. *4 FACES* was certainly not a play I would invite them to. In the second scene, Carlo is dealing with exactly what they were experiencing. I had a long talk with Rod Steiger. He'd had an extended history of manic-depression (now called bipolar). I was happy to see him warm, lucid and friendly—traits he'd never exhibited previously in all the years I knew him. The medication he was now taking was truly helping and had changed his life. At one point in our conversation, he stopped, took a hard look, and said, "How can you look the same after all these years?" I didn't want to get into a conversation right then about Subud and the latihan and how it can help to keep you young, so I thanked him and let it drop.

After two technical, one dress rehearsal, and a paid preview, the set, crew, sound, and lighting were now refined. We opened *4 FACES* in August. As I looked out at the audience, so intimately close I could touch them— and seeing so many attentive well-known faces—it only served to deepen my concentration. It was truly one of the most rewarding theatrical experiences of my life. After the curtain, I waited a few minutes then stepped out to greet everyone. Steve Allen came up to me enthused and all smiles. I'd never seen him so animated as he said all the wonderfully descriptive things every actor loves to hear, and there were sweet words from Shelley Berman, Norman Lloyd, Joe Stefano, Cliff Norton, Ruta Lee, Marie Windsor, Lee Meriwether, and Karl Malden.

"It took me back thirty years," Karl said. "You did a great job of acting and writing. Don't change it. All four pieces are so distinctive and fascinating. It's an emotional thing with me… I can't really talk about it. But you did a great service for the business. I won't forget it." What thrilled him most was the family that sticks together (Helen directing and Lucas's music). He ended by saying, "Thank you for the evening."

Of course, in everything I do in my life, in one way or another, there is always that sharp, painful cinder in the eyeball—a jagged thorn in my rear I just can't seem to remove. Before we opened, Judy Arnold, Dale Olson, and I agreed and thought it would be a great idea to again invite the critic Robert Kohler, from the *Los Angeles Times*, who'd given my acting and writing such an astounding review in Orange County. After much effort, he agreed to come on opening night in Los Angeles. If a well-intentioned mistake was ever made—that was it. This miserable worm, for reasons of his own I know not of—who'd previously lauded me explicitly for my honesty and artistry—came out with a devastatingly dreadful review hating everything about my play and my performance.

Needless to say, we were shocked. Dale and Judy kept asking me why he would do such a thing after his earlier highly favorable critique. I had no answers. How could the same critic, seeing the same play and the same actor, suddenly reverse himself and go from a rave to a pan? Now I can shake my head and laugh about it saying, *That's the way my life goes*, but then, I just wanted to clobber the miserable S.O.B. There are sick, hateful, destructive, excrement-eaters in all endeavors—he happens to be the top of the line. I was pleased when the other reviewers were gracious in their praise and I received a Dramalogue Award for my performance.

After our run at the Ventura Court Theater, we moved to the main stage at the Odyssey Theater in Los Angeles to play for another month. I was gratified to have so many of my friends and acquaintances come to see me work—especially when Leo Penn brought his son Sean. Our families have a long history together. I cherish the movies I shot of my son Howard's fifth birthday—Kelly, pushing Sean on the swing, both almost three!

Howard W. Koch, noted Paramount producer, was spearheading a drive at KCET-TV in Los Angeles to shoot a television version of *4 FACES* with Marty Pasetta directing who'd done many Academy Award shows. It looked like a "go," but then KCET suddenly changed management, killing the effort. We closed the play on October 19, but I had a feeling that this wasn't the end of the journey.

Early in 1996, Carol and Alfred were flying down from Albany to meet us at Turnberry Isle Resort, but the main reason for our flight was to visit my eighty-eight-year-old sister, Fay, now a resident in Ft. Lauderdale whom I hadn't seen in years. In the morning after a warm reunion and breakfast with Carol and Alfred, a formidable lineup of docked yachts in the background, Helen and I drove to Ft. Lauderdale and then along the beach road to the Tiffany House where Fay was living—a sun-splashed area a block from the ocean. It was a better quality retirement home, but still a sad, depressing place—the next to the last stop in the ole corral. To see my sister for the first time in seven years was a bit of a shock (time plus distance a distressing duo). I hadn't seen her since the funeral of my brother Dave in Hartford in 1989. She was standing there holding on to her walker looking small and old, a pale remnant of the sister I knew. But still—that bubbly smile and a greeting of sisterly love. Standing behind her was Henry, her second husband, all twisted over holding onto his walker. They were a sight to break your heart.

We took them out to lunch, unloading and loading two walkers in the process, then back to the Tiffany where she showed us the small room where their lives were lived. Afterward we sat by the pool, remembering and reliving our past. Just to look into her pale blue eyes once more and hear her rippling laugh, her wrinkled face tightening smooth again with the laughter, was alone worth the trip. She told me again that I was born with a caul. She was the only one who remembers that. (A caul is an additional membrane or "veil" that covers the head, rare in thousands of births. It has spiritual meaning because the child born with it is thought to have an aura of protection for his life, and will receive blessings—spiritual and otherwise. Symbolically, it means The Lord is guiding you. It is mentioned in Shakespeare's *Macbeth*.)

A sister is a sister and she was the only family left who knew me as a little boy—my Mom, Pop, Gert, Harry, and Dave were all gone. Fay expressed how special she thought I was as a child, how bright and mature. "You could talk to him about everything," she said to Helen, "and he would listen and respond like a grown person." She talked about the suffering I had to endure with Mom—the pain and anguish of a child and no real attention or care. "It was a terrible abuse to grow up that way," she said, crying. "I was never really around to do anything about it. I was married and lived far away and had my own life." Tears were stuck in my throat and dribbled down my cheeks.

We talked for four hours about our very troubled mother and the sad relationship she'd had with all of her children and our dear, sweet Pop. "He was always trying to make it work with her," she said, "but she was impossible, a real schizoid." As a child I was always trying to assuage the situation too. "Please, let's not fight today... please... let's have a nice day and go someplace for dinner... huh, Mom... huh, Pop?" (I could almost hear my little boy voice.) To look at my sister and to feel her body next to mine in an embrace was just a joy—sad and wonderful. Her once lovely blonde hair was now white, frizzy and stiff—and her beautiful skin, now a mass of wrinkles. Strangely enough, when she spoke of her mother and me, and the emotional traumas of the past and her mother being a "bone in her throat"—and the love she'd never had from Mom—and the suffering I experienced as a child and the love I'd never received, and the terrible parental conflicts I witnessed growing up, her face lost twenty years. She was animated and clear of thought and expression. Prior to that she was a bit slow getting her thoughts together and even hearing her was a problem. Helen sat quietly listening, her eyes sometimes filling up, while Henry never said a word, his thoughts, I'm sure, elsewhere. Fay told us with humor, "Living here in the Tiffany House was... actually not being in a retirement home—it was more like being in a cuckoo house." I understood immediately what she meant when I witnessed a woman in her eighties about to step into the pool who was nude. She'd neglected to put on her swimsuit correctly and it just hung from her neck to reveal her nakedness. Of course, she didn't realize it. I went over to engage her in conversation while the attendants were summoned. Oblivious, she took my arm exclaiming, "Why doesn't anybody use this lovely pool? I wouldn't have registered here if I couldn't swim. I'm a very good swimmer." And I'm standing there, holding her arm and feeling quite silly as the good Samaritan—talking to this jewelry bedecked, bright red lip- sticked eighty-year-old naked lady. I was very grateful that we came to see Fay. I loved her with all my heart and wished the distance hadn't kept us apart. I've always been sorry that she'd been unable to continue the latihan. She'd been opened in Los Angeles years ago, but when she went back to Florida, the Subud group was distant and she'd drifted away. I was struck by how much Fay looked like Mom as she had aged. She wouldn't have liked hearing that, but it was true.

The event that was to bring me to Chapman University initially finally took place. Jim Doti, the university president, gave me the "Inaugural Exhibition of The Henley Galleria." My one-man show called "A Life in Art" (a painting of Mom and Pop in Atlantic City on the brochure) would have a two-month run, and it consisted of an extensive display of my works: thirty oils, plus watercolors, collages, and computer art—fifty in all, a thirty-year retrospective. It was beautifully mounted and about 200 people came to the opening. At the festivities in the main gallery, Jim Doti made a lovely speech then introduced me. I surprised him when I presented the university with a large painting I had done depicting myself as the characters in *4 FACES*.

On a flight to Albany in May to visit Jean, Helen's mom for her ninetieth birthday, the sweetest and sharpest ninety year old I've ever met, I was deeply involved in Tony Curtis's excellent autobiography. We'd worked together on the TV show *Vegas*, and he was always charming and likable. We'd seen each other last at Drai's, a famous dinner place, where he kissed me on the cheek and said he wanted to see my show at Chapman and would call me for directions. He never did. The woman he was with was a blonde knockout—and in my reading of his book, it surprised me a bit when he mentioned how he suffered from premature ejaculation. He, of all people.

Because my children have a grandmother who is so special, they all flew in to honor her. Not only that, they put on a show that the residents of the seniors' apartment building where she lived were talking about for weeks. "The Hollywood Players—in the community room!" I was the

MC and Lucas was at the piano coordinating the whole musical program, including a show-stopper he wrote entitled "Jeanie," sung by all the kids, extolling their "Nana's" many charms. It was witnessed by a sea of gray and white-topped heads with beaming faces, their day lightened by love and warm family entertainment. It was a joy to behold and very touching. Jean's face was at least ten years younger. While in Albany, Carol, who used to work for Senator Tarky Lombardi as his assistant, arranged for me to visit the New York State Senate. Senator Bill Stachowski (we'd all traveled together on the foreign trips) met us outside the chambers and then ushered us in and sat us down up front while the senate was in session. The Chamber was, in a word, magnificent. It had been proclaimed as the "most beautiful room in America" at its dedication in 1881. The Senate was heatedly arguing about a transportation bill in Rochester. While I sat there in this historical chair close to the Speaker, many senators kept coming up to meet the familiar TV face. Senator Frank Padavan, all smiles, had just seen me as a defrosted banker on *Star Trek: The Next Generation*. We were so involved in a whispered conversation I missed the moment of my Senate introduction. The actual Senate transcript is as follows:

Acting President Kuh
   The nominees are confirmed. Senator Stachowski, why do you rise?

Senator Stachowski
   Mr. President, I know it's unusual to introduce people, but today we have a guest in the chamber from California who is observing the proceedings. We have with us an actor from Hollywood, who happens to be a friend and, if you're wondering why it's I who's introducing him, he's also a member of the Philadelphia Hall of Fame as a football player. And so, I'd just like to take the time to introduce Peter Mark Richman, observing our proceedings today from California.

Acting President Kuhl
   Welcome, appreciate your joining us in the chamber.

   (applause)

   Well! I stood up quickly, took a couple of steps forward, smiling broadly, and waved a thank you. It was quite an honor to be at a session in progress and then be introduced.

Afterward, out in the impressive "period" corridor in front of the famous antique clock, the photographer snapped photos with all the friendly Senators and I had a warm reunion with Tarky, who was responsible for those fabulous trips. Being a participant in such a setting, the frenzy of government in action—and feeling the history of the past—all these elected officials disputing, conniving, honoring and making laws, Americans all, was heady stuff, and almost storybook to think that I'd been present watching these activities in the legislature of Sacramento, California; in the Congress and Senate in Washington with ex-congresswoman Bobbi Fiedler; and, of all places, the Parliament in Bangkok, Thailand. I must say, I do feel privileged—it goes along with celebrity and the perks of being one. It's peculiar, but I've been on television for so long I'm in people's subliminal consciousness. If they can't recall my name, the TV face has stuck tenaciously in their brains like a hook. They do a double-take and say, "Didn't I meet you at my sister's wedding?" or "Aren't you Dr. Crumpkin from Cedars Maternity?" or in Albany, someone recently asked me, "God, your face is so familiar… didn't you used to live in Loudenville?"

About this time, I had a conversation with Dale Olson, my PR representative, who had been promoting my unpublished novel. He informed me that Bantam liked the book a lot and it was now going to be reread for "sales evaluation" as to whether it would sell in hard cover. But after two months they rejected it and I was back to zero. It was so bloody aggravating.

34
4 Faces—
Actors Studio—
NY

ARTHUR PENN, NOTED DIRECTOR of Broadway and the film *Bonnie and Clyde*, and an esteemed friend, was now the artistic director of the Actors Studio in New York. He'd approved my wish to open *4 FACES* in New York for a limited run as a special Studio presentation for twenty-one performances. In September 1996, Helen and I flew east and moved into our rented condo at the Essex House on Central Park West. I'd had many long-distance phone gabs setting up what I needed for the production so the first meeting went fairly smoothly. Joe Chartier, who ran the everyday Studio operation, was immeasurably helpful, and the set was already being built to my specifications by Vince Pomilio. I'd brought the tapes of Lucas's music and the necessary sound effects; so Jack Doulin, a professional stage manager, could coordinate every detail of sound and lights with the small crew who would also assist me in the on-stage costume changes. Technically, everything had to work like a clock. With Helen observantly watching, I was sure everything would. I hadn't worked at the New York Studio since I moved to the Coast and that was thirty-five years ago. As I rehearsed, it seemed strange to be standing there in that wonderful space saying my words, with powerful memories and the ghost of Lee Strasberg present wherever I turned.

It was Sunday. Helen wasn't feeling well and I needed to stretch my legs so I walked crosstown to Madison and uptown to 65th St. It was a beautiful day. So many people and so many variations of faces. There were tourists with their cameras and parents with their babies—all kinds, sweet and sleepy in carriages and bulging arms. There were Americans, Japanese, Indians, Koreans, Latinos, you name it—and always, of course, the beggars and their cups, the sidewalk peddlers of phony Gucci watches,

T-shirts, and sunglasses too. On upper Madison Avenue, the restaurants with sidewalk tables, their guests sipping white wine oblivious to the dust and noisy traffic. New York. They say if you live here long enough you get used to everything. It's a great city, but I don't think I could ever get used to it again at my age, and certainly not apartment living where I would shrivel up and die from confinement and lack of breathing space. I walked back to the hotel along Fifth Avenue adjacent to Central Park. The horses and carriages went by with the drivers hustling for a paying fare. In the street, wafting up into my shnoz with a gust of dusty wind—dried horseshit. It made me grimace. I thought, *Dry or wet, it still smells like...* In the afternoon, Helen was feeling better and joined me for a visit to

Rita Gam's apartment. I've never understood cucumber sandwiches, but that's what she served with tea. They were popular in old English films—I can picture Hermione Gingold delicately wolfing one down. Rita, a warm and beautiful woman of taste and a good actress, revealed her hellish, but victorious, bout with cancer. She looked the picture of health and was thrilled that I was doing my play at the Studio and she promised to be there opening night. I had a warm conversation with Arthur Penn. I told him that performing my play at the Actors Studio was, in a sense, "giving something back." He appreciated that and couldn't have been more welcoming. I okayed the proof of the invitational card that would be sent out to a mailing list of 2,000. John Green, a fabulous graphic designer, was creating a poster. I was so grateful that everybody was knocking themselves out for me, including some young crew members from the Actors Studio program at the New School for Social Research. I had *4 FACES* T-shirts and hats made for the whole gang. That evening, we went down to Soho to see Phyllis Diller's one-woman art show. She was so pleased to see us as the press popped away in front of her colorful "big faced" paintings—so free and fun. She is such a doll and so genuine. Cliff Gorman was there and we had a nice reunion; I hadn't seen him since a *Police Story* gig years ago. Robert Osborne, always friendly, chatted with us and said he'd come to my opening. Soho had changed so much—galleries galore, chic shops, fancy boutiques, and the roving crowds—but on every corner, beggars still jabbing their paper cups for money.

After rehearsal one day, I saw this poster on the wall in the office: Roy Schatt—Marilyn Monroe—1955, a fabulous photo of Marilyn in a camelhair coat, cigarette in hand, surrounded by some known and unknown faces—and in the back row behind Marilyn—there I am. Roy was a famous photographer who did all these shots at the Actors Studio and eventually a classic book on Jimmy Dean. In 1954 or1955, he did a study of me doing a monologue I wrote and performed, when Lee Strasberg sarcastically asked, "Do you want to be a writer or an actor?" Roy had all these negatives in his voluminous files—and in the old days I couldn't afford his photos at $3 a pop. When I had called him a few years ago—inflation, the price of fame, and an agent had taken over. He wanted $400 a print. I found his number in the phone book and thought it would be nice to say hello and maybe pick up a photo or two—at a reduced price. He was so pleased that I looked him up he insisted we come for a visit. It was kind of sad when we arrived. He was standing in the doorway holding onto a cane, looking quite old and lame—after a stroke, I assumed. He'd lived with his wife, Elaine, for forty-one years in this congested apartment on East 33rd Street with a scraggly little sunless garden that he was so proud of. It was like Willy Loman now surrounded by skyscrapers still dreaming of how it was—this pathetic square piece of worn-out dirt. He was sorry to tell me that he had no idea where to look for my film files, but he proudly signed and presented me with the Marilyn Monroe poster as a gift. He beamed when I invited him and Elaine to see *4 FACES* and said he would be there.

One evening after dinner, we were walking up Sixth Avenue when there was a sudden lengthy caravan of police cars, motorcycles, an ambulance, and long black limos—their sirens blasting away. They turned into the blocked off 58th Street entrance to the Essex House. We found out that Benjamin Netanyahu, the Prime Minister of Israel, was staying there. Security around the hotel was ferocious. Just getting to our floor was a nightmare. Police, Israeli security, and the FBI were all over the place. In the morning, there was a lot of activity outside our suite so, in my robe, I opened the door to get a peek. A SWAT Team officer was standing there holding a machine gun. A bit startled, to say the least, I noticed many more officers swarming in the hall with guns. It was weird, so I said: "Uh… Is he on this floor?"

"I'm not at liberty to say," he answered with a smile, "but there's nothing to worry about, sir… you're well protected. Did we wake you up?" "No," I said. But the thought crossed my mind: *With all the conflict and hate going on… what would happen if we had a little bomb incident…?*

The production was beginning to flow more smoothly, my young crew adapting well to working out the kinks and lighting cues. Going from a well-dressed pastor to an open-shirted Carlo in the first act—and in the second, transforming the leather-jacketed SS Nazi to a sweater and cap-wearing old Jew, was an integral part of the audience's participation, watching the characters change before I spoke, covered by Lucas's transitional music. As we progressed, I was trying some slight variations in my performance, and Helen's notes, so perceptive and loving, were invaluable. Lucas flew in for the preview, intent on making sure the sound levels were right. It was so good to have him with us, "Well, it's my play too," he said, sweetly. Indeed, his music added so much. After one preview-dress rehearsal, we opened to a receptive full house and the play went as smooth as glass. I was on—and all the colors, nuances and variations blossomed. Afterward, my son Howard, who'd also flown in, and friends and studio members whom I hadn't seen in years were effusive in their compliments about the acting and my writing. Unfortunately, there would be no reviews. It was a policy of the Actors Studio not to allow the critics to attend "workshop" productions. Many "theater" people continued to attend, and it was gratifying to hear their comments. Betsy Von Furstenberg came backstage with the extraordinary Tammy Grimes who went on and on. She was bowled over by the Pastor and asked if I'd given any thought to London. I said, "Do you know anybody?" Arthur Penn came and was very complimentary. "Wonderful work… to show what we can do in this place." That evening I got a standing ovation and I must say, it gave me a kick to see all those people standing and clapping at the Actors Studio. Arthur had some suggestions concerning the Pastor not being "specific enough." He said, "Think about the fact that the Pastor got a letter that morning that angers him before he gives his sermon." Good suggestion, but frankly, I've played that, and many variations thereof. "Angry" doesn't work on a continual basis. It gets monotonous, and I still have to give an appealing sermon. I've always had more concern with the Pastor's very complex character, the writing more difficult to act. Interestingly, Arthur Penn was the only person who didn't think I was guilty of fooling around with the ladies. Joan Copeland, a good actress (Arthur Miller's sister), came twice and so did my dear friend Sondra Lee, bubbling with enthusiasm. One night after a performance, Lee Richardson, a fine actor who'd had an aneurism in the brain and was still seriously ill, joined us for coffee at a local restaurant on 9th Avenue. I ordered my usual almond horn pastry and talked him into having one too. Mistake! He took a bite and had a frightening coughing spell and I thought he would die right there, his coughing continuing without end. It was scary as hell. When it finally abated he told us his wife was on chemo for cancer and was dying, and he had a twenty-seven-year-old institutionalized autistic son. "It's a great life, huh?" he said. On another night, Anne Jackson and Eli Wallach came. They were ecstatic, throwing words around like "extraordinary." We went out afterward and Eli said, "Peter Mark… you should be very pleased. It's quite an accomplishment." It was so good to hear real theater people express themselves. Anne, her vibrant face sparkling, talked about my writing and how I don't preach: "The work unfolds—and you say it all so naturally and honestly… and your acting is brilliant." They were both so spirited. They wanted everybody to see it and said they would call a lot of people immediately. They wanted to come again before I closed and suggested I think about moving it to another theater. "It should be seen," Eli said. "We go to a lot of plays… and your play is a real evening in the theater. We loved it." They also sent a fax to Dale Olson with all kinds of complimentary words for Dale to use PR-wise. It was delicious. Helen and I were so pleased, and I was thinking: May it only be the beginning. This play has a life of its own… and I pray it continues so my work can be seen. One of the unexpected kicks in doing my play in New York was my youngest son, Roger, a good-natured rag doll, as sweet and vulnerable as ice cream cake, flew in from Los Angeles on the "red-eye" to see me perform again (my biggest fan). And not only that. To encourage an audience, he took it upon himself to hand out 200 *4 FACES* flyers at the stand-by line on 47th and Broadway. Lee Grant, one of the finest actresses in America, came and then came backstage with Will Hare—both Studio stalwarts. "It was a gift," Lee said. "You gave us a gift." It was very gratifying to hear Lee, an actress I respect enormously, elaborate in her praise. "There is such humanity in your writing," Will Hare said, "Such wonderful characters… we thank you for bringing them to us." And then Lee said, "You belong on the stage. It's wonderful to watch you take the time on stage… we see you thinking. Such wonderful work… a lot of the kids from the new school were out there… and they were quiet because to watch a master at work… it's best to be quiet." Will had to leave, but Lee stayed and we talked and laughed for half an hour—her warmth and sweetness so pleasurable. She asked me how I did my characters— "Observation?" I told her. "It comes from my inner… my insides." She nodded, not knowing I was really talking of my spiritual insides.

We took a cab, talking all the way, to the Essex House before she dropped us off. She said she was blown away with the acting and writing of Gerhardt, but also had some reservations about the Pastor. She wanted me to be more "Hot with God!" It's interesting that most controversy comes when talking about the Pastor and how to play him. Arthur Penn, Lee Grant, and even Anne Jackson mentioned it. I wonder if it has mainly to do with God? My sermon, which is deliberate and powerful, may also irritate. No matter what, the pastor is a tough S.O.B. to solve. Many people have said the Pastor was a highlight and even affected their belief center. Joseph Stefano (*Psycho, Black Orchid*) said the scene touched him so deeply that it was a stimulus to attend church more regularly. I do think whatever uncertainty in the playing of him mainly has to do with the writing. I've made so many acting adjustments to his character—up and down and all around—emotional, angry and passionate (with God)—there always seems to be a flaw in the totality to some people. Maybe it's because there's a flaw in his character.

Helen and I took another delightful walk in Central Park. On view were the joggers, cyclers, roller skaters and old ladies with poop-scoopers in hand watching their little doggies. Just a great place to walk. The rest of the city I could never get too gaga over. Helen was enjoying it a lot more than I did. I don't get turned on by all the Broadway glitz and hullaballoo. I grew up in Philly, a big city with all the usual city crap, so New York never had any great pull on me. I never loved it when we lived here, married for eight plus years or so before moving to Los Angeles. But New York is where it's at as far as theater is concerned, and if it doesn't happen here, most likely it won't happen anywhere. That's why I was so bugged about closing down the coming Wednesday. Rita Gam called to tell me that Arthur Penn had announced at a Studio session that he'd seen *4 FACES* and it was terrific… and all studio members should go see it.

I gave my final performance that night. I tried to make it count, slowing things down a bit and incorporating every deeply fermented nuance. Jane Powell, petite and lovely, and Dickie Moore, a former child star, came back to see me, both expansive in their praise, tossing accolades at me like tasty jelly beans. An African-American studio member I didn't know was in tears as she thanked and kissed me. The crew gathered in the green room, and we opened a bottle of champagne and toasted each other in thanks and goodbyes. They were a wonderful bunch of kids who really knocked themselves out for me. At Eli Wallach's suggestion, I had tried to make a move to another small theater, but everything was booked solid and wouldn't be available until weeks ahead—impossible for me. So that was it. My venture at the Actors Studio was a major success, but it wasn't going anywhere (not unusual in my life). I suppose subconsciously I expected some moneybags to see my play and say, Hallelujah! Jumpin' hot Farina! Come to my theater and we'll run for a year! Well, it didn't happen. Now what? The star actor back to oblivion—my haven in Woodland Hills.

Or… perhaps stay in New York and opt for a refurbished career on the stage? It's possible. I've been told that many times, but could I endure this town for a really extended stay? Not to walk in my garden, not to feed rose bush, not to hug my grandchild, Jenny, and feel her kisses, and not to see the rosy, pink, and purple sky at sunset over the Santa Susannah mountains? I don't think so. After an almost six-hour flight and a drive to the Valley, we were back in our home on the top of the hill in Woodland Hills and all was well. The sprinklers had worked, the grass was green, the gardener was cleaning up, and all the mail was at the post office waiting to be picked up. In a few days, my triumph at the Actors Studio seemed like a dream. And maybe that's all it was.

Georgia Frontiere, at a luncheon in Los Angeles, had said to us, "I'm inviting you to St. Louis… when do want to come?" The Rams were now in the city where she was born after an incredible wooing and financial deal that sealed her commitment. All of St. Louis was ecstatic with Georgia, the Rams, and the fact that they were again an NFL city. However, it would take a while to get a coach and worthy team together to get them to the big prize—the Super Bowl. In November 1996 we saw what St. Louis had done for their new franchise—the spectacular Transworld Dome. The Rams home field was a high-tech indoor stadium that could comfortably seat 67,000 fans. The practice facility in Earth City, about twenty miles out of St. Louis, was a modern training headquarters of amazing proportions and included an indoor eighty-yard astroturf field and two outdoor playing fields. It was so beautiful that it seemed too pampering for football. The team at that time was floundering under a mediocre coach. I gagged watching them lose to the Carolina Panthers, an expansion team, 20-10. John Shaw revealed his frustration in a private conversation: "Not delivering a winner to this city after what they put up to get the team here is a real failure." He was unhappy with the coach and asked my opinion about the lack of motivation of some of the players. I said that the coach had "foolishly gotten rid of a whole host of fine players who were now starring for a lot of different teams: Sean Gilbert, Jerome Bettis, and more. It was stupid because we didn't get anybody any better. Getting rid is easy, acquiring is hard. The philosophy of getting a good coach is complex, and the coach brings all his assistants with him or recruits them well. If you get a defensive or offensive coordinator as a coach, that's half the whole need because he's an expert in half the game. It will be interesting to see what happens after the season." Georgia was depressed at dinner, but veiled it with smiling good will. We yakked a lot—always optimistic, she wanted desperately to have a quality team and fulfill a glorious dream for St. Louis. But at this point, that possibility seemed way down the line.

The next night we spent some time talking to a very charming Stan Kroenke and his wife, Ann—an enormously rich guy who had just purchased 30 percent of the Rams. After dinner, Georgia and all of us trudged over to Powell Hall (home to the St. Louis Symphony) to see Gregory Peck do his one-man show of old film clips and chatting with the audience. It was a wonderful, casual performance, but it was a bit shocking to see what an elderly fellow he'd become, especially after witnessing him cavort on screen a few minutes earlier. After enthralling everybody with his personal show biz stories on stage, he was just as warm and personable at the reception. As we shook hands he looked at me quizzically and said in that deep, unique voice of his, "Have we met before?"

"Yes, tangentially," I answered. "I'm on the board of the Motion Picture and Television Fund and blah, blah, blah… we both received the Silver Medallion… only years apart."

"Oh, yes," he said, "you're all doing a fine job out there." His beautiful wife, Veronique, smiled as the bulbs flashed. I didn't mention it, but he had no idea that I had had framed a Norman Rockwell painting of Judy Garland that he'd given to the Fund as a gift. It now hangs in the medical office at the hospital.

Norby Walters (party host extraordinaire) had invited us to his 1997 Academy Awards gala at the Beverly Hills Hotel. That evening, we were seated for dinner with Neil Simon, Sid Caesar and his wife Florence, Martin Landau, Norman Fell, and Mariette Hartley. I had known Sid over the years and we got into a conversation about the Academy. I was shocked when he told me that he was not a member.

"No," he said, "I'm a member of the Television Academy."

"You're kidding," I said. "You mean nobody has ever proposed you for your rightful place in the Academy of Motion Pictures Arts and Sciences? After all you've done?"

"No."

I was aghast. "You mean, not one of all your actor friends in the industry?"

"No," he said.

I leaned in close to him. "Sid, the first thing I'll do tomorrow is fill out a card and write a letter to the Academy proposing you for a long overdue membership."

Then I laughed. "I'm going to have to ask you to send me your credits." I was appalled that a legend had been overlooked, but it was finally rectified when he was admitted as a member shortly after. I did the same for Carroll O'Connor, Jack Klugman, William Daniels, Harvey Korman, and many more. To me, their presence and discerning votes for awards were essential and valuable.

Suddenly, before I could do anything about it—or even get out of bed or dance a jig—I realized, and there was no getting around it or room for rationalization, or possibility of a plea for a delay in the circumstances—like it or not—it was April 16, 1997, and I was now, oh, my God—seventy years old! And that my friends, is a millstone, I mean milestone, in anyone's life. I can't say that I was shocked because I knew it was coming, but it's sobering to know that no matter how you look at it, you're only ten years away from eighty—and that is old! Then again, I have a lot of friends who are eighty-plus and they are doing just fine, so I'm not going to fret one damned bit, but go on with what I've been doing and hope and pray that it all turns out for the best.

In the evening, all my children had thoughtfully arranged and paid for their Mom and Dad to celebrate my birthday—just the two of us—at a wonderfully intimate "Brandywine" dinner, even providing the wine for a toast. Of course, when we tipped our glasses the first time, it was to our children—how lucky and blessed can you get? Five kids, and each one deep in our hearts. The next night, unaware and out of it—my distraction totally complete—Helen and the kids again pulled off a fabulous surprise bash at the El Caballero Country Club. There I was, suspecting nothing, being pushed into this private room that I'm trying to back out of when I saw someone shooting a video and finally realized they were shooting me! All those familiar smiling faces—thirty-five of them—suddenly applauded and welcomed me into the room, which was all decked out with a spectacular arrangement of roses, lilies, and Japanese blossoms—so beautiful, and superbly designed by my dear Adrienne, Art Stone's wife. I was overwhelmed, but enjoying every moment, redundantly thankful to God for my blessings—all of them. Throughout the excellent dinner (with different laminated placemats of my old press clippings in a Kelly collage at each seat), my friends were getting up and reading things they'd written—such heart-touching words that I wondered for a moment if they were really talking about me. I had a lump in my throat the whole evening. Tender tributes from Deborah and Joel Rogosin, Louise and Ernie Frankel, Eileen and Leo Penn, Marilyn and Joseph Stefano, Rebecca and Walter

Schacht, and more. Of course, my kids Orien and Roger also declaimed how much they loved me, then Kelly and my daughter-in-law, Debbie, sang a resounding duet with Lucas at the piano—the premiere of Lucas's many faces of the "Renaissance Man" honoring his Dad. That certainly thrilled and tugged my heart. Loren, my son-in-law, had us all chuckling with his Richard Burton priceless parody of Camelot, substituting: Peter Mark! Then my Metropolitan Opera star friend Richard Fredricks sang two songs magnifi tly in my honor! The capper of the festivities was the lovely song that Helen wrote and sang to the beautiful music of Howard, now at the piano, "It's Always Been You and Me." That's when the lump in my throat turned all squishy. It's one thing to turn seventy, but having a family and friends who care, celebrate it with you—well, that's defi tely something else. Before the evening was over, I'll never forget a basket presented to me containing seventy little boxes. In each box was a child's remembrance of their Dad (fourteen each), expressing a little moral they'd absorbed from each memory and how they felt about their Dad. It affected me deeply. I allowed myself to open only three a day. I couldn't take any more.

The next day the doorbell rang at my home—an additional birthday perk. I was handed a special delivery card from Hoffman Travel: "Your vacation in Sedona awaits you, just call, make arrangements and come! Georgia and Earle." Once again, the ever-gracious Georgia had set it all up for another taste of a mountainous, red-rock view from the top of Skyline Drive too spectacular to take for granted, the sky too blue and blinding to ever forget—and in our lovely garden room a thoughtful basket of welcoming yellow roses.

I was truly gratified that my children were doing well. Howard, my eldest, was composing specialized music for health and had fifty piano students, children and professional. Kelly, starting in her garage, had created a business called Art Plates, Inc, designing artistic collages on light switch plates. It had expanded to a factory operation employing ten people under her supervision and sales nationwide. Lucas, at present, was sharing the conducting reins of the spectacular Mathew Bourne British production of *Swan Lake* (all male) at the Music Center in Los Angeles. Orien was running Cook's warehouse, sending out "spielers," himself included, selling quality restaurant cookware at fairs and convention halls across the country, while still managing to act, somehow, in commercials and low-budget films. Roger, our youngest, who looked a lot like my father, except had the size of an NFL linebacker, was holding down two jobs trying to decide what he wanted to do with his young life.

The Jeffrey Foundation, which cares for special needs children and their families, had a huge affair at the Beverly Wilshire Hotel to celebrate the twenty-fifth year of its existence. Alyce Morris, the founder and president, presented me with a "Special Friend Award" for my involvement with the organization and the many master of ceremony activities I'd performed. That evening, Fred Travalena, a wonderful comic and impersonator, sang a parody of "If I Were a Rich Man" that he'd written and dedicated to me, which was pretty funny. There are moments like that when you realize, aside from the humor, how extremely blessed you are to have healthy children free of debilitating impairments. Steve Allen, another Jeffrey Foundation helpmate and one of the sweetest men I knew, and Sybil Brand also received awards.

Marion Ross, a wonderful actress and lovely woman, joined me in a special staged reading of my play *A Medal for Murray*. It was hosted by the West Coast Jewish Theater and directed by my friend Rocky Kalish. I played the part that Eli Wallach was interested in—the zesty octogenarian in an old age retirement home who captivates a lonely, kvetchy lady (Marion) and surprisingly changes her personality and outlook. Since it was only a staged reading with five characters, not much of an attempt was made for a set or for makeup—the play holding together on its own merits. Marion was excellent—and I, wearing a soft felt hat and a sweater, played the old Jew somewhat akin to Daniel in *4 FACES* with a few variations. The audience responded enthusiastically. There was no question in my mind that I'd written a viable, commercial audience-pleaser, but the avenue is a long one and the detours and pitfalls for me are inevitable.

As a football aficionado why wouldn't I want to have a conversation with Dick Butkis, one of the most ferocious linebackers in football history? When Jack Faulkner asked me to be on the Steering Committee and attend The Gridiron Gala of the Century, a tribute in memory of Pete Rozelle, the father of the Super Bowl, of course I said yes. I get more of a charge being among great athletes than I have ever felt mingling with my theatrical peers, and talking football with Merlin Olsen and Lamar Lundy, two of the Rams "Fearsome Foursome," at my table was a special treat. Everywhere I looked in the Westin Hotel ballroom, I recognized major sports figures who'd come together to honor a man who had forever changed the face of football. During the evening, I chatted with friends Vince Ferragamo, Jackie Slater, Ernie Barnes, and Charlie Cowan and renewed acquaintances with Rams executive Don Klosterman and with Tom Hayden, a former quarterback for the Rams. The gala was also a fundraiser for NFL alumni—"to assist fallen Teammates in dire need"—a long overdue recognition that many old players were suffering infirmities without proper medical coverage. Maurie Nipp, president of the Los Angeles chapter of the NFL alumni, introduced me to the national president, Frank W. Krauser. We had a meaningful discussion about a place for old football players; based on the concept of the Motion picture and Television Fund's retirement home, that evening Georgia Frontiere wrote a check for $25,000.

In July, my son Howard got married in a fancy wedding with overflowing guests at the Bel Air Hotel. Unfortunately, the vows didn't work out, causing a lot of anguish and turmoil (seven years later they split). My beautiful grandson Oliver is the one loving and positive note from a conflicted relationship. His smile tickles my heart.

35 Subud World Congress In Spokane

THE ATMOSPHERE AND THE EXPERIENCE of the Tenth Subud World Congress, an event planned every four years and this time in Spokane, Washington, beginning August 3, 1997, put simply, was extraordinary. Three thousand four hundred people from sixty-one countries came to worship God in the latihan. The enormity of it in this age of disdain and cynicism was humbling and profound. Across the river from the convention center, on a vast hill and under a starry sky, the city dignitaries and the invited public witnessed an amazing performance of music, dancers, and a laser light show that initiated the opening ceremonies. It was written and produced by Honora and Dahlan Foah and I was honored to be the narrator, making event introductions and at embracing moments and expressing Bapak's words and explanations. It was the kick-off for a wonderful and deeply spiritual two weeks. All these men and women with their children had traveled from the Congo, South Africa, Australia, New Zealand, Great Britain, France, Spain, Portugal, Israel and many other countries to be with their international Subud family. When I first walked into this enormous convention hall space at the Doubletree Hotel and saw 1,000 to 1,200 men sitting quietly waiting to begin the latihan—it was a sight I'll never forget. The consuming power we all felt in worship was so pleasantly revivifying. Of course, Helen had the same experience with the women.

During the week, I watched my son Lucas take an amorphous group of sixty Subud members with limited choral experience (and limited English) and coax, teach, mold, and sweeten their efforts into a wonderfully cohesive body of vocal capability. Where was I? Why, I was to be the narrator in a provocative musical composition that Lucas had written for the occasion called "Seven Circles of Life… a Subud Cantata," which embraced Bapak Subuh's receivings in an orchestral palette encompassing humankind's spiritual evolution. A week later, I had one of the greatest and most satisfying experiences of my life. Standing on the stage in a tuxedo at the Spokane Opera House, I watched my son conduct the Spokane Symphony Orchestra. Helen, upstage in the chorus that had now grown to eighty voices with the addition of the Spokane Chorale, looked so proud and beautiful singing, as I waited patiently for the maestro's special cues to articulate Bapak's meaningful words in between his powerful music. I was very moved, and the vocals he'd written for soprano Sylvia McClain at a particular crescendo brought tears to my eyes. Lucas was totally in command at every precise moment and it was awe-inspiring. The 2,500 people in attendance were mesmerized. I must say, a mother, a father, and son on stage performing in front of a symphony orchestra is not an everyday occurrence.

In between all the latihans and penetrating talks by Ibu Rahayu, Bapak's daughter, we did manage to attend a workshop concerning "Translations of Bapak's Talks," which was chaired by Sharif Horthy and his wife, Tuti, Bapak's granddaughter. There was consideration being given to alter the use of some Indonesian words that could be a turnoff to potential new Subud members—words such as "Jiwa" being changed to "soul," thus eliminating needless explanations. A couple of times during the congress, we were pleased to share warm and pleasant moments sitting in the coffee shop with Ibu Rahayu and Ibu Mastuti, Bapak's widow. Helen and I reminisced with them about the time they visited us at our home and we took them to lunch at the country club. Being with Rahayu, who had assumed great responsibilities since the death of Bapak, was an honor and a blessing. She carries the weight of authoritatively responding to all the spiritual questions that come up and need to be answered. She does it with grace and a shy disarming smile that only confirms her strength. I was reading Istimah Week's book *The Man From The East*, and in one chapter someone had asked Bapak about the "messengers of God." Bapak answered: "In the past God had sent Abraham, Moses, Jesus, Muhammed—and now he had sent himself." When you think about that… it's overwhelming. And of course, it is. God is here for all to receive Him now—all you have to do is say, I want to receive Him and be opened in Subud. Prior to now only the messengers were opened to the contact. It's as simple as that. I know it must sound strange—but it's true. And it doesn't matter what religion you are. Subud strengthens your own religion. He has come to all of us. People just can't believe it—it's so profound and simple. So simple it's incomprehensible to most people—their cynical rationale gets in the way. The mind is a formidable opponent—especially a closed one.

We attended the Stella Adler Theater for a tribute to Steve Allen on his seventy-fifth birthday. It was a fun night of memories watching Steve's old *Tonight Show* videos, then hearing this funny and amazingly gifted man sing a few songs he'd written while accompanying himself on the piano. Later, while sipping champagne, we talked about his enormous list of published songs and lyrics. "How do you do that?" I asked him. That prompted him to tell me he had an ability to remember his "music" dreams and then write them down when he woke up. I also had seen him compose a song on the spot when someone plunked three random notes on the piano. He'd written thousands of songs and many books and was still phenomenally productive.

The next evening, before we could catch our breath, we were at another "Norby Walters Celebrity Night" at the Century Club in Beverly Hills. At dinner we sat with Barbara Rush, my co-star in many TV productions as well as the play *Blithe Spirit*, who never seems to lose a speck of her loveliness. Marty Landau joined us, an Actors Studio compatriot from way back. As I strolled around, I shook hands with many old friends and even hugged a few: Henry Silva, George Segal, Jack Jones, Dick Van Patten, Jan Murray, Buddy Hackett, Diane Ladd, Russ Tamblyn, Esther Williams, Mariette Hartley, and the inimitable Red Buttons. If you're in show business long enough, you really begin to know everybody—and like family, you're happy to see them, congratulate them for an achievement, and wish them well.

I wrote a letter to my dear old friend Maureen Stapleton, who now lived in Lennox, Massachusetts. Truly one of the great actresses of our time. I thought, *Wouldn't it be fabulous to have her play the old lady in* A Medal for Murray? *She would be terrific. And if Eli Wallach would do the male role... Oh, my... wouldn't that be something! Not since* The Rose Tattoo... *They were so brilliant together.* A week later she called me. It was one of those heart-tugging, sad conversations. I can still hear her voice as if it were yesterday. With all my dreams and good intentions, I had an immediate realization—time had moved on. "Mark, I haven't done a play in seventeen years," she said. "I can't do a play... I'm walking with a cane." And then she intimated how physically infirm she was, sounding so confined and lonely. She told me she had just finished her autobiography and asked, "Are you coming up to this area? If you are would you visit me? I'd love to see you." I promised her I would if I was anywhere near Lennox. When I hung up, I just sat there, thinking about our past relationship in New York and the excitement of being a young actor all those years ago. Nothing stays the same—only memories—and even they get fuzzy and fade in time.

On January 26, 1998, while Helen sat quietly, I paced the Tarzana Medical Center hallway waiting for the words "It's a boy! It's a girl!" It was a shorter wait than usual. My daughter Kelly gave birth to her second, a precious little girl with a full head of hair. Loren, movie camera in hand, survived the delivery quite well, and so did Kelly, who had a bit more to do. When it was my turn to hold that little turkey swaddled in a blanket, her lovely face so soft and peaceful, I couldn't prevent the wetness in my eyes as I stared at my new granddaughter, Lily. I loved her already.

Hisashi Ito and Cookie called from Japan, insisting we make a date and come be their house guests. They'd recently visited Los Angeles and we'd had them to our club and home for a fabulous evening. They were so appreciative of the attention they received from us. We decided to put the invitation on a "must do soon" list. We also had a call from Lucas who informed us that the Pittsburgh Symphony wanted him to be their assistant conductor and were offering him a four-year contract. We were thrilled. It certainly would be prestigious step up.

I was reading the fascinating 1940 daily journal of Clifford Odets. What an incredibly talented, innovative, and confused person. It was fun to read about Harold Clurman, Lee Strasberg, Morris Carnovsky, Luther Adler, and the whole Group Theater from a great playwright's point of view. I've known so many of the people he talks about and worked with quite a few, and my memories are vivid. I must say that his intellectual analysis of life and its conclusions are without illumination and leave me cold. It was all up in the head, especially when he quotes famous writers and their perceptions of what life is all about. But who am I to say? I met Odets in the early 1950s at the Actors Studio. Franchot Tone was with him and looked frail and dissipated. To read a daily journal written almost sixty years ago about Broadway is a trip. I immediately got a visual picture and a feeling of the time—the places and the people. I can almost taste it. Odets was a provocateur. He got me thinking about the creative process, the evolution and the machinations he went through—the torment and the sexual escapades fulfilling his every momentary impulse. He wrote about his dreams, detail after detail, every minute remembrance.

It's amazing. It was in a way what I relate of my dreams to Helen, long, generally agonized sequences. Well… Odets and I have something in common. But, I dare say, I do find him so over the edge in relation to his leftist, Marxist, socialist, communist line. In light of history it all sounds so asinine and utterly misguided.

I was obligated to fly to New York for a wedding, and it gave us an opportunity to see a few shows. Jack Klugman had arranged seats for us at the Lyceum Theater to see him in a revival of The Sunshine Boys with Tony Randall. They worked well together and it was a good show. I found it remarkable that Jack, seriously impaired with a now cured vocal cord problem, could still deliver a rousing performance, even though the range of his voice was somewhat limited. Afterward we chatted with Tony and then went for some pasta with Jack and his girlfriend, Peggy Crosby, who played the sexy nurse in the vaudeville sketch extremely well. We walked up Seventh Avenue to 52nd Street, yakking about acting and our lives since the days of South Philly. It was good to spend some quality time with a dear friend I've known for over forty years.

The following night we saw Eli Wallach in *Visiting Mr. Green* at the Union Square Theatre, playing an old man who'd lost his wife. He was superb and such a pleasure to watch—simple, honest, very real, and a great listener. It was a delicious performance by a masterful, dedicated actor. He was almost eighty-three, but alive with his age on stage. He'd had a couple of hip replacements and in his dressing room was impishly swinging a leg just to show how well it worked. He's a delightful friend, and I'll never forget how helpful he and Annie had been getting people to see me do *4 FACES* at the Actors Studio.

Estelle Parsons, who was the new artistic director of the Actors Studio, had been innovative in her approach, establishing many evenings of readings and scene performances embracing the plays of the Group Theater. We were privileged to attend such a session—warmly ushered through the crowded Studio to our front row "Reserved Richman" seats. We kissed and said hello to Joanne Woodward, the hostess for the evening, which turned out to be very special indeed. Historian Helen Krich Chinoy gave an informative talk with slides about the first summer camp of the Group Theater and subsequent camps that were the foundation for the Group under the direction of Harold Clurman, Lee Strasberg, and Cheryl Crawford. It was quite thrilling to see the blow-ups on the screen of the faces we were so familiar with and the production stills of *Waiting for Lefty*, *Awake and Sing*, *Paradise Lost*, *Men in White*, and *Golden Boy*—

the powerful plays of the young Clifford Odets. There was a short, acted scene from *Golden Boy*, then a discussion and talk by Joanne, and a "closer" by Estelle Parsons, who started this whole admirable festival. I complimented her afterward for her efforts to recapture and relive some of the past excitement. Then she surprisingly asked me, "Are you coming back?"

Yeah, sure.

I must admit—so much was always happening in New York concerning the theater, and there was so much more opportunity for a stage actor. But what was I to do? My inclination was to remain in Los Angeles. I have a good life, a certain style of living, and a family. If a play came up for me to be in New York, I would be in New York. Just to be available was not my bag. I had no desire to be in New York on the nebulous hope that something would turn up. It was all too remote at my age. Then again, it was a bit disheartening to be in Los Angeles, sitting on my butt, feeling very alienated from the Broadway scene and the mix of really talented people who are in the theater. It was always a two-coast dilemma, an odd predicament. People have asked me, "Are you still working?" I smile and say, "Yes, when there's something I want to do." In reality though, I am not working. I'm shunted aside like a used, burnt-out light bulb. When actually, all the juices are hot and there's power in my bones ready to explode.

This irritation permeates my being and I'm as frustrated as any artist would be with such restricted possibilities to express his craft. I know what I can do. Truthfully, however, nothing really happened for me professionally from doing *4 FACES*, except for fine notices and gracious compliments. I think maybe I have this penance I have to suffer in my life for past misdeeds in other lives, or something—an evolution of my soul—suffering, development, growth, and then fulfillment—in a dreadfully slow and painful process. Karma, and all that stuff.

Life is a test and how you deal with it separates the men from the boys and who falls by the wayside in hopeless agony. Or to have the balls and vigor to carry on, head held high with faith, trust and acceptance, no matter what, trippingly down life's stony and prickly path.

36 A Grandson Named Max and then, Japan!

A week after we arrived home we had a wonderful 9 pound, 2 ounce special delivery. Of course, we were expecting it, but I can't get too blasé about the situation. Having our first male grandson just doesn't happen every day of the week. Debbie, Lucas's wife, pulled the whole thing off quite well. Oh yes… they named him Max, and we have a birth announcement of the little guy in a tuxedo holding a baton in his right paw. A footnote to the blessed event—the night before, Lucas was at the piano accompanying Zoe Caldwell at the Mark Taper Theater in her one-woman show. She was brilliant. At the thunderous curtain call, she took Lucas's hand and brought him downstage and said, "We all have to stop applauding now. Lucas's wife, Debbie, is expecting a baby at any moment and he has to get to the hospital!" Then they both dashed off stage!

Hisashi Ito had finally convinced us to come to Japan for a visit, but it was a bit difficult to set a commitment date because of the many cross currents happening in my life.

The prolific, Tony award-winning producer Lester Osterman had read my play *A Medal for Murray*. He liked it a lot and had asked for some rewrites, which I was involved in doing. We were set for attending a dinner honoring dear friend Chuck Cecil, a neighbor and famous disc jockey of his perennial "The Swinging Years." (That evening we sat with great old time recording stars Bea Wayne, Gogi Grant, and Martha Tilton.) We attended Lucas's concert debut as the conductor of the Pasadena Pops Orchestra, which was fabulous but short-lived because he'd agreed to pick up the baton as assistant conductor of the Pittsburgh Symphony with a four-year contract.

I'd been working on a scene from my novel for the Actors Studio with Salome Jens, a fine actress. Mark Rydell, the moderator when we did the scene, was very complimentary. I heard the words "Renaissance Man" thrown around a few times, but I was thinking: Jesus... my damn novel is such a good read... when the hell am I ever going to get it published? This has been going on so long it's like a suppurating wound.

In August, we attended the Golden Boot Awards as guests of Roger Mayer, President of Turner Entertainment. It is always a poignant "remembrance" evening of Westerns and cowboys—the proceeds going to the Motion Picture and Television Fund. The amazingly handsome Buddy Rogers was celebrating his ninety-fourth birthday and came through again with his yearly check for $50,000 from the Mary Pickford Foundation. We visited one of our dearest old friends who was gravely ill with cancer, Leo Penn—a fine actor, director, and an absolutely sweet man. Eileen, his wife, and their boys, Michael, Sean, and Christopher hovered over their ailing dad with an outpouring of family fun, love, and devotion that was touching to share. A week later he was gone.

Lucas ended his brief tenure with the Pasadena Pops by conducting an evening "At the Movies." I had the pleasure of introducing my son, and then the night's guest star, Pat Boone, who'd made his film debut with me in *Friendly Persuasion* by singing the title song "Thee I Love" so beautifully.

In the fall of 1998, finally committed to the Itos, we were winging our way on an eleven-hour flight to Narita Airport in Tokyo. After we had gone through customs, Hisashi was waiting for us—his warm, smiling good nature giving us a lift. (The former chairman of the board of the Nikko Hotel Chain and ex prez of the airline travelled seventy miles to pick us up.) It's a good thing. Without his assistance, we would have been lost. (In Japan, there are no Red Caps. Baggage has to be sent ahead by courier.) It's fortunate that Hisashi was doing most of the talking on the speeding two-hour trip because we were falling off our seats with fatigue, although attempting to smile and occasionally mumble something intelligible. We finally arrived at Atami and piled into his waiting Subaru wagon and then drove through the resort area, circling and ascending higher up to reach his spacious hilltop home. Cookie greeted us with hugs and kisses. A quick shower offered a temporary awakening, and then a toast of champagne before Cookie's elegant dinner—but it was obvious that we were fading fast; about twenty-seven hours without any real sleep. We said goodnight (good morning), climbed the stairs to our restful Japanese haven, a cool breeze tinkling the chimes, and immediately zonked.

I woke up to an exquisite view out my window of the misty mountains, Mt. Fuji, fogged over and looking like all those Japanese prints I've always admired. I couldn't believe I was now in the country I was being trained to invade while in the Navy in 1945. Gracious Cookie served us a delicious breakfast of multiple treats and then we were off with Hisashi who wanted to show us everything our visitor's sights could bare. Atami was like a mini-Riviera, the views breathtaking high above the cove and crashing ocean. There were so many steps I thought my chewing-gum knees would collapse at any moment. Their Museum of Art was a knockout—traditional Japanese paintings, Hiroshige woodcuts, and fabulous ceramics. Hisashi just wanted to keep going, eagerly showing us his world and how he lived it—our fatigue overcome by his kindnesses and smiles. We even went shopping in the markets, maneuvering through congested Sunday traffic. The people were attractive, prosperous looking and friendly. The only difference, it seemed to me, from the States was that they were much more courteous, a bit shorter, and all the signs were in Japanese. Later, while taking a mineral bath in their rectangular wooden tub, Hisashi suddenly popped in and snapped a semi-immersed photo of me with Mt. Fuji in the distance! It was so beautiful there and everything was so laid out for us in every way that it was difficult to believe it wasn't all just a dream. I've never met such gracious and honorable people in my life, but that's what they say about the Japanese—it's in their nature. It's so complex trying to comprehend how they were taken over by such a hateful, blood-thirsty militaristic regime for so many years.

Winding around the rising countryside was almost like going up to Lake Arrowhead in California, but we were on our way to the Narukawa Art Museum in the mountainous Hakone National Park. It was a small museum that had some of the most incredible hand-blown glass and vase pieces I've ever seen—the originality, color, and sheer imagination outdoing Tiffany. When we finally got back, Hisashi made further arrangements for our visits to Kyoto and Tokyo in every specific detail. Then in the evening, they took us to Kushinobo, a fantastic eatery where we sat at the counter in front of the chef who prepared deep-fried vegetables then fish, meat, and quail eggs on a stick while our cosmopolitan host explained the process of prices and eating in Japan.

It rained like hell during the night. Heavy rains in this area do enormous damage and cause tremendous mudslides—and it was threatening again. The heavy mist hovered over the mountains and the verdant valley looked like another Japanese print. Even the cloud formation looked Japanese. At Cookie's breakfast, we had a revealing conversation from the reserved couple. Hisashi's father had been quite a playboy, wealthy from his father's money and a Geisha participant. We found out that Cookie had graduated from Rutgers University. Afterward, Hisashi wanted to show us a Japanese version of a mall, where he insisted on buying me a calculator as a gift so I could instantly figure out dollars to yen. Mingling with the crowds, I'd never seen so many beautiful, doll-like children and babies. I love babies and when I showed them attention the mothers beamed. Unfortunately, I made one baby cry and another begin to. Maybe it was the weirdness of my eyes.

It was typhoon weather—very overcast, gray-black and ominously foreboding—not a good sign. When we returned, we passed some of the previous mudslides being cleared, which wasn't encouraging. We were sipping wine and watching TV news about the impending typhoon when Hisashi came in, soaked and holding a flashlight. He'd been helping workmen cover his roof with a tarpaulin. Now it was raining a ton and the wind outside was howling frightfully. Hisashi insisted on showing us a video of Malcolm Forbe's seventieth birthday in Morocco with invited multitudes. Elizabeth Taylor, and all the notables—Kissinger, King of Morocco, etc.—and there was Hisashi, the only one allowed to use his video camera. The typhoon finally came full blast and the rain was fierce. I thought the roof was coming off. We did a latihan and prayed, but we didn't sleep all night. It was really terrifying. It quieted down about 5:30. When we finally came down for breakfast, we discovered Hisashi furiously mopping the floor in his recreation room. Thankfully, the weather had changed and the sun was trying to sneak through the clouds. Later, Hisashi dove into further arrangements for our succeeding travel plans—train, courier and taxi schedules—and even tickets to visit his grandfather's museum in Kyoto. I couldn't take any more detail, so I left it to Helen and started painting a watercolor of Cookie's hydrangeas. It turned out so well that she beamed when I gave it to her as a memento of our visit. Hisashi loved to talk and did go on a bit, but he was such an interesting man to listen to, while Cookie sat quietly and patiently saying very little, only commenting if asked—which was very Japanese. Later that night, Hisashi ushered us into his "Tatami Room" of authentic Japanese design and ambiance. Many of his parents' possessions were stored there, including art works by Seiho, his grandfather. He opened the closets and showed us scrapbooks of his mother's marriage—the dowry "parade" and photos of his mother in her wedding kimono, hand-painted on silk by Seiho. He couldn't share enough with us. We sat on pillows on the floor, our legs comfortably in the recessed hollow under the table. He even showed us his mother's photograph in seventy-year-old society magazines. Then Hisashi surprised us. He gave us a collector's item, a rare postage stamp of a Seiho painting. I kept wondering why our relationship had developed and why we were there. Another one of life's mysteries. For one moment, the wine and the hour narcotizing, I almost slid under the table recess dead asleep, but a pinch from Helen caught me just in time. The following evening, we were sartorially spruced-up for the special trip to Neumazu—a fisherman's area by the bay on the other side of Mt. Fuji. We settled into a small private motor launch for the five-minute ride and then docked at the Awashima Hotel. I'd seen fancy places in my life, but this edifice was beyond description. The modern oriental design, decor and color coordination—from the lobby to the suites—were incomparable. I was more than astonished to see the number of high-quality paintings on the walls when we stepped out of the elevator. I stared at a Camille Pissarro landscape, then, a Morisot, Chagall, Matisse, Lautrec, Dali, Vlaminck and on and on—a fortune in art and sculpture.

Sitting in the "Italian" dining room, the red sun glimmering through the dark clouds as it set on the purple bay, was unforgettable. I surprised myself when I ate my first tiny octopus and it tasted good—it even looked like an octopus with eight legs and a large head! The evening must have cost Hisashi a bundle, but money was of no concern when a guest of Mr. Ito. It was a night of intimate and wonderful conversation. As we sipped our champagne, the sky darkening dramatically, I thought how privileged we were and how memorable the experience.

The next morning Hisashi knocked on our door and said there was a phone call from home. Howard was calling and told us that Helen's mother was gravely ill and the cancer had spread and she wouldn't live long. There we were—just getting ready to leave that day for a three-day trip to Kyoto and then on to Tokyo—hotels, trains and tours—"The best laid plans of mice and men..." all arranged by our knowledgeable host. There were moments of utter madness trying to decide what we should do. We concluded that there was only one thing we must do—abort the trip and fly home immediately. Hisashi, his gentle face contorted, sadly understood and went to work with his influence, cancelling all the arrangements he'd made. We spent a frantic morning packing and had our last breakfast with darling Cookie while Hisashi was on the phone with the head of Japan Airlines to get us on a flight. Then, on a miserably rainy day, over narrow mountainous roads and along the beach, finally picking up the expressway, this gracious man drove us all the way to Tokyo! The traffic was a congested nightmare as we approached the city—the hodgepodge of buildings all squashed together in an incongruous design that defied description. We finally pulled into the Imperial Palace Hotel. Hisashi knew the hotel provided transportation to the airport. In the Frank Lloyd Wright Bar, we had a champagne farewell—thirty minutes of heartfelt thanks to one of the most wonderful characters we'd ever had the good fortune to know; a real loving bond had been cemented. He kept standing there, a solitary figure waving kisses to us as the bus pulled out. We'd been truly touched by his genuineness, and Cookie's too. Soon after, we settled in for the long flight home, to arrive sometime the next day. Helen, heavy-hearted and eager to be with her Mom, was now asleep beside me. We would have to make arrangements quickly for our flight to Albany. Only God knew how long Jean would hang on.

I was flying alone to Chicago and then to Albany. Helen had preceded me there by a few days. I couldn't stop thinking about being in Japan the previous week and how remote it all seemed now, and how hectic it had been since. Dear, sweet Jean, so near the end with her spreading cancer. Just a couple of weeks ago she was playing golf, at ninety-two! A very special woman who was so dear to me through our forty-five years of marriage. I was glad I had done a sketch of her recently on our patio. I have so many memories of her that I cherish; like the first time I saw her that year at the Grove Theater. This very attractive, dignified lady coming up to me as I sat on the cottage porch. "Pardon me, do you know where my daughter, Theodora Landess, is staying?"

I'd spoken on the phone to Carol and Alfred a few days earlier and had gotten very annoyed when I found out the doctors had Jean on morphine and basically in a vegetable state. I swear, doctors go into automatic pilot when patients go into hospice; the patient is routinely and prematurely drugged until death. I suggested they get her off morphine so she could live her last days in a more normal state until pain necessitated it. They listened and Motrin was sufficient for now, which allowed her to enjoy her grandchildren, who had all flown in to see their "Nana," and even her great-grandchildren Jenny, Lily and Max whom she'd never seen (a wonderful and moving sight to behold). When I saw her semi-asleep in her room at the St. Peters Hospital Hospice where she was receiving excellent care, she looked so frail and ethereal. I kissed her and she took my hand and kissed it, her bony hands gnarled with arthritis. She smiled a tired smile and in a short time became more animated, speaking in a whisper, strangely without pain, her mind as sharp as ever. We laughed about things of the past and told a few reminiscent stories of the children and she suddenly said, "I'm so tired. I want to go to sleep and not wake up anymore. It's time, I want to go… I've had enough."

Even though they were a distance apart, Helen was emotionally very attached to her mother—spiritually too. Even though Jean had shown no interest in Subud, we believe she'd received the opening, recovering from surgery a year earlier when Helen had quietly done the latihan in her room. Presently, a few times, Jean had approved Helen again doing latihan. The woman was a lesson and made it easy for all of us. Not one word of complaint, just acceptance. I impulsively borrowed some pencils and asked a social worker to bring me a sketch pad. A large definitive drawing of Jean's last hours was the result. She was so pleased she asked me to display it on the wall for everyone to see. In the void of being parentless, Jean and Sam had become my surrogate parents and I cherished them ever since we were first married. Our relationship had always been rock solid. They never interfered or caused friction in our lives, only giving their gracious love and wholehearted support. Sam even redid their home, adding bedrooms so we could visit comfortably with all the children.

One evening we all shared a heart-tugging experience. We played a tape of a song Lucas had composed for her birthday ten years earlier titled "That Touch of Nana."—recalling all the special little things she'd done with my kids—with Lucas at the piano and sung by all her loving grandchildren, Kelly's voice especially sticking my throat with emotion. Even the nurses stopped in to listen. I knew Jean had enjoyed it in her quiet way, and when she said her now standard mantra, "I want to go… I'm so tired." I gave her a whispered prayer. Say, "Help me, Lord, in submission to come to thee." Surprisingly, she said it a few times as I stood close to her. I suggested to Helen that she do a latihan again with her mother after everyone had left. By this time, she'd had her sleeping pills and was almost death-like, but she had such dignity. She kissed my hand again when I told her I loved her, and she mouthed, "I love you, too." It was the last time I ever saw her. I left the next day. Helen stayed on, doing what a loving daughter does to comfort a dying mother for as long as necessary.

I couldn't turn off my overactive brain or put it in barely functioning "idle." The problem for me has always been that if I wasn't creating something—acting, painting, or writing—I was doing too much thinking, living in my head and running through a repetitious litany of irritations and frustrations. There didn't seem to be much happening in my career. It was eating at me more than ever. The only respite was turning to God through the latihan—that God was guiding my life—which always worked to put everything in the proper perspective. When Helen came back from Albany—her mother laid to rest next to her father—we felt a significant chunk of our lives had been put to rest also. Carol and Alfred had moved to New York City. Albany would have no hold on us anymore—but countless unforgettable memories would—like all the warm colorful scarves that Jean had knit for me that I always wear in chilly weather. Dear Jean, close to my heart and thoughts.

Four of our children were graduates of UCLA: Howard and Lucas in music, Kelly and Orien in theater. We went to see Roger in a play at California State University at Northridge. He was majoring in theater also, God help him, and he was playing a whimsical dark-skinned gentleman from India with a convincing dialect. He was pretty good and funny too, but we weren't sure he was dedicated enough to pursue the elusive career of an actor. Only time would tell.

I began working on another scene from my novel, again playing Lucas Hollander, the studio mogul, with Claudia Stediline, a terrific actress defining my troubled daughter. We had a few rehearsals then presented it at the Actors Studio—a scene telling me she'd fallen in love with the young New York producer I'd introduced her to. I was convinced more than ever that my novel would make one hell of a picture. It had all the elements to involve. I've known many Hollywood icons and sometimes it was difficult to separate their screen persona from the person sitting next to you. I didn't have that problem with Ann Miller, a dear friend, but occasionally I slipped. I'd be casually talking to her when suddenly in my mind's eye, there she was tapping away magnificently in a glorious MGM musical. She came to dinner with the stoic-faced character actor Morgan Woodward, one of the gentlest men I know. We'd worked together in *Zuma*, a TV movie shot in Tucson. Ann, without artifice and pretensions, was as down-to-earth as a young school girl. I'll never forget that she'd come to see me twice in *4 FACES*. I even used a quote of hers for publicity releases.

At the end of the year, Lucas was again flown in from Pittsburgh. This time by Twentieth Century Fox to conduct a full orchestra on a sound stage party for the release of *The Thin Red Line*, playing Hans Zimmer's music, the composer for the film. We chatted with Sean Penn, who starred in the film, and his wife Robin and a whole host of other celebs who were there. When I introduced new home-run champ Mark McGuire to Lucas, I made a mental slip and said, "I'd like you to meet Mack McGuire!" McGuire then turned to me and said, "Mack? MACK?" He was smiling.

Another realization that time was hurtling—Mona and Karl Malden invited us to their sixtieth wedding anniversary at their daughter Myla's home. Warmth and heartfelt feelings abounded for the two genuinely exceptional and loving people we were honored to call our friends.

I've been to extravagant parties before, but I'd never attended a celebrity wedding shindig like the one held in early 1999 at Connie Stevens's palatial home and grounds, with a vast enclosed tent to hold 300-400 dinner guests! Diane Ladd, formerly married to Bruce Dern and mother of Laura Dern, got married again to entrepreneur Robert Hunter. Everywhere you turned it was wall to wall familiar faces, from James Coburn and Kathy Bates to Red Buttons and Billy Bob Thornton. I had a chat with Vilmos Zsigmond, a great academy award cinematographer (*Close Encounters of the Third Kind, The Deer Hunter*). He was rather aloof and didn't remember me—or didn't want to—and I didn't mention that he'd worked a couple of days as a sub on a stinker of a film I was starring in years ago. At that time, he'd just come from Hungary and was trying to get established in Hollywood. "Oh, Mr. Richman… I can do everything… 16 mm or whatever you want. Call me, I would like to work for you again. I just have to get into the union and maybe you could help…"

Hollywood—it's a wondrous place.

37 An Amazing Proposal

DONNA AND JOHN CREAN came to dinner at our club then visited our home. John wanted to see my new paintings so I took him into my studio. On the wall was a *4 FACES* poster from the New York Actors Studio. (John had seen the play when I premiered it at Chapman University and had given a special dinner for Helen and me prior to the opening.)

"Peter Mark, what are you doing with the play?" he asked.

"At the moment, John, nothing."

"Well, why don't you come down for lunch and we'll talk about it," he said, his smiling good-nature spilling promises.

"What do you mean, John?" I asked. He paused a moment.

"What I mean is… I could build the sets and you could do the show in my studio and we'll put it on tape." (John Crean, aside from being an inventor, designer, builder, and founder of Fleetwood Enterprises, the largest manufacturer of recreational vehicles in the world, also was the cook on his funny syndicated cooking show shot on tape in his own studio.) Two weeks later John called and asked me again… when was I coming down to visit him and talk about the taping? I was stalling because I wasn't sure what I wanted to do, but finally we made a date and I drove down to the exclusive Balboa Bay Club where he had his fabulous yacht The Donna Crean moored. When I found him, John was on his knees, drilling a screw into a bar cabinet door. He finally saw me, dusted himself off and said, "Let's go to lunch." While I was eating a deliciously prepared salmon, the waiter replenishing my cool white wine, John said, "You've seen my studio… it's fully equipped. We would just have to build the sets for you to move around in." This whole situation had been jumping around in my head. I already had a good tape of my show from the Chapman University performance; but I couldn't really do anything with it.

"John… listen," I said, "if we tape my show… what have we got? A taped one-man show. And what do we do with it?" Before he could answer, the words tumbled out of my mouth, "Why don't we make a movie!"

John took about two seconds, not a man to challenge. "You want to make a movie?" he asked.

"Yes."

"Okay… I'll give you two hundred and fifty thousand dollars. Go make a movie."

I nearly fell off my chair, I couldn't believe it. "Are you serious, John?"

"Of course, I am. But you'll have to write a screenplay first."

I had never had anybody under any circumstances put money in my lap before—and with such ease and gracious good wishes. It was astounding. I was convinced it was truly a gift from God. On the drive home, I called Helen and told her the amazing news and she was equally astonished. Lingering in the back of my brain was the crucial question: Could I put together the elements to make a quality film with such limited funds? I was already mulling over the possibilities of opening up the play. There was no getting around the fact that *4 FACES* was a one- man show of four different people at a crucial time in their lives, but I thought I might have a way to flesh out the people I only imagined on stage, visually and verbally on film. In a furious two weeks, I pounded out a film script that I thought would work, at least for a production budget breakdown and shooting schedule. I called John and he was pleased to hear it and gave me another "go ahead." In fact, he offered me more money! I agreed to take thirty of the additional fifty thousand he insisted on. To legally protect me, he even had his lawyer help me establish my company: 4 FACES PRODUCTIONS, INC. Aside from his good graces, John did not want to be involved. I was to be the owner-producer along with the other two hats I would wear as the writer and star. I had to get a director immediately and the first person I thought of was a dear friend, Ted Post, an award-winning director with over fifty years' experience. We had worked together several times (*Twilight Zone*, *Combat*) and he'd seen the play and loved it. Accepting the fact of a miniscule budget, he enthusiastically signed on. I gave him a percentage and shared producership. Next, if I could, I wanted to get top quality people in all the other key positions, especially the cinematographer. I had a list I was pursuing that was a half-page long. I took Owen Roizman, whom I knew, to dinner. One of the best cameramen in the business (Academy Award nominated for *The Exorcist*, *Tootsie*) sadly told me he had retired because of ill health. Following that, I was getting nowhere with my list when Ted said he would call John Alonzo, nominated cameraman for *Chinatown*. I sent him the script and a week later I took him to lunch. He showed the warmth of possibilities, liking the material of four different people and the short shooting schedule. He gave us a tentative yes… unless a "big" film at Paramount he was committed to suddenly went into production. Ted and I were encouraged, but, of course, the other film got going and he was quickly out of ours. I then recalled a cinematographer, Isadore Mankofsky, whose work I admired in TV films (*The Burning Bed*) and the feature *Somewhere in Time*, with Christopher Reeve, and decided to track him down. I finally got his evasive phone number, called him, and personally delivered a script to his home. He phoned me the next day to say he was going away on a lecture tour and couldn't do the film, although he'd liked my script. I was very disappointed but wished him well. Strangely enough, the following morning he called me again and said, "I couldn't sleep last night… if the job is still open, I'd like to do it."

I was ecstatic and said, "Izzy, last night you felt the hand of God on your shoulder!"

Ted asked me to call retired Jack Senter, with whom he'd worked at 20th Century Fox, and an art director with vast experience (*M*A*S*H*) who was interested in joining us. I did, made my pitch, and we were off and running. It was becoming clear to me that I was putting together solidly experienced professionals who were eighty years old or nearing it. Age discrimination is something that Hollywood unfortunately perpetuates, dismissing fabulous elderly talent as if they were decrepit incompetents. It had always irritated me, and now, as I was decidedly getting upper in my years, I was progressively realizing it too. There would be no ageism in my production! If the talent is vital and can do the job—they get hired!—and I would consider myself lucky to have them. I then proceeded to employ a senior sound mixer, and a script supervisor, Joyce King, who years earlier had worked on *Easy Rider* but was not working in film anymore (couldn't get hired). A production manager was needed posthaste, so I called Roger Mayer, my friend at Turner Network, who gave me four suggestions. Narrowing them down, I had a meeting at my home with Bob Perkis, who seemed very capable so I hired him on the spot. Getting the full cast and crew together I was responsible for employing a total of sixty-two people. One of the most valuable was my production and post production coordinator, Gary Adelman, who was extraordinarily helpful in every area. After endless discussions and planning, we set a start date for a ten-day shooting schedule.

John Crean called and suggested I talk to Pastor Robert Richards at the Lutheran Church of The Master where he was a contributor. Ted, Izzy, Jack, and I went to see the small church on Santa Monica Boulevard and marveled at how perfect it was for the church scene. Pastor Richards approved us and we were set. Again travelling in a hired van with key people, we visited other possible locations to make sure permits would allow us to shoot there, especially in Griffith Park where we needed to film an approaching city bus for Daniel to board. There was so much technical planning and thinking and decision making I thought my head would spin off its mooring, and in the midst of all this I was still trying to polish the script. However, I wasn't complaining—it was my baby and I was a couple of feet off the ground with purpose, excitement and energy—almost the kind of adrenaline rush I had felt as a player before the kickoff in a football game—all cylinders going. At an Actors Studio acting session I saw two actors that interested me. Julie Janney, a wonderful young character actress to play my wife in the Carlo segment dealing with a drug addict son, and Gabriel Dell (Junior) to play my visiting grandson in the Gerhardt scene when he comes to visit the former Nazi SS officer hiding in South America. We set up "reading" appointments and Ted agreed to my choices. Casting agent Marvin Paige found us nineteen-year-old Lane Garrison, who we read and set for the role of the drug addict son in Carlo. The only other major part was the young man in the park that the old holocaust survivor Daniel meets on his walk. My son Orien desperately wanted to play it. I read him and made him sweat a bit on purpose, but he got the role and was excellent. Before making a deal for our camera needs, another little miracle happened. Through a friend, I met Tracy Langan, a marketing executive at Panavision, who was so impressed with my credits that he contacted Kelly Simpson, who was in charge of grants. The next thing I knew I was given a "New Filmmakers Grant" that entitled me to the complete Panavision 35 mm camera package for free, saving me $8,000 on my budget. I was floating with that coup. We were a few weeks from shooting and I hadn't lined up a makeup artist; so, I called the best, an old friend who I'd worked with many times—Mike Westmore, the youngest of the great Westmore descendants. I'd worked with them all, but Mike was innovative and special. As expected, he was locked in at Paramount Studios, but as I knew he would, he gave me a first-rate recommendation, Jennifer Turchi, and we diligently worked out the four subtly different looks needed for my characters on film.

I asked my son Lucas to compose the movie score, elaborating on what he'd done so brilliantly for the play. I knew he would be in from Pittsburgh for several weeks, conducting a seminar for BMI film composers, teaching them conducting at the musicians union which he inaugurated, and at the same time serving as music director of the Young Musicians Foundation Debut Orchestra camp. His plate was stuffed, but I knew he would come through for me (many sleepless nights). For openers, he quickly composed the music for a hymn I wrote, "We are Thy Children" that was needed immediately for the opening of the church scene. And who do you think sang that hymn? Why my daughter, Kelly, of course! Alongside Debbie, Lucas's wife, and another lovely actress-singer, Ann Winkowski. An extraordinary trio of talent that set the mood for the Pastor's moving sermon, and then you find out unexpectedly that he'd been sexually fooling around with these beauties and others in the congregation. It was a peculiar reality for an actor/writer, acting out my heartfelt spiritual convictions in a real church, however deceitful, and a Christ statue framed behind me. The three-day shooting there went extremely well, everybody hustling in the set-ups. They all knew we had limited time to get it in the can—the budget couldn't tolerate screw-ups. There wasn't a whole lot of difference in the atmosphere from a multimillion dollar production and our little venture. The crew was experienced and everybody was getting paid on time, except me. I deferred payment for all my services and my script. It didn't matter. When I walked to my trailer and saw the equipment trucks lined up for a block, the signs posted with "4 FACES PRODUCTON VEHICLES," I smiled with a tickling happiness.

In the adjoining church building, we were able to shoot the Carlo sequence for two days where he reveals to a drug intervention meeting his son's drug problem. Helen, in close-up playing one of the parents, cried effectively when told of his death. In a small room that Jack Senter cleverly altered to look like a police station entry, my pal Gene Butler, as a friendly cop, scolds my boy and warns him of the consequences of remaining on drugs. When we moved to my son Orien's rented house in Hollywood, which he allowed us to use for Carlo's interiors, an old friend and a fabulous actor, Nehemiah Persoff, came down from retirement in Cambria to play the family priest. What a joyous addition to a sequence so enriched by his believable presence, deepening the reality of parents torn apart by drugs and death. Of course, in every production there are always problems that have to be nipped in the bud, otherwise it's chaos. I certainly had enough to do, even signing slews of checks in between takes, but one day I had to jump into an escalating situation with the production manager and the key wardrobe girl, sternly warning that I wanted harmony on the set! Another time I had to assuage the growing discontent between the director and cinematographer with diplomacy and sweet verbal agility. Thank God it worked.

Shooting in beautiful Griffith Park after being cooped up in a small house was indeed pleasurable. Wearing a woolen cap over white hair, my false mustache itching as I run to catch a bus and don't—Daniel, the upbeat health nut and eighty-three-year-old holocaust survivor meets a young man on a bench (Orien) and begins a friendly conversation. Playing with my son—the birds chirping, a dog barking in the distance—was a highlight for me, observing his well-played indifference, gradual interest and then involvement as I slowly relate my life to him: my obsession with walking, eating properly, my singer's background in Germany, the Nazis and concentration camps; my wife's death and a visit to her grave nearby. As the old man leaves to catch another bus he smiles and yells back, "Keep walking, every day… and you'll live a long time, I promise you!" The bus pulls away as the camera moves in close to the young man's face— the experience has changed him a little. It was June 15 and Orien's actual birthday. At lunch time the candles were lit on a strawberry cake and we all wished him a happy one. I kissed him and gave him a Daddy bear hug.

John Crean's estate in Newport Beach facing the bay was sixteen acres of magnificence, with varying buildings, offices, and workshops perfectly set among the groomed, lush landscaping. The main house, looking like "Tara," had an enormous mahogany paneled living room, ideal as the Gerhardt South American hideaway, giving an immediate visual impression of stolen Nazi wealth. When the camera pulls back from a close-up of my hands peeling an apple with a knife, revealing a turtlenecked, aristocratic gentleman—the fireplace roaring as he expounds his SS life for the first time to an inquisitive grandson—I can honestly say it was the most chilling scene I've ever put on film; horrendous mayhem, brutality, and murder—an eager specialist for the Final Solution told with justified rational logic and simplicity. Now the grandson, learning much more than he'd expected by his hesitant, but probing questions, had suddenly put his own life in jeopardy. After two days of intense shooting it was a wrap. We'd finished principal photography. Ted Post, my director, had been a doll to work with and except for a few blips it had been a harmonious shoot. Now all we had to do was put it together. Looking at bits and pieces on an Avid editing monitor hours on end is enough to drive anyone rabid. But thanks to the calming expertise of Ted Post and our editor Debbie Light, after six weeks of claustrophobic concentration and sometimes testy decision making, we were pleased with the final cut. Now we had to add the finishing embellishments in post-production. I met with Jim Corbett of Mix Magic who would handle all the re-recording and mixing of sound levels of voices, effects, and music. I met and hired Sharon McGeeney, who eventually would meticulously cut the negative. I met with Keith Allan of Title House and discussed my ideas for titles and the four computer-painted character faces I'd created for the opening credits. I liked his idea of establishing each face and then having them disappear into infinity—a classy effect for a little extra money.

In the middle of August, while all this preparatory stuff was going on, my dear son Lucas, bless his soul, was locked in my studio for two weeks glued to a computer and a video composing the score—occasionally sleeping on the couch. Then, for two days I watched this young man superbly conduct a recording session at Capitol Records, Studio #A (where Sinatra recorded) with the best musicians in Hollywood. To hear what he'd written for my film brought tears to my eyes and a lump in my throat more than once. He even wrote a tag song for the film called "Daddy's Wisdom," which was sung by my seven-year-old granddaughter, Jenny Lester (a union member!), and Jeff Austin. How blessed could I be? Lucas joined Ted and me for the long final session at Mix Magic, making the necessary adjustments to the music and sound levels. A week later, the "master print" was approved. Consolidated Film Industries (CFI) had been doing our film developing and printing. Izzy Mankofsky, my cameraman, and I met with Dan Muscarella, who was the assigned color timer, and I couldn't have been more pleased. He had rendered his incredible expertise for the film *Titanic!*—a multi-zillion dollar picture—and now, gratefully, I had him for my peanuts-priced effort. We studied three frames from each scene and set the color for the eventual final print. A week later, after many screenings of the four reels and all the corrections, I okayed the final look of the film for printing. Dale Olson, a renowned Hollywood press agent who'd been my rep during the stage run of *4 FACES*, came to a screening at CFI. He was very impressed with the film and my performance and said to me, "I think you could get an Academy Award nomination next year with the proper campaign…" That floored me, but it seemed rather remote, although Dale had been handling stars' nominations and awards for years. First, I would have to get the film released—a task I would soon face head on.

In September, Helen and I flew to Philadelphia. My niece Elaine had called and said her mother (my sister Fay) was failing and might not survive long, a victim of cancer. Fay was ninety-two. In a lucid moment, free of dementia, she suddenly had said, "I don't want to go through surgery… I've had a long life. My heart couldn't take it…" Laura, my other niece, the psychologist (Harry's daughter), and her husband, Alan, had set us up at the Rittenhouse Hotel. They, in turn, had a magnificent condo on the thirty-second floor with the most spectacular view of the city I'd ever seen. Alan, an extremely successful businessman, was a warm, genial host and a sculptor—his work impressive. The four of us spent some heartwarming moments together talking about our children and the difficulties we'd faced. Alan's line was the most telling: "We didn't get the return we expected from our kids… not relative to our investment…" Elaine and her husband, Phil, came to lunch at the hotel. We'd seen them very little over the years and it was good to renew a relationship. Elaine looked so much like Fay it was almost shocking, and Phil had aged considerably since I'd seen him last. When we drove out to see Fay I recognized very little—Philly had changed so much. Now it was zipping freeways and fifteen minutes to anywhere. We were in the reception area of the sprawling facility when Elaine wheeled in her mother. Her hair was white and her face heavily wrinkled, but her eyes still lit up with that marvelous smile and contagious laugh. We had a terrific two hours, even with her lucidity fading in and out, reminiscing, holding hands, and sharing our remembrances. Emotionally, it was a tug and a pull. I loved her deeply. There had always been a strong, caring bond. So many years, and always a distance separating us. It was a memorable visit, and Helen was so wonderful with her too. My feelings were raw. Fay was my last immediate family member. It would be the last time I would ever see my sister, God bless her. Thankfully, she'd been opened in Subud, but she didn't remember. I prayed that God would.

Shortly after returning home, Tracy Langan arranged for a screening of *4 FACES* at the Panavision Theater in Woodland Hills, California. More than a hundred guests, family and many notables attended—Karl Malden, Jane Withers, Ann Miller, and many more including my financier, John Crean and Donna. I made a little speech and then sat in the back row with Helen, my heart pounding. As soon as Lucas's lush music filled the theater I relaxed and enjoyed the event—a quality, literate "art film" that had something to say about four diverse people, the frailty of their human nature, and their tangential relationship with God. Near the end of the film, Daniel, the old Jew, holocaust survivor says, "Everybody has problems… big ones, small ones… but how we solve our problems… that's what God sees…"

In the opening credits, Daniel's line fills the screen: How we solve our problems… that's what God sees… It was the theme of the picture—and the title song. Afterward, most of the comments were good, some reserved and some raves. Many thought it was better than the play, which was heartening. The future of it? I had no idea. But I felt ecstatic about my accomplishment, bringing in a quality film for under 300 thousand—a minor miracle in anybody's league.

Kelly Simpson of Panavision called: "You must get your film in the Sundance Festival. The entry deadline is coming up this weekend." I immediately took the *4 FACES* 35 mm digital version of the film to a lab to make 100 VHS cassette copies. Thus began my frenetic search for festival acceptances all over the world—having decided it would immediately expose the film for potential theatrical release.

4 FACES was selected by The Santa Clarita Film Festival with two screenings in March 2000, the Newport Beach Film Festival in April, and the Director's Guild of America's "Finder Screening Series" (quality unreleased independent films) in May. All of the screenings were well received and I remember Maximilian Schell and Sally Kirkland saying particularly nice things. In 2002, *4 FACES* received a nomination for a Prism Award. The most elaborate festival we attended and enjoyed was the one in Newport Beach where John Crean, my financier, resided. The festival went on for a whole week with V.I.P. gatherings. Arnold Kunert, the Festival director who chose *4 FACES* as an official entry, was an exceptionally nice man and we immediately became friends. Before my screening, Arnold gave an excellent introduction lauding the "superb work." Then John Crean got up and surprised me with his remarks: "We're old and close friends… and I never saw a man work as hard on anything as Peter Mark did putting this film together…" I was touched. As the lights dimmed in the packed house, I looked to my right and saw my old friend Theodore Bikel sitting there—another heartwarming surprise. The audience seemed to love it. Afterward there was a resounding applause and then a spirited Q & A session—intelligent questions that prompted free-swinging answers concerning the three hats I was wearing as writer, producer, and actor. I enjoyed myself immensely, especially when an elderly woman said, "… it was a strong study in humanity and thought provoking… it makes you think!"

The representative for the Berlin Film festival, Al Newman, saw a video of my film and was "blown away," insisting on sending it to Berlin personally. I continued to put packages together for Venice, Milan, England, Paris, Edinburgh, Rotterdam, Australia, Houston, Chicago, Austin, San Francisco, New York, and many, many more destinations. Forty-eight in all, the considerable expense of which would have been better spent if given to charity. Unfortunately, I slowly came to the conclusion, after several months and many rejections, that a lot of festivals, although they wouldn't admit it, were in it for the buck and their entry fees were a scam. Multiply fees of $50–$100 x 2,000 entries, and you'll see that their enticing "come-ons" add up to a tempting and indecently large figure.

How to promote a festival: Print your "Blue Sky Film Festival" letterhead stationery; take an ad in several film magazines; solicit all your friends and aunt Sadie and uncle Charlie to be a film committee; and let them view the submissions (beer and booze optional) and come up with a winner (if they can get past the first five minutes). Then, rent a theater for a night or two, run a bunch of films plus the winner and runner-up you've chosen—and voilà!—you too are a Film Festival! (Many returned cassettes were never rewound, indicating only three to seven minutes were ever viewed! If they turned off the beginning of the Pastor's sermon, the first FACE, they never saw the film.) It was dispiriting. You could say that I had a bitter taste in my mouth. Most of these festivals (not all, of course) are so full of themselves, and their ridiculous committees don't really see the submissions. Contrastively, major studio submissions get all the courtesy without ever being screened because everybody want to be a starfucker—to hob knob and call attention to their miserable little group who would be nothing without a festival. The people who run these things are generally your academic-type film enthusiasts—or fourth rate failed producer types who once made an obscure 16 mm film about a cockroach biting somebody's toe. In other words, most are failed shits who sit in judgement of other people's creativity and are not qualified, squinting out from their limited, foggy and sometimes perverse perspective. Then, when you get to see some of the films that are chosen and they've gone nuts about, you wonder what planet you reside on and if there's any hope. It had become increasingly clear that the avenue for my film was not to be in a theatrical release, at least at that time. I had a good and unusual picture for sale. But it was a picture with a lot of dialogue and no visible sex and violence (a necessity in today's market), which discouraged a distributor from getting involved.

On January 26, 2000, my daughter's beautiful little girl, Lily, had a birthday. She was two years old. On the same day, my sister Fay died in Philadelphia at ninety-two. A ninety-year separation and a trunkful of life's experiences now put to rest. My sister—a loving, volatile and vibrant gem of a woman with radiant, pale blue eyes like a summer sky—is a memory seared in my soul. She remains as much a part of me as my own breathing, and her sparkling smile and laughter are in my head forever.

Then, two days later, my daughter, Kelly, gave birth to her third little girl, a magnificent eight-pound turkey dumpling with reddish hair named Julia Rose. Such a sweet, tightly wrapped little package with a tiny hand sticking out. We now had four grandchildren and couldn't have been more grateful.

38 The Super Bowl Rams

AFTER A FANTASTIC SEASON of football surprises and unbelievable performances by Kurt Warner, our quarterback, and running back Marshall Faulk, we were finally in the grandest spectacle of all. On January 29, 2000, Orien and I flew to Atlanta (Momma stayed with Kelly) to see the Tennessee Titans play the Rams. I couldn't believe after all these years of moaning, groaning, and endless disappointments in Los Angeles and Anaheim, the St. Louis Rams were now competing for the big enchilada. Orien and I were ecstatic. A festive atmosphere permeated the Crowne Paza Ravinia where the Rams and Georgia were staying. Outside the hotel there was wildness and mayhem—busses, cars, and taxis jammed all over the icy-slick streets. Inside it was rather well organized—the Rams fans jocular and cheery as we were directed to the Rams Space, a huge isolated area separated by hanging drapes and tough-looking security guys. We were welcomed warmly by assistants Ida Kaul and Mike Moyneur, who gave us our assortment of Rams paraphernalia and, thanks to Georgia, superb Super Bowl tickets. I called her in her suite and she immediately asked us for dinner. Exhausted, we hustled back to the Marriott Hotel for a nap. It was wonderful having my son Orien with me, jabbing and joking—and also getting in a few words about Subud, boring his ass, but still some of it seeping through his resistant, glib exterior. A lot going on in that boy... more than he lets on.

It was freezing cold in Atlanta, my knitted scarf tightly wrapped around my neck. The cab driver didn't know where the hell he was going and then, luckily, I saw the sign Il Fornaeo-Italiano Restaurante. Georgia's son, Chip Rosenbloom, a young film writer-director, guided us to a long table where about sixty people were being seated. During dinner Orien and I had a deeper father-son talk when I said something like, "You're a real talented guy... you can't just coast anymore, you have to get serious in your life and make some choices."

I remember him saying, "Don't you know, Dad, that I always hear your voice in my head? I do... I hear you." Then he said with a little laugh, "I'm getting your message." We'd had variations of this conversation many times before, but there was a real glimmer of positivity that I never heard before, it gave me hope he'd change.

That evening I met two delightful people: Anna and Whitney Harris. Whitney was ninety years old, ram-rod straight, white-haired handsome. He also had the distinction of serving on the staff as a prosecuting attorney at the Nuremberg Trial of Nazi war criminals in 1945–1946 when he was a Lieutenant Commander in the Navy (he received the Legion of Merit for his efforts). His book *Tyranny on Trial* is a highly respected classic. (On another visit to St. Louis, we were invited to his home where he gave us a personal copy of his book, which I've since read. It is an incredible work and should be required reading at every university.) Anna, his attractive second wife and about twenty-five years his junior, was also someone special—a pilot, an artist, and surprisingly... a pharmacist.

Later, I moved to where Georgia was sitting and she introduced me to hefty Bernie Miklasz, sports reporter for the *St. Louis Post Dispatch*. He knew me from TV and I told him I'd been reading his Rams stuff on the internet. We both defended Georgia against the continually vicious *Los Angeles Times* reporters—the two entrail-eaters Bill Plashke and T.J. Simers who inexorably resent Georgia's exit from the Los Angeles area. I sincerely complimented Georgia for what she'd accomplished and she glowed in appreciation. It had been a warm, wonderful evening, a perfect beginning for the big day—tomorrow!

In the morning, we returned to the Crowne Plaza Ravinia for a Rams brunch. The lobby was swarming with mobs of people wearing blue and gold—old friends, new ones; the banners flying, jackets and T-shirts for sale; the steady cacophony of Rams exuberance, the giggles and smiles; the tremendous excitement and anticipation tingling the bloodstream! We sat down with my buddy Jack Faulkner, who'd been the offensive coordinator when the Rams lost to Pittsburgh in the 1980 Super Bowl. Jack has a huge picture of me in a Rams uniform on his office wall (Georgia presented me the uniform when I received the Silver Medallion). When anybody asks, "Who is that guy?" Jack responds, "Don't You know him? Why he's one of the greatest Rams players that ever... blah, blah, blah!" He really tickles me.

Finally, it was time to get on the busses heading for the Georgia Dome. Orien was beside himself with enthusiasm, and my heart was pumping too with edgy suspense. We departed the bus and walked through the muddy parking lot toward the stadium. It was a crush to get in through all the security, up the escalator and ramps to the second tier and our great seats on the fifty-yard line. (Orien said scalpers would get $3,000 to $5,000 on the street.) We arrived an hour before kickoff, a tag around our necks saying: "Rams Family." Magic Johnson spotted me and came by to say hello. On the field, the 70,000 screamers witnessed a raucous show of dancers in exotic costumes, wild music, lights, fireworks, and Tina Turner; and thankfully—I had a soft pillow for the arse.

While wandering around our level where a vast variety of food was being served, we ran into Orien's friend Vince Vaughn, a hot young actor. He was with a friend of mine, Scott Wilson, another fine actor who'd come to a screening of *4 FACES* and now again wishing me luck. After gulping a sandwich, we returned to our seats for the kickoff, my blood pulsing. There is nothing like this kind of excitement to a football rooter whose team is about to face the jangling, nervous-time, joyous, depressing or exultant unknown. This game exemplified all the categories, and the heart-thumping anxiety never let up. We were biting our nails—and the last three minutes had everybody doing it in their pants! The Titans had tied the score in the last quarter with less than two minutes left. It looked bad for the Rams because the Titans suddenly had the momentum to win. Everybody was standing and wishing and praying and sweating bullets.

But suddenly, on the first play of the Rams possession, Kurt Warner unleashes a seventy-yard bomb to Isaac Bruce—and breathtakingly, we go ahead again 23–16! Hallelujah! Oh, happy day! We're gonna win this sucker! But then—with a choking gag in my throat, the Rams now limping—I watch the Tennessee bastards drive down the field again— yard by yard! They're getting it done! They're doing it—and only seconds are left— enough for one last desperation McNair pass! Oh, my God—he caught it— and then miraculously—the receiver is STOPPED by our Mike Jones with a tremendous tackle at the ONE FOOT LINE! The game was over!

Rams win the Super Bowl! 23–16! Victory, finally—after twenty-five years of tortuous losses and scabby callouses on our suffering hearts. Everybody to our right and left was kissing us and we were unashamedly kissing back. I hugged and kissed Orien who had suffered along with me, but still grew up to be a Rams stalwart. In the 1980 Super Bowl, when we lost to Pittsburgh in the fourth quarter, 31–19—our TV all gussied up with drooping blue and gold pom-poms—my eighty-year-old son Roger had cried gushing, unstoppable tears. We'd been at this a long time.

That evening Georgia gave a huge, jubilant party at the hotel and we were seated at her table with her family and John Shaw. She was beaming as she received all the effusive congratulations she so rightfully deserved. Coaches, players and friends stopped by to pay their respects. I clinked Georgia's glass and proffered a toast to her graciousness and our stupendous Rams, embraced her, and planted a happy kiss on her cheek. Orien and I wandered around, shaking hands with the whole team, sharing the victory and camaraderie. The festivities went on until 3:00 a.m. It was an unforgettable merry-go-round evening of pleasure and good will. Goodbye Atlanta! Man, it was cold! Long drooping icicles were hanging from the trees and the curling branches looked like coils of white cable. After lunch, we finally boarded the last Rams charter that would fly us to St. Louis and the awaiting parade. The excitement of the game still lingered for both of us. When we landed, Orien and I sat in the first row of the bus, a TV monitor above the driver. It was as if we were watching a television show—only we were in it!—news helicopters shooting it all above us. We saw our caravan of busses, police cars, and the motorcycle escorts zooming alongside us, controlling traffic and grinding through the streets and freeways. At a predetermined place, everybody scrambled off the busses and headed for the line-up of small trucks and cars that would be part of the parade. They were labeled with signs: KURT WARNER, MARSHALL FALK, JOHN SHAW, GEORGIA FRONTIERE, etc. I suddenly realized we had no place to be as we aimlessly wandered around past everyone else settling in. I really felt lost and stupid wondering what the hell we were doing there anyway. Suddenly I heard the Rams head trainer, Jim Anderson, yell, "Hop aboard, Peter Mark!" Without hesitation, we jumped onto his designated truck, loaded with bales of hay to sit on, and unexpectedly, we were an integral part of the parade the whole town had frozen their asses off for. It was an experience of a lifetime—inching for miles slowly past thousands of cheering, screaming Rams fans—their blue and gold banners, jackets, sweat shirts, and homemade signs waving exultantly in this football-crazed city. Orien and I were waving and yelling "We're number one!"—sticking up our thumbs in a victory sign as we moved past the sea of people eight to ten rows deep on either side, many reaching out to take my hand or slap it in a high five. I was beginning to feel as if I had played a hell of a game! I even signed autographs, uncertain if they recognized me from TV or thought I was coach Dick Vermeil.

All the while we were two trucks behind Kurt Warner, the game MVP. I couldn't believe our fortunate positioning in the parade for Super Bowl XXXIV. Then, there we were, Orien and I, suddenly up there on the stage above the City Hall steps with all the players, coaches, and the mayor—with the music going and the singing M.C. and the speeches lauding the team and Georgia—and the excited fans absolutely beside themselves, loving their team and the lady who brought them there. As we left the stage, I told offensive coordinator Mike Martz what a great job he'd done. He shyly thanked me as we shook hands.

After all those miserable years in Los Angeles and Anaheim, we were floating on a cloud and were savoring every moment. After such a long and fruitless period, winning the Super Bowl was like finding an oasis in the desert, climbing Mt. Everest, and landing on the moon rolled into one—it was that satisfying, and indeed, a memory to treasure.

Oliver Liam Richman was born on September 11, 2000—the son of Lisa and Howard Richman and our fifth grandchild. When I held him in my arms, I marveled at the beauty of his doll-like delicate face and full head of hair. I was touched, thinking how the chain of life goes on—this precious child I cradled, a blessed gift from God for my son Howard—and how Howard had been a gift to me who I still cherish, as I do with all my kids.

Edward G. Robinson's granddaughter, Francesca Robinson Sanchez, invited me to the Egyptian Theater in Hollywood for a luncheon and special dedication of a United States stamp with Eddie's unmistakable image. I hadn't seen Francesca since she was a child when I'd been commissioned by Gladys Lloyd Robinson to paint her portrait, but Gladys Lloyd died suddenly and I never did. Now she was a grown married woman who'd inherited a couple of my paintings from Gladys. The circle had been completed. Helen and I were sitting in the audience with Steve Allen and his wife, Jayne Meadows. Jayne whispered to me, "Peter Mark, Steve isn't seeing well. He's going to perform… would you help him to the stage?" Of course, I said yes. When the time came for him to play the piano, he was introduced, and we rose to make the trip down the aisle, Steve's arm firmly in my grasp, as he seemed shaky and insecure. I had to shoo away an insolent photographer lying in the aisle on his back to get a shot. "Move!" I said, through my teeth, fearing that Steve would trip as we moved to the stage and up the stairs. The reason I mention this incident is because a few days later Steve passed away. At his memorial service at the Television Academy where every known celebrity and bigwig was present—when

Jayne hugged and kissed me, she quietly said, "You helped Steve to the stage…" Months later, at some affair, she mentioned it again. It's odd how a seemingly insignificant moment had stayed with her—and me too. Steve was a dear, sweet man, and an amazingly prolific and gifted writer, composer, musician, and comedian. He was also an early Subud member and had recorded a conversation in 1959 with John Bennett who'd brought Subud to the west. (Interestingly enough, I'd given my copy of the LP record "What is Subud" to Bernardo Sagal, a well-known pianist who was interested in Subud.) Then his house burned down and everything in it in one of the Malibu fires. On opening night of *4 FACES* when I moved to the Odyssey Theater, there on my makeup table was a gift from Ron Sossi who ran the place—his copy of the LP. He also had been an early member of Subud. In October, Subud Los Angeles had arranged for Sharif Horthy to give a talk to the public called, again, "What is Subud?" In the evening, a small group of interested and receptive people gathered at our hall on Wilshire Boulevard for the friendly, informal explanation. Helen and I, and other helpers, joined Sharif after his talk for the Q & A period, which thankfully turned humorous, balancing the earnestness that permeates any discussion about God. The evening had been videotaped, and the talk was later printed in a booklet and distributed. The next afternoon we had the honor of again hosting for lunch at our country club, Bapak Subuh's daughter Ibu Rahayu, who had assumed many of his responsibilities since his death. She constantly says to all of us, "I am not Bapak." Highly evolved spiritually, with a deep and penetrating understanding of Subud, it was always a joy to be in her presence. Ibu Yati, her sister, was with her and also Sharif and his wife, Tuti. They were on another short overseas tour visiting selected Subud centers; next, Argentina. I was more than pleased when Rahayu and her party agreed to come to my home after our luncheon to view a video of my film *4 FACES*. Of course, they were gracious and kind and I felt privileged having them attend. It reminded me that I had sat with Bapak years ago when he viewed a TV airing of *Friendly Persuasion* and had said, "The Quakers had the latihan… that's why they quaked!" The following day 700 Subud people from all over came for latihan and a fabulous Rahayu talk at a hotel in the San Fernando Valley.

Virginia Mayo, a memorable friend and one of the most beautiful of Hollywood stars of the past, invited us to her eightieth birthday party at a chic Greek restaurant. When we hugged and kissed, she looked lovely, sweet, and very vulnerable. It was difficult not to see her as the magnificent youthful image forever implanted in my memory. She was now an elderly woman, but her radiance and warmth were undiminished. Helen and I sat next to other old-timers: Esther Williams, Jane Withers, and Elliott Reid, a nice guy who was also eighty. He was surprised and pleased when I told him that I had always liked him as a leading man in films, mistakenly thinking there wasn't a soul alive that would remember him. Then, Red Buttons, in an extensive toast, had us laughing convulsively and falling into our baklava with his insightful humor about getting old.

In December 2000, in the new football season, we flew to St. Louis for the crucial game with the Vikings who were boasting a winning record while the Rams were only 8 and 5 and needed to get going if they were to make the playoffs. In the evening, Georgia, of course, was entertaining—and this time there must have been a hundred guests in the trés chic "Kemoll's" downtown, including Rams scouts and their wives. As always, she was happy to see us and placed us next to her at her table. Before the dinner party broke up at 1:00 a.m., everybody was hoping, toasting, and wishing the Rams a victory in tomorrow's game. Well, something must have worked. Cheering our heads off in Georgia's palatial suite, we, along with 66,000 other screamers, watched the revivified Rams and champs that they were annihilate Minnesota 40–27. That evening, Georgia introduced us to Tennessee Williams's brother Dakin Williams, who was quite a character at eighty-one years. He told us that he performed occasionally, playing Blanche in *A Streetcar Named Desire* wearing a wig! He said that Tennessee discovered Georgia as a young talented singer in St. Louis, and Dakin had continued their relationship. Later, he recited a scene for us from *The Glass Menagerie*, playing Tom (not very well). I found him fascinating, especially his stories of threats and intrigue concerning his brother. He said their father called him Dakin (the king), and Tennessee, "Nancy!" He also told me he had locked up Tennessee for three months so he could dry out from drugs. "Tennessee hated me for doing that," he said. Then in his Missouri drawl he asked me if I wanted to hear another "Tom" soliloquy. I couldn't say no, so I suffered through it. Well, at least the Rams had won.

William Daniels, a friend from way back, had become the president of the Screen Actors Guild. It was during the time the agents (ATA) were in pre-negotiations for a new contract with the guild wanting special rights to produce films and not be limited to only representing actors. It was a time of tremendous turmoil and bad feelings between a rigid faction of the guild who wanted to succumb to the agents' wishes and those that didn't. Bill invited me to attend some high-profile meetings where celebrities could express themselves in free-wheeling discussions either pro or con. I was against it, having personally experienced a similar situation in 1962 with MCA. Simply put: An agent cannot truly represent an actor and have his best wishes at heart to achieve a proper salary if he is the also the producer holding the money strings. In one of the early meetings where many stars were present, including Warren Beatty, Patrick Stewart, Patty Duke, Albert Brooks, and Jodie Foster, I made a little speech and at the end was surprised by the spontaneous applause. I guess I hit a responsive chord. Following, a short excerpt:

"An actor gets into the acting profession with no guarantee of anything, zero, zilch. Nothing! Nothing is guaranteed his or her whole life. It is only a dream… a dream and a desire for self-expression and hope to God for a better life—maybe. I would like to know why the actors' union should guarantee the life of the agent who is supposed to represent the actor? Did anyone ever guarantee the future of the actor? Why should the actor guarantee the agent's income, future earning power and power-brokering by allowing them to become part of conglomerates and controllers of our destiny? They are supposed to represent us. Did the agent ever care how the actor would pay his mortgage, pay a doctor bill or send his kids to college? I don't think so…"

After the meeting, Warren Beatty shook my hand and said he liked my "pro-actor" words. Tyne Daly and director Paul Mazursky complimented me also. I then had a chat with Elliott Gould about the problem. The more we talked, I began thinking that maybe… just maybe… with elections in the guild coming up, I should get more involved. I thought… having paid my dues, so to speak, and having been a member of the guild since 1953, I could contribute my experience and awareness to guide and enhance an actor's benefits with greater impact if I were a member of the board of trustees. I recalled, maybe too nostalgically, all those earlier board members and presidents like James Cagney, Leon Ames, Ronald Reagan, and Charlton Heston who had done so much to improve the actors working conditions and income. I certainly had good intentions.

Well, my name was on the ballot, and to my surprise I garnered enough votes to win a seat on the board, joining like-thinking friends and new initiates Tom Bosley and Valerie Harper; I was honored. Bill Daniels was pleased to have me along in his push for changes that had stagnated for years from past administrations, especially with so much unreasonable opposition on the Hollywood board. Frankly, I was unprepared for the downright ferocious animosity and pettiness coming from this group, still "resenting-having-lost" the election when Bill became president. I was appalled. It was an eye-opener and a potent source of generated anger that started in my toes and quickly worked its way to my brain during the interminable seven- and eight-hour contentious meetings. At times, somewhat outspoken, I had a hard time controlling myself as I sat there in the James Cagney Board Room (it was certainly nothing like the cordial and civil meetings of the Motion Picture and Television Fund Board). There was always too much on the agenda and dealing with an eight-foot screen of televised New York Board members with their instant "opposition to everything"—plus phone hook-ups from other branches (Chicago, Miami etc.) was so irritating and exhaustingly enervating, it would take me a day to fully recover. I found it particularly bizarre that with 58,000 members in Hollywood and only 27,000 in New York (22,000 elsewhere), Hollywood was unfairly represented in the boardroom as to the votes on any major decision. That would have to change, along with passing RULE ONE (making SAG contract valid overseas); RUNAWAY PRODUCTION (influencing companies to remain and shoot in the U.S.A.); and immediately looming, securing a new "commercials" contract with meaningful improvements in session fees and residuals.

Bill Daniels was firm about that and threatened a strike if we couldn't make positive headway. Unfortunately, the production companies were just as adamant, demanding rollbacks and refusing to budge an inch. The strike that followed was a necessity. There was no other way to pulverize their concrete thinking. In the following five months, I found myself vociferously defending our position in interviews; at rallies all over the city (on stage with Tom Hanks); riding a fire truck in a parade with Larry Hagman (firemen were sympathetic); and walking the picket line with my strike poster held on high. As one of several recognizable actors, I flew to Cincinnati to face the press and cameras on the sidewalk and then confront an insular Procter & Gamble shareholder's meeting where we were allowed to plead our case. Two thousand hostile people who hated actors and our boycott continually booed and hissed at us for curbing their quarterly earnings. They didn't care about the dreadful hardships many actors were enduring. I was one of the speakers who got their attention when I humbly said, "Ladies and gentlemen… I want to thank you all for giving us the opportunity to present our point of view… blah, blah, blah…" Rob Schneider and Esai Morales told me I was "eloquent."

The odd thing about all this: In the lobby after the meeting, I met the chairman of the board (Mr. Laffey) and said to him, "You know, today in your presentation of Procter & Gamble commercials to your stock holders, you featured well-known faces, stars, to sell your products. How can you be an advocate of hiring non-union people, which is what you've been doing during the strike?"

He looked at me for a long moment and didn't answer.

Then he went into a meeting with other SAG representatives who made a concerted effort to bring a settlement. I've always thought that we had put a face on an abstraction by that trip, taking the strike to another level and that the weight that somehow tipped the balance. Powerhouse Procter & Gamble was the main wall of strike resistance, and suddenly, a hole opened up. Shortly afterward the strike was settled and the contract that evolved was a major improvement. The strength, unity, and dedication of the Screen Actors Guild had been more than admirable.

One day my son Orien called me and said he was going to be in a film titled *Pool Hall Junkies* and the director and writer, his close friend Mars Callahan, wanted me to be in it too—but Mars was too shy to ask. I said to Orien, "Have him call me, for God's sake… I won't bite." I knew Mars and thought him very talented, having seen another film he'd done with Orien. Mars called and expressed his wishes and also told me I would have two scenes with Christopher Walken. I told him to send me the script. It was a good piece of work—about a pool shark (who Mars would play) and all the tension and personal machinations involved in betting. I agreed to do the picture and flew to Salt Lake City, joining Rod Steiger, Chris Walken, Allison Eastwood (Clint's Daughter), and Rick Schroeder.

The next day we were shooting on location at "my mansion," where I was playing a rich dude who was giving a party—and who was a close friend of Walken's. The usual chaos ensued—greeting new people, the crew, the fuss in makeup and just getting used to where the hell you were. The first scene I shot was a major one in the film, where I make a bet with Chris that I can whip his ass again at my pool table. He takes me on, then challenges me to beat Mars, who, unbeknownst to me, is a shark and master of his game. After some hair-raising pool gymnastics, humorous taunts and tension, of course I lose. Chris and I worked very well together, but I didn't expect anything else. I've been an admirer of his performances, always spontaneous, varied and fresh—his creative motor continually alive. He was easy to be with too, and we kidded about being old Actors Studio members. Mars was happy with the day's work and Orien was tickled that his Dad was a "stud" and "awesome." I sure got a kick out of that. I liked Mars; he was a gentleman in every sense of the word. This film could be a big breakthrough for him. The following day, my son and I drove to Park City, Utah, where the next winter Olympics would take place. It was a bright and chilly day, and the countryside was absolutely magnificent—snow- capped mountains and splattered evergreens everywhere. I was happy to be doing the film, but I was happier being with Orien, sharing moments of closeness. Having the opportunity of being alone with one of my kids was a real plus—and a rarity now that they were all grown-up. We drove into the main drag and parked, then visited the colorfully painted shops on the hilly street, the art galleries, and a charming eatery. By the time we took it all in, it was really getting cold and I was beginning to sag—the day fast disappearing. We drove back to the hotel both feeling it had been a fruitful and wonderful day well spent.

The next morning, before I got into the van to drive to location, Rod Steiger was standing outside the hotel and when he saw me said, "Oh, now here we are….and you've come to save the picture, right?" We hugged and had a few laughs. He'd just married again and told me he was seventy-five. I was pleased to see his spirits were up. I'd know him for years. Before he discovered he was a manic-depressive and found the medication to alleviate his problem, he was almost impossible to be around.

I finished another scene with Chris Walken and Allison Eastwood. I come out of a building where Chris is waiting for me to go play golf, and I stall him to call my wife and give her a sorry excuse for not coming home. On completion, Mars and I embraced as the crew applauded my last shot. Chris and I hugged and exchanged nice words (he said he wished we had more scenes together) as Orien snapped some photos. Everyone had been extremely kind and I felt it had been a positive experience—and actually, it was all due to Orien. When the film was released it was fairly well received, but didn't play in theaters extensively, quickly going to video and DVD distribution.

Now that we were old-timers, Bill Daniels, with a smile on his face, asked me to become the National Chairman of the Senior's Committee. I accepted and formed a new committee and called a few meetings. I don't know how much was accomplished, but I did generate some national publicity. In November 2001 and again in August 2002, I testified before the California State Legislature, chaired by Senator John Vasconcellos, concerning a pervasive problem, "Ageism in Hollywood." Others who testifi d were Ed Asner, Kent McCord, Marvin Kaplan, and Gloria Allred.

At the microphone in one meeting I said: "… I'm seventy-four years old. I've appeared in over 500 TV shows, feature films, and on Broadway and elsewhere. I'm one of the lucky ones, I've had a successful career and I'm grateful… and I refuse to let myself think that it's over. But the industry keeps giving me unsubtle hints that it is. I have lost nothing of my talent, only gained… but the opportunities to work are becoming increasingly slim. There are thousands of actors like me, seniors, of varying type and talent waiting to work… but the call doesn't come. Why? The reason is… we are being discriminated against with a vengeance!"

Frankly, they could pass all the bills about ageism in Sacramento they can muster, but it has more to do with educating the people at the networks in the hiring capacity. Their thinking is jaded and their reliance on ratings is a joke. Some potent facts: 25 percent of the American population is over fifty years old (70 million) and own 77 percent of all the wealth in the country. Blindly, the industry still maintains its obsession with youth, intent on producing these moronic shake-and-jiggle shows with nineteen- and twenty-year-old kids, whose targeted audience doesn't have a pot to pee in. Anne-Marie Johnson, an actress and a dynamic member of the Affirmative Action/Diversity Task Force, at a committee meeting one day (after hearing that I had hired all seniors in key positions for *4 FACES*), excitedly said to me, "Peter Mark, that's your caucus!"

"What?"

"Your caucus! *4 FACES* should have a screening, a discussion afterward and a reception: 'How You Defied Ageism!'"

Smart girl that Anne-Marie. At the Director's Guild, the Affirmative Action Department of the Screen Actors Guild presented *4 FACES*. About 400 SAG and AFTRA members attended. Bill Daniels welcomed everyone and said some lovely opening remarks. Afterward there was a spirited panel discussion with the creative team: me, Ted Post, cameraman Isidore Mankofsky, and production designer Jack Senter. My additional panelists on stage were Shelly Berman, Tom Bosley, Richard Crenna, David Huddleston, and Kent McCord—seniors all. It was an extremely successful evening, the comments perceptive and positive about my film, and ageism got a good working over—the purpose of the event having been served.

Lucas Does Sondheim

PITTSBURGH USED TO BE A DARK, pollution-plagued dump, but now it was quite a restored, beautifully cleaned-up city and very culture oriented, with all the Heinz, Frick, and Mellon billions to help it along. Lucas was now the assistant conductor of the prestigious Pittsburgh Symphony under the main man, Mariss Jansons. It was early March and we were visiting to see him perform and to be with Debbie and our grandson, Max, now three, who we certainly didn't see often enough. Looking out the window from the twenty-fourth floor of the Pittsburgh Hilton, the sky was heavy with threatening snow. When we arrived at Lucas's home in Squirrel Hill, Max was a bundle of joy and playful putty, just what the grandparents needed the most. I told the beautiful boy a couple of impromptu stories and had him wide-eyed and giggly—especially the one about the little man with a red hat whose nose was so long he had put the end of it in his pocket. I broke myself up on that one. On a tour of the house, we were most impressed with the goings-on in the basement where Debbie efficiently helped run Lucas's LeDor Music Company, sending out his scores for hire. His "Holiday Festival Overture" has been played by thirty-five different orchestras across the country.

That afternoon Lucas and Debbie gave a party for the cast of his *Sondheim Tribute* we were seeing in the evening. Lucas had brought in George Hearn and Nancy Dussault for the production and it was great to see them. I hadn't been with George since he rehearsed Lucas's musical *Bonanza* at our home, and I had not seen Nancy since the adapted Ray Bradbury play we did together.

My niece Laura and her husband, Alan, flew in from Philly for the opening night. I was so pleased that they wanted to share this rather special evening with us. After dinner at the hotel, we strolled over to Heinz Hall, the cold and blustery night air pushing us along. First, we stopped in the Pittsburgh Symphony gift shop where Laura purchased several copies of Lucas's CD *Day is Done*, a collection of his tender lullabies.

Heinz Hall is the most beautiful concert auditorium I've ever been in—old-world, sparkling with charm, comfortable, and tastefully lush on a grand scale. The audience of more than two thousand saw an extraordinary and ambitious evening so difficult to achieve, but Lucas pulled it off in spades with the Pittsburgh Symphony—arranging, staging, conducting, and even playing the piano. The symphony played excerpts from many of Sondheim's musicals—*Into the Woods*, *A Little Night Music*, *Follies*, *Company*, *Pacific Overtures*, and more—done to perfection by a truly incredible cast of ensemble performers. George Hearn was spectacular reliving his dynamic and scary performance in *Sweeney Todd*, and Nancy Dussault was a great comedic and dramatic counterpart. They just put me away in their love song duet from *Follies*. I was so enthralled by the evening that I went back the next night to see it again. I trudged my way alone in a blizzard, Nana's woven scarf warming my neck as gusts of wind and snow pulled on my hair and umbrella mercilessly. It didn't matter, it was worth it. What Lucas had done was a major accomplishment on any scale. Broadway would have cheered.

Bleary-eyed, I looked out the window. The sky was still gray and gloomy, a light rain falling and the billowing steam from distant chimneys blended perfectly into the powdery fog. I was just getting my bearings while my remarkable wife, up for hours, was down in the hotel gym working out. Who would know that she would be seventy-one in ten days? It was so good to be with our son even though we knew he was up to his neck in obligations for another concert he was writing and rehearsing—a new composition with a children's choir. Hopefully, we would get to see it before we left. In the evening, I hosted our little group to an Italian dinner. George Hearn, snowbound and stranded until the weather changed, joined us. I couldn't help but tell a few definitive stories of Lucas's childhood and musical beginnings. Then George regaled us with humorous remembrances of his life and career. Such a charming and gifted man who surprised me when he said he was losing his need for performing and was retiring—at sixty-six! I knew how he felt. I told him I was seventy-three and had been "semi-retired" for eight years. Jim Sweenie, a warm, perceptive fellow in a baseball cap, interviewed me on station WQED in Pittsburgh. We talked about my lengthy career and then segued into a discussion of *4 FACES* and Lucas's score for the film. I was then given a tour of the studio, which was the oldest public radio and TV station in the country. It was where "Mr. Rogers" had originated his show and still did his broadcasts. That evening, Judi Cannova, a producer at WQED, was giving a reception in our honor at her home and we were looking forward to it.

As we drove with Lucas, the winding streets were a dark, slippery white mess. The falling snowflakes sparkled like crystals against the car window when we passed a street lamp. We finally found the house, and there were hugs and hellos from Judi Cannova and her husband, Tom, a retired gynecologist who immediately led us to his bountiful wine cellar to pour any bottle of our choice. Judi and Tom were hospitable people who loved Lucas. Many members of the orchestra, also enthusiasts of the young maestro, were invited too and were eager to share a lovely evening honoring his Mom and Dad. We were indeed touched.

In the morning, we sat in Heinz Hall watching Lucas conduct a rehearsal of his coming "Fiddlesticks" program—his own composition called "I Remember a Lullaby" with a children's choir and soloists of forty kids. It was wondrous to witness what he'd created, how he handled the Pittsburgh Symphony, and in turn, the way they responded to him with such respect. He's such a remarkable young man with so many of God's gifts—handling the orchestra, the children, and all the personnel taken in by his gentleness and genuine warmth. He's already conducted other composers' scores for their films—*Se7en*; Academy Award–nominated *As Good as It Gets*; and *Face/Off*. One day, God willing, he will be recognized for his music—and his humanity will touch the world. His sense of melody and his concept of remembrances in his lyrics tickles the emotions—childhood, family, the longing for love and fulfillment; all of the elements that affect everyone who's ever had a child or longs for one are present in his work. His themes are universal. After the rehearsal, we met the ladies who'd commissioned him to write his piece, their beaming faces expressing what Helen and I felt. Then we said our goodbyes, telling him what a joy it had been to finally experience his life in Pittsburgh. In April, the Los Angeles Jewish Symphony, under the baton of Noreen Green, performed *Remembrances—Reflections on the Holocaust*. It was a powerful evening of works by composers who had lived in horror and were now dead. Lucas had taken Herbert Zipper's slave laborer's song "Dachau Lied," based on the hated words above the concentration camp gates—Arbeit Mact Frei (Work Makes You Free)—and transformed them into a dynamic tone poem for men's chorus, narrator, and orchestra. It was bone-chilling and dissonant—like marching boots, screams, and Zeig Heil! I was honored to be the narrator for my son's stunning efforts. Richard S. Ginell of the *Los Angeles Times* wrote: "... in some cases, the composers struck a nerve. Lucas Richman's 'Dachau Lied' expanded Herbert Zipper's song into a painfully sarcastic Weillian series of marches, with a narration performed by his father, actor Peter Mark Richman."

Gary Cooper was being honored for his 100th birthday at the Academy of Motion Pictures, and I was invited to be a guest as an actor who'd been in one of his films. It was a packed-house evening hosted by a class-act guy, Robert Osborne, who does such a splendid job on Turner Classic Movies. Unfortunately, there were no clips from *Friendly Persuasion*, but I was one of only two actors introduced to the audience that evening—the other, Charlton Heston. I chatted with Maria Cooper, Gary's daughter, who was in from New York for the occasion with her extraordinarily fine pianist husband, Byron Janis. Maria, even more lovely as a mature woman, was happy to see me and wanted to get together. The next morning, we drove to Beverly Hills for a wonderful visit at Katie Johnson's home. It was an opportunity to express again how I felt about her father, and we certainly gave them an earful of our children and of course, Lucas. They seemed to know all about him, I suppose because Byron was so aware of the music scene. We took a lot of photos and then Maria surprised us with a beautiful gift; her fabulous book *Gary Cooper Off Camera: A Daughter Remembers*, a large format collection of Coop and his family. She inscribed it:

To Peter and Helen... I hope you enjoy these memories—of a special time—place and person. I look forward to more time to visit and "yak."

Love,

Maria

Jack Faulkner, who had lost his first wife several years earlier, took the vow again with Debbie, a woman who had grown boys, a lovely face, and a heart as big as her smile. Jack roared when I said, "What in hell Debbie would want with an overweight, old broken-down, ex-football player and coach, is beyond anybody's understanding!" It was a heartfelt affair and it gave me another chance to mingle and share special moments with some of my favorite football greats—Deacon Jones, Jackie Slater, and one of the greatest defensive coordinators of all time, Bud Carson.

Pat and Tom Bosley invited us to their beautiful home for dinner. It was good to spend some relaxed socializing with Tom away from the Screen Actors Guild Board, which had us so frustrated sometimes that we just shook our heads in repressed, screaming hopelessness. Marion Ross and Paul Michael were there, as well as Joanna Carson. Rosemarie and Robert Stack also—an ageless movie star looking as great as ever and one of the warmest gentlemen I've ever known.

On September 11, 2001, we were glued to our television sets, disbelieving and horrified like everybody else. A group of about twenty crazies, now known as al-Qaeda terrorists, planned and highjacked four huge American commercial airliners full of passengers. Two planes plunged into the Twin Towers in New York City, causing them to eventually crumple like playing cards. One crashed into the Pentagon in Washington, D.C., and another into an isolated meadow in Pennsylvania— thankfully, the last due to some courageous passengers. Almost three thousand people were killed and America would never be the same; it was no more the safe, untouchable haven we'd been used to and had so taken for granted. Gone forever. We were like any other country now, vulnerable and ripe for attack. President George W. Bush, in a powerful speech, rallied the country against our enemies—Bin Laden and his al- Qaeda wackos—and before long we were at war dropping bombs all over the caves of Afghanistan hoping to pulverize him, but routing the Taliban in consolation. Then into Iraq—unsuccessfully looking for Saddam Hussein's weapons of mass destruction, quickly defeating his army, and eventually capturing the rat himself in a rat hole. Fifty million people were liberated. Afghanistan was well on its way to a democracy, but in Iraq, the insurgent remnants of Hussein still remained. Their seventh-century Jihad mindset, an unholy distortion of Islam—a definite detriment to rational thought and change—was another matter entirely. "Sticking to it" seems to be the way to go, but the continual loss of our military who are like sitting ducks in a pond is extremely disheartening. But the incessant Monday morning quarterbacking and pontifical blabbing from all the talking heads in the media and in Washington isn't worth the air it heats either. It's so easy to have all the answers with no responsibility.

The Motion Picture Country Home and Hospital welcomed a new spectacular addition to the campus, The Ray Stark Villa—a residential apartment building that Broadway and Hollywood producer Ray Stark had contributed millions to complete. It would comfortably accommodate ninety elderly residents in elegant surroundings. It even had a koi pond and a walk-over bridge to observe the colorful fish. Nearby was Roddy McDowall's dedicated Rose Garden. It was a star-studded launching with many power brokers of the industry also attending. I had a chat with the always friendly Lew Wasserman who looked rather frail, his huge black horn-rimmed spectacles that accentuated his paleness. Jack Valenti was his exuberant, smiling self, and Michael Douglas introduced us to his wife, Catherine Zeta-Jones. If there is a more beautiful and gracious woman in Hollywood—I've never met her.

I received a letter from the Prism Award committee in February 2002, telling me that my film *4 FACES* had been nominated for a Prism Film Festival Award. I was particularly pleased because the awards were given to films that accurately depicted drug and alcohol addiction. There were five full length features concerning that problem I was competing against, but *4 FACES* dealt with drug addiction in only a twenty-minute segment in one of the four stories. I assumed they felt it significant enough to challenge the other films. On the evening of May 9, with cameras capturing everything for a "special" at CBS Television City—among wall-to-wall tuxed-up and severely gowned celebrities—I sat for interviews, speeches, dinner, and entertainment with my family and director Ted Post and his wife, Thelma. By the time they got through handing out all the television awards in every category, their excerpts endlessly splashed on the big screens before us, I was yawning and increasingly getting the feeling that I couldn't possibly win with a twenty-minute piece in the feature division. It wouldn't have been fair. I was right.

But I still went home gratified that I'd been nominated.

Final Cut

I'VE BEEN STRUCK RECENTLY by the inevitable truth which keeps repeating itself with depressing regularity. As you get up in years, the death of friends—older or even younger—keeps happening. In early February 2002, we went to a memorial service at the Writers Guild for a dear friend, Tracy Roberts. She was a fine actress, teacher, and someone who loved my writing, having appeared in two of my plays. In the same month, Dick Kleiner, a friend and wonderful feature writer who'd written many stories about me, was gone also. Shockingly, around the same time, Arlene Dayton, my former manager—and Edward Goldfied, an art dealer who'd given me an exhibition in 1979—and beautiful Diana Van der Vlis who had starred with me in *The Invaders*—and Otis Young, a terrific African-American actor I knew—and Sam Arkoff, who'd put his bucks up for our film *Letting Go* had also smoked his last cigar—and Fred de Cordova, a really nice man from the *Tonight Show*—and dear Dorothy McGuire, with an innate sweetness hard not to love who was so warm to me during *Friendly Persuasion*—and Paul "Tank" Younger, a Rams great and a fine man I admired—and Jane Greer, a beauty and a doll of a woman—and Kim Stanley, a truly great actress who I'd known since New York—and Ann Doran, one of the finest character actresses in Hollywood who was in *Longstreet* with me and served on the Fund board—and legendary Milton Berle, whom I enjoyed so much just being in his company—and Anthony Quinn, who was just great to work with in *Black Orchid*—and Carroll O'Connor, a friendly cohort for fifty years—and Troy Donahue—and George Sidney—and John Frankenheimer—and Jack Lemmon—and… and…

Then the strangest thing happened. I was just lying there half dozing and half dreaming—in between turning over and shifting the pillows—when the sun suddenly popped its warming rays through the shutters of our bedroom and onto my face, and I realized with a start that today was that day it had begun. It was April 16, 2002—and I was irrevocably seventy-five years old! It was difficult to believe I'd lived three quarters of a century. I'd survived a horrendous childhood; I'd been through war times and getting mangled in football; I'd learned a profession in college I briefly pursued; and with God's grace, I'd found my career and a wife that had fulfilled my life, with children and grandchildren. I felt truly blessed and thankful. What's more, I still had this sizzling certainty in my gut that I had a lot more to do before the final curtain. All these projects I'd broken my back to complete—some accomplished, some only half and some not—and my acting career inexplicably ebbing and definitely on hold, hadn't really debilitated me, thank God. Sure, I get depressed, but there's always tomorrow—and as sure as the sun will rise and my roses will unfurl and bloom, there's always hope that I will have the fortitude to do what I'm meant to do. I look upon all the changes and challenges as a reality and a test in my life for the future. There are no guarantees in life—nothing stays the same. How we deal with all this stuff and the crunching disappointments and pain only toughens the backbone. The fact that I'm writing about this is only helping me to see everything a little more clearly. And—oh, yes… I did have some heartwarming birthday celebrations. Helen took me to a fine dinner where we sat in an intimate booth and shared a lot of meaningful loving thoughts. On another evening my kids and grandchildren toasted their Dad at the Country Club, and then my kids gave me a musical seventy-fifth at the Wilshire Subud Hall where my Subud brothers and sisters enjoyed Howard, Kelly, Lucas, Orien, Roger, and son-in-law Loren singing and roasting the old man—with Lucas at the piano, fortuitously in town conducting the Young Musicians Foundation Orchestra. Hovering nearby was a three-foot-high cake, with my sculptured image on top in a Rams uniform!

Drinking in my grandchildren, Jenny, Lily, Julia, Oliver, and Max—I was so full of love for them I thought I would burst—and when I read nine-year-old Jenny's poem written on tree bark, I did:

April 16, 1927. I am here today because to my grandpa I have something to say:

> my grandpa was brought to this earth from heaven…
> my grandpa tries as hard as he can
> and always brings out the best in man…

my grandpa is someone I love so dearly...
daily, monthly and yearly.

Happy birthday,
Love, your first grandchild, Jenny Luisa Lester

It was a joyous jab to my heart.

In the last five years, whenever I could, I've adjourned to the isolation and solitude of my studio and have continued painting a series of new works; namely, figurative watercolors and inks. For my next exhibition, whenever that may be, I have about a hundred new pieces in my portfolio. I've slacked off a bit painting in oils because the undertaking is so much more complex and requires more time and energy—an over-supply I don't seem to have while writing this book. I've often thought about the creative impulses in my life, ebbing and flowing like the tide, and how each variation garners my attention and concentration. I've always felt blessed, given the talent to paint, act, and write—all contributing, in a sense, to an ability to fully express myself. But the writing, sitting down to think, is the most draining for me, perhaps because it's so personal; and it isn't immediate, it's reflective and tortuous—having to go through the myriad mind filters and the intricate ways of expressing thought, and the infinite complications of the process; although what comes out and where the thoughts come from can be magical and surprising. Painting is best when not thinking; I mean by that; after you've gotten your materials together and decided what you want to paint; once you've begun, the flow of creativity really comes from that divine source a painter unconsciously plugs into. In a way, the same can be said for acting—the best of it coming less from cerebral activity but rather the following of moment to moment unexpected impulses, real thoughts and having a sensory awareness—going with the flow—and reacting as in life, except that it's all a fiction, given credibility by the actor's individuality, expertness in craft, and experience.

Helen and I were invited to a small West Coast alumni dinner at the chic Peninsula Hotel in Beverly Hills given for the graduates of the Philadelphia College of Pharmacy and Science, now renamed The University of the Sciences. It was an evening to inform us of the fabulous new construction on campus and to raise funds. We enjoyed meeting some of the staff and the dynamic president, Dr. Philip Gerbino, who was instrumental in altering the old college's physical look way beyond the way it was when I attended. As a student, I had done extensive animal dissection art work in my freshman Zoology class. In a conversation with Dr. Gerbino (remembering I had turned down giving my requested drawings to the college as a gift), I impulsively said, "You know, Phil...I have a large collection of drawings I think the university should have in their collection for display."

He responded immediately: "Peter Mark, I'll take whatever you want to give us... just let me know when they'll be ready for shipment."

A week later, after scrounging in my garage, air freight picked up two huge cartons of my college study notes, notebooks, manuals, my drug herbarium (one hundred samples of bagged natural drugs, which as a student I had to identify on sight), and about a hundred pencil and colored drawings that the university would exhibit when appropriate. Since that time, I've felt that the Motion Picture & Television Fund and the University of the Sciences should have a relationship—the university being in the forefront of what's happening in the pharmaceutical and medical fields. Recently, I was able to arrange and join a very productive breakfast meeting with Dr. Gerbino and Dr. David Tillman, Fund president, that got the ball rolling, and I'm positive the association will be beneficial to both institutions in the future.

Georgia Frontiere had been gently coaxing us to visit her in Sedona again since our last visit a couple of years ago. Th s time she had another incentive. Her small ranch (eighteen acres) in Cornville, Arizona, had been transformed and she proudly wanted us to see the results. In June, we flew to Phoenix and then picked up a rented car for the two-hour picturesque drive to Sedona—the precipitous red buttes, so astoundingly magnifi t, announcing we'd arrived. We settled in at the guest house, rested a bit, then took off for the ranch—the scribbled directions in my pocket. I finally found sleepy Cornville and pulled into the ranch road, and were we surprised. When I'd first seen it a few years ago, I'd thought, *Why would anyone want to buy this termite-ridden dump?* Driving in now, I couldn't believe my eyes. Aside from housing eighteen horses and two mules, Georgia had let Earle, a builder with visionary ideas, go all the way in building a fantasy—an old Western town and street (like the back lot of Columbia Pictures) with many store fronts, an opera house, and an authentic "period" hotel that was still under construction. But the pièce de résistance was the opera house— replete with a small stage, a long bar, and an upper surrounding balcony where two bedrooms were decked out to resemble a bordello. Clicking our heels on the shiny hardwood floors, we congratulated them as we made our way to the ranch house across the way that had also been completely modified into a warm and cozy abode. "You did good, Earle," I said, "real good." He smiled and gave me one of his crunching bear hugs.

"We could shoot a movie out there, couldn't we?" Georgia asked. "Yes, we could," I said, "especially up in that hookers' room."

Tom Guthrie, Georgia's aide, laughed and poured us some red wine. "What color do you think the stage curtain should be?" Georgia ventured, her mind still in the unfinished opera house.

"Dark color, maybe burgundy," I said, "so it doesn't distract."

Suddenly excited, Georgia's face lit up. "Helen, Peter Mark… why don't you plan on coming back here for a week or two? We could put on a melodrama. You know, one of those stormy, old fashioned audience pleasers with a villain!"

"Yeah, I could play Rudolf Rassendale," I said, "with a twirling moustache… and you could play Nell. I once directed *He Ain't Done Right by Nell* years ago."

"You can direct it too!" she said. "Will you think about it? It would be fun."

I was kidding, but she was venturously serious. Two hours later, by the time we sauntered over to the opera house for dinner, my stomach was crying out for help. Seated at a long table facing the stage and a twenty-foot screen, while dinner was served, Earle ran a DVD movie and it was a surprise—*Friendly Persuasion*. The film looked as if it had been shot yesterday, the restoration and color in the DVD process were absolutely extraordinary. I hadn't seen it on a big screen in twenty-five years or so and I was reminded, without reservation, that Wyler's film was a classic and that forty-seven years had gone by.

One afternoon, the Arizona sun a scorcher, Earle drove us in his truck to see Georgia's 250-acre Flagstaff ranch now being developed, our butts bumping wildly for the hour ride over U.S. Forestry dirt roads and wilderness. It wasn't my favorite means of travel, but Helen had the worst of it sitting behind us holding on for dear life. *God*, I thought, *This whole area is such a fire hazard… a tinderbox ready to go.* Every twenty yards or so there were massive mounds of rotting, cut pine just lying there. Finally, we came to a padlocked gate that Earle opened. We drove in and shortly after, through the trees, an incredible structure was revealed that Earle had designed—a combination stable with living quarters above it! It was huge, a full stable to house at least twenty horses and a truck driveway on either end. (Wouldn't that be a disturbance?) We were led upstairs to the fully appointed, gorgeously planned apartment that just went on and on. It had the "Frank Lloyd Wright" look that Earle loves and was probably adapted from the plans they received from Wright's disciple who we'd met years earlier at Taliesin. It was Shangri-La in the wilderness and fabulous. But man, it was isolation. I wondered… *What in hell would Georgia do here? And friends visiting? You'd need a road map, an Indian guide, and prayer beads to ever find this place.*

The next day we drove to meet Earle in Camp Verde, Arizona, about fifty miles south of Sedona. Hooking up with him, we followed his truck through the dreamy countryside to a sheep farm. On a road adjacent, he stopped in front of a large one-story building. The sign said, "Southern Mountain Studio." Earle wanted us to meet John Soderberg, the famous sculptor. Traci, his wife, a beautiful young woman who was also an artist, came out to greet us then sweetly ushered us inside. It was inspiring and somewhat overwhelming. John Soderberg's cramped studio was packed full of powerfully impressive figurative studies of Native Americans and mythological character and colorful bronzes and paintings. Standing next to a gigantic unfinished new work of Christ and a group of children was the man himself—a sight to behold—a solid 280 pounds with a full beard and hair setting off a face of smiles and twinkles. Born in Bangkok to artist parents, he'd lived in Afghanistan and India, studying art and sculpture at a very young age. He came to America when he was eighteen. "I remember seeing Michelangelo's *Moses* in Rome when I was six and being moved," he said. I liked him instantly—almost immediately getting into a fabulous conversation about his innovative methods preparing oil-based clay and his unusual patina coloring techniques for the bronzes. His work deeply reflected his humanitarian nature. He traveled every year with his motorcycle buddies to a Mexican town, delivering food and gifts to poor children. The massive, smiling Jesus he was working on was the tenth commission from Reverend Schuller and the Crystal Cathedral. He asked us to come to the unveiling when it would be dedicated and gave us a video of his work and methods. I promised to send him a tape of *4 FACES*. Meeting John was indeed more than special, it was the beginning of a vibrant new friendship. I thanked Earle for his thoughtfulness.

In July 2002, Helen and I attended one of the most extraordinary events that had to do with a death of a well-known personality. It wasn't a movie star we went to pay tribute to, or a musician, athlete or even a revered politician (does one exist?). No, it was the memorial service for the most powerful mogul from the pinpoint top of the upper echelon of Hollywood bosses—Lew Wasserman. About six thousand people—friends, family, union representatives, stars of all sizes, and political figures—even Nancy Reagan and former president Bill Clinton—paid their respects en masse in the packed amphitheater at Universal Studios. Every one of the speakers lauded the former agent-turned-empire-builder for his honesty, fairness, dependability, and generous philanthropy.

"Lew was a tough negotiator, but his word was gold."

I sat next to Robert Wagner and Jill St. John, and it was amazing to realize how many attendees' lives had been touched by the one we were there to honor. I recalled the time as building chairman, I had strongly insisted that Lew and Edie come to the just-completed Motion Picture & Television Hospital for the placement of their dedicated plaques. The press opening was the following day and it had to be done, there was no other time. I was on a ladder meticulously sticking letters on the wall—The Edie and Lew Wasserman Wing—when the long black Wasserman limo pulled in the driveway next to the hospital entrance.

After the service, it was sad to see the always vital Edie slightly bent over and walking with a cane. An era was passing.

William Wyler was given a tribute and reception by the Academy of Motion Pictures. One of Willy's great films of the thirties, *Counselor at Law* with John Barrymore, was screened. It was a fabulous piece of work, and Barrymore was never better. The director, Vincent Sherman (now ninety-six years!), a dear friend with whom I'd worked in TV, had a featured role in it as a radical and was excellent (he'd appeared in the play on Broadway). He was one of the panelists talking about Willy after the screening along with Terrence Stamp and Carroll Baker. I was introduced in the audience by M.C. Peter Ranier, so I stood up, smiled, and waved, but thinking: I should have been up on the stage—I have a lot to say about Willy. At the reception afterward, I had a warm chat with Cathy and David Wyler. I told David how much I loved his Dad and what hiring me for *Friendly Persuasion* had meant in my life.

Every day as I read the newspapers at breakfast, I'm startled by another friend having left the scene. The incessant frequency magnified the utter fragility of life and how transient our visit here really is. I went to a memorial service given at the Actors Studio West, this time for Rod Steiger. There was a large, heartfelt turnout. Mark Rydell, executive director of the Studio, spoke as did many others, myself included, expressing our personal feelings about another legendary actor who would be sorely missed.

In December, we flew to New York and checked in at the Mayflower, an old theatrical hotel on Central Park West and a short walk around the corner to Lincoln Center and Avery Fisher Hall. Lucas was set to conduct the New York Philharmonic in a "Young People's Concert" (the kind that Leonard Bernstein used to do). Would any parent want to miss that? Lucas had also just been hired to be the music director and conductor of the Knoxville, Tennessee Symphony—his own orchestra, finally, at thirty-eight. After a restless night of uncooperative pillows, piercing sirens and fire engines, I awoke to a bright sunny day—the view of Central Park, a picture postcard. Lucas, still with the Pittsburgh Symphony, called from Harrisburg on his way here and said he would arrive at the hotel with Debbie and Max at 3:00 p.m. I couldn't wait to see my grandson who was now four. He'd shown a very early talent for sketching, his head bent over the paper intently creating from memory: monsters, ghouls, and Spider-Man! I'd brought a box of oil crayons and tubed water colors to give him—and maybe I'd squeeze in an art lesson if he's willing. The next day, this beautiful little boy with rumpled black hair had his hand in mine as we traipsed up the steps of the Museum of Natural History—a fun experience that lingers in my memory. The place was a zoo with all the school kids, but we finally got to sit down and observe the spectacular show of outer space projected on the ceiling, so thrilling and creative. On the tour through the dinosaur exhibit, the sizes overwhelming, my little partner kept asking, "Grandpa, is it real?" I was wondering that myself. Here on Earth… frolicking on 42nd and Seventh? Max told me his stomach was growling, but in the museum restaurant he only wanted the large, gingerbread cookie man on display and then proceeded to eat nothing but the icing!

In the afternoon Debbie, Helen, and I walked over to the Lincoln Center stage door, then up the stairs to Lucas's dressing room. He was rehearsing *Peter and the Wolf* with Tony Randall, who was the narrator for the concert, so I just wandered over to listen through the door. Finally, when they came out, I greeted Tony whom I'd known for years, as Lucas rushed off to rehearse the orchestra. We were then ushered to a box above the stage of magnificent Avery Fisher Hall, and there I proudly watched my son guide THE NEW YORK PHILHARMONIC—so confidently, it was riveting! The orchestra responded readily and respectfully to his pacing and nuances… and I was saying to myself: Hey, man… this is the New York Philharmonic! He'd come so far in so short a time, and God willing, there was no limit to where he would go.

Later, the rain tormenting us, we all cabbed it to 74th and Second Avenue to join Carol and Alfred at the Pamir restaurant for an Afghan dinner. We were happy to see Roger, my youngest, who'd also flown in for the concert. While we were all joyously stuffing ourselves, Max, at the end of the table with pen in hand, was obsessively concentrated, mastering another monster-masterpiece.

The Big Day. Hisashi Ito and Cookie were in from Japan sitting next to us and a prideful Debbie. So were Jack Klugman and Peggy Crosby; Brad Richman in from Philly with his two lovely daughters; my psychiatrist cousin Arthur Peck; Rebecca (Ross Martin's step-daughter); Walter Schacht; my niece Laura and hubby Alan Wechsler; and my dear friend Rita Gam. who said, "I'm just so thrilled to be invited!" We were all there to witness Lucas's debut in New York as a conductor and a composer. No small thing. There were no sweaty palms when Helen and I held hands as we watched a poised young conductor produce a wonderful performance of *Peter and the Wolf*, with Tony Randall in top form. Then Lucas's two melodic pieces, "The Hanukah Festival Overture" and "Reindeer Variations" thrilled us even more. The audience ate it up and the kids were happily demonstrative when Lucas did his "arm waving" routine, teaching them all how to conduct. It had been an extremely successful debut. Later at the convivial reception in the Green Room with Lucas standing in front of a photo of Leonard Bernstein, Tony asked me when I'd first recognized Lucas's talent. "Very early," I said. We were talking about children and then he told me he was eighty-two years old. "Well, you sure look fit and trim."

"I'm falling apart," he answered, sadly.

When the champagne was poured, I made a fatherly toast. I don't remember what I said, but I do recall my watery eyes, and when I looked at Helen, she had them too. Then a familiar face from the past came close and beamed at me. After a moment I said, "Leona?"

"Yes," she answered shyly, the years dripping away. I couldn't believe it. Standing there was my favorite cousin, my father's brother, Philip Richman's daughter—who I hadn't seen in almost fifty years, and her face hadn't changed. Just to hug her and feel a deep-rooted family tie, our parents long gone, was another moving experience of a very special day.

On the way back to Los Angeles, we had a planned layover in St. Louis to see a game. It was nothing like the giddy Super Bowl days, the Rams only 5 and 8 this time around. Paul Mason, chief of airport police, picked us up again when we arrived and drove us to the Frontenac Hilton. Mike

Moyneur had field passes for us at the stadium when we entered Georgia's suite so down we went—the "privileged" card strung around our necks—to witness the whole spectacle close up; the team, the exhilarated crowd, the sexy cheerleaders. Jackie Slater, former great tackle and now "Hall of Famer," came over to give me a warm bear hug as the team took the field for the kickoff. The Rams came back to beat Arizona 30-28 with Marc Bulger performing well in place of an injured Kurt Warner. The season ended with a 7-9 record, which is pretty stinko for a Super Bowl team. But, as they say when bleeding, "There is always next year."

Helen, wanting to get back on stage and impervious to my negatives, began rehearsing *The Vagina Monologues* by Eve Ensler. I suppose I'm a bit of a square, but the sight of a lot of women discussing their most personal and private thoughts and escapades concerning that hallowed place on a public stage was a serious affront to my sensibilities. To me, that passageway, God's short channel to a new life on Earth, is a sacred place, and to be sullied up with an exposed and blaring intimate discussion of body juices, clitoral exploration, and reaching a climax… on a stage, yet… defeats what intimacy and femininity is all about. In jest, I threatened to write The Penis Soliloquies, but I heard that fifty variations were already in the works. The production at Pierce College, staged with many women by Valerie Greer, was quite well done. Helen, playing an uptight English lady, was humorous, selective, and very ladylike under the circumstances—but through most of it I just tuned out.

Roger Mayer, the president of the Motion Picture and Television Fund, asked me to guide the needed redecoration of the main dining room, the library, and the lounge in the Country Home. Reluctant to get involved again, I finally succumbed to Roger's persuasiveness and found myself meeting with the decorator and her assistants.

Thankfully, we developed a good relationship, but it took some finessing. I have strong opinions. Colors and choices of carpeting, hall flooring, chair fabrics, and wall hangings are a major undertaking and selections are personal and subjective. When it was completed, I was pleased when members of the board viewed the facility and were impressed. But no more so than when a white-haired resident in the dining room smiled sweetly at me and said, "It's pleasant to eat here… it's so comfortable."

Remember when you were a kid and your grandmother and grandfather were celebrating their golden wedding anniversary—their fiftieth? What a remote and nebulous happening that was. Fifty years! My

God, it was something too remote to contemplate when you're pulling on your knickers and the knotted laces on your sneakers won't tighten. Actually, I don't remember if my grandparents on my mother's side ever had a fiftieth celebration. I didn't really know them. They just seemed ancient to me whenever I visited them, and it was all so depressing. They were gone before I was ten. My father's parents and relatives who remained in Lithuania were all wiped out in the Holocaust. So, the deeper significance of a golden wedding anniversary never really got to me; that is, until mine. My daughter, Kelly, and her husband, Loren, had planned to give us a golden wedding anniversary party, with one caveat—we weren't allowed to know where it would take place until the invitations went out and then not to inquire about the place when we got it! I thought that was rather peculiar, but of course I went along. The big day arrived, and as we pulled into the parking lot in Beverly Hills and took the elevator up to the proper floor, we quickly realized we were going to a new screening facility. Then my children (Lucas and Debbie had flown in from Pittsburgh with Max) and excited grandchildren greeted us with their beaming faces as we walked to the small theater, where just outside the entrance was a huge brass cart and a bartender pouring libations. Nearby, an attendant serviced another cart full of multiple goodies and delights. When all of our friends had arrived—their handshakes, hugs, and kisses a wave of warmth—we filtered into the packed, comfy screening room and sat down to witness something we'd never truly expected.

There on a big screen for an hour, our lives, our careers, our marriage and children, and many interviews of friends enveloped us with an extraordinary tapestry of personal events. Loren and Kelly had worked torturously to piece together all the material shown, editing judiciously, and adding appropriate and funny titles and music to complete a DVD of priceless quality. (Even my ten-year-old granddaughter, Jenny, in a very clever ruse a month earlier, had convinced us to do a grandparents "interview for school" on video that, of course, we were all now viewing.) We were overwhelmed, and so were the friends who shared it with us. It was so deeply touching. As they say, "There wasn't a dry eye in the house." When the evening was over I was grateful to be sleeping with my favorite grandmother.

Knoxville, Tennessee, has a lot going for it. It's a beautiful place and the people are ingratiating. More than that, they've got the University of Tennessee where they all go nutzo about their football team, the Volunteers—their stadium seating a crazed 107,000, the banners and pom-poms a sea of orange. Now, in the cultural department, Knoxville has embraced my son, Lucas, as musical director and conductor of the Knoxville Symphony Orchestra. We flew to Knoxville for his first concert since he had assumed the reins. There was a formal gala dinner at the Marriott Hotel with all the "movers and shakers." The attractive ladies were a special delight with their lilting Southern accents and who were suddenly surprised that the conductor's father was someone they'd seen on TV. I was asked to introduce my son and relished the opportunity at the podium, spouting a couple of short endearing anecdotes about the maestro everyone seemed to enjoy.

Following the dinner, we were trollied over to the cavernous auditorium, a temporary venue, while the Tennessee Theater was being renovated to be the permanent home of the orchestra. After the concertmaster completed tuning the musicians, there was a long moment of silence. Then Lucas entered; the audience greeting him warmly, and our hearts fluttered a couple of extra beats. Aaron Copland's An Outdoor Overture was the first piece and then Tchaikovsky's *Symphony No. 2*. Lucas's confidence and control were so pleasurable to watch as he guided his malleable and responsive musicians, weaving a beautiful tapestry of nuanced and glorious sounds. After the intermission, an additional treat was in store. Lucas had engaged one of the great pianists of our time, André Watts, who performed Beethoven's "Emperor" *Piano Concerto No. 5*. He was brilliant, and Lucas' accompaniment was smooth and complimentary. We were sitting close and could see how André Watts kept glancing at Lucas in total trust as the composition progressed to its climax. We'd seen this before. Performers loved working with him because he has such consideration for the soloist. After the concert, we went backstage and the accolades were flowing freely from everyone. I got a special kick when André Watts and his wife came into my son's dressing room to say goodbye and they embraced. André was smiling and said, "I was just following you!" It was truly a warm parting of great talents. The evening was a winner from start to finish, and Helen and I were bursting with pride. We felt it was a solid beginning for his new life in Knoxville. He was now the guy in charge. It was a deserved opportunity to mold and develop the orchestra to his fresh and discerning vision.

Renée Taylor and Joe Bologna invited us to their home. They were hosting an evening to introduce a charming Anthony Minghella, director of the film *Cold Mountain*, starring Nicole Kidman, to stir up Academy votes. I spotted Sid Caesar, and he waved me over so I sat and chatted with him. He'd always been a robust "workout" guy, and it was disheartening to see one of my favorites looking so thin and fragile-looking—more so than the last time I saw him, his body more twisted, his cane perched on his chair. I tried to get him to go to the exceptionally good therapy department at the Motion Picture Hospital. I thought they could alleviate some of his muscular contortions, but I couldn't make any headway. He thanked me. "For what?" I said. "For being you," he answered.

Again, sadly, another major movie icon had left us. We went to the memorial service at St. Mel's Catholic Church in Woodland Hills for our very special friend, Ann Miller. It was a love-outpouring for one of the greatest female tap dancers the screen had ever seen, who was also a good actress. She was thoughtful and kind with an interest and a smile for whomever engaged her. I'll never forget how she went out of her way to see me perform in *4 FACES*, twice. Thankfully, there's a treasury of her unique and startling work on film for all to see again and again.

I went to my first Nominating Committee meeting of the Academy of Motion Pictures. I'd been chosen by my peers—which surprised the hell out of me—out of 3,000 members. We were the group who would choose just four to represent the actors branch in all Academy decisions. Among the quorum who showed up: Tom Hanks, Henry Winkler, Kathy Bates, John Saxon, William Schallert, Ed Begley Jr., Carl Reiner, and li'l ole me.

Early in June, Helen and I went to MGM-SONY to watch Lucas conduct the scoring of the M. Night Shyamalan film *The Village*. James Newton Howard, who composed the score, wanted Lucas. Lucas was flown in from Knoxville for the engagement, primarily because the violin sequences featuring young Hilary Hahn were so crucial, and Lucas is masterful with soloists. It was thrilling to see all the musicians and technicians at their complex audio consoles concentrating under the baton of our young maestro.

I watched the spectacular tributes and funeral procession of former president Ronald Reagan—a man who really changed the world. Margaret Thatcher's laudatory comments said it all. Next to my TV screen was the autographed photo he had graciously sent thanking me for my letter after his trip to Russia when he gave a film print of *Friendly Persuasion* to Gorbachev, an amazing series of events of historical significance I somehow felt I was a part of in a tiny way.

In July, Helen, Howard, and I flew up to Oakland, California, for a few days to attend the Subud National Congress at the Berkeley Marina Hotel. Howard was going through a difficult divorce proceeding with his wife,

Lisa. We thought it would be good for Howard to have some powerful latihans to help alleviate his heavy heart and some of the sadness and pressure he was under. He agreed. It was always wonderful to see such a mixed bag of Subud people from all over, their warmth and friendliness disarming; and, of course, the worship of God through the latihan, giving us a goose-up in energy and outlook.

There were also some fun things to participate in. We attended a workshop given by old friend Richmond Shepard, a mime and improv teacher, that had us all laughing hysterically with our silly choices. Howard, a fine pianist and teacher, gave a terrific workshop called "Discovering Your Inner Composer," an innovative and imaginative effort. We were enthralled when he asked us to peck out three notes and then he created a composition—playing it in ten styles, from Broadway, Pop, and Rag to Reggae! He's such a fine son; I pray that everything will work out well for him.

Our friend Vincent Sherman, a famous Hollywood director of the past, was ninety-eight years old. The Film Department of the Los Angeles County Museum of Art honored him for his birthday and they were screening his films. Still a dapper dresser with white hair and bright blue eyes, you'd think he was twenty years younger—especially with his attractive actress friend Francine York on his arm, who was at least thirty-five years his junior. He'd directed many fine films at Warner Bros. with some of the top stars of the day: Rita Hayworth, Joan Crawford, Ann Sheridan, Errol Flynn, and even Ronald Reagan (*The Hasty Heart*). He did some of his best work on the film shown that day (when story and actors counted), the director's cut of the 1944 hit *Mr. Skeffington* with Bette Davis and Claude Rains—both Oscar-nominated. His romance with the tempestuous Ms. Davis was well explored in his marvelously revealing book *Studio Affairs*, which he inscribed and gave me as a gift—a life really worth reading about.

After the acting session at the Actors Studio West at the end of July, there was a memorial "remembrance" for one of the greatest actors of our generation, Marlon Brando, a man of such superb talent his influence was awesome and almost overwhelming to every developing young actor. Marty Landau and Mark Rydell spoke as did many, but when Shelley Winters, eighty-two, in a wheelchair and looking poorly, finished her remembrances of Marlon, Tony Franciosa, sitting next to me, prompted a smile when he whispered, "I guess I better go say hello to my ex-wife." (Two years later they would die within a week of each other.)

The times I spent with Marlon, he was cordial and conversant—but I knew I was in the presence of a personality of unique greatness. Helen remembers well the time she had a lunch date with Eva Marie Saint at the Paramount Studio commissary. Eva called and said, "I hope you won't mind if Marlon joins us." Duuuuh…! She'll never forget how he came on to her, taking her hand and saying first off, "You have such delicate and beautiful fingers… are you sure that's a wedding ring?"

So many memories of so many people who've left us.

Father and Son

WHEN LUCAS ASKED ME TO NARRATE Aaron Copland's Lincoln Portrait with the Knoxville Symphony Orchestra, I answered that it would be a privilege. Spicing the deal was another invitation: Deane Conley, a lovely Knoxville Symphony enthusiast who owns a mansion beyond imagination, invited us to stay there during our visit. Since we were going back East, I thought, *Why don't we combine it with a short visit to my niece, Laura, in Beach Haven, New Jersey?* So, in September 2004 we flew to Philly, somehow escaping the tail end of Hurricane Francis—a slight drizzle the only remnant remaining when we landed. In a rented car, we drove a circuitous route through Philly (now totally unfamiliar) over the bridge to Jersey and to Beach Haven on the ocean. It was a warm and wonderful reunion with Laura, her husband, Alan, a retired entrepreneur who had become a good sculptor—a sensuous alabaster nude in evidence. Fortuitously, when Carol and Alfred drove down from New York City to join us, an intimate gabfest transpired. We all have lots of kids and have been through the joys and pits of raising them, so there were genuine interests to share and reveal. The fabulous beach house, almost touching the ocean with a 180 degree view from the porch, was more than spectacular. Walking that windswept beach, the sand crunching under our feet, sucking in that air with the surf pounding—the seagulls screeching above—was certainly one of God's ways to revivify us. Then we rode on Alan's sailboat to Barnegat Bay, the sun blazing and Helen's wide white hat blowing in the wind. Later, we watched a DVD of Laura's seventieth birthday celebration and all of her kids paying tribute, and sadly, their son Bruce, probably fifty years old now and in a wheelchair, his head mangled from many surgeries as a child in a terrible tragedy. A bungled circumcision as an infant led to a *staphylococcus* infection in his brain. Laura and Alan have been remarkable dealing with this perpetual nightmare of a severely handicapped son, now in an institution. It really got to me when in a close-up Bruce says, "I love you, Mommy."

September 11, 2004. It's difficult to believe three years had zipped by since the crazies flew the planes into the Twin Towers in New York. (Helen and I will never forget we were on that same flight from Boston to Los Angeles three days earlier.) The horror of it all is still so vivid—the TV repetitions compounding the memory. Oddly enough, September 11 is also the actual birthday of Laura and my grandson Oliver. I knew this trip was necessary and it had planned out. Laura was the only one living who knew so much about my family—Mom and Pop and all the relationships. I even found out my brother Harry, her Dad, and Faye, her mother, were not very compatible and fought all the time. That really surprised me. I'd always assumed my brother and his wife were a prime example of harmony and togetherness. I also found out why Laura was a successful psychologist. She's a very loving person and a great listener. I had many fruitful talks with her and Alan, but Laura felt she really got to know me from my writing and was unabashedly moved (I read them twenty-five pages of the beginning of this book—my chaotic childhood).

Over the years we'd never spent as much time together. It was a blessing and so bonding. When we all toasted her birthday, I presented her with a little flower watercolor I had painted that afternoon—it kind of sealed a deeper relationship. I was a bit sorry to leave such a comfortable respite where any one the areas adjoining Beach Haven was a potential TV series—Harvey Cedars, Love Ladies (honest), Barnegat, or Surf City! But it was time to go to Knoxville—my son, the conductor was awaiting. On the flight to Dulles Airport in Washington I finished reading *The Albert Salmi Story* by Sandra Grabman, who I had given an interview to earlier. Even though I'm expecting it, I always find it somewhat startling to see my name and thoughts printed in someone's book. We had a three- hour screw-up at Dulles and finally took off and landed shortly after in Knoxville where Deane Conley's butler, Angus, picked us up and drove us to "Villa Collina." Deane, an adorable blonde with a charming southern lilt in her voice, was graciously welcoming—so pleased to have us in her "home." She was an extremely talented designer/ decorator and songwriter who was recently, I gathered, bitterly divorced. Every palace—and that's what her home is—I've ever been through in France, Germany, Spain, Austria, or Hungary doesn't come close to the opulence here. Deane designed it and it took five years to build at a cost of $29 million! Forty-two thousand square feet of magnificent majestic elegance high above the Tennessee River. We took an elevator trip down to the swirling pool level, which resembled a sexy Turkish harem. Nearby was the locked, brick passageway wine cellar where Deane toasted us with a 170-year-old bottle of Grand Marnier. Imagine, sipping a brew from 1834! It was deliciously strong.

Helen had the gold suite at the end of the mile-long hallway, with a balcony and breathtaking view of the estate, and I had the green suite at the top of the Turkish marble winding staircase. When I walked down those steps for an "Angus" served breakfast, the baroque paintings all around me, the crystal sparking chandeliers and dancing cupids on the sky-high ceilings above, I felt like Rhett Butler in *Gone with The Wind*. I've never seen anything like it—beyond belief. Now I know how the kings of the past lived—but I'm sure not as comfortably.

The tiny buttoned computer lights and the huge bed with too many pillows gave me a hard time, but I finally slept through the night. I must say that the enclosed decorative toilet in the elaborate sunken tub john was just too elegant to pee in and should've been only stared at. However, out of necessity I did manage to get over my artistic appreciation and even sat down.

The next morning Lucas and Debbie picked us up and we drove to see their new home in Whittington Creek. It was the perfect abode for the new conductor—attractive, spacious, and ideal for entertaining, with lots of greenery outside for Max to play on. When my grandson came home from school we had a ball—his cowering grandpa a good foil for the skeleton costume and the "green blanket monster!" Later in the day, I went to the Civic Auditorium for my first rehearsal. After the run-through, the orchestra graciously tapped their instruments in approval. Many people had narrated *Lincoln Portrait*, including Henry Fonda, but I'm sure none had received their conductor's cues accompanied with a smiling nod. That evening, we had a dress rehearsal that went very well, the orchestra stomping their feet in further approval. I was beginning to feel the needs and nuances for my delivery, and Copland's music was inspiring. It was exciting stuff to be on stage with my son. I was surprised at the break when a gentleman came to the apron of the stage and presented me with a gift: a worn little book published in 1906 by Scribner's called *The Perfect Tribute*, by Mary Raymond Shipman Andrews—a lot of names for such a small book. The content was extraordinary. It was a moving story about Lincoln scribbling the Gettysburg address on an odd piece of paper while he was on the train from Washington and then delivering it at the gravesite. Lincoln thought that he'd failed miserably, the audience sitting in stunned silence when he finished. But the next day on his visit to a severely wounded Confederate soldier in the prison hospital, he discovered from the dying man, who'd read Lincoln's speech in the newspaper, that his address was powerfully successful; the silence was a tribute to its greatness. This little story deepened my understanding for the narration.

The following night was the opening of the Knoxville Symphony Orchestra's new season. What a theatrical welcoming for the father-son event! Just before the concert, Lucas and I were asked to descend the stairs in the packed lobby to trumpets! The smiling crowd greeted us with warm applause as the photographer's strobes popped. It was wonderful to share that with my son. I don't believe there are many actor/father–conductor/son performances on record.

Holiday Overture, by Elliott Carter, was the first piece Lucas conducted. Then he embraced the full house with a brief salutation, finally introducing me as the audience responded enthusiastically. We stood center stage for a long moment, hugged (I may have even planted a kiss), and then I settled on a stool in front of the orchestra close to Lucas. To be on stage and hear that powerful music surrounding me was awesome—and to watch my son conducting with such fervor and control was just thrilling, and actually, goose bump time. At the appropriate moment, I rose and took my place at the music stand and microphone to begin speaking on the multiple cues from the maestro. I was ready. My voice penetrated the auditorium, clear, strong, and nuanced—the orchestra effectively accentuating and lifting the words to a lingering and poignant crescendo. There was an explosive response (the kind every actor lives for) followed by three curtain calls and a standing ovation. Lucas and I, arms around each other, beamed and bowed. It was memorable.

After the intermission, I joined Helen in the audience to watch Lucas conduct a fabulous performance of Dvorak's *Ninth Symphony (The New World)*. Even I could tell in the short time he'd been there that Lucas had elevated the level of the orchestra several notches. Afterward, there were many kudos and congrats from everybody—the crew guys even asked me to sign my name on the backstage wall. We then went to a gala dinner at LeConte, a private club, given by the symphony board. Lucas spoke and introduced me again. "I feel right at home with you all," I said. "I guess it's because I was raised in the South… South Philadelphia!" When the laughter died down, I thanked everyone for their warm hospitality. This truly had been a father-son evening, and I will cherish it always.

In October, we were again invited to the Los Angeles County Museum of Art Theater, this time to share in the tribute to one of the truly great Hollywood producers, the already highly honored Walter Mirisch. His productions, made with his brothers, Harold and Marvin, are some of the greatest films and box office smashes Hollywood has ever realized. They include *West Side Story, The Apartment, In the Heat of The Night, Some Like it Hot, The Magnificent Seven, Fiddler on the Roof,* and *The Pink Panther.* Always a warm and friendly gentleman, we've sat on the Motion Picture and Television Fund Board together for twenty-five years. I'll never forget that he was the producer and owner (with William Wyler) of my first studio contract for the film *Friendly Persuasion* at Allied Artists Studio. Occasionally we muse about that.

Many guests spoke that evening, lauding the guest of honor following the documentary shown of his life and accomplishments: Blake Edwards, Julie Andrews, Fay Kanin, and Sidney Poitier. Afterward, I was particularly touched when this gracious man spotted me, walked to where I was standing and said, "I'm thrilled to see you here and I'm honored that you came."

The memorial party for Janet Leigh, held at the Beverly Hills Hotel a week later, was an extraordinary get-together of Hollywood notables and friends. It seems as though every day without fail another unforgettable personality leaves us—and the impression they've made strongly persists in our consciousness. Or maybe I'm just more aware of what's happening because I'm… uh, getting older by the day.

Janet's beautiful daughter Jamie Lee Curtis was the hostess and Mistress of Ceremonies and her other beauty, Kelly, both spoke of their mom with tenderness and humor. Touching tributes were also given by Robert Wagner, Saul Turtletaub, and Dick Van Dyke, and movie clips were shown of her collective efforts revealing her varied and sparkling talent which brought a few tears to those who knew her—myself included.

Walter Mirisch, Jan and Tom Sarnoff, Cyd Charrise and Tony Martin, Frank Mancuso, Jay Cantor, and Edie Wasserman also attended. Debbie Reynolds sat next to us and I couldn't help telling her about Lucas being in Knoxville. Wouldn't it be exciting if Debbie appeared there in a "Pops" concert? Later as we were leaving, I told Jamie how much I adored her mother and how we'd had such a warm relationship all these years since we first met on the TV movie *House on Greenapple Road.* "I know," she said, "she felt the same about you." In 1988 Janet gave me her extremely well-written autobiography, *There Really Was a Hollywood.* Inside she inscribed: *Dear Peter Mark and Helen, And there really are friends! Love, Janet.*

Soon after, another special friend was gone. We went to the memorial service for Virginia Mayo, who was on view at the mortuary. Looking at her in the casket, she really did seem to be asleep, so peaceful and utterly beautiful, almost the way she did in films—her weight and age had vanished. I was moved. She was such a dear woman, no airs, just a loving grandmother. I loved her. As she was laid to rest on a verdant hill in Thousand Oaks, Helen and I held hands and hugged each other. It was most peculiar that in all of Hollywood, Esther Williams and I were the only actors who attended.

At a special luncheon in December 2004, the Southern California Motion Picture Council presented me with an impressive plaque—A Lifetime Achievement Award: "For Your Contribution To The Entertainment Industry and Performing Arts." Also receiving awards were Jayne Meadows and Fayard Nicholas (with brother Harold, the greatest African-American tap dancing duo in film history). After my short acceptance speech, I returned to my seat and said to my daughter, Kelly, "I'm glad I'm not dead. I still have a lot I want to do…"

Epilogue

AFTER ALL THESE YEARS, I've come to the conclusion that I'm basically the same as I was as a kid. I may have creaky joints, a hairline that escapes daily definition, and more wrinkles than I need—but I do remember as a young man thinking of other people with consideration and not wanting to harm or take advantage of anyone. If I'd heard a gossipy tale I didn't run around repeating it, especially something told to me intimately. A privacy remained private. In that sense, I haven't changed. I don't mean that I'm a Pollyanna—push me and I'll push back, harder. But I do live by a code of ethics; just as I did as a kid without knowing why. It was inbred. Loyalty, honor and respect. It runs deep—for myself and for my family.

I must say that without understanding it as a child, God has had a profound influence in my life. Looking back, growing up in a dysfunctional family and living through all the suffering and chaos, I seem to have been guided and protected. I didn't find out about that until much later, after I came into Subud when the true meaning of the molten, white light I saw as a child was revealed to me. This understanding has enabled me to reflect on my childhood and my life as a young adult and how everything has evolved.

I do believe we all come into this world with the whole package, the works. Inside of us, everything we are and are meant to be has been graciously granted to us by our creator. I'm not talking about destiny, but the potential to be. We have the tools. Of course, most of the time we have a free will to do want we please, but we do have indications from inside of us as to what path to take or walk away from in every endeavor. If we screw up, it's our fault, not God's. Our lives are like a gigantic jigsaw puzzle—all the pieces are there in our firm or hesitant grasp, but how and when we fit them all together is disconcerting and elusive. The distractions, the temptations, the doubts and insecurities, the misguided efforts, the mental games we play with ourselves, the wrong decisions and choices—it's all a necessary and painful learning process. But without a supreme power to pick us up and dust us off to continue—trying again and again to find our true way—I believe it is infinitely tougher.

As I've gotten older, there isn't any question in my mind as to how my life has been immeasurably enhanced and fulfilled by my children and now my grandchildren. Even though they're completely definitive individuals, sometimes when I look at them I can't help but see the inherited traits from Helen and myself and also our parents—even in photographs—the enthusiasm, a tender gesture, a laugh, a shy smile—the eyes—an emotional response, a sudden burst of anger. I seem to know them all more deeply—as if I'm living my life all over again in a different way, having been there and seen it all before—my remembrances of childhood dreams rekindled.

Of course, they all exist because of God's grace, but the blood feelings coursing through their veins is the golden thread of familial attachment and it's severely powerful. I'm sure that every parent feels the same.

God has been good to me, in everything. Through all the struggle and suffering, progress has been made. I've learned through my "opening" in Subud, and by doing the latihan for forty-five years how truly blessed I am. That realization hit me immediately and through the years I've never wavered in my profound gratefulness. To think that I've been granted the opportunity to truly worship God by way of Subud, tapping into His essence of power which is within all of us, is beyond intellectual understanding. Yet, it's all so simple. God put this sacred and mysterious place inside all of us—our inner life or soul—that has the capacity to come alive again—to wake up from its sleepy torpor once the button is pushed for the door to open.

And when the door is open, most of the time the sun is warm, and the birds are singing—and all things are possible.

www.ingramcontent.com/pod-product-compliance
Lightning Source LLC
Chambersburg PA
CBHW071400230426
43669CB00010B/1399